THE IMPACT OF LITERATURE-BASED READING

Donna E. Norton
Texas A&M University

Merrill, an imprint of
Macmillan Publishing Company
New York

Maxwell Macmillan Canada
Toronto

Maxwell Macmillan International
New York   Oxford   Singapore   Sydney

Editor: Linda James Scharp
Production Editor: Sheryl Glicker Langner
Art Coordinator: Raydelle M. Clement
Cover Designer: Cathleen Norz
Production Buyer: Pamela D. Bennett

This book was set in Galliard by Carlisle Communications, Ltd. and was printed and bound by
R. R. Donnelley & Sons Company. The cover was printed by New England Book Components.

Macmillan Publishing Company
866 Third Avenue
New York, NY 10022

Macmillan Publishing Company is part of the
Maxwell Communication Group of Companies.

Maxwell Macmillan Canada, Inc.
1200 Eglinton Avenue East, Suite 200
Don Mills, Ontario M3C 3N1

Library of Congress Cataloging-in-Publication Data

Norton, Donna E.
    The impact of literature-based reading / Donna E. Norton.
        p.   cm.
    Includes bibliographical references and index.
    ISBN 0-675-21369-X
    1. Reading (Elementary)—United States. 2. Literature—Study and
teaching (Elementary)—United States. 3. Children—United States—
Books and reading. I. Title.
LB1573.N66   1992
372.6′044′0973—dc20   91–30437
                                                              CIP

Printing: 1 2 3 4 5 6 7 8 9   Year: 2 3 4 5

To my husband Verland with gratitude and affection

F ollowing the completion of her doctorate at the University of Wisconsin, Madison, Donna E. Norton joined the College of Education faculty at Texas A&M University where she teaches courses in children's literature, language arts, and reading. Dr. Norton is the 1981–1982 recipient of the Texas A&M Faculty Distinguished Achievement Award in Teaching. This award is given "in recognition and appreciation of ability, personality, and methods which have resulted in distinguished achievements in the teaching and the inspiration of students." She is listed in *Who's Who of American Women*, *Who's Who in America*, and *Who's Who in the World*.

Dr. Norton is the author of three books in addition to this volume: *Through the Eyes of a Child: An Introduction to Children's Literature*, 3d ed., *The Effective Teaching of Language Arts*, 3d ed., and *Language Arts Activities for Children*, 2d ed. She is on the editorial board of several journals and is a frequent contributor to journals and presenter at professional conferences. The focus of her current research is multicultural literature, comparative education, and literature-based reading programs. The multicultural research includes a longitudinal study of multicultural literature in classroom settings. This research is supported by grants from the Meadows Foundation and the Texas A&M Research Association. In conjunction with the research in comparative education, she developed a graduate course that enables students to study children's literature and reading instruction in England and Scotland and is evaluating educational programs in several Asian and European countries. She currently has a grant from GTE Foundation to develop institutes in children's literature and literacy.

Prior to her college teaching experience, Dr. Norton was an elementary teacher in River Falls, Wisconsin and in Madison, Wisconsin. She was a Language Arts/Reading Consultant for federally funded kindergarten through adult basic education programs. In this capacity she developed, provided in-service instruction, and evaluated kindergarten programs, summer reading and library programs, remedial reading programs, learning disability programs for middle school children, elementary and secondary literature programs for the gifted, and diagnostic and intervention programs for reading disabled adults. Dr. Norton's continuing concern for literature programs results in frequent consultations with educators from various disciplines, librarians, and school administrators and teachers.

PREFACE

The Impact of Literature-Based Instruction

A revolution is upon us. Children's literature has invaded the nation's classrooms. Educators, parents, legislators, and members of the media are encouraging classroom teachers to allow the rich content of "real" literature to drive instructional programs. This renewed interest in harnessing the power of children's literature is one response to declining test scores and alarming national reports that document the fact that large numbers of students are not fulfilling their potential as readers. Furthermore, leaders of business and industry find that many high school graduates lack the reading and problem-solving abilities necessary for successful job performance.

While there seems to be general agreement that reading instruction needs to change and that teaching through primary sources like children's literature may be the answer, very few people have addressed an important question. *How* can the classroom teacher use children's literature effectively? This book offers answers to that question.

Part One begins with issues of theory and philosophy and provides an historical perspective for literature-based instruction. People who have been taught to read from basal readers or those who have taught using basal readers will find ideas that will challenge their beliefs and practices. But the primary purpose of this book is to apply and integrate reading theory to literature-based practice.

Part One continues with chapters exploring strategies for improving comprehension of whole text as well as vocabulary development. Specific approaches to literature that research has demonstrated improve students' comprehension and help them "make meaning" are discussed in Chapter 2. In addition, Chapter 2 outlines criteria for selecting literature for a literature-based program with a strong emphasis on finding appropriate literature for the diverse cultures represented in many of today's classrooms. While children's literature provides a rich context for exposure to new words, teachers are challenged to help students make full use of that exposure to build their reading and writing vocabularies. Chapter 3 focuses on strategies and activities for selecting, emphasizing, and expanding vocabulary.

Chapter 4, the final chapter in Part One, discusses a continuum of assessment with a focus on naturalistic or ecological assessment through the use of portfolios.

This chapter is placed in Part One because successful literature-based instruction requires attention to assessment from the outset—providing an appropriate environment, selecting literature, planning units and lessons, and setting up opportunities for reader responses as well as teacher reflection.

Part Two contains five chapters devoted to developing an understanding of and an appreciation for literary elements: plot development and conflict, characterization, setting, theme, and author's style and point of view. Each chapter contains lists of core books, extended books (books that amplify a theme or unit), and related books suitable for recreational reading as well as detailed lesson plans for implementing a literature-based program. Each chapter is further organized by separate lists and plans appropriate for lower elementary students, middle-elementary students, and the upper elementary and middle school students.

While these plans are presented in detail, the intent is not to be prescriptive. There is no one "right" way to implement a literature-based program. There is no one "right" list of books. The extensive lists of books and their division into core, extended, and recreational categories plus the descriptive detail in the unit and lesson plans is included to help give adequate direction to both the preservice and inservice teacher. Teachers are encouraged to use their own favorite books and follow the interests articulated by their own students. Further, teachers are encouraged to engage in the process of developing their own units or modifying the ones presented here.

Part Three contains five chapters on developing an understanding of and an appreciation for literary genre: folklore, modern fantasy, poetry, realistic fiction, and a fifth chapter that combines historical fiction, biography, and informational literature. Each chapter gives a list of core books for each particular type of literature plus sample lessons that help build understanding of the characteristics of each genre.

Model units are provided as well as methods and strategies for developing thematic and genre-based units. Some suggestions for independent projects associated with thematic units are also included. The directions for and purposes of these projects can be extrapolated to work with other units as well.

Part One provides a solid research base—the "why" teachers need to be empowered to undertake a literature-based instructional program. It is also intended as the basis for a dialogue between teachers and parents or teachers and school administrators. Parts Two and Three provide the "how." These chapters need not be studied exhaustively, but it is hoped that they will serve as a rich resource and guide.

I wish to acknowledge the teachers and administrators in the public schools in Glenview, Wheeling, Skokie, and Wilmette, Illinois for their willingness to serve as a receptive audience as ideas for this text were refined and developed. I also value the contributions of the reviewers: Martha Combs, University of Nevada–Reno; Carol J. Fisher, University of Georgia, and Pose Lamb, Purdue University. I would also like to thank my editors at Merrill, an imprint of Macmillan Publishing, Linda Scharp and Sheryl Langner for their efforts to bring yet another writing project to fruition.

CONTENTS

PART ONE
Developing a Literature-Based Reading Program   1

CHAPTER ONE
What is Literature-Based Instruction?   3

    A Historical Perspective   5

    Instructional Formats   8

    Choices for Reading Programs   10

    Issues of Program Development   12 ·

    Objectives for Literature-Based Programs   14

CHAPTER TWO
The Reading and Literature Connection:
Developing Meaning and Comprehension   17

    Balancing Efferent and Aesthetic Responses
    to Literature   19

    Applying Comprehension Research to
    Literature-Based Programs   22

    Scientific Approaches to Literature   23

    Creating Meaning Through Writing   45

    Selecting Literature for a Literature-Based Program   46

CHAPTER THREE
Vocabulary Development   57

    Selecting Vocabulary for Instruction   58

    Developing Vocabulary Through Literature   61

CHAPTER FOUR
Assessment 97

Assessing the Instructional Environment 99

Assessing Students 104

Assessing the Total Literature-Based Program 119

PART TWO
Understanding and Appreciating
Literary Elements 123

CHAPTER FIVE
Plot Development and Conflict 125

Developing Understanding and Appreciation of Plot
and Conflict 129

CHAPTER SIX
Characterization 163

Developing Understanding and Appreciation
of Characterization 164

CHAPTER SEVEN
Setting 185

Developing Understanding and Appreciation of Setting 186

CHAPTER EIGHT
Theme 213

Developing Understanding and Appreciation of Theme 214

CHAPTER NINE
Author's Style and Point of View 235

Developing Understanding and Appreciation of
Author's Style 236

Developing Understanding and Appreciation of Point
of View 257

PART THREE
Developing Understanding and Appreciation of Literary Genre — 273

CHAPTER TEN
Folklore — 275

Developing Understanding of Folklore — 277

CHAPTER ELEVEN
Modern Fantasy — 317

Developing Understandings of Modern Fantasy — 319

CHAPTER TWELVE
Poetry — 343

Developing Understandings of Poetry — 345

CHAPTER THIRTEEN
Realistic Fiction — 359

Contemporary Realistic Fiction — 360

CHAPTER FOURTEEN
Historical Fiction, Biography, and Informational Literature — 381

Historical Fiction — 382

Biography — 389

Informational Literature — 400

AUTHOR INDEX — 434

SUBJECT INDEX — 440

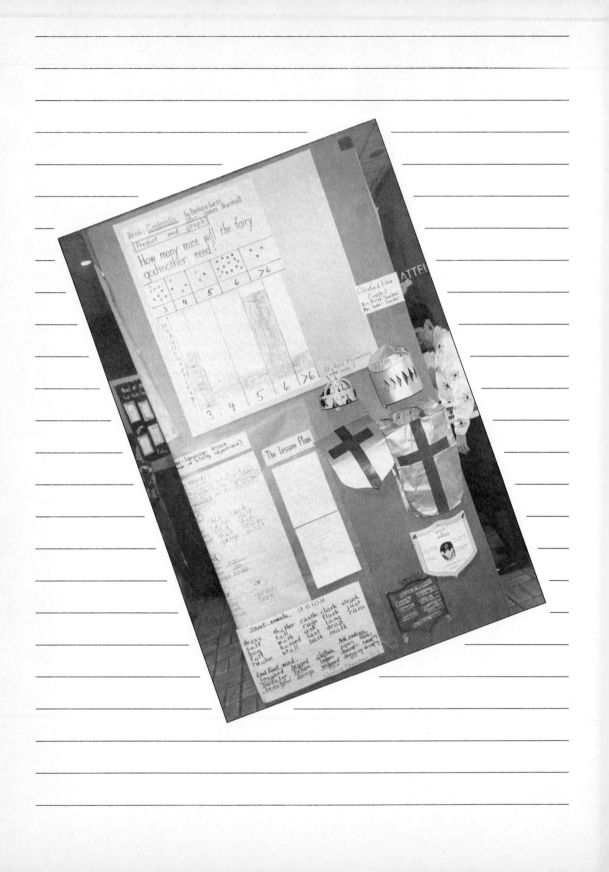

PART ONE:

DEVELOPING A LITERATURE-BASED READING PROGRAM

What Is Literature-Based Instruction?
The Reading and Literature Connection:
 Developing Meaning and Comprehension
Vocabulary Development
Assessment

CHAPTER 1

WHAT IS LITERATURE-BASED INSTRUCTION?

A HISTORICAL PERSPECTIVE

INSTRUCTIONAL FORMATS

CHOICES FOR READING PROGRAMS
  Total Literature Approaches
  Basal Programs Supported by Literature

ISSUES OF PROGRAM DEVELOPMENT

OBJECTIVES FOR LITERATURE-BASED PROGRAMS

Education in the 1990s is an exciting time for professionals who believe in the power of literature. Professional sources and popular journals and newspapers emphasize the need to make children's literature a dominant force in the school curriculum. This renewed interest in teaching through primary sources of children's literature is attributed to concerns that students are not reading up to their potentials and to realizations that the content of what is read is as important as the process involved in teaching reading.

Reports, books, and test results in the 1980s and 1990s reflect both questioning and controversy over how reading should be taught and what materials should make up the reading curriculum. For example, documents such as *Becoming a Nation of Readers* (Anderson, Hiebert, Scott & Wilkinson, 1985) recommend focusing on comprehension, reading aloud to children, reading books, and requiring fewer worksheets. Educators such as E. D. Hirsch in *Cultural Literacy: What Every American Needs to Know* (1987) maintain that elementary and secondary educators are not emphasizing the rich content on which an education should be based. Throughout his text, Hirsch argues for a strong content base that emphasizes literature, history, science, and geography. Educators responding to the decreasing verbal scores on the Scholastic Aptitude Test (SAT) attribute the decline to the erosion of reading time, students' preoccupation with television and video games, and poor-quality reading materials (Putka, 1990).

Many of the responses to these reports and test results call for the additional use of literature in classrooms. For example, when asked to respond to the latest SAT decline, the California State Superintendent of Education, William Honig, stated, "We need to revamp the curriculum toward more writing, more problem solving, and more literature" (Putka, 1990, p. B1). Honig's statement reflects the philosophy of the California State Department of Education as expressed in *Recommended Readings in Literature: Kindergarten Through Grade Eight* (California State Department of Education, 1986). Numerous states and cities are currently following the California initiative and recommending or even mandating the use of literature in the classroom. According to *Reading Today* (Miller & Luskay, 1988), the newspaper of the International Reading Association, "Everywhere you look, there seems to be a renewed interest in the use of children's literature in the school reading program. This trend is evident in increased coverage of the topic in conference presentations, journal articles, and books" (p. 1).

The article in *Reading Today* identifies both concerns and realizations that encourage this greater emphasis on literature. Many communities believe that students are neither learning to read adequately nor choosing to read independently. Of equal concern are the criticisms that many basal readers are limited in their scope and do not contain either classic or contemporary literature. On the other hand, literature-based reading programs appear to promote the fun and joy of reading; enrich students' lives; provide material that is inspiring, interesting, and informative; and increase reading ability.

In the literature-based view, reading is not the acquisition of a set of isolated skills. Instead, reading is the ability to read all types of literature with understanding, appreciation, and enjoyment. In this viewpoint, literature can be used to develop or support the reading curriculum, to teach or reinforce reading skills, and to introduce students to a variety of good and enjoyable books. Students discover that reading is more than skill lessons, workbook pages, and disconnected short stories. Through literature, students discover that reading can become a lifelong habit that brings both knowledge and enjoyment. This belief in the power of literature is reinforced by a study by Freppon (1990). This study, which investigated students' concepts related to the purposes and nature of reading, found that students in literature-based programs view reading as language and meaning based. An appreciation of language and an emphasis on meaning are certainly two of the goals of any reading and language arts curriculum.

The images that come to mind when describing a good literature-based curriculum include enthusiastic teachers and students who love to read literature in classrooms; libraries filled with colorful and varied books; librarians who help teachers and students select books that meet curricular and personal needs; and teachers who not only read enthusiastically to students, but who also encourage them to develop an understanding of and an appreciation for many types of literature. These descriptions might indicate some of the reasons that literature has both a contemporary and historical place in the school curriculum and why educators are showing a renewed interest in using children's literature, especially in the reading and language arts curriculum.

A HISTORICAL PERSPECTIVE

Literature and literature-related activities historically have had a strong place in the curriculum although educators usually have disagreed about which literature to read and what type of activities should accompany the literature. A review of the place of literature in the curriculum explains some of the disagreements. Purves and Monson (1984), for example, identify three structures that emerged during the nineteenth and twentieth centuries for teaching literature-based curriculums. Each of these structures has its own goals, objectives, and literature activities. A brief review of these structures highlights common literature activities that still are found in classrooms.

First, Purves and Monson identify the historical or imitative structure in which students read and discuss classical literature. Early advocates of this approach, such as Arnold (1895), argued that a core of literature exists, which educated people should read and recognize for its literary and historical excellence. Such literature is seen as a way to transmit the cultural and historical values of the society to the children. A canon of literature can be identified that encourages students to read the great books and to acquire standards of excellence by which they can judge other books. Many authors still assume that their readers can recognize and understand various literary and historical allusions. For example, many newspapers such as the *Washington Post* or the *New York Times* publish articles in which the writers expect their readers to understand such allusions. *Washington Post* columnist George Will's column of Thursday, September 20, 1990, is headlined "American Iliad Finds its Homer in Young Filmmaker Ken Burns." In the column, which discusses the making of the miniseries "The Civil War," Will states, "Our Iliad has found its Homer: He has made accessible and vivid for everyone the pain and poetry and meaning of the event that is the hinge of our history" (1990, p. 6A) Will expects his readers to understand the relationship between Homer's recounting of the Trojan War in poetic terms and this rendition of an important event in American history.

The contemporary influence of the historical structure also is found in book lists such as *Touchstones: A List of Distinguished Children's Books* identified by the Children's Literature Association (1985) and "Education Secretary Bennett's Suggested Reading List for Elementary-School Pupils" (1988). Standards of excellence also are reflected in the selections of literature that win awards such as the Newbery Medal and Honor Awards (Norton, 1991). Core lists of books that are read and discussed by students frequently reflect standards of excellence.

The second structure identified by Purves and Monson is the cognitive or analytic structure, which is based on the work of literary critics such as Northrop Frye (1964). In this approach teachers teach students to analyze, criticize, and classify literature. Literature activities stress the development of critical and thinking abilities as the students practice comprehending, analyzing, and responding to literature. As with the historical structure, the analytic structure is reflected in literature discussions found in many contemporary classrooms.

The third structure identified by Purves and Monson is the psychological or generative structure influenced by early psychologists and educators such as Sigmund Freud and John Dewey. This approach to literature encourages students to respond directly and personally to what they read. Rosenblatt's (1968) more contemporary writing emphasizes the relationships between the literature and the reader. Rosenblatt believes that

> teaching becomes a matter of improving the individual's capacity to evoke meaning from the text by leading him to reflect self-critically on this process. The starting point for growth must be each individual's efforts to marshal his resources and organize a response relevant to the stimulus of the printed page. The teacher's task is to foster fruitful interactions—or, more precisely, transactions between individual readers and individual literary works. (pp. 26–27)

Literature activities in the generative structure stress individual growth through reading more than the development of critical skills. This growth might take the form of unstructured inquiry in which students focus on their experiences with literature and their responses to the text.

These three structures are found in many literature programs today. Purves and Monson (1984) advocate using a combination of these structures rather than only one, because, "Each of them emphasizes a different aspect of the reader's transaction and all can be brought together into harmony" (p. 186). Teachers should consider the importance of each structure when they ask, "What books should my students read?" "What attitudes about reading and books do I want my curriculum to promote?" "What skills do I want my students to learn through the literature-based curriculum?"

If a literature-based curriculum incorporates aspects of all three structures, teachers would be likely to choose books and activities that encourage students to read and enjoy a wide variety of genres and types of books. The curriculum would include classic examples of each genre as well as contemporary works that students might use for comparisons, criticisms, and evaluations. Exposure to a variety of books also would encourage students to develop their own knowledge or schemata about literature and literature structures. Some of these books would be used for formal instruction, while many others would be used for recreational reading and incidental learning.

In addition to a wide range of books, teachers would expose students to a variety of approaches for reading literature. These approaches would help students learn to read for different purposes; understand the importance of literary elements such as plot, characterization, setting, theme, and style; critically evaluate what they read; understand the differences and requirements for such genres as folklore, fantasy, poetry, realistic fiction, biography, and informational books; and read texts for aesthetic purposes.

The literature-based curriculum would give teachers the opportunity to integrate many subject areas as well as reading and language arts. For example, the National Commission on Social Studies in the Schools (1989) recommends literature as a means of developing understanding about social studies: "Heroes and heroines ought to play a prominent part in early social studies, providing models for emulation, but common people should also be studied. Choosing figures so as to balance across the sorts of social divisions in our country is important: we need black and white, male and female, Native Americans, Asians and Hispanics, not necessarily balanced to reflect the exact ethnic composition of the class, but balanced to reflect the realities of the world and of the cultural landscape of our country" (p. 8). The National Commission warns that space limitations in textbooks can result in restricted treatment of heroes and heroines as well as the accomplishments and frustrations of ordinary people. The use of literature and other written learning materials can supplement the textbooks. Barnes (1991) reiterates the importance of literature in the social studies curriculum when he states that even young children can learn anthropological concepts. He recommends that literature be used to develop concepts related to learning about one's original culture (enculturation), to learn about a way of life different from one's original culture (acculturation), to examine the rites of passage practiced by various cultural groups, to develop knowledge about the life cycle, and to investigate the concept of race. These anthropological concepts are readily available in books for students from the lower elementary grades through middle school.

Within the total curriculum, students would have many opportunities to respond to literature as they listen to books during storytelling, discuss their personal reactions to the stories, write their own examples of various literature forms, illustrate their favorite texts, tell stories, create plays from books, develop units around genres of literature, and conduct research for various content areas. Students would learn that books can be used to expand both knowledge and pleasure. As we proceed through this text, we will develop a literature curriculum that considers the best from each of these historical approaches to literature.

INSTRUCTIONAL FORMATS

Just as different theories about literature exist that can influence book selection, literature objectives, and activities, literature-based programs have different instructional formats. Hiebert and Colt (1989) identify the varied instructional formats that can be found in effective literacy programs that focus on children's literature. As shown in Figure 1.1, these formats range from small- or large-group instruction to independent work.

One form of literature activity is led by the teacher using teacher-selected materials that relate closely to the specific objectives being taught. These lessons provide guidance in critical strategies such as reading for the theme or main idea, evaluating the author's development of characterization, understanding the author's point of view, and understanding the characteristics of particular genres. During teacher-led instruction, students can read or listen to the same text or they can read different texts but find and discuss examples that exemplify the instruction. Teachers also can develop minilessons in which they model or demonstrate how to approach a difficult concept or passage. Instruction includes considerable discussion as students explore various strategies for reading literature and try the approaches under guidance from the teacher.

Another form of instruction includes considerable teacher- and student-led interaction from materials selected by both teachers and students. Instruction usually takes place in small groups, in which students have many opportunities to share their new understanding and to respond individually to the literature. In the small groups students can practice strategies presented during teacher-led instruction. Small, flexible groups also allow teachers to group students according to interests and needs.

A third instructional format relies on independent reading from student-selected literature. At this stage students are given many opportunities to apply their reading abilities independently, and they develop their selection abilities by choosing their own books. Teachers can include Sustained Silent Reading activities as well as opportunities for recreational reading and reading for various content projects.

According to Hiebert and Colt (1989), effective literature programs include a variety of these formats because,

> When teachers focus only on independent reading of student-selected material, they fail to consider the guidance that students require for becoming expert readers. A focus on teacher-led instruction fails to develop the independent reading strategies that

FIGURE 1.1 Formats found in effective literature programs.

Two dimensions of effective literacy programs		
Instructional Format		
Teacher-led instruction	Teacher- and student-led interaction	Independent application
├──────────────────────────┼──────────────────────────┤		
Literature Selection		
Teacher-selected material	Teacher- and student-selected materials	Student-selected material
Patterns of literature-based reading instruction		
Patterns	***Examples of Implementation***	***Functions***
Teacher-led instruction/teacher-selected literature	One text for all students; strategy lessons	Guidance in critical strategies; opportunities to extend interpretations
Teacher- and student-led interaction; teacher and student selection of literature	Multiple copies of material; specific skills instruction, especially in content areas	Guidance in critical strategies; opportunities for peer interaction and cooperative selection of literature
Independent application/student-selected literature	Sustained Silent Reading; independent reading periods that are central to small- and large-group discussions and teacher guidance	Students develop selection abilities; students assume reponsibility for their own learning

underlie lifelong reading. A total reading program should contain various combinations of teacher and student interaction and selection of literature so that children develop as thoughtful, proficient readers. (p. 19)

Throughout this text we will focus on a balance of activities and literature that emphasizes teacher direction, student interaction, and independent reading.

The terminology used and the varied objectives stated in literature programs of different states also fit Hiebert and Colt's instructional formats. Teachers easily can place the type of reading suggested in state documents into this type of format. For example, documents published by the California State Department of Education, the *English-Language Arts Framework for California Public Schools: Kindergarten Through Grade Twelve* and the *Recommended Readings in Literature: Kindergarten Through Grade Eight* (1986), state literature objectives and recommend more than 1,000 titles categorized according to genre, grade span, cultural group, and the place of the literature in the curriculum. The recommended reading list also categorizes the books according to core literature, extended literature, and recreational literature.

Notice how easily these categories of books fit into the three formats shown in Figure 1.1. For example, core literature refers to books selected for in-depth analysis. Students read and discuss these books as they analyze various literary elements, identify characteristics of genres, and discuss responses to the literature. These core books could be the focus for teacher-directed minilessons in which teachers guide students through understandings of specific literary elements. The teacher would choose these books because they represent the best examples for the specific instructional purpose. These books, which are to be used in the classroom, are likely to stimulate writing and discussion.

Extended literature includes works that teachers can assign to individuals or to small groups of students. In studying these books, students apply knowledge gained during the analysis of core books. The extended books might be used for literature units, small-group interaction, and independent application. For example, after students discover the characteristics of a fable during a teacher-directed lesson, they could read other fables and discuss how their extended books meet or do not meet the criteria for fables. During this second phase of literature reading student interaction increases and students select from a wider variety of fables. Students might meet in small groups as they consider specific qualities of fables or receive more individualized guidance in reading and understanding fables. Consequently, extended reading can have characteristics of both teacher- and student-led interaction and independent application.

Recreational literature refers to the literature recommended for independent reading and for fostering enjoyment. Recreational literature includes works for individual, leisure-time reading that students select from classroom, school, and community libraries. Teachers, librarians, or parents also can recommend titles to ensure that students are reading enjoyable literature that allows them to apply specific literacy skills and extend their understandings. For example, after students complete a unit on historical fiction, many of them want to continue reading books in this genre. If the unit focuses on the pioneer family through Laura Ingalls Wilder's *Little House in the Big Woods* and other "Little House Books," students frequently enjoy reading books such as Carol Ryrie Brink's *Caddie Woodlawn*, Patricia MacLachlan's *Sarah, Plain and Tall*, Louise Moeri's *Save Queen of Sheba*, and Brett Harvey's *Cassie's Journey: Going West in the 1860s*.

CHOICES FOR READING PROGRAMS

Teachers and school districts have several options as they approach a literature-based curriculum. School districts currently are choosing total literature programs or basal programs in which literature supports the basal. Many school districts encourage their teachers to choose among the different elements of these frameworks. The criterion for selecting an approach frequently is based on how prepared the teachers are for selecting and teaching literature. Some school districts encourage their teachers to begin with a basal program in which literature supports the basal and move to the total literature approach as soon as they feel secure in selecting and using literature.

Total Literature Approaches

When teachers use literature as the core or basis of the curriculum, they identify literature selections and literature-related activities that will be used to teach various reading and language arts objectives. As they approach this task, they must be aware of the dual objectives of any literature-based curriculum: to develop both an understanding of and an appreciation for literature. It would be indefensible to use literature in such a way that students actually grow to dislike literature. Consequently, teachers might, as in the California example, identify core, extended, and recreational literature as well as literature-related activities that will allow them to enhance both the appreciation for and understanding of literature. Developing appreciation and understanding of literature usually requires a balance between aesthetic and efferent responses to literature. Aesthetic reading and literature-related activities encourage readers to focus on their feelings and other personal responses as they interact with the text. Efferent reading and literature-related activities focus on analyzing concepts, testing propositions, gaining information, and arriving at solutions.

As the primary source for teaching becomes real literature, teacher requirements expand. To choose literature that motivates students to read and that stimulates an appreciation for literature requires knowledge about literature, awareness of students' interests, and knowledge about instructional approaches that stimulate interest and appreciation. Likewise, to teach reading and other language arts areas through literature requires knowledge about appropriate literature and instructional approaches that encourage the broad development of reading skills as well as the understanding of literary elements used by authors of literature. Teachers also should consider the literary strengths of each literature selection. Common sense tells us that if Armstrong Sperry develops powerful descriptions of setting and conflict within his book *Call It Courage*, this book should be used to encourage students to appreciate and understand the author's ability to create such memorable settings and conflicts. Both aesthetic and efferent responses can be encouraged as students respond personally to the vivid descriptions and the conflicts and analyze the techniques the author uses to evoke these responses.

In addition to reading for goals such as the main idea, important details, and cause-and-effect relationships, teachers can emphasize the strengths of good literature by encouraging students to develop understanding and appreciation for setting, conflict, characterization, plot, theme, author's style, and point of view. Within the author's style are such complex areas as symbolism, metaphor, simile, personification, allegory, and allusion. In addition, each genre of literature has specific reading and writing demands. Thus, folklore, fantasy, poetry, realistic fiction, historical fiction, biography, autobiography, and informational literature have unique reading requirements. Teachers need to be able to identify some of the selections that can be used for each of these reading requirements. Fishel's (1984) warning is worthy of note: "Of the content areas, English is one of the most demanding in terms of the reading skills required to understand the various genres. In addition, appreciation of the genres is a teaching goal" (p. 9).

To develop an excellent literature-based reading program, teachers need to know how to select literature and must be skilled in the instructional strategies that highlight the best features of literature as well as excite the students. Gardner (1988) warns that literature approaches must not become basal approaches. Instead, programs should "help students select wisely, respond to literature in creative, personally meaningful ways, or help readers raise ethical issues" (p. 251). From Gardner's concerns we see that the formats and structures for literature-based instruction discussed earlier can be used to help students improve their reading and appreciation. The wise teacher balances instruction so that students have many opportunities to read and discuss quality literature.

A study of effective literature-based programs conducted by Zarrillo (1989) also emphasizes the importance of balancing the literature curriculum through selection of literature and types of instructional activities. Zarrillo identified three interpretations of literature-based reading programs that can be found in classrooms: (a) core books, (b) literature units, and (c) self-selection and self-pacing. Zarrillo concluded that effective teachers should include all three of these structures in the literature-based curriculum: "For example, in a fourth-grade classroom, a 2-week core book unit on *Ramona the Pest* could be followed by a 3-week unit on Books with School Settings. A 2- or 3-week period of self-selection and self-pacing would complete the cycle" (p. 28).

Basal Programs Supported by Literature

When teachers use literature to support the reading curriculum developed in the basal, they identify reading skills taught in the basal approach and assign literature selections that reinforce those skills. As a result, students learn that the major goal of the reading program is to understand, appreciate, and enjoy literature, not merely to complete workbook pages.

For example, a committee from Conroe Independent School District in Conroe, Texas, first identified the objectives, themes, and topics developed within the basal series of each grade level. Next, they identified literature selections that could be used to reinforce those objectives and provide independent practice. Some of the literature reinforced specific skills such as reading to understand cause-and-effect relationships. Other literature selections were related to specific genres of literature such as historical fiction or specific topics and themes that might be covered in the basal such as "Winning Moments." Then the committee identified a comprehensive list of books that could be used with the basal. Several of these curriculum documents are extensive and include ideas for using the literature during reading, listening, writing, speaking, and art activities. Some of the documents include model lessons that show teachers how to use the literature for specific purposes.

ISSUES OF PROGRAM DEVELOPMENT

Public responses to national studies, state mandates, and educational issues and concerns currently affect the development of literature-based curriculums. The most visible battles over the reading curriculum often are found in newspaper and television reports that highlight the issues and frequently analyze the efforts of local school districts to overcome any cited deficiencies. For example, results from a study by the National Endowment for the Humanities, a report requested by the U. S. Congress, were highlighted on September 1, 1987, by the *CBS Morning News*. The same study was the lead front page article in *The Dallas Morning News*. The headline read, "Teens Know Little About America's Past, Report Says." The secondary headline stated, "Public schools faulted for failing to teach literary classics, history" (Holloway, 1987). The news article contained interviews with local educators and descriptions of programs such as magnet schools and proposed new programs designed to increase knowledge of literature and history. Similar television reports and newspaper articles reacted to the latest reporting of SAT scores. For example, the headline in *The Wall Street Journal* read, "Verbal Skills Slip as SAT Scores Fall" (Putka, 1990). The article quotes various educators as saying, "Reading is in danger of becoming a lost art among too many American students," "Students spend little time reading and writing both in and out of school," and "We need more problem solving and more literature." As might be expected, public reactions to these studies and reports often lead to legislative mandates.

Some states, such as California, have mandated literature-based curriculums. In 1985 the Illinois Public Act 84-126 amended the School Code of Illinois to include specific goals and objectives for reading, listening, writing, oral communications, literature, and language functions. Likewise, the essential elements mandated by Texas law provide detailed objectives for reading and language arts teaching and assessment. Many states across the country either have similar mandates or are developing or considering such mandates. The role of legislative mandates in education is controversial, however. For example, Durkin (1990) cautions that educators need to be careful in responding to national reports because "typically they describe very complex problems and then provide simplistic solutions, such as longer days, more homework, and so on" (p. 372).

Most educators and responses from the public seem to favor adding literature to the curriculum. This response is exemplified by Giroux's comments as the keynote speaker at a 1990 "New Directions in Education Conference." Giroux told about a superintendent who was extremely happy over increased reading scores in his school district. However, when the superintendent was asked, "What are they reading?" he did not know. Giroux stated, to the approval of the audience, that we can no longer ignore the sources for reading instruction. Purves (1990) also agrees that real books are important in the classroom. He states, "The curriculum of text should include real books written by real authors and written in a variety of genres (p. 104).

Real books written by real authors are the source of considerable controversy. Basal stories written for specific age groups or adapted from primary sources of literature have caused few censorship problems. In fact, the stories usually are criticized for being too bland or uninteresting. Teachers who choose primary sources of real literature face the questions of which literature to use, and which authors to allow the students to read. Certain groups believe in censoring books or authors that they suspect are capable of subverting children's religious, social, or political beliefs, and insist that teachers not be allowed to use these materials in the classroom. According to a survey by People for the American Way, censorship attempts "increased by 20 percent during the 1986–87 school year and by 168 percent in the last five years" (Wiessler, 1987, section 1, p. 8). A report by Dronka (1987) indicates that organized groups are increasingly advocating censorship. According to Dronka, 17 percent of the censorship incidents in 1982–83 were linked to organizations. By 1985–86, 43 percent were associated with organized group efforts. Litigation efforts over text-books in Tennessee and Alabama demonstrate the power of censorship efforts. Al-though the appeals court decisions in both states upheld the rights of the school districts to use the books, we can be certain that censorship attempts will continue and will influence the literature selections in literature-based curriculums. An article in *Education Week* (Rothman, 1990) focuses on the attempts to censor classic texts and states that "school districts can protect their literature curriculum by having in place procedures that ensure that the materials selected are educationally sound" (p. 5).

As more publishers develop literature-based textbooks, they too face the chal-lenges of censors. For example, Meade (1990) describes one such series that, "de-pending on your point of view, . . . is seen as either a treasure-trove of children's literature or a passport to perdition" (p. 38). He also quotes advocates who view the literature-based series as a challenging "blend of sophistication and wholesomeness" and opponents who "detect a not-so-subtle emphasis on violence, death, and the occult" (p. 38).

As we can see from the issues related to literature, it is important for teachers to develop a rationale for the literature that will be used. With a sensible rationale, teachers should not find it difficult to defend high-quality literature.

OBJECTIVES FOR LITERATURE-BASED PROGRAMS

Objectives for literature-based programs relate to understanding and appreciating different literary genres and elements. This dual role is emphasized in endorsements by educational groups and by various state goals and objectives. For example, the National Council of Teachers of English (1983) states that students should (a) realize the importance of literature as a mirror of human experience, (b) be able to gain insights from their involvement with literature, (c) become aware of writers who represent diverse backgrounds and traditions, (d) become familiar with past and present masterpieces of literature, (e) develop effective ways of discussing and writing about various forms of literature, (f) appreciate the rhythms and beauty of the lan-guage in literature, and (g) develop lifelong reading habits.

Stated goals and objectives also can include literature objectives within the language arts and reading curriculum. For example, the literature goal for language arts in the state of Illinois *State Goals for Learning and Sample Learning Objectives: Language Arts* (1985) states, "As a result of their schooling, students will be able to understand the various forms of significant literature representative of different cul-tures, eras, and ideas" (p. 43). The sample objectives identified to encourage students to meet these goals can be divided into objectives that emphasize appreciation, objectives that relate to understanding different genres of literature, and objectives that relate to understanding literary elements. For example, at the appreciation level the third-grade objective states that students will read and enjoy appropriate literary works. At the same grade level, objectives related to genre state that children will recognize the nature of poetry, prose, and biography, and will compare versions of folktales. By the sixth grade, students are encouraged to recognize examples of historical fiction, fantasy, science fiction, realistic fiction, and folk literature. At the literary elements level, the third-grade objectives include recognizing plot sequences and actions; identifying settings; identifying important character traits and explaining how and why characters change throughout a story; recognizing the main idea of a selection; and identifying similes, personification, and onomatopoeia. By the sixth grade, this list of literary elements expands to understanding author's tone, point of view, symbolism, and other types of figurative language.

In addition to objectives related to developing appreciation, understanding genre characteristics, and understanding literary elements, the literature-based program has broader educational and personal goals. Folklore collections from around the world, the writings of Mark Twain and Louisa May Alcott, and the works of poets from Langston Hughes to Edward Lear help students understand and value their cultural and literary heritage. Historical fiction and nonfiction books that chronicle the early explorations and the frontier expansion allow students to live vicariously through world history. Books on outer space, scientific breakthroughs, and information in every field open doors to new knowledge and expand interests. Fantasy, science fiction, and poetry nurture and expand imaginations and allow students to visualize worlds that have not yet materialized or to see common occurrences through the eyes of the poet. Through realistic fiction, biography, and autobiography students can explore human possibilities and enhance their personal and social development. Interactions with many types of literature allow students to expand their language and cognitive development. The time spent with literature is among our most rewarding experiences.

Purves (1990) states that reading and writing programs should interrelate knowledge, skill, and habit. He believes that educators should start at the end rather than the beginning when planning objectives: "Rather than consider the child who enters the system, one can begin by thinking of the adult who emerges from it. Once one knows the destination, then one can consider the path" (p. 89). Purves maintains that the curriculum should be based on the concept of text because such a curriculum allows students

> to become more than literate, for they are privy to much of the mystery that seems to surround the world of the written word as it has grown. Such a curriculum focuses on the activities of reading and writing and seeks to develop the competence and preferences of the students within the confines of the scribal culture, and to allow the opportunity for them to modify that culture. It does so by giving them the requisite knowledge and the power to employ it in the complex world of the text and the scribe. (p. 102)

Knowledge and the power to use that knowledge are two strong objectives that educators want for all students as they graduate from the literature-based curriculum.

REFERENCES

ANDERSON, R.; HIEBERT, E.; SCOTT, J.; & WILKINSON, I. (1985). *Becoming a nation of readers*. Washington, D.C.: National Institute of Education.

ARNOLD, M. (1895). The Study of Poetry, *Essays in criticism: second series*. London: Macmillan.

BARNES, B. (1991). Using children's literature in the early anthropology curriculum. *Social Education*, January, pp. 17–18.

CALIFORNIA STATE DEPARTMENT OF EDUCATION. (1986) *Recommended readings in literature: kindergarten through grade eight*. Sacramento, CA: State Department of Education.

CHILDREN'S LITERATURE ASSOCIATION. (1985). *Touchstones: A List of Distinguished Children's Books*. Lafayette, IN: Purdue University, Children's Literature Association.

DRONKA, P.(1987). Forums for curriculum critics settle some disputes: Clash persists on students' thinking about controversy. *Update*, (March): 1, 6, 7.

DURKIN, D. (1990). Dolores Durkin speaks on instruction. *The Reading Teacher*, 43, 472–476.

EDUCATION SECRETARY BENNETT'S SUGGESTED READING LIST FOR ELEMENTARY SCHOOL PUPILS. (1988). *The Chronicle of Higher Education*. September, B3.

FISHEL, C. T. (1984). Reading in the content area of English. In M. M. Dupuis (Ed.), *Reading in the content areas: Research for teachers*. Newark, DE: International Reading Association.

FREPPON, P. A. (1990). An investigation of children's concepts of the purpose and nature of reading in different instructional settings. *Dissertation Abstracts International*, 50, 10A. (University Microfilms No. 85–08, 451)

FRYE, N. (1964). *The educated imagination*. Bloomington, IN: Indiana University Press.

GARDNER, M. (1988). An educator's concerns about the California initiative. *The New Advocate*, 1, 250–253.

GIROUX, H. (1990, June). *New directions in education*. Paper presented at New Directions in Education Conference, College Station, TX.

HIEBERT, E. H. & COLT, J. (1989). Patterns of literature-based reading instruction. *The Reading Teacher*, 43, 14–20.

HIRSCH, E. D., JR. (1987). *Cultural literacy: What every American needs to know*. Boston: Houghton Mifflin.

HOLLOWAY, K. (1987, August 31). Teens know little about America's past, report says. *The Dallas Morning News*, pp. 1A, 6A.

MEADE, J. (1990, November/December). A war of words. *Teacher*, pp. 37-45.

MILLER, M. & LUSKAY, J. (1988). School libraries and reading programs establish closer ties. *Reading Today*, 5, 1, 18.

NATIONAL COMMISSION ON SOCIAL STUDIES IN THE SCHOOLS. (1989). *Charting a course: Social studies for the 21st century*. Washington, DC: Author.

NATIONAL COUNCIL OF TEACHERS OF ENGLISH (1983). Forum: Essentials of English. *Language Arts*, 60, 244–248.

NORTON, D. E. (1991). *Through the eyes of a child: An introduction to children's literature* (pp. 690–694). Columbus, OH: Merrill.

PURVES, A. (1990). *The scribal society: An essay on literacy and schooling in the information age*. New York: Longman.

PURVES, A. & MONSON, D. (1984). *Experiencing children's literature*. Glenview, IL: Scott, Foresman.

PUTKA, G. (1990, August 28). "Verbal skills slip as SAT scores fall." *The Wall Street Journal*, pp. B1, B4.

ROSENBLATT, L. (1968). *Literature as exploration*. New York: Noble and Noble.

ROTHMAN, R. (1990, February). Experts warn of attempts to censor classic texts. *Education Week*, p. 5.

STATE OF ILLINOIS. *State goals for learning and sample learning objectives: Language arts*. Springfield, IL: Author.

WIESSLER, J. (1987, August 28). Book censorship attempts are soaring, group's survey says. *Houston Chronicle*, section 1, p. 8.

WILL, G. (1990, September 20). American Iliad finds its Homer in young filmmaker Ken Burns. Bryan-College Station *Eagle*, p. 6A.

ZARRILLO, J. (1988). Teachers' interpretations of literature-based reading. *The Reading Teacher*, 43, 22–28.

CHILDREN'S LITERATURE REFERENCES*

BRINK, CAROL RYRIE. *Caddie Woodlawn*. New York: Macmillan, 1935, 1963, 1973 (I: 8–12).

HARVEY, BRETT. *Cassie's Journey: Going West in the 1860s*. New York: Holiday, 1988 (I: 5–10).

MACLACHLAN, PATRICIA. *Sarah, Plain and Tall*. Harper & Row, 1985 (I: 8–12).

MOERI, LOUISE. *Save Queen of Sheba*. New York: Dutton, 1981 (I: 10–14).

SPERRY, ARMSTRONG. *Call It Courage*. New York: Macmillan, 1940 (I: 10–14).

WILDER, LAURA INGALLS. *Little House in the Big Woods*. New York: Harper & Row, 1932, 1953 (I: 8–12).

*I = Interest by age range

CHAPTER 2

THE READING AND LITERATURE CONNECTION: Developing Meaning and Comprehension

BALANCING EFFERENT AND ASETHETIC RESPONSES

APPLYING COMPREHENSION RESEARCH TO LITERATURE-BASED
  PROGRAMS

SCIENTIFIC APPROACHES TO LITERATURE
    Using Knowledge of Text: Schema Theory
    Learning to Read by Reading
    Using the Whole Text to Create Meaning
    Improving Comprehension
    Making Predictions
    Using Direct Teaching Strategies
    Responding to Widening Reading Achievement

CREATING MEANING THROUGH WRITING

SELECTING LITERATURE FOR A LITERATURE-BASED PROGRAM
    Meeting the Needs of Culturally Diverse Students
    Meeting the Interests of Students

Educators who review connections between reading, language arts, and literature stress both the importance of the literature to be read and the strategies used to teach reading through literature. For example, Sawyer (1987), an Australian educator, reviewed both Australian and British studies that support a strong literature-based reading curriculum and argues that learning to read no longer can be separated from reading to learn because the two are interwoven. Sawyer defends this position because "researchers have been unable to study how and why children learn to read through literature without at the same time addressing the question of how they acquire competence in dealing with literary structures" (p. 33). Sawyer contends that the story structures chosen to teach reading are important because the structures themselves teach the rules of narrative organization. Meeks (1983) argues that students who fail to learn to read have not learned "how to tune the voice on the page, how to follow the fortunes of the hero, how to tolerate the unexpected, to link episodes" (p. 214). Within these arguments, the materials chosen to read or to be listened to are just as important as the processes being used. This viewpoint supports Giroux's (1990) question: "But, what are they reading?" It also supports Purves' (1990) contention that the reading curriculum should be based on text and include a wide variety of literature from many genres.

Studies show that using literature in the classroom improves reading comprehension, develops understanding of story structures, increases appreciation of reading and literature, increases active use of language, and improves writing. For example, Feitelson, Kita, and Goldstein (1986) found that first graders who were read to for 20 minutes each day outscored comparable groups in decoding, reading comprehension, and active use of language. This research, however, shows that an adult needs to help students interpret the literature by elaborating beyond the text. Feitelson, Kita, and Goldstein attribute the success of their research to enriching students' information base, introducing students to language that might be unfamiliar to them, increasing students' knowledge about various story structures, exposing students to literary devices such as the metaphor, and extending students' attention spans. My own research with fifth- through eighth-grade students (Norton and McNamara, 1987) shows that combining children's literature with teaching strategies that emphasize cognitive processes, story structures, and modeling significantly increases comprehension and attitudes toward reading. Freppon (1990) concluded that students who receive instruction in literature-based programs view reading as language or meaning based. Dressel (1990) found that stories written by students who heard and discussed higher quality literature showed superior literary quality and genre development than did stories written by students who heard and discussed literature of lesser quality.

Educators who use and recommend literature-based reading instruction emphasize the dynamic nature of the environment and the desirability of developing both understanding of and appreciation for literature. For example, Taxel (1988) describes the literature-based classroom "as fluid and dynamic, . . . a place where educators see literature as central to the curriculum, not as an occasional bit of enrichment undertaken when the real work is completed" (p. 74). May (1987) describes a literature-based program in which understanding and enjoyment are the major goals.

Five (1988) uses minilessons that focus on such literary elements as characterization, setting, flashbacks, and book selection. After each lesson, the students read related literature, discuss the books, and complete writing activities. Five emphasizes that the program dramatically increases independent reading, peer discussions of literature, and student evaluation of areas such as believable characters and effective language and dialogue. The sequence of these minilessons followed by reading, discussing, and writing is similar to that recommended by Hiebert and Colt (1989) for effective literature-based programs. The sequence also has characteristics similar to Zarrillo's (1989) recommended use of core books, literature units, and self-selected literature.

Books and teacher guidance are also important in programs for very young children. In a study of early childhood education, Morrow and Rand (1991) concluded that "preschool and kindergarten children are likely to engage in more voluntary literacy behaviors during free-play periods when literacy materials are introduced and teachers guide children to use those materials" (p. 399).

BALANCING EFFERENT AND AESTHETIC RESPONSES TO LITERATURE

Developing meaning for and comprehension of literature is a complex process. In their summary of studies in reading comprehension, Calfee and Drum (1986) identify three components that are essential for reading comprehension: "A text, a reader of the text, and an interpretation of the text by the reader" (p. 834). Each of these components has unique characteristics and requirements. For example, the literature texts vary from fairly simple narrative structures in folktales to elaborate novel-length plots with interwoven themes; detailed characterizations; and vivid, complex styles of language. In addition, each of the genres of literature has unique requirements: poetry has a different form from biography; expository texts have different reading requirements and purposes than does realistic fiction; and mythology has a different fundamental belief system from fantasy. Even within expository writing, texts vary from simple, literal descriptions to structures and concepts that develop complex ideas such as cause-and-effect relationships.

Readers add another dimension as they bring their emotional, cultural, and scholastic backgrounds to the reading task. Readers approach literature with their previous knowledge of the subject, their purposes for reading that literature, and their various strategies for gaining meaning from literature. Each reader, therefore, can gain quite different meanings from the same literature. Consequently, the interpretation of the text is another complex task. Rewarding interpretations of literature require personal responses that allow readers to connect experiences, emotions, and text; to understand and appreciate the unique requirements of different literary elements and genres; and to apply various strategies to gain meaning and to comprehend numerous examples of literature.

When literary critics and authorities discuss meaning related to literature, they frequently emphasize at least two types of meaning: efferent and aesthetic. Rosenblatt (1985) distinguishes between the two when she states that efferent reading focuses attention on "actions to be performed, information to be retained, conclusions to be drawn, solutions to be arrived at, analytic concepts to be applied, propositions to be tested" (p. 70). Aesthetic reading, according to Rosenblatt, focuses on "what we are seeing and feeling and thinking, on what is aroused within us by the very sound of the words, and by what they point to in the human and natural world" (p. 70). A worthy literature-based program probably should include both efferent and aesthetic responses to literature.

Purves and Monson (1984) emphasize the relationships between the text and the reader as the reader draws meaning from a text (transactions). They describe two important functions in any literature program that prepares readers through a transactional approach. First, the program provides a literary schema that gives students a broad background of various literary genres and allows them to talk about books using words like *plot, metaphor, characterization, theme, style,* and *tone.* This function of the program encourages students to understand the reasons for deciding that one book is better than another book. The program also exposes students to a variety of approaches and critical questions that allow students to consider, "How does the literature or character affect me? What does it mean? How good is it?" These types of responses allow aesthetic involvement and individual transactions.

Notice how Purves and Monson stress both the efferent and the aesthetic responses to literature when they state

> It would seem therefore that students should be exposed to a variety of critical questions, including those which are personal and affective, those which are analytic, those which are interpretive, and those which are evaluative. Each of these questions can be answered intelligently and answering each can help a student learn to read and think and feel. And you can teach students how to answer them. (p. 189)

Throughout this chapter and this text we will include literature and literature-related activities that include efferent and aesthetic responses to literature.

Probst (1989) argues that students must learn not only to extract information from texts, but also to make their own unique meanings from the experience of reading. When reading poetry, for example, most readers seek experience not information, individual meaning not facts. Probst states that when teachers direct students' reading they "must be encouraged to attend not only to the text, but to their own experience with it as well—the emotions, associations, memories, and thoughts that are evoked during the reading of the work" (p. 180). Probst recommends the following types of questions that teachers might use to encourage students to provide aesthetic responses to their reading:

1. Questions that encourage students' immediate emotional and intellectual responses to literature:

   What is your first response or reaction to the literature?

   What emotions did you feel as you read the literature?

   What ideas or thoughts were suggested by the literature?

   How did you respond emotionally or intellectually to the literature?

   Did you feel involved with the literature or did you feel distance from the text?

2. Questions that encourage students to pay attention to the text, without ignoring their roles while reading the literature:

   What did you focus on within the text? What word, phrase, image, or idea caused this focus?

   If you were to write about your reading, upon what would you focus?

   Would you choose an association or memory, an aspect of the text, something about the author, or something else about the literature?

   Describe an image that was called to your mind by the text.

   What in the text or in your reading of the literature caused you the most trouble?

   Do you think this is a good piece of literature? Why or why not?

3. Questions that direct attention to the context in which the literature is encountered, a context of other readers, other texts, and personal history:

   What memories do you have after reading the literature: Memories of people, places, sights, events, smells, feelings, or attitudes?

   What sort of a person do you think the author is?

   How did your reading of the literature differ from that of your classmates? How was your reading similar?

   What did you observe about others in the class as they read or discussed the literature?

   Does this text remind you of any other literary work such as a poem, a play, a film, a story, or other genre? If it does, what is the literature and what connection do you see between the two works?

These questions can be added easily to the discussion of any literary work. Many literature authorities stress that students' first responses to any literary work should be personal ones. For example, Cianciolo (1990) recommends that teachers should encourage personal responses during the first sharing of a picture story book before introducing any other activities related to the literature. You will notice frequent recommendations throughout this text that students share their personal responses to the literature. These responses can take many forms as students discuss their reactions, write about their responses, create responses through art, or even create or select music that depicts their responses to the moods or content of the literature.

APPLYING COMPREHENSION RESEARCH
TO LITERATURE-BASED PROGRAMS

Reading research provides strong rationales for teaching literature and guidelines for how to teach it. Early and Ericson (1988) identify nine findings from reading research that should influence how and why we teach literature in the reading curriculum. A review of these findings shows us the importance of the literature-related activities that will be developed later in this text. As you read these findings, notice how they can be incorporated into a literature-based curriculum that focuses on core books, extended reading selections, recreational reading, and units around literature. Also notice that teachers can emphasize both efferent and aesthetic responses during many of the approaches recommended for developing meaning for and comprehension of literature.

1. Readers use their knowledge of texts and contextual cues to create meaning during reading. (Schema theory also suggests that successful readers use their knowledge of various kinds of texts, the world, and contextual cues to create meaning.) Literature provides one of the best sources for gaining and reinforcing this knowledge.

2. Readers learn to read by reading. This finding implies that students need opportunities to read a variety of literature.

3. Readers need to experience whole texts to increase understanding. Literature is an obvious choice for encouraging students to develop meaning from longer texts.

4. Good readers understand when their reading makes sense. They also are aware when their reading processes break down and can use a variety of corrective strategies. Reading different genres that include several literary elements encourages students to use a variety of reading strategies.

5. Readers improve their comprehension if teachers use such techniques as modeling, direct explanation, and questioning. These strategies work especially well with literature.

6. Good readers use cues in the text and their prior knowledge to make predictions. Again, literature is an excellent source for making predictions.

7. Students benefit from direct teaching of strategies for reading literature. Literature discussions and teaching strategies can focus on many details in literature such as characterization, setting, plot, and theme.

8. Students need help in looking for details to use in making inferences. Strategies such as modeling ways to comprehend inferences are especially valuable with literature.

9. The range of students' reading achievement grows at each successive grade level. Consequently, a variety of literature helps meet these growing needs.

When we apply the nine findings from research identified by Early and Ericson to specific literature approaches, we also meet the requirements for effective literature-based instruction. Within the activities are teacher-led lessons that can be related to the core curriculum. Many types of activities also encourage broad reading, discussing, and responding to literature through an emphasis on teacher and student interaction. Some of the approaches highlighted by the research findings emphasize self-selection of recreational reading materials. In the next section we will briefly describe how each of

Early and Ericson's findings could be applied to the literature-based curriculum. A few examples will be shown in each area, and additional detailed examples can be found in the remaining chapters of this text.

SCIENTIFIC APPROACHES TO LITERATURE

Using Knowledge of Text: Schema Theory

Implications from schema theory provide valuable reasons for using literature within the reading curriculum. According to schema theory, the basis for comprehension, learning, and remembering the ideas in stories and in other types of texts is the reader's schema, or organized knowledge of the world. In this theory readers create meaning using their prior knowledge of various kinds of texts, their knowledge of the world, and the cues supplied by the text.

According to Anderson (1985), our schema (with its sets of knowledge and expectations) provides the scaffolding that allows us to assimilate new information. When new information fits into our slots of prior knowledge, information is readily learned. When the new information does not fit into our sets of knowledge, it is neither easily understood nor readily learned. Our schema provides information for determining what is important in a text and for deciding where in the text we should pay close attention. Our schema provides the basis for making inferences that go beyond the information literally stated in the text. Our schema guides us as we search our memories for the information we need to recall, produce summaries and edit information so that only important information is retained, and generate hypotheses about the missing information. In other words, our schema is influenced by our accumulation of past experiences.

Prior knowledge and past experiences are important for comprehending and appreciating all types of literature. Students who hear stories read aloud learn to develop schema for story structures, vocabulary, and other literary elements. Reading stories aloud is important at all grade levels because many of the story structures that exist in literature might be too difficult for students to read independently. These acquired sets of knowledge and expectations about literature are valuable when students face similar structures, vocabularies, and literary elements in their independent reading. Consequently, teachers and parents should read aloud, tell stories, and talk about a wide variety of literature with children. To provide the maximum knowledge base, the literature should come from various genres and include varied language patterns. For example, after reading or listening to numerous folktales, students can recognize and understand the structure of such literature. When they read folktales independently they know what to expect and what type of plot development is typical. Likewise, if they have been introduced to many forms of nonfictional literature, they will understand the various requirements for comprehending biography, autobiography, or scientific texts. Students also should be encouraged to add to their knowledge base and to their expectations by reading a wide variety of literature independently.

Implications from schema theory emphasize the importance of activating prior knowledge and helping students fill the gaps in their knowledge before they read. Valuable instructional strategies include conducting prereading discussions that focus on students' prior knowledge, introducing information that helps students use their prior knowledge during the reading experience, and asking questions that help teachers identify gaps in students' knowledge. If gaps are identified or if prerequisite knowledge is required, it should be presented before students approach the literature selections.

Maps, pictures, films, and historical time lines all are useful when reading literature set in places or times that might be unfamiliar to students. For example, before reading historical fiction students should understand the location, the time period, and any important characteristics that will influence plot sequences, conflict, characterizations, and theme. Several of the modeling activities developed in this text show teachers how to activate prior knowledge. For example, a modeling lesson associated with Patricia MacLachlan's *Sarah, Plain and Tall* asks students to close their eyes and visualize the prairie and the settings in Maine. When students describe these settings they are activating prior knowledge as well as allowing the teacher to discover any misconceptions.

In addition, picture books and easier stories also can be used to activate students' prior knowledge or to prepare them for story structures or elements found in more difficult texts. For example, before reading a story set in pioneer America students might read Byrd Baylor's *The Best Town in the World* or Brett Harvey's *My Prairie Year: Based on the Diary of Eleanor Plaisted*. Before reading a story that takes place in medieval Europe, students might read David Macaulay's *Castle*. Before older students read Geoffrey Chaucer's *Canterbury Tales* they might read the easier versions adapted and illustrated for younger readers such as Barbara Cohen's *Canterbury Tales* and Selina Hastings' *The Canterbury Tales*. The illustrations in these books add greatly to students' understandings of the time periods.

Helping students make connections between historical literature and current events also increases their understanding and their personal responses to the characters and conflicts developed in the stories. For example, before reading Joan Lingard's *Tug of War*, set in Poland and Germany during World War II, older students could discuss the current events in the Baltic states of the U.S.S.R. as the citizens there try to regain their independence. Then they might better understand the historical reasons for both the current situation and the conflict that caused a university professor and his family to flee the oncoming Russian army in the 1940s. Is there contemporary as well as historical meaning in the professor's feelings when he thinks, "Liberated us? Well, yes, I suppose you did, but then you stayed and occupied us and did not give us back to ourselves. We would like to belong to ourselves, to be an independent nation again." (p. 61)? The same themes associated with freedom and independence are found in both historical fiction and in current reality.

Berger (1989) identifies several additional ways to help students activate prior knowledge. For example, students can use brainstorming to identify everything they know about a subject, an author, a literary element, or a genre. They can take part in a prereading activity in which they identify images or feelings associated with a word such as *poetry*. They can use a discovery learning strategy in which they answer various questions about a topic and list additional questions they would like answered before they read. After activating their prior knowledge, students can read the story and discuss any new ideas and concepts. They might use an interactive strategy in which they first list all they can recall about a topic and then use the lists to predict what might be discovered in the new reading. After reading they can discuss the merits of their predictions and what new information they learned.

Learning to Read by Reading

As we discovered under schema theory, reading widely and frequently allows students to develop sets of knowledge about the world and about literature, and to develop expectations that help them comprehend new materials. Such reading also develops an appreciation for literature and increases the likelihood that they will become lifelong readers.

Students need opportunities to read literature during both teacher-directed activities and free-choice activities that encourage them to select their own literature. Free-choice activities help students develop their own selection criteria, synthesize information from several sources, and apply their developing reading abilities. The literature on extended and recreational reading lists in this text is designed to encourage independent reading. Teachers provide time for independent reading that relies on self-selection through activities such as focus or thematic units, Uninterrupted Sustained Silent Reading (USSR), and recreational reading groups.

Focus or Thematic Units.   These units frequently are used in literature-based programs. Literature-based units are especially important because they can be developed to increase interaction among such areas as language arts, reading, science, and social studies. Units encourage students to apply their reading and language arts skills, search for information, work together in interest or research groups, share enthusiasm for books, increase knowledge in other content areas, and share their findings in creative ways. According to Norton (1982) literature units are especially beneficial because the units (1) "allow teachers to differentiate instruction by providing trade books on several reading levels, (2) let good and poor readers work together, and (3) promote integration of reading and language arts as students plan together, discuss together, and present their results to an audience of their peers" (p. 349).

The units can include both teacher-directed activities, which help students focus on specific reading and literature skills, and individualized reading as students choose literature for either unit-related projects or enjoyment. Units frequently begin with teacher-directed activities and expand to activities in which students have many opportunities for independent reading and individual responses to the literature. Units usually provide opportunities for students to integrate the total curriculum because they can include activities that require responding to literature through writing, speaking, and listening as well as reading. Literature units also can be related to other content areas such as social studies, history, science, art, and music. Diakiw (1990) emphasizes the importance of children's literature as the starting point for either a single lesson or a whole unit. He states, "The story becomes the common knowledge for the class—it is the scaffold, the schema, upon which students' understandings and interests are explored and new knowledge is added" (p. 297).

Focus or thematic units can be genre specific or they can be developed around various themes or literary elements. For example, if a unit focuses on biography, the teacher-directed activities would use specific selections from biographical writing to help students identify the characteristics of biography, consider the requirements for writing effective biography, and develop reading skills that help them comprehend a biography. Students also would develop evaluative abilities that help them analyze the authenticity of a specific biography and to compare several biographies written about the same biographical character. These teacher-directed activities could be in the form of minilessons that emphasize the specific requirements of biographical writing especially in the areas of authentic settings and characterizations. In addition, minilessons might emphasize the unique requirements for writing biography. Small-group and individual activities within the unit might focus on reading and evaluating several biographies written by different authors about the same person.

Students then could apply the criteria gained during the minilessons to their independent reading of biography. They also could provide aesthetic responses as they consider which author provides the greatest personal responses, what personal responses and emotions are generated by each author, and what attracts their attention to the biographical character. The biographical unit easily could extend to writing and research skills as students select their own biographical personages, research the lives of the personages, and write their own biographies.

The biographical unit also could relate to various content areas especially if the subjects are known for accomplishments in government, art, science, or literature. Numerous recreational reading possibilities exist as the unit base broadens to include subjects of interest to the biographical characters. For example, a biographical focus on Langston Hughes could include his poetry, a focus on Beatrix Potter could include her numerous animal tales, and a focus on Walt Disney could include books that have been adapted for Disney productions. A Disney unit also might include comparisons between the Disney texts and the original books that were chosen for adaptations.

Theme units easily can combine several genres of literature. For example, a unit developed later in this text focuses on "Times that Tried Men's Souls." This unit uses historical fiction, biography, poetry, and nonfiction from periods such as the Revolutionary War, the Civil War, World Wars I and II, the fight for freedom during the 1960s and 1970s, and the problems related to the 1990s. The unit also integrates other subjects by considering how the theme affects art, music, and theatre.

Themes also are a marvelous way to increase multicultural understanding if they are developed around specific cultures or groups. For example, a unit on Native Americans might include the traditional beliefs of Great Plains Indians as discovered through their myths and legends. It also might include insights gained from autobiographies, realistic fiction, and poetry written by Native American authors from the Great Plains.

Units can be developed around any of the literary elements. For example, exciting units might focus on such areas as memorable characterizations, settings that create obstacles, and recurring themes in history. The books listed in the extended and recreational reading lists in the chapters presenting literary elements can be grouped into interesting units.

Webbing is an excellent procedure for developing units and identifying important components within the unit. Webbing also allows the students to participate in planning the unit. Consequently, the technique can motivate students to think about topics they would like to investigate, consider possible literature they would like to read, and come up with ways of sharing their knowledge. The first step in webbing a unit is to identify a topic that can be enhanced through children's literature. "Pioneer America" might be a topic for which students would choose to integrate social studies, historical fiction, biography, and music (Figure 2.1). Second, the teacher leads a brainstorming session in which the students draw a web to identify the subtopics that might be investigated around the central theme. For example, around Pioneer America the students might identify the following subtopics: Pioneer Environment, Education of Children, Pioneer Entertainment, and Pioneer Values. These subtopics are identified on spokes of the web. Then students list questions they would like to have answered about each of the subtopics. Third, the students investigate sources and choose literature and other materials related to the subtopics on the web. They answer the questions, "What literature and other sources might discuss Pioneer America? What literature and other sources could I use to make Pioneer America exciting?" Fourth, the students read and discuss the literature and other materials. They identify what they have learned about each of the subtopics on the web and share their findings through creative means. Teachers can divide the class into groups around each of the subtopics. Each group, under the guidance of the teacher, is responsible for developing creative ways to share their findings with the rest of the class.

When the Pioneer America unit shown in Figure 2.1 was taught in a middle elementary classroom, the teacher introduced the pioneer period by creating a pioneer environment in the room using objects necessary for survival and pleasure.

As shown in the web, a strong values-clarification component can be developed around the literature of this time period. Students identified values held and problems faced by fictional characters living in pioneer America. They role-played a family's interactions during decision making similar to that found in many of the books in which families move to a new land. Students assumed different family roles as they discussed whether or not they should leave their home and move westward. In this situation the father wanted new land, another member showed fear of the unknown, another member was reluctant to leave friends, while another was excited over possible adventures. Students then considered a frontier area that might be open to residents in the 1990s and how they would approach the problems that the pioneers faced. Books about this period often illustrate human needs as family and neighbors help each other during times of crisis or provide companionship and entertainment during periods of isolation and loneliness.

Considerable discussion can be stimulated by the diverse attitudes expressed toward Native Americans in these books. Students can compare the negative attitudes

FIGURE 2.1 Pioneer America unit web: subtopics and literature.

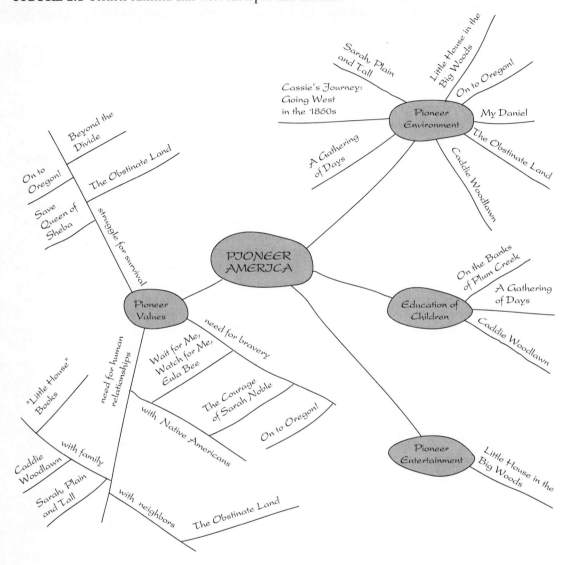

expressed in Walter Edmond's *The Matchlock Gun* with the positive attitudes found in Alice Dalgliesh's *The Courage of Sarah Noble* or Patricia Beatty's *Wait for Me, Watch for Me, Eula Bee* and then consider the consequences of both attitudes.

Other activities that can be developed during this unit include re-creating family leisure activities described in Laura Ingalls Wilder's *Little House in the Big Woods* (storytelling, square dancing, singing); re-creating a pioneer school as described in Carol Ryrie Brink's *Caddie Woodlawn* and Joan W. Blos's *A Gathering of Days* (reading and writing parables, memorizing multiplication tables, reading primers, taking part in spelling bees); building models of a country store and churning butter as described in *Little House in the Big Woods;* and writing journals from the viewpoint of pioneer characters as illustrated by Blos's writing style in *A Gathering of Days.*

As students read the pioneer books, interact with each other during discussions and activities, and create projects that depict the pioneer culture, they develop understandings related to social studies, gain enjoyment from reading historical fiction, and strengthen their language arts abilities. Students also discover that there are many similarities between people from the past and the present.

Uninterrupted Sustained Silent Reading (USSR). USSR can be used to increase independent reading in total school systems or in individual classrooms. Teachers who use this approach allow about 30 minutes each day or several periods during the week in which students silently read self-selected books. If the total school is involved, everyone employed by the school usually stops their normal duties and reads self-selected literature. Within the classroom, everyone reads including the teacher.

For a successful USSR experience, students should have access to a wide selection of literature. Teachers should have some knowledge of students' interests and reading levels as well as knowledge about a variety of books so they can recommend appropriate titles to their students.

The USSR approach can be used at all reading and grade levels because even kindergarten students can read the pictures in wordless books and picture storybooks. Easy-to-read books allow first- and second-grade students to apply their reading skills. High interest-easy reading books encourage lower ability readers to extend their knowledge and increase their enjoyment of reading. Students can select books from all genres from the school or public library or bring books from home. One school worked closely with the local Reading Is Fundamental (RIF) program. The RIF committee purchased paperback books with funds raised from business leaders and other interested citizens. This activity was especially popular with students because the books became their property and formed the beginnings of their private collections. Some teachers introduce USSR before a visit to the public library, where students sign up for library cards and borrow their first books. These books then become the sources for USSR.

The classroom structure for USSR is simple: Everyone takes out a book during this specified time and reads. Enjoyment is emphasized because students are not expected or even permitted to read other types of assignments during this time. Teachers model reading for enjoyment by joining in with their own self-selected reading.

Recreational Reading Groups. Recreational reading groups have some of the same characteristics of USSR except they usually contain more structure, can encourage students to select literature around a specific theme or topic, and include opportunities for students and teachers to verbally respond to their reading experience. Students can select books from a wide range of literature or from a narrower range of topics, genres, or characteristics of literature. If topics provide the focus, students are grouped according to interest in those topics rather than on their reading achievement levels. Consequently, teachers should be sure to include a range of literature that meets reading levels of all the students in the group.

If the materials are totally self-selected, the teacher divides the class into about three groups with a leader designated for each group. The students bring their books to one of these three reading circles, read for about 30 minutes (the time varies according to attention spans and reading interests), and then tell something interesting about the books they have been reading. If the students are unfamiliar with the concept of recreational reading groups, teachers might begin with one large group with the teacher as leader. Teachers model independent reading behavior for the total group and begin the discussion by telling something interesting about the books they are reading. When students understand the procedures, however, smaller groups can be formed, encouraging more interaction among students. By placing competent readers next to less efficient readers, for example, students quietly can get help with unknown words. These groups might contain different students each time they are formed or might retain the same students until the books are finished. Teachers usually change groups after each session.

My favorite recreational reading groups are structured around specific topics. This grouping encourages students to read a wider variety of materials and genres than they might otherwise select. This approach also encourages literary appreciation and aesthetic responses as students and teachers consider why they like or do not like the literature they have selected.

For example, the topic of humor appeals to almost all students, contains enough books to allow self-selection, and encourages students to develop appreciation for how authors develop humor in literature. Students could begin by selecting, reading, and sharing incidents of humor in picture books. Within this category they can share their enjoyment of the humor developed by both the author and the illustrator. For example, they might consider the word play and nonsense in Dr. Seuss' *If I Ran the Zoo,* in Bill Peet's *No Such Things,* and Margaret Mahy's *17 Kings and 42 Elephants.* Unexpected situations provide the humor in Margot Zemach's *It Could Always Be Worse: A Yiddish Folktale,* in Margaret Mahy's *The Great White Man-Eating Shark: A Cautionary Tale,* and in Jon Agee's *The Incredible Painting of Felix Clousseau.* Exaggeration is the source of humor in James Stevenson's *Could Be Worse!* and Patricia Polacco's *Meteor!.* Ridiculous and foolish situations provide humor in David Small's *Imogene's Antlers,* Glen Rounds' *I Know An Old Lady Who Swallowed a Fly,* and Eric Kimmel's *The Chanukkah Tree.*

Recreational reading groups can focus on any of the subjects developed during teacher-directed minilessons. For example, after a lesson in characterization from a core book, teachers could encourage students to select literature from numerous books that have strong characterizations. Students can increase their aesthetic responses by highlighting why they like or do not like the characterization in their self-selected books. They can emphasize how they personally respond to the characters and even how they might have responded if they were that character. A similar approach can be used with any of the literary elements or genres of literature. For example, after in-depth discussions of a myth, students could gather in recreational reading groups and read and respond to examples of mythology. Throughout this text, there will be recommended lists of books that could be used for recreational reading within specific interest areas.

When students select their materials, read for pleasure, and share what attracts them about the literature or the author, they are encouraged to learn to read by reading. This approach also has a strong motivational factor because students frequently choose books that are recommended by their peers.

Using the Whole Text to Create Meaning

Literature is one of the best means of encouraging students to consider longer segments before judging meaning. Characterizations change over the course of a story; themes are often drawn from the whole book; and conflicts gradually develop until problems are overcome or personal conflicts are resolved. Good readers use several effective strategies to make these connections. Poor readers have fewer effective strategies from which to choose.

Shorter picture story books help students understand the desirability of reading a total text to gain meaning. Many of these books are excellent choices because the stories are developed sooner and the books can be reread if necessary to trace how themes or conflicts are developed throughout the text. Books such as Denys Cazet's *A Fish in His Pocket* show even the youngest listener or reader the steps a young bear goes through to solve his problems and realize that it is important to care for others and to be responsible for your actions. Books such as Ann Grifalconi's *Darkness and the Butterfly* help younger students identify two important themes: (1) We all can have fears that cause us problems and (2) we can and must overcome our own fears. Within this shorter text students can identify both illustration and textual support for these themes. Books such as Virginia Lee Burton's *The Little House* help older students trace the developing theme: Social and environmental changes have considerable effects on life. Lessons that use these whole books to enhance an understanding of theme are developed later in this text. Using the whole text to develop plot structures also helps in gaining meaning from the whole text. Lessons showing plot structures are developed later in this text.

Improving Comprehension

Improving comprehension of text is usually one of the most important goals of any reading program. Literature is an excellent source for developing approaches that help students comprehend the text. Again, implications from schema theory stress the importance of using knowledge of text when reading literature. Students should receive instruction and experiences that encourage them to use their knowledge of text when trying to comprehend a new selection. For example, through a variety of reading experiences, students can discover how to approach the reading of different genres such as folktale, fantasy, biography, and poetry. In this text we develop guidelines to help students read, comprehend, and respond to different genres of literature. Other approaches such as semantic mapping or webbing, modeling, and questioning strategies are excellent for developing comprehension of text.

Semantic Mapping or Webbing.   Semantic mapping or webbing graphically displays relationships among ideas and concepts, emphasizes cognitive processes, and encourages problem solving. Semantic mapping encourages higher thought processes, fosters ideas, and stimulates oral interactions among students and teachers as they complete the web. Research indicates the value of this technique and shows how semantic mapping can increase comprehension. For example, semantic mapping procedures increase vocabulary development (Johnson & Pearson, 1984; Toms-Bronowski, 1983); enhance literary discussions that highlight plot development, setting, characterization, and theme (Norton, 1991); improve reading comprehension (McNamara & Norton, 1987; Prater & Terry, 1985); enhance the development of instructional units (Norton, 1982, 1991); stimulate the composition process (Myers & Gray, 1983); encourage interaction and understanding in various content areas (Heimlich & Pittelman, 1986); and encourage the integration of reading, literature, writing, listening, and oral discussion (McNamara & Norton, 1987). These different uses of semantic mapping will be developed throughout this text. Specific examples will show how to use the semantic mapping of literature for each of these purposes.

Figure 2.2 illustrates how the semantic mapping or webbing technique can be used to enhance understanding of various literary elements. The web was developed on the chalkboard with a group of students after they had investigated each of the literary elements. The students identified the important examples under each category and used webbing for both group and individual activities related to literature. Notice how the web integrates the important elements within the story. The web also enhances discussions as students think about each of the subtopics.

Modeling.   Pearson and Camperell (1985) identify important implications from comprehension research that relate to modeling. They state, "If teachers want students to get the author's message, they are well advised to model for students how to figure out the author's general structure" (p. 338). Early and Ericson (1988) reinforce this view when they state that research shows that teachers neglect modeling the process and explaining or describing what students should do during a comprehension lesson. These modeling strategies are especially important in teaching students how to make inferences because failure to make inferences is "frequently the cause for faulty comprehension" (p. 37). Modeling also encourages readers to think about why they are responding personally to literature or a question in a certain way. The approach can be used to increase both efferent and aesthetic responses to literature.

Modeling related to literature follows a sequence in which the teacher first identifies a skill such as inferring characterization or appreciating and understanding similes. Second, the teacher analyzes the requirements needed for gaining meaning. For example, if the teacher is developing students' ability to infer characterization, the teacher needs to go beyond the information the author provides in the text; use clues from the text to hypothesize about a character's feelings, actions, relationships, beliefs, values, hopes, fears; and use background knowledge gained from other experiences. Third, the teacher identifies a text and portions of the text from which characterization can be inferred. Fourth, the teacher develops ways to review the students' prior knowledge (schema) related to both the literary element and the setting for the book.

FIGURE 2.2 Web of literary elements.

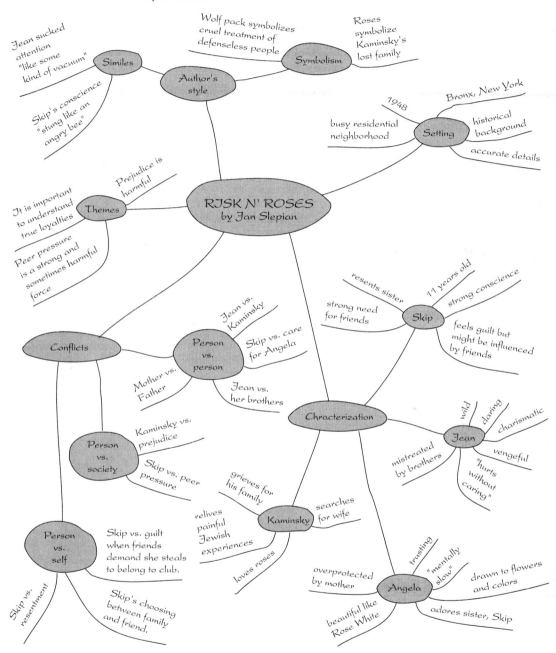

Fifth, the teacher introduces or reviews the specific element that will be modeled and introduces the text. The students also discuss why understanding that element is important to them. Next, the teacher models the whole sequence by reading from the text, stopping at an appropriate place and asking the inference question, answering the question, providing evidence that supports the answer, and exploring the reasoning process. This last part is extremely important because it allows the teacher to explain how the task was approached. It also allows for an aesthetic response as the teacher explains the personal feelings, past experiences, and previous knowledge that entered into the thought processes. Finally, when the students understand the process, they join in by answering the question, citing the evidence, and exploring their own thought processes.

The extensive modeling approaches developed later in this text are based on research conducted by Roehler and Duffy (1984) and Gordon (1985). The modeling lessons were developed for my own consultations with school districts. Consequently, the examples have been field tested with students and teachers from New York to California.

Questioning Strategies.   Various questioning strategies are well-known techniques within the reading program, although critics of comprehension instruction believe that questions too often encourage students to respond at the lowest levels of the thought process. Ambrulevich (1986), for example, found that questions in literature anthologies focused on the two lowest types of thinking on Bloom's Taxonomy. Most basal series, however, use questioning strategies based on a Taxonomy of Comprehension to make sure that all levels of comprehension are covered within the reading program. Not all literature selections should be accompanied by questioning. Many educators warn that teachers should not basalize literature selections by using extensive questioning strategies to accompany each chapter in a literature selection. Many of the strategies developed in this text show teachers how to develop comprehension through techniques that are more appropriate for a specific literature selection. However, if children's literature is used to reinforce and strengthen a basal reading program, teachers frequently will want to lead discussions of the literature that focus on some of the same comprehension levels developed in the basal series.

A taxonomy of comprehension can be used to develop questions that might accompany a literature selection or the questioning strategies could encourage students to focus on setting, plot development, characterization, theme, and style. The following examples were developed by students in my college classes (Norton, 1989). They divided into groups and used either Barrett's Taxonomy of Comprehension (1972) or focused on developing appreciation of the literary elements of setting, plot development, characterization, theme, and author's style. Both groups developed questions around Beverly Cleary's *Dear Mr. Henshaw*. After the students developed their questioning strategies they compared their questions. They discovered that both approaches to questioning helped them discover vital information about developing their own questioning techniques. As you read the following questions, consider the advantages and disadvantages of each approach. How would the development of both series of questions help students and teachers improve their questioning strategies and their ability to focus on important literary elements?

The first series of questions illustrates how questioning strategies can be developed around Barrett's four levels of reading comprehension: Literal recognition or recall, inference, evaluation, and appreciation. The questions listed exemplify each level on the taxonomy. Depending on the book and the instructional purpose, students might want to develop more or fewer questions. (In both examples here, the college students provide numerous questions because they were exploring the various types of questions they could develop. It is not necessary to use all of these questions when discussing the book.)

Literal recognition requires students to identify information provided in the literature. Teachers can require students to recall the information from memory after reading or listening to a story or to locate the information while reading a literature selection. Literal-level questions such as the following often use words such as who, what, where, and when:

1. *Recall of details:* How old was Leigh Botts when he first wrote to Mr. Henshaw? What is the name of Leigh's dog? What is Leigh's father's occupation? Where does the story *Dear Mr. Henshaw* take place?

2. *Recall of sequence of events:* What was the sequence of events that caused Leigh to place an alarm on his lunch box? What was the sequence of events that caused Leigh to write to Mr. Henshaw and to write in his diary?

3. *Recall of comparisons:* Compare the way that Leigh thought of his mother and the way that he thought of his father.

4. *Recall of character traits:* Describe Leigh's response to Mr. Henshaw when Mr. Henshaw asks Leigh to answer 10 questions about himself.

When students infer an answer to a question, they go beyond the information the author provides and hypothesize about such things as details, main ideas, sequence of events that might have led to an occurrence, and cause-and-effect relationships. Inference is usually considered a higher-level thought process; the answers are not specifically stated within the text. Examples of inferential questions include the following:

1. *Inferring supporting details:* At the end of the book Leigh says that he "felt sad and a whole lot better at the same time." What do you think he meant by this statement?

2. *Inferring main idea:* What do you believe is the theme of the book? What message do you think the author is trying to express to the reader?

3. *Inferring comparisons:* Think about the two most important characters in Leigh's life, his mother and his father. How do you believe they are alike and how do you believe they are different? Compare Leigh at the beginning of the book when he is writing to Mr. Henshaw with Leigh at the end of the book when he is writing in his diary and writing true stories for school.

4. *Inferring cause-and-effect relationships:* If you identify any changes in Leigh, what do you believe might have caused those changes?

5. *Inferring character traits:* On page 73 Leigh decides that he cannot hate his father anymore. What does this tell us about Leigh and about his father? Why do you think Leigh's father sent him $20?

6. *Inferring outcomes:* At one point in the story, Leigh wishes that his mother and father would get back together. What do you think would have happened to the story if they

had? How would Leigh's life have changed? How would his mother's life have changed? What might have been the outcome of the writing contest at school if Leigh had not had the advantages of his advice from Mr. Henshaw?

Evaluation questions require students to make judgments about the content of the literature by comparing it with external criteria such as what authorities say about a subject or internal criteria such as the reader's own experience or knowledge. The following are examples of evaluative questions:

1. *Judgment of adequacy or validity:* Do you believe that an author would take time to write to a child and take such an interest in him? Why or why not?

2. *Judgment of appropriateness:* Do you believe that Leigh's story, "A Day on Dad's Rig" was a good story for the Young Writers' Yearbook? Why or why not?

3. *Judgment of worth, desirability, or acceptability:* Do you believe that Leigh had the right to feel the way he did toward his father? Why or why not? Do you believe that Leigh was right in his judgment that his father did not spend enough time with him? Why or why not? Was Leigh's mother's judgment correct at the end of the book? What would you have done?

Appreciation of literature requires a heightening of sensitivity to the techniques that authors use to evoke an emotional response from their readers. Questions can encourage students to respond emotionally to the plot, identify with the characters, react to an author's use of language, and react to an author's ability to create a visual image through the choice of words in the text. The following are examples of questions that stimulate appreciation:

1. *Emotional response to plot or theme:* How did you respond to the plot of *Dear Mr. Henshaw?* Did the author hold your attention? If so, how? Do you believe the theme of the story was worthwhile? Why or why not? Pretend you are either recommending this book to someone else or recommending that this book not be read; what would you tell that person?

2. *Identification with characters and incidents:* Have you ever felt, or known anyone who felt like Leigh? What caused you or the person to feel that way? How would you have reacted to the theft of an excellent lunch?

3. *Imagery:* How did the author encourage you to see Leigh's home, his neighborhood, and his school? Close your eyes and try to describe your neighborhood or town. How would you describe it so that someone else could "see" it?

These examples are not organized according to any sequence for presentation to students, but they do exemplify the range of questions that are considered when the teacher's focus is on strengthening students' reading comprehension abilities.

The next series of questions was written about the same book, *Dear Mr. Henshaw.* They focus on and are grouped according to specific literary elements within the text:

1. *Setting:* How have Leigh's living conditions changed as a result of his parents' divorce? What are some of the positive and negative aspects of where he is now living? Leigh's mother describes their new home by saying, "At least it keeps the rain off, and it can't be hauled away on a flatbed truck." How does this statement reflect her opinion of their past living conditions? What is the importance of having a stable environment in which to live? How did you respond to Leigh and his mother's

descriptions of his home? What did you think was the author's purpose for developing the setting? Was the purpose effective for you? Why or why not?

2. *Plot development:* What problem is causing conflict for Leigh and his family? Why does Leigh write his first letter to Mr. Henshaw? Why does he continue to write letters even after the assigned letter is completed? What does Mr. Henshaw suggest that Leigh do? How do Mr. Henshaw's suggestions help Leigh accept the divorce? What causes Leigh to stop writing "Dear Mr. Pretend Henshaw"? What was the significance of this title when he first began his journal? Why does Leigh have such a problem with his lunch box? What plan does he devise to overcome the lunch-box thief? Is this a good plan? Why or why not? What happens as a result of his lunch-box plan? What does Mrs. Badger say to Leigh that makes him feel good? What did Leigh learn from Mrs. Badger? What helps Leigh understand his mother's point of view about the divorce? How do we know he now understands his mother's point of view? What happens to help Leigh understand his father's point of view? What does Leigh do to show that he understands his father's point of view? How does Leigh feel about himself and his family at the end of the story? How did you react to the outcome of the story? If you could continue the plot, what would happen in the next chapter? If you could rewrite the plot, how would you change the story?

3. *Characterization:* How does Leigh view himself in comparison with the other children in his school? What three events help improve Leigh's self-image? How does Leigh's self-image change as a result of these events? How does the following passage reflect Leigh's growth and the changes in his character? "I don't have to pretend to write to Mr. Henshaw anymore. I have learned to say what I think on a piece of paper. And I don't hate my father either. I can't hate him. Maybe things would be easier if I could" (p. 73). How does Leigh's real father differ from the father of his dreams? In what ways does Leigh's father disappoint him? How do we know that Leigh's father still cares about Leigh and Leigh's mother? How does the character of Leigh's mother differ from that of his father? What actions show that Leigh's mother wants to care for and to provide for her son? Who was your favorite character in the story? What caused you to respond to this character in a favorable way? Who was your least favorite character? What caused you to respond to this character in an unfavorable way? What did the author do to make these characters real for you? Do you know any people who reminded you of these characters?

4. *Theme:* Why do you believe that Beverly Cleary wrote *Dear Mr. Henshaw* in a diary-and-letter format? Why was this an effective way to present this book? What important message did the letters and diary reveal about Leigh and the problems that he was facing within himself and his family? How did either the real or the imaginary exchange of letters and ideas with Mr. Henshaw allow the author to develop this message? How did Leigh change because of these exchanges? At what point do you think Leigh started to accept his parents' divorce? At what point in the story does Leigh begin to understand that his parents are not going to get back together? How do we know that divorce cannot be blamed on one person in the family? Based on the theme of the book, what do you think would be another good title for this book? Was the theme meaningful to you? Is the theme important in our own lives? Why or why not? What other books can you think of that have a similar theme? How did the author of the other book develop the theme?

5. *Style:* From whose point of view is this story told? How do you know that the story is written from the point of view of a young boy? How does the format of *Dear Mr. Henshaw* differ from most other fictional books? How did the diary-and-letter format

allow the author to develop the theme, the conflict, and the characterization? How did the author's style make you believe that you were or were not reading the writing of a real boy who was facing believable problems? This book deals with some painful and serious emotions. At the same time, the author is able to make the reader laugh. How does she accomplish this? What was the most important element of the author's style for you?

Questions that Emphasize Story Grammar.   Educators frequently emphasize the importance of developing students' understanding of story grammars through questioning strategies. For example, Pearson (1984) identifies a common story grammar that proceeds from the setting, to the problem, to the goal and the events that occur as the character pursues the goal, and the resolution of the problem. He then provides a guide for questioning strategies that are developed around this story grammar. For example, Pearson recommends that the lesson begin with questions that focus students' attention on background experiences that are necessary for gaining meaning from the story. Second, ask students to use their background knowledge to predict what might happen in the story and to think about how they might react if a similar problem happened to them. Third, set a purpose that lasts as long as possible throughout the story. Fourth, during or after the reading, ask questions that tie in the important elements from the story map. Fifth, after the reading, return to the purpose-setting questions. Sixth, discuss the story by asking the students to retell the story map, to compare this story with their own experience or with another story, to speculate about how the characters might react in a new situation, and to appreciate the author's ability as a storywriter. Pearson stresses that this final discussion can include many different formats, such as dramatizing a story, making a time line of events, and providing aesthetic responses that emphasize responses to dialogue, colorful language, and favorite characters.

Researchers who investigate story structures and story grammars often emphasize the importance of developing students' comprehension of the plot and their ability to ask and answer questions about the plot structure. In a similar approach, Barr and Sadow (1985) show that many stories have a specific plot sequence. They found that most stories begin with a setting that places the story in a time and place and describes the normal circumstances of the story and the characters. Second, a problem occurs that changes the normal circumstances, usually for the worse. Third, the main character reacts to the incident, frequently undergoing an emotional change. Fourth, the main character takes corrective action. Fifth, most stories end with a resolution of the problem or a description of the new circumstances after the problem is corrected. In addition to the importance of understanding such story grammars, educators frequently emphasize the need to transfer questioning strategies about such plot structures from the teacher to the students.

Developing Active Comprehension.   Singer and Simonsen (1989) found that comprehension of story grammars such as the one described in the previous paragraph increases when students are actively involved in their own comprehension. They found that comprehension improves if students gradually progress from answering questions developed by the teacher about the story grammar to formulating and answering their own questions. Singer and Simonsen state that development of active comprehension takes 6 to 12 training sessions. During these sessions the students begin by answering teacher-developed generic questions associated with the setting and the normal circumstances, the problem, the character's reactions to the problem, the character's actions as the problem is solved, and resolution of the problem. During the first few sessions the teacher models the questioning strategies by asking the questions, pointing out where in the story each part of the story grammar begins and ends, and answers the questions. Gradually the students become actively involved until they can ask story-specific questions, point out in the story where each phase of the story grammar takes place, and answer their own questions.

The following example illustrates how active comprehension can be developed with students. The example discusses a two-week sequence in which folktales are used as the primary literature source:

First day: Explain story grammar and generic questions to the class. Discuss a list of generic questions such as:

1. *Setting and normal circumstances:* Where and when does the story take place? What are the circumstances surrounding the characters?
2. *Problem or adverse incident:* What is the problem? What causes the main character to take action?
3. *Characters' reactions:* How does the main character act after encountering the problem? Is there someone to help or advise the character? How does the character change?
4. *Corrective action:* What does the main character do to solve the problem? What keeps the main character from solving the problem? Does the main character receive help?
5. *Resolution of the problem and new circumstances:* How does life change for the characters at the end of the story? What do the characters learn as a consequence of their experience? What is the final effect of the experience on the characters?

After explaining and discussing story grammar and generic questions, read a short story such as Grimm's *Rumpelstiltskin* (Caldecott Honor) to the class. Stop and point out the beginning of each part of the story grammar to the class. For example, at the beginning of the tale point out the setting and the normal circumstances. Second, point out the beginning of the problem or upsetting incident in which the girl is forced to try to spin straw into gold. Third, point out the main character's reactions in which she goes through a series of emotions including being frightened and weeping. Fourth, identify how the main character takes action to solve the problem such as promising her necklace and her ring, and finally her first born child to the little man who spins the gold. The corrective action also includes thinking of names to identify the little man and the help she requires as she sends a faithful servant into the woods to look for the man. Finally, point out the resolution of the problem and the new circumstances that show the girl telling Rumpelstiltskin his name and supposedly living happily ever after in the palace. Discuss how the story grammar changed the normal circumstances of the main character from a rural setting for a poor miller's daughter to a palace for the queen.

Second day: Read another story to the class, but this time form story-specific questions at the beginning of each story-grammar stage. As in a modeling approach, the teacher answers the questions as the information appears in the story. (Notice that, as the teacher, you model your own active comprehension process associated with stages in plot development by asking and answering all the questions related to story grammar.) For example, when reading Katherine Paterson's *The Tale of the Mandarin Ducks* ask and answer the following story-specific questions as you proceed through the story:

1. *Setting and normal circumstances:* "Where and when does *The Tale of the Mandarin Ducks* take place?" Answer: "The story takes place a long time ago in Japan. The storyteller calls it the Land of the Rising Sun, but I know from my own knowledge that this is another name for Japan. The normal circumstances show a male and female duck living peacefully in the country."

2. *Problem or adverse incident:* "What is the problem that causes the ducks to change their circumstances?" Answer: "A cruel lord sees the beautiful drake swimming in the pond, demands that he be captured, places him in a bamboo cage, and takes him to the manor house. The female duck is left behind in the woods."

3. *Characters' reactions:* "How does the duck respond to his new circumstances?" Answer: "The duck shows worry for his mate and sadness for his loss of home. The text does not tell us exactly but we can infer that he is worried because he thinks about his mate sitting alone on her eggs and not knowing what happened to him. The text tells us that he droops his head and loses his luster. We also can infer that these are his reactions to his confinement and his change of setting."

4. *Corrective action:* "What keeps the duck from returning home? Who helps him get his desire? What happens to the people who try to help him?" Answers: "The lord orders the cage with the duck to be cast into the kitchen garden. A kitchen maid feels sorry for the duck and releases him. Then the lord blames a male servant for releasing the bird. Both the male and female servants are eventually sentenced to death for their actions."

5. *Resolution of the problem and new circumstances:* "Does life return to the way it was before for both the ducks and the servants? What final effect does the incident have on the ducks and the servants?" Answers: "The duck returns to his home but does not forget the people who saved him. We must infer this information from the actions of the reunited ducks when they transform themselves into Imperial messengers, save the servants from execution, take them to a new hut in the woods, and finally reveal themselves to the now happy man and woman. The illustrations at the end of the book showing an elderly couple suggest that the man and woman live happily in freedom."

Third day: Read another folktale such as Robert D. San Souci's *The Talking Eggs: A Folktale from the American South* (Caldecott Honor, Black). This time, stop at the beginning of each new stage in the story grammar and ask an appropriate generic question such as, "Where and when does the story take place? What are the normal circumstances?" Immediately ask the students to provide questions that are specific to the story, such as, "Where and when does *The Talking Eggs* take place? What are the circumstances of the characters in the beginning of *The Talking Eggs*?" Stop at the end of that stage in the story grammar and ask the students to provide answers to the previous question. For example, *"The Talking Eggs* takes place a long time ago on a very poor farm. We know that the farm is very poor because the author says it looks like 'the tail end of bad luck.' That means that bad things have happened to the farm and it is probably run down and does not produce much food or many animals. The farm is in a southern setting because palm trees are shown in the illustrations. The normal circumstances include Blanch, a sweet girl who does all the work; Rose, her bad-tempered sister who is lazy and wants to be rich; and their mother who prefers Rose and Rose's dreams of wealth without working." Continue stopping at the beginning of each phase, ask a generic question, ask students to provide a story specific question, read to the end of the stage, and ask the students to answer the question.

Fourth and fifth days: Follow the same procedures with additional folktales, but do not ask the generic questions at the beginning of each stage. As you read the story, stop in the appropriate places and ask the students what they would like to know. Allow the students to ask and answer their own questions.

Sixth and seventh days: Give more responsibility to the students for their active comprehension by dividing the class into groups of four or five students. Ask each group to read additional stories, generate their own questions, and answer their questions. Observe the groups and help them when required.

Eighth and ninth days: Follow the same procedure as for days six and seven except divide the class into pairs.

Tenth day: Each student works individually, reads a story, writes down questions, and answers questions.

The above comprehension strategy developed by Singer and Simonsen emphasizes the transfer of responsibility for questioning from the teacher to the students. Anthony and Raphael (1989) reinforce this concept of transferring questioning strategies when they state, "Research in classrooms confirms that the most effective way to bring about student control of a strategy is through an instructional sequence in which independent use is preceded by direct and guided practice" (p. 254). This approach begins with direct instruction and modeling in which teachers explain the strategy and then perform or model the task while thinking aloud, making their mental processes visible to the students. Then teachers consider how they created their own meaning by asking and answering questions such as, "What do I know about this question from my own personal experiences and from my previous reading? How should I use my own experiences to gain meaning from the text?" Students then take part in guided practice until they are able to ask and answer most of their own questions.

Making Predictions

Good readers use cues in the text and their own prior knowledge to make predictions. Texts can be in the form of predictable books in which story structures, repetitive phrases, language style, various literary devices, and illustrations encourage students to predict what will happen next. Stories such as "The Three Billy Goats Gruff" have predictable story structures and plot developments. Books such as Mem Fox's *Hattie and the Fox* and Michael Rosen's *We're Going on a Bear Hunt* include repetitive phrases that encourage students to join in the story. Books such as Chris Van Allsburg's *The Z Was Zapped* encourage students to use their knowledge of the alphabet to predict the line that will follow each illustration. Books such as Keith Baker's *The Magic Fan* encourage students to use both knowledge of text and knowledge gained through illustrations to predict the actions of the main character. Before students can make predictions, however, they need to experience many different story structures, language styles, and literary devices so that they will know what forms to expect in the text.

Some predictions require knowledge of literary devices. For example, foreshadowing is a device that allows authors to suggest plot development before it occurs. A detail in an illustration, the mood of the story, the author's choice of words, a minor episode, or a symbol presented early in the story might foreshadow later action. Poets might use specific formats that are followed consistently through their poems. Authors might use allusions to develop insights into themes, characterizations, or conflicts.

Predictable books frequently are introduced for oral language activities and then used for reading activities. Tompkins and Weber (1983) describe the following five-step teaching strategy to direct students' attention to repetitive and predictable features of a book:

1. The teacher reads the title aloud, shows the cover illustration, and asks the students what they think the story is about.
2. The teacher reads through the first set of repetitions, stopping where the second set of repetitions begins and asking the students to predict what will happen next or what a character will say.
3. The teacher asks the students why they made their specific predictions.
4. The teacher reads the next set of repetitive patterns to allow the students to confirm or reject their predictions.
5. The teacher continues reading the selection, repeating steps 2, 3, and 4.

For example, to use this technique with Mem Fox's cumulative tale *Hattie and the Fox,* read the title, pointing to each word. Point to the cover illustration and ask students what they think the story will be about. Through discussion, encourage the students to predict that Hattie is a hen because a hen's picture is on the cover, that the story is about a fox and a hen because the word *fox* is in the title, and that the story includes a confrontation between the fox and the hen because we know from other stories that the fox and hen are usually enemies. Expand the predictions by recalling other stories that are in the students' backgrounds that give hints to the possible characterizations of fox and hen such as "The Cock and the Mouse and the Little Red Hen" (a folktale found in Anne Rockwell's *The Three Bears and 15 Other Stories).* To help confirm these initial predictions, turn to the title page, which shows a fox lurking behind a tree.

During the second step, read the first three pages of the text. These pages introduce the main character, a big black hen named Hattie; the beginning of a cumulative description of the hidden fox; and the repetitive responses of the various farm animals. Read the beginning of the fourth page of the text, "And Hattie said, . . ." Stop here and ask the students what they think Hattie will say. Tell the students to look at the illustrations because the illustrator is providing hints about what Hattie will say. Turn the page and ask the students to predict the responses of the goose, pig, sheep, horse, and cow.

During the third step, ask the students to provide reasons for their predictions. The students should notice that the illustrator helps with the predictions by showing only a hidden nose in the first series of illustrations and increasing the view to a nose and eyes in the second series. Likewise, if students have had frequent experiences with repetitive text, they will expect that the animals will use the same language during the second series.

Next, read the text to allow the students to confirm or reject their predictions. Continue the process, because with each repetition Hattie sees a little more of the fox's body. Students enjoy this book because they quickly catch on to the cumulative action and the repetitive responses of the animals. They easily predict the conclusion in which the fox acts in a predictable manner and the animals change their complacent responses.

Hattie and the Fox is equally successful with the beginning reading approach recommended by McCracken and McCracken (1986). After reading a predictable book several times to students, they encourage the students to join in the reading. They use pictures to help the students follow the sequence. Then, they introduce the students to the text by printing the repetitive portion on the chalkboard or word cards in a pocket chart. They point to the words as the students say the lines.

Next, the students match the words on the word chart or chalkboard with a second, identical set of word cards. If the words form a refrain, they either place the whole refrain on the chart while the students match the words by placing identical words on top of the cards, or they create the first line of the refrain while the students produce the next lines. They repeat this activity several times, to provide many opportunities for the students to read the text.

Finally, they place the story on phrase cards in the pocket chart, and have the children match the phrases to pictures that represent each phrase. They continue this activity as the students build and rebuild the entire story, providing many opportunities for individual and group reading practice.

Additional books that can be used for these activities, because they contain either predictable plots or repetitive language, include: Arnold Lobel's *A Rose in My Garden,* Michael Rosen's *We're Going on a Bear Hunt,* Glen Rounds' *I Know An Old Lady Who Swallowed a Fly* and *Old MacDonald Had a Farm,* and Nicki Weiss' *Where Does the Brown Bear Go?*

This text develops lessons that encourage students to make predictions. Some of these lessons will be appropriate for the beginning reader, while other lessons will show how to encourage older students to use their knowledge of literary devices and to make educated predictions.

Using Direct Teaching Strategies

As shown in chapter 1, students need both teacher-led instruction and opportunities to read and respond to literature independently. The core books are frequently identified as the texts that encourage teachers and students to analyze the literature. Research cited earlier showed the advantages of presenting lessons in which teachers help students comprehend the various structures, genres, and elements.

Research in both reading and writing show the desired effects of some teacher-led instruction. For example, many of the research studies that Hillocks (1986) identifies as the most effective approaches for teaching writing include approaches in which the teacher introduces a concept in a short, structured lesson and then asks the students to apply that concept during writing and revision. As an example of an effective strategy, Hillocks points to Sager's (1973) study in which she increases the ability of sixth-grade students to elaborate details. Throughout this text we will develop examples of teacher-directed strategies that improve understanding of literature and help students make the reading and writing connections.

Looking for Details to Help in Making Inferences.   Developing an understanding of inferences is one of the most difficult tasks of the reading teacher. Literature is full of inferences through such techniques as describing actions of characters, dialogue among characters, and thoughts of characters to develop characterizations. These characterizations are rarely stated literally. Instead students must use clues developed by the author to understand the many facets of a character's personality. Authors also use similes and metaphors to make comparisons and to enrich understanding of poetry and other types of literature. Cause-and-effect relationships can be inferred in historical fiction, biography, and other nonfiction. Numerous lessons developed in this text encourage students to search for important details they need to make inferences. The modeling activities are especially valuable for improving this ability.

Responding to Widening Reading Achievement

As students progress into the upper grades, the reading achievements within a specific grade usually become wider. For example, after testing the reading achievements in five sixth-grade classes, a group of researchers and I discovered that the reading levels ranged from second grade through high school. These vast differences provide challenges for any teacher. The program must include a wide range of literature from each genre, which can be read to and by students, and which meet the instructional goals for developing literary appreciation and understanding. Books designated as core books, extended books, and recreational books also need to cover these varied reading abilities. Many upper-grade and middle-school teachers find that they must include considerable oral reading in their programs, especially if the students are to have opportunities to enjoy the classics and Newbery Medal and Honor Award books. This text will provide examples of lessons and books for lower-elementary, middle-elementary, upper-elementary, and middle-school students. Recommended books are included for core selections as well as for extended and recreational books.

CREATING MEANING THROUGH WRITING

Literature is often a springboard for writing as students write personal, critical, and analytical responses to literature, and create their own literary forms such as short stories, poems, and autobiographies. Studies such as those conducted by Daniels (1990) and Konopak and Martin (1990) report that writing associated with literature programs improves the achievement of the students and their attitudes toward various content subjects.

Educators who recommend practices associated with writing and literature emphasize several types of writing. For example, Swope and Thompson (1986) state that after students read literature, "they need to connect the literature to their own experience" (p. 76). They suggest a reader-response journal that allows students to make three types of responses to each selection they read: emotional, associative, and figurative. For the emotional response, students emphasize their immediate feelings about the literature and analyze their reactions. For the associative response, students relate the reading to various subconscious experiences. Swope and Thompson recommend that students make at least five associations to ensure sufficient personal connections. For the figurative response, students identify a feature of the literature such as a word, phrase, theme, or motif and explore why that feature attracted their attention.

Fiderer (1986) recommends a personal written reaction to literature by encouraging students to write directly on the page. She duplicates pages from the reading assignment and asks students to write their immediate reactions. In this way, students have an active, written dialogue with the author as they read. They might ask questions that are not answered for them, respond favorably or unfavorably to content, respond to certain words or phrases, agree or disagree with statements, or share their own experiences related to the subject.

Students can respond to literature in many more ways through writing. For example, they might choose a character from a book and keep a dialogue journal with that character. They can write questions they would like to ask about the character's feelings, beliefs, motives, or actions. They might respond to the character's actions and feelings by telling the character how they felt when they read about the character. They also can tell the character how they might have acted or felt in the same situation or even give advice to the character. Students frequently enjoy giving a character advice in the early part of a book and then analyzing how closely their advice fits the changing plot of the story. They also can decide if the early advice would have helped or hindered the character.

Throughout this book, there will be numerous recommendations for writing associated with literature. Some suggestions will involve expressive writing in which students write an aesthetic response to the literature. Other suggestions will encourage students to use literature to motivate imaginative and poetic writing or to develop expository writing especially related to nonfictional literature.

How important is the quality of the literature that is used before any of these writing activities? Research indicates that the quality of the literature that precedes the writing assignment influences the quality of the writing. For example, Dressel (1990) found that the stories written by fifth-grade students who heard and discussed higher quality literature had higher literary quality and genre development than did stories written by students who heard and discussed lesser quality literature. Consequently, the literature selected for any of the facets of the literature-based program is critical.

SELECTING LITERATURE FOR A LITERATURE-BASED PROGRAM

When selecting the literature for a school curriculum, teachers should consider students' development, reading abilities, listening abilities, and interests as well as literary standards, curricular needs, and genre and cultural balance. Throughout this book we will try to recommend literature that will best develop the objectives of the literature-based reading program. Consequently, the strengths of the specific literature to develop the objectives will be considered as well as the interest levels of the students. In this section we will briefly review some of the additional sources that you can use to select literature that meets the needs of your students.

The following are some examples of major children's literature texts, which are the best sources of literature.

1. *Through the Eyes of a Child: An Introduction to Children's Literature* (Norton, 1991): Provides evaluative criteria; recommendations for literature; and classroom applications for picture books, traditional literature, fantasy, poetry, contemporary realistic fiction, historical fiction, multicultural books, biography, and informational literature. The works discussed range from books for younger children to books for students through the middle school.
2. *Children's Literature* (Huck, Hepler, and Hickman, 1987): Contains chapters on the major literature genres.
3. *Children and Books* (Sutherland and Arbuthnot, 1991): Discusses the major authors who write in each of the genres.
4. *Literature and the Child* (Cullinan. 1989): Contains chapter on the major literature genres.

The following are examples of books that look at specific areas or specific needs of students:

1. *For Love of Reading: A Parent's Guide to Encouraging Young Readers from Infancy Through Age 5* (Rudman and Pearce, 1988): Explores various stages in the development of young children and recommends books that enhance that development.
2. *Picture Books for Children* (Cianciolo, 1990): Focuses on illustrated texts.
3. *Choosing Books for Children: A Commonsense Guide* (Hearne, 1990): Provides recommendations for parents.
4. *Children's Literature: An Issues Approach* (Rudman, 1984): Discusses and recommends books in areas such as sibling relationships, death, special needs, adoption, and gender.

5. *High Interest, Easy Reading* (Matthews, 1988): Recommends books with high interest and lower vocabulary for junior and senior high school students.

6. The journal *Social Education:* Publishes notable Children's Trade Books in the Field of Social Studies each year.

7. *Best Books for Children* (Gillespie and Gilbert, 1990): Provides brief annotations for books according to subject.

8. *The New Read-Aloud Handbook* (Trelease, 1989): Provides guidelines for selecting and reading books to students up to age 12.

Literature journals are good sources for current books as well as for specialized lists. *Booklist, Hornbook, School Library Journal,* and *Bulletin of the Center for Children's Books* include reviews. They star reviews of books that the editors think are of exceptional quality. *Booklist* also publishes special lists of books in various editions. These lists focus on varied subjects such as storytelling sources, picture books for older students, books published in foreign languages, and contemporary issues. *The School Library Journal* publishes a best-books list each year as well as lists of specific subjects. Other helpful journals include *The Reading Teacher, Language Arts,* and *The New Advocate.* A list of "Children's Choices" is published each year in *The Reading Teacher.*

Award-winning books and classics, whether they are read to or by students, are of special interest in reading programs. These books encourage students and teachers to explore and discuss selections considered the best in their fields. For example, the Caldecott Medal and Honor Awards, presented annually since 1938, are awarded to the illustrators of the most distinguished books published in the United States. The Newbery Medal and Honor Awards, presented annually since 1922, are awarded for the most distinguished contributions to children's literature published in the United States. The Children's Book Award, presented since 1975, is awarded by the International Reading Association to a children's author whose work shows unusual promise. The Coretta Scott King Award is presented to a black author and a black illustrator for outstanding inspirational contributions to children's literature. In Canada, the Canadian Library Award is given annually to a children's book of literary merit written by a Canadian citizen and to a book of literary merit published in French. In Britain, the Kate Greenaway Medal is awarded to the most distinguished work in illustration and the Carnegie Medal is awarded to an outstanding book first published in the United Kingdom.

A list of Touchstone Books is available from the Children's Literature Association, publisher of the *Children's Literature Association Quarterly.* These books are considered so noteworthy that they should be used as the standards by which to evaluate all literature. Following are examples of classics that appear on the Touchstone list:

1. Folktales of the Brothers Grimm and Charles Perrault.

2. Picture books such as Robert McCloskey's *Make Way for Ducklings* and Kate Greenaway's *A Apple Pie.*

3. Realistic fiction such as Frances Hodgson Burnett's *The Secret Garden* and L. M. Montgomery's *Anne of Green Gables.*

4. Fantasy such as E. B. White's *Charlotte's Web* and Kenneth Grahame's *The Wind in the Willows.*

5. Poetry such as Stephen Dunning, Edward Lueders, and Hugh Smith's *Reflections on a Gift of Watermelon Pickle . . . And Other Modern Verse.*

6. Historical fiction such as Esther Forbes' *Johnny Tremain* and Laura Ingalls Wilder's "The Little House" series.

Meeting the Needs of Culturally Diverse Students

America is a multicultural nation, including people with European backgrounds, Native Americans, Black Americans, Hispanics, and Asians, and the selection of books should reflect our varied cultural and literary heritage. A heightened sensitivity to the needs of all people in American society has led to the realization that the curriculum should heighten self-esteem and create a respect for the individuals, contributions, and values of all cultures.

Experts in multicultural education frequently emphasize the importance of using literature to increase cultural awareness. For example, Tway (1989) maintains that multicultural literature is essential in the classroom because it meets the needs of students and helps them grow in understanding of themselves and others. Piper (1986) found that using traditional folklore from various cultural sources helps students develop awareness of different language and cultural backgrounds. Barnes (1991) emphasizes the importance of using children's literature from numerous cultures to teach anthropological concepts such as enculturation, acculturation, rites of passage, life cycle, and race.

Through carefully selected and shared literature, students learn to understand and appreciate a literary heritage that comes from many backgrounds. Through this literature, students learn to identify with people who created the stories. From the past, they discover folktales, fables, myths, and legends that clarify the values and beliefs of the people. They discover the stories on which whole cultures have been founded. From the present they discover the threads that weave the past with the present and the themes and values that continue to be important.

Of equal value are the personal gains acquired by students when they read great works from their own cultural backgrounds and those of other cultures. They gain understandings about different beliefs and value systems. They develop social sensitivity to the needs of others and realize that people have similarities as well as differences. Students gain aesthetic appreciation as they learn to understand and respect the artistic contributions of people from many cultural backgrounds. Multicultural literature helps students expand their understanding of geography and natural history, increase their understanding of historical and sociological change, broaden their appreciation for literary techniques used by authors from different cultural backgrounds, and improve their reading, writing, and thinking abilities.

Providing information about European and white American cultures is not difficult. The majority of the books listed on the Newbery, Caldecott, Carnegie, Greenaway, and Touchstone lists reflect these two cultural backgrounds. Several concerns should be noted, however, when selecting literature from other cultural backgrounds. Three problems face teachers who are choosing literature about blacks, Native Americans, Hispanics, and Asians. First, although the number of books in these areas is increasing, there is still a disproportionately small number that deals in any way with minorities (Frederick, 1990). Native American and black literature is easier to locate because more books are available.

Second, fewer books exist that are written in English about Hispanic cultures or the native cultures of Spanish-speaking regions, and the books that are available tend to go out of print quickly (Norton, 1986). An analysis of two recent lists of notable books shows the difficulty in locating high quality multicultural literature. The 55 titles on The Best Books of the Year 1989 (Jones, Toth & Gerhardt, 1989) include one black, one Native-American, and no Hispanic works. The 67 titles on the 1990 Notable Children's Books for 1990 (Booklist Committee, 1990) include seven black, two Native-American, and no Hispanic works.

Third, careful evaluation is necessary to avoid choosing books that contain stereotypic views of minority cultures and individuals. A brief review of children's literature written before the late 1960s suggests stereotypes for each minority. For example, books about blacks frequently characterized them as physically unattractive, musical, dependent on whites, religious with superstitious beliefs, and required to select life goals that benefit black people. Native Americans often were characterized as savage, depraved, and cruel or noble, proud, silent, and close to nature. Their culture often was shown as inferior and not worth retaining. Hispanic literature often contained recurring themes related to poverty, intervention of Anglos in problem-solving situations, and superficial treatment of problems. Finally, Asian-American literature frequently suggested that Asians looked alike, lived in quaint communities in the midst of large cities, and clung to outworn, alien customs. Because of these negative stereotypes, literature, especially the literature published before the late 1960s, must be carefully evaluated. Lists of evaluation criteria for black, Native-American, Hispanic, and Asian literature are found in Norton's *The Effective Teaching of Language Arts* (1989, pp. 561–564). Recommended lists of books are published in Norton's *Through the Eyes of a Child: An Introduction to Children's Literature* (1991) and in Norton's "Teaching Multicultural Literature in the Reading Curriculum" (1990).

Meeting the Interests of Students

Understanding why students read what they read is necessary if we are to help them select books that stimulate their interests and enjoyment. This is especially important when helping students choose texts for individual, recreational reading. To learn about students' interests, teachers can review studies of student interests and prefer-ences, talk to students, and evaluate student responses on interest inventories.

Each year a joint project of the International Reading Association and the Children's Book Council allows about 10,000 students from around the United States to evaluate children's books published during that year. Their reactions are recorded, and a research team uses this information to compile a list of Children's Choices. A look at these lists of favorites can give teachers a better idea of the characteristics of books that appeal to students. Sebesta (1979) identified characteristics of some of these books. His evaluation produced the following conclusions:

1. Plots of the Children's Choices are faster paced than those found in other books.

2. Young children enjoy reading about nearly any topic if the information is presented in detail. The topic itself might be less important than interest studies have indicated; specifics rather than topics seem to underlie children's preferences.

3. Children like detailed descriptions of settings; they want to know exactly how the place looks and feels before the main action occurs.

4. Children like different plot structures. Some stories on the Children's Choices lists have a central focus with a carefully arranged cause-and-effect plot; others have plots that meander, with unconnected episodes.

5. Children do not like sad books.

6. Children seem to like some books that explicitly teach a lesson, even though critics usually frown on didactic books.

7. Warmth was the most outstanding quality of books that children preferred. Children enjoy books in which the characters like each other, express their feelings in things they say and do, and sometimes act selflessly.

Sebesta believes this information should be used to help students select books and to stimulate reading and discussions. For example, students' attention can be drawn to the warmth, pace, or descriptions in a story to encourage them to become involved with the story.

The Children's Choices lists also suggest particular types of stories that appeal to young readers. For example, analysis of a recent list showed that the "beginning independent reading" category contains comical stories about more-or-less-realistic family situations, humorous animal stories, stories that develop emotional experiences, action-filled fantasies, traditional stories, counting books, rhymes, and riddles. The "younger reader" category includes realistic stories about families, friends, school, and personal problems; animal stories; fantasies; fast-paced adventures; folktales; and humorous stories. Stories chosen by students in the middle grades include realistic stories about sibling rivalry, peer acceptance, fears, and not conforming to stereotypes; fantasies; suspense; and humorous stories. Popular information books include factual and nonsensical advice about human health, factual information about animals, and biographical information about sports stars. The Children's Choices includes books from a wide variety of genres. Notice how easily these categories of books could be used for focus during Recreational Reading Groups.

Research also indicates that students' reading interests are influenced by their reading ability. Swanton's (1984) survey comparing gifted students with students of average ability reports that gifted students prefer mysteries (43 percent), fiction (41 percent), science fiction (29), and fantasy (18 percent). The top four choices for students of average ability were mysteries (47 percent), comedy/humor (27 percent), realistic fiction (23 percent), and adventure (18 percent). Gifted students indicated that they liked "science fiction and fantasy because of the challenge it presented, as well as its relationship to Dungeons and Dragons" (p. 100). Gifted students listed Lloyd Alexander, J. R. R. Tolkien, C. S. Lewis, and Judy Blume as favorite authors. Average students listed Judy Blume, Beverly Cleary, and Jack London. As you can see, there are similarities and differences within these favorites. Many additional types of literature might become favorites if an understanding and knowledgeable teacher provides opportunities for students to listen to, read, and discuss literature.

Although information from research and Children's Choices provides general ideas about what subjects and authors students of certain ages and reading abilities prefer, teachers should guard against developing stereotypical views about preferences and supplement their information by asking questions of their students. Such questions, perhaps during an informal conversation, can uncover students' specific and unusual interests. Ask students what they like to do and read about, note the information on cards, and find several books that might meet these interests. Teachers usually need some way of recording the information when they are working with several students. Teachers can develop interest inventories in which students answer questions about their favorite hobbies, books, authors, sports, television shows, and other interests. Teachers can write down young students' answers, and older students usually can read the questionnaire themselves and write their own responses. Such an inventory might include some of the questions asked in Figure 2.3. (Changes should be made according to age levels, and additional information can be discovered by asking students why they like certain books.) After the interest inventory is complete, the findings can serve as the basis for helping students select books that interest them and extend their enjoyment of literature.

FIGURE 2.3 An informal interest inventory.

1. What do you like to do when you get home from school?
   _____

2. What do you like to do on Saturday?
   _____

3. Do you like to watch television? _____ If you do, what are the names of your favorite programs?
   _____

4. Do you have a hobby? _____ If you do, what is your hobby? _____
   _____

5. Do you like to make or collect things? _____ If you do, what have you made or collected? _____
   _____

6. What is your favorite sport? _____

7. What games do you like best? _____

8. Do you like to go to the movies? _____
   If you do, what was your favorite movie? _____
   _____

9. Do you have a pet? _____ If you do, what is your pet? _____

10. Where have you spent your summer vacations? _____
    _____

FIGURE 2.3 *continued*

11. Have you ever made a special study of rocks? _____ space? _____

    plants? _____ animals? _____ travel? _____ dinosaurs? _____

    other? _____

12. What are your favorite subjects in school?

    art? _____ handwriting? _____ social studies? _____

    physical education? _____ science? _____ music? _____

    creative writing? _____ spelling? _____ arithmetic? _____

    other? _____

13. What subject is the hardest for you? _____

14. What kinds of books do you like to have someone read to you?

    animal stories? _____ fairy tales? _____ true stories? _____ science fiction? _____

    adventure? _____ mystery stories? _____ sport stories? _____ poems? _____

    humorous stories? _____ other kinds of stories? _____

15. What is your favorite book that someone read to you? _____

16. What kinds of books do you like to read by yourself?

    animals? _____ picture books? _____ fairy tales? _____

    true stories? _____ science fiction? _____ adventures? _____

    mystery stories? _____ sport stories? _____ poems? _____

    funny stories? _____ other kinds of stories? _____

17. What is your favorite book that you read by yourself? _____

18. Would you rather read a book by yourself or have someone read to you?

    _____

19. Name a book that you read this week.

    _____

20. What books or magazines do you have at home?

    _____

21. Do you ever go to the library? _____

    How often do you go to the library? _____

    Do you have a library card? _____

From: *The Effective Teaching of Language Arts* (p. 377) by D.E. Norton, 1989 Columbus, OH: Merrill.

REFERENCES

AMBRULEVICH, A. K. (1986). An analysis of the levels of thinking required by questions in selected literature anthologies for grades eight, nine, and ten. *Dissertation Abstracts International, 47,* 03A (University Microfilms No. 86–13, 043)

ANDERSON, R. C. (1985). Role of the reader's schema in comprehension, learning, and memory. In H. Singer and R. Ruddell (Eds.), *Theoretical models and processes of reading* (3rd ed.). Newark, DE: International Reading Association.

ANTHONY, H. & RAPHAEL, T. (1989). Using questioning strategies to promote students' active comprehension of content area material. In D. Lapp, J. Flood, and N. Farnam (Eds.), *Content area reading and learning.* Englewood Cliffs, NJ: Prentice Hall.

BARR, R. & SADOW, M. (1985). *Reading diagnosis for teachers.* New York: Longman.

BARRETT, T. (1972). Taxonomy of reading comprehension. *Reading 360 Monograph.* Lexington, MA: Ginn.

BARNES, B. R. (1991, January). Using children's literature in the early anthropology curriculum. *Social Education,* 17–18.

BERGER, A. (1989). Ways of activating prior knowledge for content area reading. In D. Lapp, J. Flood, and N. Farnam (Eds.), *Content area reading and learning* (pp. 270–282). Englewood Cliffs, NJ: Prentice Hall.

BOOKLIST COMMITTEE. (1990). Notable children's books, 1990. *Booklist, 86,* pp. 1478–1479.

CALFEE, R. & DRUM, P. (1986). Research on teaching reading. In M. C. Wittrock (Ed.), *Handbook of research on teaching* (3rd ed.) (pp. 804–849). New York: Macmillan.

CIANCIOLO, P. (1990). *Picture books for children* (3rd ed.) Chicago: American Library Association.

CIANCIOLO, P. (1990, November). Responding to picture books. Paper presented to the National Council of Teachers of English, Atlanta.

CULLINAN, B. (1989). *Literature and the child.* San Diego: Harcourt Brace Jovanovich.

DANIELS, J. P. (1990). Reading and writing to learn: The effects of a literature program and summary writing strategies on achievement in and attitude toward social studies content among fourth-grade students. *Dissertation Abstracts International, 50,* 11A (University Microfilms No. 90–00, 793).

DIAKIW, J. W. (1990). Children's literature and global education: Understanding the developing world. *The Reading Teacher, 43,* 296–300.

DRESSEL, J. H. (1990). The effects of listening to and discussing different qualities of children's literature on the narrative writing of fifth graders. *Research in the Teaching of English, 24,* 397–414.

EARLY, M. & ERICSON, B. O. (1988). The act of reading. In B. F. Nelms (Ed.), *Literature in the classroom: Readers, texts, and contexts* (pp. 31–44). Urbana, IL: National Council of Teachers of English.

FEITELSON, D.; KITA, B.; & GOLDSTEIN, Z. (1986). Effects of listening to series stories on first graders' comprehension and use of language. *Research in the Teaching of English, 20,* 339–355.

FIDERER, A. (1986). Write on the reading! In J. Golub (Ed.), *Classroom practices in teaching English: Activities to promote critical thinking* (pp. 97–101). Urbana, IL: National Council of Teachers of English.

FIVE, C. L. (1988). From workbook to workshop: Increasing children's involvement in the reading process. *The New Advocate, 1,* 103–113.

FREDERICK, H. V. (1990, February 21). In search of multi-ethnic books. *Christian Science Monitor.*

FREPPON, P. A. (1990). An investigation of children's concepts of the purpose and nature of reading in different instructional settings. *Dissertation Abstracts International, 50,* 10A, (University Microfilms No. 85–08, 451).

GARDENER, M. (1988). An educator's concerns about the California initiative. *The New Advocate, 1,* pp. 250–253.

GILLESPIE, J. & GILBERT, C. (1985). *Best books for children.* New York: R. R. Bowker.

GIROUX, H. (1990, June). New directions in education. Paper presented at New Directions in Education Conference, College Station, TX.

GORDON, C. J. (1985). Modeling inference awareness across the curriculum. *Journal of Reading, 28,* 444–447.

HEARNE, B. (1990). *Choosing books for children: A commonsense guide.* New York: Delacorte.

HEIMLICH, J. E. & PITTELMAN, S. D. (1986). *Semantic mapping: Classroom applications.* Newark, DE: International Reading Association.

HIEBERT, A. & COLT, J. (1989). Patterns of literature-based reading instruction. *The Reading Teacher, 43,* pp. 14–20.

HILLOCKS, G. (1986). *Research on written composition: New directions for teaching.* Urbana, IL: National Conference on Research in English.

HUCK, C., HEPLER, S., & HICKMAN, J. (1987). *Children's literature.* New York: Holt, Rinehart & Winston.

JOHNSON, D. D. & PEARSON, P. D. (1984). *Teaching reading vocabulary.* New York: Holt, Rinehart & Winston.

JONES, T., TOTH, L., & GERHARDT, L. (1989). Best books of the year. *School Library Journal, 35,* 36–41.

KONOPAK, B. C., MARTIN, S. H., & MARTIN, M. A. (1990). Using a writing strategy to enhance sixth grade students' comprehension of content material. *Journal of Reading Behavior, 22,* 1–18.

MATTHEWS, D. & COMMITTEE TO REVISE HIGH INTEREST-EASY READING. (1988). *High interest-easy reading.* Urbana, IL: National Council of Teachers of English.

MAY, J. P. (1987). Creating a school wide literature program: A case study. *Children's Literature Association Quarterly, 12,* pp. 135–137.

McCRACKEN, R. & McCRACKEN, M. (1986). *Stories, songs, and poetry to teach reading and writing: Literacy through language.* Chicago: American Library Association.

McNAMARA, J. & NORTON, D. E. (1987). *An evaluation of the multiethnic reading/language arts program for low achieving elementary and junior high school students.* Final research report, College Station: Texas A&M University College of Education.

MEEKS, M. (1983). *Achieving literacy: Longitudinal case studies of adolescents learning to read.* London: Routledge & Kegan Paul.

MORROW, L. M. & RAND, M. K. (1991). Promoting literacy during play by designing early childhood classroom environments. *The Reading Teacher, 44,* pp. 396–402.

MYERS, M. & GRAY, J. (1983). *Theory and practice in teaching of composition: Processing, distancing, and modeling.* Urbana, IL: National Council of Teachers of English.

NORTON, D. E. (1982). Using a webbing process to develop children's literature units. *Language Arts, 59,* pp. 348–356.

NORTON, D. E. (1986). The rise and fall of ethnic literature. Paper presented at the annual meeting of the National Conference of Teachers of English, Phoenix, AZ.

NORTON, D. E. (1989). *The effective teaching of language arts.* Columbus, OH: Merrill.

NORTON, D. E. (1990). Teaching multicultural literature in the reading curriculum. *The Reading Teacher, 44,* pp. 28–40.

NORTON, D. E. (1991). *Through the eyes of a child: An introduction to children's literature,* Columbus, OH: Merrill.

NORTON, D. E. & McNAMARA, J. (1987). *An evaluation of the BISD/TAMU multiethnic reading program.* College Station: Texas A&M University, College of Education.

PEARSON, P. D. (1984). Asking questions about stories. In A. J. Harris & E. R. Sipay (Eds.), *Readings on reading instruction* (pp. 274–283). New York: Longman.

PEARSON, P. D. & CAMPERELL, K. (1985). Comprehension of text structures. In H. Singer & R. Ruddell (Eds.), *Theoretical Models and Processes of Reading* (pp. 323–342). Newark, DE. International Reading Association.

PIPER, D. (1986). Language growth in the multiethnic classroom. *Language Arts, 63,* pp. 23–36.

PRATER, D. C. & TERRY, C. A. (1985). The effects of a composing model on fifth grade students' reading comprehension. Paper presented at the American Educational Research Association, (ERIC Document Reproduction Service No. ED 254 825).

PROBST, R. (1989). Teaching the reading of literature. In D. Lapp, J. Flood, & N. Farnan (Eds.), Content area reading and learning: Instructional strategies (pp. 179–186). Englewood Cliffs, NJ: Prentice Hall.

PURVES, A. (1990). *The scribal society: An essay on literacy and schooling in the information age.* New York: Longman.

PURVES, A. & MONSON, D. (1984). *Experiencing children's literature.* Glenview, IL: Scott, Foresman.

ROEHLER, L. & DUFFY, G. G. (1984). Direct explanation of comprehension processes. In L. R. Roehler & J. Mason (Eds.), *Comprehension instruction* (pp. 265–280). New York: Longman.

ROSENBLATT, L. (1985). Language, literature, and values. In S. N. Tchudi (Ed.), *Language, schooling, and society* (pp. 64–80). Upper Montclair, NJ: Boyton/Cook.

RUDMAN, M. K. (1984). *Children's literature: An issues approach.* New York: Longman.

RUDMAN, M. K. & PEARCE, A. M. (1988). *For the love of reading: A parent's guide to encouraging young readers from infancy through age 5.* Mount Vernon, NY: Consumers Union.

SAGER, C. (1973). Improving the quality of written composition through pupil use of rating scale. *Dissertation Abstracts International, 34,* 04A.

SAWYER, W. (1987). Literature and literacy: A review of research. *Language Arts, 64,* pp. 33–39.

SEBESTA, S. (1979). What do young people think about the literature they read? *Reading Newsletter, 8,* Rockleigh, NJ: Allyn & Bacon.

SINGER, H. & SIMONSEN, S. (1989). Comprehension and instruction in learning from text. In D. Lapp, J. Flood, & N. Farnan (Eds.), *Content area reading and learning: Instructional strategies* (pp. 43–57). Englewood Cliffs, NJ: Prentice Hall.

SUTHERLAND, Z. & ARBUTHNOT, M. H. (1991). *Children and books.* Glenview, IL: Scott, Foresman.

SWANTON, S. (1984). Minds alive: What and why gifted students read for pleasure. *School Library Journal, 30,* 99–102.

SWOPE, J. W. & THOMPSON, E. H. (1986). Three R's for critical thinking about literature: Reading, 'riting, and responding. In Jeff Golub (Ed.), *Classroom practices in teaching english: Activities to promote critical thinking.* (pp. 75–79). Urbana, IL: National Council of Teachers of English.

TABA, H., LEVINE, S., & ELZEY, F. F. (1964). *Thinking in elementary school children: Cooperative research project number 1574.* Washington, DC: U.S. Department of Health, Education, and Welfare, Research Program of the Office of Education.

TAXEL, J. (1988). Notes from the editor. *The New Advocate, 1,* pp. 73–74.

TOMPKINS. G. & WEBER, M. (1983). What will happen next? Using predictable books with young children. *The Reading Teacher, 36,* pp. 498–502.

TOMS-BRONOWSKI, S. (1983). An investigation of the effectiveness of selected vocabulary teaching strategies with intermediate grade level students. *Dissertation Abstracts International, 44,* 1405A (University Microfilms No. 83–16, 238).

TRELEASE, J. (1989). *The new read-aloud handbook.* New York: Penguin.

TWAY, E. (1989). Dimensions of multicultural literature for children. In M. K. Rudman (Ed.), *Children's literature: Resource for the classroom* (pp. 109–138). Needham Heights, MA: Christopher-Gordon.

ZARRILLO, J. (1989). Teachers' interpretations of literature-based reading. *The Reading Teacher, 43,* pp. 22–28.

CHILDREN'S LITERATURE REFERENCES*

AGEE, JON. *The Incredible Painting of Felix Clousseau.* New York: Farrar, Straus & Giroux, 1988 (I: 5–8).

BAKER, KEITH. *The Magic Fan.* San Diego: Harcourt Brace Jovanovich, 1989 (I: 5–8).

BAYLOR, BYRD. *The Best Town in the World.* Illustrated by Ronald Himler. New York: Scribner's, 1983 (I: all).

BEATTY, PATRICIA. *Wait for Me, Watch for Me, Eula Bee.* New York: Morrow, 1978 (I: 12+).

BLOS, JOAN W. *A Gathering of Days: A New England Girl's Journal, 1830–32.* New York: Scribner's, 1979 (I: 8–14).

BRINK, CAROL RYRIE. *Caddie Woodlawn.* Illustrated by Trina Schart Hyman. New York: Macmillan, 1935, 1963, 1973 (I: 8–12).

BURNETT, FRANCES HODGSON. *The Secret Garden.* Illustrated by Tasha Tudor. Philadelphia, 1911, 1938, 1962 (I: 8–14).

BURTON, VIRGINIA LEE. *The Little House.* Boston: Houghton Mifflin, 1942 (I: 5–8).

CAZET, DENYS. *A Fish in His Pocket.* New York: Watts, 1987 (I: 5–8).

CHAUCER, GEOFFREY. *Canterbury Tales.* Adapted by Barbara Cohen. Illustrated by Trina Schart Hyman. New York: Lothrop, Lee & Shepard, 1988 (I: 8–14).

CHAUCER, GEOFFREY. *The Canterbury Tales.* Retold by Selina Hastings. Illustrated by Reg Cartwright. New York: Henry Holt, 1988 (I: 8–14).

CLEARY, BEVERLY. *Dear Mr. Henshaw.* Illustrated by Paul O. Zelinsky. New York: Morrow, 1983 (I: 9–12).

CONRAD, PAM. *My Daniel.* New York: Harper & Row, 1989 (I: 10+).

DALGLIESH, ALICE. *The Courage of Sarah Noble.* Illustrated by Leonard Weisgard. New York: Scribner's, 1954 (I: 6–9).

DUNNING, STEPHEN; LUEDERS, EDWARD; & SMITH, HUGH. *Reflections on a Gift of Watermelon Pickle . . . And Other Modern Verse.* New York: Lothrop, Lee & Shepard, 1967 (I: all).

EDMOND, W. *The Matchlock Gun.* Illustrated by John Schoenherr. Boston: Little, Brown, 1971 (I: 10+).

FORBES, ESTHER. *Johnny Tremain.* Illustrated by Lynd Ward. Boston: Houghton Mifflin, 1943 (I: 10–14).

FOX, MEM. *Hattie and the Fox.* Illustrated by Patricia Mullins. New York: Bradbury, 1987 (I: 5–8).

GRAHAME, KENNETH. *The Wind in the Willows.* Illustrated by Ernest H. Shepard. New York: Scribner's, 1908, 1933, 1953, 1983 (I: 8–14).

GREENAWAY, KATE. *A Apple Pie.* London: Warne, 1886 (I: 5–8).

GRIFALCONI, ANN. *Darkness and the Butterfly.* Boston: Little, Brown, 1987 (I: 5–8).

GRIMM, BROTHERS. *Rumpelstiltskin.* Retold and Illustrated by Paul O. Zelinksy. New York: Dutton, 1986 (I: all).

HARVEY, BRETT. *Cassie's Journey: Going West in the 1860s.* Illustrated by Deborah Kogan Ray. New York: Holiday, 1988 (I: 7–9).

_____. *My Prairie Year: Based on the Diary of Eleanor Plaisted.* Illustrated by Deborah Kogan Ray. New York: Holiday, 1986 (I: 5–10).

HOWARD, ELLEN. *Edith Herself.* New York: Atheneum, 1987 (I: 7–10).

IVIMEY, JOHN. *The Complete Story of Three Blind Mice.* Illustrated by Paul Galdone. New York: Clarion, 1987 (I: 2–8).

KEITH, HAROLD. *The Obstinate Land.* New York: Crowell, 1977 (I: 12+).

KIMMEL, ERIC. *The Chanukkah Tree.* Illustrated by Giora Garmi. New York: Holiday, 1988 (I: 5–8).

*I = Interest by age range

LASKY, KATHRYN. *Beyond the Divide*. New York: Macmillan, 1983 (I: 9+).

LINGARD, JOAN. *Tug of War*. New York: Lodestar, 1990 (I: 12+).

LOBEL, ARNOLD. *A Rose in My Garden*. Illustrated by Anita Lobel. New York: Greenwillow, 1984 (I: all).

MACAULAY, DAVID. *Castle*. Boston: Houghton Mifflin, 1977 (I: all).

MACLACHLAN, PATRICIA. *Sarah, Plain and Tall*. New York: Harper & Row, 1985 (I: 7–10).

MAHY, MARGARET. *The Great White Man-Eating Shark: A Cautionary Tale*. Illustrated by Jonathan Allen. New York: Dial, 1989 (I: 5–9).

———. *17 Kings and 42 Elephants*. New York: Dial, 1987 (I: 5–8).

MCCLOSKEY, ROBERT. *Make Way for Ducklings*. New York: Viking, 1941 (I: 5–8).

MONTGOMERY, L. M. *Anne of Green Gables*. New York: Grosset & Dunlap, 1908, 1935, 1983 (I: 10–14).

MORROW, HONORE. *On to Oregon!* Illustrated by Edward Shenton. New York: Morrow, 1926, 1948, 1954 (I: 10+).

PATERSON, KATHERINE. *The Tale of the Mandarin Ducks*. Illustrated by Leo and Diane Dillon. New York: Lodestar, 1990 (I: all).

PEET, BILL. *No Such Things*. Boston: Houghton Mifflin, 1983 (I: 5–8).

POLACCO, PATRICIA. *Meteor!* New York: Dodd, Mead, 1987 (I: 5–10).

ROCKWELL, ANNE. *The Three Bears and 15 Other Stories*. New York: Crowell, 1975 (I: 3–8).

ROSEN, MICHAEL. *We're Going on a Bear Hunt*. Illustrated by Helen Oxenbury. New York: Macmillan, 1989 (I: 5–8).

ROUNDS, GLEN. *I Know An Old Lady Who Swallowed a Fly*. New York: Holiday, 1990 (I: 3–7).

———. *Old MacDonald Had a Farm*. New York: Holiday, 1989 (I: 3–6).

SAN SOUCI, ROBERT D. *The Talking Eggs: A Folktale from the American South*. Illustrated by Jerry Pinkney. New York: Dial: 1989 (I: all).

SEUSS, DR. *If I Ran the Zoo*. New York: Random House, 1950 (I: 5–10).

SMALL, DAVID. *Imogene's Antlers*. New York: Crown, 1985 (I: 5–8).

STEVENSON, JAMES. *Could Be Worse!* New York: Greenwillow, 1977 (I: 5–8).

VAN ALLSBURG, CHRIS. *The Z Was Zapped*. Boston: Houghton Mifflin, 1987 (I: 5–8).

WEISS, NICKI. *Where Does the Brown Bear Go?* New York: Greenwillow, 1989 (I: 2–6).

WESTCOTT, NADINE. *Peanut Butter and Jelly: A Play Rhyme*. New York: Dutton, 1987 (I: 3–7).

WHITE, E. B. *Charlotte's Web*. Illustrated by Garth Williams. New York: Harper & Row, 1952 (I: 8–10).

WILDER, LAURA INGALLS. *On the Banks of Plum Creek*. Illustrated by Garth Williams. New York: Harper & Row, 1937, 1953 (I: 8–12).

———. *The Little House in the Big Woods*. Illustrated by Garth Williams. New York: Harper & Row, 1932, 1953 (I: 8–12).

ZEMACH, MARGOT. *It Could Always Be Worse: A Yiddish Folktale*. New York: Farrar, Straus & Giroux, 1976 (I: 5–8).

CHAPTER 3

VOCABULARY DEVELOPMENT

SELECTING VOCABULARY FOR INSTRUCTION
DEVELOPING VOCABULARY THROUGH LITERATURE
 Reading Aloud
 Writing Activities
 Context Clues
 Webbing and Plot Structures
 Semantic Feature Analysis
 Building Student Responsibility for Vocabulary Development

One of the greatest concerns of teachers as they develop a literature-based curriculum is how to develop, reinforce, and expand the vocabularies of their students. Many teachers find this task especially challenging because, unlike in the basal series, the vocabulary words in literature selections are not identified. Nonetheless, literature and literature-related activities are marvelous sources for helping students gain understandings of vocabulary. Like the various effective structures for literature-based programs discussed in chapter 1, vocabulary can be increased through teacher-directed activities around core literature, through units and discussions during extended reading activities, and through extensive recreational reading of self-selected books.

This chapter discusses such concerns as selecting vocabulary for literature-based instruction and developing effective strategies to help students understand and expand their vocabularies. Numerous examples are included that can be used in both direct instruction and incidental learning.

SELECTING VOCABULARY FOR INSTRUCTION

One of the characteristics of many basal reading series is that only a few new words are introduced with each carefully constructed story. These stories are developed on the belief that students should not be expected to read many words that are unfamiliar to them. Consequently, the vocabularies are carefully controlled to include high frequency words that are believed to be familiar. This control, especially in the basals published for primary grades, limits the words that can be used within the stories. The accompanying instructional manual identifies both the new words and words that have been previously taught but are being reviewed through the specific story and the accompanying lesson.

Calfee and Drum (1986) describe how the vocabulary words are introduced in most basal series. For example, a list of words judged to be difficult to pronounce or that occur infrequently are presented at the beginning of the lesson. Instruction proceeds as students are asked to define or make up a sentence using each word. This type of activity often is followed by worksheet or workbook lessons in which students are asked to do tasks such as match words to synonyms, place words in sentence blanks, or look up words in glossaries or dictionaries. Calfee and Drum are critical of such vocabulary practices because the vocabulary instruction lacks both intensity and scope and the materials rely on rote practice.

In contrast to the carefully controlled vocabularies in basal series, the selections that form literature-based reading programs use primary sources of literature in which the authors do not control the scope or sequence of words to be introduced. Each literary selection might contain many new words, some of which are already in the reader's listening or speaking vocabulary. These words require minimal teaching, especially if context clues within the story allow students to identify the words and the appropriate meanings. Other words, however, might present new concepts and require instruction.

Reading authorities disagree on whether vocabulary should be taught through direct instruction or through incidental learning during extensive reading. Research supports both approaches to vocabulary acquisition. Ruddell (1986), for example, emphasizes the teacher's role in developing vocabulary instruction. He describes reading as a complex interactive process that requires readers to respond to text features that are enhanced by teacher-initiated discussion and instructional strategies. Ruddell states, "The teacher-directed reader environment serves to orient the student to the text, assess and activate prior student knowledge, and use instructional strategies to develop new concepts. The interaction between the teacher, text, and student should establish a clear goal direction for the vocabulary instruction" (p. 582).

According to Ruddell, the reader environment includes features of the text to be read, features of the discussion between students and teacher, and features of the instruction in which the vocabulary is developed. Encouraging students to assess and activate prior knowledge allows them to examine knowledge developed during previous instruction and other experiences. Students create goals, plan their actions for approaching the reading task, and monitor and evaluate their progress. Meaning is processed and further elaborated when reading results in comprehension, word recognition, oral output, written output, and new knowledge.

Ruddell shows the importance of both the features and the teacher for vocabulary development when he states:

> These features are heavily influenced by the teacher in selecting appropriate text, conversational interaction with the student, and the use of effective vocabulary development strategies. In effect, the teacher controls the reader environment to a significant degree and so doing should assist the reader in forming purpose. . . . Activation of the reader's previous knowledge related to the text and new concepts is of vital importance, as is the activation of strategies to process new meanings ranging from the use of context to word reference sources. The importance of the learning product must not be overlooked in helping the student understand the value of comprehending the text and in acquiring new vocabulary. (p. 586)

Additional support for teacher-directed instruction of vocabulary is found in Stahl and Fairbanks' (1986) review of vocabulary research. They found that direct instruction of vocabulary improves understanding of the words taught and increases comprehension of the texts in which the words are contained. McKeown et al. (1985) found that effective vocabulary instruction needs to be extensive and multifaceted and include frequent encounters with the words. Multifaceted instruction includes associating new words with a variety of concepts, contrasting words to discover relationships, and grouping words into semantic categories.

Other studies support the acquisition of vocabulary through incidental reading and that wide reading enhances vocabulary development. For example, Nagy, Anderson, and Herman (1987) conclude that students learn many new words from reading them in context. In addition, they learn more words through incidental experiences than through direct instruction.

After reviewing the research on direct instruction and incidental learning of vocabulary, Marzano and Marzano (1988) conclude, "A safe middle position appears to be that wide reading should be the primary vehicle for vocabulary learning, yet some selected words can be the focus of direct vocabulary instruction" (p. 11). Other researchers point out that the ease of gaining incidental vocabulary knowledge through wide reading depends on the quality of the writing. Sternberg, Powell, and Kaye (1983) state, "Some contexts essentially define the word; others leave its meaning murky. . . . A vocabulary training program that uses learning from context is incomplete if it fails to provide instruction in how to use context" (pp. 128–129).

A research review conducted by Carr and Wixson (1986) provides four guidelines for vocabulary instruction and suggests some beneficial strategies. First, they state that instruction should help students relate new vocabulary to their previous experience and background knowledge. (Notice how this principle for vocabulary development is similar to our earlier discussion of schema theory.) Activities in which students are asked to think about personal experiences with the word and to respond through written or oral associations are effective. For example, students can make individual vocabulary cards on which they associate the words and their definitions with clues from their own experiences.

Second, vocabulary instruction should help students develop word knowledge that extends beyond learning a word in a single context or memorizing a definition. Techniques that allow students to elaborate their word knowledge include examining relationships among new words, introducing words in multiple contexts, introducing new vocabulary and related concepts together, grouping words for semantic categories, developing vocabulary webs, and comparing features of words to decide if the words are mutually exclusive.

Third, instruction should encourage students to become actively involved as they learn the new vocabulary and construct meanings for the new words. Such activities allow students to discuss and explore the meanings of the words rather than to merely memorize definitions given to them by the teacher.

Fourth, instruction should develop strategies that students can use to learn the meanings of new words when they are reading independently without adult involvement. Effective strategies teach students a variety of methods for acquiring word meanings, enhance students' abilities to monitor their own understanding of new words, and encourage students to change or modify their strategies for understanding new words when necessary. Carr and Wixson state that "students become independent learners through instruction that gradually shifts the responsibility for developing new word meanings from the teacher to the student" (p. 592). For example, teachers could instruct students in how to use context cues when the students read independently and then teach them ways to make sure that they actually know what a word means.

If we assume that some vocabulary words should be the focus of instruction, the question remains, "Which words should be selected from a literature selection?" Points made by Anders and Bos (1986) in their discussion of content area reading also apply to literature-based programs. They state, "We suggest that vocabulary instruction based on criteria of either difficulty or frequency is not appropriate; rather we argue that vocabulary should be taught because it is related to the major ideas presented in the text" (p. 610). They recommend selecting words that encourage students to identify the relationships among the conceptual vocabulary and the main ideas in the text. In this way, students interact with and extend their understandings of words through the study of vocabulary that is functionally and conceptually related.

The various genres of literature provide many opportunities to focus on words that are important to the story, encourage students to increase their understandings of relationships, and expand students' knowledge to include multiple meanings for words. For example, younger students can expand their understandings of concept words and things that relate to those concepts through books such as Tana Hoban's *Of Colors and Things, Round & Round & Round,* and *Shapes, Shapes, Shapes.* When older students are reading Selina Hastings' retelling of the legend, *Sir Gawain and the Loathly Lady,* a vocabulary lesson could focus on words related to the age of chivalry and to the characters, setting, and plot of the story. Studying words such as knight, quest, armour, honor, challenge, and enchantment can help students develop understandings of the time period and the eventual theme of the story. Likewise, a nonfictional selection such as Patricia Lauber's *Volcano: The Eruption and Healing of Mount St. Helens* might include a vocabulary lesson that focuses on geological terms such as volcano, eruption, crater, geologist, earthquake, magma, pressure, and pumice.

DEVELOPING VOCABULARY THROUGH LITERATURE

In this section we will apply the guidelines from research to specific examples of literature. As suggested by the research, vocabulary activities should allow students to apply a variety of techniques to several literary forms. Some activities are useful during teacher-directed instruction using core books. Others are useful with extended reading during unit activities and other small-group sessions. Still others emphasize individualized responses to vocabulary development and are especially beneficial during independent reading assignments and recreational reading. The importance of enhancing vocabulary through a variety of visual, oral, written, and reading activities is supported by a research summary by Marzano and Marzano (1988). As you read these conclusions consider how you might apply these principles to developing vocabulary through literature. The following conclusions suggest the importance of both incidental learning and teacher-directed instruction:

1. Wide reading and language-rich activities should be the primary vehicles for vocabulary learning. Given the large number of words students encounter in written and oral language, general language development must be encouraged as one of the most important vocabulary development strategies.

2. Direct vocabulary instruction should focus on words considered important to a given content area or to general background knowledge. Since effective direct vocabulary instruction requires a fair amount of time and complexity, teachers should select words for instruction that promise a high yield in student learning of general knowledge or of knowledge of a particular topic of instructional importance.

3. Direct vocabulary instruction should include many ways of knowing a word and provide for the development of a complex level of word knowledge. Since word knowledge is stored in many forms (mental pictures, kinesthetic associations, smells, tastes, semantic distinctions, linguistic references), direct vocabulary instruction should take advantage of many of these forms and not emphasize one to the exclusion of others.

4. Direct vocabulary instruction should include a structure by which new words not taught directly can be learned readily. Again, given the large number of words students encounter and the limited utility of direct instruction, some structure must be developed to allow the benefits of direct vocabulary instruction to go beyond the words actually taught. (pp. 11–12)

Reading Aloud

As discussed in chapter 2, reading aloud to students increases their vocabulary knowledge, improves their comprehension, and provides important background knowledge that prepares them for independent reading. Research that identifies effective oral reading strategies also provides guidelines for improving students' vocabularies and comprehension.

For example, earlier research conducted by Lamme (1976) provides valuable guidelines for reading aloud and highlights some of the reasons that oral reading by adults is related to vocabulary development and comprehension improvement. Lamme found that in addition to carefully selected stories and enthusiastic reading, the following factors contribute to the quality of the oral reading experience:

1. Child involvement—including reading parts of a selection with an adult, predicting what will happen next, or filling in missing words. It is the most influential factor during oral reading.

2. Eye contact between the reader and the audience.

3. Adults who read with expression rather than a monotonous tone.

4. Oral readers who try to put variety into their voices. The pitch should be neither too high nor too low, and volume should be neither too loud nor too soft.

5. Readers who point to meaningful words or pictures in the book as they read, rather than merely read the story and show the pictures.

6. Adults who know the story and do not need to read the text verbatim.

7. Readers who select picture books large enough for children to see and appealing enough to hold their interest or elicit their comments.
8. Grouping children so that all can see the pictures and hear the story.
9. Adults who highlight the words and language of the story by making the rhymes apparent, discussing unusual vocabulary words, and emphasizing any repetition.

As you read this list notice especially those factors related to vocabulary development: Involving children by asking them to fill in missing words or to predict what will happen next; pointing to meaningful words or pictures; and highlighting words and language by making the rhymes apparent, discussing unusual vocabulary words, and emphasizing any repetition. Also notice that many of Marzano and Marzano's (1988) points related to effective vocabulary development can be enhanced through oral reading. This is especially true with the conclusion that wide reading and language-rich activities should be the primary vehicles for vocabulary learning. Oral presentations of stories are required through all grades. This is especially important for students who would not have access to the literature unless it is read by an adult. Let us consider how these effective strategies can be developed with examples of books appropriate for different grade levels.

Lower Elementary Grades. While reading Michael Rosen's *We're Going on a Bear Hunt* to kindergarten or first-grade students, emphasize the repetitive language and the descriptive words. Show the students that the illustrator, Helen Oxenbury, places the repetitive verses on black and white backgrounds and the descriptive action words on colored backgrounds. Ask the students: "Why would an illustrator choose both black-and-white and colored backgrounds in the same book? How should we read this story to show the differences between black-and-white and colored backgrounds?" After orally reading the first series of repetitive text, encourage the students to join in the reading. On the colored action pages ask them to predict the sounds that the family will make as they go through each obstacle. Ask them to notice that each action is repeated three times and that each line increases in size. Ask the students: "Why would an author increase the size of the letters? How could we use our voices and actions to show this increasing size?" Then have the students read and act out the lines such as:

Splash splosh!
Splash splosh!
Splash splosh!

Students enjoy acting out this whole rhyme as they start the bear hunt, swishy swashy through the grass, splash splosh through the river, squelch squerch through the mud, stumble trip through the forest, hoooo wooooo through the snowstorm, tiptoe through the cave, discover the bear and then go back through each obstacle until they reach the safety of home and bed. This book encourages students to become involved in the text and their own vocabulary development as they join in the repetitive language, act out the action words, and discover how an author and an illustrator might show how words should be spoken by changing the size of the text or by alternating the backgrounds.

After students have responded through voice and actions to the increasing letter sizes in *We're Going on a Bear Hunt,* they enjoy joining in the oral reading of other books in which the authors change the letter size for emphasis. Mem Fox's *Night Noises* highlights the descriptive words by printing them in large red letters. The remainder of the text is printed in smaller black print. Students can join in the reading as they predict the appropriate noise and then imitate each sound. For example, the book shows an illustration of someone walking on dirt and the text reads: "Feet tiptoed up the garden path" (p. 9, unnumbered). Students can predict the sound and try to create the sound with their voices. The sound shown in the text is, "CRINCH, CRUNCH."

In *Old MacDonald Had a Farm,* Glen Rounds changes the letter sizes and uses capital letters to emphasize the animals and the sounds that they produce. Rounds uses a similar technique in *I Know An Old Lady Who Swallowed A Fly.* Poems such as Mary Ann Hoberman's "Fish" found in Jack Prelutsky's *Read-Aloud Rhymes for the Very Young* can be used to show students that poets also can use letter size to show vocabulary meaning and to indicate how a word should be read. The poem ends with the line "But none of them making the tiniest

tiniest

tiniest

sound."

Students enjoy joining in the reading of the poem and showing what "tiniest" means by making voices softer and softer to correspond with the tiny letters in the poem.

Mother Goose rhymes and other rhymes are enjoyable sources for predicting words and filling in missing words. Three good sources for rhymes for lower elementary students include Tomie dePaola's *Tomie dePaola's Mother Goose,* Lucy Cousins' *The Little Dog Laughed and other Nursery Rhymes,* and Arnold Lobel's *The Random House Book of Mother Goose.* Students enjoy producing the words in rhymes such as "Hush, Little Baby, Don't Say a Word" and "There Was an Old Woman Who Lived in a Shoe." The lesser known rhymes in Iona and Peter Opie's *Tail Feathers From Mother Goose: The Opie Rhyme Book* provide more challenge for students. John Ivimey's *Three Blind Mice* is a longer version of the popular rhyme and encourages students to become involved in the repetitive language as well as to predict the rhyming words. Paul Galdon's illustrations encourage students to predict the next plight of the mice.

Anthologies of poetry such as Jack Prelutsky's *Read-Aloud Rhymes for the Very Young, The Random House Book of Poetry for Children,* and *Something Big Has Been Here* and Laura Whipple's *Eric Carle's Animals Animals* are excellent sources for poems that encourage students to fill in the missing words. Poetic texts such as Jane Yolen's *The Three Bears Rhyme Book* and Bill Martin, Jr. and John Archambault's *Up and Down on the Merry-Go-Round* provide many opportunities for students to hypothesize about rhyming words and to fill in the missing words.

Middle Elementary Grades.   When adults read orally to students in the middle grades, they can select works that expand the students' understanding of vocabulary and provide important background knowledge. Some of the books are longer texts in which one or two chapters are read during each experience, while other books are shorter, illustrated texts. Teachers can discuss unusual vocabulary, highlight important understandings, and emphasize relationships developed through the literature.

Books that have vivid descriptions of setting encourage students to visualize these settings and to understand why authors need to select words carefully if they want to set the stage for their books. One of my favorite techniques is to ask students to close their eyes and listen to a passage. As they listen to the passage, they try to visualize the setting and then describe what they see. For example, while reading Natalie Babbitt's *Tuck Everlasting* ask the students to visualize the following paragraph:

> On the other side of the wood, the sense of easiness dissolved. The road no longer belonged to the cows. It became, instead, and rather abruptly, the property of people. And all at once the sun was uncomfortably hot, the dust oppressive, and the meager grass along its edges somewhat ragged and forlorn. On the left stood the first house, a square and solid cottage with a touch-me-not appearance, surrounded by grass cut painfully to the quick and enclosed by a capable iron fence some four feet high which clearly said, 'Move on—we don't want you here.' So the road went humbly by and made its way, past cottages more and more frequent but less and less forbidding, into the village. But the village doesn't matter, except for the jailhouse and the gallows. The first house only is important; the first house, the road, and the wood. (p. 5–6)

After listening to the passage, ask the students to describe their visions in as much detail as possible. "What does it look like to be uncomfortably hot, to be surrounded by oppressive dust and meager grass, and to see grass that is ragged and forlorn? What does the "touch-me-not" house look like? What does grass look like if it is cut painfully to the quick? How did they visualize a humble road or a capable iron fence? What did they picture for gallows?" Ask them if they noticed the technique that the author uses to make the setting seem real and vivid—encourage them to identify the author's use of personification. Ask them to consider why the author describes the setting in personified terms. If they have not noticed the terms, read the paragraph a second time, have them note these terms, and ask them if the personification makes a difference in their ability to visualize the setting. Also, note that the word gallows helps readers identify the setting as taking place in an earlier time period.

Numerous books have vivid paragraphs that can be used for visualization and discussion. In *Call It Courage,* Armstrong Sperry describes nature's harsh law of survival and a sea that is a vivid monster. In *The Wish Giver,* Bill Brittain uses rich and colorful imagery to create a memorable story. Pointing out the author's use of similes and metaphors helps students expand their understanding of the story and comprehend the text.

When reading heavily illustrated books such as Blaise Cendrars' *Shadow,* teachers can point out how Marcia Brown's illustrations reinforce the spooky mood of the poem in which shadow staggers, steals back like a thief, and sprawls on the ground. Students can discuss how the poet's choice of words and use of language are heightened by the collage illustrations, especially the ones in which black silhouettes are on the same page with white ghostly images. After reading *Shadow,* teachers can read Edward Lear's *The Scroobious Pip,* pointing out the effect of the soft pastel drawings on the mood of the poem. Students can focus on Lear's style of writing and discuss whether the pastel drawings are more appropriate for this poem than would be the predominantly black shapes found in *Shadow.* Highlighting moods created by illustrations helps students develop backgrounds for texts and analyze the appropriateness of relationships between the authors' choice of words and the illustrators' choice of drawings.

Upper Elementary and Middle School. As the texts become harder and more complex teachers should take special care to point out difficult concepts and vocabulary to their students. A similar visualization technique as described with *Tuck Everlasting* can be used to help students focus on unusual words, figurative meanings, and important relationships. The vocabularies in books such as Jamake Highwater's *Anpao: An American Indian Odyssey* might seem deceptively easy at first glance. But because the author uses much simile, metaphor, personification, and mythological symbolism, many readers might not comprehend the story or fully appreciate how the author's techniques add to the enjoyment of the story unless these features are pointed out by the teacher. For example, after providing background about the book, teachers can ask students to close their eyes and visualize the first paragraph of the chapter "In the Days of the Plentiful:"

> In the days before the people fled into the water, the wind held leaves aloft in the sky like dragonflies. There was no war and people were at peace. The buffalo-people lived in the world of the sweet grass below, and the sky above was filled with birds of many colors and of many songs. The air was blue and the earth was green and each thing rested upon the other. In the forest the leaves fell slowly. There was no fear. The birds did not leap into flight when the cats awoke. And the wild flowers changed colors to amuse themselves. (p. 15)

After reading the paragraph orally ask the students to describe their visualization in as much detail as possible. Ask them how they visualized the time period as reflected in "before the people fled into the water." If the students have not studied Native American mythology they might not know that this is an allusion to an earlier time period at the beginning of Native American mythological history. Ask the students how they visualized the people who live in this early time. "Who are the buffalo-people?" Again, they might not be aware that the buffalo-people belonged to one of the Great Plains tribes, who lived in harmony with the buffalo. The buffalo provided food and other necessities for the people. These understandings can improve students' abilities to visualize the setting. How do leaves appear if they are compared to dragonflies? What does a setting look and sound like if the author describes sweet grass below, colorful birds singing in the sky, and leaves falling slowly? How is the visualization of the setting influenced by the description of birds who are not afraid of the cats? How did they visualize wild flowers that change colors to amuse themselves?

This is not a text that should be read rapidly. Instead, it should be savored for the language and the effect of the comparisons on the listener and the reader. Students' enjoyment and comprehension of the text is enhanced if teachers highlight the importance of similes, personification, and mythological symbolism as they read. Teachers can point out and discuss comparisons developed by the author and why these comparisons are appropriate in a text based on Native American legend and mythology.

Other excellent examples of symbolism and figurative language in Native American literature can be found in Jan Hudson's *Sweetgrass,* an award-winning Canadian historical fiction book set in the northern prairies of the 19th century. Again, the author's frequent use of similes, metaphors, and mythological beliefs should be pointed out as students listen to the reading.

Numerous classic texts include vocabulary or concepts that are difficult for contemporary students to understand. Some of these books originally were considered appropriate for younger students but now are difficult for them to understand because of outdated references to times and places. Many of these books should be read orally by teachers who can help students understand and appreciate the texts. For example, as a middle school teacher read Kenneth Grahame's *The Wind in the Willows* to her students, she highlighted the references to history; the allusions to the British Industrial Revolution; the terminology that reflected the English background; and the author's fascination with the Thames river, the woods, and the fields around his home. By highlighting such information the teacher tied together literature and history. Another teacher used Martin Gardner's *The Annotated Alice* to highlight important historic and literary information when reading Lewis Carroll's *Alice's Adventures in Wonderland* and *Through the Looking Glass.*

Writing Activities

Writing activities—both formal assignments and informal responses in journals—provide rich opportunities for students to use their developing vocabularies. In this section we will consider ways to expand vocabulary knowledge through poetry writing, learning logs, and individualized dictionaries.

Poetry.   Writing poetry about specific characters, incidents, or themes in books encourages students to expand their vocabulary as they consider the best words to present an image. Specific forms of poetry also stress certain types of vocabulary. For example, a cinquain uses descriptive words and action words. When creating their own cinquains students first read or listen to numerous cinquains. Next, they discuss the structure of the cinquain and then use the structure to write their own poems.

During this activity teachers should review the following structure for the cinquain and note the requirements for each line:

Line 1:   A word for a title
Line 2:   Two words to describe the title
Line 3:   Three words to express action
Line 4:   Four words to express feeling
Line 5:   The title again, or a word like the title

Teachers and students can draw a diagram for the cinquain:

title
describe title
action, action, action
feeling about the title
title

Before writing their own cinquains students should read several published examples of cinquains. Students also can discuss the kinds of words that make up each line and brainstorm examples.

Various characters in literature provide excellent sources for exploring descriptive words and action words. For example, after reading Munro Leaf's *The Story of Ferdinand* students could describe the characterization of this unusual bull who does not want to fight the matadors. A group of second-grade students created the following cinquain:

Ferdinand
Happy, strong
Sitting, smelling, growing
Loves to smell flowers
Independent

The following are additional books that provide interesting characterizations and cinquain writing for students in the lower elementary grades:

1. Virginia Lee Burton's *The Little House* and *Mike Mulligan and His Steam Shovel*
2. Leo Lionni's *Swimmy*
3. Patricia McKissack's *Mirandy and Brother Wind*
4. Hans Rey's *Curious George*
5. Robert San Souci's *The Talking Eggs*
6. Maurice Sendak's *Where the Wild Things Are*
7. Dianne Snyder's *The Boy of the Three-Year Nap*
8. Judith Viorst's *Alexander and the Terrible, Horrible, No Good, Very Bad Day*
9. Rosemary Wells' *The Little Lame Prince*

After reading Patricia MacLachlan's *Sarah, Plain and Tall,* students in the middle elementary grades could create cinquains that describe Sarah, Anna, Calab, and Papa. The following cinquain was developed with a fourth-grade class:

Sarah
Adventurous, intelligent
Hardworking, caring, singing
Pulls the family together
Confident

The following are additional books that provide sources for characterizations and cinquain writing for students in the middle elementary grades:

1. Beverly Cleary's *Dear Mr. Henshaw* and the Ramona books
2. Jean Fritz's *What's the Big Idea, Ben Franklin?* and *Where Was Patrick Henry on the 29th of May?*
3. E. L. Konigsburg's *From the Mixed-Up Files of Mrs. Basil E. Frankweller*
4. C. S. Lewis's *The Lion, the Witch, and the Wardrobe*
5. Mary Norton's *The Borrowers*
6. George Selden's *The Cricket in Times Square*
7. E. B. White's *Charlotte's Web* and *Stewart Little*

The characters in books appropriate for upper elementary and middle school students provide numerous sources for cinquains as students read legends, fantasy, contemporary fiction, historical fiction, and biography. For example, after reading Esther Forbes's *Johnny Tremain* a group of sixth-grade students developed the following cinquain:

Johnny
Brave, patriotic
Daring, delivering, riding
Made a strong commitment
Apprentice

Johnny Tremain provides numerous subjects for cinquains. Students also wrote about Revolutionary War heroes such as Paul Revere and Samuel Adams, the Boston setting, and historical occurrences such as the Boston Tea Party.

The following are additional books that are especially good for writing cinquains for upper elementary and middle school students:

1. Russell Friedman's *Lincoln: A Photobiography*
2. Joseph Krumgold's . . . *And Now Miguel*
3. Scott O'Dell's *Sing Down the Moon*
4. Uri Orlev's *The Island on Bird Street*

Legendary characters such as Robin Hood and King Arthur and the heroes of mythology also provide interesting sources.

The diamante is a more complex form of poetry that requires students to provide contrasting terms. This form of poetry is especially useful in helping students explore changes in characters or conflicts. The diamante has the following requirements for each line:

Line 1:	Noun
Line 2:	Two adjectives
Line 3:	Three participles
Line 4:	Four nouns or phrase
Line 5:	Three participles indicating change
Line 6:	Two adjectives
Line 7:	Contrasting noun

Like the cinquain, the diamante should be drawn out to show the structure and the terms should be discussed and examples presented. Thus, in line 1, the teacher presents examples of a noun; in line 2, examples of adjectives related to the first line noun; in line 3, examples of participles, as verb forms ending in *-ing, -ed, en*. The nouns in the line 4 contrast with the first noun, so that readers' thoughts move from the subject of the first noun to the subject of the contrasting noun on line 7. Line 5 contains three participles that correspond with the noun on line 7, and indicate change from the first noun. Line 6 contains two adjectives that correspond with the final noun and, thus, contrast with line 2. The final noun contrasts with line 1.

A diagram of the diamante looks like this:

noun
describing, describing
action, action, action
transition nouns or phrase
action, action, action
describing, describing
noun

In addition to illustrating the parts of speech used in this poetry, teachers also must clarify the concept of contrasts. Contrasting nouns are necessary, in addition to contrasting adjectives and contrasting verb forms that correspond with appropriate nouns. An instructional activity leading up to this form of poetry begins with identifying the form and suggesting contrasting nouns, such as war-peace, freedom-slavery, and fantasy-reality.

Because the diamante is a more complex form of poetry it is not as appropriate for younger students. Many of the books that are loved by younger readers, however, make excellent sources for developing insights into the vocabulary of character change. For example, after reading Margery Williams' *The Velveteen Rabbit or How Toys Become Real* a group of fourth graders developed the following diamante:

Toy
Stuffed, velveteen
Sitting, lying, riding
Love made him real
Walking, running, leaping
Real, furry
Rabbit

Leo Buscaglia's story that progresses from life to death, *The Fall of Freddie the Leaf,* is another picture story book that can help students consider opposites. Many of the characters in literature appropriate for older students change as they proceed through the story. The following books provide excellent sources as students focus on vocabulary terms that characterize the differences between characters at the beginning and the end of stories:

1. Paula Fox's *One-Eyed Cat*
2. Jean Craighead George's *The Talking Earth*
3. Virginia Hamilton's *The Planet of Junior Brown*
4. Armstrong Sperry's *Call It Courage*
5. Cynthia Voigt's *Dicey's Song* and *A Solitary Blue*
6. Maia Wojciechowska's *Shadow of a Bull*

Journal Writing and Learning Logs.   Journal writing is used at all levels to encourage students to express ideas and react in personal ways. Some teachers use short daily writing times to have students write about topics of their choosing. These topics easily can be related to literature that is currently being read for class or recreation.

Journal writing can encourage students to brainstorm with themselves, to consider what they already know or think about a subject, and to list or categorize ideas and vocabulary that can be used to develop writing projects.

Teachers can provide ideas for journal writing such as listing favorite characters and describing them from different points of view within the story, identifying the setting for a story, listing vocabulary words and phrases that develop that setting, and listing examples of language that the students particularly appreciate. Students can collect vivid examples of dialogue, unusual examples of contrasts or comparisons, and meaningful similes and metaphors that enhance their understanding of vocabulary.

Nonfictional sources provide excellent materials for learning logs because students can focus on specific content and vocabulary knowledge gained from informational books, biographies, and autobiographies. Teachers can encourage students to write about what they liked best in a book, what information they believe is important, how they will use that information in the future, what new vocabulary words and concepts will be important to them, and what questions still need to be answered or researched.

Learning logs help students retain material and focus on the development of understandings. Learning logs also personalize learning as students identify the specific information they learned from the text and use the vocabulary developed as part of the subject.

Individualized Dictionaries and Vocabulary Notebooks. Individualized dictionaries or vocabulary notebooks can accompany teacher-directed instruction with core books, extended reading activities such as unit involvement, or individualized or recreational reading activities. These dictionaries can take numerous forms; therefore, students can choose their own approaches for highlighting interesting words to add to their vocabularies. Features such as illustrations, personal responses to words, synonyms, antonyms, phrases, and sentences that show interesting or unusual ways to use the words can be placed in the dictionaries. The following examples show how students from lower elementary, middle elementary, and upper elementary and middle school levels have developed their individualized dictionaries.

Because students in the lower grades gain considerable vocabulary knowledge from picture books, these students enjoy adding illustrations to their own dictionaries. Concept books provide excellent sources for individualized dictionaries and suggest ways that students might illustrate their own words. For example, Figure 3.1 shows an entry developed by a first-grade student after reading Dayle Ann Dodds' concept book, *Wheel Away!*

Other entries focused on different concepts found in this book: down, through, in, over, under, across, between, on top of, in front of, in back of, climbing, slowing, and coming back.

Additional picture books that develop concepts through illustrations can be used for similar entries. For example, Linda Banachek's *Snake In, Snake Out* develops spatial concepts. Donald Crews' *Freight Train* follows trains that go across trestles, through cities, and into tunnels. Pat Hutchins' *What Game Shall We Play?* develops concepts such as across, among, over, under, in, near, on top of, around, behind, and

FIGURE 3.1
Individual
vocabulary card.

through. Sally Noll's *Watch Where You Go* follows a mouse as it goes through, up, among, down, between, onto, and into various settings. Bruce McMillan's *Here a Chick, There a Chick* develops spatial concepts and opposites as the chicks are pictured in such positions as inside and outside. Tana Hoban's *Exactly the Opposite* also develops opposites such as open-closed, large-small, and push-pull through the illustrations.

Specialized vocabularies are illustrated in some picture books. These books are especially appealing to students who have specific interests. For example, Gail Gibbons' *Trains* could stimulate the development of dictionary entries that emphasize types of trains, names of train cars, purposes for trains, and specialized terms such as *cargo* and *couplers*. Using a similar subject, Helen Sattler's *Train Whistles* explains the meanings of signals used by train whistles.

Individualized dictionaries can be related easily to personal responses with the vocabulary words. For example, after reading Anne Rockwell's *First Comes Spring*, a second-grade student related vocabulary associated with the seasons to his own experiences with the words. Figure 3.2 shows how one student felt about summer.

In the middle and upper elementary grades students are expanding their vocabularies and increasing their understandings of multiple meanings for words. Some of these meanings might even be conflicting. Figure 3.3 shows an individualized dictionary entry developed by a student after reading Rudolf Frank's *No Hero for the Kaiser*.

FIGURE 3.2
Individual
vocabulary card.

I love summer.
I swim in the pool.

I play baseball.

FIGURE 3.3 Individualized dictionary entry.

Contrasting Meanings for *No Hero for the Kaiser*
Bull's eye: Peaceful meaning—hitting the center in a dart game or when aiming a bow and arrow.
Bull's eye: war-time meaning—hitting a target and destroying property or people.
In the field: peaceful meaning—planting and plowing the crops.
In the field: war-time meaning—soldiers going into battle.

Haggard (1986) recommends a self-collection technique for vocabulary instruction that encourages students to enhance their vocabularies by using their own interests and knowledge. This technique is especially appropriate for core books or for units in which students are reading books related to central themes or topics. Students first identify words they believe the class should learn. (Whether words are chosen by individuals or by student teams will depend on the number of students in the group. If a whole class is involved, the list might be too long if everyone chooses a word.) Teachers also choose words they believe are important. Second, teachers or students write each word on the chalkboard, and each student or team provides definitions for each word, emphasizing the context from which the word is taken. Third, class members add information about each word and definition. Fourth, teachers and students consult references to supplement definitions that are incomplete or unclear, and the group agrees on the definitions. Students and teachers narrow the list to a predetermined number that will make up the class list. Students record the class list with the agreed-upon definitions in their vocabulary journals. They record any additional words on their personal vocabulary lists. The class lists are used during various follow-up activities, and the words become part of the unit activities. Words can be tested according to the instructional goals of the unit.

Literature selections are excellent sources for such an activity as students choose, define, and defend the importance of their words for class knowledge. The words are now personal choices and, therefore, are perceived as important. If these words are related to a theme or topic, they lend themselves to activities such as contextual analysis, webbing, and semantic feature analysis, which are developed in the next sections.

Context Clues

Teaching students to use context clues within the literature helps them during both teacher-led activities and independent reading. Rakes and Choate (1989) believe that teaching context clues is especially vital when working with students with special needs. To help these students, the authors state:

> Because all of the word-recognition skills should be presented and applied in meaningful context, contextual analysis should be taught as an integral part of word recognition and meaning from the very first day of reading instruction. The utility of contextual analysis is not confined to reading alone but is also important to mastering the content and concepts of all other subjects as well. Effective corrective instruction must include demonstrations, discussions, and explanations of the thinking strategies involved in predicting and verifying with context. (p. 98)

Most reading-methods books emphasize the development of context clues. Many of these discussions are based on the earlier work of McCullough (1944) in which she identified the following six types of context clues found in texts:

1. *Definition:* The word is defined within the content of the book.
2. *Comparison:* Contrasting words help the reader identify unfamiliar words.
3. *Summary:* The unfamiliar word is a summary of the ideas that precede the word.
4. *Familiar expression:* Knowledge of a familiar expression helps the reader identify the unknown word.
5. *Experience:* The reader's background aids in identifying an unknown word.
6. *Synonym:* A known synonym can help the reader identify an unknown word.

All these types of context clues are found within literature. When reading books, teachers can identify particularly good examples of these context clues and give students opportunities to use the clues and explore meanings related to these context clues. Some books are especially well written and encourage students to consider both the textual clues and the illustrations when attacking meanings. In the next section we will identify examples of books that can be used to help students identify and use these context clues.

Books that Develop Definitions.   Nonfictional texts are especially good for showing students how authors develop meanings of words through definitions. In addition, technical terms in books often are reinforced through labeled illustrations that define and clarify concepts. These illustrations help students verify unfamiliar meanings. In addition, some authors italicize important words that are defined within the context. Some authors also boldface words in the text and define them in the glossary. These multiple techniques help students explore meanings and verify their meanings within that context.

Nonfictional books for students in the lower elementary grades often use numerous illustrations to help students define and understand new concepts. For example, Millicent Selsam and Joyce Hunt's *A First Look at Animals With Horns* asks the question: "What is a horn?" The text then describes different types of horns; the illustrations show these horns; and a labeled illustration shows the components of a horn including bone, outer covering, and hair. The authors use a similar technique as they introduce, define, and illustrate animals with horns. Other books in this series that can be used to introduce definitions to younger readers include *A First Look at Animals that Eat Other Animals, A First Look at Bird Nests, A First Look at Caterpillars,* and *A First Look at Seals, Sea Lions, and Walruses.* These books help students verify their knowledge by answering questions and analyzing illustrations that are shown within the text.

Definitions commonly are developed in books written for students in the middle elementary grades. For example, in *The News About Dinosaurs* Patricia Lauber uses italics to introduce the technical terms and provides the meanings for those terms through an exact definition, a description, and an illustration. Teachers can use the following paragraph to show students how Lauber develops the meaning of the italicized word *baryonyx:*

> Baryonyx was 30 feet long, with 15-inch claws and a snout like a crocodile's. It probably lived along rivers and used its claws and snout to catch fish. It was discovered near London, England, by a plumber whose hobby was searching for fossils, traces of ancient life preserved in rock. Baryonyx means "heavy claw." (p. 6)

In this example, students can focus on both the exact definition and the descriptions developed through the text and reinforced through the illustrations. Lauber uses similar techniques throughout her book—notice how she also defines fossils within the text.

Teachers in the middle and upper elementary grades can use Heiderose and Andreas Fischer-Nagel's *The Life of the Honeybee* and Sylvia Johnson's *Potatoes* to show students how authors develop technical vocabulary through context definitions, illustrations, and glossary entries. The following paragraphs illustrate how the Fischer-Nagels introduce technical vocabulary that is not defined in the glossary and terms (such as *beeswax* and *pollinate*) that are included in the glossary:

> Honeybees belong to the scientific order "Hymenoptera." This term comes from Greek words meaning "membrane wing" and describes the bees' thin, transparent wings. Of the many species, or kinds, of bees, honeybees are of the species "Apis mellifera." The Latin "Apis" means "bee," and "mellifera" means "honey-bearer."

In this example, notice how the terms are defined within the context of the book.

> Honeybees are very helpful to humans. As their name suggests, they produce the sweet, delicious honey we enjoy as food. They also produce "beeswax," which is used to make candles, lipsticks, lotions, and many other useful items. One of the honeybee's most important job is to "pollinate" flowers so that they can produce seeds and fruit. In this book, we will learn more about how honeybees perform their important duties. (p. 3)

In this example, notice that the highlighted words are not defined; instead uses are given for beeswax and an effect is provided for pollinate. These words are, however, defined in the glossary.

In *Potatoes,* Johnson uses highlighted terms, illustrations to support the meanings of the terms, a glossary, and an index to help students locate key information. For example, the text, illustrations, and glossary develop the meaning of *eyes* and *buds:*

> If you look at a sprouting potato closely, you will notice that the sprouts grow only from certain spots. They emerge only from the "eyes," the small indentations scattered over the surface of the potato. Located in each eye are several tiny "buds." These are the parts of the seed potato that produce sprouts. The sprouts in turn will develop into the stems of a new potato plant. (p. 8)

Now, if students turn to the glossary they will discover that buds are "small plant structures that develop into stems, leaves, or flowers" and that eyes are "small indentations on a potato that contain buds" (p. 46).

Students and teachers will find similar techniques in many examples of nonfictional texts written for upper elementary and middle school students. One class made a list of books in which authors develop technical vocabularies through definitions, labeled illustrations, and glossaries. The documentation included examples to show how the authors defined their terms. Then the students evaluated how effective each text was in developing the technical terms that were considered important for the subject. This activity encouraged the students to read for definitions, to apply their knowledge, and to evaluate the effectiveness of the definitions provided by the authors.

Books that Develop Comparisons.   Authors use many interesting relationships within books to help readers understand meanings. They might use context clues to develop cause-and-effect relationships as they emphasize the consequences related to specific terms. Words are often associated with several concepts. Authors might use contrasting words such as opposites to encourage readers to discover relationships. Again illustrations can help readers understand these associations and comparisons.

For example, I have used the following activity with Tomie dePaola's *The Legend of the Bluebonnet* to show how context clues and illustrations develop both cause-and-effect relationships and opposite meanings. This approach is appropriate for lower elementary and middle elementary students. My colleagues and I also have used it in remedial reading classes at the upper elementary grades. The following example is developed in detail to show how effective certain books can be in helping students identify and use illustrations and textual clues to verify meanings.

When teaching the context clues within *The Legend of the Bluebonnet,* write excerpts from the text on the chalkboard or on transparencies. For example, the first paragraph is written on the chalkboard with the vocabulary word *drought* underlined:

> "Great Spirit, the land is dying. Your People are dying, too," the line of dancers sang. "Tell us what we have done to anger you. End this *drought*. Save your people. Tell us what we must do so you will send the rain that will bring back life." (p. 1 unnumbered)

After reading the paragraph the students identify, circle, and discuss the words that mean drought: "The land is dying." Next, they identify, circle, and discuss the words that indicate why the drought must end and that show the dangerous consequences of the drought: "Save your people," "bring back life." Now the students explore the consequences of drought and think about how terrible drought must be if the most powerful being for the tribe is asked to intervene. Next, the students discuss the importance of picture clues that show the hot, yellow sun and the brown, dry earth. They consider, "What do the pictures add to the meaning of *drought?*"

To understand the opposite concept, they identify, circle, and discuss the words that mean the opposite of drought: "The rains will come and the earth will be green and alive."

As the reading of the story continues, the meaning of *drought* is extended as students identify other comparisons related to drought. These comparisons include additional cause-and-effect relationships such as:

> drought→famine, starving

and opposite meanings:

> drought→rain, earth will be green and alive, buffalo will be plentiful

These meanings are printed on the board and the supporting illustrations are discussed.

This procedure continues as additional paragraphs are printed and context clues and illustrations are used to identify and explore the meanings for *plentiful, selfish, healing, famine, valued, sacrifice,* and *restored.*

Finally, additional cause-and-effect relationships are identified, such as:

> rain→grass, plenty
> healing→rains came, brought back life
> plentiful→people will be rich again
> famine→very young and very old died
> sacrifice→offering a most valued possession

Additional opposite meanings are identified, printed on the board, and discussed.

These cause-and-effect relationships can be extended to the descriptions of the characters and the settings. Students can identify the "before-miracle" and "after-miracle" consequences to the people and the setting. For example:

Comanche people
> Before the miracle→unhappy, hungry, starving, living with famine, selfish, taking from the land
> After the miracle→happy, thankful

She-Who-Is-Alone
  Before the miracle→unselfish, loves her parents, loves her people, loves the land
  After the miracle→becomes beloved and respected One-Who-Dearly-Loved-Her
  People
Setting
  Before the miracle→dry, drought, dying earth, brown, no food or animals, famine
  After the miracle→bluebonnets, green, plentiful, restored

In this example, notice how the associations develop several concepts related to the vocabulary. Through both the associations and illustrations students discover vocabulary that is functionally and conceptually related.

Books that Develop Summaries.   Authors of nonfictional books frequently use summaries to develop related ideas associated with a geographic location or animal characteristics. Students can discuss these summaries and describe what they know about the unknown words. For example, students in the lower and middle elementary grades might consider how Downs Matthews introduces the Arctic and the North Pole with the following summary from *Polar Bear Cubs:*

> Picture a place so cold that oceans freeze . . . a place where tall trees can't grow . . . a place where the sun never shines in winter nor sets in summer. There is such a place. It is called the Arctic. It is the world of snow and ice at the North Pole. Polar bears live there. (p. 1 unnumbered)

Jane Goodall, in *The Chimpanzee Family Book,* uses summaries to develop meanings related to the various characteristics of chimpanzees. For example, students can identify and discuss how Goodall summarizes the meaning of *fierce* and *charging display* in the following paragraph:

> All at once Goblin charges towards an adult male who has appeared at the edge of the clearing. Goblin stamps the ground, hits on tree trunks and hurls a rock. He leaps up and shakes the vegetation. All these things make him look very large and fierce. This was how he challenged the other males when he was working his way towards the top position. It is called the charging display. (p. 8 unnumbered)

In the following paragraph, students can consider how Goodall summarizes decision making by listing examples of decisions that need to be made:

> They are always having to make decisions, such as what to do next, or where to go, or who to spend time with. Do they also think about things which have happened to them, or things they would like to happen? I suspect they do. (p. 38 unnumbered)

Books that Develop Familiar Expressions.   Authors of books written for younger readers often develop vocabulary through familiar expressions. In *City Sounds,* Rebecca Emberley uses numerous familiar urban expressions such as "pop" to show the sound of a toaster, "zoom" to illustrate the noise of a jet, and "rat-a-tat-a-tat" to duplicate the sound of an air hammer. In *Jungle Sounds,* she uses a similar technique to represent common sounds found in the jungle. Children who are familiar with the language of machinery will be able to understand Byron Barton's *Machines At Work.*

If they are familiar with space travel they will have no difficulty with Barton's vocabulary in *I Want to Be an Astronaut.* Likewise, in *One Crow: A Counting Rhyme,* Jim Aylesworth relies on many familiar expressions as puppies "romp" in the yard and "wag" their tails, pigs "wallow" in a muddy hole, and sheep "nibble" grass in the meadow.

Books that Use Experience to Aid Identification.   Authors of nonfictional books frequently help readers understand new concepts and technical terms by relating the unknown terms to information the reader knows. This technique should be pointed out to readers so that they will try to visualize the new terms in relationship with knowledge from their previous experience.

For example, when reading the following quotes in Peter and Connie Roop's *Seasons of the Cranes,* students can visualize the relationships and discuss how their understanding of a baby crane is improved because the authors relate the crane to known information:

> A second egg is laid the following morning. The two eggs, twice as long as chicken eggs, lie side by side in the shallow bowl of bulrushes. (p. 6)
>   A little later the chick emerges. A warm breeze fluffs her to a reddish ball no bigger than a robin. The newborn crane is so weary from her struggle to hatch that she can stand for only a few minutes. (p. 8)

Note how the authors also develop an understanding of the cranes' nest by describing it as a "shallow bowl" of bulrushes. Students usually know what a shallow bowl looks like so they can visualize the nest made of bulrushes.

In *Storms,* Seymour Simon encourages readers to use their knowledge of jet planes and vacuum cleaners to understand a tornado and to clarify the actions of a tornado:

> Sometimes a thunderstorm gives birth to a tornado. The wind blows hard and trees bend. Heavy rains or hailstones fall. Lightning and thunder rip the dark sky, and a howling roar like hundreds of jet planes fills the air. (p. 20 unnumbered)
>   Like the hose of an enormous vacuum cleaner, the tornado picks up loose materials and whirls them aloft. In less than fifteen minutes, the funnel cloud becomes clogged with dirt and air and can no longer suck up any more. (p. 22 unnumbered)

Helen Roney Sattler and Roy Gallant use similar techniques in books written for older readers. In *The Book of Eagles,* Sattler uses students' knowledge of different types of eggs to help them understand the characteristics of eagle eggs:

> All eagle eggs are large. The smallest is no smaller than a chicken egg. A Bald Eagle's eggs are the size of goose eggs. The largest—those of Harpy, Verreaux's, and Golden Eagles—are as big as the plastic egg used to package some pantyhose. Eagle eggs also vary in shape, texture, and color. Some have rough surfaces, others are smooth. Most are white, but some are mottled or splotched with brown, lilac, or red. The shells are very thick and some are blue on the inside. (p. 21)

In *Before the Sun Dies: The Story of Evolution,* Gallant uses readers' understanding of their own bodies and our own solar system to develop understandings of the orderliness of a galaxy. Using the following example, students can discuss how these relationships help them understand a galaxy:

What about the orderliness of the collection of atoms that is you? Your body contains millions of hydrogen atoms, along with more complex atoms of oxygen, nitrogen, phosphorous, carbon, potassium, and sodium, for example. All of these atoms are arranged in a certain orderly fashion and are made to work together as a human being. The work is done by electrical energy that makes your nerves send messages throughout your body; by chemical energy that digests the food you eat; and by the mechanical energy of your muscles that enables you to walk, pedal a bicycle, or turn the pages of this book.

What about the orderliness of a galaxy? The hundreds of billions of stars, planets and their moons, comets, and gas and dust between the stars that form a galaxy also are made up of atoms. In a galaxy there are the same kinds of atoms that are in you, and many other kinds as well. . . . Gravitational energy is what holds a galaxy together and keeps it orderly. Gravity also keeps the Solar System orderly by holding the planets and their moons in orbit around the Sun instead of letting them fly off into space in every which direction. (p. 2)

Books that Use Synonyms.   Authors of books for readers of all ages increase understandings through synonyms. Authors often repeat a term or idea by referring to a synonym. Sometimes the first word is known and the synonym is unknown, although authors can change this order.

In *Dragonflies,* Molly McLaughlin uses numerous synonyms to develop understandings of new vocabulary related to dragonflies. For example, "From a special pouch at the front of the male's abdomen, she receives some of his reproductive cells, or sperm" (p. 14); "This larva, or nymph, is quite different from its colorful flying parents (p. 16); "This remarkable lip, or labium, is one of the tools that make the 'pond monster' such a fearsome hunter" (p. 19); and "As the time for the big change, or metamorphosis, comes closer, the nymph's behavior changes, too" (p. 22). Teachers should point out this technique to students to help them understand the meanings of words.

Many nonfictional texts use several of the contextual techniques discussed above. After students focus on the importance of each technique, they can read books and search for examples in which authors use context clues to increase understanding of vocabulary. For example, in Seymour Simon's *Storms,* a book appropriate for middle elementary grades, students will find definitions, illustrations that support the definitions, comparisons, synonyms, and examples that encourage them to use previous experience to understand new concepts.

Students can analyze the work of one author and locate the various contextual techniques used by that author. Because Simon writes for students in different grade levels and his work reflects considerable use of context clues, students in both middle and upper elementary grades have focused on his techniques in works such as *Danger from Below: Earthquakes—Past, Present and Future; Galaxies; Jupiter; Little Giants; The Long Journey from Space; Saturn; The Smallest Dinosaurs;* and *Volcanoes.*

Additional authors who have written many nonfictional texts include Franklyn Branley, Vicki Cobb, Joanna Cole, Ron and Nancy Goor, Kathryn Lasky, Patricia Lauber, Bianca Lavies, Hershell and Joan Nixon, Dorothy Patent, Laurence Pringle, Helen Roney Sattler, Jack Denton Scott, and Millicent Selsam. Students enjoy locating and evaluating the techniques used by the authors and can apply these techniques in their own writing. This type of activity is often associated with work in science or history.

Webbing and Plot Structures

Webbing, a method for visually displaying relationships among ideas and concepts, is an excellent technique for expanding students' understandings of the multiple meanings of words. Webbing can accompany the vocabulary in a single book or can suggest related words in a unit or theme approach. A web can be drawn as a prereading vocabulary activity or it can be a follow-up approach. Students can identify prior knowledge on the web before they read and then add to and even change the web after they have read a book. Vocabulary words also can be placed on a plot diagram to help students understand the relationships among vocabulary and action. (See chapter 5 for a discussion of plot diagramming.) Diagramming the plot structure helps students relate comprehension and vocabulary.

Webbing and Plot Structures with One Book. Webbing and plot structures are appropriate for any grade level. For example, in the lower elementary grades the teacher might use Jan Brett's retelling of *Goldilocks and the Three Bears* to expand students' understandings of size concepts. The context could be used to develop understandings of words such as *wee, middle-sized,* and *huge.* Next the words can be drawn onto a web and the students can expand their knowledge of the words by identifying related words. The web in Figure 3.4 was completed with first- and second-grade students who focused on the words *wee, middle-sized, huge, woods,* and *porridge.*

After placing the words on the web, the students identified the important instances in the story (Figure 3.5). They tried to use as many of their vocabulary words as possible as they developed the plot structure.

If a web accompanies a single book such as dePaola's *The Legend of the Bluebonnet,* the teacher can choose the words that were identified under context clues. The title of the book is placed in the center of the web and the vocabulary words *drought, famine, selfish, healing, plentiful, restored, valued,* and *sacrifice* are extended from the center. If the web is introduced as a prereading activity, students can identify definitions or synonyms that they think are related to the words. Students then can verify these definitions and synonyms as they read the text and explore the context clues. If the web is a follow-up activity the students can identify definitions and synonyms after reading the text. Teachers frequently use a combination of these activities as they discover what students know about the vocabulary and then add to or even change this information as the book is read. The web in Figure 3.6 was developed with a group of lower-achieving fifth- and sixth-grade students. (This book also is appropriate for regular reading students in lower grades.)

The vocabulary words emphasized in the web also can be placed on a plot diagram. Students then identify the sequence of actions developed in the story by using as many of the vocabulary words as possible. This reinforces the importance of the vocabulary within the story. If the vocabulary words cannot be associated with the most important incidents in the story, the words might not be crucial to the story. The plot diagram of *The Legend of the Bluebonnet* (Figure 3.7) was developed with the same group of children as the web. The students identified the sequence of actions that are important in the story using as many of their vocabulary words as possible. The

FIGURE 3.4 Web of *Goldilocks and the Three Bears.*

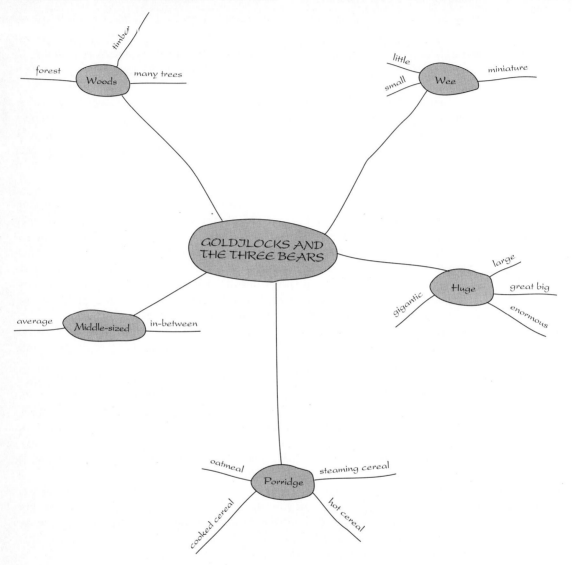

underlined words were identified by the students during the teacher-led activity. The words in parentheses are vocabulary words that had to be drawn out by the teacher during the plotting experience. For example, when the group did not identify *drought* in the beginning problem, the teacher said, "What word did you use for the land is dying?" When the group did not identify *famine* the teacher said, "What word did you use for the people are dying?" The students were able to use more of the vocabulary words as the activity proceeded.

FIGURE 3.5 Plot structure of *Goldilocks and the Three Bears.*

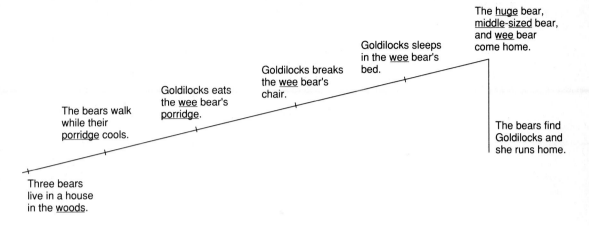

FIGURE 3.6 Vocabulary web of *The Legend of the Bluebonnet.*

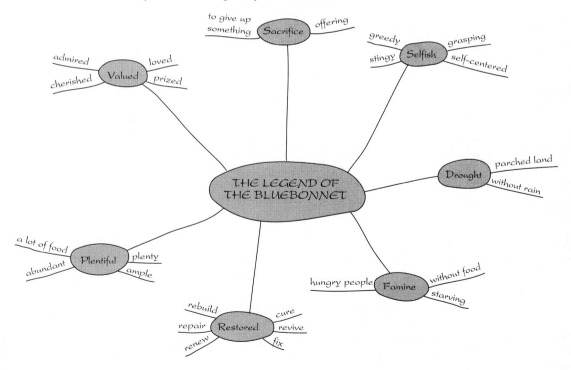

FIGURE 3.7 Plot diagram for *The Legend of the Bluebonnet.*

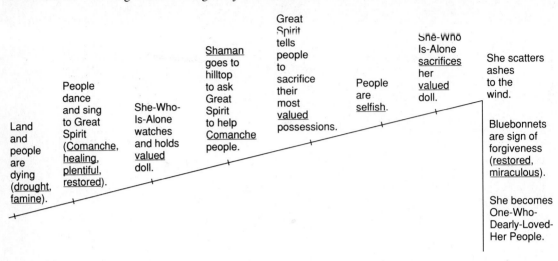

Webbing and plot diagrams are equally effective with students in the upper grades and middle school. The web in Figure 3.8 was developed with Selina Hastings' legend, *Sir Gawain and the Loathly Lady.* The vocabulary was selected because the words related to legendary quests and the age of chivalry. Students were then asked to develop plot diagrams in which they used as many of the vocabulary words as possible. The diagram in Figure 3.9 represents one of these examples.

After students developed webs and plot diagrams for *Sir Gawain and the Loathly Lady* they extended their understandings of the vocabulary of legendary quests and the age of chivalry by reading, webbing, and diagramming other books, such as Margaret Hodges' *Saint George and the Dragon* and various versions of the King Arthur legend. Finally, they compared the webs and diagrams as they looked for similarities.

Webbing with Units and Themes.   A similar webbing activity can accompany a unit or theme approach to literature. For example, a first-grade teacher developed a unit around books that stressed the seasons. The students read, listened to, and looked at the pictures in a variety of books including Jane Chelsea Aragon's *Winter Harvest,* Susi Gregg Fowler's *When Summer Ends,* and Anne Rockwell's *First Comes Spring.* Next, the teacher drew a web with the word *seasons* in the center and *spring, summer, autumn,* and *winter* on the arms extending from the center. The students brainstormed words that they associated with each season. The web in Figure 3.10 is a partial example of the one developed by these first-grade students.

Students frequently benefit from identifying the words that they would like to learn in a unit. A second-grade teacher used Haggard's (1986) approach for self-collection of vocabulary during a unit on problem solving. The students read, listened to, and discussed the following books:

FIGURE 3.8 Vocabulary web of *Sir Gawain and the Loathly Lady.*

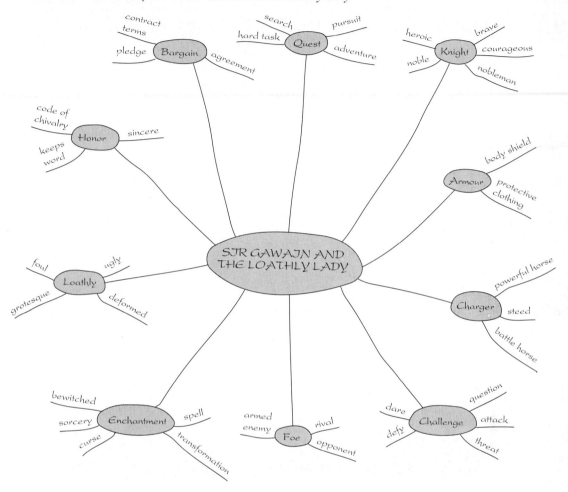

AUTHOR	TITLE	PROBLEM TO OVERCOME
Eve Bunting	*The Wednesday Surprise*	Teaching grandmother to read
Denys Cazet	*A Fish in His Pocket*	Overcoming an accident
Lisa Ernst	*When Bluebell Sang*	Plotting an escape
Ina Friedman	*How My Parents Learned to Eat*	Eating with chopsticks, eating with forks
Amy Hest	*The Purple Coat*	Choosing the color for a coat
Ezra Jack Keats	*Peter's Chair*	Overcoming jealousy
Dayal Khalsa	*I Want A Dog*	Wanting a pet dog
Petra Mathers	*Theodor and Mr Balbini*	Selecting the right dog
Eve Rice	*Peter's Pockets*	Finding a place for treasures
Mildred Walter	*Brother to the Wind*	Dreaming of flying

FIGURE 3.9 Plot diagram for *Sir Gawain and the Loathly Lady.*

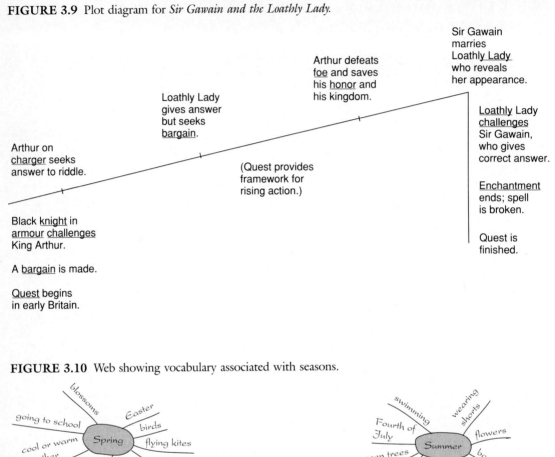

FIGURE 3.10 Web showing vocabulary associated with seasons.

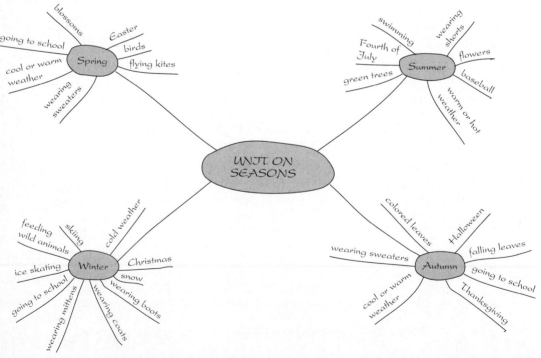

Next, the teacher drew a web on the chalkboard with "Characteristics of Problem Solvers" written in the center, and the students selected vocabulary words to place on the first extensions of the web. They chose the words by discussing and voting on the characteristics of people who are able to solve problems. Then the students identified definitions and synonyms that extended the meanings.

The students eventually drew the web on a bulletin board and placed the appropriate literature on a table under the bulletin board. As the students discovered additional books in which the characters solved problems, they added the books to the reading table. For each new book, they described how the characters overcame their problems and if the characters had any of the characteristics previously identified. Other units that result in interesting vocabulary webs for lower elementary students include weather, animals, family relationships, and friendship.

A fifth-grade teacher used a similar webbing approach during a unit about heroes and heroines. The unit included legendary and folktale heroes, historical heroes, and contemporary heroes. The following books were read and discussed by the students:

AUTHOR	TITLE	TYPE OF HERO
Richard Chase	*The Jack Tales*	Folk
Padraic Colum	*The Golden Fleece*	Legendary
Harold Courlander	*The Crest and the Hide*	Legendary
Margaret Hodges	*Saint George and the Dragon*	Legendary
Julius Lester	*The Tales of Uncle Remus*	Folk
Robin McKinley	*The Outlaws of Sherwood*	Legendary
Steve Sanfield	*The Adventures of High John the Conqueror*	Legendary
Rosemary Sutcliff	*The Sword and the Circle*	Legendary
Virginia Hamilton	*Anthony Burns: The Defeat and Triumph of a Fugitive Slave*	Historical
Nancy Smiler Levinson	*Christopher Columbus: Voyager to the Unknown*	Historical
Milton Meltzer	*George Washington and the Birth of Our Nation*	Historical
Douglas Miller	*Frederick Douglass and the Fight for Freedom*	Historical
Carol Pearce	*Amelia Earhart*	Historical
Beatrice Siegel	*Lillian Wald of Henry Street*	Historical
Rose Sobol	*Woman Chief*	Historical
Jay Tuck and Norma Vergara	*Heroes of Puerto Rico*	Historical
Beverly Cleary	*A Girl from Yamhill*	Contemporary
Jima Haskins and Kathleen Benson	*Space Challenge: The Story of Guion Bluford*	Contemporary
Lillie Patterson	*Martin Luther King, Jr. and the Freedom Movement*	Contemporary
Elliott Roosevelt	*Eleanor Roosevelt, With Love*	Contemporary

The students read and discussed their individual books. Next they drew a web identifying the vocabulary that represented the various characteristics of heroes in-

FIGURE 3.11 Web showing characteristics of heroes and heroines.

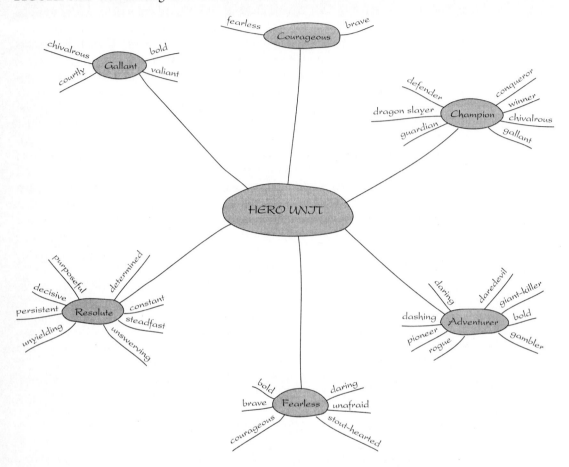

cluding champion, adventurer, fearless, resolute, gallant, and courageous. Then they added terms that expanded each characteristic. Finally, they identified characters from the books that exemplified each of the characteristics. They stated why they thought their character should be placed under the specific characteristics. The web in Figure 3.11 shows part of the extended web developed by the students.

Through the webbing activities and the accompanying discussions, students are encouraged to relate vocabulary development and comprehension of text. Some of the webbing activities, such as the one that accompanies heroes and heroines and the activity that associates characteristics of problem solvers with vocabulary, also relate characterization and vocabulary development.

Semantic Feature Analysis

Semantic feature analysis is another method for associating vocabulary development with text comprehension. According to Anders and Bos (1986) semantic feature analysis is closely related to schema theory because the procedure helps students activate prior knowledge by encouraging them to associate personal experiences with the concepts discussed. The approach also helps students understand the semantic relationships or hierarchical organization of words so that readers can create bridges between ideas and acquire deeper understandings of what is read. Anders and Bos state, "When semantic feature analysis is used before, during, and after reading, it encourages students to predict relationships, read for confirmation, and integrate new and old learning" (p. 611). The approach can be used with a full book, a unit, or a chapter.

Anders and Bos recommend that teachers first read the material to determine the major ideas that will be gained from that reading. Then teachers should list words and phrases that are related to those ideas. Next, they should examine the list and determine which words or phrases represent the most important ideas and concepts. Then they can identify words and phrases that represent details (the vocabulary words) that are related to the ideas and concepts. These ideas and concepts and important vocabulary are then placed on a chart with the important ideas across the top and the related vocabulary listed down the side. The chart in Figure 3.12 was developed with sixth-grade students who were reading Patricia Lauber's *Volcano: The Eruption and Healing of Mount St. Helens.*

The chart should be duplicated so that each student can complete the chart, add to it, and refer to it during reading and discussion. It is helpful if the teacher displays a model chart on an overhead projector to introduce the procedure, the topic, and the vocabulary and ideas that will be studied. Students are encouraged to add their personal experiences or understandings during this discussion.

Students then use the chart to determine the relationships between each of the important ideas and the important vocabulary. If the relationship is positive, the students place a (+) sign in the square. If the relationship is negative, they place a (−) sign in the square. A zero (0) represents no relationship and a question mark (?) shows that an answer cannot be reached without more information.

During class, the teacher leads a discussion in which students chart the relationships and justify their choice of markings. Anders and Bos state:

> Student involvement during the discussion is critical to the success of the semantic feature analysis strategy. One key to a successful discussion is to ask students why they reach a certain relationship rating. This seems to encourage them to use their prior knowledge regarding the topic. This, in turn, seems to encourage other students to activate what they already know about the vocabulary. (p. 614)

In this example notice how closely the semantic feature analysis can be related to content areas and comprehension of key ideas and vocabulary within the various content areas. A semantic feature analysis easily could accompany history books such as Jean Fritz's *Shh! We're Writing the Constitution,* Carolyn Meyer and Charles Gallenkamp's *The Mystery of the Ancient Maya,* or Judith St. George's *The White House: Cornerstone of a Nation.* Students who are studying ancient reptiles might complete a semantic feature analysis around Patricia Lauber's *The News About Dinosaurs.* In science class students might study the dangers of animal extinction and then develop a chart around Margery and Howard Facklam's *And Then There Was One: The Mysteries*

FIGURE 3.12 Semantic feature analysis.

Related vocabulary	Signs of waking volcano	Mount St. Helens is an old volcano	Molten rock turns to lava	Volcanoes have bowl-shaped craters at the top	The Cascade Range is a chain of volcanoes	Volcanoes are to be feared	There is a need to predict volcanic eruptions
earthquake							
eruptions							
magma							
pumice							
gas and steam							
explosions							
swelling and cracking							
geologists							
measuring the bulge							
instrument recording							
avalanche							
seismometer							
pressure							
mudflows							

of Extinction or Laurence Pringle's *Saving Our Wildlife*. Interesting semantic feature analysis might accompany Heiderose and Andreas Fischer-Nagel's *The Life of the Honeybee* or Helen Roney Sattler's *Giraffes, the Sentinels of the Savannas*.

Building Student Responsibility for Vocabulary Development

Helping students activate prior knowledge, use context clues, and become involved in strategies that help them verify meanings is important. Many of the approaches presented in this chapter stress discovering what students know about words through discussions, brainstorming, and various types of analysis.

Researchers in vocabulary development also stress that students should be encouraged to use a variety of strategies and to verify when meanings are making sense within a specific context. Blachowicz (1986) identifies a five-step strategy that helps students activate prior knowledge and become involved in their own vocabulary development. First, when approaching vocabulary, have students ask themselves,

"What do I already know about these words?" Second, ask the students to preview the text and predict the meanings of the words. They should ask themselves, "What clues do I see when previewing the text that will give me ideas about the meanings of the words? What is my best guess?" Third, have the students read the text and consider the context of the words. Fourth, ask the students to use the initial cues and the cues from the selection to confirm and clarify their preliminary decisions about meanings. At this point they should understand that they can predict meanings of words and then read to confirm or clarify the accuracy of their predictions. Fifth, ask the students to use the words in their own writing and to search for the words in additional readings. Such an approach can be used with any type of literature selection.

Students need many opportunities to develop and expand their vocabularies. The techniques developed in this chapter include learning vocabulary through incident experiences and through teacher-led instruction. Most of the strategies emphasize the importance of wide reading and discussions that encourage students to activate prior knowledge and to relate new words to understandable contexts. In the next chapters we will develop many other techniques such as understanding author's style that also help students increase their understanding of vocabulary.

REFERENCES

ANDERS, P. & BOS, C. (1986). Semantic feature analysis: An interactive strategy for vocabulary development and text comprehension. *Journal of Reading, 29,* 610–616.

BLACHOWICZ, C. (1986). Making connections: Alternatives to the vocabulary notebook. *Journal of Reading, 29,* 643–649.

CALFEE, R. & DRUM, P. (1986). Research on teaching reading. In Merlin Wittrock (Ed.), *Handbook of research on teaching.* New York: Macmillan.

CARR, E. & WIXSON, K. (1986). Guidelines for evaluating vocabulary instruction. *Journal of Reading, 29,* 588–595.

HAGGARD, M. R. (1986). The vocabulary self-collection strategy: Using student interest and word knowledge to enhance vocabulary growth. *Journal of Reading, 29,* 634–642.

LAMME, L. L. (1976). Reading aloud to young children. *Language Arts, 53,* pp. 886–88.

MARZANO, R. & MARZANO, J. (1988). *A cluster approach to elementary vocabulary instruction.* Newark, DE: International Reading Association.

McCULLOUGH, C. (1944). Recognition of context clues in reading. *Elementary English Review, 22,* pp. 1–5.

McKEOWN, M., BECK, I., OMANSON, R., & POPLE, M. (1985). Some effects of the nature and frequency of vocabulary instruction on the knowledge and use of words. *Reading Research Quarterly, 20,* pp. 522–535.

NAGY, W., ANDERSON, R., & HERMAN, P. (1987). Learning words from context during normal reading. *American Educational Research Journal, 24,* pp. 237–270.

RAKES, T. & CHOATE, J. (1989). *Language arts: Detecting and correcting special needs.* Needham Heights, MA: Allyn & Bacon.

RUDDELL, R. (1986). Vocabulary learning: A process model and criteria for evaluating instructional strategies. *Journal of Reading, 29,* 581–587.

STAHL, S. & FAIRBANKS, M. (1986). The effects of vocabulary instruction: A model based meta-analysis. *Review of Educational Research, 56,* pp. 72–110.

STERNBERG, R. J., POWELL, J. S., & KAYE, D. B. (1983). Teaching vocabulary-building skills: A contextual approach. In A. C. Wilkinson (Ed.), *Classroom computers and cognitive science.* New York: Academic Press.

CHILDREN'S LITERATURE REFERENCES*

ARAGON, JANE CHELSEA. *Winter Harvest.* Boston: Little, Brown, 1988 (I: 5–8).

AYLESWORTH, JIM. *One Crow: A Counting Rhyme.* Illustrated by Ruth Young. New York: Lippincott, 1988 (I: 2–7).

*I = Interest by age range

BABBITT, NATALIE. *Tuck Everlasting.* New York: Farrar, Straus and Giroux, 1975 (I: 8–12+)

BANACHEK, LINDA. *Snake In, Snake Out.* Illustrated by Elaine Arnold. New York: Crowell, 1978 (I: 3–7).

BARTON, BYRON. *Machines At Work.* New York: Crowell, 1987 (I: 2–6).

_____. *I Want to Be an Astronaut.* New York: Crowell, 1988 (I: 2–6).

BRETT, JAN, retold by. *Goldilocks and the Three Bears.* New York: Dodd, Mead, 1987 (I: 5–8).

BRITTAIN, BILL. *The Wish Giver.* Illustrated by Andrew Glass. New York: Harper & Row, 1983 (I: 8–12).

BUNTING, EVE. *The Wednesday Surprise.* Illustrated by Donald Carrick. New York: Clarion, 1989 (I: 6–9).

BURTON, VIRGINIA LEE. *The Little House.* Boston: Houghton Mifflin, 1942 (I: 3–8).

_____. *Mike Mulligan and His Steam Shovel.* Boston: Houghton Mifflin, 1939 (I: 3–8).

BUSCAGLIA, LEO. *The Fall of Freddie the Leaf.* New York: Holt, Rinehart & Winston, 1982 (I: all).

CARROLL, LEWIS. *Alice's Adventures in Wonderland.* Illustrated by John Tenniel. New York: Macmillan, 1866; Knopf, 1984 (I: 8+).

CARROLL, LEWIS. *Through the Looking Glass.* Illustrated by John Tenniel. New York: Macmillan, 1972; Knopf, 1984 (I: 8+).

CAZET, DENYS. *A Fish in His Pocket.* New York: Orchard, 1987 (I: 3–7).

CENDRARS, BLAISE. *Shadow.* Illustrated by Marcia Brown. New York: Scribner's, 1982 (1: 8–12+).

CHASE, RICHARD. *The Jack Tales.* Illustrated by Berkeley Williams, Jr. Boston: Houghton Mifflin, 1943 (I: all).

CLEARY, BEVERLY. *Dear Mr. Henshaw.* Illustrated by Paul O. Zelinsky. New York: Morrow, 1983 (I: 9–12).

_____. *A Girl from Yamhill.* New York: Morrow, 1988 (I: 8+).

COLUM, PADRAIC. *The Golden Fleece.* Illustrated by Willy Pogany. New York: Macmillan, 1921, 1949 (I: 9+).

COURLANDER, HAROLD. *The Crest and the Hide.* Illustrated by Monica Vachula. New York: Coward, McCann & Geoghegan, 1982 (I: 8+).

COUSINS, LUCY. *The Little Dog Laughed and Other Nursery Rhymes.* New York: Dutton, 1990 (I: 3–8).

CREWS, DONALD. *Freight Train.* New York: Greenwillow, 1978 (I: 3–7).

DEPAOLA, TOMIE. *The Legend of the Bluebonnet.* New York: Putnam, 1983 (I: all).

_____. *Tomie dePaola's Mother Goose.* New York: Putnam's, 1985 (I: 3–7).

DODDS, DAYLE ANN. *Wheel Away!* Illustrated by Thacher Hurd. New York: Harper & Row, 1989 (I: 3–7).

EMBERLEY, REBECCA. *City Sounds.* Boston: Little, Brown, 1989 (I: 5–8).

_____. *Jungle Sounds.* Boston: Little, Brown, 1989 (I: 5–8).

ERNST, LISA. *When Bluebell Sang.* New York: Bradbury, 1989 (I: 6–9).

FACKLAM, MARGERY & FACKLAM, HOWARD. *And Then There Was One: The Mysteries of Extinction.* Illustrated by Pamela Johnson. Sierra Club, 1990 (I: 10+).

FISCHER-NAGEL, HEIDEROSE & FISCHER-NAGEL, ANDREAS. *Life of the Honeybee.* Minneapolis: Carolrhoda, 1986 (I: 8–10).

FORBES, ESTHER. *Johnny Tremain.* Illustrated by Lynd Ward. Boston: Houghton, Mifflin, 1943 (I: 10+).

FOWLER, SUSI GREGG. *When Summer Ends.* Illustrated by Marisabina Russo. New York: Greenwillow, 1989 (I: 5–8).

FOX, MEM. *Night Noises.* Illustrated by Terry Denton. San Diego: Harcourt Brace Jovanovich, 1989 (I: 5–8).

FOX, PAULA. *One-Eyed Cat.* New York: Bradbury, 1984 (I: 10+).

FRANK, RUDOLF. *No Hero for the Kaiser.* New York: Lothrop, Lee & Shepard, 1986 (I: 10+).

FRIEDMAN, INA. *How My Parents Learned to Eat.* Illustrated by Allen Say. Boston: Houghton Mifflin, 1984 (I: 5–9).

FRIEDMAN, RUSSELL. *Lincoln: A Photobiography.* New York: Clarion, 1987 (I: 8+).

FRITZ, JEAN. *Shh! We're Writing the Constitution.* Illustrated by Tomie dePaola. New York: Putnam, 1987 (I: 7–10).

_____. *What's the Big Idea, Ben Franklin?* Illustrated by Margot Tomes. New York: Coward, McCann, 1978 (I: 7–10).

_____. *Where Was Patrick Henry on the 29th of May?* Illustrated by Margot Tomes. New York: Coward, McCann, 1975 (I: 7–10).

GALLANT, ROY. *Before the Sun Dies: The Story of Evolution.* New York: Macmillan, 1989 (I: 10+).

GARDNER, MARTIN. *The Annotated Alice.* New York: Bramhall House, 1960 (I: 10+).

GEORGE, JEAN CRAIGHEAD. *The Talking Earth.* New York: Harper, 1983 (I: 10+).

GIBBONS, GAIL. *Trains.* New York: Holiday, 1987 (I: 3–8).

GOODALL, JANE. *The Chimpanzee Family Book.* Photographs by Michael Neugebauer. Saxonville, MA: Picture Book Studio, 1989 (I: 8–12).

GRAHAME, KENNETH. *The Wind in the Willows.* Illustrated by Ernest Shepard. New York: Scribner's, 1908, 1983 (I: 8 +).

HAMILTON, VIRGINIA. *Anthony Burns: The Defeat and Triumph of a Fugitive Slave.* New York: Knopf, 1988 (I: 10 +).

_____. *The Planet of Junior Brown.* New York: Macmillan, 1971 (I: 10 +).

HASKINS, JIM & BENSON, KATHLEEN. *Space Challenger: The Story of Guion Bluford.* Minneapolis: Carolrhoda, 1984 (I: 8–12).

HASTINGS, SELINA, retold by. *Sir Gawain and the Loathly Lady.* Illustrated by Juan Wijngaard. New York: Lothrop, Lee & Shepard, 1985 (I: 10 +).

HEST, AMY. *The Purple Coat.* Illustrated by Amy Schwartz. New York: Four Winds, 1986 (I: 6–9).

HIGHWATER, JAMAKE. *Anpao: An American Indian Odyssey.* New York: Lippincott, 1977 (I: 10 +).

HOBAN, TANA. *Exactly the Opposite.* New York: Greenwillow, 1990 (I: 3–8).

_____. *Of Colors and Things.* New York: Greenwillow, 1989 (I: 3–8).

_____. *Round & Round & Round.* New York: Greenwillow, 1983 (I: 3–8).

_____. *Shapes, Shapes, Shapes.* New York: Greenwillow, 1986 (I: 3–8).

HODGES, MARGARET, retold by. *Saint George and the Dragon.* Illustrated by Trina Schart Hyman. Boston: Little, Brown, 1984 (I: 10 +).

HUDSON, JAN. *Sweetgrass.* New York: Philomel, 1989 (I: 10 +).

HUTCHINS, PAT. *What Game Shall We Play?* New York: Greenwillow, 1990 (I: 3–7).

IVIMEY, JOHN. *Three Blind Mice.* Illustrated by Paul Galdone. New York: Clarion (I: 5–8).

JOHNSON, SYLVIA. *Potatoes.* Photographs by Masaharu Suzuki. Minneapolis: Lerner, 1984 (I: 8–12).

KEATS, EZRA JACK. *Peter's Chair.* New York: Harper & Row, 1967 (I: 5–8).

KHALSA, DAYAL. *I Want a Dog.* New York: Crown, 1987 (I: 5–8).

KONIGSBURG, E. L. *From the Mixed-Up Files of Mrs. Basil Frankweiler.* New York: Atheneum, 1970, 1980 (I: 9–12).

KRUMGOLD, JOSEPH. *. . . And Now Miguel.* Illustrated by Jean Charlot. New York: Crowell, 1953 (I: 10 +).

LAUBER, PATRICIA. *The News About Dinosaurs.* New York: Bradbury, 1989 (I: 8–10).

_____. *Volcano: The Eruption and Healing of Mount St. Helens.* New York: Bradbury, 1986 (I: 8–12).

LEAF, MUNROE. *The Story of Ferdinand.* Illustrated by Robert Lawson. New York: Viking, 1936, 1964 (I: 5–8).

LEAR, EDWARD. *The Scroobious Pip.* Illustrated by Nancy Ekholm Burkert. New York: Harper & Row, 1968 (I: all).

LESTER, JULIUS, retold by. *The Tales of Uncle Remus: The Adventures of Brer Rabbit.* Illustrated by Jerry Pinkney. New York: Dial, 1987 (I: all).

LEVINSON, NANCY SMILER. *Christopher Columbus: Voyager to the Unknown.* New York: Lodestar, 1990 (I: 10 +).

LEWIN, HUGH. *Jafta.* Illustrated by Lisa Kopper. Minneapolis: Carolrhoda, 1983 (I: 5–8).

_____. *Jafta's Mother.* Illustrated by Lisa Kopper. Minneapolis: Carolrhoda, 1983 (I: 5–8).

LEWIS, C. S. *The Lion, the Witch, and the Wardrobe.* Illustrated by Pauline Baynes. New York: Macmillan, 1950 (I: 9 +).

LIONNI, LEO. *Swimmy.* New York: Pantheon, 1963 (I: 2–6).

LOBEL, ARNOLD. *The Random House Book of Mother Goose.* New York: Random House, 1986 (I:3–8).

MACLACHLAN, PATRICIA. *Sarah, Plain and Tall.* New York: Harper & Row, 1985 (I: 7–10).

MARTIN, BILL, JR. & ARCHAMBAULT, JOHN. *Up and Down the Merry-Go-Round.* Illustrated by Ted Rand. New York: Henry Holt, 1988 (I: 3–8).

MATHERS, PETRA. *Theodor and Mr. Balbini.* New York: Harper & Row, 1988 (I: 6–9).

MATTHEWS, DOWNS. *Polar Bear Cubs.* Photographs by Dan Guravich. New York: Simon & Schuster, 1989 (I: 5–10).

McKISSACK, PATRICIA. *Mirandy and Brother Wind.* Illustrated by Jerry Pinkney. New York: Knopf, 1988 (I: 6–9).

McKINLEY, ROBIN. *The Outlaws of Sherwood.* New York: Greenwillow, 1988 (I: 10 +).

McLAUGHLIN, MOLLY. *Dragonflies.* New York: Walker, 1989 (I: 7–12).

McMILLAN, BRUCE. *Here A Chick, There A Chick.* New York: Lothrop, Lee & Shepard, 1983 (I: 3–7).

MELTZER, MILTON. *George Washington and the Birth of Our Nation.* New York: Watts, 1986 (I: 10 +).

MEYER, CAROLYN & GALLENKAMP, CHARLES. *The Mystery of the Ancient Maya.* New York: Atheneum, 1985 (I: 10 +).

MILLER, DOUGLAS. *Frederick Douglass and the Fight for Freedom.* New York: Facts On File, 1988 (I: 10 +).

NOLL, SALLY. *Watch Where You Go.* New York: Greenwillow, 1990 (I: 3–7).

NORTON, MARY. *The Borrowers.* Illustrated by Beth and Joe Krush. Orlando: Harcourt Brace Jovanovich, 1952 (I: 7–12).

O'DELL, SCOTT. *Sing Down the Moon.* Boston: Houghton Mifflin, 1970 (I: 10 +).

OPIE, IONA & OPIE, PETER. *Tail Feathers From Mother Goose: The Opie Rhyme Book.* Boston: Little, Brown, 1988 (I: 5–8).

ORLEV, URI. *The Island on Bird Street.* Boston: Houghton Mifflin, 1984 (I: 10+).

PATTERSON, LILLIE. *Martin Luther King, Jr. and the Freedom Movement.* New York: Facts On File, 1989 (I: 10+).

PEARCE, CAROL. *Amelia Earhart.* New York: Facts On File, 1988 (I: 8+).

PRELUTSKY, JACK, selected by. *The Random House Book of Poetry for Children.* Illustrated by Arnold Lobel. New York: Random House, 1983 (I: all).

_____. selected by. *Read-Aloud Rhymes for the Very Young.* Illustrated by Marc Brown. New York: Knopf, 1986 (I: 3–8).

_____. *Something Big Has Been Here.* Illustrated by James Stevenson. New York: Greenwillow, 1990 (I: 3–10).

PRINGLE, LAURENCE. *Saving Our Wildlife.* Hillside, NJ: Enslow, 1990 (I: 10+).

REY, HANS. *Curious George.* Boston: Houghton Mifflin, 1941, 1969 (I: 2–7).

RICE, EVE. *Peter's Pockets.* Illustrated by Nancy Winslow Parker. New York: Greenwillow, 1989 (I: 5–8).

ROCKWELL, ANNE. *First Comes Spring.* New York: Crowell, 1985 (I: 5–8).

ROOP, PETER, & ROOP, CONNIE. *Seasons of the Cranes.* New York: Walker, 1989 (I: 8–12).

ROOSEVELT, ELLIOTT. *Eleanor Roosevelt, With Love.* New York: Dutton, 1984 (I: 10+).

ROUNDS, GLEN. *I Know An Old Lady Who Swallowed a Fly.* New York: Holiday, 1990 (I: 3–7).

_____. *Old MacDonald Had a Farm.* New York: Holiday, 1989 (I: 3–6).

ROSEN, MICHAEL. *We're Going on a Bear Hunt.* Illustrated by Helen Oxenbury. New York: Macmillan, 1989 (I: 3–6).

SANFIELD, STEVE, retold by. *The Adventures of High John the Conqueror.* Illustrated by John Ward. New York: Orchard, 1989 (I: 8+).

SAN SOUCI, ROBERT. *The Talking Eggs.* Illustrated by Jerry Pinkney. New York: Dial, 1989 (I: 6–9).

SATTLER, HELEN R. *The Book of Eagles.* Illustrated by Jean Zallinger. New York: Lothrop, Lee & Shepard, 1989 (I: 8+).

_____. *Giraffes, The Sentinels of the Savannas.* Illustrated by Christopher Santoro. New York: Lothrop, Lee & Shepard, 1990 (I: 8+).

_____. *Train Whistles.* Illustrated by Giulio Maestro. New York: Lothrop, Lee & Shepard, 1985 (I: 3–9).

SELDEN, GEORGE. *The Cricket in Times Square.* Illustrated by Garth Williams. New York: Farrar, Straus & Giroux, 1969 (I: 7–12).

SELSAM, MILLICENT & HUNT, JOYCE. *A First Look at Animals With Horns.* Illustrated by Harriet Springer. New York: Walker, 1989 (I: 5–8).

_____. *A First Look at Animals that Eat Other Animals.* Illustrated by Harriet Springer. New York: Walker, 1990 (I: 5–8).

_____. *A First Look at Bird Nests.* Illustrated by Harriet Springer. New York: Walker, 1985 (I: 5–8).

_____. *A First Look at Caterpillars.* Illustrated by Harriet Springer. New York: Walker, 1987 (I: 5–8).

_____. *A First Look at Seals, Sea Lions, and Walruses.* Illustrated by Harriet Springer. New York: Walker, 1988 (I: 5–8).

SENDAK, MAURICE. *Where the Wild Things Are.* New York: Harper & Row, 1963 (I: 3–8).

SIEGEL, BEATRICE. *Lillian Wald of Henry Street.* New York: Macmillan, 1983 (I: 10+).

SIMON, SEYMOUR. *Danger from Below: Earthquakes—Past, Present, and Future.* New York: Four Winds, 1979 (I: 10+).

_____. *Galaxies.* New York: Morrow, 1988 (I: 5–8).

_____. *Jupiter.* New York: Morrow, 1985 (I: 5–8).

_____. *Little Giants.* Illustrated by Pamela Carroll. New York: Morrow, 1983 (I: 7–12).

_____. *The Long Journey from Space.* New York: Crown, 1982 (I: 9+).

_____. *Saturn.* New York: Morrow, 1985 (I: 5–8).

_____. *The Smallest Dinosaurs.* Illustrated by Anthony Rao. New York: Crown, 1982 (I: 5–9).

_____. *Storms.* New York: Morrow, 1989 (I: 8–12).

_____. *Volcanoes.* New York: Morrow, 1988 (I: 8–12).

SNYDER, DIANNE. *The Boy of the Three-Year Nap.* Illustrated by Allen Say. Boston: Houghton Mifflin, 1988 (I: 5–9).

SOBOL, ROSE. *Woman Chief.* New York: Dell, 1976 (I: 8+).

SPERRY, ARMSTRONG. *Call It Courage.* New York: Macmillan, 1940 (I: 9–12).

ST. GEORGE, JUDITH. *The White House: Cornerstone of a Nation.* New York: Putnam's, 1990 (I: 9+).

SUTCLIFF, ROSEMARY. *The Sword and the Circle.* London: Bodley Head, 1981 (I: 10+).

TUCK, JAY & VERGARA, NORMA. *Heroes of Puerto Rico.* New York: Fleet, 1969 (I: 8+).

VIORST, JUDITH. *Alexander and the Terrible, Horrible, No Good, Very Bad Day.* Illustrated by Ray Cruz. New York: Atheneum, 1972 (I: 3–8).

VOIGT, CYNTHIA. *Dicey's Song.* New York: Atheneum, 1982 (I: 10+).

_____. *A Solitary Blue.* New York: Atheneum, 1983 (I: 10+).

WALTER, MILDRED. *Brother to the Wind.* Illustrated by Diane and Leo Dillon. New York: Lothrop, Lee & Shepard, 1985 (I: all).

WELLS, ROSEMARY. *The Little Lame Prince.* New York: Dial, 1990 (I: 5–8).

WHIPPLE, LAURA, compiled by. *Eric Carle's Animals, Animals.* New York: Philomel, 1989 (I: all).

WHITE, E. B. *Charlotte's Web.* Illustrated by Garth Williams. New York: Harper & Row, 1952 (I: 7–12).

———. *Stewart Little.* Illustrated by Garth Williams. New York: Harper & Row, 1945 (I: 7–12).

WILLIAMS, MARGERY. *The Velveteen Rabbit: Or How Toys Become Real.* Illustrated by William Nicholson. New York: Doubleday, 1958 (I: 6–9).

WOJCIECHOWSKA, MAIA. *Shadow of a Bull.* New York: Atheneum, 1983 (I: 10+).

YOLEN, JANE. *The Three Bears Rhyme Book.* Illustrated by Jane Dyer. San Diego: Harcourt Brace Jovanovich, 1987 (I: 3–8).

CHAPTER 4

ASSESSMENT

ASSESSING THE INSTRUCTIONAL ENVIRONMENT
    Physical Environment and Materials
    Teacher Behaviors

ASSESSING STUDENTS
    A Portfolio Approach
    Assessing Interests and Background Information
    Assessing Comprehension
    Assessing Reading Processes Through Self-Evaluation
    Assessing Reader Response to Literature

ASSESSING THE TOTAL LITERATURE-BASED PROGRAM

One of the cardinal rules for developing evaluation schemes and choosing assessment instruments is that the evaluation scheme and the assessments need to match the objectives for the program and for instruction. Consequently, teachers and administrators need to consider the overall objectives of their literature-based program, note the information that would help them improve their students' achievement, and identify assessment measures to evaluate students' gains in literacy.

The need to match instructional objectives and assessment instruments is one of the issues in evaluating literature-based programs. But the standardized tests used in many school districts do not measure the scope of a literature-based program. After reading, analyzing, and responding to literature, students have many understandings about reading and literature that are not measured on the tests. Pikulski (1989) argues that assessment must be broadened significantly, that tests and other assessment materials must reflect the purposes of the program, that assessment of reading needs to be teacher- and pupil-centered rather than test-centered, and that the form of assessment must reflect the goals of instruction and the dynamic nature of the reading process. Valencia (1990) maintains that assessment should meet the following criteria: (a) It is developed from authentic reading instruction and reading tasks; (b) it is continuous and ongoing; (c) it samples a wide range of texts and purposes and assesses various cognitive processes, affective responses, and literacy activities; and (d) it provides for active, collaborative reflection by both teacher and student. The recommendations of Pikulski and Valencia illustrate the need for assessment that goes beyond results found in most standardized tests that use short reading passages and multiple-choice formats.

Although most school districts and states require standardized tests, many educators are searching for and developing assessment measures that more closely match the objectives of literature-based instruction. For example, Mathews (1990) focuses on many of the issues facing teachers and school districts when she describes the approach used by Orange County, Florida, in its search for a literacy-assessment program that meets the needs of students in both basal and literature-based programs. After numerous discussions and evaluations, the planning group decided to use a portfolio approach to literacy assessment. This portfolio, a folder kept on each student, contains information that teachers and students think illustrates the literacy growth of the students. Each portfolio includes a reading-development checklist, several writing samples taken during different times of the year, a list of books read by the students, and the results of a reading-comprehension test. In addition to these core items, the portfolios might include self-evaluations, examples of various assignments that focus on literature, and personal responses to books. Mathews states that identifying a test of comprehension has been the most difficult task because

> We are still looking at commercially available tests and hope to find one that will have authentic texts and quality questions. We are also considering using a science or social studies passage at each grade level and writing appropriate assessment questions.
> Three different tests at each grade level will allow for trimester testing and allow us to include different kinds of passages. (p. 421)

This brief discussion of the process used by the Orange County school district highlights many of the problems facing teachers as they attempt to assess an approach to reading that might teach different processes and understandings than have previous approaches.

Some useful guidelines for assessment are provided by researchers who analyze effective evaluation of content-area instruction. For example, Farr, Tulley, and Pritchard (1989) state that teachers in content areas need to know students' reading levels, strategies that students employ to identify vocabulary, students' competency with different levels of comprehension, students' background knowledge related to the subject, and students' interests and attitudes. Notice how closely these items relate to the literature curriculum. According to Farr, Tulley, and Pritchard, informal tests including checklists, inventories, and surveys of specific student abilities are among the most useful instruments for determining students' strengths and weaknesses. They highlight six informal measures that are reliable and valid in content-area settings: (a) exploring background data, (b) self-assessments, (c) observations, (d) informal reading inventories, (e) cloze tests, and (f) content-area reading inventories.

Farr, Tulley, and Pritchard state that these methods

> allow teachers to sample reading behaviors at different times and under different conditions. Second, they typically allow teachers to sample a much larger set of behaviors using a variety of item types. And, third, the results of these methods are certain to be useful for instructional decision making since they are likely to be based on specific classroom materials and activities. (p. 349)

This chapter focuses on some informal assessment measures that relate to literature-based curriculums. The evaluation includes the assessment of the instructional environment, the assessment of the students in the literature program, the assessment of student responses to literature, and the assessment of student and teacher responses to literature-based programs.

ASSESSING THE INSTRUCTIONAL ENVIRONMENT

According to Lipson (1990), the instructional environment or setting related to reading and literacy includes instructional context, methods, texts, and tasks. She states that the focus for assessing this environment should be on the "elements of the context that are most likely to impact specific students' performance in reading and writing" (p. 330). According to Lipson, these important elements include both an analysis of the materials used by the students and the teacher's use of various literacy activities. An assessment of materials should include information about the materials, the tasks associated with the materials, and the demands being placed on the students by the materials and the tasks. An assessment of the teacher should include an examination of the teacher's use of time spent in such activities as interaction with literature, teacher- and student-initiated talk, and student reading of connected texts.

Physical Environment and Materials

From the discussions in the previous chapters, the lists of literature, and recommendations for various teaching strategies that encourage both efferent and aesthetic responses to literature, it is clear that the assessment of the physical environment and the materials that make up that environment is important. If students are to read and respond to literature they must have opportunities to select literature for group and independent activities. They need both an in-class library and a school library that give them the chance to read a variety of genres of literature. They need access to all types of literature including fictional and expository materials. These materials should reflect the evaluation criteria developed earlier in this book. In addition, Peters (1991) stresses the importance of selecting the various expository materials that are used within the content fields. He provides five guidelines for the selection of expository materials with authentic content: (a) The materials should reflect important themes and ideas because themes and ideas guide the integration of facts, concepts, generalizations, and theories; (b) the materials should be consistent with the goals of the subject-area curriculum; (c) the materials should be rooted in real-world experiences and be applicable to the world in and out of school; (d) the materials should be sensitive to the developmental progress of the students; and (e) the materials should encourage students to engage in higher order thinking.

One of the first assessments related to the evaluation of the literature-based program should focus on the quality of the environment, the motivational and stimulation quality of the setting, the quality of the materials available within the environment, and the accessibility of these materials. This last point is important. Even the best equipped libraries are inadequate if the students are not encouraged to use the materials or taught how to use the sources.

Two types of assessments are helpful. One type analyzes the types of materials that are available to the students. This assessment might include a listing of available books, tapes, magazines, and films. The second type considers the quality of the environment and materials. Figure 4.1 shows an example of an inventory that could be used to evaluate the quality of the physical features and materials provided for the students and teachers.

Students themselves also should be encouraged to assess the quality of the environment and the materials. Frequently they make suggestions that could increase the attractiveness or the accessibility of the environment. Encouraging students to assess the books they read is an excellent way to stimulate interest in reading literature, especially for recreation. For example, teachers in the lower elementary grades can

FIGURE 4.1 Inventory of room and school environment.

	High Quality	Average Quality	Low Quality
1. The room has a library corner with a variety of literature that can be read for group and individual assignments, and for recreational reading.	_____	_____	_____
2. The library corner is attractive. It includes a place to display books, read books, and display responses to the books.	_____	_____	_____
3. The room and the school reflect a love for literature. There are many places to display books and students' creative works related to literature.	_____	_____	_____
4. The main school library has a wide range of quality literature that reflects various genres, subjects, and cultures.	_____	_____	_____
5. The literature collection reflects the needs of the various content areas so that students can integrate literature into the content areas.	_____	_____	_____
6. The main library attracts students to select and read literature. Students are encouraged to use the library.	_____	_____	_____
7. The librarian provides book talks that stimulate students' interests in books and encourages them to find books that meet their interests and their needs.	_____	_____	_____

construct easy rating charts made of tagboard or other firm material, to be placed near the classroom library. When a student reads a book, the student writes the name of the book on the chart, signs his or her name next to the book, and gives the book either a smiley face, a neutral face, or a frowning face. Students also can write a brief sentence explaining their rating. As might be expected, such a rating chart interests other students to read and assess the same books. Books that are rated highly by several students are especially popular.

Students in the upper grades and middle school also should be encouraged to rate books they read. Students in one class developed a rating system similar to those used by movie critics. They gave books numbers according to how well they liked the books, how well the books were written, and how highly they should be recommended to other students. When new books arrived in the library, they had several students read them and present their views. Just as with the movie critics, the students often had opposing views, which stimulated more interest as students read the books to decide which critic they thought was correct.

In addition to assessing the physical environment and the quality of the books available to the students, teachers should assess the quality of the instructional tasks related to the literature. Lipson (1990) recommends that teachers ask questions such as, "Do the activities access background knowledge and set purposes for reading? Do the activities foster independence in the use of reading strategies? Do the activities reflect the most important aspects of what is being taught in the reading program? Are student response modes the closest possible to authentic reading and writing activities?" (p. 330).

In addition to these questions, teachers can assess their ability to encourage both efferent and aesthetic responses. For example, Figure 4.2 shows an informal way to keep track of the various instructional tasks that accompany literature. Teachers can use such a list to make sure they are encouraging both efferent and aesthetic responses to literature.

This check list allows teachers to analyze the various activities used in their literature programs and to evaluate if the instructional programs include activities that encourage both efferent and aesthetic responses to literature. After completing such a check list many teachers discover that they are not balancing their literature instruction or encouraging students to give many different responses.

FIGURE 4.2 Assessing a variety of instructional tasks that encourage efferent and aesthetic responses to literature.

1. List examples of instructional tasks that encourage students to understand the literary elements:
   a. Instructional tasks designed to help students understand and analyze setting.
   b. Instructional tasks designed to help students understand and analyze plot and conflict.
   c. Instructional tasks designed to help students understand and analyze characterization.
   d. Instructional tasks designed to help students understand and analyze theme.
   e. Instructional tasks designed to help students understand author's style.

2. List examples of instructional tasks that encourage students to give personal responses to the literature, to describe how they responded, and to think about why they responded in certain ways.
   a. Instructional tasks designed to help students give a personal response to setting.
   b. Instructional tasks designed to help students give a personal response to plot and conflict.
   c. Instructional tasks designed to help students give a personal response to characterization.
   d. Instructional tasks designed to help students respond to theme.
   e. Instructional tasks designed to help students respond to author's style.

3. List examples of instructional tasks that encourage students to understand the literary genres:
   a. Instructional tasks designed to help students understand and analyze folklore.
   b. Instructional tasks designed to help students understand and analyze modern fantasy.
   c. Instructional tasks designed to help students understand and analyze poetry.
   d. Instructional tasks designed to help students understand and analyze contemporary realistic fiction.
   e. Instructional tasks designed to help students understand and analyze historical fiction.
   f. Instructional tasks designed to help students understand and analyze biography.
   g. Instructional tasks designed to help students understand and analyze nonfictional informational literature.

4. List examples of instructional tasks that encourage students to give personal responses to the literature genres:
   a. Instructional tasks designed to encourage students to respond to folklore.
   b. Instructional tasks designed to encourage students to respond to modern fantasy.
   c. Instructional tasks designed to encourage students to respond to poetry.
   d. Instructional tasks designed to encourage students to respond to contemporary realistic fiction.
   e. Instructional tasks designed to encourage students to respond to historical fiction.
   f. Instructional tasks designed to encourage students to respond to biography.
   g. Instructional tasks designed to encourage students to respond to nonfictional informational literature.

5. List examples of instructional tasks that integrate literature into the other content areas.

Teacher Behaviors

Most educators would agree that the teacher is the most important element in an effective educational program. Lipson (1990) states that the assessment of the literacy environment must assess the role of the teacher. She maintains that the assessment must examine the teacher's use of time in the classroom; for example, how much time is spent on such tasks as interacting with literature, teacher- and student-initiated talk, student reading of connected text, and management.

My experiences with literature-based programs show that teachers frequently benefit from completing self-evaluation inventories in which they assess their own behaviors and analyze how well these behaviors enrich a literature-based curriculum and help students understand and appreciate literature. The self-evaluation inventory in Figure 4.3 has been used by many teachers to help them clarify and identify behaviors that should enrich a literature-based curriculum.

Teachers can use such self-evaluation inventories to brainstorm ideas together as a means of thinking through how they can improve their literature-based curriculums.

FIGURE 4.3 Inventory for self-evaluation of teacher behaviors.

1. I create an attractive environment that encourages students to read and enjoy literature.
   (*List examples of attractive literature environment.*)

2. I frequently read aloud to the students from a wide genre of literature.
   (*List examples of books read orally.*)

3. I am a role model because I show my students how important reading is to me.
   (*List examples of behaviors.*)

4. I provide opportunities for students to share their enthusiasm for books with other students through such activities as students reading to students, students discussing books with other students, and students working together on literature-related projects.
   (*List examples of sharing enthusiasm.*)

5. I develop literature-related activities in which I model how students should think through the literature.
   (*List examples of modeling activities.*)

6. I encourage my students to give personal responses to the literature.
   (*List examples of personal responses.*)

7. I try to discover what my students know about the literature, genre, or setting before I expect them to read, analyze, and respond to the literature.
   (*List examples of discovering background information.*)

8. I consider recreational reading to be important. I encourage students to do recreational reading and I plan school time for recreational activities.
   (*List examples of recreational reading activities.*)

9. I know the needs of my students and I prepare minilessons that teach them about elements of literature and other techniques that readers and writers need to know.
   (*List examples of minilessons.*)

10. I integrate literature into the total curriculum. I use literature when teaching the various content areas.
    (*List examples of integrating literature into the curriculum.*)

11. I consider literature to be central to the curriculum and not just something to be added once in a while for enrichment.
    (*List examples of how I make literature central to the curriculum.*)

12. I use additional ways to develop my students' understanding of and appreciation for literature.
    (*List examples of additional ways.*)

School librarians also can develop self-evaluation inventories and join the teachers in their brainstorming. Teachers always should remember that knowledgeable librarians are among their most important sources.

ASSESSING STUDENTS

Several types of student information can be of special value to teachers in literature-based programs. The information can be kept in individual portfolios and most reading authorities agree that the information should be flexible and useful and reviewed periodically by the teachers and the students. Flexibility is especially important to avoid allowing the portfolio contents and review to become another mandatory assessment that takes valuable time away from the reading curriculum. Teachers can make better assessments if they have information about students' interests, backgrounds (such as home reading habits and data found in cumulative files), comprehension levels, processes for gaining comprehension, and responses to different types of literature and literacy activities.

A Portfolio Approach

According to Pikulski (1989),

> One of the most dynamic assessment concepts currently being discussed in our field is that of a portfolio approach to the assessment of reading and literacy. Since there are no tests or test materials that are specifically associated with this approach, it has the potential for placing teachers and students—not tests and test scores—at the very center of the assessment process. (p. 81)

In a portfolio approach, teachers and students collect and assess diverse samples of literacy events over a longer period of time. These samples, which are collected as students interact with different types of literature, become what Pikulski refers to as "the fullest, most ecologically valid approach that can be taken to assessment" (p. 81).

When teachers and students are considering the development of a portfolio approach, it is helpful if they imagine themselves in a profession in which portfolios have been popular and extremely useful. For example, they might think of themselves as artists, photographers, or authors who want to demonstrate their talents and breadth of experience. They might ask, "What examples would best show our talents? What examples might show how we have progressed in our chosen fields?" Then they can think about what might be included in a portfolio of reading and literature to illustrate their growing understanding of and appreciation for literature.

Valencia (1990) provides guidelines for the development and management of portfolios, beginning with the selection of large expandable folders to hold samples of work that reflect the goals of the program. She states that school districts, teachers, or states should develop goals for instruction and then decide what information would help teachers assess those goals. The folders usually include samples of work chosen by the teacher or the student, the teacher's observational notes, the student's self-evaluations, and the progress notes contributed collaboratively by the student and the teacher. The portfolio also can include results from classroom tests, various written responses to literature, checklists, and audio or video tapes. What is selected should relate closely to the instructional goals. For example, if understanding literary elements and plot structures are important goals, then literary webs and plot diagrams should be included in the portfolios. Valencia next describes how to manage the contents of a portfolio. For example, by stating goals and priorities for instruction, teachers can select samples that reflect these goals; by assessing continuously, teachers can collect and assess several indicators related to reading and literacy; and by collecting both required evidence and supporting evidence, teachers can look systematically at the progress of the students and the effectiveness of the literature program. Valencia maintains that supporting evidence is especially important because it shows the depth and variety of a student's literacy abilities. In addition to collecting and assessing information in the portfolios, Valencia recommends that teachers and students meet every few weeks to discuss progress, add notes, and decide what additional materials should be in the portfolios. At the end of the year teachers and students can decide which materials will be taken home and which will be kept to show progress into the next year. The portfolios also can be used during conferences with parents and administrators.

Assessing Interests and Background Information

Teachers can draw on several sources to assess students' interests and gather background information. They can use inventories to discover students' interests related to literature and reading. They can ask parents to complete surveys that provide information about the students' reading habits at home. They also can check students' records in the school's cumulative files.

Interest Inventories. The informal interest inventory presented in Figure 2.1 in Chapter 2 provides a method of asking students questions about their interests and recording the information for future use. The inventory asks questions about such topics as hobbies, sports, pets, special studies, and favorite types of books. For younger students, teachers read the questions and write the responses. Older students can read the questions and write their own responses. The responses on the interest inventory can be used to help students find recreational reading that interests them, group students for research and interest projects, and stimulate additional interests. Teachers and librarians frequently use such lists to help students locate authors who have similar interests to their own. In one school, the librarians kept files on the interests of each student which impressed the students because they realized that the librarians and teachers cared about their interests and tried to help them find appropriate materials.

Parent Surveys.   Teachers can discover considerable information about their students' reading habits and preferences by surveying the parents. Some teachers have parents fill out short surveys during PTA meetings or other school visits. Other teachers send home the surveys and ask parents return them in self-addressed, stamped envelopes that are provided by the school. Figure 4.4 includes some items and questions that could be included on a parent survey.

Background Information in Cumulative Files.   Cumulative files provide information that can influence each student's achievement. For example, the cumulative files usually include previous grades, standardized test scores, anecdotal records, attendance records, and other data such as tests performed by other professionals. Although caution should be used when evaluating such information, teachers can discover information that alerts them to a student's strengths and weaknesses. For example, a simple analysis of attendance records could show that a student's reading problems might be caused by infrequent attendance, since it is difficult to become an excellent reader or writer without many opportunities to develop and use those capabilities.

Assessing Comprehension

Several techniques can be used to assess comprehension of students in literature-based programs. This section stresses informal techniques that are closely related to the

FIGURE 4.4 Parent survey of student's interests.

---

1. What is your child's favorite after school activity?
2. List any hobbies or sports that are of special interest to your child.
3. Check any of the following types of reading that your child does at least once a week:

       Newspapers _____   Library books _____

        Sports pages _____   Comic books _____

        Comics _____   Television guide _____

        News articles _____   Cookbooks _____

       Magazines _____   How-to books _____

       Other reading _____
4. What are your child's favorite books?
5. What book topics might be especially interesting for your child?
6. Does your child have a library card? _____ If so, how often does your child

   go to the library? _____
7. Is there any information you could tell me that would help me improve your child's reading? If so, please explain briefly.
8. If you would like a conference to discuss your child's reading ability, please indicate a time after school that would be the most convenient.

---

objectives of the literature-based program—such as informal reading inventories, self-evaluations, cloze techniques, webs to assess comprehension of stories and vocabulary, plot structures to assess understandings of story structures, and writing samples collected from using wordless books.

Informal Reading Inventories (IRIs). Whether constructed by the teacher or created by a publisher, IRIs long have been popular with reading teachers. They are especially valuable for assessing the reading ability of students in literature-based programs because the IRIs can be constructed from passages and questions that are similar to those in the materials read by the students. IRIs usually analyze word-recognition abilities and oral and silent reading comprehension levels of individual students. Graded paragraphs are used for individual oral and silent reading. When the student reads a selection orally, the teacher marks all errors on the test, then asks the student a list of questions to assess comprehension levels. If the student reads the selection silently, the teacher asks the accompanying questions afterward and records the answers.

Teachers usually continue individual testing until they can identify three levels of reading ability: (a) the independent level, at which a student is able to pronounce 98 percent to 100 percent of the words in the selection and answer 90 percent to 100 percent of the comprehension questions; (b) the instructional level, at which a student is able to pronounce 94 percent to 97 percent of the words in the selection and answer 70 percent to 89 percent of the comprehension questions; and (c) the frustration level, at which the student pronounces fewer than 94 percent of the words in the selection and answers fewer than 70 percent of the comprehension questions. Teachers also note consistent areas of strengths and weaknesses to evaluate students' understanding of what is read. The obvious disadvantage of the IRI is that it is individually administered and requires more time than a group-administered test. Many teachers, however, believe the advantages far outweigh any disadvantages.

Pikulski (1990) provides a useful description of four published IRIs: The Analytic Reading Inventory (Woods & Moe, 1989), the Basic Reading Inventory (Johns, 1988), the Classroom Reading Inventory (Silvaroli, 1989), and the Informal Reading Inventory (Burns & Roe, 1989). Pikulski includes a chart that allows teachers to readily compare the four inventories, and his conclusion includes strengths and weaknesses for each inventory. If teachers choose to use the published informal reading inventories, they should analyze each inventory and decide which inventory provides them the most useful information.

Assessing Reading Processes Through Self-Evaluation

Several activities developed in this text can teach students self-questioning strategies that help them read a folktale or decide if a story belongs to a specific genre. Teachers easily can assess students' ability to use such strategies by observing their reading and reactions as they try to apply the strategies.

Wixson (1991) describes a scaffolding or support approach to assessment in which teachers present students with reading activities, observe their responses, and introduce modifications in the form of prompts. For example, if a student is unable to answer a question or a series of questions, the teacher adds prompts and records the point at which the student can answer the question. The following are examples of such questions:

1. What could you do to answer that question?
2. Do you know the answer to the question?
3. Can you figure it out?
4. Is the information you need in the selection?
5. Where in the selection could you find that information? (p. 421)

After asking these questions, the teacher begins instruction designed to help the student answer the question or solve the problem. In this way the teacher can analyze how much support the student needs to successfully perform the task.

Wixson also recommends that teachers interview students after questioning or prompting. The teacher can ask questions such as, "How did you figure out that answer? Which activity helped you the most? Why did it help you? What did you learn today? When will you use what you learned today?"

Developing Cloze Techniques.   Cloze procedures are used to assess students' ability to read particular materials. The cloze technique is closely related to literature-based reading because students read passages taken directly from their reading materials. Farr, Tulley, and Pritchard (1989) recommend this approach and show how closely it relates to the literature selection because, "from the ability to provide a correct response for a deleted word, it can be assumed that the student has synthesized background knowledge, syntactic knowledge, the use of context clues, and knowledge of an author's style" (p. 352).

Teachers can construct a cloze test by selecting a passage of 250 to 300 words. Passages should be selected from the front of the book so that the content is not loaded with concepts that will be developed later in the book. The first and last sentences of the passage should be left whole. Throughout the remainder of the passage, every fifth word should be deleted. This leaves about 50 blanks to be completed by the students.

Before the students complete a cloze activity, allow them to practice using another example. After students have finished the practice passage, give them the prepared passage. Allow them as much time as they need to complete the passage. Grade the passage by counting the number of exact word replacements (some educators allow synonyms). Scores of 44 percent to 57 percent correct mean that the materials are on the students' instructional levels. Scores of 58 percent and above signify independent reading levels. Scores of 43 percent and below reflect frustrational reading levels.

Cloze tests have several advantages. Teachers can develop them using the exact literature that students will be reading. Tests can be constructed easily from both narrative and expository books, can be group-administered, and are easy to grade. Teachers can develop cloze tests from a variety of literature selections, keep the results in the students' portfolios, and evaluate changes in reading comprehension according to changes in cloze results over time.

The following is an example of the beginning of a cloze test using an expository text:

From *The Clover & the Bee, A Book of Pollination* by Anne Ophelia Dowden, a nonfictional information book recommended for students in grades 5 through 10.

The Flowers

For the million years man has lived on earth, flowers have been the glory of the green world around him. Their blossoming delights us _____ , from the youngest child _____ the oldest philosopher. But _____ do not exist for _____ delight, and their great _____ , in spite of what _____ say, is not "its _____ excuse for being." All _____ , large or small, dull _____ spectacular, exist for one _____ only—to make new _____ .

Flowers are the reproductive _____ of a plant. They _____ the male and female _____ , and they provide ways _____ those male cells to _____ those female cells in _____ to produce seeds. The _____ and color of every _____ , its scent, its texture, _____ opening and closing, all _____ the precise and wonderful _____ by which plants reproduce _____ .

Continue using the same approach until 250 to 300 words have been included. Leave the final sentence whole.

The following is an example of a cloze test using a narrative text:

From Lewis Carroll's *Through the Looking-Glass, and What Alice Found There,* a fantasy published in 1872.

"Do you know, I was so angry, Kitty," Alice went on, as soon as they were comfortably settled again, "When I saw all the mischief you had been doing, I was very nearly opening the window, and putting you out into the snow! And you'd have deserved _____ , you little mischievous darling! _____ have you got to _____ for yourself? Now don't _____ me!" she went on, _____ up one finger. "I'm _____ to tell you all _____ faults. Number one: you _____ twice while Dinah was _____ your face this morning. _____ you can't deny it, _____ : I heard you! What's _____ you say?" (pretending that _____ kitten was speaking.) "Her _____ went into

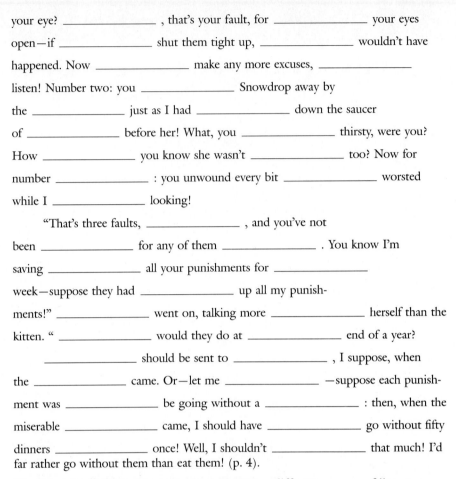

your eye? _____ , that's your fault, for _____ your eyes open—if _____ shut them tight up, _____ wouldn't have happened. Now _____ make any more excuses, _____ listen! Number two: you _____ Snowdrop away by the _____ just as I had _____ down the saucer of _____ before her! What, you _____ thirsty, were you? How _____ you know she wasn't _____ too? Now for number _____ : you unwound every bit _____ worsted while I _____ looking!

"That's three faults, _____ , and you've not been _____ for any of them _____ . You know I'm saving _____ all your punishments for _____ week—suppose they had _____ up all my punishments!" _____ went on, talking more _____ herself than the kitten. " _____ would they do at _____ end of a year? _____ should be sent to _____ , I suppose, when the _____ came. Or—let me _____ —suppose each punishment was _____ be going without a _____ : then, when the miserable _____ came, I should have _____ go without fifty dinners _____ once! Well, I shouldn't _____ that much! I'd far rather go without them than eat them! (p. 4).

Teachers can develop cloze tests to accompany different genres of literature, or to accompany different levels of books. Students also improve their ability to use context clues and to notice sentence structures.

Using Webs to Assess Comprehension and Vocabulary.   The webs developed in this book around the literary elements and vocabulary related to a book also can be used to assess students' comprehension. By keeping examples of individually developed webs in each student's portfolio, teachers can observe and evaluate changes in the student's ability to analyze literature according to setting, characterization, conflict, and theme. Webs collected during different time periods also show changes in the student's ability to identify important details associated with each area. The vocabulary webs are easily turned into assessment instruments.

This type of assessment should be used only after students are familiar with the webbing technique. To use this approach, give the students a web with the name of the book in the center and setting characterization, conflict, and theme drawn on the spokes of the web. Have the students fill in the web using as much detail as they can from the story. The webs can be evaluated for accuracy and insightfulness as well as for details that the students place on their webs. Teachers discover that they quite rapidly develop their own rating scales as they analyze the information placed on the webs. For example, Figures 4.5 and 4.6 are literary webs accompanying Katherine Paterson's *The Tale of the Mandarin Ducks*. The two webs, however, present quite different levels of literary analysis. Notice how the student who developed Figure 4.5 analyzed the book rather superficially. The answers are correct, but there is no depth to the literary analysis.

In contrast, the student who developed Figure 4.6 shows a deeper understanding of the literature and the literary elements. Notice that this student focused on numerous characteristics of each of the characters, subdivided the types of conflict developed in the story, and identified several important themes.

Assessment webs also can be developed for a single literary element such as a detailed analysis of setting, characterizations, conflict, theme, author's style, or point of view. Students place one of these areas at the center of the web and identify as much supporting information as they can. These single webs should be individually

FIGURE 4.5 Web of *The Tale of the Mandarin Ducks*.

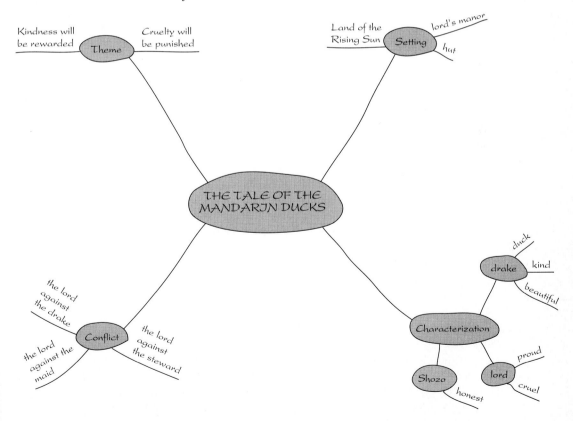

FIGURE 4.6 Web of *The Tale of the Mandarin Ducks.*

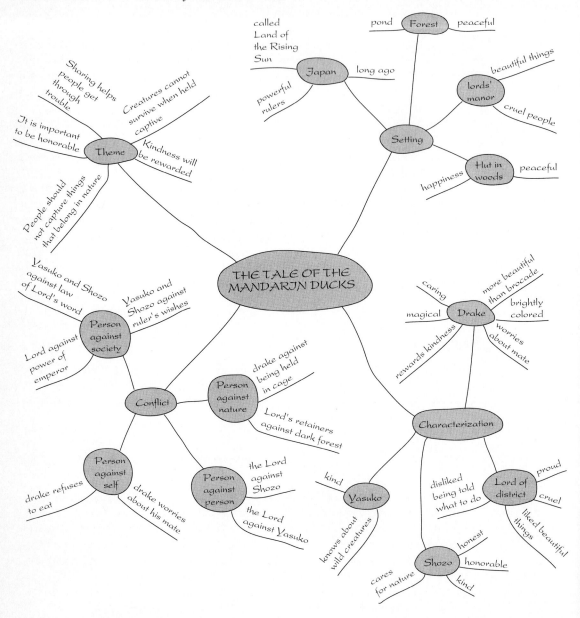

developed. Figure 4.7 is an example of an assessment web developed by a student in the third grade after reading Claus Stamm's *Three Strong Women: A Tale From Japan.*

This type of assessment can be collected at different times during the year and placed into each student's portfolio. Students and teachers then can analyze how understandings of literary elements progress throughout the year.

FIGURE 4.7 Assessment web for characterization with *Three Strong Women*.

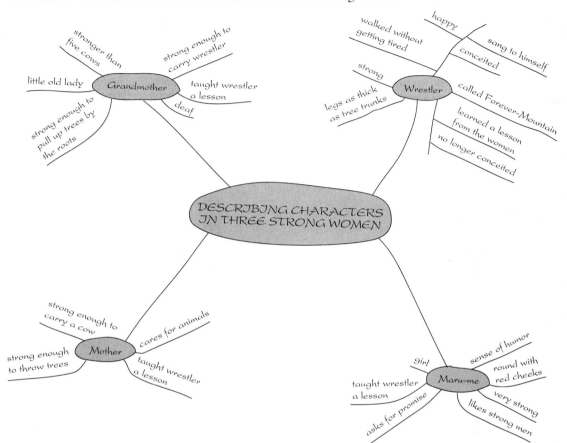

Webs are also excellent ways to assess vocabulary knowledge and development. Several different successful methods are available. As a prereading assessment, teachers can develop a vocabulary web to assess students' vocabulary knowledge before they read a book. Teachers can use the same type of web after students read the book to assess the students' use of story structures and context clues to develop understanding. For either of these approaches, teachers should give individual students vocabulary webs with the meanings of the words deleted. Students then fill in as much information as possible. They can define the words, use synonyms, give examples, and so forth. Or, teachers can use a vocabulary web with the focused vocabulary words deleted. This approach is frequently used to assess vocabulary knowledge after students have read and discussed a book and have explored the vocabulary found in the book.

Figure 4.8 is an example of a vocabulary assessment web used by a teacher to accompany "Treasure Mountain," a folktale found in *Treasure Mountain: Folktales from Southern China*, retold by Catherine Edwards Sadler.

FIGURE 4.8 Vocabulary web used as assessment.

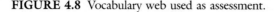

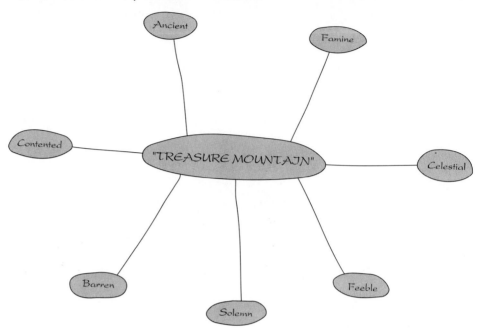

Figure 4.9 shows how the same vocabulary web can be used to assess vocabulary knowledge after students have read and discussed the book and explored the vocabulary. At this point, the meanings and synonyms are included, but students fill in the main vocabulary.

Webs make excellent additions to students' portfolios because the webs are easy to obtain and evaluate, and show changes in students' understandings of both literary elements and vocabulary. The webs also relate closely to the objectives for literature-based programs.

Using Plot Structures to Assess Comprehension of Stories.   The plot diagrams recommended throughout this text also can be used to assess students' understandings of plot and story structures. After students have completed and discussed several plot diagrams so that they understand the procedure, they can individually develop plot diagrams that teachers can use to assess the student's understanding of the important instances in a plot. Younger students might be asked to identify only the important instances. Older students, however, can relate these instances to the specific incidents that reveal character and problem identification, increasing conflict, climax, turning-point incident, and end of conflict or resolution. Teachers also can use the diagram recommended for person-against-self conflict to assess students' understandings of this type of conflict.

Figure 4.10 shows a plot diagram used to assess understandings of students in the lower elementary grades. The plot structure was completed with Emily Arnold

FIGURE 4.9 Vocabulary web used as assessment.

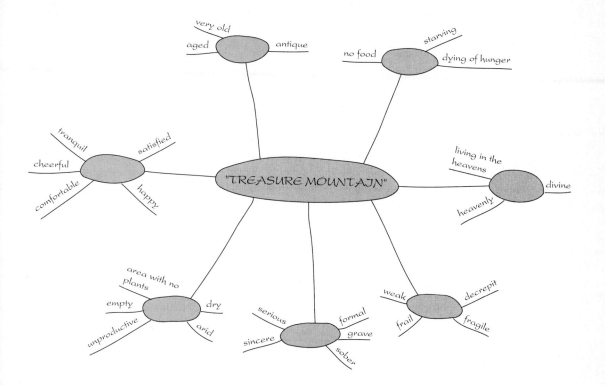

FIGURE 4.10 Plot diagram used as assessment.

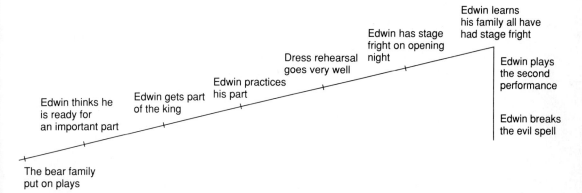

McCully's *The Evil Spell.* Depending on the students' reading abilities, the story can be read by or to the students. If students have not yet learned to write the necessary words, they can draw pictures to show the important incidents or dictate the information to the teacher.

Plot structures can be collected during different times of the year and placed in students' portfolios for use as assessments. Like webs, plot structures are easy to obtain and evaluate, and relate closely to the objectives of the literature-based program.

Using Students' Writing Samples that Accompany Wordless Books.   Wordless books provide excellent sources for developing writing samples that teachers can use when evaluating students' comprehension of a story, use of observational skills, level of language usage and vocabulary, and ability to develop a logical structure that reflects the framework developed in the book. For such evaluations, the teacher chooses a wordless book with a subject that appeals to students and matches their experiential backgrounds, a sequential organization that provides a framework for the plot, and the depth of detail appropriate for the students' age levels.

Depending on the age of the students, wordless books can stimulate dictated stories or individually written stories. Teachers who use wordless books with younger children, for example, can follow procedures similar to dictating language-experience stories. For example, teachers choose an appropriate wordless book such as Peter Collington's *The Angel and the Soldier Boy;* Pat Hutchins' *Changes, Changes;* Emily Arnold McCully's *School;* and Mercer Mayer's *A Boy, A Dog, and A Frog.* Students are told that they will have an opportunity to become authors and tell the story that accompanies the pictures. Allow the students plenty of time to look through the book and think about the story they would like to tell. When they are ready, ask them to tell the story that accompanies the book—they may use the book to prompt their story. The teacher writes down each student's story word for word.

These dictated stories can give teachers several types of information. Teachers can observe whether the student watches as the words are written, paces the dictation according to the teacher's ability to write the story, pauses at the end of a phrase or sentence, or attempts to read the story back to the teacher. This information is especially important when assessing beginning readers, because teachers are able to determine how much knowledge students have about print and the relationship between words and writing. Teachers also can assess the stories themselves to determine whether the students have developed a logical sequence, provided details associated with setting, described characters, or expressed themselves through a vivid and well-developed vocabulary. Figure 4.11 is an adaptation of a student profile used with language-experience stories.

Teachers should collect samples of stories accompanying wordless books from different periods during the school year. These samples, along with the evaluations, can be kept in the students' portfolios. Teachers and students can assess changes in writing ability as the school year progresses.

A similar approach for collecting and assessing stories can be used with older students. The students write their own stories to accompany wordless books such as Henrik Drescher's *The Yellow Umbrella,* Emily Arnold McCully's *Picnic,* Chris Van Allsburg's *The Mysteries of Harris Burdick,* and David Wiesner's *Free Fall.* Teachers can use the chart shown in Figure 4.11, leaving blank the items that deal with dictation.

FIGURE 4.11 Student profile to accompany a story told from a wordless book.

	Yes	Sometimes	No
Name _____ Date _____			
Grade _____ Wordless book _____			

Name _____

Grade _____

Date _____

Wordless book _____

	Yes	Sometimes	No
1. Watches while the teacher writes the words	_____	_____	_____
2. Paces dictation according to writing	_____	_____	_____
3. Pauses at the end of a sentence	_____	_____	_____
4. Attempts to read the story back to the teacher	_____	_____	_____
5. Child is confident during the dictation experience	_____	_____	_____
6. Dictates complete sentences	_____	_____	_____

Example _____

_____

	Yes	Sometimes	No
7. Tells the story in a logical, sequential order	_____	_____	_____
8. Uses the picture clues to develop the plot	_____	_____	_____
9. Uses the picture clues to describe the characters	_____	_____	_____
10. Uses the picture clues to describe the setting	_____	_____	_____
11. Dictated story demonstrates a rich vocabulary	_____	_____	_____
12. Dictated story has coherent arrangement of words	_____	_____	_____
13. Dictated story includes all words needed for understanding	_____	_____	_____
14. If child gives a new title, the title indicates grasp of the main idea	_____	_____	_____
15. The story shows that the child has background knowledge	_____	_____	_____

From: *The Effective Teaching of Language Arts* (p. 62) by D. E. Norton, 1989, Columbus, OH: Merrill.

Or, they can choose a holistic scoring scale for writing such as the one shown in Figure 4.12.

A holistic scoring scale can be used to assess any of the writing assignments that accompany literature. As with the dictated stories collected from younger students, the portfolios of older students should contain numerous samples of writing about literature. Teachers and students can analyze each student's writing progress throughout the year.

Assessing Reader Response to Literature

Various reader response activities developed throughout this text can be added to the students' portfolios several times during the year. These activities can be written responses or responses developed through art and can be used to help students evaluate their own responses to literature and the reasons for any changes in those

FIGURE 4.12 Holistic scoring scale for writing.

Score	Characteristics
6	Has a thesis Uses concrete details effectively Is fluent in words and ideas Uses varied sentence structure Delivers satisfactory closing statement Has generally clear mechanics
5	Has a central idea Relays specific facts, details, or reasons Develops story consistently Is less insightful, imaginative, concrete, or developed than one who scores a 6 Has generally clear mechanics; errors do not interfere with overall effectiveness
4	Has several clear ideas Relays relevant and specific details Shows evidence of fluency, but not of unified development Can be overly general or trite Can have simple sentence structure or vocabulary Has mechanical errors, but they do not affect readability
3	Has at least one idea but few, if any, supporting details Is less fluent, developed, or detailed than one who scores a 4 Exhibits simplistic sentences, vocabulary, and thoughts Has mechanical errors, but they do not affect readability
2	Has no thesis Has a sense of order, but that order might be only that of plot summary Displays minimal fluency and thought Has at least one relevant idea Might have many mechanical errors but paper is readable
1	Has no thesis Has no sense of organization Uses simplistic or vague language Has mechanical problems in areas such as spelling and handwriting, which might render the paper unreadable

From: "Effects on Student Writing of Teacher Training in the National Writing Project Model" by R. J. Pritchard, 1987, *Written Communication*, *4*, p. 58. Reprinted by permission.

responses. For example, teachers can keep examples of the three types of aesthetic responses recommended by Many (1990):

1. Examples from the students' free-association journals in which they write comments as they read or listen to the books. These responses can include such topics as emotions felt by the students, questions the students would like to ask the characters or the authors, reactions to the characters and plot situations, personal memories that the book stimulates, responses to vivid language, reactions to point of view, and overall judgments about the literature.

2. Examples of students' responses to probes after completing an entire book. For example, they might write about the emotions they felt in response to the book and what prompted these emotions. They also can list the associations that come to mind as they read the book, or focus on memorable features and explain why they are memorable.

3. Examples in which students choose the form of response such as painting a picture, writing a poem, writing a sequel to the book, or keeping a diary while reading.

Students discover interesting information about themselves and their changing appreciation of literature as they assess the results of activities that encouraged their responses. Students often are amazed when they compare responses written at the beginning of the year with those written later in the year. As one sixth-grade student stated, "My reactions to literature have changed a lot this year. I think it is because I know a lot more about literature. I know many of the techniques authors use and I enjoy trying to decide if the author is successful. I have tried to use some of these techniques in my own writing."

ASSESSING THE TOTAL LITERATURE-BASED PROGRAM

Both students and teachers can provide many suggestions that can be helpful in assessing the effectiveness of a literature-based curriculum (Norton and McNamara, 1987). In addition to measures of comprehension, the evaluation of a literature-based program that focused on using multicultural literature with students in upper elementary and middle school included interviews with students and teachers who were part of the program. For example, the responses to the following four questions were tabulated from the students:

1. "Think for a moment about this school year. What three things did you like best about your reading and writing classes?"
2. "What three things helped you most to improve your reading and writing skills?"
3. "To help your reading and writing teacher get better, what are the three most important things you could tell (him/her)?"
4. "Assume friends will start this reading and writing class next year. What would you tell them to help them do well?"

In answer to the first question, fifth-grade students preferred oral reading activities, reading folklore stories, doing creative writing activities that accompanied literature, and using webs to identify literary elements. In answer to the same question, eighth-grade students preferred reading stories silently, listening to the teacher read books to the class, acting out parts of the stories they read, and participating in various composition activities stimulated by literature.

In answer to the second question, students responded that reading and discussing stories in groups, reading a lot of books, writing their own stories, doing vocabulary activities, webbing story structures, and diagramming plot structures helped them the most. When asked to identify how their teachers could help them, the students responded that teachers should read more stories to the classes; do a lot of activities with folklore; allow students to write books and write in journals; and use more vocabulary, webbing, and plot-diagramming activities. In addition to these specific suggestions, the students recommended that teachers give individual help and provide detailed explanations about what was expected of the students. The teachers had used many modeling activities, which the students indicated were beneficial.

In answer to the fourth question, students advised new students to practice reading by reading a lot, reading books you like, and reading aloud. They also suggested that new students take responsibility for listening and studying, listen to the teacher, study the stories each day, and "get on the books." It is interesting to note that listening to stories read by the teacher, acting out stories, reading many books silently and orally, webbing literary elements and vocabulary, diagramming story structures, and getting explanatory details through modeling were identified as some of the best and most beneficial elements in the literature-based program.

The teachers in the program were asked to respond to the following questions:

1. "Given your involvement in the literature-based reading/language arts program, what do you believe are the three most important benefits of the program?"
2. "Given your involvement in the literature-based reading/language arts program, what do you believe are the three most important ways to improve this program?"
3. Assume another colleague is assigned to teach next year in the literature-based reading/language arts program. What are the three most important ideas you would like to share at the beginning of the year?"

In answer to the first question, the teachers focused on the students' achievement and success, the webbing strategies that enhanced enjoyment of teaching story parts and building vocabulary, the literature activities that integrated all of the language arts, and the students' interest in the literature. Teacher responses for the second question indicated that they would like to have more literature available for group and individual use. They also emphasized the need to select teachers with positive attitudes and to use literature-based approaches in earlier grades.

Responses to the third question showed that teachers highly recommended the in-service training that was given before teaching in the program. They especially emphasized using the techniques such as webbing and modeling that helped students understand and appreciate literature. They also stated that teachers needed to become familiar with the literature, provide many opportunities for independent reading, and keep up the excitement that a literature-based program generates among the students.

These responses indicate that both students and teachers can give valuable advice for evaluating and improving a literature-based program. They clearly enjoy such a program and see benefits in both the literature and literature-related activities. The responses also indicate that teacher training, student and teacher enthusiasm, and availability of materials are important.

REFERENCES

BURNS, P. & B. R. (1989). *Informal Reading Inventory* (3rd ed.). Boston: Houghton Mifflin.

FARR, R., TULLEY, M. A., & PRITCHARD, R. (1989). Assessment instruments and techniques used by the content area teacher. In D. Lapp, J. Flood, & N. Farnam, (Eds.), *Content area reading and learning: Instructional strategies,* (pp. 346–356). Englewood Cliffs, NJ: Prentice Hall.

JOHNS, J. (1988). *Basic Reading Inventory* (4th ed.). Dubuque, IA: Kendall/Hunt.

LIPSON, M. Y. (1990). Evaluating the reading context. *The Reading Teacher, 44,* pp. 330–332.

MANY, J. (1990, November). Encouraging aesthetic responses to literature. Paper presented at the GTE Conference on Children's Literature and Literacy, College Station, TX.

MATHEWS, J. (1990). From computer management to portfolio assessment. *The Reading Teacher, 43,* pp. 420–421.

NORTON, D. E. & McNAMARA, J. F. (1987). An evaluation of the BISD/TAMU multicultural literature reading program. Research Report, College Station: Texas A&M University, College of Education.

PETERS, C. W. (1991). You can't have authentic assessment without authentic content. *The Reading Teacher, 44,* pp. 590–591.

PIKULSKI, J. J. (1989). The assessment of reading: A time for change? *The Reading Teacher, 43,* pp. 80–81.

PIKULSKI, J. J. (1990). Informal reading inventories. *The Reading Teacher, 43,* pp. 514–516.

SILVAROLI, N. (1989). *Classroom Reading Inventory.* Dubuque, IA: William Brown.

VALENCIA, S. (1990). A portfolio approach to classroom reading assessment: The whys, whats, and hows. *The Reading Teacher, 43,* pp. 338–340.

WIXSON, K. K. (1991). Diagnostic Teaching. *The Reading Teacher, 44,* pp. 420–422.

WOODS, M. L. & MOE, A. (1989). *Analytic Reading Inventory* (4th ed.). Columbus, OH: Merrill.

CHILDREN'S LITERATURE REFERENCES:*

CARROLL, LEWIS. *Through the Looking-Glass, and What Alice Found There.* London: Macmillan, 1872 (I: 8+).

*I = Interest by age range

COLLINGTON, PETER. *The Angel and the Soldier Boy.* New York: Knopf, 1987 (I: 3–7).

DOWDEN, ANNE OPHELIA. *The Clover & the Bee: A Book of Pollination.* New York: Crowell, 1990 (I: 10+).

DRESCHER, HENRIK. *The Yellow Umbrella.* New York: Bradbury, 1987 (I: all).

HUTCHINS, PAT. *Changes, Changes.* New York: Macmillan, 1971 (I: 2–6).

MAYER, MERCER. *A Boy, a Dog and a Frog.* New York: Dial, 1967 (I: 5–9).

McCULLY, EMILY ARNOLD. *The Evil Spell.* New York: Harper, 1990 (I: 5–9).

_____. *Picnic.* New York: Harper & Row, 1984 (I: all).

_____. *School.* New York: Harper & Row, 1987 (I: 3–8).

PATERSON, KATHERINE. *The Tale of the Mandarin Ducks.* Illustrated by Leo and Diane Dillon. New York: Lodestar, 1991 (I: all).

SADLER, CATHERINE EDWARDS, retold by. *Treasure Mountain: Folktales from Southern China.* Illustrated by Cheng Mung Yun. New York: Atheneum, 1982 (I: 8+).

STAMM, CLAUS. *Three Strong Women: A Tale from Japan.* New York: Viking, 1990 (I: 3–8).

VAN ALLSBURG, CHRIS. *The Mysteries of Harris Burdick.* Boston: Houghton Mifflin, 1984 (I: all).

WIESNER, DAVID. *Free Fall.* New York: Lothrop, Lee & Shepard, 1988 (I: all).

PART TWO

UNDERSTANDING AND APPRECIATING LITERARY ELEMENTS

Plot Development and Conflict
Characterization
Setting
Theme
Author's Style and Point of View

CHAPTER 5

PLOT DEVELOPMENT AND CONFLICT

DEVELOPING UNDERSTANDING AND APPRECIATION OF PLOT AND CONFLICT
    Core Books and Sample Lessons for Lower Elementary Students
    Extended Books for Lower Elementary Students
    Recreational Books for Lower Elementary Students
    Core Books and Sample Lessons for Middle Elementary Students
    Extended Books for Middle Elementary Students
    Recreational Books for Middle Elementary Students
    Core Books and Sample Lessons for Upper Elementary and Middle School Students
    Extended Books for Upper Elementary and Middle School Students
    Recreational Books for Upper Elementary and Middle School Students

When we ask ourselves what it is that we like about a piece of literature we usually remember the literary elements. A strong plot and a believable conflict allow us to vicariously join the main character in Gary Paulsen's *Hatchet* as he fights for physical and spiritual survival in the Canadian wilderness. The memorable character of Laura in Laura Ingalls Wilder's *Little House in the Big Woods* is so well developed that we care about her and wish she could be our friend. The detailed setting in Esther Forbes' *Johnny Tremain* encourages us to vicariously walk down the streets of Boston and to see, feel, and hear the Revolutionary War environment. The theme in Lois Lowry's *Number the Stars* lets us consider how important it is to have friends who would risk their lives for worthy principles. The style of writing in Eve Merriam's *Rainbow Writing* colors our minds and inspires us to look at nature as if through a kaleido-scope. One of the strengths of the literature-based curriculum is that students are exposed to and respond to books that allow them to have these experiences.

How important are the literary elements in a literature-based program? Answers to this question are found in both children's literature textbooks and in the writings of authors who describe literature-based programs. Most authors of children's liter-ature textbooks and reviewers in journals such as *Hornbook*, *School Library Journal*, and *Booklist* emphasize an author's ability to develop literary elements. A brief review of some of the children's literature textbooks also reveals the importance of literary elements. For example, in my own text, *Through the Eyes of A Child: An Introduction to Children's Literature* (Norton, 1991) literary elements are discussed in a chapter titled, "Evaluating and Selecting Literature for Children." The literary elements are used as a focus for discussion in each of the genre chapters. In *Children and Books*, Sutherland and Arbuthnot (1991) emphasize the literary elements in their discussions of authors and genre. In *Children's Literature in the Elementary School*, Huck, Hepler, and Hickman (1987) introduce some of the values of children's literature by defining and discussing the various literary elements. Both Stewig (1988) and Cullinan (1989) refer to literary elements in their discussions of children's books, and Lukens struc-tures *A Critical Handbook of Children's Literature* (1990) around the literary elements.

Authors of articles about literature-based programs frequently emphasize the importance of the literary elements as they relate to developing instruction and en-hancing interactions of teachers and students with the literature. For example, Rud-man (1989) argues, "One of the problems with questions in basal manuals is that they too often have little relationship to the sense of the story or are the type that send the child looking for a particular word or sentence without much thought required on the child's part" (p. 197). Rudman believes that the instructional approaches should allow students to respond to the story and the characters rather than to questions that tend to isolate responses from the literature. She then describes a literature-based curriculum in which students read different books and then join groups to "talk about the interesting characters they are reading about and what makes them interesting. Another group might be able to discuss the settings of the various stories and the part the setting plays in conveying the sense of the book" (p. 199).

Watson and Davis (1988) describe literature study groups in which fifth-grade

> students are expected to read, read, read—a great many books. But just as important as *extensive* reading is *intensive* reading. The literature study group program does more than add another title to a list of books read or another segment to the bookworm elongating itself around the room. Children are asked to slow down, move back and forth between their lives and the text life, to consider meaning embedded in characterization, mood, pattern, ordering of time, circumstance of setting, even conventions of print. In other words, they are encouraged to participate in higher order thinking—anything that helps them live through the literature experience, learn from it, and value it. (p. 61)

In the previous examples, notice how important the literary elements are in helping students read intensively.

Purves, Rogers, and Soter (1990), in their discussion of a response-centered literature curriculum, emphasize the difference between reading a message and reading literature. In the following description of a literature curriculum notice the emphasis on literary elements:

> Don't be fooled by the fact that reading tests include stories and poems. You are after the thoughtful articulation of the imaginative vision of a story or a poem. Cherish the experience for its own sake. Don't look for a quick answer to a simple question like those in the teacher's guide. Don't treat *The Old Man and the Sea* as a descriptive account of how to catch marlin, but rather the story of an old man, a boy, a fish, the sea, and their complex relationship. Remember this is a literature curriculum, one that has its own goals and pursuits. It is not designed to get people to read reports fast or to help them answer multiple-choice questions. It is designed to help students think about their experiences, to deepen them, to challenge their assumptions. (p. 70)

Children's literature authorities also emphasize the use of illustrated books; in fact, picture books and discussions focusing on picture books now are considered important for all age groups. Cianciolo (1990) develops a strong argument for using picture books with students at all grade levels, from the three-year-old child who cannot yet read to the sophisticated young adult who analyzes the illustrations and grasps new meaning and significance. Cianciolo states

> In these picture books the illustrations are superbly accomplished works of visual and graphic art, and the texts are written in beautifully expressive language . . . in addition to bringing out and emphasizing the text, they convey other meanings and impressions that readers would not have envisioned from the verbal information on its own. They encourage higher-level thinking and imaginative thinking. Readers can and do grasp their meaning and significance and can go well beyond what the illustrator and author suggested. (p. 2)

These quotes suggest that developing students' understanding of and appreciation for the literary elements in both the text and the illustrations should be the heart of the literature-based curriculum. In addition, the procedures and books that can be used to accomplish these goals easily meet the characteristics of literature-based programs discussed in Chapters 1, 2, and 3. For example, instructional formats can include teacher-directed activities with core books, extended reading during smaller discussion groups, and numerous opportunities for recreational reading with books chosen by the teacher or the students. The related procedures and activities allow teachers to use the effective techniques discussed in Chapter 2, such as using knowledge of texts and contextual cues to create meaning, reading a variety of books, experiencing whole texts to create meaning, using a variety of reading strategies, improving comprehension through modeling and questioning, using cues in the text and prior knowledge to make predictions, and focusing on details that help students understand literary elements and make inferences (Early and Ericson, 1988). The procedures and activities also allow teachers to integrate the total curriculum.

Let us consider a situation in which students read numerous books that include both teacher-directed lessons and independent reading, and that integrate language arts and other content areas. When exploring setting, for example students, can take part in teacher-led discussions of core books in which they discover the purposes for setting, how to evaluate setting, and the techniques authors use to develop believable settings. In small study groups the students read numerous books from the extended list that contain vivid settings. During discussions they emphasize the settings and analyze how their chosen authors developed settings that were integral to the book. During recreational reading they apply what they know about setting and savor the works for their own enjoyment. In addition to the integration between reading and oral language developed during the discussions, the teacher integrates reading and writing by asking the students to create their own vivid settings and respond to settings in their writing logs. To integrate literature and art, the students draw their favorite settings and create backdrops for plays and puppet productions developed from literature. To integrate literature and music, the students identify music that they believe should accompany a particular vivid setting and set the mood for the location and action. To integrate literature and social studies, history, or geography, the students evaluate the appropriateness of settings developed in specific time periods or locations.

In this chapter and in the next four chapters on literary elements, we will organize the teaching of literary elements in two ways. First, we will follow the format: (a) teacher-directed core book lessons, (b) extended books that have a similar focus and can be used for reading and application of knowledge during individual as well as small group discussions, and (c) recreational reading books. This discussion also will be divided according to lower elementary, middle elementary, and upper elementary and middle school. Second, we will explore additional ways to integrate literature, language arts, and other content areas of the curriculum during activities that allow students to search for meaning in literature through reading, listening, speaking, and writing.

I have used this structure during in-service instruction for public schools, in institutes on literature-based instruction, and in graduate classes in literature-based instruction. The participants have evaluated this format and concluded that it is one of the most beneficial. It includes a variety of teaching strategies as well as numerous opportunities for individual and small group responses. Consequently, teachers can select books and activities that meet their own needs, the needs of their students, and their preferred teaching styles. Numerous books are included so that teachers will not have difficulty finding them.

The next three chapters also use three core books to develop activities around the literary elements: Ann Grifalconi's *Darkness and the Butterfly* for lower elementary grades, Byrd Baylor's *Hawk, I'm Your Brother* for middle elementary grades, and Selina Hastings' *Sir Gawain and the Loathly Lady* for upper elementary grades and middle school. These books emphasize such strategies as plot structures, webbing literary elements, and analyzing theme.

DEVELOPING UNDERSTANDING AND APPRECIATION OF PLOT AND CONFLICT

The plot of a story develops the action. A good plot lets readers share the action, feel the conflict, recognize the climax, and respond to a satisfactory ending. The development of events usually follows a chronological order, although flashbacks might be used to fill in a character's background or reveal information about a previous time or experience. Excitement in a story occurs when the main character experiences a struggle or overcomes a conflict. When conflict is added to the sequence of events, the result is a plot. Authors develop plots through four kinds of conflict: (a) person against person, (b) person against society, (c) person against nature, and (d) person against self. This section presents activities that help students understand plot sequence and different types of conflict.

Core Books and Sample Lessons for Lower Elementary Students

LESSON ONE: Understanding Plot Structure

OBJECTIVES

To develop an understanding of plot structure by acting out the sequence of actions that occur in a story; by drawing and illustrating the plot diagram of a story; and by writing stories that include a beginning, a middle, and an end.

To develop an understanding that many plots include person-against-person conflict.

CORE BOOKS: A nursery rhyme collection such as Tomie De Paola's *Mother Goose* or Arnold Lobel's *The Random House Book of Mother Goose*; a folktale in which the sequence is easily recognizable, such as "Three Billy Goats Gruff" or Jan Brett's retelling of *Goldilocks and the*

Three Bears; and a wordless book that contains easily identified plot and conflict, such as Peter Collington's *The Angel and the Soldier Boy.*

PROCEDURES: This core lesson includes a sequence of activities that will take several days or weeks to accomplish. The sequence begins with activities that introduce students to plot structure and person-against-person conflict through creative drama. The next activities encourage students to draw plot diagrams. The final activities allow students to apply their knowledge of plot diagrams and person-against-person conflicts in their own writing and story creations.

Creative drama activities provide an enjoyable way for children to discover that plot provides the framework for a story. Students learn that stories have a beginning in which the conflict and characters are introduced, a middle that moves the action toward a climax, and an ending that offers a resolution to the conflict. Through dramatization children discover that stories must have a logical sequence that gradually builds until the conflict is resolved.

For the first drama activity, choose a nursery rhyme that contains definite actions that cannot be interchanged and still retain a logical sequence. For example, "Humpty Dumpty" has such a sequence: (a) A beginning—"Humpty Dumpty sat on a wall," (b) a middle— "Humpty Dumpty had a great fall," and (c) an end—"All the king's horses and all the king's men couldn't put Humpty together again." Read the rhyme to the students and ask them to identify the actions and the characters. Ask them, "What is the order of events in the nursery rhyme? What happened first, second, and third? Do you think there are reasons for that order? What would happen if we tried to change the order of 'Humpty Dumpty?'"

To verify the importance of a logical order in "Humpty Dumpty," print each of the three parts of the nursery rhyme on strips of paper. Put these strips in the wrong order and ask the students to try to act out the story. Ask them, "What happens if the final incident is placed first? Do we still have a story? Why not?"

After students have tried to act out the wrong sequence, have them act out the correct sequence. Encourage them to extend their parts by adding dialogue or characters to beginning, middle, and ending incidents. Ask them, "Is our story better? What makes the story better?" Encourage the students to act out other nursery rhymes such as "Tom, Tom, the Piper's Son," "Jack and Jill," "Little Miss Muffet," and "Rock-a-Bye Baby." After they act out each rhyme, ask them to discuss the importance of a beginning, a middle, and an end in a logical story.

Dramatizations and plot diagrams can be used to help students at any grade level understand plot structure and the important components of a story. After students understand the importance of beginning, middle, and ending incidents, introduce a simple folktale such as "Three Billy Goats Gruff" or *Goldilocks and the Three Bears.* First, read the story to the students. Ask them to concentrate on the order and importance of the events. Next, ask them to list the important events and the order in which they occurred. For example, after listening to "Three Billy Goats Gruff," a group of second-grade students listed the following events:

1. A little billy goat, a middle-sized billy goat, and a big billy goat want to cross the bridge and eat grass.
2. A terrible troll is under the bridge.
3. The little billy goat is threatened by the troll but talks his way out of trouble.
4. The middle billy goat is threatened by the troll but talks his way out of trouble.
5. The big billy goat is threatened by the troll and he fights the troll.
6. The big billy goat knocks the troll off the bridge.
7. The three goats eat grass across the bridge.

Next, ask the students to think about how they might dramatize the story. Ask them, "Who are the major characters? What is the problem that is introduced at the beginning of the story? How could we divide the story to show beginning actions, middle actions, and ending actions?" Finally, divide the class into groups and ask each group to dramatize the beginning actions, the middle actions, or the ending actions. After the class has dramatized the play, change the order of events so that the group depicting the ending actions are first. Ask the students, "What is wrong with this sequence? What would happen if the ending incidents come first in the story?"

Next, ask the students to consider the type of conflict that they just dramatized in their story as well as who is in conflict. Ask them to list these major conflicts: (a) The little billy goat against the troll, (b) the middle billy goat against the troll, and (c) the big billy goat against the troll. Now ask them, "How might we identify this kind of conflict?" Help the students understand that this is an animal-against-animal conflict but then point out that, in literature, when two characters are in conflict we call it person-against-person conflict.

Next, show the students how to place their actions from a story onto a plot diagram. Draw the shell of the diagram from Figure 5.1 on the chalkboard. Ask the students to either place their list of actions from the story onto this diagram or draw illustrations that show each major action from the story and place the drawings on the plot diagram. The diagram in Figure 5.1 shows drawings developed by lower elementary students. (Some teachers choose to use the terms *conflict, climax, turning point,* and *end of conflict* on the diagram. For a diagram showing these terms, see the lesson for middle elementary students.)

Next, introduce Peter Collington's wordless book, *The Angel and the Soldier Boy.* Because there are no words, the students will need to create their own text that includes conflict and important incidents that make up the story. Encourage them to look at the pictures and discuss the plot that follows the actions in a young girl's dream. The plot proceeds as a toy soldier and angel come to life and challenge the pirates who rob the girl's piggy bank, capture the solider, and return to their ship on top of the piano. The illustrations include enough detail to enhance storytelling. Ask the students to identify the plot structure

FIGURE 5.1 Plot diagram with drawings of "Three Billy Goats Gruff."

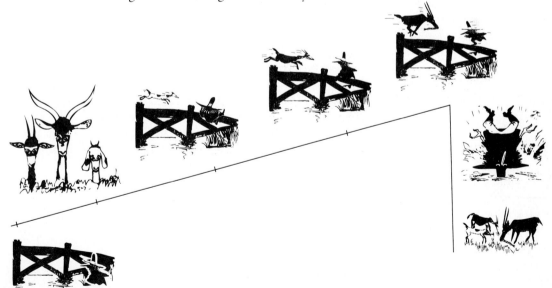

and the type of conflict. Then have them write a story that accompanies the illustrations, including the important foundations for plot structure. These stories can be dictated, individually written or written in a group.

Finally, ask the students to think of a story they would like to write and to draw a plot diagram that could accompany this story. Have the students write the story to accompany their diagram. After they have written their stories have them refer to their plot diagrams and ask them, "Does each story have a beginning, a middle, and an end? Is there conflict between characters that develops in the story?" Ask the students to have a classmate read their stories. "Do the stories follow a logical sequence? Are each of the parts of the story developed? Does any part of the story need to be changed? How could the story be changed to create a better sequence?" As part of the writing process, allow students to change their stories as needed to improve them.

LESSON TWO: Drawing a Plot Diagram for *Darkness and the Butterfly*

OBJECTIVES
> To identify the problem or conflict within the story.
> To draw the plot structure for the book.

CORE BOOK: Ann Grifalconi's *Darkness and the Butterfly* (Picture Story Book, African).

PROCEDURES: Introduce *Darkness and the Butterfly*. Ask students to look at the illustrations and to identify where they think the story takes place, who the characters are, and what type of problem the main character might need to overcome. Read the book and encourage students to respond to the story, to the problem of overcoming fear, and to the way that the main character overcomes her problem.

Next, ask the students to listen again as they identify the sequence of events in the story. Place the sequence of events on a plot structure. The plot structure in Figure 5.2 was developed by students in the lower grades.

Extended Books for Lower Elementary Students

The following books provide many opportunities for students in small group discussion to create dramas, respond to plot and conflict, and identify plot structures and person-against-person conflict. All the books contain easily recognizable plots that allow students to identify a logical sequence of events, to understand that stories have beginning incidents, middle incidents, and ending incidents in which the characters overcome some type of problem. The major conflicts in the books listed result because the main character is in conflict with another character. These characters can be people, animals, or inanimate objects. Many of these stories are folktales, which have easily identifiable plots and conflicts. Students can dramatize these stories, draw the important incidents within the story, and place the stories on plot diagrams.

Folktales

PAUL GALDONE's retelling of *The Three Bears*. The plot follows a girl as she tries out various items in the bears' house before she is finally discovered by the bears.

PAUL GALDONE's retelling of *What's in Fox's Sack? An Old English Tale*. The plot follows a woman who outsmarts a fox when she puts a bulldog in fox's sack.

MIRRA GINSBURG's retelling of *Two Greedy Bears* (Hungarian). Two greedy bears fight over cheese, but a fox solves the problem by eating the cheese.

BROTHERS GRIMM *The Wolf and the Seven Little Kids*, translated by Anne Rogers. Seven little goats have a conflict with a wolf when their mother leaves the house.

FIGURE 5.2 Plot structure for *Darkness and the Butterfly.*

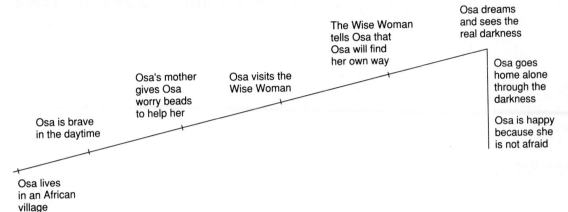

JAMES MARSHALL's retelling of *Hansel and Gretel.* The plot follows the children as they try to survive in the forest and finally outwit the witch.

ANNE ROCKWELL's retelling of *The Three Bears & 15 Other Stories.* This collection includes tales such as "The Three Bears," "The Gingerbread Man," and "The Three Little Pigs," which are especially good for plot development. The cumulative language in "The Gingerbread Man" is especially good for highlighting plot structure. Each time the Gingerbread Man meets a new character the sequence of conflict is repeated.

Wordless Books

MARTHA ALEXANDER's *Bobo's Dream.* Bobo dreams that he becomes large and rescues his master's football from a group of big boys.

MERCER MAYER's *Frog Goes to Dinner.* The boy puts Frog into his pocket and takes him along when the family goes to a fancy restaurant.

Modern Fantasy

HANS CHRISTIAN ANDERSEN's *The Ugly Duckling,* retold by Lorinda Bryan Cauley. The plot follows an ostracized duckling who turns into a beautiful swan.

BEATRIX POTTER's *The Tale of Peter Rabbit* (Touchstone). The plot follows Peter as he disobeys his mother, enters the garden, and tries to escape from Mr. McGregor.

Picture Story Books

GRACE CHETWIN's *Box and Cox.* The plot follows two men as they both rent the same room without knowing about each other. One works in the daytime and the other works at night.

EZRA JACK KEATS' *Goggles!* (Caldecott Honor). Two boys outwit the bullies in their neighborhood.

MERCER MAYER's *There's a Nightmare in My Closet.* A young boy confronts the nightmare that he believes is in his closet.

PHYLLIS REYNOLDS NAYLOR's *Keeping a Christmas Secret.* A young boy reveals a secret and then redeems his action.

CHRIS VAN ALLSBURG's *Jumanjii* (Caldecott Medal). A boy and a girl go through a series of unusual adventures after they find a game.

ROSEMARY WELLS' adaptation of *The Little Lame Prince*. In a retelling for younger children, the prince's uncle seizes the throne and exiles the prince before the prince eventually returns to the throne.

Recreational Books for Lower Elementary Students

The following books have easily recognizable plot structures:

Folktales

TONY JOHNSTON'S *The Badger and the Magic Fan* (Japanese)
JAMES MARSHALL'S *Goldilocks and the Three Bears* (Caldecott Honor)
JAN ORMEROD AND DAVID LOLLYD'S *The Frog Prince*

Easy-To-Read

NATHANIEL BENCHLEY'S *Oscar Otter*
DR. SEUSS' *The Cat in the Hat*
DR. SEUSS' *The Cat in the Hat Comes Back*

Picture Story Books

LISA CAMPBELL ERNST'S *Ginger Jumps*
RUSSELL HOBAN'S *Monsters*
MILDRED PITTS WALTER'S *Two and Too Much* (Black)

Core Books and Sample Lessons for Middle Elementary Students

This section includes lessons that introduce or review plot structures and lessons that explore the different types of conflicts that are developed within literature. The lessons on different types of conflict include both illustrated books in which the conflict is emphasized through the illustrations and the text and stories in which the conflict is developed primarily through the text.

LESSON ONE: Plot Structure and Person-Against-Person Conflict

OBJECTIVES

To develop an understanding of plot structure by acting out the sequence of actions in a story, drawing the plot diagram of a story, and writing stories that include a beginning, a middle, and an end.

To develop an understanding that characters in a person-against-person conflict can respond differently to the same sequence of actions.

CORE BOOKS: Choose folktales such as John Steptoe's *Mufaro's Beautiful Daughters: An African Tale* (Caldecott Honor) and other stories in which the plot is easily recognizable, such as Ed Young's *Lon Po Po: A Red-Riding Hood Story from China* (Caldecott Medal); Dianne Snyder's *The Boy of the Three-Year-Nap* (Japanese, Caldecott Honor); Susan Cooper's retelling of *The Silver Cow: A Welsh Tale*; Marianna Mayer's retelling of *The Twelve Dancing Princesses* (German); Isaac Bashevis Singer's *Mazel and Shlimazel, or the Milk of the Lioness* (Jewish); Arthur Ransome's *The Fool of the World and the Flying Ship* (Russian, Caldecott Medal); and Francisco Hinojosa's *The Old Lady Who Ate People* (Mexican).

PROCEDURES: As in the lesson for lower-elementary students, this core lesson includes a sequence of activities that takes several days to accomplish. When you introduce and review the concept of plot, ask the students to think about a story that was so exciting that they could not put it down. Ask them, "What did the author do to make it exciting?" Have the students give you examples of exciting stories and explain why the stories were exciting for them. Through discussion, develop the concept that exciting stories usually have a structure in which the characters overcome some type of conflict. The students usually decide that an interesting plot contains generous amounts of action, excitement, suspense, and conflict. Excitement occurs when the main character experiences a struggle or overcomes a conflict. The author must describe and develop the conflict so that it is believable. A good plot lets readers share the action, feel the conflict, recognize the climax, and respond to a satisfactory ending.

Dramatizations as described for the lower-elementary grades work equally well for students in the middle-elementary grades. Choose a story that the students identified as being so exciting it was difficult to put it down or a familiar folktale. Help the students identify the incidents they would like to dramatize. Encourage them to include beginning incidents in which the characters and the problems are introduced, middle incidents that increase the conflict and lead to the climax, and ending incidents that include a turning point and a conclusion to the conflict. Tell the students that these incidents provide the structure for their story. After they have identified the happenings in each part of the story, allow them to dramatize the story.

Next, draw the plot diagram shown in Figure 5.3 on the board. Review with the students how they included each part of this diagram in their drama. Ask them, "What would happen to our story if we left out any of these parts? What would happen to the story if the beginning, middle, and ending incidents were mixed?" Have them identify the incidents from their drama that correspond to each part of the diagram.

Now introduce the core book *Mufaro's Beautiful Daughters: An African Tale*. During a first reading of the story ask the students to listen for the conflict and the characters in the story. Encourage them to discuss their reactions to the conflict and the characters. Next, have the students diagram the story according to the previously discussed plot diagram.

Ask the students, "Did each of the characters respond in the same way to the major incidents in the story? Why do you believe that there were differences between the responses of the greedy, selfish sister and the generous, kind sister? What do we call this type of conflict in literature?" Be sure that they understand that this is a person-against-person conflict because

FIGURE 5.3 Plot diagram showing conflict.

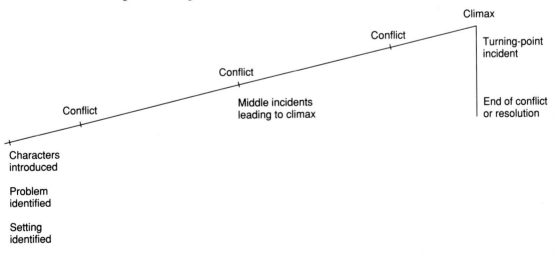

the two main characters have different motives and desires that are in conflict. Ask the students to not only plot the major incidents in the story, but also identify how each of the two characters responds to the incidents. This activity will allow the students to better understand the motivation of the characters and how the characters' motives relate to the conflict in the story. You can reread the story orally or allow students to reread the story themselves. The diagram in Figure 5.4 was completed with middle-elementary students. Notice how the students identified both the common plot structures and the different character responses to each incident.

Next, choose one of the other stories identified in the core materials. Ask the students to develop plot diagrams (either in small groups or individually) that show the structure of the story. When possible, ask them to consider how different characters respond to the same incidents. Have the students share their diagrams.

After students identify the plot structure and differences in responses among the main characters in several books, ask them to draw out a structure for a story they would like to write. Ask them to consider how each of the characters in the story might respond to a similar incident. These plot development models can be used during different phases of the writing process to help students focus on the key elements in plot development. For example, during prewriting students listen to stories, develop the model, and apply the model to other stories. During the writing phase they refer to the model to develop stories with beginning, middle, and ending incidents and to include rising action. After writing their first drafts they refer to the models during teacher conferences and peer editing groups. The models encourage students to focus on areas that are well-developed as well as areas that need to be revised for clarity. The models encourage self-evaluation because students are able to consider elements in plot development and to analyze whether their writing includes these elements.

LESSON TWO: Person-Against-Nature Conflict

OBJECTIVES

To develop an appreciation for and an understanding of person-versus-nature conflict as developed by illustrators and authors. To encourage an aesthetic response to person-versus-nature conflict during a drawing activity.

To understand the importance of illustrations in developing person-versus-nature conflict.

FIGURE 5.4 Plot diagram for *Mufaro's Beautiful Daughters*.

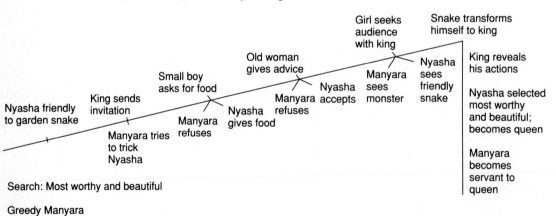

CORE BOOKS: Books that show the various frightening forces of nature such as Marcia Brown's *Shadow* (Picture Story Book, Caldecott Medal); Eve Bunting's *Ghost's Hour, Spook's Hour* (Picture Story Book); Paul Goble's *The Girl Who Loved Wild Horses* (Picture Story Book, Caldecott Medal); Keizaburo Tejima's *Fox's Dream* (Picture Story Book). Several contrasting books that depict a more benevolent side of nature such as Donald Hall's *The Ox-Cart Man* (Caldecott Medal) and Cynthia Rylant's *When I Was Young in the Mountains* (Caldecott Honor). Armstrong Sperry's *Call It Courage* (Realistic Fiction, Newbery Medal), in which the author uses language to develop the conflict with nature.

PROCEDURES: When nature is the antagonist the illustrator must present the environment or the author must describe nature in such a way that readers understand that characters are in danger from something in that environment. It might be the description of a mighty storm that threatens the life of a boy at sea, a cold and cruel terrain that brings starvation to a young girl, or a frightening, shadowy woods that encourages the emergence of the terror within our souls.

Begin an exploration of person-against-nature conflict by encouraging students to look closely at several illustrated books in which the illustrators develop nature as the antagonist. For example, ask the students to look at the effect of line and color in *Shadow*. Ask them, "What do you feel when you look at the introductory illustration showing a black collage figure, a long black shadow, and the ghostly white figures that are almost transparent? How do you react to the long spindly fingers and the elongated shadow? From this first illustration, do you believe that the world of shadow will be a safe and secure place?" Encourage the students to provide their own responses to this illustration and to consider what message about nature is being supported by the illustrations.

Next, read Marcia Brown's introduction in which she asks, "What is Shadow?" Ask the students what they would expect in the illustrations when the illustrator states that, "The beliefs and ghosts of the past haunt the present as it stretches into the future. The eerie, shifting image of Shadow appears where there is light and fire and a storyteller to bring it to life." Next, do a dramatic reading of *Shadow* in which you encourage the students to immerse themselves in their own reactions caused by the illustrations and the accompanying text. Ask them, "How did you respond to the illustrations and to the poet's choice of words? What emotions did you feel? Did the illustrations or text remind you of any past experiences? Were these experiences frightening or peaceful? How did you react to the illustrator's use of vivid blacks, bright reds, and transparent whites?" Point out to the students that illustrators use both lines and colors to create a mood and depict the environment. Help them see how Brown uses both line and color to create an antagonistic environment. Ask them, "Which words in the poem help us visualize nature as the antagonist?" They should identify frightening words such as "prowler," "thief," "staggers," "body dragging," and "teeming snakes, scorpions and worms." Ask them, "What memories do each of these words evoke in you? Do these memories correspond with the illustrations?"

To further the readers' reaction to both line and color, introduce *The Girl Who Loved Wild Horses*. To prepare, look carefully at Paul Goble's use of line and color. Notice how Goble's use of line supports and develops the conflict developing in the text. For example, Goble introduces readers to the main character as the character goes down to the river at sunrise to watch the wild horses. The illustration shows a calm, non-threatening scene. The lines of the horses' legs are vertical, because the horses are quietly drinking from the river. The calm is enhanced by the reflections in the water; not even a ripple breaks the tranquillity. (Vertical and horizontal lines suggest calm, sleep, stability, and an absence of strife.)

On the next page, the girl rests in a meadow close to home. Goble illustrates the triangular shapes of teepees sitting securely on the ground. (Triangular shapes suggest safety and the horizontal ground suggests tranquillity.) The text relates, however, that a rumble of thunder can be heard while the girl sleeps. The outlines of the clouds suggest this break in a peaceful afternoon: they are still rounded, but are also heavy, with protrusions jutting into the sky. (Curved lines are fluid and seem less definite and predictable than straight lines. Jagged lines have connotations of breakdown and destruction, suggesting danger.)

As the story progresses the movement in the story and the illustrations become more pronounced as lightning flashes and the horses rear and snort in terror. Sharp lines of lightning extend from black, rolling clouds to the ground. Even the lines of the plants are diagonal, suggesting the power of the dangerous wind as the horses gallop away in front of the storm. (Diagonal lines suggest loss of balance and uncontrolled motion—unless they form a triangle that rests on a horizontal base, which suggests safety. Jagged lines such as those found in the lightning suggest danger.) When night falls and the storm is over, the tired girl and horses stop to rest. Horizontal and vertical lines return, suggesting the new feeling of safety and shelter under the moon and the stars.

Share the illustrations and text from *The Girl Who Loved Wild Horses* with the students. Encourage them to note the use of both line and color especially in the scenes that go from tranquillity to storm to tranquillity.

Share several other books with the class in which illustrators depict nature as an antagonist. For example, ask the students to look at the illustrations in *Fox's Dream*. They can note that the illustrator uses shades of black and cold blues and whites when Fox is alone, lonely, and probably hungry in the woods. When he closes his eyes and remembers the warmth of summer and the nearness of his family, the illustrations are in warm yellows and browns. Share *Ghost's Hour, Spook's Hour* and ask the students to notice the changing lines and colors as the boy is frightened by the storm and then relieved by the appearance of his parents. Ask them to notice how the illustrator depicts this new security through yellow light and horizontal and vertical lines.

To show contrasts in nature, show and discuss several illustrated books in which nature is not the antagonist, such as *The Ox-Cart Man* and *When I Was Young in the Mountains*. Ask students to respond to the illustrators' use of pastels, muted hues of darker colors, and gentle curves that can produce a feeling of tranquillity. Ask the students to consider if this feeling is appropriate for each of the books. "If you were the author of either of these books, is this the feeling you would want expressed in the illustrations? Why or why not? What words did the author use to develop the nature of the environment within the text? How do these words differ from the ones that were used by authors who were developing person-against-nature conflicts?" Ask the students to draw some conclusions about what they have learned about the role of illustrations and text in developing person-against-nature conflicts.

Finally, introduce *Call It Courage* in which the author develops person-against-nature conflicts through vivid descriptions that allow readers to visualize nature through words. A dramatic reading of Chapters 1 and 2 helps students respond to Sperry's vivid descriptions of the sea and understand that nature is indeed a harsh antagonist. Read these two chapters once and ask the students to describe their own reactions to the story, the boy's fear, and the threatening sea.

After students have expressed their own reactions, ask them to listen a second time to excerpts from the story. This time they are to listen for the techniques that the author uses to make readers believe that nature is dangerous and that the boy is in conflict with nature. The following paragraphs are especially appropriate for this discussion:

> A storm was making, moving in out of those mysterious belts which lie north and
> south of the equator, the home of hurricanes. The wind shifted a point, bringing with
> it a heavy squall. Mafatu lowered the sail on the run and gripped the steering paddle

with hands that showed white at the knuckles. All around him now was a world of tumbling water, gray in the hollows, greenish on the slopes. The wind tore off the combing crests and flung the spray at the sky. Like advance scouts of an oncoming army, wind gusts moved down upon the canoe, struck at it savagely. So busy was Mafatu with the paddle that there was no time for thought. He called a prayer to Maui, God of the Fishermen: "Maui e! E matai tu!" (p. 21)

. . . This sea that he had always feared was rising to claim him, just as it had claimed his mother. How rightly he had feared it! Moana, the Sea God, had been biding his time. . . . "Someday, Mafatu, I will claim you!" (p. 23)

There was a wave lifting before the canoe. Many the boy had seen, but this was a giant—a monster livid and hungry. Higher, higher it rose, until it seemed that it must scrape at the low-hanging clouds. Its crest heaved over with a vast sigh. The boy saw it coming. He tried to cry out. No sound issued from his throat. Suddenly the wave was upon him. Down it crashed. Chaos! Mafatu felt the paddle torn from his hands. Thunder in his ears. Water strangling him. Terror in his soul. The canoe slewed round into the trough. The boy flung himself forward, wound his arms about the mid-thwart. It was the end of a world. (p. 24)

After reading these selections for the second time—or third or fourth, if necessary—ask the students, "What did the author do to make you understand that the sea is dangerous and that it is Mafatu's enemy?" Help the students identify that Mafatu's actions reveal how frightened he is of the sea: He grips the paddle with hands that are white at the knuckles, desperately prays to Maui, remembers that the sea had claimed his mother and would someday claim him, tries to cry out but cannot, winds his arms around the mid-thwart, and concludes that it is the end of his world. The author's use of personification helps readers understand the dangerous nature of the storm: The wind flings the spray at the sky, the storm is compared to the dangerous advance scouts of an oncoming army, and the storm is referred to as a hungry and livid monster. Finally, the author's sentence structures show the increasing climax of the storm: The sentences become shorter and shorter as the crest approaches until the author uses only one word, "Chaos!"

Allow the students to respond to this conflict with nature by illustrating the setting in which Mafatu faces the oncoming storm. Ask them to pretend that they are an illustrator such as one they analyzed in the earlier illustrated books. Ask them to try to portray a setting in which the character is afraid for his life and the sea is something to be feared.

As they finish reading *Call It Courage*, ask the students to consider how Mafatu overcomes his fear of the sea. Tell the students that there are two conflicts in this book. Nature is revealed first as an antagonist, but fear is also an antagonist. When Mafatu must overcome his fear we refer to this conflict as person-against-self conflict. Ask the students, "How does the author reveal the conflict and the nature of the conflict for this boy? How do we know that he has overcome his fear of the sea?" This question can lead directly into Lesson Three, person-against-self conflict.

LESSON THREE: Person-Against-Self Conflict

OBJECTIVES

To develop an appreciation for and an understanding of person-against-self conflict as developed by illustrators and authors.

To encourage an aesthetic response to person-against-self conflict during a drawing activity.

To understand the importance of illustrations in developing person-against-self conflict.

To understand the plot structure that frequently accompanies person-against-self conflict. To write a person-against-self conflict that follows the plot structure.

CORE BOOKS: Books that show the personal conflict that might accompany the main character, such as Arthur Yorinks' *Hey, Al* (Picture Story Book, Caldecott Medal) and Denys Cazet's *A Fish in His Pocket* (Picture Story Book). Armstrong Sperry's *Call It Courage* (Realistic Fiction, Newbery Medal).

PROCEDURES: The illustrator or the author must depict person-against-self conflict so that readers understand what is causing the inner turmoil, why the characters are experiencing this turmoil, and what alternatives might be open to the characters. Authors can develop the attitudes of peers or family and then develop different beliefs of the main character so that readers understand why these beliefs, values, and feelings might be causing problems for the main character. Person-against-self conflicts are usually credible to readers because many of these conflicts occur in their own lives. These conflicts frequently reflect the hidden terrors that are just below the surface in many children's lives. The type of conflict also can change with age. For example, young children might experience jealousy and inner conflicts resulting from the birth of a sibling or they might try to undo an action that they know is wrong. Older children might face even harsher turmoils as they try to reconcile peer pressures and what they believe to be right. Ask the students to explore the various person-against-self conflicts that they have experienced or that they have read about in literature. Ask them to consider how these conflicts might change in books written and illustrated for younger children and in books written for older children.

Introduce *A Fish in His Pocket*, an illustrated book written for younger children. Ask the students to notice how the illustrator encourages readers to understand that the bear has a person-against-self conflict after he accidently causes the death of a fish. Ask them to follow the bear as he worries about his problem, conceives a satisfactory solution, executes his actions, and changes back into a happy bear after he completes the solution that does not conflict with his strong respect for life. Encourage the students to notice that because this book is intended for younger children, the bear's emotions and actions are depicted in the illustrations. For example, the illustrations show him reading a book upside down and offering his lunch to a friend. These illustrations extend the ideas in the text beyond what is actually stated.

Next, share *Hey, Al*, an illustrated text in which the main character must decide if it is better to live and play in paradise as a bird or to live and work hard in his dilapidated city apartment. Read the book to the students and allow them to look carefully at the illustrations. Ask them to respond to Al's conflict: "How would they react if they were in a similar situation? Do they believe that Al made the correct decision?"

Read and share the illustrations in the book a second time. Point out that the Caldecott Award illustrations provide an excellent example of how illustrators can show the rising action in the plot through increasing the size of the illustrations. Color and facial expressions also are used to support a satisfactory solution to a person-against-self conflict. Encourage students to notice that, as the plot develops, the illustrations increase in size to double-page spreads at the height of the action. The illustrations return to normal size after Al overcomes his personal struggle and creates a satisfactory ending. Also encourage students to notice that the illustrator uses color to reflect differences between reality and fantasy and to show that a satisfactory conclusion has been reached. For example, the introductory pages and the early environment are in drab colors. Bright colors enter the pictures when the bird entices Al into a new way of life and Al reaches the fantasy island. The drab colors return after Al makes his decision to go back to human form and to the existence that means hard work. These drab colors do not remain, however. In the last picture Al is wearing a bright shirt and painting his apartment yellow. The end pages of the book also are colored bright yellow. Ask the students, "How does the illustration size and the use of color reinforce the developing conflict and the last line of the story, 'Paradise lost is sometimes Heaven found'? How do these same techniques help readers respond to a person-against-self conflict?"

Next, tell students that when characters try to overcome problems caused by inner conflicts they can use the same type of plot structure that they used for person-against-person conflict, except with different terminology. Cohen (1985) identifies four major components in the development of person-against-self conflicts: Problem, struggle, realization, and achievement of peace or truth. Cohen states, "The point at which the struggle wanes and the inner strength emerges seems to be the point of self-realization. The point leads immediately to the final sense of peace or truth that is the resolution of the quest. The best books are those which move readers and cause them to identify with the character's struggle." (p. 28)

Draw the diagram in Figure 5.5 on the board. Then ask the students, "How should we plot the struggles in *A Fish in His Pocket* and *Hey, Al*?" Have them place the important incidents from these books on separate plot diagrams.

Next, reintroduce Sperry's *Call It Courage*. Remind the students that, earlier, they were considering the person-against-nature conflict that Mafatu faced. But the text also said that he was in conflict with his own fear. The two adversaries are interwoven in the plot as Mafatu sails from his island to prove that he is not a coward. Ask the students, "What are the implications of the following quote found toward the end of the book?"

> "Moana, you Sea God!" he shouted violently. "You! You destroyed my mother. Always you have tried to destroy me. Fear of you has haunted my sleep. Fear of you turned my people against me. But now—" he choked; his hands gripped his throat to stop its hot burning, "now I no longer fear you, Sea!" His voice rose to a wild note. He sprang to his feet, flung back his head, spread wide his arms in defiance. "Do you hear me, Moana? I am not afraid of you! Destroy me—but I laugh at you. Do you hear? I laugh!" (p. 112).

Ask the students, "What has happened between the second chapter and the final chapter?"

As the students read *Call It Courage*, ask them to identify the person-against-self problem, the incidents that reveal Mafatu's inner struggle, the point of self-realization, and the point at which they know he has achieved peace and truth. Remind the students that each time

FIGURE 5.5 Plot diagram for person-against-self conflict.

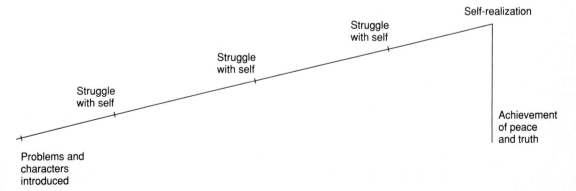

Mafatu wins a victory over nature, he comes closer to his main goal, victory over his fear. Without that victory, he cannot be called by his rightful name Mafatu (Stout Heart), nor can he have the respect of his father, his Polynesian people, and himself.

To complete the study of this novel encourage students to pretend that they have been asked by Armstrong Sperry to create a picture book version of *Call It Courage*. Sperry wants them to highlight the incidents that show how Mafatu overcomes his person-against-self conflict. They can use any artistic technique for this assignment.

Finally, ask students to develop their own example of a person-against-self conflict. Encourage them to think through the plot structure in which they identify the problem, the struggles that lead to self-realization, and the conclusion in which the character achieves peace and truth. Have the students write their stories as part of the writing process described earlier. After they have finished, encourage them to illustrate their stories and to share them with an audience.

LESSON FOUR: Person-Against-Society Conflict

OBJECTIVES

To develop an appreciation for and an understanding of person-against-society conflict as developed by illustrators and authors.

To encourage an aesthetic response to person-against-society conflict during a drawing activity.

To understand the importance of illustrations in developing person-against-society conflict.

To write a personal response to a person-against-society conflict.

CORE BOOKS: Illustrated books that depict person-against-society conflicts, such as Virginia Lee Burton's *The Little House* (Picture Story Book, Caldecott Medal); Monro Leaf's *The Story of Ferdinand* (Picture Story Book, Touchstone); and Dr. Seuss' *The Lorax* (Picture Story Book). Jane Yolen's *The Devil's Arithmetic* (Modern Fantasy).

PROCEDURES: Students might have more difficulty understanding and identifying person-against-society conflicts. The antagonist is not a specific person but a whole group of people who express similar values and beliefs. When authors develop person-against-society conflicts, the main character's actions, desires, or values differ from those of the surrounding society. This conflict might result because the main character is different from the majority in terms of race, religion, values, or physical characteristics. Numerous survival stories set in wartime develop person-against-society conflicts as the main character survives in a hostile world. Sometimes person-against-society conflict is caused by environmental changes such as pollution or industrial expansion. For the conflict to be believable, the personal values of the main character must be developed and the social setting and society's values must be presented in accurate detail. Readers must understand why the character is in conflict with society. Share this information with the students and ask them to identify any person-against-society conflicts that they have read about or experienced. Ask them, "How did you know that there was a conflict between someone and society? If the conflict was in a book, how did the author make you believe in the conflict?" Finally, ask them to list some current person-against-society conflicts that authors might write about. Suggest that they consider information from the news that shows this type of conflict.

Introduce the three illustrated books. Tell the students that illustrators also can show various types of person-against-society conflicts and ask them how illustrators might do this. Tell the students that two of the illustrated books show conflict caused by environmental changes and one of the books develops conflict through differences between one character's values and society's expectations. Ask the students, "How do you think an illustrator might show these conflicts?"

First, look at and read *The Little House*. Ask the students, "What techniques does the illustrator use to let viewers know that the little house is really in conflict with the approaching city?" Encourage the students to compare the illustrations at the beginning of the text that show the happy house surrounded by rolling fields and the illustrations that show the bleakness of the structures that eventually surround and overshadow her. Ask them to identify the first picture that shows that societal changes will not have a benevolent influence on the house. Ask them to discuss the effect of this illustration, which shows a brown slash going across the tranquil rural setting. Ask them, "What do you think Burton is showing with the brown road that includes a steam shovel, trucks, and other road equipment? What is the visual effect of this picture. What does it imply for the future? Look again at the illustrations that follow this picture. Is this the point that suggests the person-against-society conflict for the little house? How does the illustrator reveal the problems that come with time and environmental change? How does the illustrator resolve the problems and return the little house to a happy existence? What techniques does the illustrator use to reveal that the house is happy again? How does this final change reveal that the little house's main conflict was person-against-society?"

Next, ask the students to look at the illustrations in *The Lorax*. Ask them, "What is Dr. Seuss' reason for writing and illustrating this book? What is the message about society that he is trying to achieve? How does he make us understand that lack of concern for the environment causes considerable conflict?"

Next, share *The Story of Ferdinand*. As the students look at the illustrations and listen to the text, ask them to think about Ferdinand's conflict. "What is the nature of the society that causes his conflict? What techniques do the illustrator and the author use to reveal the differences in values and beliefs between Ferdinand and the society that has certain expectations for a bull? How does Ferdinand resolve this conflict?"

Next, return to the list of contemporary person-against-society conflicts that the students identified at the beginning of this lesson. In groups, ask the students to choose one of these conflicts and to brainstorm how they would develop the conflict in a picture-book format. As their first task, have them identify the characteristics of both a main character and the society that might be in conflict with the beliefs and values of the character. Next, ask them to plot the structure of the story so that readers will understand the beliefs of the main character and the conflicting values of a societal group. As part of the writing process ask them to write their stories and then illustrate them so that the illustrations also reflect the person-against-society conflict.

Finally, introduce *The Devil's Arithmetic*. Read the back cover of the text in which Jane Yolen reveals her reasons for writing this book about a Jewish girl's experiences during the Holocaust. Give the students some background information about the 1940s setting and the nature of the conflict for Jewish people living in Europe. You also might tell the students that this is a time-warp story in which a contemporary American Jewish girl finds herself in Europe during the 1940s. Her previously safe world changes to the violent world of the Holocaust. The vivid descriptions, fear, and personal reactions to losing friends while in a concentration camp reveal the nature of the society.

Because students frequently report highly personal reactions to this book, it is an excellent source for aesthetic responses through writing or art. Allow the students to select how they would like to respond to this book. The following are a few suggestions chosen by students: (a) Write a personal response to this book in your writing journal. Include what you liked or did not like about a character or characters, the plot and conflict of the story, and the language in the book. What scenes affected you? How and why did they affect you? (b) Choose one of the characters in the book and keep a dialogue journal with that character. Write questions you would like to ask that character about the character's feelings, reactions, beliefs, motives, or actions. Exchange your dialogue journal with someone else in the class. Ask the person to write the answers to your questions as if he or she were that character. (c) Keep a diary as if you were one of the characters in the book. Include your personal reactions to things that happened to you in the story. (d) Respond to the person-against-society conflict in *The Devil's Arithmetic* through an artistic response. Using any technique you choose, such as collage or paint, try to create the feelings you had as you read the book.

LESSON FIVE: Webbing Conflict

OBJECTIVES

To identify the various types of conflict developed in a book.

To web the major conflicts and the evidence for those conflicts.

CORE BOOK: Byrd Baylor's *Hawk, I'm Your Brother* (Caldecott Honor, Native American).

PROCEDURES: Review plot diagrams and the four different types of conflict that can be found in a book: person against person, person against nature, person against society, and person against self. Introduce *Hawk, I'm Your Brother* by telling students that it is a book about a Native American boy who has an important dream. Ask the students to think of some desire they have had. "What would you do to make your dream possible? What conflicts might you cause as you try to make your dream come true?" Share the book and discuss the students' reactions to the boy and to his dream.

Next, ask the students to identify the major incidents in the story and to place those incidents on a plot diagram. If necessary, reread the story. The plot diagram in Figure 5.6 was developed by students in the middle elementary grades.

Next, draw a web on the board with *conflict* written in the center. Ask the students to identify the types of conflicts they encountered in *Hawk, I'm Your Brother*. Place these conflicts on the spokes from the center of the web. Most students identify all four of the

FIGURE 5.6 Plot diagram for *Hawk, I'm Your Brother*.

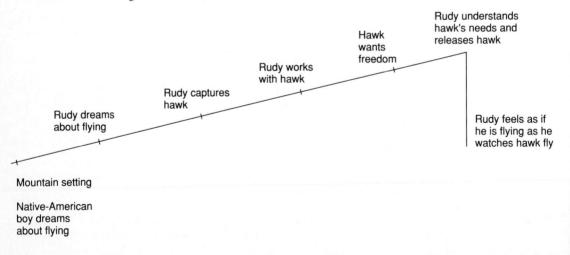

major conflicts. If they do not, explore the unidentified conflicts. Ask, "Did anything happen in the story that could be classified as a _____ conflict?" Then add that conflict to the web.

Next, reread the book. Ask the students to locate evidence and examples of each type of conflict. Place these examples on the web. The web in Figure 5.7 was developed by middle-elementary students.

Extended Books for Middle Elementary Students

The books identified in this section are excellent for dramatizing, developing plot structures, motivating artistic interpretations, and stimulating ideas for writing. The illustrated books allow students to consider the importance of pictures when depicting plot structure and conflict. The person-against-person, person-against-nature, and person-against-society conflicts can be depicted on a plot structure that emphasizes the problem, the conflicts that support the rising action, the climax, the turning-point incident, and the resolution of conflict. The person-against-self books frequently are more appropriate for a structure that follows the problem, the increasing struggle, the self-realization, and the achievement of peace and truth. Because many books include person-against-self conflicts as well as one or more of the other conflicts, it is interesting to diagram the different types of plot structures. Students then can compare the

FIGURE 5.7 Webbing conflict in *Hawk, I'm Your Brother*.

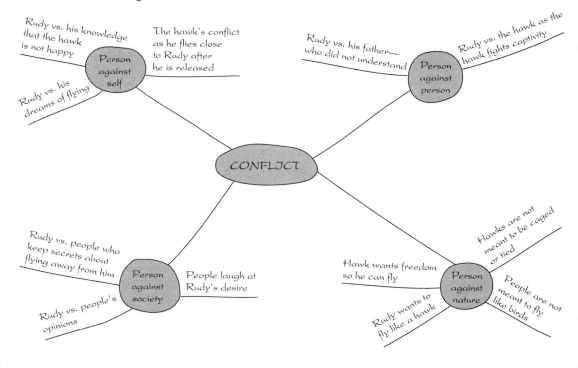

structures and see how the different types of conflict are interwoven in the story and how they influence the character.

The books also can be used to develop webs showing conflict and can be compared, especially within a specific genre of literature.

Folktales

JAN CAREW's *The Third Gift* (African). The plot follows the Jubas as they gain the gifts of work, beauty, and imagination.

SELMA LAGERLÖF's *The Legend of the Christmas Rose* (Swedish). The plot follows an abbot as he observes a miraculous garden in the forest.

BROTHERS GRIMM's *The Water of Life* (German). The plot follows the youngest son as he completes a quest that saves his father.

JOSEPHA SHERMAN's *Vassilisa the Wise: A Tale of Medieval Russia*. The plot follows a clever and courageous woman as she saves her husband's life.

SUMIKO YAGAWA's *The Crane Wife* (Japanese). The plot follows a man whose greed causes him to lose his wife.

Modern Fantasy

LLOYD ALEXANDER's *The Town Cats and Other Tales*. In person-against-person conflicts, cats succeed in outwitting humans.

HANS CHRISTIAN ANDERSEN's *The Red Shoes*. In a person-against-self conflict a girl dances as punishment for her pride.

HANS CHRISTIAN ANDERSEN's *The Snow Queen*. Errol LeCain's illustrations show the evil queen against a dark blue background.

CARLO COLLODI's *The Adventures of Pinocchio: Tale of a Puppet* (Touchstone). In person-against-person and person-against-self conflicts, the wooden marionette eventually learns to be a real boy. It is interesting to compare the consequences of seeking idleness and pleasure found in this book with the same consequences in Arthur Yorinks' highly illustrated book, *Hey, Al* (Caldecott Medal).

IAN FLEMING's *Chitty Chitty Bang Bang*. In a person-against-person conflict a car has remarkable properties that help save the family from gangsters.

Realistic Fiction

JUDY BLUME's *Blubber*. In a person-against-society conflict a girl is ostracized by her classmates because she is overweight.

EVE BUNTING's *The Empty Window*. In a person-against-self conflict a boy cannot face the approaching death of his best friend.

SHEILA BURNFORD's *The Incredible Journey*. Three animals face a person-against-nature story as they travel through 250 miles of Canadian wilderness.

CONSTANCE GREENE's *The Ears of Louis*. In a person-against-self conflict a boy discovers that he has many desirable characteristics that are not related to his physical appearance.

DENNIS HASELEY's *The Scared One* (Native American). In person-against-society and person-against-self conflicts a boy faces and overcomes fear and ridicule.

NICHOLASA MOHR's *Felita* (Puerto Rican). In person-against-society and person-against-self conflicts a girl is unhappy when her family moves to a new neighborhood.

Historical Fiction

CAROL CARRICK's *Stay Away from Simon!* In a person-against-society conflict two children discover the true worth of the mentally retarded boy who is feared by the village.

MARGUERITE DEANGELI's *The Door in the Wall* (Newbery Medal). In a person-against-self conflict a disabled boy discovers that he must find his own way to overcome his problems.

JANET HICKMAN's *Zoar Blue.* In person-against-society and person-against-self conflicts a young man discovers that his religious convictions will not let him fight in the Civil War.

LAURA INGALLS WILDER's *The Long Winter* (Touchstone). In a person-against-nature conflict the family must face a blizzard that causes them great discomfort and hardships.

Biography

JAMES DEKAY's *Meet Martin Luther King, Jr.* (Black). Considerable person-against-society conflict is developed as the text stresses the reasons that King fought against injustice.

JERI FERRIS' *Go Free or Die: A Story of Harriet Tubman* (Black). In a person-against-society conflict the biographer describes Tubman's experience during slavery and the Underground Railroad.

ELOISE GREENFIELD's *Rosa Parks* (Black): In a person-against-society conflict the biographer describes the woman who refused to give up her bus seat in Montgomery, Alabama.

Recreational Books for Middle Elementary Students

Folktales

AFANASYEV, ALEXANDER NIKOLAYEVICH *The Fool and the Fish: A Tale from Russia*
ARIANE DEWEY's *The Thunder God's Son* (Peruvian)
ALAN GARNER's *A Bag of Moonshine* (British)
MARILEE HEYER's *The Weaving of a Dream* (Chinese)
JANE IKE AND BARUCH ZIMMERMAN's *A Japanese Fairy Tale* (Japanese)
CAROLE KISMARIC's *The Rumor of Pavel and Paali: A Ukrainian Folktale* (Russian)
MERCER MAYER's *East of the Sun and West of the Moon* (Norwegian)

Modern Fantasy

HANS CHRISTIAN ANDERSEN's *The Wild Swans*
LUCY M. BOSTON's *An Enemy at Green Knowe*
ROALD DAHL's *James and the Giant Peach*
ALEXANDER KEY's *The Forgotten Door*
RUDYARD KIPLING's *The Jungle Book*
O. R. MELLING's *The Singing Stone*
MARY RODGERS' *Summer Switch*
DAVID WISNIEWSKI's *The Warrior and the Wise Man*

Realistic Fiction

BETSY BYARS' *The Animal, The Vegetable, and John D. Jones*
BETSY BYARS' *The 18th Emergency*
BEVERLY CLEARY's *Ramona and Her Father* (Newbery Honor)
BEVERLY CLEARY's *Ramona Quimby, Age 8* (Newbery Honor)
JEAN CRAIGHEAD GEORGE's *My Side of the Mountain* (Newbery Honor)
VIRGINIA HAMILTON's *Zeely* (Black)
LOIS LOWRY's *Anastasia Krupnik*
BERNIECE RABE's *The Balancing Girl*

Historical Fiction

MARIE MCSWIGAN's *Snow Treasure*
JOYCE ROCKWOOD's *Groundhog's Horse* (Native American)
MILDRED TAYLOR's *The Gold Cadillac* (Black)

Biography

Arnold Adoff's *Malcolm X* (Black)
Ruth Franchere's *Cesar Chavez* (Hispanic)
Jean Fritz's *Why Don't You Get a Horse, Sam Adams?*
John Jakes' *Susanna of the Alamo*
Betsy Lee's *Charles Eastman: The Story of an American Indian*
Carol Ann Pearce's *Amelia Earhart*

Core Books and Sample Lessons for Upper Elementary and Middle School Students

The sample lessons in this section include tasks that are similar to those developed for the middle grades. While many of the lessons and books presented for middle-elementary students also are appropriate for students in upper elementary and middle school, the lessons in this section are based on books geared toward older students. Teachers should choose the books according to their students' previous knowledge, reading ability, and interests. Many use both series of lessons and books, which can be especially important if students have had little experience with literature.

Teachers in the upper grades frequently emphasize the terminology related to conflict. For example, they want their students to understand that conflict occurs when a protagonist or main character struggles against an antagonist or an opposing force.

As in the previous section, the sample lessons introduce or review various types of plot structures and explore the different types of conflicts developed within literature. The lessons include the use of both books in which the conflict is emphasized through illustrations and stories in which the conflict is developed primarily through the text. Many picture books are quite appropriate for this age range, which often surprises older students, especially if they have had few experiences with illustrated texts.

LESSON ONE: Person-Against-Person Conflict

OBJECTIVES

To develop an understanding of plot structure and the requirements of a person-against-person conflict.

To diagram a person-against-person conflict.

To compare the plot structures and the characteristics of the protagonist and the antagonist in two legends that contain noble knights and evil foes.

CORE BOOKS: Selina Hastings' *Sir Gawain and the Loathly Lady* (Legend) and Margaret Hodges' *Saint George and the Dragon* (Legend, Caldecott Medal).

PROCEDURES: Review the information about plot structures and person-against-person conflict presented in Lesson One for Middle-Elementary Grades. Make sure students understand that a credible person-against-person conflict requires that both the antagonist and the protagonist be developed so that readers understand why they are in conflict with each other. Tell the students that they will analyze the plot structure and identify the conflict in two legends: *Sir Gawain and the Loathly Lady* and *Saint George and the Dragon*. Tell them that they also will use illustrated books so they can discover the effect of the illustrations in depicting the person-against-person conflict.

First, read and discuss *Sir Gawain and the Loathly Lady*. Ask the students to list characteristics of the protagonist and antagonist and to consider why characters with these characteristics might be in conflict. For example, they probably will identify King Arthur versus the Black Knight. Characteristics of King Arthur include that he is honorable, honest, noble, and king of England. In contrast, the Black Knight is developed as an evil foe, angry, and desirous of Arthur's crown. Ask the students, "Why would we expect characters with such opposite descriptions to be in conflict with each other? Is this a believable conflict? Why or why not?" Next ask them to consider the effect of the illustrations, "How does the illustrator depict King Arthur versus the Black Knight? How do the illustrations support the person-against-person conflict?" (Several conflicts are developed in this book. For an expanded analysis of literary elements see the completed conflict web developed in Lesson five—Figure 5.9.)

Next, place the plot diagram from Figure 5.3 on the board or on a transparency. Discuss or review each part of the plot structure. Ask the students to place the major conflict developed in *Sir Gawain and the Loathly Lady* on this diagram. The plot diagram in Figure 5.8 was developed by upper-elementary students.

Next, ask the students to read and identify the characteristics of the protagonist and antagonist in *Saint George and the Dragon*. They should identify the characteristics of the noble Saint George and the evil dragon. Ask them to analyze the illustrations and identify how the illustrations support the conflict and the natures of the protagonist and the antagonist. Then have them place the developing conflict on the plot diagram. After they have completed this task, ask them to compare the characteristics of the protagonists and the antagonists and the plot structures for *Sir Gawain and the Loathly Lady* and for *Saint George and the Dragon*. Ask the students, "Are there any similarities between the two stories? If there are, what do you believe accounts for the similarities? If we read another legend would you expect to discover any similarities? Why or why not?"

FIGURE 5.8 Plot diagram for *Sir Gawain and the Loathly Lady.*

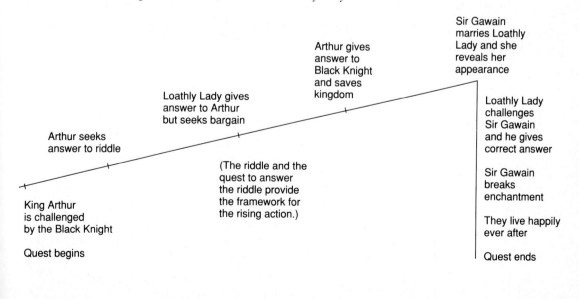

LESSON TWO: Person-Against-Nature Conflict

OBJECTIVES

To develop an appreciation for and an understanding of person-against-nature conflict as developed by illustrators and authors.

To understand that authors must carefully develop the dangerous forces of nature if readers are to believe that the protagonist is in conflict with this dramatic force.

To understand that personal experience can influence the way an author develops a person-against-nature conflict.

To understand the importance of illustrations and detailed descriptions in developing person-against-nature conflicts.

To write a description of nature that makes the reader believe in the dangerous forces of nature.

CORE BOOKS: Books that include photographs or illustrations of the dangerous forces of nature, such as Patricia Lauber's *Volcano: The Eruption and Healing of Mount St. Helens* (Nonfiction Informational, Newbery Honor); Ron and Nancy Goor's *Pompeii: Exploring a Roman Ghost Town* (Nonfiction Informational); Seymour Simon's *Storms* (Nonfiction Informational); Downs Matthews' *Polar Bear Cubs* (Nonfiction Informational); and Holling Clancy Holling's *Paddle to the Sea* (Nonfiction Informational, Caldecott Honor). Gary Paulsen's *Hatchet* (Realistic Fiction, Newbery Honor) and *Woodsong* (Autobiography).

PROCEDURES: Review the information about person-against-nature conflict presented in the middle-elementary grades. If desired, the illustrated books under that section can be discussed. Ask the students to think about various natural settings and natural phenomena that could cause conflict for a character. List these examples and ask the students to describe each example so that they understand that nature is a dramatic force.

Next, look at and discuss the photographs and illustrations in the nonfictional sources. Ask the students to choose one of these books or illustrations and to describe nature so that readers understand how dangerous that setting might be if a person is caught there. Share the descriptions in class and discuss how each writer made the destructive force of nature believable.

Introduce Paulsen's *Hatchet* by explaining to the students that this is a survival-in-nature story in which a boy must make correct decisions if he is to survive alone in the Canadian wilderness. Ask the students to look at the illustration on the jacket cover. Have them note and discuss the importance of the wilderness, the wolf, the hatchet, and the lone boy. They should remember the illustrations of the wilderness in *Paddle to the Sea* and consider their chances of survival in such an environment. Show them a map of the Canadian wilderness so that they can see and appreciate the abundance of trees and lakes and the shortage of settlements and towns.

As the students read this book ask them to consider the importance of how Brian approaches critical, often life-and-death problems. Ask the students to consider their responses when Paulsen reveals Brian's reasoning processes as he tries to survive in nature. For example, ask the students to discuss the effect of each of the following experiences as Brian thinks about the pros and cons of various actions:

1. Brian thinks through the various actions he could take after the pilot has a heart attack and Brian realizes he is alone (pp. 17–30).

2. Brian contemplates the reasons that he should not fear the bear and should return to the raspberry patch (p. 75).

3. Brian considers the reasons a water animal would come up to the sand (pp. 98–99).
4. Brian analyzes a way to create a weapon to effectively catch fish (pp. 111–115).
5. Brian thinks about ways to capture birds for meat (pp. 140–141).
6. Brian logically considers a way to make a raft and reach the plane after a tornado reveals the location of the plane (pp. 166–183).

Ask the students to consider the importance of each of these problem-solving situations in a person-against-nature conflict. Ask them to notice how Paulsen encourages readers to understand the gravity and the consequences of many of the problems. For example, Brian compares his experiences in the wilderness with experiences he has had at home. Readers understand that the search for and the storage of food is more than a simple trip to the grocery store; unlike Brian's home experiences, the actions in the wilderness are life-and-death matters.

After the students have read and discussed the person-against-nature conflict in this book, ask them to consider the experiences that the author might have had. Ask, "How do you think Gary Paulsen was able to describe the wilderness and the character's conflicts so that we believed they were really true? What experiences do you think he has had?" Now introduce Paulsen's autobiography, *Woodsong*. Have the students read the book and identify any information that verifies their speculations about Paulsen's experiences. Or, read portions of the book to the students and ask them to compare Paulsen's descriptions of the Minnesota wilderness with the descriptions of the Canadian wilderness in *Hatchet*. They also should consider what Paulsen learned as he ran with his sled dogs in the Minnesota wilderness and on the Iditarod dogsled race across Alaska.

After students have discussed the person-against-nature conflict in both of Paulsen's books, ask them to imagine themselves in a conflict with nature. Have them consider the characteristics of nature that would cause them problems, the actions that must be taken if they are to survive, and the problem-solving approaches that they might use. Have them use *Hatchet* or *Woodsong* as a model and to write a short story in which they must make major decisions. Like Brian or Paulsen, ask the students to verbalize their reasoning processes as they document their problem-solving approaches. Have the students share their stories.

LESSON THREE: Person-Against-Self Conflict

OBJECTIVES

To develop an appreciation for and an understanding of person-against-self conflict as developed by illustrators and authors.

To encourage an aesthetic response to person-against-self conflict during a drawing activity and a writing activity.

To understand the plot structure that frequently accompanies person-against-self conflict.

To understand and appreciate how the author's use of language enhances a person-against-self conflict.

CORE BOOKS: Illustrated books and book-cover illustrations that show the personal conflict that might accompany the main character, such as the covers of Paula Fox's (Realistic Fiction, Newbery Honor); Cynthia Rylant's *A Fine White Dust* (Realistic Fiction, Newbery Honor); and Marion Dane Bauer's *On My Honor* (Realistic Fiction, Newbery Honor).

PROCEDURES: Review the information about person-against-self conflict presented in Lesson Three for middle-elementary grades. After students understand the requirements for a person-against-self conflict, ask them to look carefully at the covers of the three core books that develop this type of conflict. Ask the students, "How do you know from looking at the cover illustrations that each of these characters will be in conflict with himself?" Encourage the students to discuss such information as the dark, brooding colors used on Fox's cover, the transparent look of the boy holding the air rifle, and the placement of the one-eyed cat as if it dominates the story and Ned's thoughts. On Rylant's cover they will notice the solid image of a boy with a transparent image of a character who again seems to dominate his conscience. Finally, on Bauer's cover they will notice the look of desperation on the boy's face and the position of his hand, suggesting severe agitation. Ask the students to hypothesize about the cause of each person-against-self conflict.

Next, draw the plot diagram from Figure 5.5 on the board. Discuss each of the four major components, including problem, struggle, realization, and achievement of peace or truth. Allow students to share books and experiences that reflect person-against-self conflicts. Place the important incidents from these conflicts on the plot diagram.

Ask the students, "Why do you believe that many authors write books for older students that have person-against-self conflicts?" Tell the students that they will be reading about a boy who must overcome feelings of guilt in *One-Eyed Cat.* As they read this book they will discover what the air rifle and the cat have to do with this boy's conflict. As they read the book ask the students to identify incidents in the book that show the problem, Ned's struggle with himself, his self-realization, and his achievement of peace or truth. Ask the students to identify powerful incidents that affected them as they read the book. The following list was identified by a group of seventh-grade students:

1. Papa asks Ned to trust him and to not use the air rifle (p. 36).
2. Ned sneaks up into the attic, takes the rifle, and fires it outside (pp. 43–46).
3. Ned shows fear when he sees the cat with a hole where the eye should be (p. 66).
4. Ned remembers past feelings of guilt and the consequences of his actions (p. 68).
5. The description of the cat: "He'd seen the gap, the dried blood, the little worm of mucus in the corner next to the cat's nose where the eye had been" (p. 70).
6. "The gun was like a splinter in his mind" (p. 90).
7. "If he could keep the cat alive, it wouldn't matter so much that he had disobeyed Papa, sneaked into the attic and taken out the gun. . . . But if the cat disappeared . . . then his taking the gun would matter more than anything in the world" (p. 100).
8. Ned was disgusted with himself. Bullies might not know they were bullies, but a liar must know when he lied. Ned did (p. 113).
9. "It was as if he'd moved away, not to the parsonage next to the church . . . , but a thousand miles away from home. . . . Each lie he told made the secret bigger, and that meant even more lies. He didn't know how to stop" (p. 117).
10. Ned's guilt caused him to refuse a trip at Christmas. He had to feed the wounded cat (p. 154).
11. Ned's guilt is relieved when the cat begins to eat (p. 156).
12. "All the lies he had told, the subterfuge, were piled up over the gun like a mountain of hard-packed snow. He felt his secret had frozen around him. He didn't know how to melt it" (p. 162).
13. Ned feels relived when he confesses his guilt to the critically ill Mr. Scully (p. 186).
14. "Mr. Scully was going to die, he was leaving Ned perched on the top rung of a ladder built out of lies; the ladder was leaning against nothing" (p. 189).

15. Ned shows his increasing feelings of guilt: "He nearly told Papa then—he felt about to burst with all that he'd hidden" (p. 197).

16. Ned's happy reactions to the cat family (p. 210).

17. Ned and his mother have a conversation. He discovers that his mother had some of his same feelings and she had actually run away because, "I was afraid of your father's goodness." He confesses to his mother and feels complete relief. Together they go in to tell his father (p. 212).

Ask the students to tell why they chose the incidents they did. Students can agree on the most important incidents and place them on the plot diagram.

Have students respond to the book through drawing or writing. They might create a collage, a poster, or a painting that reflects their aesthetic response to the character and his conflict. They might create another cover for the book or illustrate one of the major incidents in which Ned shows or overcomes his conflict. They might write a journal response to the character and his problems or they might write a poem that traces their feelings about the character and how he overcame his problem.

Students also can read Bauer's *On My Honor* and Rylant's *A Fine White Dust,* which can be used for developing person-against-self plot diagrams and personal responses to the conflict.

LESSON FOUR: Person-Against-Society Conflict

OBJECTIVES

To develop an appreciation for and an understanding of person-against-society conflict as developed by illustrators and authors.

To encourage an aesthetic response to person-against-society conflict during a dramatization.

To increase the aesthetic response to person-against-society conflict through music, writing, and drawing.

To write a personal response to a person-against-society conflict.

CORE BOOKS: Several illustrated books or book jackets that show the harmful consequences of a person-against-society conflict that is caused by society's prejudice or misunderstanding such as Taro Yashima's *Crow Boy* (Picture Story Book, Caldecott Honor); Carol Carrick's *Stay Away from Simon!* (Historical Fiction); and Elizabeth George Speare's *The Witch of Blackbird Pond* (Historical Fiction, Newbery Medal).

PROCEDURES: Review the information about person-against-society conflict developed in the middle-elementary grades. Be sure that students understand that society means the attitudes and beliefs of a group of people and not one individual. They also should understand that a person-against-society conflict develops when the main character's actions, desires, or values differ from those of the surrounding society. To be believable the actions, desires, or values of both the main character and the society must be well developed. Otherwise, readers do not understand why the main character is in conflict with that society.

Next, ask the students to identify various person-against-society conflicts that might be caused by prejudices or misunderstandings in a society. Encourage the students to use their knowledge of history as well as contemporary issues to identify conflicts caused by misunderstandings about people who differ from the norms of society, conflicts caused by racial differences, and conflicts caused by differing attitudes toward males and females.

Next, share the illustrated books. Have the students look at Yashima's illustrations and ask them, "How do you know that the boy is in conflict with and afraid of the school children and the teacher? How do the illustrations show that he is ostracized by his peers? How do the illustrations depict the acceptance of society?" The students should identify the way the author separates Chibi from society through white or yellow spaces, the faces made by the school children, and the activities chosen by Chibi that place him in isolation from society. The students should identify the changes in attitudes after Chibi's aptitudes are finally accepted and admired. Now, have them look at the cover for Carrick's text. Ask, "How do you know there will be conflict in this book?" Have them look through the illustrations and describe how the illustrator shows that, during the early 1800s, there was considerable fear of and prejudice toward people with mental disabilities. Ask them to identify how the illustrator shows that the main characters overcome their fear of Simon and learn to value his abilities.

Introduce *The Witch of Blackbird Pond* by telling the students that unreasonable fears about people and unjustified persecutions appear throughout history. Provide some background information such as, "In the New England colonies of the late 1600s, strict Puritan beliefs governed every aspect of social life. Any kind of nonconformity was viewed as the work of the devil. The famous witch hunts of 1692 in Salem, Massachusetts, began when a doctor stated that the hysterical behavior of several teenage girls was due to the 'evil eye.' Within six months, 20 persons had been sentenced to death and 150 had been sent to prison. The conflict in stories set in this period of American history is usually person-against-society. Authors often place their characters in a hostile environment, where their unusual behaviors create suspicion. For example, in *The Witch of Blackbird Pond*, the author contrasts the people in Kit's early childhood environment and the people in New England. These contrasts encourage readers to anticipate the conflict. On Barbados, Kit is raised by a loving grandfather, who encourages her to read history, poetry, and plays. After the death of her grandfather, Kit travels to New England to live with her aunt. Several experiences on the ship suggest that her former life-style will not be appropriate for her new world. When Kit's actions in the Puritan village remain consistent with her earlier behavior, she raises the suspicions of the townspeople because she goes against that society's values."

This book lends itself to numerous discussion, dramatization, writing, and personal-response activities. The following activities can help increase students' personal responses to the book and their understanding of person-against-society conflict.

Discussion
1. Compare the jewel-like setting of Barbados with Kit's description of the colorless Puritan village. Why do you think the author described both locations?
2. Why did Kit's grandfather want her to read and discuss plays? Why do you think the Puritans reacted so differently to her desire to read such material?
3. Why do you believe that Kit enjoyed going to the meadow and visiting Hannah Tupper? Why were the villagers afraid of both the meadow and Hannah Tupper? What makes Hannah Tupper different from the villagers? Why would people fear her? What makes Kit different from the villagers? Why would people fear her?
4. How do the following people see Kit and feel about her: Kit's grandfather, Matthew Wood, Aunt Rachel, Reverend Gershom Bulkeley, William Ashby, Goodwife Cruff, Hannah Tupper, Nat Eaton, and Kit herself? What do these feelings reveal about the society in which Kit is now living?
5. What was the difference between the way Goodwife Cruff felt about her daughter Prudence and the way Kit felt about Prudence? Who do you think was right?

6. How would Prudence's life have been different if Kit had not helped her? Why do you think Kit did not speak out in court about Prudence, even if her answer might have helped her own case?

7. Why do you believe Kit's friend, "dear dependable William," did not come to her defense at the trial? Why did Nat Eaton risk his own liberty to testify for her?

Dramatization
1. Dramatize Kit's first meeting with her relatives.
2. Recreate the dame's school and Kit's providing instruction for her six students.
3. Role-play the conversations between Kit and the Quaker woman, Hannah Tupper, who lives in the meadow.
4. Dramatize the scenes during which Kit is accused of witchcraft, is held prisoner in the shed, stands trial for witchcraft, and is freed because Prudence demonstrates her reading skills.

Personal response through art, writing, and music
1. Through an artistic interpretation compare the setting on Barbados with the Puritan village. What music might you choose to depict each setting?
2. Pretend you are a "court reporter" and sketch the various people that are involved when Kit is accused of witchcraft. Remember how Taro Yashima illustrated the characters in *Crow Boy*. Could you use any of these techniques to emphasize the personal feelings at the trial?
3. Pretend you are Kit. Choose a period of time from the story and write your experiences in a journal format.
4. Pretend to be someone living in Puritan New England who has relatives in England. Write a letter to these relatives telling them about what has been happening in your village.
5. Pretend to be a 20th-century writer developing a script for a television "You Are There" program. Write the script for a reenactment of the trial. Choose the music that you believe best depicts the action and the feelings of the various people.
6. If Kit were to think of her life through music, what music do you believe she would choose? Where would each of these musical selections fit into the story?
7. If you had been Kit, would you have risked your safety to help Hannah Tupper and Prudence Cruff? Why or why not?
8. Do you believe that a story about personal persecution could be written about a person today? What would be the cause of the persecution? How might the person solve the problem?

LESSON FIVE: Webbing the Conflict in Literature

OBJECTIVES

To identify the types of conflict developed in a literary selection.

To identify and web the details connected with that type of conflict.

CORE BOOK: Selina Hastings' *Sir Gawain and the Loathly Lady* (Legend).

PROCEDURES: Review *Sir Gawain and the Loathly Lady* and ask the students to identify the types of conflict found in the book. Draw conflict in the center of a web and identify the types of conflict on the spokes of the web: person against person, person against self, and person against society. Next, identify the examples from the text. The web in Figure 5.9 was developed by seventh-grade students.

FIGURE 5.9 Webbing of conflict in *Sir Gawain and the Loathly Lady.*

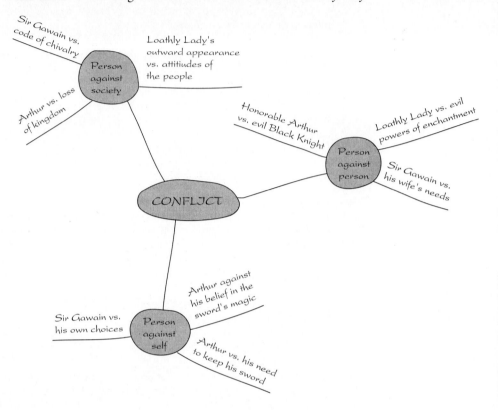

Extended Books for Upper Elementary and Middle School Students

The books in this section include well-developed plots that show the various types of conflicts emphasized through the core lessons. Many of the books provide excellent sources for comparative studies. For example, after reading, analyzing, and discussing the person-against-society conflict in *The Witch of Blackbird Pond,* students could compare Ann Petry's *Tituba of Salem Village* with Speare's text. Or, they could compare other books in which prejudice causes the person-against-society conflict such as Janet Lunn's *Shadow in Hawthorn Bay,* Scott O'Dell's *Sing Down the Moon,* or Mildred Taylor's *Roll of Thunder, Hear My Cry.* Likewise, they might respond to the similarities and differences in person-against-self conflicts in the core book, *One-Eyed Cat,* and Marion Dane Bauer's *On My Honor.*

Modern Fantasy

JOHN CHRISTOPHER'S *The White Mountains.* In a future world a fourteen-year-old boy battles a society in which machines have taken over and free will has diminished.

MONICA HUGHES' *The Keeper of the Isis Light.* In a person-against-society conflict, the protagonist faces the intolerance of humans toward people who do not conform to accepted standards.

ROBIN MCKINLEY's *The Hero and the Crown* (Newbery Medal). Both person-against-person and person-against-self conflicts develop as the protagonist battles the forces of evil and questions her heritage.

Realistic Fiction

MARION DANE BAUER's *On My Honor* (Newbery Honor). A boy experiences a person-against-self conflict when he breaks his word to his father.

JEAN CRAIGHEAD GEORGE's *Julie of the Wolves* (Newbery Medal, Eskimo). A 13-year-old girl faces person-against-nature and person-against-self conflicts as she tries to survive on the North Slope of Alaska.

NICHOLASA MOHR's *Going Home* (Puerto Rican). A 12-year-old girl experiences person-against-society and person-against-self conflicts when she spends the summer with relatives in Puerto Rico.

SCOTT O'DELL's *Island of the Blue Dolphins* (Newbery Medal, Native American). In a person-against-nature conflict a girl survives alone on a Pacific Island.

KATHERINE PATERSON's *Jacob Have I Loved* (Newbery Medal). A complex person-against-person conflict develops between two sisters.

Historical Fiction

JANET LUNN's *Shadow in Hawthorn Bay* (Canadian). A person-against-society conflict develops in the early 1800s when a girl with second sight moves from Scotland, where people accept her powers, to Ontario, where people are suspicious of her powers.

SCOTT O'DELL's *The Captive* (Hispanic). In person-against-self and person-against-society conflicts, a young, idealistic Jesuit seminarian faces conflicts associated with greed and exploitation of the Mayas and the Aztecs.

SCOTT O'DELL's *Sing Down the Moon* (Newbery Honor, Native American). The Navahos face a person-against-society conflict as they are forced to leave the beautiful Canyon de Chelly and move into Fort Sumner.

ANN PETRY's *Tituba of Salem Village* (Black): An enslaved black woman faces a person-against-society conflict in 1600s Salem.

LAURENCE YEP's *Dragonwings* (Newbery Honor, Asian American). In 1903, a boy and his father face prejudice in the United States and build the father's dream.

Biography

BRENT ASHABRANNER's *To Live in Two Worlds: American Indian Youth Today.* Native American youths describe the conflicts facing them as they try to adjust to white society while retaining their own culture.

Recreational Books for Upper Elementary and Middle School Students

Modern Fantasy

ANN CHEETHAM's *The Pit*

JOHN CHRISTOPHER's *The City of Gold and Lead* and *The Pool of Fire*

MARIA GRIPE's *Agnes Cecilia*

MONICA HUGHES' *The Guardian of Isis* and *The Isis Pedlar*

ANNE MCCAFFREY's *Dragonsong*

JOAN PHIPSON's *The Watcher in the Garden*

Realistic Fiction

JUDY BLUME's *Tiger Eyes*
ANN NOLAN CLARK's *To Stand Against the Wind* (Vietnamese)
VERA AND BILL CLEAVER's *Lady Ellen Grae*
ELEANOR CLYMER's *The Get-Away Car*
PAULA FOX's *The Moonlight Man*
VIRGINIA HAMILTON's *The House of Dies Drear* (Black)
NORMA FOX MAZER's *After the Rain* (Newbery Honor)
HUYNH QUANG NHUONG's *The Land I Lost: Adventures of a Boy in Vietnam*
VIRGINIA DRIVING HAWK SNEVE's *High Elk's Treasure* (Native American)

Historical Fiction

PATRICIA BEATTY's *Wait for Me, Watch for Me, Eula Bee* (Native American)
PATRICIA CLAPP's *I'm Deborah Sampson: A Soldier in the War of the Revolution*
DALE FIFE's *Destination Unknown*
PAUL FLEISCHMAN's *Path of the Pale Horse*
LEON GARFIELD's *The December Rose* (English)
ESTHER HAUTZIG's *The Endless Steppe: A Girl in Exile* (Jewish)
WILLIAM HOOK's *Circle of Fire*
JUDITH KERR's *When Hitler Stole Pink Rabbit*
CAROLYN REEDER's *Shades of Gray*
ROSEMARY SUTCLIFF's *Song for a Dark Queen* (England)
YOSHIKO UCHIDA's *Journey Home* (Japanese American)

Nonfiction

ALBERT PRAGO's *Strangers in Their Own Land: A History of Mexican-Americans*

REFERENCES

CIANCIOLO, P. J. (1990). *Picture books for children* (3rd ed.). Chicago: American Library Association.

COHEN, C. L. (1985). The quest in children's literature. *School Library Journal, 31,* 28–29.

CULLINAN, B. (1989). *Literature and the child.* San Diego: Harcourt Brace Jovanovich.

EARLY, M. & ERICSON B. O. (1988). The act of reading. In B. F. Nelms (Ed.), *Literature in the classroom: Readers, texts, and contexts,* (pp. 31–44). Urbana, IL: National Council of Teachers of English.

HUCK, C., HEPLER, S., & HICKMAN, J. (1987). *Children's literature in the elementary school.* New York: Holt, Rinehart & Winston.

LUKENS, R. J. (1990). *A critical handbook of children's literature* (4th ed.). Glenview, IL: Scott, Foresman.

NORTON, D. E. (1991). *Through the eyes of a child: An introduction to children's literature.* Columbus, OH: Merrill.

PURVES, A., ROGERS, T., & SOTER, A. (1990). *How porcupines make love II: Teaching a response centered literature curriculum.* New York: Longman.

RUDMAN, M. (1989). Children's literature in the reading program In M. Rudman (Ed.), *Children's literature: Resource for the classroom* (pp. 177–205). Needham Heights, MA: Christopher-Gordon, 1989.

STEWIG, J. (1987). *Children and literature.* Boston: Houghton Mifflin.

SUTHERLAND, Z. & ARBUTHNOT, M. H. (1991). *Children and books.* Glenview, IL: Scott, Foresman.

WATSON, D. & DAVIS, S. (1988). Readers and texts in a fifth-grade classroom. In B. Nelms (Ed.), Literature in the classroom: Readers, texts, and contexts (pp. 59–67). Urbana, IL: National Council of Teachers of English.

CHILDREN'S LITERATURE REFERENCES*

ADOFF, ARNOLD. *Malcolm X.* New York: Crowell, 1970 (I: 7–12).

*I = Interest by age range

AFANASYEV, ALEXANDER NIKOLAYEVICH. *The Fool and the Fish: A Tale From Russia*, retold by Lenny Hort. Illustrated by Gennady Spirin. New York: Dial, 1990.

ALEXANDER, LLOYD. *The Town Cats and Other Tales.* Illustrated by Laszlo Kubinyi. New York: Dutton, 1977 (I: 8–12).

ALEXANDER, MARTHA. *Bobo's Dream.* New York: Dial (I:3–8).

ANDERSEN, HANS CHRISTIAN. *The Red Shoes*, translated by Anthea Bell. Illustrated by Chihiro Iwasaki. Natick, MA: Neugebauer, 1983 (I: 6–10).

_____ . *The Snow Queen*, adapted by Naomi Lewis. Illustrated by Errol LeCain. New York: Viking, 1979 (I: 6–9).

_____ . *The Ugly Duckling*, retold and illustrated by Lorinda Bryan Cauley. Orlando: Harcourt Brace Jovanovich, 1979 (I: 6–8).

_____ . *The Wild Swans*, retold by Amy Ehrlich. Illustrated by Susan Jeffers. New York: Dial, 1981 (I: 7–10).

ASHABRANNER, BRENT. *To Live in Two Worlds: American Indian Youth Today.* Photographs by Paul Conklin. New York: Dodd, Mead, 1984 (I: 10+).

BAUER, MARION DANE. *On My Honor.* New York: Clarion, 1986 (I: 10+).

BAYLOR, BYRD. *Hawk, I'm Your Brother.* Illustrated by Peter Parnall. New York: Scribner's, 1976 (I: all).

BEATTY, PATRICIA. *Wait for Me, Watch for Me, Eula Bee.* New York: Morrow, 1978 (I: 12+).

BENCHLEY, NATHANIEL. *Oscar Otter.* Illustrated by Arnold Lobel. New York: Harper & Row, 1966 (I: 5–9).

BLUME, JUDY. *Blubber.* New York: Bradbury 1974 (I: 10+).

_____ . *Tiger Eyes.* New York: Bradbury, 1981 (I: 12+).

BOSTON, LUCY M. *An Enemy At Green Knowe.* Illustrated by Peter Boston. Orlando: Harcourt Brace Jovanovich, 1964 (I: 8–12).

BRETT, JAN, retold by. *Goldilocks and the Three Bears.* New York: Dodd, Mead, 1987 (I: 3–8).

BROWN, MARCIA. *Shadow.* New York: Scribner's, 1982 (I: all).

BUNTING, EVE. *The Empty Window.* Illustrated by Judy Clifford. New York: Warne, 1980 (I: 7–10).

_____ . *Ghost's Hour, Spook's Hour.* Illustrated by Donald Carrick. New York: Clarion, 1987 (I: 2–7).

BURNFORD, SHEILA. *The Incredible Journey.* Illustrated by Carl Burger. Boston: Little, Brown, 1960 (I: 8+).

BURTON, VIRGINIA LEE. *The Little House.* Boston: Houghton Mifflin, 1942, 1969 (I: 3–7).

BYARS, BETSY. *The Animal, the Vegetable, and John D. Jones.* Illustrated by Ruth Sanderson. New York: Delacorte, 1982 (I: 9–12).

_____ . *The 18th Emergency.* Illustrated by Robert Grossman. New York: Viking, 1973 (I: 8–12).

CAREW, JAN. *The Third Gift.* Illustrated by Leo and Diane Dillon. Boston: Little, Brown, 1974 (I: 7+).

CARRICK, CAROL. *Stay Away From Simon!* Illustrated by Donald Carrick. New York: Clarion, 1985 (I: 7–10).

CAZET, DENYS. *A Fish in His Pocket.* New York: Orchard, 1987 (I: 3–6).

CHEETHAM, ANN. *The Pit.* New York: Holt, 1990 (I: 10+).

CHETWIN, GRACE. *Box and Cox.* Illustrated by David Small. New York: Bradbury, 1990 (I: 5–8).

CHRISTOPHER, JOHN. *The City of Gold and Lead.* New York: Macmillan, 1967 (I: 10+).

_____ . *The Pool of Fire.* New York: Macmillan, 1968 (I: 10+).

_____ . *The White Mountains.* New York: Macmillan, 1967 (I: 10+).

CLAPP, PATRICIA. *I'm Deborah Sampson: A Soldier in the War of the Revolution.* New York: Lothrop, Lee & Shepard, 1977 (I: 9+).

CLARK, ANN NOLAN. *To Stand Against the Wind.* New York: Viking, 1978 (I: 10+).

CLEARY, BEVERLY. *Ramona and Her Father.* Illustrated by Alan Tiegreen. New York: Morrow, 1977 (I: 7–10).

_____ . *Ramona and Her Mother.* Illustrated by Alan Tiegreen. New York: Morrow, 1979 (I: 7–10).

_____ . *Ramona Quimby, Age 8.* Illustrated by Alan Tiegreen. New York: Morrow, 1981 (I: 7–10).

CLEAVER, VERA & BILL CLEAVER. *Lady Ellen Grae.* Illustrated by Ellen Raskin. Philadelphia: Lippincott, 1968 (I: 8–12).

CLYMER, ELEANOR. *The Get-Away Car.* New York: Dutton, 1978 (I: 8–12).

COLLINGTON, PETER. *The Angel and the Soldier Boy.* New York: Knopf, 1987 (I: 3–7).

COLLODI, CARLO. *The Adventures of Pinocchio: Tale of a Puppet*, translated by M. L. Rosenthal. Illustrated by Troy Howell. New York: Lothrop, Lee & Shepard, 1983 (I: 9+).

COOPER, SUSAN, retold by. *The Silver Cow: A Welsh Tale.* Illustrated by Warwick Hutton. New York: Atheneum, 1983 (I: 5–10).

DAHL, ROALD. *James and the Giant Peach.* Illustrated by Nancy Ekholm Burkert. New York: Knopf, 1961 (I: 7–11).

DeANGELI, MARGUERITE. *The Door in the Wall.* New York: Doubleday, 1949 (I: 8–12).

DeKay, James. *Meet Martin Luther King, Jr.* Illustrated by Ted Burwell. New York: Random, 1969 (I: 7–12).

De Paola, Tomie. *Mother Goose.* New York: Putnam, 1985 (I: 3–8).

Dewey, Ariane, retold by. *The Thunder God's Son.* New York: Greenwillow, 1981 (I: 6–10).

Ernst, Lisa Campbell. *Ginger Jumps.* New York: Bradbury, 1990 (I: 5–8).

Ferris, Jeri. *Go Free or Die: A Story of Harriet Tubman.* Minneapolis: Carolrhoda, 1988 (I: 7–10).

Fife, Dale. *Destination Unknown.* New York: Dutton, 1981 (I: 10+).

Fleischman, Paul. *Path of the Pale Horse.* New York: Harper & Row, 1983 (I: 10+).

Fleming, Ian. *Chitty Chitty Bang Bang.* Illustrated by John Burmingham. New York: Random, 1964 (I: 7–11).

Forbes, Esther. *Johnny Tremain.* Illustrated by Lynd Ward. Boston: Houghton Mifflin, 1943. (I: 10–14).

Fox, Paula. *The Moonlight Man.* New York: Bradbury, 1986 (I: 12+).

_____ . *One-Eyed Cat.* New York: Bradbury, 1984 (I: 10+).

Franchere, Ruth. *Cesar Chavez.* Illustrated by Earl Thollander. New York: Crowell, 1970 (I: 7–9).

Fritz, Jean. *Why Don't You Get A Horse, Sam Adams?* Illustrated by Trina Schart Hyman. New York: Coward, McCann, 1974 (I: 7–10).

Galdone, Paul. *The Three Bears.* Seabury, 1972 (I: 3–7).

_____ . *What's in Fox's Sack? An Old English Tale.* New York: Clarion, 1982 (I: 3–7).

Garfield, Leon. *The December Rose.* New York: Viking Kestrel, 1986 (I: 10+).

Garner, Alan. *A Bag of Moonshine.* Illustrated by Patrick James Lynch. New York: Collins, 1986 (I: 5–9).

George, Jean Craighead. *Julie of the Wolves.* Illustrated by John Schoenherr. New York: Harper & Row, 1972 (I: 10+).

_____ . *My Side of the Mountain.* New York: Dutton, 1959 (I: 10+).

Ginsburg, Mirra. *Two Greedy Bears.* Illustrated by Jose Aruego and Ariane Dewey. New York: Macmillan, 1976 (I: 3–6).

Goble, Paul. *The Girl Who Loved Wild Horses.* New York: Bradbury, 1978 (I: all).

Goor, Ron & Nancy Goor. *Pompeii: Exploring A Roman Ghost Town.* New York: Crowell, 1986 (I: 10+).

Greene, Constance. *The Ears of Louis.* Illustrated by Nola Langer. New York: Viking, 1974 (I: 8–12).

Greenfield, Eloise. *Rosa Parks.* Illustrated by Eric Marlow. New York: Crowell, 1973 (I: 7–10).

Grifalconi, Ann. *Darkness and the Butterfly.* Boston: Little, Brown, 1987 (I: 5–8).

Griffith, Helen. *Grandaddy's Place.* Illustrated by James Stevenson. New York: Greenwillow, 1987 (I: 4–8).

Grimm, Brothers. *The Water of Life*, retold by Barbara Rogasky. Illustrated by Trina Schart Hyman. New York: Holiday (I: 4–9).

_____ . *The Wolf and the Seven Little Kids*, translated by Anne Rogers. Illustrated by Otto S. Svend. Larousse, 1977 (I: 4–8).

Gripe, Maria. *Agnes Cecilia.* Translated by Rika Lesser. New York: Harper & Row, 1990 (I: 10+).

Hall, Donald. *Ox-Cart Man.* Illustrated by Barbara Cooney. New York: Viking, 1979 (I: all).

Hamilton, Virginia. *The House of Dies Drear.* New York: Macmillan, 1968 (I: 10+).

_____ . *Zeely.* Illustrated by Symeon Shimin. New York: Macmillan, 1967 (I: 8–12).

Haseley, Dennis. *The Scared One.* Illustrated by Deborah Howland. New York: Warne, 1983 (I: 5–9).

Hastings, Selina, retold by. *Sir Gawain and the Loathly Lady.* Illustrated by Juan Wijngaard. New York: Lothrop, Lee & Shepard, 1985 (I: 10+).

Hautzig, Esther. *The Endless Steppe: A Girl in Exile.* New York: Harper, 1968 (I: 12+).

Heyer, Marilee. *The Weaving of a Dream.* New York: Viking, 1986 (I: 8+).

Hickman, Janet. *Zoar Blue.* New York: Macmillan, 1978 (I: 9–14).

Hinojosa, Francisco. *The Old Lady Who Ate People.* Illustrated by Leonel Maciel. Boston: Little, Brown, 1984 (I: all).

Hoban, Russell. *Monsters.* Illustrated by Quentin Blake. New York: Scholastic, 1989 (I: 6–8).

Hodges, Margaret, retold by. *Saint George and the Dragon.* Illustrated by Trina Schart Hyman. Boston: Little, Brown, 1984 (I: all).

Holling, Holling Clancy. *Paddle to the Sea.* Boston: Houghton Mifflin, 1941 (I: all).

Hooks, William H. *Circle of Fire.* New York: Atheneum, 1983 (I: 10+).

Howard, Ellen. *Edith Herself.* New York: Atheneum, 1987 (I: 7–10).

Hughes, Monica. *The Guardian of Isis.* New York: Atheneum, 1984 (I: 9+).

_____ . *The Isis Pedlar.* New York: Atheneum, 1983 (I: 9+).

_____ . *The Keeper of the Isis Light.* New York: Atheneum, 1984 (I: 9+).

Iké, Jane & Baruch Zimmerman. *A Japanese Fairy Tale.* New York: Warne, 1982 (I: 5–9).

JAKES, JOHN. *Susanna of the Alamo.* Illustrated by Paul Bacon. Orlando: Harcourt Brace Jovanovich, 1986 (I: 7–12).

JOHNSTON, TONY. *The Badger and the Magic Fan.* Illustrated by Tomie De Paola. New York: Putnam, 1990 (I: 3–8).

KEATS, EZRA JACK. *Goggles!* New York: Macmillan, 1969 (I: 5–9).

KERR, JUDITH. *When Hitler Stole Pink Rabbit.* New York: Coward McCann, 1972 (I: 8–12).

KEY, ALEXANDER. *The Forgotten Door.* Louisville, KY: Westminister, 1965 (I: 8–12).

KIPLING, RUDYARD. *The Jungle Book.* New York: Doubleday, 1894, 1964 (I: 8–12).

KISMARIC, CAROLE. *The Rumor of Pavel and Paali: A Ukrainian Folktale.* Illustrated by Charles Mikolaycak. New York: Harper & Row, 1988 (I: 6–9).

LAGERLÖF, SELMA. *The Legend of the Christmas Rose,* retold by Ellin Greene. Illustrated by Charles Mikolaycak. New York: Holiday, 1990 (I: 8–12).

LAUBER, PATRICIA. *Volcano: The Eruption and Healing of Mount St. Helens.* New York: Bradbury, 1986 (I: all).

LEAF, MONRO. *The Story of Ferdinand.* Illustrated by Robert Lawson. New York: Viking, 1936 (I: 4–10).

LEE, BETSY. *Charles Eastman: The Story of an American Indian.* Minneapolis: Dillon, 1979 (I: 8–12).

LOBEL, ARNOLD. *The Random House Book of Mother Goose.* New York: Random, 1986 (I: 3–8).

LOWRY, LOIS. *Anastasia Krupnik.* Boston: Houghton Mifflin, 1979 (I: 8–12).

_____ . *Number the Stars.* Boston: Houghton Mifflin, 1989 (I: 10+).

LUNN, JANET. *Shadow in Hawthorn Bay.* New York: Scribner's, 1986 (I: 10+).

MARSHALL, JAMES. *Goldilocks and the Three Bears.* New York: Dial, 1988 (I: 3–8).

_____ . *Hansel and Gretel.* New York: Dial, 1990 (I: 4–6).

MATTHEWS, DOWNS. *Polar Bear Cubs.* Photographs by Dan Guravich. New York: Simon and Schuster, 1989 (I: 5–10).

MAYER, MARIANNA, Retold by. *The Twelve Dancing Princesses.* Illustrated by K. Y. Craft. New York: Morrow, 1989 (I: 8+).

MAYER, MERCER. *East of the Sun and West of the Moon.* New York: Four Winds, 1980 (I: 8–10).

_____ . *Frog Goes to Dinner.* New York: Dial, 1974 (I: 6–9).

_____ . *There's a Nightmare in My Closet.* New York: Dial, 1969 (I: 3–7).

MAZER, NORMA FOX. *After the Rain.* New York: Morrow, 1987 (I: 12+).

McCAFFREY, ANNE. *Dragonsong.* New York: Atheneum, 1976 (I: 10+).

McCLOSKEY, ROBERT. *Make Way for Ducklings.* New York: Viking, 1941 (I: 4–8).

McKINLEY, ROBIN. *The Hero and the Crown.* New York: Greenwillow, 1984 (I: 10+).

McSWIGAN, MARIE. *Snow Treasure.* Illustrated by Mary Reardon. New York: Dutton, 1942 (I: 8–12).

MELLING, O. R. *The Singing Stone.* New York: Viking Kestrel, 1986 (I: 8+).

MERRIAM, EVE. *Rainbow Writing.* New York: Atheneum, 1976 (I: all).

MOHR, NICHOLASA. *Felita.* Illustrated by Ray Cruz. New York: Dial, 1979 (I: 9–12).

_____ . *Going Home.* New York: Dial, 1986 (I: 10+).

NAYLOR, PHYLLIS REYNOLDS. Keeping a Christmas Secret. Illustrated by Lena Shiffman. New York: Atheneum, 1989 (I: 4–8).

NHUONG, HUYNH QUANG. *The Land I Lost: Adventures of a Boy in Vietnam.* Illustrated by Yo-Dinh Mai. New York: Harper & Row, 1982 (I: 8–12).

O'DELL, SCOTT. *The Captive.* Boston: Houghton Mifflin, 1979 (I: 10+).

_____ . *Island of the Blue Dolphins.* Boston: Houghton Mifflin, 1960 (I: 10+).

_____ . *Sing Down the Moon.* Boston: Houghton Mifflin, 1970 (I: 10+).

ORMEROD, JAN & DAVID LOLLYD. *The Frog Prince.* New York: Lothrop, Lee & Shepard, 1990 (I: 5–8).

PATERSON, KATHERINE. *Jacob Have I Loved.* New York: Crowell, 1980. (I: 10+)

PAULSEN, GARY. *Hatchet.* New York: Bradbury, 1987 (I: 10+).

_____ . *Woodsong.* New York: Bradbury, 1990 (I: 10+).

PEARCE, CAROL ANN. *Amelia Earhart.* New York: Facts on File, 1988 (I: 8+).

PETRY, ANN. *Tituba of Salem Village.* New York: Crowell, 1964 (I: 11+).

PHIPSON, JOAN. *The Watcher in the Garden.* New York: Atheneum, 1982 (I: 10+).

POTTER, BEATRIX. *The Tale of Peter Rabbit.* New York: Warne, 1902 (I: 3–7).

PRAGO, ALBERT. *Strangers in Their Own Land: A History of Mexican-Americans.* New York: Four Winds, 1973 (I: 10+).

RABE, BERNIECE. *The Balancing Girl.* Illustrated by Lillian Hoban. New York: Dutton, 1981 (I: 7–9).

RANSOME, ARTHUR. *The Fool of the World and the Flying Ship.* Illustrated by Uri Shulevitz. New York: Farrar, Straus & Giroux, 1968 (I: 6–10).

REEDER, CAROLYN. *Shades of Gray.* New York: Macmillan, 1989 (I: 10+).

ROCKWELL, ANNE. *The Three Bears and 15 Other Stories.* New York: Crowell, 1975 (I: 3–8).

ROCKWOOD, JOYCE. *Groundhog's Horse.* Illustrated by Victor Kalin. New York: Holt, Rinehart & Winston, 1978 (I: 7–12).

RODGERS, MARY. *Summer Switch.* New York: Harper & Row, 1982 (I: 8–12).

RYLANT, CYNTHIA. *A Fine White Dust.* New York: Bradbury, 1986 (I: 11+).

_____ . *When I Was Young in the Mountains.* Illustrated by Diane Goode. New York: Dutton, 1982 (I: all).

SENDAK, MAURICE. *Where the Wild Things Are.* New York: Harper & Row, 1963 (I: 4–8).

SEUSS, DR. *The Cat in the Hat.* New York: Random, 1957 (I: 4–7).

_____ . *The Cat in the Hat Comes Back.* New York: Random, 1958 (I: 4–7).

_____ . *The Lorax.* New York: Random, 1971 (I: all).

SHERMAN, JOSEPHA, retold by. *Vassilisa the Wise: A Tale of Medieval Russia.* Illustrated by Daniel San Souci. Orlando: Harcourt Brace Jovanovich, 1988 (I: 8+).

SIMON, SEYMOUR. *Storms.* New York: Morrow, 1989 (I: 8–12).

SINGER, ISAAC BASHEVIS. *Mazel and Shlimazel, or the Milk of the Lioness.* Illustrated by Margot Zemach. New York: Farrar, Straus & Giroux, 1967 (I: 8–12).

SNEVE, VIRGINIA DRIVING HAWK. *High Elk's Treasure.* Illustrated by Oren Lyons. New York: Holiday, 1972 (I: 8–12).

SNYDER, DIANNE. *The Boy of the Three-Year Nap.* Illustrated by Allen Say. Boston: Houghton Mifflin, 1988 (I: all).

SPEARE, ELIZABETH GEORGE. *The Witch of Blackbird Pond.* Boston: Houghton Mifflin, 1958 (I: 9+).

SPERRY, ARMSTRONG. *Call It Courage.* New York: Macmillan, 1940 (I: 9+).

STEPTOE, JOHN. *Mufaro's Beautiful Daughters: An African Tale.* New York: Lothrop, Lee & Shepard, 1987 (I: all).

SUTCLIFF, ROSEMARY. *Song for a Dark Queen.* New York: Crowell, 1978 (I: 10+).

TAYLOR, MILDRED. *The Gold Cadillac.* Illustrated by Michael Hays. New York: Dial (I: 8–10).

_____ . *Roll of Thunder, Hear My Cry.* Illustrated by Jerry Pinckney. New York: Dial, 1976 (I: 10+).

TEJIMA, KEIZABURO. *Fox's Dream.* New York: Philomel, 1985 (I: all).

UCHIDA, YOSHIKO. *Journey Home.* Illustrated by Charles Robinson. New York: Atheneum, 1978 (I: 10+).

VAN ALLSBURG, CHRIS. *Jumanjii.* Boston: Houghton Mifflin, 1981 (I: 5–8).

WALTER, MILDRED PITTS. *Two and Too Much.* Illustrated by Pat Cummings. New York: Bradbury, 1990 (I: 4–7).

WELLS, ROSEMARY, adapted by. *The Little Lame Prince.* Based on story by Dinah Maria Mulock Craik. New York: Dial, 1990 (I: 5–8).

WILDER, LAURA INGALLS. *Little House in the Big Woods.* Illustrated by Garth Williams. New York: Harper & Row, 1932, 1953, (I: 8–12).

_____ . *The Long Winter.* Illustrated by Garth Williams. New York: Harper & Row, 1940, 1953 (I: 8–12).

WISNIEWSKI, DAVID. *The Warrior and the Wise Man.* New York: Lothrop, Lee & Shepard, 1989 (I: 6–10).

YAGAWA, SUMIKO, retold by. *The Crane Wife.* Illustrated by Suekichi Akaba. New York: Morrow, 1981 (I: all).

YASHIMA, TARO. *Crow Boy.* New York: Viking, 1955 (I: all).

YEP, LAURENCE. *Dragonwings.* New York: Harper & Row, 1975 (I: 10+).

YOLEN, JANE. *The Devil's Arithmetic.* New York: Viking Kestrel, 1988 (I: 8+).

YORINKS, ARTHUR. *Hey, Al.* Illustrated by Richard Egielski. New York: Farrar, Straus & Giroux, 1986 (I: all).

YOUNG, ED. *Lon Po Po: A Red-Riding Hood Story From China.* New York: Philomel, 1989 (I: all).

CHAPTER 6

CHARACTERIZATION

DEVELOPING UNDERSTANDING AND APPRECIATION OF
CHARACTERIZATION

Core Books and Sample Lessons for Lower Elementary Students
Extended Books for Lower Elementary Students
Recreational Books for Lower Elementary Students
Core Books and Sample Lessons for Middle Elementary Students
Extended Books for Middle Elementary Students
Recreational Books for Middle Elementary Students
Core Books and Sample Lessons for Upper Elementary and Middle School Students
Extended Books for Upper Elementary and Middle School Students
Recreational Books for Upper Elementary and Middle School Students

In the previous chapter we looked at techniques that help students understand plot. We began with plot because most students can identify and understand the sequence of actions in a story easier than they can understand the more complex techniques that authors use to develop characterization. Plot and characterization, however, are related closely because characters perform actions and overcome the various conflicts. Consequently, characterization and plot work well together in memorable stories.

DEVELOPING UNDERSTANDING AND APPRECIATION OF CHARACTERIZATION

We enjoy stories in which we can identify with the characters, recognize their feelings, and understand why they act in certain ways. A believable, enjoyable story needs main characters who seem lifelike and who develop throughout the story. Believable and convincing characters can be found in books for all ages. Young children respond to Beatrix Potter's *Peter Rabbit* because, like themselves, he is not always the perfect child. Instead he is sometimes greedy, mischievous, and frightened. Like many young children, he is also adventurous and able to accept his punishment when he knows that he has misbehaved.

Slightly older students respond to Sarah, Anne, and Caleb in Patricia McLaughlin's *Sarah, Plain and Tall* because they understand the feelings, fears, inner conflicts, and dreams that motivate the characters. Older students enjoy the well-developed characters in Cynthia Voigt's *Dicey's Song* and *A Solitary Blue* because these characters develop and change as they face conflicts similar to those faced by many teenagers.

Two types of characters are found in literature. Flat characters such as the princess or the prince in folk tales are not well developed. They are easily characterized in one or two sentences and they do not change within the story. For example, the princess is usually beautiful, kind, and generous, and the prince is usually handsome, noble, and brave.

As the name implies, round characters are more interesting. They are complex and many-sided, and they develop within the story. Authors use numerous techniques to develop the natures of round characters: They might use a direct method, and literally tell us about the characters. Through their narration they describe the appearance of the characters, where the characters live, and other important information about the characters' lives. This direct method of revealing characterization is easily identified by readers. Authors also might use indirect methods that require readers to infer information about the characters. These methods include showing the actions of the characters, revealing the speech of the characters through their dialogue, developing the thoughts of the characters, and disclosing the thoughts of others about the characters. These indirect methods require readers to ask questions such as, "What do these actions tell us about the characters? What do the speech patterns and the actual words used by the characters tell us about the characters? What additional information do we have when we know what other people think about these characters? What do the thoughts of the characters reveal about the characters?" Because most of the information about the characters is implied rather than stated directly, many students require assistance as they approach characterization, especially the complex characterization developed in many books for older students. The modeling technique shown in the lessons for middle elementary and upper elementary and middle grades can be helpful as students develop the thought processes that allow them to appreciate and understand complex characterizations.

Authors also frequently allow their rounded characters to change within their stories. For example, Mary Lennox in Frances Hodgson Burnett's *The Secret Garden* changes from a spoiled, bad-tempered little girl to a cheerful, caring person. Certain requirements exist for the change to be convincing. According to Perrine (1983), convincing change in characterization must meet three conditions: "(1) it must be within the possibilities of the character who makes it, (2) it must be sufficiently motivated by the circumstances in which the character is placed, and (3) it must be allowed sufficient time for a change of its magnitude believably to take place. Basic changes in human character seldom occur suddenly" (p. 69). Again, students need assistance as they explore and respond to the changes and the believability of the changes within the characters.

The lessons in this section range from lessons for younger students in which they interact with, dramatize, and illustrate their favorite characters to modeling lessons that encourage middle-grade students and above to infer characterization by identifying aspects of characterization, providing the evidence for those aspects, and exploring their reasoning for their decisions. One lesson encourages older students to explore symbolism and to relate the symbolism to characterization.

Core Books and Sample Lessons for Lower Elementary Students

LESSON ONE: Developing an Understanding of Characterization

OBJECTIVES

To develop an understanding of characterization by pantomiming the actions and feelings of the characters in a story.

To add dialogue to the story and to explore how dialogue can develop understanding of the characters.

To draw the different characterizations depicted by an author.

To write a description of a character by looking at the illustrations in a wordless book.

CORE BOOKS: Beatrix Potter's *The Tale of Peter Rabbit* (Modern Fantasy, Touchstone); Ezra Jack Keats' *The Snowy Day* (Picture Story Book, Caldecott Medal); Hans Christian Andersen's *The Ugly Duckling* (Modern Fantasy); and Emily Arnold McCully's *School* (Wordless Book).

PROCEDURES: The activities in the lesson require several days to complete. The format of the lessons also can be used with numerous additional books. Begin the lesson on characterization by reading *The Tale of Peter Rabbit* to the students. Allow them to look at the illustrations and share their personal responses to the story and the characters.

Next, tell the students that they will have an opportunity to play each of the characters in *The Tale of Peter Rabbit* as you read the story to them. Introduce the concept of pantomime by telling the students that it is a way of acting that uses gestures, facial features, body movements, and actions instead of words. Reread *The Tale of Peter Rabbit,* and have students pretend to be each of the characters in the story to show what the characters are doing and feeling. Before asking students to do this pantomime, ask them to identify different emotions such as fear, happiness, and sadness and to show how they could express these emotions without using words.

Next, read the book slowly to the students. Ask them to pretend to be each of the characters in the story: Mrs. Rabbit warning her children; Flopsy, Mopsy, and Cotton-tail contentedly gathering blackberries; disobedient Peter squeezing into Mr. McGregor's garden and happily eating the vegetables; Mr. McGregor angrily chasing Peter with a rake; frightened Peter trying to escape and losing his jacket; desolate Peter crying; Mr. McGregor hanging up Peter's jacket for a scare-crow; Peter running home and becoming ill; concerned Mrs. Rabbit dosing Peter with camomile tea; and Flopsy, Mopsy, and Cotton-tail eating blackberries for supper.

Next, ask the students to think about what they know about each of the characters and how they showed this information in their pantomime. Allow them to discuss these characters and to think about what they know about each character. Ask them, "Which character do we know the most about?" They should identify Peter. "How do we know this much about Peter?" Encourage the students to think about Peter's responses during the various parts of the story and to consider the range of feelings and emotions that Peter expressed. At this point many students enjoy acting out *The Story of Peter Rabbit.* They frequently choose to add dialogue to the story and create a total play. They might even want to add additional speaking parts.

To develop an additional aesthetic response to Peter's characterization, ask the students to select at least two emotions expressed by Peter or another character and to illustrate how they felt when they were pantomiming that character's actions. After the students have completed these drawings, ask them to look again at the illustrations. Ask them, "How did Beatrix Potter show the different emotions of the characters in the illustrations? How do we know when Peter is adventuresome, happy, frightened, disobedient, and sorry for his actions? A similar set of pantomime, discussion, and drawing activities can be used to accompany *The Snowy Day* and *The Ugly Duckling.*

Finally, encourage students to write about a character after looking at the illustrations and discussing the story in the wordless book, *School.* Introduce the book by telling the students that everything they know about the characters and the plot are shown in the illustrations. Share the book by showing them the illustrations, and encourage them to orally tell the story that accompanies the illustrations. Next, ask the students to consider the characters shown in the story: the mouse children who go to school, little mouse who wants to go to school and then satisfies his curiosity by sneaking off to school, mother mouse who comes to school to get little mouse, and the teacher who makes little mouse feel welcome. Ask the students, "What do we know about each of these characters? How would you feel if you were any of these characters and you were in the same situation?" Ask the students to choose one of these characters and describe the character so that readers know as much as possible about that character. Ask them to describe the character's appearance, actions, feelings, thoughts, and how other characters respond to that character. This writing activity can be in the form of a group chart story or individual stories.

LESSON TWO: Webbing Characterization with *Darkness and the Butterfly*

OBJECTIVES

To identify major characters in a book.

To web descriptions of characterization in a book.

CORE BOOK: Ann Grifalconi's *Darkness and the Butterfly*

PROCEDURES: Review the story *Darkness and the Butterfly*. Remind the students that they have already developed a plot structure for the book. Review this plot structure. (Placing completed plot structures and webs on transparencies makes reviewing books easy.) Ask the students, "Who were the major people in the story?" Draw a web on the board in which you identify these characters. Most students identify Osa as the main character, and her mother and the Wise Woman as important secondary characters. Some students want to separate Osa's character on the web. This can be done by identifying "Osa Before" and "Osa After" her experience with the Wise Woman.

Reread the story asking the students to focus on the characters and descriptions of the characters. The web in Figure 6.1 was developed with lower-elementary students:

Extended Books for Lower Elementary Students

The books listed in this section include believable and memorable characters developed in stories for younger students. These books encourage students to respond to characterization as developed by both authors and illustrators. Most of the stories—whether they are about people, animals, or inanimate objects—encourage students to understand that believable characters have many of the characteristics, feelings, and emotions that children also experience. All the stories stimulate personal responses to the characters, discussions, creative dramatizations, and art interpretations.

Modern Fantasy

BEATRIX POTTER's *The Tale of Squirrel Nutkin*. Through his actions and his dialogue, the squirrel is shown as disrespectful, rude, resourceful, intelligent, and frightened.

Realistic Fiction

EVE BUNTING's *The Wednesday Surprise*. The characterizations show the needs and relationships between a grandmother and a granddaughter.

SID FLEISCHMAN's *The Scarebird*. A lonely farmer discovers that he needs a friend.

SHIRLEY HUGHES' *Dogger* (English). A boy experiences a series of emotions as he shows his love for a toy, loses the toy, and then regains the toy because his sister performs an unselfish act.

MAVIS JUKES' *Like Jake and Me* (Newbery Honor). The author develops characteristics of a boy and his stepfather as they make discoveries about each other.

FIGURE 6.1 Webbing characterization in *Darkness and the Butterfly*.

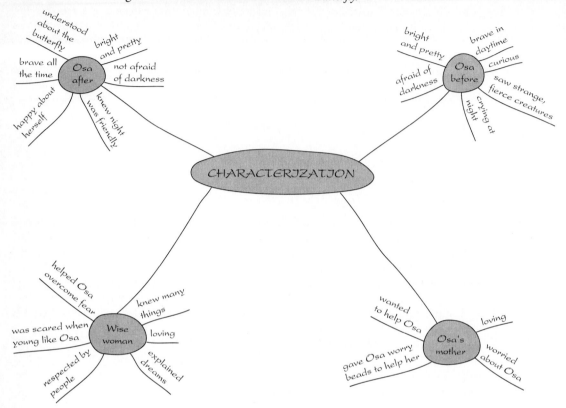

EZRA JACK KEATS' *Peter's Chair* (Black). Many sides of Peter's character are developed as he shows jealousy for his new sister and then decides that it is good to have a baby sister.

EVALINE NESS' *Sam, Bangs & Moonshine* (Caldecott Medal). A girl discovers that her imagination can be harmful.

JOHN STEPTOE'S *Daddy Is A Monster...Sometimes* (Black): The text and illustrations develop several sides of a father's character.

Picture Story Books

MARGARET WISE BROWN'S *The Runaway Bunny*. The interactions between a rabbit and the mother show that all young characters need to feel independent and loved.

RUSSELL HOBAN'S *Best Friends for Frances*. Frances the badger experiences needs that are similar to those of human children.

Recreational Books for Lower Elementary Students

Modern Fantasy

BEATRIX POTTER'S *The Tale of Mrs. Tiggy-Winkle*

Realistic Fiction

BERNARD WOLF'S *Anna's Silent World*

CHARLOTTE ZOLOTOW'S *My Grandson Lew* and *William's Doll*

Picture Story Books

TOMIE DE PAOLA's *Oliver Button Is A Sissy*

HELEN V. GRIFFITH's *Grandaddy's Place*

SHIRLEY HUGHES' *Alfie Gives A Hand* (English)

EZRA JACK KEATS' *Louie*

RONI SCHOTTER's *Captain Snap and the Children of Vinegar Lane*

AMY SCHWARTZ's *Annabelle Swift, Kindergartner*

GABRIELLE VINCENT's *Smile, Ernest and Celestine, Ernest and Celestine's Picnic*, and *Feel Better, Ernest!*

VERA WILLIAMS' *A Chair for My Mother* (Caldecott Honor)

Core Books and Sample Lessons for Middle Elementary Students

The first sample lesson in this section develops a modeling lesson that teaches students how to become actively involved in and aware of their thought processes. Researchers such as Roehler and Duffy (1984) have shown that learning can be enhanced using a modeling approach that places the teacher in an active learning role with the students. In this role, the teacher shows the students how to approach thought processing. I have developed and used modeling examples (Norton, 1991) that help students understand the learning process necessary for understanding literary elements such as inferring characterization. Making inferences about the characters through their actions, dialogues, and thoughts is difficult for many students. Teachers can help students understand the often complex nature of inferences by modeling activities in which they analyze evidence from the text and speculate about the characters.

The example in this core lesson uses the historical fiction book *Sarah, Plain and Tall*. Some of the characterizations in the book are stated, while others are implied. Students frequently need assistance analyzing the implied characterizations.

The following example develops the important instructional sequences in a modeling lesson: First, the teacher identifies the requirements for effective reasoning. Second, the teacher develops an introduction to inferring characterization. Third, the teacher identifies the importance of making inferences. Fourth, the teacher introduces the story. Fifth, the teacher proceeds with the modeling examples and brings the students into the discussion. Although this lesson is placed under the middle-elementary grades, it has been used with students from third grade through eighth grade.

LESSON ONE: Modeling the Process of Inferring Characterization

OBJECTIVES

To be involved in a modeling activity designed to show students how to analyze evidence from the text and to speculate about characters.

To understand the requirements for effective reasoning.

To appreciate and understand the author's use of implication when developing characterization.

To write a response that shows that the students understand the authors' implications.

CORE BOOK: Patricia MacLachlan's *Sarah, Plain and Tall* (Historical Fiction, Newbery Medal).

PROCEDURES: First, identify the requirements for effective reasoning so that the lesson will help students understand those requirements. For example, effective inferring of characterization requires that readers go beyond the information an author provides in a text. Readers must use clues from the text to hypothesize about a character's emotions, beliefs, actions, hopes, and fears. Readers also must be aware that authors develop characters through dialogue between characters, narration, a character's thoughts or the thoughts of others about the character, and a character's actions. The lesson must be developed so that students understand these requirements for effective reasoning.

Second, develop an introduction to the inferential process of characterization. For example, review characterization by asking the students to identify how authors develop three-dimensional, believable characters. Share examples of each type of characterization as part of this review. Ask the students to listen to a series of statements about a person. Then discuss what the students have learned about this person after reading or listening to each of the following statements:

1. Jimmy is the best football player on the team. He is a fast runner and he is able to block his opponents. (Narrative)
2. Jimmy's sister thought to herself, "I like to watch Jimmy play football, but I wish he would be my partner for the tennis match." (Thoughts of others about the character)
3. Jimmy thought to himself, "I don't like that bully who is trying to make the kids vote for him in the school election." (Thoughts of the character)
4. Jimmy got off his bike to see why his dog was limping. He carried the dog home. (Character's actions)
5. Jimmy said to his sister, "I don't have time to do my math assignment. I'll play tennis with you Saturday if you'll do my homework for me tonight." His sister answered, "Play tennis with me first, you have tricked me before." (Dialogue)

Explain to the students that in this modeling activity, they will listen to you ask a question, answer the question, provide evidence from the story that supports the answer, and share the reasoning process you used to reach the answer. Tell the students that after they have listened to you proceed through the sequence, they will use the same process to answer questions, identify evidence, and explore their own reasoning processes. As part of this introduction, discuss the meanings of evidence and reasoning. Encourage the students to identify evidence about a character in literature and to share how they would use this evidence.

Third, develop the importance of inferring. Ask the students to explain why it is important to be able to make inferences about characters in literature. Encourage them to discuss how understanding characterization makes a story more exciting, enjoyable, and believable. They also should understand that they can imply characterization in their own writing.

Fourth, develop an introduction to the story. *Sarah, Plain and Tall* has two important settings: (a) the pioneer setting in one of the prairie states, and (b) the pioneer setting in Maine. To identify the students' understandings of these locations and time periods, have them close their eyes and pretend they are sitting on the front porch of a cabin in one of the prairie states in the 1800s. Ask them to look away from the cabin and describe what they see. Make sure they describe prairie grass, wheat fields, few trees, a dirt road, and flat or gently rolling land. Ask them to describe the colors they see. Then ask them to turn around and describe what they see through the open door of the cabin. Again, make sure that they describe a small space, a fireplace, and characteristic furnishings, such as wooden chairs and a wooden table.

The Maine setting is also important to this story because Sarah's conflict results from her love of a different setting. Ask the students to close their eyes and pretend they are sitting on the coast of Maine. Have them look out at the ocean and describe what they see. Ask them to turn toward the land and describe the setting. Ask them to discuss the differences between the prairie and the Maine coast and to consider how the differences in these settings might cause conflicts for a character.

Fifth, provide the first modeling example. Read orally from the beginning of the book through the line, "That was the worst thing about Caleb," on page 5. Ask, "What was Anna's attitude toward her brother Caleb when he was a baby?" Answer, "Anna disliked her brother a great deal. We might even say she hated him." Provide the evidence from the text: "Anna thinks Caleb is homely, plain, and horrid smelling. Anna associates Caleb with her mother's death." Provide the reasoning that you used to reach your answer. For example, "The words Anna uses, especially *horrid,* often are associated with things we do not like. I know from my own experience that I do not tell someone something if I am thinking something bad about the person. I know from the reference to the happy home that Anna loved her mother. When she says her mother's death was the worst thing about Caleb, I believe that she blamed him for the death."

Provide the second modeling example. At this point, verify that the students understand the procedure. If they do not, model another example completely. When the students understand the process, let them join the discussion by providing an answer, the evidence, and the reasoning. It is advisable to have the students jot down brief answers to the questions, evidence, and reasoning. These notes will increase the quality of the discussion that follows each question.

The next logical discussion point comes at the bottom of page 5. Read through the lines, "Slowly, one by one, they left. And then the days seemed long and dark like winter days, even though it wasn't winter. And Papa didn't sing." Ask the question, "What is Anna really telling us about her inner feelings?" Ask the students to answer the question. They should provide answers similar to this one: "She believes that nothing can replace her lost mother and that the home will not be happy again." Ask the students to provide evidence, such as, "The author tells us that the relatives could not fill the house. The days are compared to long, dark winter days even though it is not winter. The author states that Papa did not sing." Ask the students to provide reasoning, such as "The author created a very sad mood. We see a house filled with relatives that do not matter to Anna. I know from my own experience what long, dark, winter days are like. I can visualize a house without singing. I think Anna is very unhappy and it might take her a long time to get over her loss."

Continue this process, having the students discuss the many instances of implied characterization in the book. The letters written by Sarah to Mr. Weaton (p. 9), to Anna (pp. 9– 10), and to Caleb (p. 11) are especially good for inferring characterization because students need to infer what was in the letters written to Sarah by Anna and Caleb. To help the students infer the contents of the letters, ask the students to write the letters themselves.

Longer stories, such as *Sarah, Plain and Tall,* lend themselves to discussions according to chapters. Students can read and discuss several chapters each day. After each session, ask the students to summarize what they know about Sarah, Anna, Caleb, and Papa. Ask them, "What do you want to know about these characters?"

The following is a list of logical places in *Sarah, Plain and Tall* to ask questions about implied characterization and some questions that might be asked and answered. Remember to have students also provide evidence for their answers and explore their reasoning. The references are grouped by chapters because many teachers use two chapters at a time when they have students read and discuss the characterization in this book.

Chapters 3 and 4

Text: "Caleb slipped his hand into mine as we stood on the porch, watching the road. He was afraid" (p. 17). *Question:* Why was Caleb afraid? What does this fear reveal about Caleb's character?"

Text: "The cat will be good in the barn, said Papa. For mice. Sarah smiled. "She will be good in the house, too" (p. 19). *Question:* "What does Sarah's statement about the cat reveal about her character?"

Explore the characterization revealed by Anna's statement, "I wished we had a sea of our own" (p. 21); the characterization implied by the flower-picking incident (p. 23); the characterization of Papa implied by the hair-cutting incident (p. 25); and the implication about Sarah's conflicting emotions in the discussion of seals and singing (p. 27).

Chapters 5 and 6

Text: The sheep incident on page 28. *Question:* "What type of a person is Sarah? Do you believe that she will make a good mother for Caleb and Anna? Why or why not?"

Explore the implications of the haystack incident and the comparison to sand dunes on page 32; and the inferences that can be made from Anna's dream described on page 37.

Chapters 7, 8, and 9

Text: The description of a squall and the family's reactions to the storm on page 49. *Question:* "What do Sarah's actions and her statement, 'We have squalls in Maine too. Just like this. It will be all right, Jacob,' tell you about Sarah's character? What do you believe Sarah has decided to do?"

Explore the inferences that can be made from the reactions of the children when Sarah rides to town alone on page 52 and the inference that can be drawn from Anna's comparison of Sarah driving away in the wagon by herself to her mother leaving in a pine box on page 54.

The chart in Figure 6.2 can be helpful when developing a modeling lesson.

LESSON TWO: Webbing Characterization

OBJECTIVES

To identify the main characters in a book.

To identify the characteristics of the main characters.

CORE BOOK: Byrd Baylor's *Hawk, I'm Your Brother* (Caldecott Honor, Native American).

PROCEDURES: Review the book *Hawk, I'm Your Brother.* Ask the students, "Who are the main characters in the book?" Most students will identify Rudy Soto and the hawk. Draw a web on the board with the word *characterization* in the center. Place Rudy Soto and Hawk on the spokes of the web. Next, reread *Hawk, I'm Your Brother.* Ask the students to identify important characteristics of both of these characters. The web in Figure 6.3 was developed by students in the middle elementary grades:

Extended Books for Middle Elementary Students

The books listed in this section develop strong characterizations. Students can respond to these characters, identify how the characterizations are developed by the authors, and identify and defend the books they believe have the strongest character-

FIGURE 6.2 Chart for modeling.

Modeling for _____

Requirements for understanding:

Examples showing:

Introduction to text (associating schema):

Why is _____ important for developing understanding?

Text Examples:	Question:	Answer:	Evidence Cited:	Reasoning Process:

---

izations. Like the books identified for lower elementary grades, the characters lend themselves to art interpretations and dramatizations. Modeling and webbing activities also can be developed.

Modern Fantasy

George Selden's *The Cricket in Times Square* (Newbery Honor). A personified cricket experiences the city.

E. B. White's *Charlotte's Web* (Newbery Honor, Touchstone). Wilbur the pig develops with the help of Charlotte, the spider, and Templeton, the rat.

Realistic Fiction

Eleanor Cameron's *That Julia Redfern*. Characterization is revealed through a girl's various exploits.

Beverly Cleary's *Dear Mr. Henshaw* (Newbery Medal). A boy learns about himself as he communicates with his favorite author.

FIGURE 6.3 Webbing characterization in *Hawk, I'm Your Brother.*

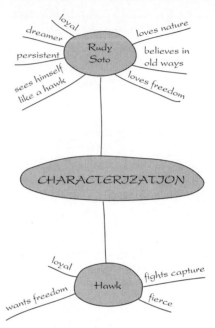

Beverly Cleary's *Ramona and Her Mother.* The characterization is revealed as Ramona tries to help her father through a trying period after he loses his job.

Kevin Crossley-Holland's *Storm* (English). A girl makes discoveries about herself as she faces her fear and gets a doctor for her sister.

Jean Little's *Different Dragons.* A boy makes discoveries about himself and his family when he overcomes his fear of dogs.

Patricia MacLachlan's *The Facts and Fictions of Minna Pratt.* Many sides of a girl's character are revealed as she learns to appreciate herself and her family.

Historical Fiction

Ellen Howard's *Edith Herself.* A girl with epilepsy learns to value herself in the 1890s.

Recreational Books for Middle Elementary Students

Realistic Fiction

C. S. Adler's *Ghost Brother*

Betsy Byars' *Bingo Brown, Gypsy Lover*

Elizabeth Enright's *Thimble Summer* (Newbery Medal)

Fred Gipson's *Old Yeller* (Newbery Medal)

Beverly Keller's *No Beasts! No Children!*

Suzy Kline's *Herbie Jones and the Monster Ball*

Lois Lowry's *Anastasia on Her Own*

Barbara Park's *The Kid in the Red Jacket*

Historical Fiction

Marguerite De Angeli's *The Door in the Wall* (English, Newbery Medal)

Core Books and Sample Lessons
for Upper Elementary and Middle School Students

The modeling lesson and many of the books suggested for middle elementary students also can be used with students in the upper grades. As stated earlier, the lesson with *Sarah, Plain and Tall* has been used with students through middle school. The modeling lesson developed in this section uses a more difficult book. A separate lesson focuses on symbolism as it relates to characterization. The section concludes with webbing of characterization.

LESSON ONE: Modeling the Process of Inferring Characterization

OBJECTIVES

To be involved in a modeling activity designed to show students how to analyze evidence from the text and speculate about characters.

To understand the requirements for effective reasoning.

To appreciate and understand author's use of implication when developing characterization.

CORE BOOKS: Jean Fritz's *The Great Little Madison* (Biography) and Alice Provensen's *The Buck Stops Here: The Presidents of the United States* (Informational).

PROCEDURES: Review the requirements for effective reasoning developed in the lesson that accompanies *Sarah, Plain and Tall*. The same introduction to inferring characterization can be used with this lesson.

Next, develop an introduction to the biography, *The Great Little Madison*. Students should understand Madison's time period, 1751–1836, and the role he played in both the Continental Congress and as the fourth president of the United States. Share maps with the students to show them the locations of the original Colonies. Also share illustrations that depict the historical setting of the United States during Madison's lifetime. The highly illustrated *The Buck Stops Here: The Presidents of the United States* can be used to introduce students to the accomplishments of the previous presidents and to the contributions of the fourth president, James Madison. Spend as much time as necessary to help students become familiar with this important time period in history.

Students also might find it helpful to understand Fritz's philosophy in relation to writing biography. To provide such background information, read from "Biography: Readability Plus Responsibility" (Fritz, 1988) or "Through the Eyes of an Author: On Writing Biography" (Fritz, 1991). Discuss the implications of Fritz's viewpoints on her development of biographical characters.

Tell the students that the modeling activity will focus on the first two chapters of *The Great Little Madison*. During this modeling activity they will identify as much information as possible about James Madison and explore how Fritz develops believable characterization. After they have read and discussed the first two chapters, they will continue reading the book and add to their knowledge of Madison's character.

Next, provide the first modeling example. Read from the beginning of the book on page 7 through the second paragraph on page 8. Stop with, "In any case, sickness didn't often keep him from reading. Nothing ever would." Ask, "What does Fritz tell us about Madison's character from the references to his father's library and the listing of some of these books?" Provide the answer: "I think Fritz is telling us that Madison was an excellent and avid reader who was also sick a great deal. Madison was a member of a wealthy and highly educated family. Madison had an insatiable curiosity and asked many questions that could be answered through reading. The titles of the books show some of Madison's interests in reading, such as political responsibility, science, and children's diseases." Provide the evidence from the text. Say, "Madison was reading by age 9 and he had read all of his father's books by age 11. His father had 85 books. The books provided answers to his questions as well as to new questions that Madison had not thought of asking. The books in his father's library included *The Duty of Man, The Employment of the Microscope,* and books on children's diseases. The author tells us that neither sickness nor anything else could keep Madison from reading." Provide the reasoning that you used to reach your answer. For example, "I believe that Madison must have been an avid and an excellent reader because he had read all of these complex books by the time he was 11. In the 1700s, it was unusual for any family to have so many books. Books were expensive and only a few people could read. Consequently, I believe that Madison's family was both wealthy and well educated. I also noted the titles of the books that Madison read. These titles showed me that Madison read books on different subjects. Consequently, he must have had a wide interest and considerable curiosity. I know from my own experience that I read books that interest me or that answer questions. I also know from my own experience that books frequently open doors to new ideas and provide stimulation to learn new things about various subjects. When Fritz tells us that nothing could keep Madison from reading, I think she is telling us more than that Madison was a sickly child. She is telling us that reading was one of the more important aspects of Madison's life."

Next, provide the second modeling example. At this point, verify that the students understand the procedure. If they do not, model another example completely. When the students understand the process, let them join the discussion by providing an answer, the evidence, and the reasoning. It is advisable to ask the students to jot down brief answers to the questions, evidence, and reasoning. These notes will increase the quality of the discussion that follows each question.

The next logical discussion point comes at the end of the next paragraph on page 9. Ask, "What can we infer about James Madison from the courses and subjects that he studied in school? What do we know about Madison's attitude toward his education?" The students should provide answers similar to this one: "We can infer that Madison was not satisfied with the knowledge available through his father's library. We know that he was well educated in languages, geometry, algebra, and history. He was interested in subjects beyond his own world. He must have been a student who could respond with logic and reasoning. Madison enjoyed learning about subjects that went beyond his previous knowledge." Ask the students to provide evidence, such as, "The author tells us that Madison's father sent him to a school where he had access to all the books he wanted to read. Madison learned French, Latin, and Greek. He also studied subjects such as geometry, algebra, and history, which broadened his understanding of the universe. He drew friendly features on his planets. His teacher taught him to use logic and reason." Ask the students to provide reasoning, such as, "I think Fritz describes the learning environment of a student who wanted to learn languages so that he could read books written in those languages and discover what men thought hundreds of years ago. These subjects suggest that Madison was a demanding scholar who wanted to learn through the best sources. I think he enjoyed his education because he made his universe more friendly by drawing features on the planets. When Fritz describes Madison's teacher's questioning techniques as "best of all", I think that Madison must have enjoyed learning through the kinds of questions that caused him to use logic and reasoning. This suggests to me that Madison would use logic and reasoning in all of his pursuits."

Continue this process, asking the students to discuss the many instances of implied characterization in chapter 1. For example, pages 10 and 11 describe Madison's reactions to Princeton, the types of learning and even the pranks that excited him, and the affairs of the country that interested him. On page 13 Fritz frequently uses the word *perhaps.* Ask, "Why would Fritz use this term rather than a more definite one?" On page 16 the author explores Madison's physical weaknesses and notes that they did not deter him. On page 16 the author uses the term *probably*. This is another place that students can explore the reasons for using an indefinite term in a biography. Ask, "Why is the author using *probably* instead of making a definite statement? What is the effect on the reader of using *perhaps* and *probably?*"

Chapter 2 includes numerous examples in which Fritz develops Madison's beliefs. Fritz also uses terms such as *must have* when she develops her characterization through implication rather than from documentation. For example, refer to page 18 and ask students, "What is Fritz implying about Madison when she states, "Just looking at the famous orator Patrick Henry must have made him uneasy?" To answer this question, provide evidence, and explore reasoning, students must think about earlier statements Fritz made about Madison's slight stature and weak voice. They also need to know something about Patrick Henry's ability as a speaker.

On page 19 students can analyze Madison's actions and words to infer his beliefs. Referring to the same page, ask the students, "What is Fritz saying about Madison's character when she states, 'Now at the Virginia convention James found himself objecting to the way the resolution on religion was worded. It stated that all men should enjoy the fullest toleration in the exercise of religion. Toleration! That wasn't enough for James. He couldn't abide such weak wording, so he wrote out his proposed version. 'All men are equally entitled to enjoy the free exercise of religion.' His revision was approved." To answer this question students must consider the differences in meaning between *toleration* and *free exercise* and think about how earlier information about Madison would fit into this description of Madison's actions and beliefs.

On page 20 students can make inferences in characterization through Madison's actions when he unsuccessfully ran for a seat in the Continental Congress. On page 21, students can consider, "Why did Madison produce writing that was strong and persuasive?" Now they must think back to references to his schooling that described how he was taught to use logic and reason. On page 21, students also can consider the characterizations that are developed as Fritz compares Jefferson and Madison. In this chapter, Fritz's descriptions of Madison's jokes on himself and the humorous antidotes provide additional ways to infer characterization. After completing these two chapters, ask students to list all of the characteristics they know about Madison. Ask them, "What information do you still want to know about Madison? From what you know at this point, do you think Madison will make a good president? Why or why not?"

Students can search for additional evidence of Madison's characterization as they complete the book. They also can trace the development of characterization through various incidents that happen to him throughout his life. They can consider, "How does Madison change as he grows older and acquires additional experiences and obligations? Are any actions and beliefs consistent throughout his life? If so, what are they?"

LESSON TWO: Developing Understanding of Characterization Through Symbolism

OBJECTIVES

To develop an understanding of characterization through the author's use of symbolism.

To review the meaning of symbolism and to discuss how a symbol could be related to characterization.

To illustrate the symbols and demonstrate through illustration how the symbols are related to characterization.

CORE BOOK: Cynthia Voigt's *Dicey's Song* (Realistic Fiction, Newbery Medal).

PROCEDURES: This book, the author's use of symbolism in relation to characterization, and the discussion that accompanies the book are excellent for developing divergent thinking and creative problem solving. As a first step, either review or introduce the concept of symbolism. Students should understand that a literary symbol is "something that means more than what it is. It is an object, a person, a situation, an action, or some other item that has a literal meaning in the story but suggests or represents other meanings as well" (Perrine, 1983, p. 196). For example, authors might use names to suggest something about their characters. Ask the students to suggest character names or nicknames that they might use in their own stories to suggest important characterizations. Sometimes authors compare characters to objects in nature. Ask the students, "What would an author mean if one character is compared to an oak tree and another character is compared to a weeping willow?"

After this discussion, share several guidelines for symbolism in literature. For example, Perrine (1983) provides useful guidelines that help students understand symbolism. Perrine states that the story must furnish clues that a detail is to be taken symbolically; the meaning of the symbol must be established and supported by the story; the item must suggest a meaning that is different from its literal meaning; and a symbol can have more than one meaning.

Next, introduce Voigt's *Dicey's Song*. Ask the students to speculate about the possible meanings for the title, "What could the author mean by naming the book *Dicey's Song*? Look at the illustration on the book cover. How do you think a boat or a song could be related to the main character in the book? Could either songs or a boat reveal information about a character? What do you think songs or a boat might tell you about a character?" To further the understanding that music could be related to characterization, ask the students to think of songs that might be used to reveal their characters or to show information about someone that they know. Ask them, "Would one song tell all about you, or would you need to refer to different songs to show changes in your personality?"

Tell the students that Cynthia Voigt uses references to music, a sailboat, the sea, and the farm to help readers understand characterization, character development, and how the characters face conflict. As they read this book they should note these references and trace how the author reveals characterization and character development through these symbols. Ask them to find specific quotes in the book that reveal the importance of these symbols. For example, a group of seventh-grade students traced the references to music and the sailboat and discussed the implications of each. They found that the following references to music were used to support the characters' fears, dreams, and beliefs:

> *Music:* Specific titles reflect various characters' feelings:
> "When First Into This Country a Stranger I Came"
> "Pretty Polly"—like Dicey's mother, this is a ballad about a woman who is deserted by a man.
> "Amazing Grace" is considered Dicey's family song.
> "The Water Is Wide, I Cannot Get Over" is Dicey's mother's favorite song.
> A quote toward the end of the book reinforces the importance of music in Dicey's life: "The pictures her memory made had songs in them, clearer than the noise of the train. All the songs seemed to be blending together, into music as complicated as some of Maybeth's piano pieces. But Dicey could pick them out, each one, each separate melody" (p. 186).

After locating the references to music, the group found the words to the songs. These words were then read to highlight what the music was revealing about the various characterizations.

The group drew the following conclusions about the relation of the sailboat to Voigt's development of Dicey's characterization:

1. When Dicey found the boat, it was not ready to face the sea.
2. Like the boat, Dicey was not ready to face life.
3. After many long hours of work, the boat was seaworthy.

4. Although seaworthy, the boat still had some problems and required work.

5. By the end of the story Dicey was like the boat. She was able to face life even though she still might have felt battered and in need of more work before she could face all of the responsibilities associated with life.

6. A quote toward the end of the book supports the relationship between Dicey and the boat: "As if Dicey were a sailboat and the sails were furled up now, the mainsail wrapped up around the boom, and she was sitting at anchor. It felt good to come to rest, the way it felt walking up to their house on a cold evening, seeing the yellow light at the kitchen window and knowing you would be warm inside while the darkness drew in around the house. But a boat at anchor wasn't like a boat at sea" (p. 187).

Students also can trace the resemblances between the wind-blown sea and Dicey's life and the representation of Grandmother's farm as a stability in life.

After students have finished reading and discussing this book, encourage them to develop an illustrated response to the symbolism and characterization in the book. Allow them to choose any art medium to develop the representation. It might be a collage or a painting. Point out that specific colors can be used to represent the changes in characterization. Many students enjoy selecting music as a background for their art.

A similar relationship between symbolism and characterization can be developed using Voigt's *A Solitary Blue* (Newbery Honor). Students can trace the author's use of symbolism associated with the blue heron and the implications for character development as the main character progresses from feelings of low self-esteem and anger because of his mother's behavior to self-discovery and feelings of self-worth.

LESSON THREE: Webbing Characterization

OBJECTIVES

To identify the main characters in a story.

To web the details that describe the characters.

CORE BOOK: Selina Hastings' *Sir Gawain and the Loathly Lady* (Legend).

PROCEDURES: Review the plot development and conflict in *Sir Gawain and the Loathly Lady* developed in a previous lesson. Draw a web on the board with the word *characterization* in the center. Ask the students to identify the main characters in the story. Most students identify King Arthur, the Black Knight, Sir Gawain, and the Loathly Lady. Place these characters on the spokes of the web. Then ask the students to reread the story and to identify as many characteristics as they can that describe each of the characters. The web in Figure 6.4 was developed with a group of students in middle school.

Extended Books for Upper Elementary and Middle School Students

The books listed in this section develop strong characterizations, encourage students to identify various techniques that authors use to develop characterizations, and encourage personal responses to the characterizations within the books.

Modern Fantasy

NATALIE BABBITT's *Tuck Everlasting*. The characterization shows the Tuck family as they face the problems associated with everlasting life and a girl who must decide if she wants to join the Tuck family in everlasting life.

FIGURE 6.4 Webbing characterization in *Sir Gawain and the Loathly Lady.*

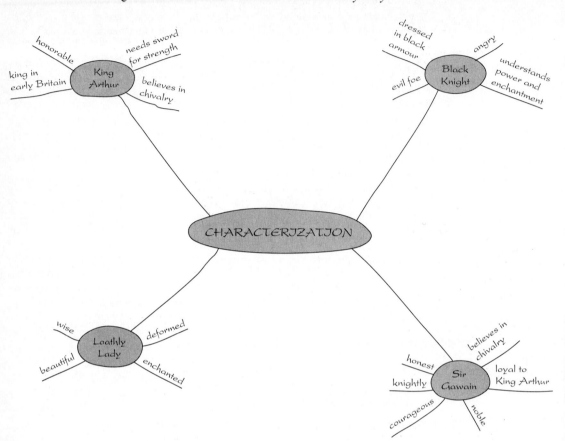

ROBIN MCKINLEY's *The Hero and the Crown* (Newbery Medal). The characterization of a
  girl develops as she faces the forces of evil during a quest.

Realistic Fiction

BRUCE BROOKS' *The Moves Make the Man* (Newbery Honor, Black). Characterization is
  revealed as two boys relate to basketball and to each other. Symbolism is associated with
  basketball terms.

FRANCES HODGSON BURNETT's *The Secret Garden* (English, Touchstone). Working in the
  garden changes the characters of a lonely girl and a sick boy.

BETSY BYARS' *Cracker Jackson.* A boy makes discoveries about himself as he tries to save his
  former baby sitter from abuse by her husband.

BROCK COLES' *The Goats.* A boy and a girl develop strength of character after they are
  marooned on an island by their peers at camp.

JEAN CRAIGHEAD GEORGE's *Julie of the Wolves.* (Eskimo, Newbery Medal). Characterization
  is revealed as a girl overcomes the harshness of nature on the North Slope of Alaska.

JANET TAYLOR LISLE's *Afternoon of the Elves* (Newbery Honor). Two girls gain understanding as they work on a miniature village.

KATHERINE PATERSON's *Bridge to Terabithia* (Newbery Honor). A boy and a girl who are
  different from their classmates create their own special kingdom.

Historical Fiction

URI ORLEV'S *The Island on Bird Street* (Jewish): A 12-year-old boy's character develops as he survives World War II in Warsaw.

ELIZABETH GEORGE SPEARE'S *The Sign of the Beaver* (Native American, Newbery Honor). A pioneer boy makes self-discoveries when an Indian friend teaches him survival techniques.

MAIA WOJCIECHOWSKA *Shadow of a Bull* (Spanish, Newbery Medal). A boy discovers that true bravery is not always found in the bull ring.

Recreational Books for Upper Elementary and Middle School Students

Realistic Fiction

VICKI GROVE'S *The Fastest Friend in the West*

VIRGINIA HAMILTON'S *The Planet of Junior Brown* (Black, Newbery Honor)

LOIS LOWRY'S *Rabble Starkey*

WALTER DEAN MYERS' *Scorpions* (Black, Newbery Honor)

KATHERINE PATERSON'S *Come Sing, Jimmy Jo*

KATHERINE PATERSON'S *The Great Gilly Hopkins* (Newbery Honor)

GARY PROVOST AND GAIL LEVINE-PROVOST'S *David and Max* (Jewish)

ALFRED SLOTE'S *Hang Tough, Paul Mather*

Historical Fiction

JAMES ALDRIDGE'S *The True Story of Spit MacPhee* (Australian)

PAM CONRAD'S *My Daniel*

REFERENCES

FRITZ, J. (1988, November/December). Biography: Readability plus responsibility. *The Horn Book,* pp. 759–760.

FRITZ, J. (1991). Through the eyes of an author: On writing biography. In D. E. Norton's *Through the eyes of a child: An introduction to children's literature* (p. 610). Columbus, OH: Merrill.

NORTON, D. E. (1991). *Through the eyes of a child: An introduction to children's literature.* Columbus, OH: Merrill.

PERRINE, L. (1983). *Literature: Structure, sound, and sense* (4th ed.). San Diego: Harcourt Brace Jovanovich.

ROEHLER, L. & DUFFY, G. (1984). Direct explanation of comprehension processes. In L. R. Roehler & J. Mason, (Eds.), *Comprehensive Instruction,* (pp. 265–280). New York: Longman.

CHILDREN'S LITERATURE REFERENCES*

ADLER, C. S. *Ghost Brother.* Clarion, 1990 (I: 9–12).

ALDRIDGE, JAMES. *The True Story of Spit MacPhee.* New York: Viking Kestrel, 1986 (I: 10+).

*I = Interest by age range

ANDERSEN, HANS CHRISTIAN. *The Ugly Duckling,* retold and illustrated by Lorinda Bryan Cauley. Orlando: Harcourt Brace Jovanovich, 1979 (I: 6–8).

BABBITT, NATALIE. *Tuck Everlasting.* New York: Farrar, Straus & Giroux, 1975 (I: 8–12).

BAYLOR, BYRD. *Hawk, I'm Your Brother.* Illustrated by Peter Parnall. New York: Scribner's, 1976 (I: all).

BROOKS, BRUCE. *The Moves Make the Man,* New York: Harper & Row, 1984 (I: 10+).

BROWN, MARGARET WISE. *The Runaway Bunny.* Illustrated by Clement Hurd. New York: Harper & Row, 1972 (I: 2–7).

BUNTING, EVE. *The Wednesday Surprise.* Illustrated by Donald Carrick. New York: Clarion, 1989 (I: 3–9).

BURNETT, FRANCES HODGSON. *The Secret Garden.* Illustrated by Tasha Tudor. Philadelphia: Lippincott, 1911, 1938, 1962 (I: 8–12).

BYARS, BETSY. *Bingo Brown, Gypsy Lover.* New York: Viking, 1990 (I: 8–12).

——— . *Cracker Jackson.* New York: Viking, 1985 (I: 10+).

CAMERON, ELEANOR. *That Julia Redfern.* Illustrated by Gail Owens. New York: Dutton 1982 (I: 9–12).

CLEARY, BEVERLY. *Dear Mr. Henshaw.* Illustrated by Paul O. Zelinsky. New York: Morrow, 1983 (I: 9–12).

_____. *Ramona and Her Mother.* Illustrated by Alan Tiegreen. New York: Morrow, 1979 (I: 7–10).

COLE, BROCK. *The Goats.* New York: Farrar, Straus & Giroux, 1987 (I: 10+).

CONRAD, PAM. *My Daniel.* New York: Harper & Row, 1989 (I: 10+).

CROSSLEY-HOLLAND, KEVIN. *Storm.* Illustrated by Alan Marks. London: Heinemann, 1985 (I: 7–10).

DEANGELI, MARGUERITE. *The Door in the Wall.* New York: Doubleday, 1949 (I: 8–12).

DEPAOLA, TOMIE. *Oliver Button Is a Sissy.* Orlando: Harcourt Brace Jovanovich, 1979 (I: 5–8).

ENRIGHT, ELIZABETH. *Thimble Summer.* Orlando: Holt, Rinehart & Winston, 1938, 1966 (I: 7–12).

FLEISCHMAN, SID. *The Scarebird.* Illustrated by Peter Sis. New York: Greenwillow, 1988 (I: 5–9).

FRITZ, JEAN. *The Great Little Madison.* New York: Putnam, 1989 (I: 9+).

GEORGE, JEAN CRAIGHEAD. *Julie of the Wolves.* Illustrated by John Schoenherr. New York: Harper & Row, 1972 (I: 10+).

GIPSON, FRED. *Old Yeller.* Illustrated by Carl Burger. New York: Harper & Row, 1956 (I: 10+).

GRIFALCONI, ANN. *Darkness and the Butterfly.* Boston: Little, Brown, 1987 (I: 5–8).

GRIFFITH, HELEN V. *Grandaddy's Place.* Illustrated by James Stevenson. New York: Greenwillow, 1987 (I: 4–8).

GROVE, VICKI. *The Fastest Friend in the West.* New York: Putnam, 1990 (I: 10+).

HAMILTON, VIRGINIA. *The Planet of Junior Brown.* New York: Macmillan, 1971 (I: 12+).

HASTINGS, SELINA, retold by. *Sir Gawain and the Loathly Lady.* Illustrated by Juan Wijngaard. New York: Lothrop, Lee & Shepard, 1985 (I: 10+).

HOBAN, RUSSELL. *Best Friends for Frances.* Illustrated by Lillian Hoban. New York: Harper & Row, 1969 (I: 4–8).

HOWARD, ELLEN. *Edith Herself.* New York: Atheneum, 1987 (I: 7–10).

HUGHES, SHIRLEY. *Alfie Gives a Hand.* New York: Lothrop, Lee & Shepard, 1983 (I: 3–6).

_____. *Dogger.* London: Bodley Head, 1977 (I: 3–8).

JUKES, MAVIS. *Like Jake and Me.* Illustrated by Lloyd Bloom. New York: Knopf, 1984 (I: 6–9).

KEATS, EZRA JACK. *Louie.* New York: Greenwillow, 1975 (I: 3–8).

_____. *Peter's Chair.* New York: Harper & Row, 1967 (I: 3–8).

_____. *The Snowy Day.* New York: Viking, 1962 (I: 2–7).

KELLER, BEVERLY. *No Beasts! No Children!* New York: Lothrop, Lee & Shepard, 1983 (I: 8–12).

KLINE, SUZY. *Herbie Jones and the Monster Ball.* Illustrated by Richard Williams. New York: Putnam, 1988 (I: 8+).

LISLE, JANET TAYLOR. *Afternoon of the Elves.* New York: Watts, 1989 (I: 10+).

LITTLE, JEAN. *Different Dragons.* Illustrated by Laura Fernandez. New York: Viking, 1986 (I: 8–10).

LOWRY, LOIS. *Anastasia on Her Own.* Boston: Houghton Mifflin, 1985 (I: 8–12).

_____. *Rabble Starkey.* Boston: Houghton Mifflin, 1987 (I: 10+).

MACLACHLAN, PATRICIA. *The Facts and Fictions of Minna Pratt.* New York: Harper & Row, 1988 (I: 7–12).

_____. *Sarah, Plain and Tall.* New York: Harper & Row, 1986 (I: 7–10).

MCCULLY, EMILY ARNOLD. *School.* New York: Harper & Row 1987 (I: 3–9).

MCKINLEY, ROBIN. *The Hero and the Crown.* New York: Greenwillow, 1984 (I: 10+).

MYERS, WALTER DEAN. *Scorpions.* New York: Harper & Row, 1988 (I: 10+).

NESS, EVALINE. *Sam, Bangs & Moonshine.* Orlando: Holt, Rinehart & Winston, 1966 (I: 5–9).

ORLEV, URI. *The Island on Bird Street,* translated by Hillel Halkin. Boston: Houghton Mifflin, 1984 (I: 10+).

PARK, BARBARA. *The Kid in the Red Jacket.* New York: Knopf, 1981 (I: 9–12).

PATERSON, KATHERINE. *Bridge to Terabithia.* Illustrated by Donna Diamond. New York: Crowell, 1977 (I: 10+).

_____. *Come Sing, Jimmy Jo.* New York: Dutton, 1985 (I: 10+).

_____. *The Great Gilly Hopkins.* New York: Crowell, 1978 (I: 10+).

POTTER, BEATRIX. *The Tale of Mrs. Tiggy-Winkle.* New York: Warne, 1905, 1986 (I: 3–7).

_____. *The Tale of Peter Rabbit.* New York: Warne, 1902 (I: 3–7).

_____. *The Tale of Squirrel Nutkin.* New York: Warne, 1903, 1986 (I: 3–7).

PRAGO, ALBERT. *Strangers in Their Own Land: A History of Mexican-Americans.* New York: Four Winds, 1973 (I: 10+).

PROVENSEN, ALICE. *The Buck Stops Here: The Presidents of the United States.* New York: Harper & Row, 1990 (I: all).

PROVOST, GARY & GAIL LEVINE-PROVOST. *David and Max.* Philadelphia: Jewish Publication Society, 1988 (I: 10+).

SCHOTTER, RONI. *Captain Snap and the Children of Vinegar Lane.* Illustrated by Marcia Sewall. New York: Orchard, 1989 (I: 5–9).

SCHWARTZ, AMY. *Annabelle Swift, Kindergartner.* New York: Orchard, 1988 (I: 4–7).

SELDEN, GEORGE. *The Cricket in Times Square*. Illustrated by Garth Williams. New York: Farrar, Straus & Giroux, 1960 (I: 7–11).

SLOTE, ALFRED. *Hang Tough, Paul Mather*. Philadelphia: Lippincott, 1973 (I: 9–12).

SPEARE, ELIZABETH GEORGE. *The Sign of the Beaver*. Boston: Houghton Mifflin, 1983 (I: 8–12).

STEPTOE, JOHN. *Daddy Is a Monster...Sometimes*. Philadelphia: Lippincott, 1980 (I: 4–7).

VINCENT, GABRIELLE. *Ernest and Celestine's Picnic*. New York: Greenwillow, 1982 (I: 3–7).

———. *Feel Better, Ernest!* New York: Greenwillow, 1988 (I: 3–7).

———. *Smile, Ernest and Celestine*. New York: Greenwillow, 1982 (I: 3–7).

VOIGT, CYNTHIA. *Dicey's Song*. New York: Atheneum, 1982 (I: 10+).

———. *A Solitary Blue*. New York: Atheneum, 1983 (I: 10+).

WHITE, E. B. *Charlotte's Web*. Illustrated by Garth Williams. New York: Harper & Row, 1952 (I: 7–11).

WILDER, LAURA INGALLS. *The Long Winter*. Illustrated by Garth Williams. New York: Harper & Row, 1940, 1953 (I: 8–12).

WILLIAMS, VERA. *A Chair for My Mother*. New York: Greenwillow, 1982 (I: 3–7).

WOJCIECHOWSKA, MAIA. *Shadow of a Bull*. Illustrated by Alvin Smith. New York: Atheneum, 1964, 1983 (I: 10+).

WOLF, BERNARD. *Anna's Silent World*. Philadelphia: Lippincott, 1977 (I: 5–10).

ZOLOTOW, CHARLOTTE. *My Grandson Lew*. Illustrated by William Péne du Bois. New York: Harper & Row, 1974 (I: 5–8).

———. *William's Doll*. Illustrated by William Péne du Bois. New York: Harper & Row, 1972 (I: 4–8).

CHAPTER 7

SETTING

DEVELOPING UNDERSTANDING AND APPRECIATION OF SETTING
    Core Books and Sample Lessons for Lower Elementary Students
    Extended Books for Lower Elementary Students
    Recreational Books for Lower Elementary Students
    Core Books and Sample Lessons for Middle Elementary Students
    Extended Books for Middle Elementary Students
    Recreational Books for Middle Elementary Students
    Core Books and Sample Lessons for Upper Elementary and Middle School Students
    Extended Books for Upper Elementary and Middle School Students
    Recreational Books for Upper Elementary and Middle School Students

$\mathbf{I}$n the previous chapters we considered the important literary elements of plot development, conflict, and characterization. In this chapter we will consider books that encourage students to understand and appreciate the functions of setting. We will explore the role of setting in memorable books as it develops the mood for the story, creates an antagonist, provides the historical background, and creates symbolic meanings that underscore the events in the story. We also will analyze how authors develop the underlying idea—or theme—that ties the plot, characters, and setting together.

Like previous chapters, this chapter provides core lessons, extended readings, and recreational selections for students in lower, middle, and upper elementary and middle school. The activities also will include many types of responses for literature, including discussions, writing, aesthetic responses, and integration of the humanities and other subjects. This chapter will continue concluding each section, where appropriate, with a literary web using *Darkness and the Butterfly; Hawk, I'm Your Brother;* and *Sir Gawain and the Loathly Lady.*

DEVELOPING UNDERSTANDING AND APPRECIATION OF SETTING

Setting is the geographic location and the time—past, present, or future—during which the story takes place. Setting can vary, from the historical depiction of an early Roman town to the carefully detailed world of a futuristic planet. If the story takes place in the world as we know it, the events should be consistent with what actually occurred during that period, and if the location is a real place, it should be presented accurately. Authors of historical fiction, for example, must make the background for their stories as authentic as possible. Readers should be able to vicariously accompany the characters as they see, feel, and hear their environment. Authors of fantasy also must develop believable settings by describing them in such detail that readers can visualize the world Alice experiences as she enters Wonderland or the world of Middle Earth as experienced by Bilbo Baggins in *The Hobbit.*

In addition to depicting a complete historical background, setting can provide an instantly recognizable background (such as that found in folktales), create a mood, develop conflict, or suggest symbolism. Illustrations in books have a similar function. They should reinforce the text by detailing the historical background, setting the mood, establishing the conflict, or reinforcing the symbolism.

Picture storybooks, with their vivid illustrations, are among the best sources for developing observational and writing skills related to setting. An activity that encourages writing about setting can vary from the younger student's simple description to the older student's creation of a setting that conveys its purposes. Settings can enhance students' understanding of other cultures and worlds. Diakiw (1990) identifies the role of picture storybooks in global education well when he states, "They are like poems, reducing an issue, scene, or emotion to its essence, thus permitting one to see the whole more clearly" (p. 298).

Art activities are an obvious extension of the study of setting. Some books lend themselves to mood pieces such as abstract paintings with colors that reflect the moods. Other books have detailed descriptions of settings that encourage students to draw the settings from the textual descriptions. Students can create their own interpretations of Wonderland, Middle Earth, or Wilbur's barn and barnyard.

Music can add another dimension to the study of setting and theme. What music might highlight the mood of the setting? What music depicts the theme of the story? What music evokes the same response as the developments in the story? Musical interpretations can take many forms, from students singing and playing instruments to guest musicians sharing their musical abilities. Lamme (1990) describes a class that read Karen Ackerman's *Song and Dance Man* and then invited parents to share their musical talents.

Core Books and Sample Lessons for Lower Elementary Students

LESSON ONE: Describing and Writing Descriptions of Familiar Settings

OBJECTIVES

To develop oral descriptive skills associated with setting and to write descriptions that accompany settings.

To compare the settings in books with settings known to the students.

CORE BOOKS: Include a variety of books with settings that are familiar to the students. The choices will vary, of course, with the backgrounds and experiences of the students. Books could include Millicent Selsam and Joyce Hunt's *Keep Looking!* (Informational); Michael Garland's *My Cousin Katie* (Informational); William George's *Box Turtle At Long Pond* (Informational); Susi Gregg Fowler's *When Summer Ends* (Informational); Amy Hest's *The Crack-of-Dawn Walkers* (Picture Story Book); Ezra Jack Keats' *Goggles!* (Picture Story Book, Caldecott Honor); Dayal Khalsa's *I Want a Dog* (Picture Story Book), Jan Mark's *Fun* (Picture Story Book); and Amy Schwartz's *Annabelle Swift, Kindergartner* (Picture Story Book).

PROCEDURES: Share several of the books with familiar settings. Read the stories while encouraging students to look carefully at the settings, and then describe these settings in detail. This discussion also can emphasize students' reactions to the settings, as well as descriptive words and phrases they think describe the settings. Finally, ask students to write or dictate their own descriptions of the settings that include the points made during the discussion.

After students have written the descriptions, ask them to describe and illustrate a similar setting that they have experienced. Then ask them to compare the settings in the book with the settings and illustrations from their own experiences.

LESSON TWO: Responding to Illustrations That Create A Warm, Happy Mood

OBJECTIVES

To develop observational powers and to respond to an illustrator's depiction of a warm, happy, and peaceful mood.

To describe and illustrate a setting that the students would consider a warm, happy, and peaceful mood.

CORE BOOK: Valerie Flournoy's *The Patchwork Quilt* (Realistic Fiction, Black)

PROCEDURES: Introduce *The Patchwork Quilt* by telling the students that this is a story about a family that includes a grandmother and a little girl who loves her grandmother very much. Ask the students to identify their feelings as they listen to the story carefully. After they have listened to the story, ask them to share their responses. (Although the text and illustrations are meant to develop a warm, peaceful, and nostalgic mood, the students do not need to agree with these feelings.)

Next, share the following information on the book jacket, "All the trust and sharing between a young girl and her treasured grandmother is captured in Valerie Flournoy's story, lovingly illustrated in Jerry Pinkney's evocative paintings." Now go back through the text and the illustrations and ask the students to identify specific examples from the setting that the students think the author and illustrator were using to create their mood. For example, a group of second-grade students identified the following examples:

1. Mother baking in the kitchen. (One child said, "The house smells good.")
2. Grandmother sitting in a comfortable chair.
3. Grandmother's warm hugs.
4. The family party at Christmas.
5. Mother and Tanya working on the quilt for Grandmother.
6. Quilt made out of family clothing.
7. Everyone was part of the quilt.
8. Quilt given to Tanya.
9. Taking care of Grandmother.
10. Papa said he felt happiness in the house.

After students have completed this discussion and identified how an author and an illustrator developed the warm, happy mood, ask the students to think about how they would describe and illustrate a warm, happy mood. Ask them to describe and illustrate this setting.

LESSON THREE: Exploring the Imagination Through Setting

OBJECTIVES

To develop appreciation of illustrations that depict the imaginative settings created in children's minds.

To create imaginative settings through an art experience.

CORE BOOKS: Books that show how the imagination can change the settings, such as Nancy Evans Cooney's *The Umbrella Day* (Picture Story Book); Ezra Jack Keats' *The Trip*

(Picture Story Book); Barbro Lindgren's *The Wild Baby Goes to Sea* (Picture Story Book); Rafe Martin's *Will's Mammoth* (Picture Story Book); and Joanne Ryder's *White Bear, Ice Bear* (Picture Story Book).

PROCEDURES: The books in this core lesson all develop plots and settings that show the power of the imagination. In *The Umbrella Day* and *The Wild Baby Goes to Sea*, simple objects such as an umbrella and a box stimulate imaginative settings and fantastic experiences. In *The Trip*, a boy constructs a shoe-box scene so that he can visit his friends. In *Will's Mammoth* and *White Bear, Ice Bear*, the characters use their imaginations to turn a snowy scene into an imaginative experience that includes animals.

This lesson takes several days as students experience each story and respond to the imaginative experiences expressed in the texts and the illustrations. Read each story to the students as they look at the illustrations. Allow them to respond through their own feelings and imaginations. Many younger students might have had similar experiences as they changed their environments through their imaginations.

After the students have responded to *The Umbrella Day* and *The Wild Baby Goes to Sea*, ask the students to think about other everyday objects that could be turned into imaginative experiences or to think about other adventures that they could have with an umbrella or a box. Have them share these ideas and create their own imaginative stories through illustrations.

After they have responded to *The Trip*, ask the students to create their own boxes that allow them to go on a fantasy trip. After reading and discussing *Will's Mammoth* and *White Bear, Ice Bear*, encourage the students to place themselves in a setting where they could have a fantasy experience. Ask them, "If you could do anything that your imaginations could create, what would you do? Who would be in your settings? What might you become?"

LESSON FOUR: Interacting With Music

OBJECTIVES

To extend enjoyment of literature through music.

To respond to the rhythm of a text through music and creative movement.

CORE BOOKS: Books that include music, such as Walter Crane's *The Baby's Opera* (Picture Story Book, Touchstone) and Dan Fox's *Go In and Out the Window: An Illustrated Songbook for Young People* (Picture Story Book). Books with rhythmical texts that stimulate creating music and movement, such as Joyce Maxner's *Nicholas Cricket* (Picture Story Book); Margaret Mahy's *17 Kings and 42 Elephants* (Picture Story Book); and Wanda Gag's *Millions of Cats* (Picture Story Book, Touchstone, Newbery Honor).

PROCEDURES: These enjoyable books can be used any time to add music and creative rhythm to the classroom. The first two books include simple musical accompaniments. Encourage the students to sing the nursery rhymes and folk songs. The other three books are written in rhythmic language that encourages creating music or movement. For example, Nicholas Cricket plays every night in the "Bug-a-Wug Cricket Band." Students can create the sounds that are heard in the night and that accompany the rhyming and repetitive text. The other two books have rhythmical texts that encourage involvement and movement.

LESSON FIVE: Webbing the Setting for a Book

OBJECTIVE

To identify important aspects of setting through a literary web.

CORE BOOK: Ann Grifalconi's *Darkness and the Butterfly* (Picture Story Book, African).

PROCEDURES: Draw a web with setting placed in the center. Now ask the students to identify the important settings in *Darkness and the Butterfly*. (For example, a group of second-grade students identified fears of nighttime Africa and daytime Africa.) Next, place these settings on the spokes of the diagram. Ask the students to identify the details that could be included to describe each of these settings. The web in Figure 7.1 was completed by the second-grade students.

Extended Books for Lower Elementary Students

The books in this section create various moods and backgrounds. Most of the books are picture story books in which the settings are reinforced through the illustrations. Students need many opportunities to respond to the illustrations in books. Some books have detailed illustrations that carefully depict a specific location. Others have more abstract illustrations that create moods and feelings through colors. Some books encourage imaginative responses as characters change their settings. Most of the books can be used to develop webs associated with settings.

> Picture Story Books
> DEBRA AND SAL BARRACCA's *The Adventures of Taxi Dog*. The settings follow a taxicab through a city.
> MARC BROWN's *Arthur's Baby*. The settings follow an animal child as he adjusts to a new baby in the home.
> MARGARET WISE BROWN's *The Runaway Bunny*. The beautiful illustrations show warmth and love as a young bunny places himself in several settings.

FIGURE 7.1 Web of setting for *Darkness and the Butterfly*.

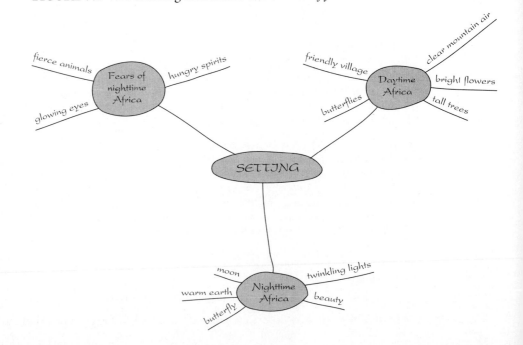

TOMIE DEPAOLA'S *An Early American Christmas*. The setting is in New England in the early 1800s.

HELEN GRIFFITH'S *Grandaddy's Place*. The setting is a rural farm.

PAT HUTCHINS' *The Wind Blew*. The setting shows what happens when the wind blows objects away from people.

EZRA JACK KEATS' *Pet Show!* Bright colors and collages provide the setting for a children's pet show.

HOLLY KELLER'S *Geraldine's Big Snow*. The settings contrast inside activities and outside activities in winter.

ROBERT MCCLOSKEY'S *Blueberries for Sal* (Caldecott Honor). A rural setting follows a bear cub and a young girl.

ROBERT MCCLOSKEY'S *One Morning in Maine* (Caldecott Honor) and *Time of Wonder* (Caldecott Medal). The settings in these books show the joys of living on an island and the storms that can threaten.

ALICE AND MARTIN PROVENSEN'S *The Year at Maple Hill Farm*. The illustrations trace the seasons of the year.

DR. SEUSS' *And to Think That I Saw It on Mulberry Street*. An ordinary setting becomes a fantastic experience through a boy's imagination.

Wordless Picture Books

EMILY ARNOLD MCCULLY'S *School*. The setting presents home and school when a little mouse wants to visit school.

MERCER MAYER'S *A Boy, A Dog and A Frog; A Boy, A Dog, A Frog, and A Friend; Frog Goes To Dinner; Frog, Where Are You?;* and *One Frog Too Many*. This series of humorous books encourage students to describe settings and write story lines.

Recreational Books for Lower Elementary Students

Picture Story Books

JOSE ARUEGO AND ARIANE DEWEY'S *We Hide, You Seek*

BARBARA COONEY'S *Island Boy*

LOUISE FATIO'S *The Happy Lion*

SUSAN JEFFERS' *Three Jovial Huntsmen* (Caldecott Honor)

EZRA JACK KEATS' *Regards to the Man in the Moon*

ROBERT MCCLOSKEY'S *Make Way for Ducklings* (Caldecott Medal)

CLEMENT MOORE'S *The Night Before Christmas* (illustrated poem)

LISA WESTBERG PETERS' *Good Morning, River!*

MAURICE SENDAK'S *Where the Wild Things Are* (Caldecott Medal)

CHRIS VAN ALLSBURG'S *The Garden of Abdul Gasazi* (Caldecott Honor)

LYND WARD'S *The Biggest Bear* (Caldecott Medal)

AUDREY WOOD'S *King Bidgood's in the Bathtub* (Caldecott Honor)

CHARLOTTE ZOLOTOW'S *Mr. Rabbit and the Lovely Present* (Caldecott Honor)

Core Books and Sample Lessons for Middle Elementary Students

This section incudes lessons that introduce and explore the four functions of settings: (a) to design appropriate moods, (b) to develop antagonists, (c) to create historical and geographical backgrounds, and (d) to suggest symbolic interpretations. Although the lessons analyze each of these purposes individually, authors and illustrators often develop more than one purpose in the same text. Picture books are used in many of the lessons to help students understand that both the illustrations and the text develop settings.

LESSON ONE: Developing Appreciation for Settings That Create Moods

OBJECTIVES

To develop an understanding that, through word choices and the pictures created by words, authors create moods ranging from humorous to frightening.

To develop an understanding that illustrators create moods through illustrations that match the text.

To develop an appreciation for text and illustrations by responding to the moods in books and by creating stories and illustrations that suggest certain moods.

To relate the moods created in words and illustrations with the moods created by music.

CORE BOOKS: Books that develop various moods through both the text and the illustrations, such as Cynthia Rylant's *When I Was Young in the Mountains* (Picture Story Book, Caldecott Honor), warm, gentle nostalgic mood; David McPhails' *The Dream Child* (Poetry), warm, happy mood; Eve Merriam's *Halloween ABC* (Poetry), frightening mood; and Patricia Polacco's *Meteor!* (Picture Story Book), funny, absurd mood.

PROCEDURES: Introduce the illustrated books by asking the students, "Do all books create the same feelings within the readers? How would an author or an illustrator let readers know that a book is meant to be humorous, happy, or frightening?" Ask them to look at the covers of the books or at the first illustration in each book. With each book, ask the students to predict the mood and explain the reasons for their prediction. Write their predictions on the board.

Next, ask the students to listen or look for words that support the mood in each of the stories. Also ask them to consider the illustrators' use of color or type of illustration to create a specific mood. For example, a group of fourth-grade students identified the following frightening words in *Halloween ABC* and warm, happy words in *When I Was Young In the Mountains*:

FRIGHTENING MOOD	WARM, HAPPY MOOD
Merriam's *Halloween ABC*	Rylant's *When I Was Young in the Mountains*
malicious, creepy crawlers, horrible touchers, fiend, ghost, trembling, terrifying, victim, lunging, nightmare, vicious.	kiss the top of my head, held my hand, smelled of sweet milk, giggling, heated cocoa, braided my hair.

Next, they looked at the illustrations to see whether the illustrations matched the moods of the words and to consider what techniques the illustrators used to create the appropriate moods. For example, for *Halloween ABC* they decided that the dark, eerie colors in the illustrations matched the mood of the poems and created a frightening feeling. They also found that the warm tones and the actions depicted in illustrations for *When I Was Young in the Mountains* created just the right mood for that text. They did a similar analysis and evaluation for the rest of the books in the core lesson.

Finally, the students divided into groups, chose one of the books, and identified music that they thought would add to the mood of the book. They prepared dramatic readings of the stories and accompanied the readings with music.

LESSON TWO: Developing Appreciation for Settings That Develop Antagonists
The setting as an antagonist is similar to person-against-nature conflict. For these core lessons and books refer to the sample lesson on person-against-nature conflict in Chapter 5.

LESSON THREE: Developing Appreciation for Settings That Create Geographical Backgrounds

OBJECTIVES

To observe the settings in illustrations and to identify the geographical backgrounds associated with the settings.

To create appropriate geographical backgrounds for additional people.

To relate geography and literature.

CORE BOOK: Edith Baer's *This Is the Way We Go to School: A Book About Children Around the World* (Informational).

PROCEDURES: The core book in this lesson introduces the settings and the modes of transportation used by students in 23 locations around the world as they go to school. Introduce the book to the students and ask them to look carefully at each illustration. They should consider the details in each illustration, including vegetation, clothing, buildings, and modes of transportation. They should observe what types of climates are required for the vegetation, the clothing, and even some of the modes of transportation. In some instances, they can find clues in the names of the students.

After looking at each illustration, list the clues that indicate where the setting might be. After the students have identified as many clues as possible, ask them where they think the setting is located. Mark the setting on a map of the world. Students can argue for more than one location if they can justify the setting. After the book has been read, verify the locations with the listings at the back of the book. (The illustrator includes a world map that shows each of the locations.)

Finally, look at the world map and identify several settings that are not included in the book. Encourage students to research that setting and draw a picture that shows the setting and the mode of transportation that a student might use to go to school.

LESSON FOUR: Developing Appreciation for Settings That Create Historical or Geographical Backgrounds

OBJECTIVES

To create maps and illustrations depicting well-defined settings in literature.

To evaluate the effectiveness of an author's textual description by using the description to create a map or other illustration.

CORE BOOK: C. S. Lewis's *The Lion, the Witch and the Wardrobe* (Modern Fantasy, Touchstone).

PROCEDURES: After the students have read this book, divide them into groups and ask each group to develop a map of Narnia. Ask the students to support where they draw specific features by providing quotes from the book. Interesting comparisons can be developed among the groups as they defend their reasons for placing landmarks in certain locations. Some groups might want to change their maps after they hear the arguments of other students. After they have completed and defended their maps, ask them to evaluate Lewis's ability to create a believable fantasy world with a carefully developed geographical background.

Additional books that are excellent for this type of activity include Lewis Carroll's *Alice's Adventures in Wonderland* (Modern Fantasy, Touchstone) and E. B. White's *Charlotte's Web* (Modern Fantasy, Newbery Honor, Touchstone). In addition to reading for details throughout the book, students often must make inferences as they decide where to place specific landmarks.

LESSON FIVE: Developing Appreciation for Settings That Have Symbolic Interpretations

OBJECTIVES

To develop an understanding that settings often have symbolic meanings that underscore the events in a story.

To develop an appreciation for the symbolic settings that are common in traditional folktales.

To compare the symbolic settings in folktales from different cultures and to understand that such symbolic settings of time and place are universal in folktales.

To understand the purpose of symbolic settings in folktales that originally were told through the oral tradition.

To relate geography and symbolic settings in a folktale by illustrating a folktale.

CORE BOOKS: Include several anthologies of folktales collected from various cultures. For example, *The Blue Fairy Book* (Touchstone) and *The Red Fairy Book*, edited by Andrew Lang (British); Naomi Lewis's *The Twelve Dancing Princesses and Other Tales From Grimm* (German); A. E. Johnson's *Perrault's Complete Fairy Tales* (French, Touchstone); Jacqueline Onassis's *The Firebird and Other Russian Fairy Tales;* John Bierhorst's *The Monkey's Haircut and Other Stories Told by the Maya;* He Liyi's *The Spring of Butterflies and Other Chinese Folk Tales;* Julius Lester's *The Knee-High Man and Other Tales* (Black); and Virginia Haviland's *North American Legends* (Native American). Also include numerous highly illustrated folktales in which the illustrator develops the setting for one folktale.

PROCEDURES: To introduce the symbolic settings in traditional folktales, ask the students to close their eyes while you read the introduction to a folktale such as "The Sleeping Beauty in the Wood" from *Perrault's Complete Fairy Tales:* "Once upon a time there lived a king and queen who were grieved, more grieved than words can tell, because they had no children" (p. 1). Ask the students to describe the setting in which the story takes place. "What setting did you see in your imagination? Where do the king and queen live? What does the castle look like? What surrounds the castle? How did you know that the setting was in a castle? What words told you immediately what to expect?" Next, read an introduction to a tale with a different symbolic setting, such as that found in "Little Tom Thumb": "Once upon a time there lived a wood-cutter and his wife, who had seven children, all boys" (p. 26). Ask the students to describe this setting. "What setting did you see in your imagination? Where does the wood-cutter and his family live? What surrounds the hut? What words told you immediately what to expect? What type of literature do we call stories that began with 'Once upon a time?'"

If the students do not already know that you were reading the introductions to two folktales, share with them the information that folktales were told orally for centuries before the stories were collected and written down. Ask the students, "Why would oral storytellers not introduce their stories with detailed settings? What would be the advantage of using symbolic settings that immediately place the audience in a far-distant time, in a castle or deep in the woods? Why would tellers of folktales choose settings such as castles and woods? What kinds of adventures can happen in castles and woods?" Have them list various enchantments and adventures that seem possible in these settings.

Next, challenge the students to discover if folktales from different cultures usually include settings that symbolically take place in the far-distant past and in locations such as great forests, mysterious castles, and mystical mountains. Divide the students into groups and ask each group to analyze the time and place settings in folktales collected from specific countries. For example, they can complete charts such as those in Figure 7.2.

After students have analyzed folktales from numerous cultures, ask them to compare and discuss the information on their charts. Ask, "What have you learned about the settings in folktales from around the world? What does this tell us about the similarities in settings for folktales from different cultures? What does this reveal about people and their oral stories?"

Now, ask students to look at several highly illustrated single editions of folktales. Ask, "How do the illustrators depict the time and place? Compare the words in the text and the illustrations. Does the text provide the detailed information for the setting? How do you think the illustrators chose the settings?"

Finally, ask the students to choose one of the folktales from the collections. Allow them to create their own detailed illustrations that depict the settings. This also would be an excellent opportunity to relate geography and folktales. Students can research the geographic settings that would be appropriate for the various folktales and then illustrate the tales accordingly. They should investigate the appropriate architecture, vegetation, land forms, and animal life. They should understand the geographic and cultural requirements of a particular area, for example, before they try to illustrate settings such as the one found in the first line of the German "Iron Hans:" "There was once a mighty king who owned a great forest filled with all kinds of wild animals" (p. 57). They need to know what types of wildlife live in the forest, what types of vegetation grow in the forest, what types of land forms are found in Germany, and what type of castle in which the king would live.

LESSON SIX: Webbing the Setting

OBJECTIVES

To identify the settings in a realistic fiction selection.

To web the details that develop the setting.

FIGURE 7.2 Analyzing settings in folktales.

Country: *Germany, Brothers Grimm*		
Story	*Time*	*Place*
"The Twelve Dancing Princesses"	"There once was"	Great castle, enchanted land
"Hansel and Gretel"	"Once long ago"	Great forest
"Iron Hans"	"There was once"	Great forest
"The Golden Bird"	"Long, long ago"	Beautiful garden, golden castle, woods
Country: *China*		
Story	*Time*	*Place*
The Wonderful Brocade"	"Once upon a time"	On the plain at the foot of a huge mountain
"The Spring of Butterflies"	"Long ago"	The peak where the clouds play, a pond
"Never Heard of This Before"	"Long, long ago"	Palace

CORE BOOK: Byrd Baylor's *Hawk, I'm Your Brother* (Caldecott Honor).

PROCEDURES: Write the word *setting* in the middle of the web. Ask the students to identify the different settings found in *Hawk, I'm Your Brother.* Draw these settings from spokes projecting from the center. Then ask the students to identify details from the text and illustrations that are associated with each of these settings. Students also may add details from their own knowledge of southwestern mountains. (The web in Figure 7.3 was created by fourth-grade students.) After students have completed the web, ask them to speculate about the purpose for setting in *Hawk, I'm Your Brother.*

Extended Books for Middle Elementary Students

The following books contain settings that designate moods, develop antagonists, create historical and geographical backgrounds, and suggest symbolic interpretations. In small groups and individually, students can describe and discuss the settings, illustrate the settings, create backdrops for creative dramas, draw travel posters that might accompany the settings for the books, create book covers that focus on the setting, identify appropriate music that could accompany the books, create murals and friezes that depict the settings, and develop webs that depict the settings. Many of the traditional folktales in this section are excellent for extending an understanding of symbolic settings within different cultures. All the books can be used to develop webs for the settings.

Folktales

Aleksandr Nikolaevich Afanasev's *Russian Folk Tales.* Seven folktales include symbolic settings from folklore.

Peter Asbjornsen and Jorgen Moe's *Norwegian Folk Tales* (Touchstone). The folktales allow students to explore settings in Norwegian folklore.

FIGURE 7.3 Web of setting for *Hawk, I'm Your Brother.*

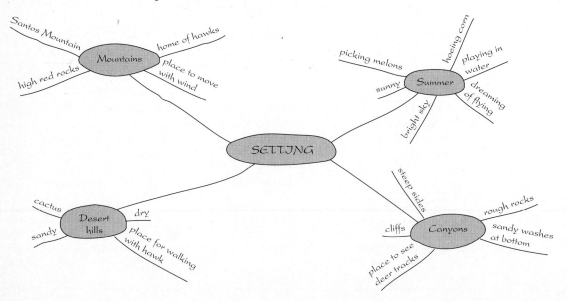

EMERSON COATSWORTH AND DAVID COATSWORTH's *The Adventures of Nanabush; Ojibway Indian Stories* (Native American). This collection includes 16 traditional tales.

DAVID CONGER's *Many Lands, Many Stories: Asian Folktales for Children*. The stories encourage representation of settings from Korea, Japan, China, Thailand, and India.

KEVIN CROSSLEY-HOLLAND's *British Folk Tales*. The stories have settings in the British Isles.

KEVIN CROSSLEY-HOLLAND's *The Fox and the Cat: Animal Tales from Grimm* (Germany): The settings allow students to explore stories about animals characteristically found in Germany.

M. A. JAGENDORF AND R. S. BOGGS' *The King of the Mountains: A Treasury of Latin American Folk Stories*. This collection incudes settings from 26 countries.

MAURICE METAYER's *Tales from the Igloo* (Native American). These settings are from a collection of Eskimo tales.

BARBARA K. WALKER's *The Dancing Palm Tree and Other Nigerian Folktales*. The settings include 11 tales from Nigeria.

Modern Fantasy

JAMES BARRIE's *Peter Pan*. The details in the book allow students to imagine and draw the fantasy Never Land.

FRANK BAUM's *The Wizard of Oz*. The details in the book support a well-developed fantasy land.

LEWIS CARROLL's *Alice's Adventures in Wonderland* (Touchstone). Students can illustrate Wonderland from the detailed settings.

ROBERT LAWSON's *Rabbit Hill* (Newbery Medal). Students can illustrate the detailed settings around the hill.

Realistic Fiction

HELEN CRESSWELL's *Bagthorpes Unlimited* and *Ordinary Jack*. A humorous mood is created as the family tries to outdo each other.

JUDY DELTON's *Angel's Mother's Wedding*. A mood of humor is developed through mistaken interpretations.

Historical Fiction

CAROL RYRIE BRINK's *Caddie Woodlawn* (Newbery Medal). The setting provides historical background for a story set on the Wisconsin frontier in 1864.

SIBYL HANCOCK's *Old Blue*. The purpose of the setting is to provide historical background for a trail drive in 1878.

NATALIE KINSEY-WARNOCK's *The Canada Geese Quilt*. The setting provides historical background for a story set in 1940s Vermont.

Biography

ALICE FORD's *John James Audubon*. The setting provides historical background for the naturalist and painter of birds.

JEAN FRITZ's *Where Do You Think You're Going, Christopher Columbus?* The setting provides historical background for the four voyages of Columbus.

BETSY LEE's *Charles Eastman, The Story of an American Indian* (Native American). The setting provides historical background for the life of a famous doctor, writer, and worker for Indian rights.

Recreational Books for Middle Elementary Students

Folktales

VERNA AARDEMA's *The Riddle of the Drum: A Tale from Tizapán, Mexico*

PURA BELPRÉ's *Once in Puerto Rico* (Hispanic)

BROTHERS GRIMM *Rumpelstiltskin* (German, Caldecott Honor)
BROTHERS GRIMM *Snow White and the Seven Dwarfs* (German, Caldecott Honor)
ELIZABETH ISELE's *The Frog Princess* (Russian)
MARGOT ZEMACH's *It Could Always Be Worse* (Jewish, Caldecott Honor)
Modern Fantasy
HANS CHRISTIAN ANDERSEN's *The Nightingale*
MICHAEL BOND's *A Bear Called Paddington* and *Paddington Abroad* (English)
BEVERLY CLEARY's *Ralph S. Mouse*
RUDYARD KIPLING's *The Jungle Book* (India, Touchstone)
MARY NORTON's *The Borrowers Afloat* (English)
Poetry
BYRD BAYLOR's *The Other Way to Listen* (Native American)
ELOISE GREENFIELD's *Under the Sunday Tree* (Bahamas)
Historical Fiction
ALICE DALGLIESH's *The Courage of Sarah Noble* (Newbery Honor)
GAIL E. HALEY's *Jack Jouett's Ride*
VIRGINIA HAMILTON's *The Bells of Christmas* (Black)
LAURA INGALLS WILDER's *The Long Winter*

Core Books and Sample Lessons for Upper Elementary and Middle School Students

The core books and sample lessons in this section extend the lessons developed in the middle elementary grades. The lessons explore how authors use settings to design moods, develop antagonists, create historical and geographical backgrounds, and suggest symbolic interpretations. If students in upper elementary and middle school have not had extensive experiences with setting, they will benefit from many of the activities and books recommended for middle elementary students. Again, numerous picture books exist that can encourage students to appreciate how illustrators can create settings though illustrations.

LESSON ONE: Developing Appreciation for Settings That Create Moods

OBJECTIVES

To develop understandings that, through word choices and the pictures created by words, authors create moods ranging from humorous to frightening.

To develop understandings that illustrators create moods that match the text.

To develop an appreciation for text and illustrations by responding to the moods in books and by creating stories and illustrations that suggest certain moods.

To relate the moods created in words and illustrations with the moods created by music.

CORE BOOKS: Books that develop various moods through both the text and the illustrations, such as Julian Scheer's *Rain Makes Applesauce* (Caldecott Honor); Ogden Nash's *Edward Lear's The Scroobious Pip* (Fantasy); Charles Perrault's *Cinderella* (Fantasy, Caldecott Medal); Judith Hendershot's *In Coal Country* (Historical); Jane Yolen's *Owl Moon* (Caldecott Medal); Chris Van Allsburg's *The Polar Express* (Caldecott Medal); Toshi Maruki's *Hiroshima No Pika*; and Alfred Noyes's *The Highwayman*.

PROCEDURES: Introduce the illustrated books by asking the students, "Do all books create the same feelings or moods within the readers? How would an author or an illustrator let readers know that the book is meant to be humorous, nostalgic, mystical, frightening, or ghostly?" Encourage students to suggest such techniques as using light and dark colors to create different moods, using heavy and light lines to influence moods, and using words to suggest moods.

Next, ask the students to look at the illustrations for the three books that have lighter, humorous, or fanciful moods: *Rain Makes Applesauce, The Scroobious Pip,* and *Cinderella.* Encourage students to feel the mood of the stories as they look at the illustrations and listen to the text. After sharing each book, ask the students to respond with their feelings and to suggest any techniques used by the illustrators and authors to reinforce those feelings. For example, in *Rain Makes Applesauce* many students identify a light, nonsense mood because the words tumble across the page, the pastel colors create a light fanciful feeling, and the nonsense phrases such as "The stars are made of lemon juice" create a happy, whimsical mood. Likewise, in *The Scroobious Pip,* the pastel colors and iridescent lines and colors suggest fanciful animals rather than dangerous ones. Even the settings such as the distant "Jellybolee" and the animal noises such as "Chippetty flip!" and "Flippetty chip!" reinforce this light, humorous mood. Marcia Brown's use of delicate lines and soft pastels in her illustrations for *Cinderella* bring a shimmering radiance to the fairy-tale quality of the pictures. Finally, ask students to identify some of the language that corresponds with these light, fanciful moods. Ask them to draw some conclusions about how illustrators and authors can create light, humorous, and fanciful moods for their settings. Ask, "Are these moods appropriate for the texts? Why or why not?"

For the next series, ask the students to respond emotionally to the illustrations and texts in the books that create nostalgia and changing moods from cold and isolation to warmth and togetherness: *In Coal Country, Owl Moon,* and *The Polar Express.* As they interact with each of the books ask them to write down their feelings. Ask "What moods did you feel? What techniques did the illustrators and authors use to develop those feelings?" For example, students might say that when reading or listening to *In Coal Country* the illustrations made them feel as if they were looking through a landscape filtered through coal dust. This is a nostalgic setting, however, because the children seem happy and they love Papa who works in the coal mine. In *Owl Moon,* they might feel the cold and silence of the winter night that is heightened by the shades of white snow and dark green and black trees. They also might respond to the illustrator's use of light that focuses attention on the two people as they search for and finally see the owl that is the happy culmination for their trip together into the woods. With *The Polar Express* most students feel both the coldness of the forest and the warmth and nostalgia created by the light focusing on the boy, the warm light emerging from the train windows, the steam from the hot cocoa, and the light flowing from the windows at the North Pole. As in the first example, ask the students to identify words that highlight the moods and summarize how authors and illustrators created these moods. You might ask the students to consider why *The Polar Express* has been on *The New York Times* best seller list of books for the past few Christmas seasons. "How could this information support the belief that many adults obtain a nostalgic feeling from this book?"

Finally, ask students to respond to the moods in *Hiroshima No Pika* and *The Highwayman.* Both of these books create terrifying, ghostly moods and settings. For example the illustrator in *Hiroshima No Pika* (The Flash of Hiroshima) uses expressionistic paintings, color, and shape to reinforce the emotional effect of horrific devastation, as a mother and child experience the aftereffects of the atomic bomb. Swirling red flames pass over the forms of fleeing people and animals. Black clouds cover the forms of huddling masses and destroyed buildings. In *The Highwayman,* stark black lines create ghostly, terrifying subjects and suggest the sinister and disastrous consequences in the tale. After students have had an opportunity to respond emotionally to these two books, ask them to summarize the techniques used by the authors and illustrators to develop these emotions and moods. Also ask them to compare the different moods created by the three sets of books.

Next, divide the class into smaller groups and allow each group to select one of the sets of books. Ask the students to identify music that they think will fit the moods created by the settings. Have them prepare dramatic readings of the books accompanied by their music choices, and share the readings and the music with the class.

Through their creative writings, encourage students to use their knowledge of how authors use settings to create moods. Allow students to create short mood pieces that reflect a specific feeling. They also can illustrate their writing to reinforce the mood.

LESSON TWO: Developing Appreciation for Settings That Develop Antagonists
For these lessons refer to the activities shown for the person-against-nature conflict in Chapter 5.

LESSON THREE: Developing Appreciation for Settings That Create Geographical and Historical Backgrounds: Modern Fantasy

OBJECTIVES

To create detailed maps of the geographical setting for an imaginary world.

To contrast safe and perilous geographical settings within one book.

To develop written descriptions of that world that include information about the geography, the history, the culture, and the people.

CORE BOOK: J. R. R. Tolkien's *The Hobbit* (Modern Fantasy, Touchstone). (Chapter 11 also contains a core lesson on this book emphasizing the mythological connections in Tolkien's work. That lesson helps students understand the bridge between mythology and high fantasy.) A useful, though nonessential, reference is Manguel and Guadalupi's *The Dictionary of Imaginary Places* (1980).

PROCEDURES: Introduce this lesson by explaining to students that several genres of literature develop believable settings through detailed geographical and historical backgrounds. For example, if modern fantasy is set in a fantasy world the author must make readers suspend their disbelief by carefully describing the setting, providing historical background for the world, and developing cultural information that makes readers believe that if they were only living in the right time and the right place they would be able to visit this imaginary world. The only way that imaginary worlds can be verified is through these detailed descriptions that cause readers to believe in the possibilities. Authors of both historical fiction and biography have quite different requirements as they create settings that are accurate for the time periods. The actions of the characters and the conflict in the story can be influenced by the time period and the geographical location, and unless authors describe the settings carefully, readers probably will not comprehend unfamiliar historical periods or the stories that unfold in them. In addition, the verification of geographical and historical backgrounds in historical fiction and biography requires evaluation using various nonfictional sources. (Lesson Four emphasizes the geographical and historical backgrounds in biography.)

The detailed settings in *The Hobbit* lend themselves to numerous responses to setting. For example, students can draw a map of Bilbo's journey as he leaves the safety of his home, crosses the Misty Mountains, proceeds through Mirkwood, and finally reaches The Lonely Mountain, home of the terrible Smaug. As part of this activity they should identify quotes from the book that support their drawings on the map.

Another activity focuses on the contrasts between safe and perilous settings within the book. Students can respond to these settings through drawings and descriptions of their feelings as the settings change from the safety of Bilbo's house in a carefully controlled landscape to the increasingly strange, eerie and frightening settings as the quest approaches The Lonely Mountain. For example, by Chapter 4, the setting incudes deceptive paths that lead nowhere or to dangerous places. A seemingly safe cave is the entrance to the wicked goblins' lair; the Great River of Wilderland induces forgetfulness; Mirkwood contains cannibalistic spiders; and The Lonely Mountain is the home of the fearsome dragon, Smaug. When these settings were discussed with a group of middle school students, the students concluded that the settings serve two purposes. They prepare the readers for the unexpected, like the sudden introduction of stone-giants who added to the dramatic effect of the thunderstorm and provide a reason for seeking the cave. The settings also show the increasing danger of the quest as Bilbo enters the underworld and eventually finds the ring that changes his destiny. The students decided that these settings and experiences were necessary to change Bilbo Baggins from a shy hobbit to an unlikely hero with legendary characteristics.

Another response to these detailed settings can be motivated by *The Dictionary of Imaginary Places*. The text of this book includes detailed maps of numerous fantasy kingdoms and encyclopedic descriptions of the lands. The information for the maps and the written entries were obtained from the careful reading of numerous fantasies. For example, the entry for Middle Earth, the land of Bilbo's quest, begins: "Middle-Earth lies on the eastern side of the Belegaer, the great sea which separates it from Aman in the north-west of the known world. The irregular coastline runs north-west to east for thousands of miles, from the bleak snowy wastes around Forochel to the great Bay of Belfalas in the south" (p. 240). The information collected from *The Hobbit* and *The Lord of the Rings* includes descriptions of geography, history, culture, and inhabitants. If *The Dictionary of Imaginary Places* is not available, any geography text or encyclopedia could be used as a model.

After reading numerous fantasies, students in one middle school class developed their own "Dictionary of Imaginary Places." The extended book list following these core lessons includes many books that are excellent for this purpose. The only requirement for the fantasy is a carefully detailed and developed setting.

LESSON FOUR: Developing Appreciation for Settings That Feature Geographic and Historical Backgrounds: Biography

OBJECTIVES

To evaluate and develop an appreciation for settings that develop accurate geographic and historical backgrounds.

To draw a time line of Franklin Delano Roosevelt's life.

To identify specific locations on maps.

To research the accuracy of specific historical happenings detailed in a biography. (Chapter 14 contains detailed lessons on authenticating historical fiction and biography.)

CORE BOOK: Russell Freedman's *Franklin Delano Roosevelt*.

PROCEDURES: Review the information presented in the previous lesson. Make sure that students understand that biographical authors must authenticate the settings in their books. Because these are actual people, who lived during real times and accomplished specific deeds, the settings must reflect these historical backgrounds.

Introduce the time period for Franklin Delano Roosevelt, 1882–1945, and the historical significance of his life as president during the Depression and World War II. Ask the students, "Why is it necessary that the setting for this book include historically accurate information? What might happen if the setting is not accurate? What are some ways that we can authenticate the accuracy of the historical setting?"

Students frequently suggest that a biography usually contains numerous dates and occurrences that can be verified through library research. Students also might suggest drawing a time line that includes specific dates and events to help them identify the important historical happenings in a person's life.

Ask the students to look briefly at the text and photographs in *Franklin Delano Roosevelt*. Ask, "Do you notice dates, happenings, and locations that can be verified? Do you think this book would be an easy book to verify? Why or why not?" Make sure the students understand that the historical background for this book covers two of the most dynamic occurrences in American life: The Depression and World War II. They also should understand that information about these time periods and Roosevelt's actions during those periods is found in numerous nonfictional sources.

As students read this book have them, individually or in groups, develop time lines of the most important occurrences in Roosevelt's life. Some teachers have each group draw time lines from the whole book, other teachers ask students to draw time lines for specific chapters. The time line in Figure 7.4 was drawn by a group of seventh-grade students.

After the students draw the time lines, have them share these important historical happenings with the class. Ask them to state why they chose certain times and occurrences. Next, ask them to verify the accuracy of these dates and occurrences through library research. They may use sources such as history books, other biographies about Roosevelt, and newspaper and magazine stories from the time periods. They also might find it valuable to interview people who lived during this time period. Have a map of the world available so that students can locate the important geographical settings in the book.

After students have completed this analysis of the historical setting, ask them to evaluate Russell Freedman's ability to create an accurate biography that includes authentic historical and geographical settings. Ask, "Is this a well-written and carefully researched biography about Roosevelt? Why or why not?"

LESSON FIVE: Developing Appreciation for Settings That Have Symbolic Interpretations

OBJECTIVES

To appreciate and understand that settings can have symbolic purposes that underscore the events in the story.

To show that symbolic settings in literature frequently accentuate plot or character development.

To compare and contrast the symbolic settings in folktales and in realistic fiction.

To create a symbolic setting that would enhance plot or character development.

CORE BOOKS: Frances Hodgson Burnett's *The Secret Garden* (Realistic Fiction, Touchstone), a collection of folktales in which great forests and fantasy kingdoms create symbolic kingdoms where magical occurrences take place. Use Barbara Rogasky's retelling of the Brothers Grimm's *The Water of Life* (Folktale) for comparison.

PROCEDURES: Introduce symbolic settings by reviewing symbolic settings in folktales (see the lesson on symbolic settings for middle elementary grades). Ask the students to speculate about why tellers of folktales placed their stories in settings in which magical occurrences seem

FIGURE 7.4 Time line of Franklin D. Roosevelt's life.

1882	Growing up	1896+	1900+	1913+	1933+	1941+	1945
Born: Hyde Park, New York	Spent time with adults, traveled to Europe 8 times	Groton Boarding School: Learned about social responsibility	Harvard University: Major in history and government, minor in English and public speaking	Assistant Secretary of Navy	President of the United States:	W.W.II: Signs declaration of war with Japan after Pearl Harbor	Died: Warm Springs, Georgia
	Hobbies: photography and stamps	Manager of baseball team	Editor of Harvard Crimson	Victim of polio	Fireside Chats	War with Germany	
	Sports: tennis and boating		Columbia Law School	Governor of New York during stock market crash and Depression	New Deal CCC WPA	Meeting of the Big Three: Stalin, Churchill, and Roosevelt	
	Summers at Campobello		Married Eleanor Roosevelt		Social Security		

possible and where heroes and heroines can overcome overwhelming odds. After the students have discussed the reasons for symbolic settings in folktales, ask them to consider if these types of settings also would be important in realistic fiction. Ask, "When might authors want to place their characters in such a setting? What might be the consequences if a realistic character is placed in a setting that stimulates overcoming overwhelming odds? Remember that the authors of realistic books cannot use magic to help their characters overcome problems. What types of modern settings might help real characters overcome their problems? Try to describe a modern setting that you think would help you overcome a problem."

Introduce *The Secret Garden*. Ask the students, "What do you believe is the importance of the title? Why do you believe an author of a realistic book would develop such a setting?" Prepare the students for reading this book by telling them that they should pay attention to the characteristics of the people and the changing settings developed in the book. Ask them to note what happens to the people when they interact with the secret garden.

The chart in Figure 7.5 can be used to focus discussion for this lesson and to develop comparisons between the importance of symbolic settings in folktales and some realistic stories.

After students have completed this discussion and comparison of symbolic settings, ask them to think of a contemporary setting that would help a real person overcome a problem. Encourage them to write a story in which they describe this setting, the problem it might

FIGURE 7.5 Comparing symbolic settings.

	The Water of Life	**The Secret Garden**
Describe the changing settings.	Castle filled with sadness. Great forest. Deep ravine. Enchanted castle.	Dreary cold mansion. Garden that needs nurturing. Garden full of beauty.
What is the problem of overwhelming odds that must be overcome?	King is dying of terrible sickness. Must find Water of Life.	Father grieved after death of his wife. Son is ill. Father and son are emotionally estranged. Lonely and unhappy girl.
Why do characters go into the setting?	Quest for the Water of Life. Only youngest is pure of heart.	Need for secret place. Need for something of their own.
Is there any being within the setting that helps them?	Dwarf.	Robin seems to show way into the garden.
What, if any, are the objects that symbolize power and change?	Sword. Miraculous loaf of bread.	Key to garden. Garden door.
What happens to the characters as result of their interactions with the setting?	Father, King, is saved. Youngest Prince and father are reunited. Prince gains kingdom.	Health restored to the boy. Happiness to girl. Father and son reunited.

overcome, and the changes in the characters as a result of their interactions with the settings. Students can get ideas by looking at pictures of settings such as beautiful gardens, majestic mountains, forests, and islands.

LESSON SIX: Webbing the Setting for *Sir Gawain and the Loathly Lady*

OBJECTIVES

To identify the setting for a legend.

To develop a web of the setting that provides details from that setting.

To discuss the purposes of the setting after developing the web.

CORE BOOK: Selina Hastings' *Sir Gawain and the Loathly Lady.*

PROCEDURES: Develop a web with the word *setting* placed in the center. On the spokes of the web place the important settings identified by the students. For example, a group of middle school students identified Legendary Setting, King Arthur's Court, and Inglewood. Next, ask the students to place details from the text and the illustrations on the web. (The web in Figure 7.6 was developed by the middle school students.)

FIGURE 7.6 Webbing setting for *Sir Gawain and the Loathly Lady.*

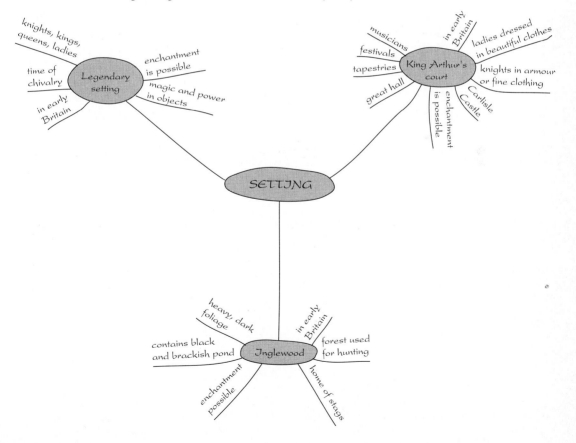

After the web is complete, ask the students to consider the purpose for the setting in *Sir Gawain and the Loathly Lady.* This group of students decided that they could identify mood, historical and geographical background, and symbolism as reflected in the enchantment, chivalry, and magical objects.

Extended Books for Upper Elementary and Middle School Students

The settings in these books include many works that can be read, discussed, and enjoyed to improve students' understanding of and appreciation for the different purposes for setting. Books for older students frequently include several purposes for setting. Many of the settings are also more detailed. The major purpose for setting is identified for each book. Many of the books provide excellent sources for drawing maps of imaginary worlds. Others have detailed geographic and historical backgrounds that are excellent for authenticating backgrounds. All the books can be used to create webs of the settings.

Modern Fantasy

LLOYD ALEXANDER's "Prydain Chronicles:" *The Book of Three, The Black Cauldron* (Newbery Honor), *The Castle of Llyr, Taran Wanderer,* and *The High King* (Newbery Medal, Touchstone). The carefully detailed settings create the imaginary world of Prydain.

VIRGINIA HAMILTON's *Justice and Her Brothers, Dustland,* and *The Gathering.* The setting is a futuristic land visited by people with psychic powers.

ANNETTE CURTIS KLAUSE's *The Silver Kiss.* This suspenseful novel tells the story of a contemporary girl and a vampire who seeks revenge for his mother's murder more than 300 years ago. The setting creates a suspenseful and often frightening mood.

URSULA K. LEGUIN's *A Wizard of Earthsea, Tombs of Atuan* (Newbery Honor), *The Farthest Shore,* and *Tehanu: The Last Book of Earthsea.* The author develops vivid descriptions of the imaginary Earthsea, its inhabitants, and a culture permeated with magic.

C. S. LEWIS's *The Lion, the Witch and the Wardrobe* (Touchstone). The magical kingdom of Narnia is carefully developed and detailed.

CARL SANDBURG's *Rootabaga Stories.* The settings provide humorous moods and imaginary backgrounds.

Realistic Fiction

ROBBIE BRANSCUM's *The Adventures of Johnny May.* The mood is one of mystery and tension as a girl tries to solve a mystery that will prove a friend innocent and relieve Johnny May's conscience.

BETSY BYARS's *The Cybil War.* The setting develops a humorous mood as a boy experiences a crush on a girl. The humor develops when the advances are intentionally misinterpreted by the boy's best friend.

VIRGINIA HAMILTON's *The House of Dies Drear* (Black). The mood is one of suspense in a tale about a house on the Underground Railroad.

JANET TAYLOR LISLE's *Afternoon of the Elves* (Newbery Honor). The symbolic settings include a dilapidated house and a miniature village that one character maintains was built by elves. Working together in the garden village helps two girls understand each other. (Compare with *The Secret Garden.*)

KATHERINE PATERSON's *Bridge to Terabithia* (Newbery Medal). A secret kingdom in the woods symbolizes the "other world" shared by two young people who do not conform to the values of rural Virginia. (Compare with *The Secret Garden.*)

Historical Fiction

Leon Garfield's *The December Rose*. The setting provides a mysterious mood and the historical background for a story set in Victorian London.

Janet Hickman's *Zoar Blue*. The setting provides the historical background for a story set in the Civil War.

Harold Keith's *Rifles for Watie* (Newbery Medal). The setting provides the historical background for a story set in the Civil War which also involves a Cherokee raider.

Evelyn Lampman's *White Captives*. The setting provides historical background and a Native American viewpoint in a story about two captives of the Apache.

George Ella Lyon's *Borrowed Children*. The setting provides historical background for a story set in Kentucky during the Depression.

Els Pelgrom's *The Winter When Time Was Frozen*. The setting provides historical background for a World War II story set in Holland.

Elizabeth George Speare's *The Bronze Bow* (Newbery Medal). The setting provides historical background for a story set in Roman times.

Rosemary Sutcliff's *Sun Horse, Moon Horse*. The setting provides historical background for story set in tribal Britain.

Laurence Yep's *Dragonwings* (Asian American, Newbery Honor). The setting provides historical background for a story set in 1903 California.

Biography

Sheila Black's *Sitting Bull and the Battle of the Little Bighorn* (Native American). The setting provides historical background.

Polly Schoyer Brooks' *Queen Eleanor: Independent Spirit of the Medieval World*. The setting provides historical background for a story set in the 12th century.

Jane Goodsell's *Daniel Inouye* (Japanese American). The setting provides historical background about the first Japanese-American member of Congress.

Virginia Hamilton's *Paul Robeson: The Life and Times of a Free Black Man* (Black). The setting provides historical background.

David Kherdian's *The Road from Home: The Story of an Armenian Girl* (Newbery Honor). The setting provides historical background for a story set in 1915 when an Armenian girl experiences the horrors of the Turkish persecution of Christian minorities.

Douglas Miller's *Frederick Douglass and the Fight for Freedom* (Black). The setting provides historical background for a story about the black leader who escaped slavery to become a political leader.

Judie Mills's *John F. Kennedy*. The setting provides historical background for the life of the 35th American president.

Rebecca Stefoff's *Ferdinand Magellan and the Discovery of the World Ocean*. The setting provides historical background for the voyages of the Portuguese sea captain.

Recreational Books for Upper Elementary and Middle School Students

Modern Fantasy

Joan Aiken's *The Wolves of Willoughby Chase*

Vivien Alcock's *The Stone Walkers*

Nancy Bond's *A String in the Harp*

Bill Brittain's *Dr. Dredd's Wagon of Wonders*

Alan Garner's *Elidor*

Robert Westall's *Ghost Abbey*

Realistic Fiction

GILLIAN CROSS's *On the Edge* and *Roscoe's Leap*

PAULA FOX's *The Village by the Sea*

JEAN CRAIGHEAD GEORGE's *River Rats, Inc.*

LYNN HALL's *Danza!* (Puerto Rican)

ROBERT NEWMAN's *The Case of the Baker Street Irregular* and *The Case of the Vanishing Corpse*

SCOTT O'DELL's *Black Star, Bright Dawn* (Eskimo)

ELLEN RASKIN's *The Westing Game* (Newbery Medal)

KEITH ROBERTSON's *In Search of a Sandhill Crane*

Historical Fiction

LAURENCE YEP's *The Serpent's Children* (Chinese)

Biography

LILLIE PATTERSONS' *Martin Luther King, Jr. and the Freedom Movement* (Black)

REFERENCES

DIAKIW, J. Y. (1990). Children's literature and global education: Understanding the developing world. *The Reading Teacher, 43,* pp. 296–300.

LAMME, L. L. (1990). Exploring the world of music through picture books. *The Reading Teacher, 44,* pp. 294–300.

MANGUEL, A. & GUADALUPI, G. (1980). *The dictionary of imaginary places.* Illustrated by Graham Greenfield. New York: Macmillan.

CHILDREN'S LITERATURE REFERENCES*

AARDEMA, VERNA. *The Riddle of the Drum: A Tale from Tizapán, Mexico.* Illustrated by Tony Chen. New York: Four Winds, 1979 (I: 6–10).

AFANASEV, ALEKSANDR NIKOLAEVICH. *Russian Folk Tales.* Translated by Robert Chandler. Illustrated by Ivan I. Bilibin. New York: Random, 1980 (I: all).

AIKEN, JOAN. *The Wolves of Willoughby Chase.* Illustrated by Pat Marriott. New York: Doubleday, 1963 (I: 7–10).

ALCOCK, VIVIEN. *The Stone Walkers.* New York: Delacorte, 1981 (I: 9+).

ALEXANDER, LLOYD. *The Black Cauldron.* Orlando: Holt, Rinehart & Winston, 1965 (I: 10+).

———. *The Book of Three.* Orlando: Holt, Rinehart & Winston, 1964 (I:10+).

———. *The Castle of Llyr.* Orlando: Holt, Rinehart & Winston, 1966 (I:10+).

———. *The High King.* Orlando: Holt, Rinehart & Winston, 1968 (I: 10+).

———. *Taran Wanderer.* Orlando: Holt, Rinehart & Winston, 1967 (I:10+).

ANDERSEN, HANS CHRISTIAN. *The Nightingale,* translated by Eva Le Gallienne. Illustrated by Nancy Ekholm Burkert. New York: Harper & Row, 1965 (I: all).

ARUEGO, JOSE & ARIANE DEWEY. *We Hide, You Seek.* New York: Greenwillow, 1979 (I: 2–6).

ASBJORNSEN, PETER & JORGEN MOE. *Norwegian Folktales.* Illustrated by Erik Werenskiold and Theodor Kittleson. New York: Viking, 1960 (I: all).

BAER, EDITH. *This Is the Way We Go to School: A Book About Children Around the World.* New York: Scholastic, 1990 (I: 7–10).

BARRACCA, DEBRA & SAL BARRACCA. *The Adventures of Taxi Dog.* New York: Dial, 1990 (I: 3–8).

BARRIE, JAMES. *Peter Pan.* Illustrated by Nora S. Unwin. New York: Scribner's, 1911, 1929, 1950 (I: 8–10).

BAUM, L. FRANK. *The Wizard of Oz.* Illustrated by Michael Hague. Orlando: Holt, Rinehart & Winston, 1982 (I: 8–11).

BAYLOR, BYRD. *Hawk, I'm Your Brother.* Illustrated by Peter Parnall. New York: Scribner's, 1976 (I: all).

———. *The Other Way to Listen.* Illustrated by Peter Parnall. New York: Scribner's, 1978 (I: all).

BELPRÉ, PURA. *Once in Puerto Rico.* Illustrated by Christine Price. New York: Warne, 1973 (I: 8–12).

BIERHORST, JOHN. *The Monkey's Haircut and Other Stories Told by the Maya.* Illustrated by Robert Andrew Parker. New York: Morrow, 1986 (I: 8+).

BLACK, SHEILA. *Sitting Bull and the Battle of the Little Bighorn.* Illustrated by Ed Lee. Silver Burdett, 1989 (I: 10+).

*I = Interest by age range

BOND, MICHAEL. *A Bear Called Paddington.* Illustrated by Peggy Fortnum. Boston: Houghton Mifflin, 1960 (I: 6–9).

———. *Paddington Abroad.* Illustrated by Peggy Fortnum. Boston: Houghton Mifflin, 1972 (I: 6–9).

BOND, NANCY. *A String in the Harp.* New York: Atheneum, 1976 (I: 10+).

BRANSCUM, ROBBIE. *The Adventures of Johnny May.* Illustrated by Deborah Howland. New York: Harper & Row, 1984 (I: 8+).

BRINK, CAROL RYRIE. *Caddie Woodlawn.* Illustrated by Trina Schart Hyman. New York: Macmillan, 1935, 1963, 1973 (I: 8–12).

BRITTAIN, BILL. *Dr. Dread's Wagon of Wonders.* Illustrated by Andrew Glass. New York: Harper & Row, 1987 (I: 9–12).

BROOKS, POLLY SCHOYER. *Queen Eleanor: Independent Spirit of the Medieval World.* Philadelphia: Lippincott, 1983 (I: 10+).

BROWN, MARC. *Arthur's Baby.* Boston: Little, Brown, 1987 (I: 3–7).

BROWN, MARGARET WISE. *The Runaway Bunny.* Illustrated by Clement Hurd. New York: Harper & Row, 1972 (I: 3–7).

BURNETT, FRANCES HODGSON. *The Secret Garden.* Illustrated by Tasha Tudor. Philadelphia: Lippincott, 1911, 1938, 1962 (I: 9+).

BYARS, BETSY. *The Cybil War.* Illustrated by Gail Owens. New York: Viking, 1981 (I: 9–12).

CARROLL, LEWIS. *Alice's Adventures in Wonderland.* Illustrated by John Tenniel. New York: Macmillan, 1866, Knopf, 1984 (I: 8+).

CLEARY, BEVERLY. *Ralph S. Mouse.* Illustrated by Paul O. Zelinsky. New York: Morrow, 1982 (I: 7–11).

COATSWORTH, EMERSON & DAVID COATSWORTH. *The Adventures of Nanbush: Ojibway Indian Stories.* Illustrated by Francis Kagige. New York: Atheneum, 1980 (I: all).

CONGER, DAVID. *Many Lands, Many Stories: Asian Folktales for Children.* Illustrated by Ruth Ra. Rutland, VT: Tuttle, 1987 (I: 8+).

COONEY, BARBARA. *Island Boy.* New York: Viking, 1988 (I: 3–8).

COONEY, NANCY EVANS. *The Umbrella Day.* Illustrated by Melissa Mathis. New York: Philomel, 1989 (I: 3–8).

CRANE, WALTER. *The Baby's Opera.* New York: Simon & Schuster, 190?, 1981 (I: all).

CRESSWELL, HELEN. *Bagthorpes Unlimited.* New York: Macmillan 1978 (I: 8–12).

———. *Ordinary Jack.* New York: Macmillan, 1977 (I: 8–12).

CROSS, GILLIAN. *On the Edge.* New York: Holiday, 1987 (I: 10+).

———. *Roscoe's Leap.* New York: Holiday, 1987 (I: 10+).

CROSSLEY-HOLLAND, KEVIN. *British Folk Tales.* New York: Orchard, 1987 (I: all).

———. *The Fox and the Cat: Animal Tales from Grimm.* Illustrated by Susan Varley. New York: Lothrop, Lee & Shepard, 1986 (I: 7–10).

DALGLIESH, ALICE. *The Courage of Sarah Noble.* Illustrated by Leonard Weisgard. New York: Scribner's, 1954 (I: 6–9).

DELTON, JUDY. *Angel's Mother's Wedding.* Boston: Houghton Mifflin, 1987 (I: 8–10).

DE PAOLA, TOMIE. *An Early American Christmas.* New York: Holiday, 1987 (I: 4–7).

FATIO, LOUISE. *The Happy Lion.* Illustrated by Roger Duvoisin. Englewood Cliffs, NJ: McGraw-Hill, 1954 (I: 3–7).

FLOURNOY, VALERIE. *The Patchwork Quilt.* Illustrated by Jerry Pinkney. New York: Dial, 1985 (I: 5–8).

FORD, ALICE. *John James Audubon.* Abbeville, 1988 (I: 8+).

FOWLER, SUSI GREGG. *When Summer Ends.* Illustrated by Marisabina Russo. New York: Greenwillow, 1989 (I: 4–9).

FOX, DAN. *Go In and Out the Window: An Illustrated Songbook for Young People.* New York: Metropolitan Museum of Art/Holt, 1987 (I: all).

FOX, PAULA. *The Village by the Sea.* New York: Watts, 1988 (I: 10+).

FREEDMAN, RUSSELL. *Franklin Delano Roosevelt.* New York: Clarion, 1990 (I: 10+).

FRITZ, JEAN. *Where Do You Think You're Going, Christopher Columbus?* Illustrated by Margot Tomes. New York: Putnam, 1980 (I: 7–12).

GAG, WANDA. *Millions of Cats.* New York: Coward-McCann, 1928, 1956 (I: 3–7).

GARFIELD, LEON. *The December Rose.* New York: Viking Kestrel, 1986 (I: 10+).

GARLAND, MICHAEL. *My Cousin Katie.* New York: Crowell, 1989 (I: 4–8).

GARNER, ALAN. *Elidor.* Walck, 1967 (I: 10+).

GEORGE, JEAN CRAIGHEAD. *River Rats, Inc.* New York: Dutton, 1979 (I: 10+).

GEORGE, WILLIAM T. *Box Turtle At Long Pond.* Illustrated by Lindsay Barrett George. New York: Greenwillow, 1989 (I: 3–8).

GOBLE, PAUL. *Buffalo Woman.* New York: Bradbury, 1984 (I: all).

GOODSELL, JANE. *Daniel Inouye.* New York: Crowell, 1977 (I: 7–10).

GREENFIELD, ELOISE. *Under the Sunday Tree.* Illustrated by Amos Ferguson. New York: Harper & Row, 1988 (I: all).

GRIFALCONI, ANN. *Darkness and the Butterfly.* Boston: Little, Brown, 1987 (I: 5–8).

GRIFFITH, HELEN. *Grandaddy's Place.* Illustrated by James Stevenson. New York: Greenwillow, 1987 (I: 5–8).

GRIMM, BROTHERS. *Rumpelstiltskin,* retold and illustrated by Paul O. Zelinsky. New York: Dutton, 1986 (I: all).

_____. *Snow White and the Seven Dwarfs,* translated by Randall Jarrell. Illustrated by Nancy Ekholm Burkert. New York: Farrar, Straus & Giroux, 1972 (I: all).

HALEY, GAIL E. *Jack Jouett's Ride.* New York: Viking, 1973, 1976 (I: 6–10).

HALL, LYNN. *Danza!* New York: Scribner's, 1981 (I: 10–14).

HAMILTON, VIRGINIA. *The Bells of Christmas.* Illustrated by Lambert Davis. Orlando: Harcourt Brace Jovanovich, 1989 (I: 8+).

_____. *Cousins.* New York: Putnam, 1990 (I: 10+).

_____. *Dustland.* New York: Greenwillow, 1980 (I: 10+).

_____. *The Gathering.* New York: Greenwillow, 1981 (I: 10+).

_____. *The House of Dies Drear.* Illustrated by Eros Keith. New York: Macmillan, 1968 (I: 11+).

_____. *Justice and Her Brothers.* New York: Greenwillow, 1978 (I: 10+).

_____. *Paul Robeson: The Life and Times of a Free Black Man.* New York: Harper & Row, 1974 (I: 10+).

HANCOCK, SIBYL. *Old Blue.* Illustrated by Erick Ingraham. New York: Putnam, 1980 (I: 7–9).

HASTINGS, SELINA. *Sir Gawain and the Loathly Lady.* Illustrated by Juan Wijngaard. New York: Lothrop, Lee & Shepard, 1985 (I: 10+).

HAVILAND, VIRGINIA. *North American Legends.* Illustrated by Ann Stugnell. New York: Philomel, 1979 (I: all).

HENDERSHOT, JUDITH. *In Coal Country.* Illustrated by Thomas B. Allen. New York: Knopf, 1987 (I: all).

HEST, AMY. *The Crack-of-Dawn Walkers.* Illustrated by Amy Schwartz. New York: Macmillan, 1984 (I: 5–9).

HICKMAN, JANET. *Zoar Blue.* New York: Macmillan, 1978 (I: 9–14).

HUTCHINS, PAT. *The Wind Blew.* London: Bodley Head, 1974 (I: 3–8).

ISELE, ELIZABETH, retold by. *The Frog Princess.* Illustrated by Michael Hague. New York: Crowell, 1984 (I: 6–10).

JAGENDORF, M. A. & R. S. BOGGS. *The King of the Mountains: A Treasury of Latin American Folk Stories.* Toronto: Copp, Clark, 1960 (I: all).

JEFFERS, SUSAN. *Three Jovial Huntsmen.* New York: Bradbury, 1973 (I: 4–8).

JOHNSON, A. E. *Perrault's Complete Fairy Tales.* Illustrated by W. Heath Robinson. New York: Dodd, Mead, 1961 (I: 8+).

KEATS, EZRA JACK. *Goggles!* New York: Macmillan, 1969 (I: 4–8).

_____. *Pet Show!* New York: Macmillan, 1972 (I: 4–8).

_____. *Regards to the Man in the Moon.* New York: Four Winds, 1981 (I: 4–8).

_____. *The Trip.* New York: Greenwillow, 1978 (I: 4–8).

KELLER, HOLLY. *Geraldine's Big Snow.* New York: Greenwillow, 1988 (I: 4–8).

KEITH, HAROLD. *Rifles for Watie.* New York: Crowell, 1957 (I: 12+).

KHALSA, DAYAL. *I Want a Dog.* Clarkson, 1987 (I: 4–8).

KHERDIAN, DAVID. *The Road from Home: The Story of an Armenian Girl.* New York: Greenwillow, 1979 (I: 12+).

KINSEY-WARNOCK, NATALIE. *The Canada Geese Quilt.* Illustrated by Leslie W. Bowman. New York: Dutton, 1989 (I: 8+).

KIPLING, RUDYARD. *The Jungle Book.* New York: Doubleday, 1894, 1964 (I: 8–12).

KLAUSE, ANNETTE CURTIS. *The Silver Kiss.* New York: Delacorte, 1990 (I: 11+).

LAMPMAN, EVELYN SIBLEY. *White Captives.* New York: Atheneum, 1975 (I: 11+)

LANG, ANDREW, edited by. *The Blue Fairy Book.* Illustrated by H. J. Ford and G. P. Hood. New York: Dover, 1965 (I: 8+).

_____. *The Red Fairy Book.* Illustrated by Reisie Lonette. New York: Random, 1960 (I: 8+).

LAWSON, ROBERT. *Rabbit Hill.* New York: Viking, 1944 (I: 7–11).

LEE, BETSY. *Charles Eastman, The Story of an American Indian.* New York: Dillon, 1979 (I: 8–12).

LEGUIN, URSULA K. *The Farthest Shore.* Illustrated by Gail Garraty. New York: Atheneum, 1972 (I: 10+).

_____. *Tehanu: The Last Book of Earthsea.* New York: Atheneum, 1990 (I: 10+)

_____. *Tombs of Atuan.* Illustrated by Gail Garraty. New York: Atheneum, 1971, 1980 (I: 10+).

_____. *A Wizard of Earthsea.* Illustrated by Ruth Robbins. New York: Parnasus, 1968 (I: 10+).

LESTER, JULIUS. *The Knee-High Man and Other Tales.* Illustrated by Ralph Pinto. New York: Dial, 1972 (I: all).

LEWIS, C. S. *The Lion, the Witch and the Wardrobe.* Illustrated by Pauline Baynes. New York: Macmillan, 1950 (I: 9+).

LEWIS, NAOMI, edited by. *The Twelve Dancing Princesses and Other Tales from Grimm*. Illustrated by Lidia Postma. New York: Dial, 1985 (I: all).

LINDGREN, BARBRO. *The Wild Baby Goes to Sea*. Illustrated by Eva Eriksson. New York: Greenwillow, 1981 (I: 2–7).

LISLE, JANET TAYLOR. *Afternoon of the Elves*. New York: Watts, 1989 (I: 10 +).

LIYI, HE. *The Spring of Butterflies and Other Chinese Folktales*. New York: Lothrop, Lee & Shepard, 1985 (I: 8 +).

LYON, GEORGE ELLA. *Borrowed Children*. New York: Watts, 1988 (I: 10 +).

MAHY, MARGARET. *17 Kings and 42 Elephants*. Illustrated by Patricia MacCarthy. New York: Dial, 1987 (I: all).

MARK, JAN. *Fun*. Illustrated by Michael Foreman. New York: Viking Kestrel, 1988 (I: 4–8).

MARTIN, RAFE. *Will's Mammoth*. Illustrated by Ste-phen Gammell, New York: Putnam, 1989 (I: 3–8).

MARUKI, TOSHI. *Hiroshima No Pika*. New York: Lothrop, Lee & Shepard, 1980 (I: all).

MAYER, MERCER. *A Boy, A Dog and a Frog*. New York: Dial, 1967 (I: 5–9).

_____. *A Boy, A Dog, A Frog, and A Friend*. New York: Dial, 1971 (I: 5–9).

_____. *Frog Goes to Dinner*. New York: Dial, 1974 (I: 5–9).

_____. *Frog, Where Are You?* New York: Dial, 1969 (I: 5–9).

_____. *One Frog Too Many*. New York: Dial, 1975 (I: 5–9).

MAXNER, JOYCE. *Nicholas Cricket*. Illustrated by William Joyce. New York: Harper & Row, 1989 (I: all).

McCLOSKEY, ROBERT. *Blueberries for Sal*. New York: Viking, 1948 (I: 4–8).

_____. *Make Way for Ducklings*. New York: Viking, 1941, 1969 (I: 4–8).

_____. *One Morning in Maine*. New York: Viking, 1952 (I: 4–8).

_____. *Time of Wonder*. New York: Viking, 1957 (I: 5–8).

McCULLY, EMILY ARNOLD. *School*. New York: Harper & Row, 1987 (I: 3–8).

McPHAIL, DAVID. *The Dream Child*. New York: Dutton, 1985 (I: 3–7).

MERRIAM, EVE. *Halloween ABC*. Illustrated by Lane Smith. New York: Macmillan, 1987 (I: all).

METAYER, MAURICE. *Tales from the Igloo*. Illustrated by Agnes Nanogak. Edmonton: Hurtig, 1972 (I: all).

MILLER, DOUGLAS. *Frederick Douglass and the Fight for Freedom*. New York: Facts on File, 1988 (I: 10 +).

MILLS, JUDIE. *John F. Kennedy*. New York: Watts, 1988 (I: 12 +).

MOORE, CLEMENT. *The Night Before Christmas*. Illustrated by Tomie De Paola. New York: Holiday, 1980 (I: all).

NASH, OGDEN. *Edward Lear's the Scroobious Pip*. Illustrated by Nancy Ekholm Burkert. New York: Harper & Row, 1968 (I: all).

NEWMAN, ROBERT. *The Case of the Baker Street Irregular*. New York: Atheneum, 1978 (I: 10 +).

_____. *The Case of the Vanishing Corpse*. New York: Atheneum, 1980 (I: 10 +).

NORTON, MARY. *The Borrowers Afloat*. Orlando: Harcourt Brace Jovanovich, 1961 (I: 7–11).

NOYES, ALFRED. *The Highwayman*. Illustrated by Charles Keeping. New York: Oxford, 1983 (I: 8 +).

O'DELL, SCOTT. *Black Star, Bright Dawn*. Boston: Houghton Mifflin, 1988 (I: 8 +).

ONASSIS, JACQUELINE, edited by. *The Firebird and Other Russian Fairy Tales*. Illustrated by Boris Zvorykin. New York: Viking, 1978 (I: all).

PATERSON, KATHERINE. *Bridge to Terabithia*. Illustrated by Donna Diamond. New York: Crowell, 1977 (I: 10 +).

PATTERSON, LILLIE. *Martin Luther King, Jr. and the Freedom Movement*. New York: Facts on File, 1989 (I: 10 +).

PELGROM, ELS. *The Winter When Time Was Frozen*. Rudnik, 1980 (I: 8–12).

PERRAULT, CHARLES. *Cinderella*. Illustrated by Marcia Brown. New York: Scribner's, 1954 (I: 5–8).

PETERS, LISA WESTBERG. *Good Morning, River!* New York: Arcade, 1990 (I: 5–8).

POLACCO, PATRICIA. *Meteor!* New York: Dodd, Mead, 1987 (I: 6–10).

PROVENSEN, ALICE & MARTIN PROVENSEN. *The Year At Maple Hill Farm*. New York: Atheneum, 1978 (I: 4–9).

RASKIN, ELLEN. *The Westing Game*. New York: Dutton, 1978 (I: 10 +).

ROBERTSON, KEITH. *In Search of a Sandhill Crane*. Illustrated by Richard Cuffari. New York: Viking, 1973 (I: 10 +).

ROGASKY, BARBARA, retold by. *The Water of Life*. Illustrated by Trina Schart Hyman. New York: Holiday, 1986 (I: all).

RYDER, JOANNE. *White Bear, Ice Bear*. Illustrated by Michael Rothman. New York: Morrow, 1989 (I: 4–9).

RYLANT, CYNTHIA. *When I Was Young in the Mountains*. Illustrated by Diane Good. New York: Dutton, 1982 (I: all).

SANDBURG, CARL. *Rootabaga Stories*. Illustrated by Micheal Hague. Orlando: Harcourt Brace Jovanovich, 1922, 1988 (I: 8–11).

SCHEER, JULIAN. *Rain Makes Applesauce.* Illustrated by Marvin Bileck. New York: Holiday, 1964 (I: 3–8).

SCHWARTZ, AMY. *Annabelle Swift, Kindergartner.* New York: Orchard, 1988 (I: 5–9).

SELSAM, MILLICENT & JOYCE HUNT. *Keep Looking!* Illustrated by Normand Chartier, New York: Macmillan, 1989 (I: 4–9).

SENDAK, MAURICE. *Where the Wild Things Are.* New York: Harper & Row, 1963 (I: 4–8).

SEUSS, DR. *And to Think That I Saw It on Mulberry Street.* New York: Vanguard, 1937 (I: 3–9).

SPEARE, ELIZABETH GEORGE. *The Bronze Bow.* Boston: Houghton Mifflin, 1961 (I: 10+).

STEFOFF, REBECCA. *Ferdinand Magellan and the Discovery of the World Ocean.* New York: Chelsea, 1990 (I: 12+).

SUTCLIFF, ROSEMARY. *Sun Horse, Moon Horse.* Illustrated by Shirley Felts. New York: Dutton, 1978 (I: 10+).

TOLKIEN, J. R. R. *The Hobbit.* Boston: Houghton Mifflin, 1938 (I: 9–12).

VAN ALLSBURG, CHRIS. *The Garden of Abdul Gasazi.* Boston: Houghton Mifflin, 1979 (I: 5–8).

_____. *The Polar Express.* Boston: Houghton Mifflin, 1985 (I: all).

WALKER, BARBARA K. *The Dancing Palm Tree And Other Nigerian Folktales.* Texas Tech University, 1990 (I: 8+).

WARD, LYND. *The Biggest Bear.* Boston: Houghton Mifflin, 1952 (I: 5–8).

WESTALL, ROBERT. *Ghost Abbey.* New York: Scholastic, 1989 (I: 10+).

WHITE, E. B. *Charlotte's Web.* Illustrated by Garth Williams. New York: Harper & Row, 1952 (I: 7–11).

WILDER, LAURA INGALLS. *The Long Winter.* Illustrated by Garth Williams. New York: Harper & Row, 1940, 1953 (I: 8–12).

WOOD, AUDREY. *King Bidgood's in the Bathtub.* Illustrated by Don Wood. Orlando: Harcourt Brace Jovanovich, 1988 (I: 6–9).

YEP, LAURENCE. *Dragonwings.* New York: Harper & Row, 1975 (I: 10+).

_____. *The Serpent's Children.* New York: Harper & Row, 1979 (I: 10+).

YOLEN, JANE. *Owl Moon.* Illustrated by John Schoenherr. New York: Philomel, 1987 (I: all).

ZEMACH, MARGOT. *It Could Always Be Worse.* New York: Farrar, Straus & Giroux, 1977 (I: 5–9).

ZOLOTOW, CHARLOTTE. *Mr. Rabbit and the Lovely Present.* Illustrated by Maurice Sendak. New York: Harper & Row, 1962 (I: 3–8).

CHAPTER 8

THEME

DEVELOPING UNDERSTANDING AND APPRECIATION OF THEME
  Core Books and Sample Lessons for Lower Elementary Students
  Extended Books for Lower Elementary Students
  Recreational Books for Lower Elementary Students
  Core Books and Sample Lessons for Middle Elementary Students
  Extended Books for Middle Elementary Students
  Recreational Books for Middle Elementary Students
  Core Books and Sample Lessons for Upper Elementary and Middle School Students
  Extended Books for Upper Elementary and Middle School Students
  Recreational Books for Upper Elementary and Middle School Students

In the previous chapters we asked questions such as "What happened next in the story?" (plot); "Why did something occur?" (conflict); "Who were the people in the story and what were they like?" (characterization); and "Where and when did the story take place?" (setting). In this chapter we will explore answers to the question, "What does the story mean?" (theme).

DEVELOPING UNDERSTANDING AND APPRECIATION OF THEME

The theme of a book is not the plot or a summary of the story. Instead, the theme is the underlying idea that ties the plot, conflict, characters, and setting together into a meaningful whole. Consequently, the theme or themes should apply to all the major characters and events in the story. The theme is also a statement that the author wants to convey about life or society. This statement goes beyond topics such as "friendship" or "love." Instead, the theme of a story presents the author's viewpoint about a topic, such as: "Friendship helps people through times of adversity."

Lukens (1989) defines theme as "a significant truth expressed in appropriate elements and memorable language. The significant truth is an element that is essential to turn a simple narrative into literature. This truth goes beyond the story and comments on human beings. This discovery holds the story together so that long after details of plot are forgotten, the theme remains" (p. 111). Lukens maintains that this unification and illumination gives the reader pleasure. She states, "The reader gains one pleasure from the discovery of the simplest of truths, and another from the discovery that truth is not simple" (p. 111). This idea that theme is not simple provides the focus for exciting discussions as students bring their own understandings and experiences into the discovery of a theme that is meaningful to them.

Perrine (1983) provides several useful guidelines for teachers who are helping students understand theme. Perrine states, "There is no prescribed method for discovering theme. Sometimes we can best get at it by asking in what way the main character has changed in the course of the story and what, if anything, the character has learned before its end. Sometimes the best approach is to explore the nature of the central conflict and its outcome. Sometimes the title will provide an important clue" (p. 110). Then Perrine provides the following principles that relate to theme:

1. Theme must be expressible as a statement with a subject and a predicate.
2. Theme must be stated as a generalization about life. In stating theme we do not use the names of the characters or refer to precise places or events.
3. We must be careful not to make the generalization larger than is justified by the story.
4. Theme is the central and unifying concept of a story. Therefore, it must account for all the major details of the story, must not be contradicted by any detail of the story, and must not rely upon facts not actually stated or clearly implied by the story.
5. There is no one way of stating the theme of a story.
6. One should avoid any statement that reduces the theme to a familiar saying or trite expression.

Perrine shows that the concept of theme is more complex and abstract than the concept of main idea. Teachers frequently indicate that they believe theme is too difficult for their students to understand. However, research and my experience with students indicate that students can indeed identify theme, especially if they are guided through the learning experience. For example, Lehr (1988) found that kindergarten, second-, and fourth-grade students could identify theme. She states: "Ability to identify theme appears to develop early; kindergarten children were able to identify thematically matched books for 80 percent of the realistic books and 35 percent of the folktales. Children's ability to generate thematic statements correlated highly with exposure to literature; those in the low-exposure group frequently gave responses that were too concrete or too vague" (p. 337).

My experience in guiding kindergarten through middle school students in the identification of theme shows that students can identify theme, provide evidence for the theme they have identified, and choose and compare books with similar themes if the lessons allow them to use previous knowledge, encourage them to understand theme through simple examples, and allow them to explore the various ways that authors develop and reinforce themes. The procedures in the following lessons begin with simple books in which themes are clearly stated and easily understood. The themes in the books are also understandable to students in the particular age group. For example, young children can relate easily to the girl in the African tale *Darkness and the Butterfly.* She is afraid of the dark and must overcome her own fear. The theme lessons also use many illustrated books because illustrations often help students reflect on the theme, and the shorter format of a picture book allows students to study all aspects of the story. Research indicates that picture books also improve understandings and discussions with older children. For example, Weston (1990) found that the discussions of fourth graders were more fully developed when background information was presented through picture books that had similar themes.

Core Books and Sample Lessons
for Lower Elementary Students

LESSON ONE: Introduction to Theme Through Simple Fables

OBJECTIVES

    To understand that a fable includes a message that the teller believes should make a
      difference in our lives.

    To write an original fable.

CORE BOOK: Arnold Lobel's *Fables* (Caldecott Medal).

PROCEDURES: To introduce the concept of theme share several fables such as those found
in *Fables*. Although *moral* and *theme* are not exactly alike, students can readily identify the
author's message in a fable. Consequently, fables provide an easy introduction to theme and
provide a bridge between the moral in the fable and the theme in longer, more complex
literature. Perrine (1983) distinguishes between *moral* and *theme* when he maintains that
sometimes the words are interchangeable, but *moral* is usually too narrow a concept to
illuminate the central insights for most pieces of literature.

    Lobel's tales are not authentic fables because they were created by Lobel, but they do,
however, follow the fable format. Each fable has a moral that is identified at the close of
the fable. After reading each fable, encourage the students to discuss the meaning of the
moral. Help them understand that the moral is an important message that the author is
trying to give the readers. Point out that *theme* is another name for this important
message. Through discussions, help the students understand that the theme is a message
that the author believes should make a difference in our lives. Ask them, "What happened
in each fable to make you believe that _____ is the important message that
should make a difference in our lives?"

    At this point, many teachers like to bring writing into the lesson. Encourage the students
to identify the characteristics of a fable: It is a short piece of fiction, it usually has animal
characters who act like people, and it has a lesson that can be learned from the story. Allow
students to write and share their own fables that develop a moral.

LESSON TWO: Expanding an Understanding of Theme into Folktales

OBJECTIVES

    To identify the themes in folktales.

    To understand the different ways that authors can develop themes.

CORE BOOKS: Illustrated folktales with easily recognizable themes such as Trina Schart
Hyman's retelling of Grimm's *Little Red Riding Hood* (Caldecott Honor).

PROCEDURES: After discussing the fables, the teacher should read a simple folktale such as
Little Red Riding Hood in which the themes are easily recognizable. Ask the students, "What
do you believe is the important message in *Little Red Riding Hood?*" After they have listed one
or two messages such as "It is important to mind your mother," or "Do not talk to strangers,"
ask them to think about how they know that these statements were important messages in the
story. Through discussions, encourage students to identify the following ways that authors can
develop themes in books:

1. The illustrations can support the theme.
2. The character's actions can reveal the theme.

3. The character's thoughts can reveal the theme.

4. The way the story ends, especially who and what is rewarded or punished, can reveal the theme.

5. The author can tell the reader.

Ask the students to think of other folktales in which they can use this list to identify theme. Ask them to think about experiences in their own lives: "How many of these ways might also be true in real life?"

LESSON THREE: Developing Understanding of Theme in a Realistic Picture Story Book

OBJECTIVE

To develop an understanding of theme by showing how an author develops theme, by identifying several appropriate themes within a story, and by providing proof that those themes are developed within the story.

CORE BOOK: Ann Grifalconi's *Darkness and the Butterfly* (Picture Story Book, African)

PROCEDURES: This lesson originally was taught to second-grade students because the themes are important to young children. The lesson also has been used to introduce theme to older students who have had less exposure to literature. To begin the lesson, make sure that the students understand the meaning of theme and have shown that they understand several ways that an author can develop theme. Then read Grifalconi's *Darkness and the Butterfly*. After the first reading, ask the students to identify what they believe are the themes developed by the author. Most students will identify the following two themes: "It is all right to have fears. We all might have fears that cause us problems." "But, we can and must overcome our fears." Write each of these themes on the chalkboard or on a chart. Ask the students to consider if these themes are also important in their lives. "Have they ever been afraid? How did they try to overcome their fear?" Teachers also can share experiences in which they were able to overcome their fears.

During the second reading of *Darkness and the Butterfly*, ask the students to identify evidence from the book that supports each of the themes. Ask, "How do we know that 'It is all right to have fears' is an important message that the author wants us to understand? How do we know that 'We can and must overcome our fears' is another important message given us by the author?" The students usually identify the following proof:

"It is all right to have fears."
1. The illustrations show the monsters that Osa thinks about at night.
2. The mother's actions show that she is understanding when she gives Osa beads to help her overcome fear.
3. The mother loves Osa even when she is afraid.
4. Osa is a normal child who does brave things in the daytime.
5. The wise woman tells Osa that she was once afraid at night.

"But, we can overcome our fears."
1. The proverb of the yellow butterfly shows that something that is very small also flies into the darkness.
2. The wise woman tells Osa, "You will find your own way."
3. The dream shows the beauty of the night when there is nothing to fear.
4. The actions of the butterfly show that it is not afraid.
5. Osa tells herself, "I can go by myself. I'm not afraid anymore."

6. The author states that Osa, the smallest of the small, "found the way to carry her own light through the darkness."

Remember that there is no one way to state theme. These themes and proofs should be written in the students' own words.

Extended Books for Lower Elementary Students

Students can read the following examples of literature in small groups or independently, identify the themes, support the themes with proof from the stories, and defend their reasons for selecting the themes and the proofs. This list includes a variety of books from different genres and reading levels. It also includes books from a variety of cultures. Any of these books can be used for a teacher-directed lesson similar to that shown for the core book.

Folktales

JAN BRETT's retelling of *Beauty and the Beast* (European). The themes "Love conquers all obstacles" and "Good wins over evil" are developed through the actions of both the female character and the beast and by what happens at the end of the story when the beast is returned to his true form after the female character shows her love. The illustrations foreshadow the ending by showing the characters before they were transformed into animals.

Modern Fantasy

HANS CHRISTIAN ANDERSEN's *The Ugly Duckling* (Animal Story). The themes "Growing up sometimes has hurtful experiences" and "Take pride in who you are" are developed through the actions of the animals as they respond to someone who is different and through the conclusion of the story that shows the ugliest being is now the most beautiful.

MARGERY WILLIAMS' *The Velveteen Rabbit.* The theme "Love is powerful and can make the impossible possible" is developed through such conversations as "Once you are Real, you can't be ugly, except to those who don't understand." The actions of the characters reveal that outward appearances might not be important; true beauty and love are found in the heart. The end of the story shows that love is powerful because the toy rabbit is turned into a real rabbit.

ARTHUR YORINKS' *Hey, Al* (Caldecott Honor). The themes "It is better to be yourself than to live in another form" and "Discontent will result in disaster" are developed through the illustrations, the consequences of the characters' actions, and the conclusion of the story. One of the illustrations foreshadows the ending by showing a bird with human hands.

Realistic Fiction

IAN WALLACE's *Chin Chiang and the Dragon's Dance* (Chinese Canadian). The themes "Always try to do your best" and "It is important to have confidence in yourself" are developed through the grandfather's desires for his grandson, the need to practice to obtain a dream, the actions of the characters, and the happy reactions of the characters after the boy succeeds.

TARO YASHIMA's *Crow Boy* (Oriental). The theme "Do not judge others before you get to know them" is developed through the painful actions of the boy's schoolmates, through the boy's responses, and through the ending of the book in which the boy demonstrates his considerable ability.

Nonfiction

TRICIA BROWN's *Hello, Amigos!* (Mexican American). The themes "It is important to be special" and "It is important to have family and friends who love you" are developed through the photographs that accompany a boy as he celebrates his birthday, the reactions of family and friends, and the joy of the boy as he experiences his special day.

Picture Story Books

DENYS CAZET'S *A Fish in His Pocket*. The themes "It is important to respect life," "We can solve our own problems," and "Solving problems might require some creative problem solving" are developed through the young bear's responses when he accidently kills a little fish, though the illustrations that show his problem solving, and through his satisfactory solution to his problem.

LEO LIONNI'S *Swimmy* (Animal Story). The themes "You can accomplish anything once you believe that you can," "No problem is too big to solve if we work together," "Size has nothing to do with intelligence," and "It is all right to be different" are developed through the illustrations, the actions of the little red fish, and the outcome of the story when the little black fish solves the problem by showing the fish how to work together to outwit the large fish. The little black fish, who is different, is also the leader because he becomes the "eye" of the huge fish.

WATTY PIPER'S *The Little Engine That Could*. The theme "If you try your best to do something you can succeed" is developed through the use of the repetitive language in which the engine repeatedly states, "I think I can, I think I can" and the conclusion of the story in which, after many trials, the little engine succeeds.

Recreational Books for Lower Elementary Students

Folktales

BROTHERS GRIMM *Hansel and Gretel* (German)
SAMUEL MARSHAK'S *The Month-Brothers* (Russian)
JOHN STEPTOE'S *The Story of Jumping Mouse* (Native American)

Realistic Fiction

TOMIE DE PAOLA'S *Nana Upstairs & Nana Downstairs* (Realistic Fiction)
SID FLEISCHMAN'S *The Scarebird* (Realistic Fiction)
VALERIE FLOURNOY'S *The Patchwork Quilt* (Realistic Fiction, Black)
SHIRLEY HUGHES' *Dogger* (Realistic Fiction, England)
MISKA MILES' *Annie and the Old One* (Realistic Fiction, Native American)
CAROL PURDY'S *Least of All* (Realistic Fiction, Historical, Vermont)

Picture Story Books

MWENYE HADITHI'S *Greedy Zebra*
MUNRO LEAF'S *The Story of Ferdinand* (Spanish)
CHARLOTTE POMERANTZ'S *Flap Your Wings and Try*
PETER SIS'S *Rainbow Rhino*

Core Books and Sample Lessons
for Middle Elementary Students

LESSON ONE: Developing Understanding of Theme

OBJECTIVE

To develop an understanding of theme by identifying how an author develops theme, by identifying several appropriate themes within a story, by providing proof that those themes are developed within the story, and by comparing how different authors develop similar themes in several books.

CORE BOOKS: *Aesop's Fables*, illustrated by Heidi Holder; Tomie De Paola's *The Legend of the Bluebonnet* (Native American, Traditional Literature); and Paul Goble's *Buffalo Woman* (Native American, Traditional Literature).

PROCEDURES: To introduce or to review the concept of theme, read "The Country Mouse and the City Mouse" from *Aesop's Fables*. Ask the students, "What truth about life is Aesop developing in this fable?" Then share the moral stated at the end of the story. Ask the students, "Is this moral similar to the truth about life that you identified?" Read another fable from the same source such as "The Marriage of the Sun." Ask the students, "What truth about life is Aesop developing in this fable?" Then read and discuss the moral stated at the end of the text. Explain to the students that they are discovering a literary element called *theme* and that a moral of a fable is a good representation of a theme. Explain to the students that the theme of a story reflects the purpose that an author has for writing a story; it is a message that the author is stating about life. After reading several more fables and thinking about folktales and other stories that the students have read, develop a list of ways that authors can reveal theme. (See the list in the core lesson for lower elementary students.)

Have the students search for themes and evidence for the themes in a Native American legend. Remind the students that folklore has been passed down through many generations from storyteller to storyteller and that the stories that endured are the ones that are significant to the storytellers and their audiences. Tell the students that themes are important in Native American folklore because they help us understand the priorities of the people and discover what is considered important within the culture.

Before reading *The Legend of the Bluebonnet*, write three questions on the board and tell the students that they will be searching for the answers to them: (a) "What is the author trying to tell us that will make a difference in our lives? (b) "What do you believe is the author's purpose for writing the story, or what is the author's message?" (c) "What proof do we find in the story that makes us believe that the author is telling us _____ ?" Ask the students to list again the evidence that they might find in a book to support the theme, such as the characters' actions and thoughts, the ending of the story, who is rewarded or punished and why, the illustrations, and the narrative in which the author tells the reader.

Introduce *The Legend of the Bluebonnet* by telling the students that this is a Comanche story set in Texas. To identify prior knowledge ask them questions such as: "What does the word *legend* mean in the title? How will our knowledge that this is a legend influence our reading and understanding? What does the fact that this is a legend tell us about the time of the story? Who are the Comanche people? What do we know about the Comanche people? What do we know about the setting for the story? What could be the significance of the bluebonnet in the title?" This also would be an excellent opportunity to locate the setting on a map or globe.

Read the story aloud as the students consider the three questions listed on the board. Whether you read the story once or twice depends on the students in your class. Some teachers read the story aloud twice. Some teachers read the story aloud the first time and then ask students to reread the story themselves. Other teachers find that their students can identify both the themes and the proof after the first reading.

Write the themes on the board that the students identify. One fifth-grade class identified the following themes: "It takes an unselfish heart to make a sacrifice" and "A willing sacrifice by one brings benefits to many."

Next, ask the students to identify proof from the book that supports each theme. The fifth-grade students identified the following evidence for each theme:

"It takes an unselfish heart to make a sacrifice."

1. The shaman said the people were selfish and that is why the drought had occurred.
2. Even though the selfish people knew what they must do to save the land and themselves, they would not sacrifice their prized possessions such as the bow or the blanket.
3. She-Who-Is-Alone heard the message and gave up her only prized possession because she was not selfish.
4. She-Who-Is-Alone's good heart is recognized in her new name, One-Who-Dearly-Loved-Her People.
5. Most of the illustrations show the people with their backs turned, as if they and their selfish hearts are turned away from the Great Spirit's message.
6. The illustrations show She-Who-Is-Alone facing the reader as if she has nothing to hide.
7. Unselfish She-Who-Is-Alone did not have to make the sacrifice; she could have rationalized her thoughts and gone to sleep like everyone else.
8. She-Who-Is-Alone's sacrifice was accepted.

"A willing sacrifice by one brings benefits to many."

1. The legend tells us that the sacrifice caused all of the ground in Texas to be covered with bluebonnets.
2. The change was not just where She-Who-Is-Alone lived.
3. All of the Comanches shared in the forgiveness because they all saw the flowers, experienced the rain, and profited from the restored land.
4. All people in the future benefited from the sacrifice because the rewards came back each year and not just during the year of the sacrifice.

After completing this reading and discussion, the students read several additional books and searched for comparable themes. For example, they read Paul Goble's *Buffalo Woman*, identified the themes and the proofs and then compared how the themes related to sacrifice and unselfish actions are developed in both books. They also drew some conclusions about the importance of harmony in nature in Native American folklore.

LESSON TWO: Webbing Theme

OBJECTIVES

To identify the themes in a book.

To identify and web details that support the theme.

CORE BOOK: Byrd Baylor's *Hawk, I'm Your Brother* (Caldecott Honor, Native American).

PROCEDURES: Review the story as developed in previous lessons. Place the word *theme* on the center of a web. Ask the students to identify the major themes in the book and place them on the spokes of the web. A group of students identified the following three themes: "It is important to have dreams," "Both birds and people need freedom," and "Loyalty is important." After the main themes have been identified, place important details associated with the themes on the web. The web in Figure 8.1 was developed by middle elementary students.

Extended Books for Middle Elementary Students

Students can read the following examples of literature in small groups or independently, identify the themes, support the themes with proof from the stories, and

FIGURE 8.1 Web for theme for *Hawk, I'm Your Brother.*

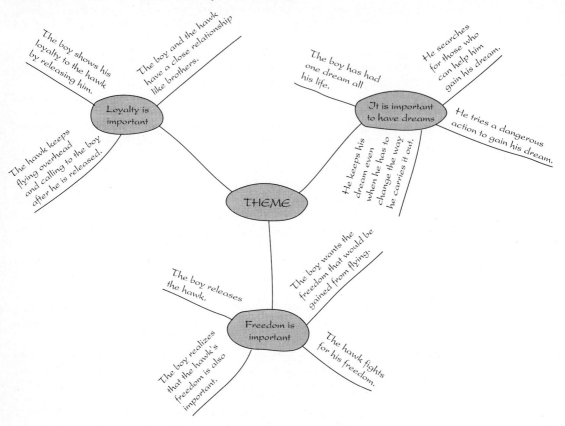

The boy shows his loyalty to the hawk by releasing him.

The boy and the hawk have a close relationship like brothers.

Loyalty is important

The hawk keeps flying overhead and calling to the boy after he is released.

The boy has had one dream all his life.

He searches for those who can help him gain his dream.

It is important to have dreams

He tries a dangerous action to gain his dream.

THEME

He keeps his dream even when he has to change the way he carries it out.

The boy releases the hawk.

The boy wants the freedom that would be gained from flying.

Freedom is important

The boy realizes that the hawk's freedom is also important.

The hawk fights for his freedom.

defend their reasons for selecting the themes and proof. The books also can be used for webbing themes. Many of these books are excellent for making comparisons in themes, within and across cultures and genres.

Folktales

FRANK CUSHING's retelling of "The Poor Turkey Girl" in *Zuni Folk Tales* (Traditional Literature, Native American). The theme "It is important to honor another's wishes and to keep your word" is developed through the actions of the turkeys as they repay the Turkey Girl for her kindness to them, but then leave her in worse poverty than she was in before when she fails to keep her word and return to them at a certain time. The theme related to keeping one's word can be compared with Sumiko Yagawa's *The Crane Wife*.

MOMOKO ISHII's *The Tongue-Cut Sparrow* (Oriental). The themes "Kindness will be rewarded" and "Greed and cruelty will be punished" are developed through the actions of and the rewards given to the kind husband and the actions of and the punishment given to the greedy wife. The theme related to greed can be compared with Sumiko Yagawa's *The Crane Wife*.

YUZO OTSUKA's *Suho and the White Horse: A Legend of Mongolia.* The themes "Good eventually will overcome evil" and "Jealousy and greed have disastrous consequences" are developed through the actions of the good and evil characters and through the conclusion of the story in which good eventually triumphs.

ISAAC BASHEVIS SINGER's *Mazel and Shlimazel, or the Milk of the Lioness* (Jewish). The theme "Good luck follows those who are diligent, honest, sincere, and helpful" is developed through the characteristics of the main characters and the outcome of the story.

JOHN STEPTOE's *Mufaro's Beautiful Daughters* (African, Caldecott Honor) The themes "Greed and selfishness are harmful personal characteristics" and "Kindness and generosity are beneficial personal characteristics" are developed through the contrasting actions of the greedy, selfish girl and the kind, generous girl. The greedy, selfish girl is punished by becoming servant to the kind, generous girl who becomes wife to the king. The consequences of greed and generosity are found in many folktales from various lands. Consequently, students can locate these themes in folklore from all cultures.

SUMIKO YAGAWA's *The Crane Wife* (Oriental). The themes "It is important to honor another's wishes and to keep your word" and "Greed will be punished" are developed through the request of the transformed crane, her actions, and the consequences of the greedy responses of her husband when he does not honor her wishes.

Modern Fantasy

HANS CHRISTIAN ANDERSEN's *The Steadfast Tin Soldier.* The theme "It is important to be steadfast and to retain our values," is developed through the characterization and actions of the soldier. Even though he goes through many trials and tribulations, he remains positive about life and the challenges before him. He retains his values even during the most difficult experiences.

MILDRED PITTS WALTER's *Brother to the Wind* (Black). The themes "Dreams are important," "It is important to keep your beliefs," and "Some people will help you obtain your dream, while some people will hinder you" are developed through the boy's actions as he completes difficult tasks that finally allow him to fly.

E.B. WHITE's *Charlotte's Web* (Newbery Honor, Touchstone). The themes "Friendship is important to all beings" and "Death is a natural way of life" are developed through the interactions of the animals as they try to help Wilbur overcome his fear. The importance of friendship is especially developed through Charlotte when she is shown as a kind, caring, and giving person who strives to help Wilbur. Death as a natural way of life is revealed through the farm animals and through the end of the story in which Charlotte dies but some of her babies return to the farm.

Realistic Fiction

BYRD BAYLOR's *Hawk, I'm Your Brother* (Caldecott Honor, Native American). The themes "Dreams are important in our lives" and "Freedom is important for both humans and animals" are developed through the boy's actions and the hawk's actions. This is a good book to compare with Mildred Pitts Walter's modern fantasy about a black character (*Brother to the Wind*), because both books show main characters who have strong dreams. By using both books, students can understand the importance of dreams for all people within diverse cultures.

SHARON BELL MATHIS's *The Hundred Penny Box* (Black). The themes "We need objects in our lives that help us remember our histories" and "Warm relationships between people of different generations are important" are developed through the box of pennies and what each penny signifies in the life of a 100-year-old woman and through the warm relationship developed between the woman and her nephew.

Recreational Books for Middle Elementary Students

Folktales

OLAF BAKER's *Where the Buffaloes Begin* (Caldecott Honor, Legend, Native American)

TOMIE DE PAOLA's *The Lady of Guadalupe* (Legend, Mexican)

MARILEE HEYER's *The Weaving of a Dream* (Chinese)

NONNY HOGROGIAN's retelling of Grimm's *The Devil with the Three Golden Hairs* (Germany)

VAN DYKE PARKS' adaptation of Joel Chandler Harris' *Jump! The Adventures of Brer Rabbit* (Black)

HARVE ZEMACH's *Duffy and the Devil* (English)

Modern Fantasy

HANS CHRISTIAN ANDERSEN's *The Nightingale*

ERIC A. KIMMEL's *Hershel and the Hanukkah Goblins* (Jewish)

ROBERT LAWSON's *Rabbit Hill* (Newbery Medal)

JANE YOLEN's *The Acorn Quest*

SHEL SILVERSTEIN's *The Giving Tree* (Poetic Style)

Realistic Fiction

JUDY BLUME's *Tales of a Fourth Grade Nothing*

LARRY CALLEN's *Sorrow's Song*

BEVERLY CLEARY's *Ramona and Her Mother*

PAULA FOX's *How Many Miles to Babylon?* (Black)

HELEN GRIFFITHS' *Running Wild*

VIRGINIA HAMILTON's *Zeely* (Black)

JEAN LITTLE's *Different Dragons*

MARILYN SACHS' *A Secret Friend*

SYDNEY TAYLOR's *All-of-a-Kind Family*

Historical Fiction

CAROL RYRIE BRINK's *Caddie Woodlawn* (Newbery Medal)

CAROL CARRICK's *Stay Away From Simon!*

ALICE DALGLIESH's *The Courage of Sarah Noble* (Newbery Honor)

CONSTANCE GREENE's *Dotty's Suitcase*

VIRGINIA HAMILTON's *The Bells of Christmas* (Black)

ELLEN HOWARD's *Edith Herself*

ANNE PELLOWSKI's *Winding Valley Farm: Annie's Story*

JOAN SANDIN's *The Long Way to a New Land*

LAURA INGALLS WILDER's *Little House in the Big Woods* (Touchstone)

Biography

MARGARET DAVIDSON's *The Golda Meir Story* (Jewish)

JERI FERRIS' *Go Free or Die: A Story of Harriet Tubman* (Black)

JEAN FRITZ's *The Great Little Madison*

ELOISE GREENFIELD's *Rosa Parks* (Black)

BETTY LOU PHILLIPS' *The Picture Story of Nancy Lopez* (Hispanic)

CLARENCE WHITE's *Cesar Chavez, Man of Courage.* (Hispanic)

Core Books and Sample Lessons
for Upper Elementary and Middle School Students

At the upper elementary and middle school levels you can develop core lessons that are similar in structure and content to those shown for the lower and middle grades. If the students have a good understanding of theme, however, and have discussed and located themes in the lower grades, they probably will enjoy the challenge of discovering and analyzing comparative themes in several books, in literature by one author, and in different times within our history. The following lessons show some of the most successful comparative studies that I have done with students in the upper grades.

LESSON ONE: Developing Understanding of Thematic Similarities Between Folktales and Literary Folktales

OBJECTIVE

To trace the similarities in theme between folktales (stories that have been handed down for generations through the oral tradition) and literary folktales (original works by authors whose stories include many of the characteristics of folktales).

CORE BOOKS: Anthologies of folktales such as *The Complete Brothers Grimm Fairy Tales* or *Household Tales* collected by the Brothers Grimm. Anthologies of literary folktale collections by Hans Christian Andersen such as *Hans Christian Andersen: Eighty Fairy Tales.* (Some students like the highly illustrated single versions, while other students consider the anthologies to be more adult in nature.) Wilhelm Grimm's *Dear Mili.*

PROCEDURES: Review how authors develop theme with the students (See the previous discussions). Prepare the students for the lesson by asking them to consider what they already know about folktales: "What is a folktale? How does a folktale differ from other types of literature? What are the characteristics of a folktale? What do we expect for setting, characterization, plot development, and themes? What are some themes that are common in folktales?" Now ask them, "What do you think is meant when we refer to a work as a literary folktale? How does the word *literary* influence the story? What is meant by the word *folktale*? What characteristics should we expect in a literary folktale?" During this discussion make sure that the students understand that a literary folktale is a story written by an author in which the writer develops characteristics that are similar to a folktale in setting, characterization, plot development, and theme. List these similarities.

Explain to the students that they will be analyzing the literary folktales of Hans Christian Andersen to identify how closely Andersen was influenced by the writing of the folktales collected by the Brothers Grimm. Have them first identify the themes found in traditional tales collected by the Brothers Grimm. Next, ask them to read and identify the themes in Hans Christian Andersen's literary folktales. Finally, have them compare the themes in the two collections and decide if there are similarities in theme across the two genres. On the chalkboard write, "Themes in Folktales Collected by the Brothers Grimm" and "Themes in Literary Folktales Written by Hans Christian Andersen." As the students read and identify the themes, list the themes under the appropriate titles. Compare the two lists. Ask, "What are the similarities? How was Hans Christian Andersen influenced by the folktales collected by the Brothers Grimm.

After this task is completed (it will take several days), provide the students with an additional challenge. Show the students *Dear Mili* written by Wilhelm Grimm and illustrated by Maurice Sendak. Tell the students that the text for the story was discovered in 1983. It originally was written in a letter to a girl in 1816 and remained in the family's possession until it was rediscovered in 1983. Explain to the students that the publishers of the book do not know if *Dear Mili* is a folktale collected by Wilhelm Grimm (who was one of the Brothers Grimm) or if it was written by him. Ask them to read or listen to *Dear Mili* and to consider all of the Grimms' tales that they have read. "How is the story similar to the other tales? How is it different? Do you believe that the story is one of the folktales that was part of the oral tradition, or do you believe that Wilhelm Grimm used characteristics of the folktales to write his own literary folktale? Justify your answer." (There are no right or wrong answers. Students enjoy debating this issue and presenting their own viewpoints. You also might explain to them that *Dear Mili* is a popular book. The first printing was 250,000 volumes.)

This is an excellent opportunity to encourage students to use the format of the folktale to write their own literary folktales. Maybe they will be as successful as Hans Christian Andersen or Wilhelm Grimm (if they decided that he wrote *Dear Mili)*.

LESSON TWO: Identifying the Themes in Works of One Author

OBJECTIVES

To identify the themes developed in the works of one author and to compare the themes in the author's work across several genres.

To develop a stronger understanding of Native American culture.

CORE BOOKS: Jamake Highwater's *Anpao: An American Indian Odyssey* (Legend, Newbery Honor); *Moonsong Lullaby* (Poetry); and *Legend Days* (Realistic Fiction).

PROCEDURES: Discuss with students the importance of traditional literature and traditional beliefs in the writings of many authors. Explain that values and beliefs expressed in the traditional literature of a culture often are found in the contemporary writings from authors who are members of that cultural group. This might be especially true if they read the works of one author that include both traditional and contemporary writing. Ask the students, "If you were going to select or retell traditional folktales, myths, or legends that are important to you and to your culture, what literature would you select? What message would you want the literature to convey? If you were to write a contemporary story, would you still want to convey the same message? If this message is important in one form of literature, would it also be important in another form of literature?"

Explain to the students that they will be reading several books written by Jamake Highwater, a Native American author. They will be searching for the themes that might be important to that author. As they read the books they will begin with the traditional literature, then read a poem, and finally read a contemporary story. Through each of the forms of literature they will search for any similarities in themes and threads that are found throughout the writings of one author.

Introduce *Anpao: An American Indian Odyssey* by explaining to the students that Anpao is a Native American character who combines several traditional Indian myths. Anpao travels across the great prairies, through deep canyons, and along wooded ridges in search of his destiny. Along the way, he observes the cultures and customs of many different tribes. Read the comments written by Highwater (1991), "Through the Eyes of An Author: Traditional Native American Tales," found in Norton's *Through the Eyes of a Child: An Introduction to Children's Literature*. After reading this essay, ask the students to speculate about the themes they would be likely to find in Highwater's writing. For example, one group decided that, "Highwater and the Native American people have a strong unity with and respect for nature" and "Highwater and the Native American people retain their foundations in traditional values and beliefs." Now ask the students to read or listen to *Anpao*. As they read the book they should identify the themes that are important to Anpao. List these themes on the board and discuss the proof and importance of each theme.

After the important themes have been identified in *Anpao*, introduce Highwater's poem, *Moonsong Lullaby*. Ask the students, "After listening to the title and looking at the cover of the book, what do you expect this poem to be about? Using your knowledge of themes that might be important to Highwater, what messages do you expect to gain from this poem?" After students have hypothesized their answers, list them on the board. Now read the poem and verify the themes or messages that are in the poem. Ask the students, "What themes are found in both *Anpao* and *Moonsong Lullaby*? Why do you think Highwater chose to develop these themes in a poem? Did the themes and the poem reflect Highwater's Native American heritage? In what ways was the heritage developed?"

Finally, introduce Highwater's *Legend Days*. Explain to the students that *Legend Days* is a contemporary story that accompanies a Native American girl as she matures and faces the conflicts that result in her life. Ask the students, "What is the significance of the title, *Legend Days*? What do you expect the book to be about? Is this a good title for a book about a Native American? Why or why not? Using your knowledge about Jamake Highwater gained from reading the previous two books, what messages and themes would you expect to see in this contemporary work? Do you believe that this contemporary girl's life will be like the life reflected by the boy in *Anpao*? How might the life be the same and how might it be different? How would you account for both the similarities and differences?"

Ask the students to read the book and identify the themes in *Legend Days*. Have them discuss the themes and present proof for the themes. Then ask them to look for any consistencies across themes found in Highwater's writing. "What themes are found in all of the books? If there are significant differences, what might account for those differences? What do we know about Jamake Highwater after reading these books? What is important in his life? What would he like to share with his readers? What do you know about Native American people? Do you think any of the themes, values, and beliefs might be found in other Native American literature?"

LESSON THREE: Developing a Web Associated With Theme

OBJECTIVES

To identify important themes in a legend.

To web the details that develop the theme.

CORE BOOK: Selina Hastings' *Sir Gawain and the Loathly Lady* (Legend)

PROCEDURES: Review the story of *Sir Gawain and the Loathly Lady* from previous lessons. Ask students to identify the themes developed in the story. Write the word *theme* in the center of the web and place the themes identified by the students on the spokes of the web. One group of students identified the following themes: "Honor and loyalty will overcome evil" and "People like to make their own choices." Place these themes on the spokes of the web. Ask students to identify the details that support each theme on the web. The web in Figure 8.2 was created by a group of seventh-grade students.

Extended Books for Upper Elementary and Middle School Students

In this section we will continue identifying books that are excellent for comparisons of themes. These books are grouped around specific themes or topics. The themes and

FIGURE 8.2 Webbing theme in *Sir Gawain and the Loathly Lady.*

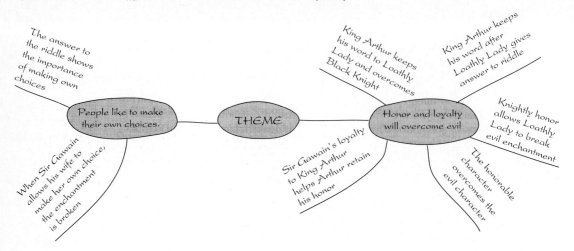

topics can include books from several genres. The first two examples continue the type of analysis conducted with the works of one author. These books assist in a multi-cultural analysis and help students understand and appreciate the writings from members of a specific cultural group. Other examples are chosen for themes that are found in the writings of numerous authors.

Virginia Hamilton

Trace and compare the themes found in Hamilton's writings:

> *In the Beginning: Creation Stories from Around the World* (Newbery Medal, select the creation stories from the African culture)
>
> *The People Could Fly: American Black Folktales*
>
> *The House of Dies Drear* (Realistic Fiction)
>
> *Junius Over Far* (Realistic Fiction)
>
> *M. C. Higgins the Great* (Realistic Fiction, Newbery Medal)

Laurence Yep

Trace and compare the themes found in Yep's writings:

> *The Rainbow People* (Folktales collected from Chinese Americans living in California)
>
> *Dragonwings* (Historical Fiction, Newbery Honor)
>
> *Child of the Owl* (Realistic Fiction)
>
> *Sea Glass* (Realistic Fiction)

Nature

Trace and compare themes related to the healing force of nature in works in which the characters are physically or emotionally healed as they interact with nature. Gardens are especially important in much of this literature. Students can identify the importance of a garden or a secret place in nature to the characters and to the outcomes of the story in:

Frances Hodgson Burnett's *The Secret Garden* (Realistic Fiction, England, Touchstone)

Katherine Paterson's *Bridge to Terabithia* (Realistic Fiction, Newbery Medal)

Philippa Pearce's *Tom's Midnight Garden* (Modern Fantasy, Touchstone, England)

Joan Phipson's *The Watcher in the Garden* (Modern Fantasy)

Persecution

Trace and compare themes related to the idea that "prejudiced persecution of others is a frightening and destructive social phenomenon" in historical fiction from different time periods. Ask the students to analyze how the themes are developed in each historical time period and to consider, "Why and how are the themes related to specific happenings in the time periods? Are these themes relevant in other periods of history? Are they relevant today?" The following books develop themes related to the destructive nature of persecution:

Elizabeth George Speare's *The Bronze Bow* (Newbery Medal, Israel, Roman rule)

The Witch of Blackbird Pond (Newbery Medal, Salem, late 1600s)

Janet Lunn's *Shadow in Hawthorn Bay* (Canada, early 1800s)

James and Christopher Collier's *Jump Ship to Freedom* (Civil War)

Kathryn Lasky's *Beyond the Divide* (Frontier, 1800s)

Mildred D. Taylor's *Roll of Thunder, Hear My Cry* (Newbery Medal, South, early 1900s)

Johanna Reiss's *The Upstairs Room* (Newbery Honor, World War II)

Recreational Books for Upper Elementary and Middle School Students

The following books can be suggested for independent reading and for applying students' understanding and appreciation of theme:

Legends

NINA BAWDEN's *William Tell* (Legend)

MARCIA BROWN's *Backbone of the King: Story of Pakaa and His Son Ku* (Legend)

KATE SEREDY's *The White Stag* (Newbery Medal)

Modern Fantasy

JOHN CHRISTOPHER's *The White Mountains*

RUDYARD KIPLING's *The Jungle Book* (Touchstone)

MADELEINE L'ENGLE's *A Swiftly Tilting Planet* and *A Wrinkle in Time* (Newbery Medal)

C. S. LEWIS's *The Lion, the Witch and the Wardrobe* (Touchstone)

Realistic Fiction

MARION DANE BAUER's *On My Honor*

BROCK COLE's *The Goats*

NICHOLASA MOHR's *Felita* and *Going Home* (Puerto Rican American)

WALTER DEAN MYERS's *Scorpions* (Black, Newbery Honor)

Historical Fiction

JANET HICKMAN's *Zoar Blue*

WILLIAM HOOKS' *Circle of Fire*

ANN PETRY's *Tituba of Salem Village*

MILDRED D. TAYLOR's *Let the Circle Be Unbroken* (Black)

YOSHIKO UCHIDA's *Journey Home* and *Journey to Topaz* (Japanese American)

REFERENCES

HIGHWATER, J. (1991). Through the eyes of an author: Traditional native american tales. In D. E. Norton's *Through the eyes of a child: An introduction to children's literature* (p. 255). Columbus, OH: Merrill.

LEHR, S. (1988). The child's developing sense of theme as a response to literature. *Reading Research Quarterly, 23,* pp. 337–357.

LUKENS, R. J. (1989). *A critical handbook of children's literature* (4th ed). Glenview IL: Scott, Foresman.

MANGUEL, A. & GUADALUPI, G. (1980). *The dictionary of imaginary places.* Illustrated by Graham Greenfield. New York: Macmillan.

PERRINE, L. (1983). *Literature: Structure, sound, and sense* (4th ed.). San Diego: Harcourt Brace Jovanovich.

WESTON, L. H. (1990). The evolution of a literature study in a fourth grade across four modes: Oral, written, artistic, and dramatic. *Dissertation Abstracts International, 51,* 01A. (University Microfilms No. 90–14, 513)

CHILDREN'S LITERATURE REFERENCES*

AESOP. *Aesop's Fables.* Illustrated by Heidi Holder. New York: Viking, 1981 (I: 9–12).

ANDERSEN, HANS CHRISTIAN. *Hans Christian Andersen: Eighty Fairy Tales,* translated by R. P. Keigwin. New York: Pantheon, 1976, 1982 (I: 9 +).

_____. *The Nightingale,* translated by Eva Le Gallienne. Illustrated by Nancy Ekholm Burkert. New York: Harper & Row, 1965 (I: all).

_____. *The Steadfast Tin Soldier.* Illustrated by Thomas Digrazia. Englewood Cliffs, NJ: Prentice-Hall, 1981 (I: 6–8).

_____. *The Ugly Duckling.* Illustrated by Lorinda Bryan Cauley. Orlando: Harcourt Brace Jovanovich, 1979 (I: 6–8).

BARRACCA, DEBRA & SAL BARRACCA. *The Adventures of Taxi Dog.* New York: Dial, 1990 (I: 3–8).

BAUER, MARION DANE. *On My Honor.* New York: Clarion, 1986 (I: 10 +).

BAWDEN, NINA. *William Tell.* Illustrated by Pascale Allamand. New York: Lothrop, Lee & Shepard, 1981 (I: 6–9).

BAYLOR, BYRD. *Hawk, I'm Your Brother.* Illustrated by Peter Parnall. New York: Scribner's, 1976 (I: all).

BAKER, OLAF. *Where the Buffaloes Begin.* Illustrated by Stephen Gammell. New York: Warne, 1981 (I: all).

*I = Interest by age range

BLUME, JUDY. *Tales of a Fourth Grade Nothing.* Illustrated by Roy Doty. New York: Dutton, 1972 (I: 7–12).

BRETT, JAN, retold by. *Beauty and the Beast.* New York: Clarion, 1989 (I: 8–12).

BRINK, CAROL RYRIE. *Caddie Woodlawn.* Illustrated by Trina Schart Hyman. New York: Macmillan, 1935, 1963, 1973 (I: 8–12).

BROWN, MARCIA. *Backbone of the King: Story of Pakaa and His Son Ku.* University of Hawaii Press, 1966 (I: 10 +).

BROWN, TRICIA. *Hello, Amigos!* Photographs by Fran Ortiz. Orlando: Holt, Rinehart & Winston, 1986 (I: 3–8).

BURNETT, FRANCES HODGSON. *The Secret Garden.* Illustrated by Tasha Tudor. Philadelphia: Lippincott, 1911, 1938, 1962 (I: 9 +).

CALLEN, LARRY. *Sorrow's Song.* Boston: Little, Brown, 1979 (I: 8–10).

CARRICK, CAROL. *Stay Away From Simon!* Illustrated by Donald Carrick. New York: Clarion, 1985 (I: 7–10).

CAZET, DENYS. *A Fish in His Pocket.* New York: Watts, 1987 (I: 3–6).

CHRISTOPHER, JOHN. *The White Mountains.* New York: Macmillan, 1967 (I:10 +).

CLEARY, BEVERLY. *Ramona and Her Mother.* Illustrated by Alan Tiegreen. New York: Morrow, 1979 (I: 7–10).

COLE, BROCK. *The Goats.* New York: Farrar, Straus & Giroux, 1987 (I: 10 +).

COLLIER, JAMES & CHRISTOPHER COLLIER. *Jump Ship to Freedom.* New York: Delacorte, 1981 (I: 10 +).

CUSHING, FRANK HAMILTON. *Zuni Folk Tales.* University of Arizona Press, 1901, 1986 (I: 10 +).

DALGLIESH, ALICE. *The Courage of Sarah Noble.* Illustrated by Leonard Weisgard. New York: Scribner's, 1954 (I: 6–9).

DAVIDSON, MARGARET. *The Golda Meir Story.* New York: Scribner's, 1981 (I: 9–12).

DE PAOLA, TOMIE. *The Lady of Guadalupe.* New York: Holiday, 1980 (I: 8 +).

_____. *The Legend of the Bluebonnet.* New York: Putnam, 1983 (I: all).

_____. *Nana Upstairs & Nana Downstairs.* New York: Putnam, 1973 (I: 3–7)

FERRIS, JERI. *Go Free or Die: A Story of Harriet Tubman.* Minneapolis: Carolrhoda, 1988 (I: 7 +).

FLEISCHMAN, SID. *The Scarebird.* Illustrated by Peter Sis. New York: Greenwillow, 1988 (I: 5–9).

FLOURNOY, VALERIE. *The Patchwork Quilt.* Illustrated by Jerry Pinkney. New York: Dial, 1985 (I: 5–8).

FOX, PAULA. *How Many Miles to Babylon?*. Illustrated by Paul Giovanopoulos. New York: Bradbury, 1967 (I: 8+).

FRITZ, JEAN. *The Great Little Madison*. New York: Putnam, 1989 (I: 9+).

GOBLE, PAUL. *Buffalo Woman*. New York: Bradbury, 1984 (I: all).

GREENE, CONSTANCE. *Dotty's Suitcase*. New York: Viking, 1980 (I: 8–12).

GREENFIELD, ELOISE. *Rosa Parks*. Illustrated by Eric Marlow. New York: Crowell, 1973 (I: 7–10).

GRIFALCONI, ANN. *Darkness and the Butterfly*. Boston: Little, Brown, 1987. (I: 5–8).

GRIFFITHS, HELEN. *Running Wild*. Illustrated by Victor Ambrus. New York: Holiday, 1977 (I: 10+).

GRIMM, BROTHERS. *The Complete Brothers Grimm Fairy Tales*, edited by Lily Owens. New York: Avenel, 1981 (I: all).

———. *The Devil with the Three Golden Hairs*, retold and illustrated by Nonny Hogrogian. New York: Knopf, 1983 (1: 5–9).

———. *Hansel and Gretel*, retold and Illustrated by Paul O. Zelinsky. New York: Dodd, Mead, 1984 (I: all).

———. *Household Tales*. Illustrated by Mervyn Peake. London: Methuen, 1973 (I: 8+).

———. *Little Red Riding Hood*, retold and illustrated by Trina Schart Hyman. New York: Holiday, 1983 (I: 6–9).

GRIMM, WILHELM. *Dear Mili*. Illustrated by Maurice Sendak. New York: Farrar, Straus & Giroux, 1988 (I: all).

HADITHI, MWENYE. *Greedy Zebra*. Illustrated by Adrienne Kennaway. Boston: Little, Brown, 1984 (I: 4–8).

HAMILTON, VIRGINIA. *In the Beginning: Creation Stories From Around the World*. Illustrated by Barry Moser. Orlando: Harcourt Brace Jovanovich, 1988 (I: all).

———. *The Bells of Christmas*. Illustrated by Lambert Davis. Orlando: Harcourt Brace Jovanovich, 1989 (I: 8+).

———. *The House of Dies Drear*. Illustrated by Eros Keith. New York: Macmillan, 1968 (I: 11+).

———. *Junius Over Far*. New York: Harper & Row, 1985 (I: 10+).

———. *M. C. Higgins, The Great*. New York: Macmillan, 1974 (I: 12+).

———. *The People Could Fly: American Black Folktales*. Illustrated by Leo and Diane Dillon. New York: Knopf, 1985 (I: all).

———. *Zeely*. Illustrated by Symeon Shimin. New York: Macmillan, 1967 (I: 8–12).

HARRIS, JOEL CHANDLER. *Jump! The Adventures of Brer Rabbit*, adapted by Van Dyke Parks. Illustrated by Barry Moser. Orlando: Harcourt Brace Jovanovich, 1986 (I: all).

HASTINGS, SELINA. *Sir Gawain and the Loathly Lady*. Illustrated by Juan Wijngaard. New York: Lothrop, Lee & Shepard, 1985 (I: 10+).

HEYER, MARILEE. *The Weaving of a Dream: A Chinese Folktale*. New York: Viking, 1986 (I: 8+).

HICKMAN, JANET. *Zoar Blue*. New York: Macmillan, 1978 (I: 9–14).

HIGHWATER, JAMAKE. *Anpao: An American Indian Odyssey*. Illustrated by Fritz Scholder. Philadelphia: Lippincott, 1977 (I: 12+)

———. *Legend Days*. New York: Harper & Row, 1984 (I: 12+).

———. *Moonsong Lullaby*. Photographs by Marcia Keegan. New York: Lothrop, Lee & Shepard, 1981 (I: all).

HOOKS, WILLIAM. *Circle of Fire*. New York: Atheneum, 1983 (I: 10+).

HOWARD, ELLEN. *Edith Herself*. New York: Atheneum, 1987 (I: 7–10).

HUGHES, SHIRLEY. *Dogger*. London: Bodley Head, 1977 (I: 3–8).

ISHII, MOMOKO. *The Tongue-Cut Sparrow*, translated by Katherine Paterson. Illustrated by Suekichi Akaba. New York: Dutton, 1987 (I: 7–10).

KIMMEL, ERIC A. *Hershel and the Hanukkah Goblins*. Illustrated by Trina Schart Hyman. New York: Holiday, 1989 (I: all).

KIPLING, RUDYARD. *The Jungle Book*. New York: Doubleday, 1894, 1964 (I: 8–12).

LASKY, KATHRYN. *Beyond the Divide*. New York: Macmillan, 1983 (I: 9+).

LAWSON, ROBERT. *Rabbit Hill*. New York: Viking, 1944 (I: 7–11).

LEAF, MUNRO. *The Story of Ferdinand*. Illustrated by Robert Lawson. New York: Viking, 1936 (I: 4–10).

L'ENGLE, MADELEINE. *A Swiftly Tilting Planet*. New York: Farrar, Straus & Giroux, 1978 (I: 10+).

———. *A Wrinkle in Time*. New York: Farrar, Straus & Giroux, 1962 (I: 10+).

LEWIS, C. S. *The Lion, the Witch and the Wardrobe*. Illustrated by Pauline Baynes. New York: Macmillan, 1950 (I: 9+).

LEWIS, NAOMI, edited by. *The Twelve Dancing Princesses and Other Tales from Grimm*. Illustrated by Lidia Postma. New York: Dial, 1985 (I: all).

LIONNI, LEO. *Swimmy*. New York: Pantheon, 1963 (I: 3–8).

LITTLE, JEAN. *Different Dragons*. Illustrated by Laura Fernandez. New York: Viking, 1986 (I: 8–10).

LOBEL, ARNOLD. *Fables*. New York: Harper & Row, 1980 (I: all).

LUNN, JANET. *Shadow in Hawthorn Bay*. New York: Scribner's, 1986 (I: 10+).

MARSHAK, SAMUEL, retold by. *The Month Brothers*, translated by Thomas Whitney. Illustrated by Diane Stanley. New York: Morrow, 1983 (I: 5–9).

MATHIS, SHARON BELL. *The Hundred Penny Box*. Illustrated by Leo and Diane Dillon. New York: Viking, 1975 (I: 6–9).

MILES, MISKA. *Annie and the Old One*. Illustrated by Peter Parnall. Boston: Little, Brown, 1971 (I: 6–8).

MOHR, NICHOLASA. *Felita*. Illustrated by Ray Cruz. New York: Dial, 1979 (I: 9–12).

_____. *Going Home*. New York: Dial, 1986 (I: 10+).

MYERS, WALTER DEAN. *Scorpions*. New York: Harper & Row, 1988 (I: 11+).

NASH, OGDEN. *Edward Lear's the Scroobious Pip*. Illustrated by Nancy Ekholm Burkert. New York: Harper & Row, 1968 (I: all).

OTSUKA, YUZO. *Suho and the White Horse: A Legend of Mongolia*, adapted from Ann Herring's translation. Illustrated by Suekichi Akaba. New York: Viking, 1981 (I: 5–8).

PATERSON, KATHERINE. *Bridge to Terabithia*. Illustrated by Donna Diamond. New York: Crowell, 1977 (I: 10+).

PEARCE, PHILIPPA. *Tom's Midnight Garden*. Illustrated by Susan Einzig. Philadelphia: Lippincott, 1958 (I: 8+).

PELLOWSKI, ANNE. *Winding Valley Farm: Annie's Story*. Illustrated by Wendy Watson. New York: Philomel, 1982 (I: 9–12).

PETRY, ANN. *Tituba of Salem Village*. New York: Crowell, 1964 (I: 11+).

PHILLIPS, BETTY LOU. *The Picture Story of Nancy Lopez*. Messner, 1980 (I: 8+)

PHIPSON, JOAN. *The Watcher in the Garden*. New York: Atheneum, 1982 (I: 10+).

PIPER, WATTY. *The Little Engine that Could*. Illustrated by George and Doris Hauman. New York: Platt, 1954 (I: 3–8).

POMERANTZ, CHARLOTTE. *Flap Your Wings and Try*. Illustrated by Nancy Tafuri. New York: Greenwillow, 1989 (I: 3–7).

PURDY, CAROL. *Least of All*. Illustrated by Tim Arnold. New York: Macmillan, 1987 (I: 5–8).

REISS, JOHANNA. *The Upstairs Room* New York: Crowell, 1972 (I: 11+).

SACHS, MARILYN. *A Secret Friend*. New York: Doubleday, 1978 (I: 8–12).

SANDIN, JOAN. *The Long Way to a New Land*. New York: Harper & Row, 1981 (I: 7–9).

SEREDY, KATE. *The White Stag*. New York: Viking, 1937, 1965 (I: 10+).

SILVERSTEIN, SHEL. *The Giving Tree*. New York: Harper & Row, 1964 (I: all).

SINGER, ISAAC BASHEVIS. *Mazel and Shlimazel, or the Milk of the Lioness*. Illustrated by Margot Zemach. New York: Farrar, Straus & Giroux, 1967 (I: 8–12).

SIS, PETER. *Rainbow Rhino*. New York: Knopf, 1987 (I: 4–8).

SPEARE, ELIZABETH GEORGE. *The Bronze Bow*. Boston: Houghton Mifflin, 1961 (I: 10+).

_____. *The Witch of Blackbird Pond*. Boston: Houghton Mifflin, 1958 (I: 9–14).

STEPTOE, JOHN. *Mufaro's Beautiful Daughters: An African Tale*. New York: Lothrop, Lee & Shepard, 1987 (I: all).

_____. *The Story of Jumping Mouse*. New York: Lothrop, Lee & Shepard, 1984 (I: all).

TAYLOR, MILDRED D. *Let the Circle Be Unbroken*. New York: Dial, 1981 (I: 10+)

TAYLOR, MILDRED D. *Roll of Thunder, Hear My Cry*. Illustrated by Jerry Pinckney. New York: Dial, 1976 (I: 10+).

TAYLOR, SYDNEY. *All-Of-A-Kind Family*. Illustrated by Helen John. New York: Follett, 1951 (I: 7–10).

UCHIDA, YOSHIKO. *Journey Home*. Illustrated by Charles Robinson. New York: Atheneum, 1978 (I: 10+).

_____. *Journey to Topaz*. Illustrated by Donald Carrick. New York: Scribner's, 1971 (I: 10+).

WALLACE, IAN. *Chin Chiang and the Dragon's Dance*. New York: Atheneum, 1984 (I: 6–9).

WALTER, MILDRED PITTS. *Brother to the Wind*. Illustrated by Diane and Leo Dillon. New York: Lothrop, Lee & Shepard, 1985 (I: 7–10).

WHITE, CLARENCE. *Cesar Chavez, Man of Courage*. Dallas: Garrard, 1973 (I: 8+).

WHITE, E. B. *Charlotte's Web*. Illustrated by Garth Williams. New York: Harper & Row, 1952 (I: 7–11).

WILDER, LAURA INGALLS. *Little House in the Big Woods*. Illustrated by Garth Williams. New York: Harper & Row, 1932, 1953 (I: 8–12).

WILLIAMS, MARGERY. *The Velveteen Rabbit: Or How Toys Become Real*. Illustrated by William Nicholson. New York: Doubleday, 1958 (I: 6–9).

YAGAWA, SUMIKO. *The Crane Wife*. Illustrated by Suekichi Akabas. New York: Morrow, 1981 (I: all).

YASHIMA, TARO. *Crow Boy*. New York: Viking, 1955 (I: 4–8).

YEP, LAURENCE. *Child of the Owl*. New York: Harper & Row, 1977 (I: 10+).

_____. *Dragonwings*. New York: Harper & Row, 1975 (I: 10+).

_____. *The Rainbow People*. Illustrated by David Wiesner. New York: Harper & Row, 1989 (I: 8+).

_____. *Sea Glass*. New York: Harper & Row, 1979 (I: 10+).

YOLEN, JANE. *The Acorn Quest*. Illustrated by Susanna Hatti. New York: Crowell, 1981, (I: 7–10).

YORINKS, ARTHUR. *Hey Al*. Illustrated by Richard Egielski. New York: Farrar, Straus & Giroux, 1986 (I: all).

ZEMACH, HARVE. *Duffy and the Devil*. Illustrated by Margot Zemach. New York: Farrar, Straus & Giroux, 1973 (I: 8–12).

CHAPTER 9

AUTHOR'S STYLE AND POINT OF VIEW

DEVELOPING UNDERSTANDING AND APPRECIATION OF
  AUTHOR'S STYLE
    Core Books and Sample Lessons for Lower Elementary Students
    Extended Books for Lower Elementary Students
    Recreational Books for Lower Elementary Students
    Core Books and Sample Lessons for Middle Elementary Students
    Extended Books for Middle Elementary Students
    Recreational Books for Middle Elementary Students
    Core Books and Sample Lessons for Upper Elementary and Middle School Students
    Extended Books for Upper Elementary and Middle School Students
    Recreational Books for Upper Elementary and Middle School Students
DEVELOPING UNDERSTANDING AND APPRECIATION OF POINT
  OF VIEW
    Core Books and Sample Lesson for Lower Elementary Students
    Extended Books for Lower Elementary Students
    Recreational Books for Lower Elementary Students
    Core Books and Sample Lessons for Middle Elementary Students
    Extended Books for Middle Elementary Students
    Recreational Books for Middle Elementary Students
    Core Books and Sample Lesson for Upper Elementary and Middle School Students
    Extended Books for Upper Elementary and Middle School Students
    Recreational Books for Upper Elementary and Middle School Students

Authors choose words to describe their settings and their characters, sentence structures to enhance their ideas, and points of view to develop insights into their stories and their characters. Authors may use figurative language in ways that encourage readers to see, to hear, and to feel the world in new ways. Eve Merriam (Janeczko, 1990) emphasizes this importance of words when she states, "Sounds of words were enthralling: I was captivated by their musicality, and by the fact that you could have alliteration, so that if you said, 'Peter, Peter, Pumpkin Eater,' it was very funny. Or if you recited 'The Highway Man came riding, riding, up to the old inn door,' it was exciting; you could hear a whole orchestra in your voice." (p. 65). Students also can experience an excitement in the sound of language as they listen to and share literature that has especially appealing language.

This chapter will focus on the important areas of author's style and point of view. As in the previous chapters on literary elements, the chapter includes core lessons and lists of related books that can be used for literature discussions and recreational reading.

DEVELOPING UNDERSTANDING AND APPRECIATION OF AUTHOR'S STYLE

Many of the discussions and activities developed around plot, characterization, setting, and theme emphasized an author's style. By selecting appropriate words and sentence structures, authors create visual images that reflect moods or increase tension. Authors might use similes or metaphors to encourage readers to make new comparisons and to visualize the world in new ways. Making new comparisons however is difficult for many students. Daane (1990) found that although college freshmen used common metaphors in their writing, fresh metaphors were extremely rare. Fresh metaphors developed in books could encourage students to develop their own uncommon comparisons. Authors of books, especially books for younger readers, frequently use personification to make the nonhuman characters and objects more meaningful to the reader. Illustrator and author Arnold Lobel emphasizes the importance of personification in both his illustrations and his text (Shannon, 1989). An author's style can be enhanced through the illustrations.

The sound of a story also should appeal to the senses and should be appropriate for the content of the story. Reading stories aloud, especially carefully crafted stories, is an excellent way to teach students to evaluate and appreciate an author's style. In this section we will focus on lessons that help students appreciate and understand personification and various types of figurative language. Several techniques will be used including identification, analysis, discussion, dramatization, writing, illustration, and modeling. Several of the lessons follow an approach I developed (Norton 1989b) in which students (a) identify personification during listening and observation, (b) discuss and analyze personification after listening and observation, and (c) perform tasks that enhance understanding and appreciation of personification. Many additional lessons on author's style are presented in Chapter 12 on poetry.

Core Books and Sample Lessons for Lower Elementary Students

LESSON ONE: Developing an Appreciation of Personification

OBJECTIVES

To stimulate the imagination.

To develop an understanding and appreciation of personification in text and illustrations.

To perform pantomime and create dramatizations using personification.

To write a story using personification.

To draw personified objects and animals.

CORE BOOKS: Virginia Lee Burton's *The Little House* and Emily Arnold McCully's *Picnic*

PROCEDURES: This lesson will take more than one day. In fact, most teachers spend several days on the activities accompanying *The Little House* and several additional days on *Picnic*.

Begin the lesson by clarifying the meaning of personification through examples. Students should understand that when authors and illustrators use personification they are giving human characteristics—feelings, actions, and life styles—to objects and animals. Ask students to describe their toys and pets so they can use examples of personification and relate personification to personal experiences. The students usually give human characteristics to objects and animals that are close to them. Ask them to list actions and feelings that are similar to their own actions and emotions.

First, read *The Little House* aloud for appreciation and enjoyment of the total story. Encourage the students to react to the house and her emotions. Before reading the story a second time, ask the students to listen for examples of personification. For example, the discussion can focus on the following questions:

1. What pronoun does the author use when writing about the house? Could you use this pronoun when writing about a person?
2. What actions can the house perform that are similar to your actions?
3. What feelings does the house have that are similar to your feelings?
4. What causes the house to have these feelings? When have you had similar feelings?
5. How do the illustrations help you understand the house's feelings and character?

This discussion either can follow the second reading of the whole book or can accompany individual pages. The decision will depend on the students. The discussion should emphasize that the house is always called "she;" that the personified actions include watching, thinking, waiting, feeling, hearing, and dreaming; that the personified emotions include curiosity, happiness, surprise, sadness, loneliness, and fear; that the bright, cheery country made the house happy, while the dirty, crowded city caused opposite feelings; that children often experience similar feelings; and that the illustrations show the house with corresponding expressions and rely on colors to enhance the mood.

During a performing activity, students can pantomime the feelings expressed by the house and create conversations that might occur between the house and her city or country neighbors. Interesting conversational partners for the house might include the horseless carriages, the subway, and the moving truck. Ask students, "How would you feel if you were the _____ ? What would you want to say to the house?" Encourage the students to create different combinations of conversations and to act out their roles.

The wordless book *Picnic* is enjoyable for developing understanding of personification because it encourages students to observe the detailed illustrations and produce their own text that includes the personified mice responding to setting, conflict, plot development, characterization, and point of view. Most students find this book so rich with detail that it requires several "readings."

After the second "reading," students can consider the following questions:

1. How do the illustrations let you know that the mice will have some personified or human characteristics?

2. What actions of the mice are similar to your actions? How do the illustrations show these actions? How would you describe these actions in personified terms?

3. What feelings or emotions do these mice seem to be expressing? How do the illustrations show these feelings? How would you describe these feelings in personified terms?

This discussion should emphasize that the illustrations show mice living in a house, riding or driving in a truck, preparing to play baseball, preparing the picnic setting, strumming an instrument, hugging each other, and crying. The illustrations also show the mice expressing happiness by jumping for joy, loneliness and maybe fear through tears, determination and self-reliance through hunting for food, worry through searching for a missing son, and love through responses when finding the lost child.

After this discussion, students can dramatize the story, create a written story to accompany the illustrations, or create dialogues among the various mice characters. After these experiences with personification, students often enjoy creating their own personified stories in which they develop both the illustrations and the text. They can create their own library corner of original personified stories.

LESSON TWO: An Introduction to Similes

OBJECTIVES

To respond to similes developed through both illustrations and text.

To dramatize and discuss the meanings of the comparisons.

To identify and illustrate similes that have meaning in the students' lives.

CORE BOOK: Hugh Lewin's *Jafta* (Picture Story Book, South African).

PROCEDURES: The similes are developed through both the text and the illustrations. Introduce the book by telling the students that the author wrote the book because he wanted to introduce his own children to South Africa and he used animals and people characteristic of South Africa. Show the students South Africa on a map or globe.

Read *Jafta* orally. Provide enough opportunity for students to view the illustrations that accompany the text. For example, the text states," 'When I'm happy,' said Jafta, 'I purr like a lioncub' " (p. 2 unnumbered). The accompanying illustration shows a smiling boy holding an equally happy lioncub. After reading the book once for enjoyment and personal response, read the book again and ask the students to describe how Jafta skips, laughs, jumps, dances, nuzzles, acts tired, shows he is cross, shows he is strong, wants to be tall, wants to be long, runs, swings through trees, and flies. Ask the students to dramatize each of these actions.

Finally, tell the students that the author is using similes to make readers visualize and understand Jafta's actions and feelings. Reread several of these similes and point out the comparisons and the author's use of *like*. Tell the students that because the story takes place in South Africa the comparisons between Jafta and the animals are all from Jafta's environment. Ask the students how they might describe their own feelings and actions if they were to compare them to those of animals in their own environment. Ask, "What feelings or actions would you include? What animals are in your environment that you could use to show how you feel and act?" Encourage the students to write and illustrate descriptions of themselves using similes that compare themselves to animal characteristics.

LESSON THREE: Developing an Understanding an Appreciation of Similes

The sample lesson in this section encourages understanding of similes through a modeling lesson that teaches students how to become actively involved in and aware of their thought processing. The steps are similar to the modeling lesson on inferring characterization with *Sarah, Plain and Tall* in Chapter 6. This lesson on similes follows the instructional sequences in a modeling lesson: (a) the teacher identifies the requirements for effective reasoning, (b) the teacher develops an introduction to similes, (c) the teacher identifies the importance of similes to the students, (d) the teacher introduces the story, and (e) the teacher proceeds with the modeling examples and brings the students into the thought processes and discussions.

OBJECTIVES

To be involved in a modeling activity designed to show students how to analyze evidence from the text and speculate about similes.

To understand the requirements for effective reasoning when thinking about similes.

To appreciate and understand the author's use of similes.

CORE BOOK: Leo Lionni's *Swimmy* (Picture Story Book, Caldecott Honor).

PROCEDURES: First, identify the requirements for effective reasoning so that the lesson helps students understand those requirements. For example, effective understanding of similes requires that students (a) go beyond information authors provide in the text, (b) know that similes are comparisons that authors make between something in the text and something that is not in the text, (c) know that similes are introduced with the clue words *like* and *as,* (d) know that authors use similes to develop more vivid descriptions and characterizations, and (e) think about how one object is like another object (sometimes the comparisons are between an object that is known and another object that is not known).

Second, develop an introduction to similes. For example, tell the students that "sometimes authors use a special kind of writing called figurative language. This kind of language allows authors to use fewer words but to write more vividly. Similes are a kind of figurative language in which an author compares one thing to another thing. Today we will be listening for ways that authors use similes to make us see pictures in our minds."

Expand the introduction to similes by providing examples of similes. For example, "Similes are comparisons in which the author tells us how two things are alike. We know when an author is using a simile because it is introduced with the clue words *like* or *as*. Many times the comparison will be between one object that you know, and one object that you do not know. The author is trying to make you see objects in new ways. For example, if we say, 'Sandy is as quiet as a mouse,' we know that the author is using a simile because of the clue word, *as*. We also know that we need to compare a mouse's characteristics and Sandy's characteristics. We know that a mouse is quiet and shy around people. So we know that the author is telling us that Sandy is quiet and even shy around people. We know that Sandy is not a mouse, but we can picture her with some of the same characteristics as a shy, quiet mouse. In another example, if we read that 'Giraffes have ears like giant leaves,' we know the author is making a comparison because of the clue word *like*. We know even without seeing a giraffe that its ears are shaped like big leaves. We know that big leaves hang down so we can imagine the giraffe with big, floppy ears that hang down alongside its head. We must listen or read carefully, however, because an *as* or a *like* in a sentence does not always signal a comparison and a simile. For example, does the sentence 'I stumbled as I was walking down the street' include a simile? Why not? Does the sentence 'I like ice cream' include a simile? Why not?" Ask the students to give you examples of similes and to discuss what the similes mean.

Explain to the students that in this modeling activity they will listen as you read portions of a story and then ask a question about a simile, answer the question, provide evidence or clues from the story that tell why you gave that answer, and share how you thought about the story and the simile to reach the answer. Tell the students that after they have listened to you go through these questions and answers, they will use the same process to answer questions, identify evidence, and explore their own reasoning or thought processes. As part of this introduction, discuss the meanings of *evidence* and *reasoning*.

Third, develop the importance of understanding and using similes. For example, "We need to know how similes work, and what they can tell us as we read so that we understand more about what we read. Similes help us appreciate the author's story. Authors use similes to paint a vivid picture with words just as an artist paints a vivid picture with paints." Ask the students, "Why do you think it is important to understand similes? When could you use similes?"

Fourth, develop an introduction to the story. *Swimmy* is a little fish who lives at the bottom of the sea. To introduce this setting ask the students to close their eyes and imagine that they are a small fish swimming around in a large ocean. Ask them to look around. "What do you see when you swim in the ocean? What does the bottom of the ocean look like? What other fish are in the ocean with you? How do you feel when you see these fish?" After the students have described what they saw, tell them that today you will read a story about a fish. They will listen for the similes, tell what the comparison means, and explain how they reached their answers. Tell them to listen carefully as you do the first one for them. By listening to how you think through the simile they will know what to do when it is their turn.

Fifth, provide the first modeling example. For this lesson do not show the illustrations before you read the book. You want the students to use the similes, not the illustrations, to work through the process. Read orally through page 1. Ask the students, "What does Swimmy look like?" Answer the question: "Swimmy is shiny and deep black." Provide the evidence: "The author used the simile clue *as*. The author says that only one of the fish is 'As black as a mussel shell.' Provide your reasoning to reach the answer. For example, "I know that the author is telling me to think about more information because I saw a simile. I know the comparison is between Swimmy's color and a black mussel shell. I know from my own experience that there are many shades of black. Also, I know from seeing a mussel shell in the water at the beach that it is dark black and shiny. If I close my eyes I can see a small, black, shiny fish swimming among many other fish who are not black." (For this lesson you might want to have on hand a dry mussel shell and a cup of water. Show the students the dry shell and then place it in water. It immediately turns from dull gray to dark, shiny black.) After completing this modeling example, ask the students to listen to the text again with their eyes closed. Ask, "Can you see Swimmy's color?" Now share the picture and compare the students' visualizations with the actual illustration. Students often envision a much shinier fish than the one in the illustration. You might want to explain to them that the illustration is not shiny because the paper it is printed on is dull.

Provide the second modeling example, but first make sure the students understand the procedure. If they do not, model another example completely. If the students understand the process, let them join the discussion by providing an answer, the evidence, and the reasoning. Read pages 4 through 10. Stop after "a lobster, who walked about like a water-moving machine." Ask the students, "How does the lobster move?" Ask the students to provide answers. They probably will provide answers similar to this one: "The lobster walks mechanically through the water. He walks slowly, pushing the water ahead of him." Ask the students to demonstrate how the lobster walks like a water-moving machine. Ask the students to provide evidence such as, "The author used the simile clue *like*. The author describes the lobster as walking about like a water-moving machine." Ask the students to provide reasoning such as, "I can see a water-moving machine that will move water. It will not swim easily like a fish. It will push forward. I can almost imagine it moving like a robot with its claws moving the water and its feet pushing along." After discussing this page show the illustration and compare the illustrator's interpretation with that of the students.

Read orally pages 11 through 17. Stop after "sea anemones looked like pink palm trees swaying in the wind." Ask the students, "What do the sea anemones look like?" Answers should be similar to this: "The sea anemones are pink and have a thin body (trunk). They have a top of thin, stringy arms that wave in the water." Encourage students to provide evidence such as "The author used the simile clue *like*. The author says that sea anemones look like 'pink palm trees swaying in the wind.'" Encourage students to provide reasoning such as, "The author tells me to think about more information because he uses a simile. The comparison is between sea anemones and pink palm trees. I know what a palm tree looks like so I can imagine the shape and actions of the anemone. The body of the anemone is like the trunk of a tree and its top is like a palm tree. I know from my own experience what palm trees look like as they move in the air." This is another good place to have students demonstrate how the anemone moves. Again, show the illustration and ask students to compare the illustration with their visualization. After looking at this illustration, students often want to draw their own example. Because the illustration is more coral in color, many students point out that they do not believe the picture is really pink.

Continue reading the book, asking and answering questions, and providing evidence and reasoning. Read page 18. Say to the students, "Describe what Swimmy sees. Why is this important to the story? How is this school different from Swimmy's school?" Encourage answers and discussion. Read from page 19 through end of text. Ask, "What was Swimmy's plan?" After students have completed this last model, ask them, "What messages is the author telling us?" Even the youngest students understand that the messages are "It is important to work together, it is important to have a plan, and being different is not bad." Finally, reread the story and let students enjoy the similes with their new understandings.

Extended Books for Lower Elementary Students

The books listed in this section are excellent for reading aloud, developing appreciation of author's style through discussions and dramatizations, and modeling activities that emphasize higher thought processes. Many of the books include personification and many of the personified actions, behaviors, and emotions are similar to those experienced by younger students. Consequently, many students enjoy sharing experiences when they felt similar emotions. Similes and metaphors are also common. Several of the books are easy to read and appeal to students with beginning reading abilities.

These books contain personification.

Picture Story Books

ANTHONY BROWNE's *Gorilla*. Personification develops as a toy gorilla comes to life and accompanies a girl to the zoo.

VIRGINIA LEE BURTON's *Katy and the Big Snow*. A red tractor is personified as she responds to pleas for help during a snow storm.

JEAN deBRUNHOFF's *Babar's Anniversary Album: 6 Favorite Stories* and *The Story of Babar*. The personified elephant experiences many human emotions and behaviors.

LISA CAMPBELL ERNST's *Ginger Jumps*. The personified dog experiences need for companionship, need to be loved, and need to overcome fear.

RUSSELL HOBAN's *A Baby Sister for Frances, A Bargain for Frances, Best Friends for Frances*, and *Bread and Jam for Frances*. The personified badger experiences emotions and behaviors that are similar to those of a human child.

ROBERT KRAUS's *Leo the Late Bloomer*. The personified young tiger experiences problems similar to those of young children.

LEO LIONNI's *Alexander and the Wind-up Mouse*. A toy mouse and a real mouse become friends and make discoveries about being themselves.

LEO LIONNI's *Tillie and the Wall*. Personified field mice are curious about what is on the other side of a wall.

ARNOLD LOBEL's *Frog and Toad All Year, Frog and Toad Are Friends, Frog and Toad Together* (Newbery Honor), *Grasshopper on the Road, Owl at Home* and *Uncle Elephant* (Easy to Read). The personified animals develop human behaviors, actions, and feelings. These are favorites of many teachers and students.

ROBERT McCLOSKEY's *Time of Wonder* (Caldecott Medal). The text includes personification, pleasing images, similes, and rhythm.

CYNTHIA RYLANT's *Henry and Mudge, Henry and Mudge and the Bedtime Thumps, Henry and Mudge and the Forever Sea, Henry and Mudge and the Happy Cat, Henry and Mudge Get the Cold Shivers, Henry and Mudge in the Green Time, Henry and Mudge in the Sparkle Days, Henry and Mudge in Puddle Trouble*, and *Henry and Mudge Under the Yellow Moon*. (Easy to Read). This series develops personification through the adventures of a boy and his dog. The dog and other animals in the stories express human emotions.

DR. SEUSS's *The Cat in the Hat* and *The Cat in the Hat Comes Back* (Easy to Read). Through rhyming dialogue, the personified cat develops humorous adventures.

GABRIELLE VINCENT's *Ernest and Celestine's Picnic, Feel Better, Ernest!*, and *Smile, Ernest and Celestine*. The young mouse experiences human emotions such as jealousy and worry.

MARGERY WILLIAMS' *The Velveteen Rabbit: Or How Toys Become Real* (Fantasy). The toys are personified and the toy rabbit becomes a real rabbit.

These books contain similes.

HUGH LEWIN's *Jafta's Mother* (South African). The text compares characteristics of Jafta's mother to nature. In the morning she is "like the sun rising in the early morning, lighting up the dark corners and gently coaxing us awake" (unnumbered), but if she finds the children cheating or teasing she "sounds like thunder in the afternoon and her eyes will flash like the lightning out of the dark clouds" (unnumbered).

Nonfiction

ALICE AND MARTIN PROVENSEN's *The Glorious Flight Across the Channel With Louis Bleriot, July 25, 1909* (Illustrated, Caldecott Honor). Text includes similes such as flying through the air "like swallows," "flaps like a chicken," and hops "like a rabbit."

Narrative Poem

CLEMENT MOORE's *The Night Before Christmas* (Illustrated). The poem is filled with similes such as "flew like a flash" and "cheeks were like roses."

Recreational Books for Lower Elementary Students

Many of these books include personification.

Picture Story Books

JANET AND ALLEN AHLBERG's *Each Peach Pear Plum: An I-Spy Story*
CATHERINE AHNOLT's *Truffles Is Sick*
MARC BROWN's *Arthur's Baby*
MARGARET WISE BROWN's *The Runaway Bunny*
ROGER DUVOISIN's *Petunia*
DIANA ENGEL's *Josephina Hates Her Name*
MARY ANN HOBERMAN's *Mr. and Mrs. Muddle*
LEO LIONNI's *The Biggest House in the World*
JAMES MARSHALL's *George and Martha One Fine Day*
BILL PEET's *The Gnats of Knotty Pine*
MARY RAYNER's *Garth Pig and the Ice Cream Lady*
HANS REY's *Curious George*
DR. SEUSS's *Horton Hatches the Egg*
JAMES STEVENSON's *Monty*
ROSEMARY WELLS's *Timothy Goes to School*

Core Books and Sample Lessons for Middle Elementary Students

LESSON ONE: Developing an Appreciation of Personification

OBJECTIVES

To develop an understanding and appreciation of personification of animals in text and illustrations.

To compare characteristics of personified animals in fantasy to the characteristics of animals in nonfictional sources.

CORE BOOKS: For the core books for this lesson select a group of personified fantasy and realistic fictional and nonfictional books about the same type of animal. For example: Ursula K. LeGuin's *Catwings* and *Catwings Return* (Fantasy) and Joanna Cole's *A Cat's Body* (Nonfiction); Robert O'Brien's *Mrs. Frisby and the Rats of NIMH* or Dick King-Smith's *Martin's Mice* (Fantasy) and William J. Weber's *Care of Uncommon Pets* (Nonfiction); Michael Bond's *A Bear Called Paddington* (Fantasy) and Downs Matthews's *Polar Bear Cubs* (Nonfiction); E. B. White's *Charlotte's Web* (Fantasy, Newbery Honor, Touchstone) and Jack Denton Scott's *The Book of the Pig* (Nonfiction); and Robert Lawson's *Rabbit Hill* (Fantasy, Newbery Medal) and Lilo Hess's *Diary of a Rabbit* (Nonfiction).

PROCEDURES: For this lesson divide students into groups according to an animal of their choice. Each group should read both the fantasy and the nonfiction selections about their animals. As they read each book, ask them to identify the characteristics of the personified animal characters and the nonfictional animals. Have them compare the personified characteristics with human characteristics and the nonfictional characteristics with real animals that they have seen. "Do the characteristics match human and animal characteristics?" After they have developed their lists, ask the students to consider, "How do personified animals differ from nonfictional animals? When do you think it is appropriate to personify animals and when is it not appropriate?" Students should conclude that it is appropriate to personify characters in fantasy stories but it is not appropriate in nonfictional sources. They should realize that nonfictional books should contain only accurate information.

Finally, ask the students to develop a chart in which they summarize the characteristics of personified animal fantasies and nonfictional animal stories. This chart can include information on characters, types of settings, plot and content, and illustrations. Leave room on the chart for the students to include examples that support each of the summaries. The basic information for the chart in Figure 9.1 was developed by a group of fourth-grade students. Each

FIGURE 9.1 Summary of characteristics of personified animal fantasies and nonfictional animal stories.

	Personified Fantasy	**Nonfiction**
Characters:	Animals speak, act, and feel like people. Animals can have human motives.	Animals behave like animals. Actions agree with animal behavior.
Examples:		*Examples:*
Setting:	Can be imaginary or seem real.	Must be real as we know it.
Examples:		*Examples:*
Plot and Content:	Animal conflicts can be same as those experienced by people.	Animal behaviors that can be seen. Often follows life cycle of animal.
Examples:		*Examples:*
Illustrations:	Animals can be dressed like people, live in human surroundings, and show emotions.	Photographs and drawings of animals living in real surroundings.
Examples:		*Examples:*

group filled in examples from their stories and then compared information and drew conclusions about evaluating the appropriateness of personification in literature.

 LESSON TWO: Developing an Understanding and Appreciation of Similes and Other Figurative Language

OBJECTIVES

To identify similes and other descriptive language and to discuss the visual images created by the author's use of language.

To develop higher reasoning abilities through a modeling lesson that has students provide evidence and reasoning to reach their answers.

To respond to the similes and figurative language in a book through art.

To develop a creative writing story that uses similes or other examples of figurative language.

CORE BOOK: Bill Brittain's *The Wish Giver* (Modern Fantasy, Newbery Honor).

PROCEDURES: Review the procedures for developing and introducing a modeling lesson about similes described for *Swimmy* in the previous section for lower elementary students. You may use the same requirements for effective reasoning, introductory examples of similes, and rationale for the importance of similes. If students have had no previous introduction to similes, the books *Jafta* and *Jafta's Mother* are also useful.

If students have taken part in the modeling lesson for inferring characterization (*Sarah, Plain and Tall*) developed in a previous chapter they will understand the structure of the lesson. If they have not, present the structure (review the information in the *Sarah, Plain and Tall* modeling lesson). If they have already completed a modeling lesson, review the approach that you will use as you first read the text example, ask a question, answer the question, provide the evidence that supports the answer, and share the reasoning that you used to reach the answer. Remind the students that after you show them how you approached this process, you will expect them to join in with the answers, the evidence, and their reasoning process.

Introduce *The Wish Giver* by telling the students that the author of this Newbery Honor book uses numerous similes and other figurative language to depict character traits and reveal information about rural life. Ask the students how they might use similes to reveal character traits or to describe nature.

Teachers have several options when using this modeling lesson with students. The book is written in sections: The prologue or "The Strange Little Man"; "Jug-a-Rum"; "The Tree Man"; "Water, Water, Everywhere"; and the epilogue or "At Stew Meat's Store." Some teachers read the prologue orally and encourage personal responses from the students. Then they reread the prologue and model a discussion about similes or begin the modeling lesson with the second story. Other teachers prefer beginning the modeling lesson with the first reading and then allowing students to read each of the remaining stories independently. After the students have read each story, teachers lead a discussion related to the vivid language and the influences of the similes on characterization and setting. Still other teachers prefer to read the whole book orally and to model the book during a series of lessons. This choice depends on the preferences of students and teachers. Whichever approach is used, this is a favorite book with many middle elementary students. In fact, one group of fourth-grade students voted it their favorite book of the year.

To make this modeling lesson useful for any of the above approaches, the lesson includes a detailed model for the first story and then identifies examples of similes and vivid descriptions that can be highlighted in the second story. To conduct a modeling lesson for the prologue, read to page 6, stopping after "The man who'd drawn back the tent flaps was short and fat, like a big ball on two legs." Ask the question, "What does the man look like?" Answer the question, "The man is short and fat with skinny legs attached to a huge, round body." Provide the evidence, "The author described the man as short and fat. He used the simile clue *like* to compare the fat man to a big ball on two legs." State your reasoning to reach your answer, "I know what a big ball looks like. In my mind I could see a funny picture of a huge, round ball. I thought that if the ball had legs they would look skinny compared with the ball. I also saw a person who was mostly round body, even his head and his legs were not that important." After completing this first modeling example, read the passage again and have the students close their eyes. After reading, ask the students to describe their image of Thaddeus Blinn. Next, show them the picture of Thaddeus Blinn on page 11 and have them compare it with their mental image.

Make sure that the students understand the modeling process. If they do, they may join in with answers, evidence, and reasoning during this second example. If they do not understand the process, model a second example completely. Before beginning the second example and discussion, ask the students to jot down their answers and their evidence. They also should think about their reasoning processes. These notes will improve the discussions.

Continue reading from page 6 to the middle of page 7. Stop after "Thaddeus Blinn's eyes glowed . . . like a cat when lantern light reaches the dark corner where it's sitting. . . .The pupils. . . .narrow like the eyes of a snake." Ask the students, "How would you describe Thaddeus Blinn's eyes?" Their answers should be similar to this one: "His eyes glow with a bright yellow color that outshines anything around them. The pupils are also narrow and slender." Ask the students to provide evidence such as, "The author used the simile clue *like* to compare the glow in Thaddeus Blinn's eyes to a cat's eyes and he compared the pupils to the eyes of a snake." Ask the students to explore their reasoning. Students might give you examples such as, "I have a pet cat. I have seen the cat outside at night. Once I was driving up to the house at night and the car's headlights shone on a cat. The only thing I could see was two bright, glowing eyes. I have seen a snake's eyes. They are narrow slits. I got a creepy feeling when I thought of the eyes. The cat's eyes reminded me of a hunter. The snake's eyes made me frightened. I don't think I would trust a man with eyes like that."

Continue, using this same approach. The following list includes text examples and questions that can be used for modeling the prologue and the first story. Ask the students to provide answers, evidence, and their reasoning:

1. *Text:* Stop after "Blinn moved his hand . . . like a church collection plate . . . full of coins" (p. 7). *Question:* How would you describe the way Blinn moved his hands?
2. *Text:* "The words tumbled . . . like wasps from a burning nest" (p. 13). *Question:* How did the words come out of Thaddeus Blinn's mouth?
3. *Text:* " . . . he snapped the tent flaps . . . like a magician doing a disappearing act" (p. 15). *Question:* How did Thaddeus Blinn close the tent flaps?

At the close of the prologue (p. 16), ask the students to summarize what they know about Thaddeus Blinn. They might relate their summaries to the author's use of similes. Ask, "What do these similes reveal about Thaddeus Blinn? Are these positive or negative comparisons? Why? Do all of the images work together to give you a better picture of the person? How do you think a person like this will influence the outcome of the rest of the stories? How did you react to Thaddeus Blinn? Would you trust this man? Why or why not? What would you still like to know about Thaddeus Blinn?"

Continue with the second story:

1. *Text:* "They were as shy as wild foxes . . . " (p. 21). *Question:* How did the twins act?
2. *Text:* " . . . the spot . . . glowed like a burning coal" (p. 30). *Question:* How would you describe the spot on the card?

3. *Text:* "You sound like a bullfrog" (p. 35). *Question:* What did Leland mean when he said that Polly sounded like a bullfrog? How did she sound?

4. *Text:* " . . . as still as stones" (p. 41). *Question:* What did the students sound like when their teacher spoke?

5. *Text:* "Both girls started giggling like little imps" (p. 54). *Question:* How would you describe the girls' giggling?

6. *Text:* " . . . like a long-lost friend" (p. 55). *Question:* How did the girls greet Polly?

7. *Text:* "like she and Eunice . . were Siamese twins . . ." (p. 60). *Question:* How does Polly describe the characters of Eunice and Agatha?

8. *Text:* " . . . like water rolling off a duck's back" (p. 63). *Question:* What does the author tell you about Polly and how she listened to the words?

Students enjoy several types of response activities. They can choose a character in a story or a description of a setting and illustrate the character or setting using the visual images created by the author's choice of words. One group of students discussed the appropriateness of the nature-related similes in this book because the stories have rural and small town settings. Then they created their own short stories that had different settings and used similes for their comparisons that corresponded with the settings. For example, an inner-city setting and an outer-space setting would require different comparisons if the stories were to seem believable.

LESSON THREE: Relating the Author's Use of Similes to the Development of Characterization

OBJECTIVES

To develop an appreciation for the use of similes to enhance characterization.

To evaluate the appropriateness of similes used to develop characterization.

To write character sketches that use similes.

CORE BOOK: Sid Fleischman's *The Midnight Horse* (Modern Fantasy).

PROCEDURES: This lesson should follow the introduction or review of similes as developed in the previous lesson. Introduce the book by placing the students in the time and place: Middle to late 1800s, after the Civil War (the war is briefly referred to as having taken place before this story); Cricklewood, New Hampshire, population 217 ("216 fine folks and 1 infernal grouch"). Encourage the students to visualize the conditions of this time period, especially the transportation (horse-drawn coach).

Next, review the effect of similes and how similes are used to enhance various literary elements and create vivid visual images. Tell the students that the author of *The Midnight Horse* uses numerous similes to describe the settings and enhance his characters. Read the introduction orally: "It was raining bullfrogs. The coach lurched and swayed along the river road like a ship in rough seas. Inside clung three passengers like unlashed cargo. One was a blacksmith, another was a thief, and the third was an orphan boy named Touch" (p. 1). Ask the students to describe how they visualized the setting, the coach, and the passengers. Then ask, "What similes did the author use to describe the coach and the ride of the passengers? Why do you think the author chose these comparisons? Are these good comparisons? Why or why not?"

Now ask the students to consider the three passengers in the coach. Ask, "If the author used two similes in the very first paragraph to describe the setting, do you think he probably will continue to use similes to describe his characters?" Encourage the students to speculate about similes that would describe the blacksmith, the thief, and Touch, the orphan boy. Ask,

"How would your similes reveal whether the characters are good or bad? How would your similes show the physical characteristics of the people?" Tell the students that they will be searching for similes that the author uses in *The Midnight Horse* to describe the good and bad characters in the story.

Ask the students to list the similes and other figurative language they find for the following characters and to consider what these similes reveal about the characters: Touch (the orphan boy), Otis Cratt (the thief), Sally (the innkeeper), and Judge Henry Wigglesforth (Touch's great-uncle).

The following list includes examples of similes related to characterization:

Touch, the orphan:
1. "Touch was skinny and bareheaded, with hair as curly as wood shavings" (p. 1).
2. "He chose to bring himself up, free as a sail to catch any chance wind that came along" (p. 29).

Otis Cratt, the thief:
1. This long-armed man had his face wrapped with a muffler so that he looked "like a loosely wrapped mummy" (p. 3).
2. When Otis saw the blacksmith's billfold, his eyes were "drawn to it like a compass needle to true north." His arm started to weave "like a snake stalking its prey" (p. 4).
3. Otis loped into the woods "like a wolf returning to its den" (p. 29).
4. His tattered overcoat had "pockets deep as graves."
5. The sheriff pulled Otis out of the river "like a flapping trout" (p. 79).

Sally, the innkeeper:
1. She brightened when she saw the visitor, "the way a morning glory opens to the sunlight" (p. 31).

Judge Henry Wigglesforth, Touch's great-uncle:
1. Touch says, "My great-uncle is tighter'n a wet shirt" (p. 32).
2. He stood in front of the fireplace "warming his hands as if stealing all the heat he could, free of charge" (p. 32).
3. The blacksmith refers to the judge: "Lad, he'll stick to you like a fishhook until he's swindled you legal out of what's coming to you" (p. 39).
4. When chasing the characters in his black buggy, the judge "was bearing down like a windstorm" (p. 72).

After the students have identified and listed as many similes as possible, ask them to consider how these similes relate to the actions of each character within the story. Ask, "How did the similes reveal the type of characters? Which characters were good? Which characters were bad? How did the similes enhance these characteristics? Give examples of how the characters lived up to the author's comparisons? Do you think the comparisons were justified by the way the story ended? Why or why not? How did these comparisons help you respond to the various characters in the story?" An additional discussion can be developed by tracing the changes in Touch as he proceeds from "bad luck on two legs" (p. 16) to "good luck on two legs" (p. 81).

After identifying the similes and discussing their relationships to characterization in *The Midnight Horse,* ask the students to think about characters they have read about in other books or characters they would like to write about. Ask them to develop short character descriptions in which they use similes to describe the character's physical appearance, behaviors, and attitudes.

LESSON FOUR: Developing a Journal of "Quotable Quotes"

OBJECTIVE

> To identify and record examples of author's style that bring pleasure, appreciation, and understanding to the reader.

CORE BOOKS: Any book that contains pleasing examples of author's style. Many of the books listed in the extended and recreational book lists can be used for this purpose. Students also can select examples from the core books of lessons in this chapter.

PROCEDURES: This core lesson easily can extend throughout the school year. Some students start their journals in one grade and continue using them throughout school and into adult life. Some students, particularly those who are interested in literature or writing, enjoy comparing the examples they have chosen in different grades. One student said, "It is interesting to see how my taste in literature has changed."

Begin this activity by sharing with students examples of the styles of your favorite authors. Try to include examples of vivid language; exciting sentence structure; and pleasing descriptions of settings, characterizations, and moods from a variety of literary genres. Encourage students to write down only examples that are particularly pleasing to them or to which they respond vividly. Some students enjoy drawing illustrations to accompany their quotes. This assignment does not need to be graded or even shared. Students should, however, be encouraged to share examples that please them. One teacher had students keep both individual and group journals. For the group journals, students brought examples of author's style to the group and explained why they thought the examples should be included in the journal.

Extended Books for Middle Elementary Students

The books listed in this section can be used for several activities such as oral reading, discussions of author's style, modeling, illustrating figurative language, and journal writing. Particularly vivid passages can be selected for oral interpretations. (For additional sources, see the recommendations for poetry in Chapter 12.)

> Traditional
>
> SAMUEL MARSHAK's *The Month-Brothers* (Slavic). Vivid images are created through similes such as "light gleamed from between the trees like a star caught in the branches" (unnumbered).
>
> Modern Fantasy
>
> KENNETH GRAHAME's *The Wind in the Willows* (Touchstone). The text personifies both nature and animals.
>
> A. A. MILNE's *Winnie-the-Pooh* (Touchstone). The text includes personification of toy animals, sensory imagery, and considerable rhyme.
>
> Poetry
>
> RICHARD MARGOLIS's *Secrets of a Small Brother*. These poems that correspond with feelings include personification, similes, alliteration, and rhyming.
>
> JACK PRELUTSKY's *The Random House Book of Poetry for Children*. This anthology contains poems that include numerous examples of personification, simile, metaphor, and vivid imagery.
>
> Nonfiction
>
> KATHRYN LASKY's *Sugaring Time*. The text is written with strong visual images that describe nature and maple sugar time.

Biography

ALICE DALGLIESH's *The Columbus Story*. Similes, repetition, and personification provide a vivid author's style.

Recreational Books for Middle Elementary Students

Folktales

VERNA AARDEMA's *Bringing the Rain to Kapiti Plain: A Nandi Tale* (African)
VERNA AARDEMA's *Why Mosquitoes Buzz in People's Ears* (Caldecott Medal, African)
BYRD BAYLOR's *Moonsong* (Native American)
ASHLEY BRYAN's *Beat the Story-Drum, Pum-Pum* (African)
HARVE ZEMACH's *Duffy and the Devil* (Caldecott Medal, English)

Modern Fantasy

A. A. MILNE's *The House at Pooh Corner* (Touchstone)
GRAHAM OAKLEY's *The Church Mice in Action*
J. R. R. TOLKIEN's *Farmer Giles of Ham*
JANE YOLEN's *The Hundredth Dove and Other Tales*

Poetry

MYRA COHN LIVINGSTON's *Space Songs*
JACK PRELUTSKY's *Something Big Has Been Here*
JUDITH VIORST's *If I Were in Charge of the World and Other Worries: Poems for Children and Their Parents*
VALERIE WORTH's *All the Small Poems*

Core Books and Sample Lessons for Upper Elementary and Middle School Students

LESSON ONE: Developing an Understanding and Appreciation of Personification of Nature

OBJECTIVES

To develop appreciation for and understanding of personification of nature.

To develop an appreciation for the rhythm, imagery, and alliteration in a poem about Native American culture.

To develop a literary web or map showing personification, imagery, alliteration, and rhythm.

To create a reader's theatre and a choral arrangement of a poem that highlights the poetic style.

To evaluate the responses to and the effectiveness of two illustrated versions of the same poem.

CORE BOOKS: Henry Wadsworth Longfellow's *Hiawatha,* illustrated by Susan Jeffers and *Hiawatha's Childhood,* illustrated by Errol LeCain.

PROCEDURES: The two illustrated versions of this poem can be enjoyed several times. Select one of the texts and read the poem orally, encouraging the students to respond with pleasure and their general feelings about the rhythm and imagery created by the poet's choice of words and the illustrator's images. Students frequently say they enjoy the rhythm that sounds like drum beats and can create visual pictures easily in their minds.

Before reading the poem a second time, draw the beginning of a web on the board. Place *Hiawatha* in the center of the spoke and draw spokes going to *Personification, Imagery, Rhythm,* and *Alliteration*. Review the meanings of each of these terms. Tell the students that they will listen for examples of each of these poetic elements as they listen to or read the poem a second time. Ask the students to look for answers to the following questions:

1. How is nature personified in the poem? What words does Longfellow use to personify nature?
2. What image does this personification create in your mind?
3. What images are created by the descriptive terms?
4. What examples of alliteration do you hear? How do these words enhance the poem?
5. Listen to the rhythm of the poem. What words reinforce the rhythm? What impression does the rhythm create? Why is it effective for this poem?
6. How do the illustrations match or enhance the personification and the imagery of the poem?

During the discussion of this poem fill in the information on the web and discuss the images created or enhanced by each literary element. Share with the students the fact that LeCain's *Hiawatha's Childhood* won the 1985 Kate Greenaway Medal for illustration in Great Britain. Ask them to consider whether LeCain's sense of visual imagery might have influenced that choice. The web in Figure 9.2 was developed by a group of middle school students.

Next, use the texts from the two illustrated versions of *Hiawatha* to develop reader's theatre and choral speaking arrangements. For example, reader's theatre arrangements emphasize personification and characterization through narrator and character roles. Select students to develop character roles by reading lines for Nokomis, Hiawatha, pine trees, water, fireflies, owl and owlet, and Hiawatha's animal brothers. Both reader's theatre and choral speaking arrangements enhance students' appreciation of the rhythmic quality of Longfellow's poem. Students also might enjoy accompanying the oral readings with a drum beat.

Choral arrangements can be used to analyze the effectiveness of poem divisions. Although the words are the same for both of the illustrated texts, LeCain and Jeffers chose different divisions of the text. Consequently, different lines are grouped together. For example, the LeCain version places the lines about fiery tresses and the spirits' death-dance on one page with an illustration in hot reds and oranges; the next page shows the frosty nights of winter and crowds of ghosts in icy whites and dark greens. In contrast, the Jeffers version places all of these lines on one page accompanied by shadowy ghostly figures. Develop a page-per-group choral arrangement that enhances the analysis of the two texts. For LeCain's version divide the class into 14 groups; for Jeffers' version, divide the class into 10 groups. Ask the students to practice their assigned pages, present the total book as a choral arrangement, and consider the effectiveness of each division. Groups can try different divisions if they decide that neither text is the more effective.

After completing the literary web, the reader's theatre, the choral speaking arrangements, and the analysis of page divisions, encourage the students to observe the illustrations in the two texts again. Ask, "Which illustrations do you believe most

FIGURE 9.2 Web of Hiawatha.

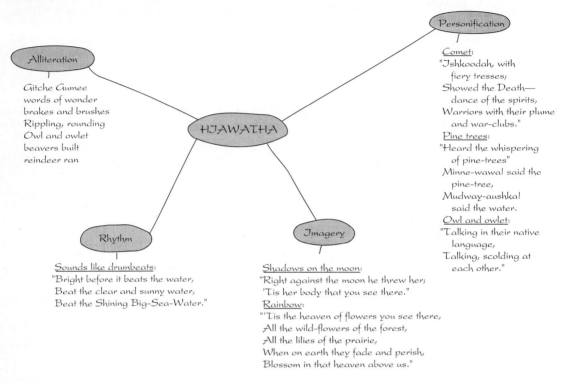

effectively develop the images of the poem? Why? If you were Henry Wadsworth Longfellow, which illustrations would you prefer? Why?" Encourage students to understand that there are no right or wrong answers to these questions. They might want to try developing their own illustrations that reflect the vivid imagery of the poem.

LESSON TWO: Developing an Understanding and Appreciation of Similes, Symbolism, Allusions, and Contrasts in a Historical Novel

OBJECTIVES

To improve an understanding of author's style.

To infer the author's meaning through the use of figurative language.

To be involved in a modeling activity that stimulates higher thought processes.

CORE BOOK: Rudolf Frank's *No Hero for the Kaiser* (This is a carefully detailed example of historical fiction and it is used in another core lesson in Chapter 14. That lesson explores authenticating historical fiction and evaluating and responding to setting as historical background, characterization related to wartime, conflict, and theme.)

PROCEDURES: This modeling lesson is related to inferring the author's meaning through the use of figurative language. The steps include those previously identified for modeling. First the teacher reviews the requirements for effective reasoning: To identify a non-literal comparison; to realize that figurative language is meant to clarify and enlighten by developing relationships that we might not have considered; to identify the similarities or differences between two things; to go beyond the information the author provides in the text; to use clues from the text to hypothesize about the relationships between figurative language and setting, characterization, conflict, and theme; and to use background knowledge gained from other experiences and stored in memory (Norton, 1989a).

Next, the teacher identifies text examples that can be used to discuss various types of figurative language. Frank's book contains many examples of figurative language, such as similes on pages 2, 12, 44, and 46; contrasts (paradox) on pages 45, 46, and 65; symbolism on page 2 (Plum Tree), page 18 (Wild Goat), and page 59 (Lance Corporal Poodle); and allusions on pages 42 and 49–51 (Napoleon), and pages 21, and 70–71 (Skull of African Sultan). Review the meanings of each of these types of figurative language by presenting examples. Review the sequence in a modeling lesson that proceeds from text example, to question, to answer, to evidence, and to reasoning process. Teachers who are developing and teaching modeling lessons should also follow the recommendations for effective modeling identified by Dole, Duffy, Roehler, and Pearson (1991):

1. Modeling that provides explicit, unambiguous information is more effective than vague or jumbled information.
2. Modeling that demonstrates flexible adjustment to text cues is more effective than modeling that emphasizes rigid rules.
3. If teachers merely ask questions without explaining the reasoning employed to answer those questions, many students will have difficulty understanding how the questions were answered.

If students do not understand how the questions were answered, they will not gain control of the process associated with answering questions. Consequently, the comprehension suffers.

Introduce the book by providing background information for the setting, which takes place in Europe during World War I. Using a map of Europe, show the students the important locations: Poland, Germany, and Russia. Next, read the students this information about the author: "Rudolf Frank was born in Germany and he was a military correspondent during World War I. After the war he wrote his first novel, *No Hero for the Kaiser*. At the time it was published in 1931, the book was described as an anti-war novel to warn young people. When Hitler came to power in Germany in 1933, Frank was arrested and the book was publicly burned. When he was released from prison, he fled to Switzerland. The book was published again in Germany in the 1970s. After this second publication, the book was awarded numerous awards for literature. In 1986, the book was first translated into English. This translation also won awards for literature." After sharing this information with the students, ask, "What could possibly be in this text that would cause the book to be banned by Hitler and the author to be imprisoned?"

After the students have speculated about the content of the book, ask them to place themselves in a situation in which they are to celebrate their 14th birthday. Ask, "What would you want to do on this important day? What could possibly happen to make you forget your birthday?" After they have answered, tell the students that they are joining a boy on his birthday and that something has happened to make him forget this important day.

The modeling examples are for the first chapter. Begin reading the book orally. Stop after this paragraph on page two: "The distant thud of cannon came closer, like a thunderstorm brewing. And as if the storm had already broken, women, boys, girls, and soldiers began to rush around in confusion; trumpets sounded, and suddenly the Russians had swept out of the village like the wind. Now they were firing down from the low hills into the village. It sounded like the high-pitched whine of mosquitoes as they fly past your ear looking for a place to settle and bite: zzzzzz—a thin, sharp noise, full of sly malice" (p. 2).

Now ask the inference question or questions. (Following is a series of questions, but you may choose just one of the questions.) "What is the author telling us about the setting in the Polish village? What is the author telling us about war? How does the author's use of simile increase your ability to visualize the setting and the war that will follow? Do you believe that these are good comparisons? Why or why not?"

Answer the questions: "The town is, or will be, the setting for a noisy and destructive battle. Soldiers who once enjoyed the town are running to take their places on the battlefield. People in the town are also running. The author tells us that war is terrible and destructive. The author's use of similes helps us hear the battle, see the movement, and feel the danger. I believe the similes are good comparisons."

Next, cite the evidence: "The author describes the normal activity and appearance of the town and then describes changes. The sound of cannon is compared to a thunderstorm. The rapidly advancing Russian soldiers are compared to wind sweeping through the town. The sound of bullets is compared to the whine of a mosquito."

Next, explore your own reasoning process. For example, "The author describes the village and then shows what happens to it when two forces are about to fight. I know from my own experience that a thunderstorm and a cannon sound alike. I also know from my own experience and from other reading that a thunderstorm can bring terrible destruction in the form of lightning or high winds. I believe that this is a good comparison for an approaching battle. I can close my eyes and see and hear the battle. I also know from my own experience that when wind sweeps through the streets it moves everything in front of it. I can close my eyes and see people rushing away from the army as it sweeps through the town without thinking of the consequences of its actions. In this way the army is also like the wind. I also know from my own experience that bullets and mosquitoes sound somewhat alike. I know that mosquitoes have a nasty bite. When the author uses a phrase such as *sly malice,* I think he is saying that bullets are much worse than mosquito bites. The author also might be saying that mosquitoes and bullets are alike in that they both hit innocent victims. I believe from these comparisons that the author is telling us that war is terrible for all people including innocent bystanders." After developing this first modeling sequence, encourage students to hypothesize about the theme of the book.

After completing one modeling example, encourage the students to join in the discussion. Ask them to jot down brief responses. The next logical discussion point is at the bottom of page 2. Ask, "What does the symbolism of the plum tree reveal about the author's attitude toward war?" Encourage the students to answer the question, provide the evidence, and explore their reasoning processes.

Continue reading through page 11. Stop after "There was no milk left in it, but it was a very happy memory for both Jan and Flox" (p. 11). Ask, "What does the incident with the birthday party reveal about Jan? What is the message related to war?"

Read the remainder of the first chapter, stopping at the end of page 12: "As the noise grew, so did Jan's fear. He climbed, shaking, onto the big stove and crept onto the backmost corner. Now it's all over, he thought. Like an insect playing dead when a pursuer approaches, Jan pressed himself flat on top of the stove. He pulled Flox up beside him. He was now his only defense. . . .'Anyone here?' called a hoarse voice. Jan did not move. The dog also played dead. A miserable heap of rags with one human and one animal soul waited for the end" (p. 12). Ask the students, "What do the simile and the author's vivid descriptions reveal about Jan and his attitude toward war?" Ask the students to provide the answers, the evidence and their reasoning processes.

The remainder of the book can be discussed in a similar manner. Some teachers continue reading each chapter orally as the students discuss the various types of figurative language. Other teachers prefer to have their students read the remainder of the book independently, locate their own examples of figurative language, and discuss the examples in a discussion group. Either approach can be effective.

LESSON THREE: Helping Students Understand other Literary Elements by Introducing Concepts Through Picture Books and Short Stories

OBJECTIVES

To locate and discuss examples of other literary elements such as allegory, irony, and foreshadowing found in picture story books.

To evaluate the illustrations that depict these elements.

To be involved in an aesthetic response that encourages students to create illustrations that reflect allegory, irony, and foreshadowing.

CORE BOOKS: Illustrated books, short stories, and more difficult novels that develop the same element through the illustrations and text. For example, for allegory in picture books: Aesop's *Aesop's Fables,* illustrated by Heidi Holder; *Belling the Cat and Other Aesop's Fables,* retold by Tom Paxton; and *Anno's Aesop: A Book of Fables by Aesop and Mr. Fox,* retold by Mitsumasa Anno. For allegory in novels: W. J. Corbett's *The Song of Pentecost* (Modern Fantasy); C. S. Lewis's "Chronicles of Narnia" (Modern Fantasy, Touchstone); and George Mac-Donald's *At the Back of the North Wind.* For irony in picture books: Graham Oakley's *The Church Mice in Action;* Frank Asch and Vladimir Vagin's *Here Comes the Cat!;* and Natalie Babbitt's "The Bus for Deadhorse," in Ann Durell and Marilyn Sachs's *The Big Book of Peace.* For irony in a novel: Bill Brittain's *The Wish Giver.* For foreshadowing in picture books: Jan Brett's retelling of *Beauty and the Beast;* Audrey Wood's *Heckedy Peg;* and Arthur Yorinks' *Hey, Al* (Caldecott Medal).

PROCEDURES: Either review each of the elements before students look at the picture books, or encourage them to read or listen to the books and discover their own definitions for the elements. For example, allegory is a description of one thing under the image of another. In an allegorical story, people, things, and happenings have another meaning. The story suggests another story such as one found in a fable or parable. Allegories are often used for teaching or explaining (Frye, Baker, & Perkins, 1985). Ask students to look at the illustrations in the fables and to listen to or read the texts. Ask them to consider if and how the illustrations and the texts develop the idea of allegory. Ask, "What lessons are taught in these fables?" After students have discussed the allegory in the picture book fables, ask them to read one of the novels and to identify any incidents of allegory. Before reading Corbett's text, students should note the author's comment, "I hope that children will read *The Song of Pentecost* as a straight adventure story. Adults, I hope, might appreciate the allegory. I wrote it tongue in cheek, but with enjoyment, and never cynically" (endnote). Ask the students to place themselves in the role of adults and to identify and respond to the author's use of allegory. They might consider, "What does the title mean? Why is the leader of the mice named Pentecost? What allegorical implications are found in the author's characterizations, settings, problems, resolutions of problems, and morals?"

An ironic statement is one that means the opposite of its stated meaning. In an ironic depiction of events, the events turn out to be the opposite of what is expected or what normally should happen (Frye, Baker, & Perkins, 1985). Introduce the illustrated books by asking the students to consider what should normally happen in each of the situations. For example, both *The Church Mice in Action* and *Here Comes the Cat!* are stories about a cat and mice. Ask, "From your own experiences and knowledge, what would you expect to happen in a story about a cat and mice. How would you expect the story to end? Now read both of these books and see if the stories end as might be predicted. How do the illustrations develop the irony of the situation?" Next read Babbitt's short story after asking, "How would you expect grown children to act when their father is taken ill." Read the story and ask the students to respond to the irony of both the children's fate and the Home for Wandering Cats. Finally, ask them to read *The Wish Giver* and discuss the irony developed in each of the stories.

Foreshadowing is a technique in which a plot development is suggested before it occurs. For example, a minor episode might foreshadow a major event, a subplot might parallel and foreshadow a main plot, a dialogue might suggest later action, a symbol might suggest the ending, or the atmosphere might foreshadow the total work (Frye, Baker, & Perkins, 1985). Illustrations in texts also can emphasize each of these roles in foreshadowing. Sometimes the illustrator's choice of color sets a mood that foreshadows the ending, or the illustrator might provide even greater foreshadowing clues by depicting or warning in the illustrations what will happen later. Ask the students to look carefully at the illustrations in each of the books. The illustrations provide foreshadowing clues, often long before the final ending. For example, in *Beauty and the Beast* the human forms of the animal characters are revealed in the tapestries. The tapestries foreshadow both the enchantment and the breaking of the enchantment. In *Heckedy Peg* the girl feeds the bird that later leads her mother to the witch so she can rescue the children. The approaching witch is seen in the illustrations through the window before the text discloses the interactions with the witch. The colors used by the illustrator also foreshadow plot changes. In *Hey, Al,* an illustration shows a bird with hands and Al landing in the tree and flapping like a bird. Both of these points certainly foreshadow Al's final condition if he chooses to stay on the island. Ask students to discuss any examples of foreshadowing they discover in other books.

Finally, allow students to write or illustrate their own examples of allegory, irony, and foreshadowing. They might wish to create their own stories or they might choose to illustrate a scene from one of the non-illustrated novels.

Extended Books for Upper Elementary and Middle School Students

The books listed in this section encourage students to identify, discuss, and respond to vivid language and author's style. (For additional sources, see the recommendations for poetry in Chapter 12.)

Legends

MARGARET HODGES' *Saint George and the Dragon* (Caldecott Medal). The text includes such vivid similes as "wings stretched like two sails when the wind fills them" and "fire flew from the dragon's coat like sparks from an anvil."

Poetry

BYRD BAYLOR'S *The Desert Is Theirs* (Caldecott Honor, Native American). The poetic text personifies nature.

ALFRED NOYES' *The Highwayman*. Metaphors develop the ghostly and tragic setting.

Historical Fiction

ELIZABETH GEORGE SPEARE'S *The Sign of the Beaver* (Newbery Honor, Native American). Numerous similes help readers visualize the time period. A gun is described as having a "walnut stock as smooth and shiny as his mother's silk dress" (p. 5). Similes also make comparisons with literary characters such as "as big a hero as Jack the Giant Killer" (p. 23) and "Robinson Crusoe had lived like a king" (p. 66).

Informational

KATHRYN LASKY's *Sugaring Time* (Newbery Honor Book, Informational): The author's imagery paints pictures of milky-white settings, ghost trees, and swirling fog. Similes describe nature: "Icicles that have hung like scepters since December suddenly begin dripping like popsicles in August" (p. 4).

Recreational Books for Upper Elementary and Middle School Students

Folktales

JULIUS LESTER's *Further Tales of Uncle Remus: The Misadventures of Brer Rabbit, Brer Fox, Brer Wolf, the Doodang and Other Creatures*

Legends

KATE SEREDY's *The White Stag* (Newbery Medal)

Modern Fantasy

SUSAN COOPER's *The Grey King* (Newbery Medal)

W. J. CORBETT's *Pentecost and the Chosen One*

Poetry

R. R. KNUDSON AND MAY SWENSON's *American Sports Poems*

NANCY WILLARD's *A Visit to William Blake's Inn: Poems for Innocent and Experienced Travelers* (Newbery Medal, Caldecott Honor)

Realistic Fiction

GARY PAULSEN's *Dogsong* (Eskimo)

DEVELOPING UNDERSTANDING AND APPRECIATION OF POINT OF VIEW

Writers have several options when they tell their stories. For example, who tells the story? How much information about the characters and the incidents is this person allowed to know? Consequently, the description of an incident can differ depending on the feelings, viewpoints, motives, and beliefs of the person telling about the incident. The point of view is this angle of vision from which the story is told. For example, who tells the story in Beatrix Potter's *Peter Rabbit*? Is the storyteller sympathetic to the rabbit family or to Mr. McGregor? How would the story change if it were told from the gardener's point of view? We might be more likely to empathize with Mr. McGregor's need to safeguard his garden. We might even sympathize with Mr. McGregor as he tries to catch the rabbit.

Authors have four options when selecting point of view:

1. First person. This point of view speaks through the "I" of one of the characters. If the author chooses the first-person point of view, the author must decide which charac-

ter's actions and feelings should influence the story. Contemporary realistic fiction stories often are told from the viewpoint of a child.

2. Omniscient. This point of view allows the author to tell the story in the third person, with the author referring to "they," "he," or "she." The author is not restricted to the knowledge, experience, and feelings of one person. An omniscient point of view is considered the most flexible because the knowledge is unlimited. The author can interpret all behaviors, understand all motives, and even look into numerous characters' thoughts.

3. Limited omniscient. The author concentrates on the experiences of one character, but can be all-knowing about other characters.

4. Objective. The author reports what the characters do and say, but does not explain why characters act in certain ways.

No one point of view is preferred for all literature. The choice of point of view, however, can affect how much children of different ages believe and enjoy a story. Students can discuss the author's point of view and describe their responses to the point of view. One of the better ways to develop students' understanding of point of view is to have them write stories from the point of view of one of the other characters in the story. They must consider how the incidents, the plot, and even the characterizations might change if the viewpoint is altered.

The illustrations also reflect and enhance a point of view. This is especially important if the artist and author are not the same person. Eichenberg (1990) highlights some of an artist's concerns when he approaches illustration. The following quote suggests additional areas of discussion that could be developed around point of view: "What is illustration if the artist does not approach the written word and its author with great reverence? What is illustration if it doesn't add 'luster' to the book, enhance the written text, fulfill the expectations of the author as well as of the reader? Even if the author has long gone to his reward, as the saying goes, he is there and he looks over your shoulder. You have made friends with him, you have studied his life, reverently, often sadly; you have tried to slip under his skin, to fathom his intentions and motivations in order to do justice to the author's greatness" (p. 62). Notice how this quote emphasizes the need for the illustrator to consider the author's point of view as well as all of the other literary elements.

Core Books and Sample Lesson for Lower Elementary Students

LESSON ONE: Developing an Understanding and Appreciation of Point of View

OBJECTIVES

To develop an understanding of and an appreciation for point of view.

To write a story from the point of view of another character in a story.

CORE BOOKS: Reeve Lindbergh's *The Day the Goose Got Loose* (Picture Story Book); Eric A. Kimmel's *The Chanukkah Guest* (Picture Story Book); and Beatrix Potter's *The Tale of Peter Rabbit* (Modern Fantasy, Touchstone).

PROCEDURES: The three different books can be used to enhance an understanding of point of view and to stimulate creative writing from a different point of view. Consequently, the lesson will take several days to complete.

For each book, follow approximately the same procedures. For example, read Lindbergh's humorous *The Day the Goose Got Loose* to the students. Allow them to respond to the humorous situations and illustrations. After they have discussed their responses to the book, ask them, "Who is telling the story about the goose—a human or the goose? How can you tell?" Now reread the page in which grandmother asks, "I wonder what thoughts went through her head?" (p. 21 unnumbered). Tell the students that the grandmother is asking this question about the goose. Now ask them, "How could we write this story if we were to tell the story through the goose's point of view? Why did she do these actions? What was she thinking about as she _____ ? How did she see each of the people and animals who chased her? How did she feel when she _____ ?" Finally encourage the students to write their own story about *The Day the Goose Got Loose* but to tell the incidents through the goose's point of view. (Notice that this lesson also emphasizes personification as students retell the story through the goose's point of view.)

On another day share Kimmel's *The Chanukkah Guest*. After sharing and discussing the book, ask the students to think about what the bear must have been thinking as the old woman (Bubba Brayna) mistakes him for the rabbi, feeds him potato latkes, and gives him a warm woolen scarf. The students can rewrite or retell the story from the time that the bear approaches the house or they can tell the story through the dreams that the bear has after he returns to his den in the deep forest and falls asleep with his stomach full of potato latkes and his neck wrapped in the warm woolen scarf.

After reading and sharing the third book in this lesson, *The Tale of Peter Rabbit,* encourage students to think about how the story would change if it were told through Mr. McGregor's point of view. Ask, "What would be important to Mr. McGregor? How would he tell the story so that we would sympathize with his need to keep rabbits out of the garden? How would each of the incidents in the story change?" Now encourage students to write or tell a story that emphasizes Mr. McGregor's point of view. Share the stories and compare them with Beatrix Potter's original tale. Ask, "How did the story change when it is told by the gardener?"

Extended Books for Lower Elementary Students

The books listed in this section can be used to discuss and react to point of view. The books also can be used to stimulate extended writings and discussions as students write or tell stories from another character's point of view. The wordless books are especially useful because students must choose a point of view and then tell the story that is developed through the illustrations.

Wordless Books

MARTHA ALEXANDER's *Bobo's Dream*. Bobo dreams that he becomes large and rescues his master's football from a group of bigger boys.

RAYMOND BRIGGS' *The Snowman*. A snowman comes to life and takes his young creator on a tour of strange lands.

PETER COLLINGTON's *On Christmas Eve*. Tiny fairies guide Santa to the home of a little girl who does not have a chimney.

JOHN GOODALL's *Paddy Under Water*. A pig discovers a treasure chest.

MERCER MAYER's wordless books, such as *Frog Goes to Dinner*. The boy secretly places Frog into his pocket and takes him to a fancy restaurant.

EMILY ARNOLD MCCULLY'S *Picnic*. A young mouse is lost on the day of the family picnic.

DAVID WIESNER'S *Free Fall* (Caldecott Honor). A boy experiences a fantasy dream.

Picture Story Books

KAREN ACKERMAN'S *Song and Dance Man* (Caldecott Medal). The story follows a grand-father as he relives his days of vaudeville for his grandchildren.

SARA JOSEPHA HALE'S *Mary Had A Little Lamb*. Photographs by Bruce McMillan. Stu-dents can discuss the loving relationships developed in the text and the photographs. They can write or tell the story focusing on the lambs's point of view.

FLORENCE PARRY HEIDE AND JUDITH HEIDE GILLILAND'S *The Day of Ahmed's Secret* (Egyp-tian). The story is told through the point of view of a young boy who takes pride in his work and cannot wait to tell his secret. He can write his name. Students can discuss the story and then write or tell a story through their own point of view in which they reveal a secret about themselves.

VERA B. WILLIAMS' *"More More More," Said the Baby* (Caldecott Honor). Teachers can extend this story that develops interactions between a baby and father, a baby and grandmother, and a baby and mother to the early elementary years. Students can write a story through the point of view of either the growing child or the adult who still is interacting with the child. Students also can write a story from their point of view when they were babies.

AUDREY WOOD'S *King Bidgood's in the Bathtub* (Caldecott Honor). The humorous text follows a king who wants to do all types of activities in the bathtub. A young boy finally is able to get the king to leave the tub.

Recreational Books for Lower Elementary Students

Wordless Books

SYD HOFF'S *Chester* and *Sammy the Seal*

ARNOLD LOBEL'S *Frog and Toad All Year, Grasshopper on the Road, Owl at Home*, and *Uncle Elephant*

DR. SEUSS' *The Cat in the Hat* and *The Cat in the Hat Comes Back*

BERNARD WISEMAN'S *Morris Goes to School* and *Morris Has a Cold*

Picture Story Books

JOANNA COLE AND STEPHANIE CALMENSON'S compilation of *Ready . . . Set . . . Read!: The Beginning Reader's Treasury* (Easy to read)

CYNTHIA RYLANT'S *Henry and Mudge Get the Cold Shivers, Henry and Mudge and the Forever Sea*, and *Henry and Mudge in the Sparkle Days* (Easy to Read)

NANCY TAFURI'S *Have You Seen My Duckling?* (Caldecott Honor)

JEAN VAN LEEUWEN'S *More Tales of Amanda Pig, Oliver, Amanda, and Grandmother Pig,* and *Oliver and Amanda's Christmas,* (Easy to Read)

VERA WILLIAM'S *A Chair for My Mother* (Caldecott Honor)

MARGOT ZEMACH'S *It Could Always Be Worse* (Jewish, Caldecott Honor)

Core Books and Sample Lessons for Middle Elementary Students

Before presenting this lesson, review the concept of point of view with the students. Teachers can choose to use some of the same books discussed in the lesson for students in the lower elementary grades. Students also can rewrite these easier stories so that the stories reflect another point of view.

LESSON ONE: Developing an Understanding and Appreciation of Point of View

OBJECTIVES

To develop an appreciation for and an understanding of author's point of view.

To develop an understanding that point of view must be consistent within the story.

To write a transformation story in which the transformed character retains his or her point of view.

CORE BOOK: Mary James' *Shoebag* (Modern Fantasy). Also, nonfictional books about animals that are chosen by the students.

PROCEDURES: *Shoebag* is a humorous fantasy story that shows what might happen if a cockroach suddenly were transformed into a boy. Introduce the book by asking the students, "What would it be like if you were suddenly changed from a cockroach into a human? What would be your feelings? How would you respond to everyday incidents? Would you retain your cockroach beliefs or would you change to human beliefs? What types of beliefs would cause you the most problems?"

After you have discussed this introduction, tell the students that they will be searching for evidence in this story that answers these questions: "What is the point of view in *Shoebag*, cockroach or human? Does the point of view change when the main character is transformed from cockroach to a human?"

Now ask the students to provide evidence for a human or a cockroach point of view. For example, the following are a few of the examples that could be used to support each point of view:

HUMAN POINT OF VIEW	COCKROACH POINT OF VIEW
Drainboard, mother cockroach says that people want to step on cockroaches (p. 5).	After the transformation Shoebag says, "You are the only family I have" (p. 5).
	"I promise—I can handle it" (p. 6).
	Shoebag promises not to hurt his family (p. 6).
	Shoebag waits until his family is hidden before he turns on the lights (p. 8).
	Shoebag does not reveal his former self because humans would not like him (p. 18).
	Shoebag is happy that he can still see a cockroach in his reflection (p. 23).
Girl says cockroaches are filthy and should be exterminated (p. 27).	Shoebag argues that cockroaches do not harm people, are not filthy, and have been around for 250 million years (p. 27).
	Shoebag defends and tries to help his cockroach mother (p. 34).
	Shoebag writes "I miss my home sweet home" in his diary (p. 40).
Classmates scream when they see cockroach in the lunchbag (p. 49).	His cockroach mother offers to go to school in his lunchbag (p. 41).
	His friend reveals that he does not step on things (p. 51).

Girl says cat tries to catch bugs (p. 49).

Shoebag is afraid when the cat follows him (p. 64).

Shoebag argues for animals that people do not like (p. 78).

When Shoebag is unhappy he sings his favorite cockroach song (p. 78).

Shoebag feels happy when he saves his cockroach mother (p. 104).

Shoebag chooses to be transformed back into a cockroach (p. 126).

After collecting as much evidence as possible, ask the students to decide if the main point of view is told from a cockroach or a human perspective and to defend their answers. Ask the students, "Did the author develop a consistent point of view? Why or why not?"

Next, ask the students to choose an animal and investigate its characteristics. Have them write a story in which the animal is transformed into a human. Ask them to try to retain the point of view of the animal as the animal overcomes various problems in its now-human life.

LESSON TWO: Writing from a Different Point of View

OBJECTIVES

To recognize differences in literature depending on the author's point of view.

To write a story from a different point of view.

CORE BOOK: Byrd Baylor's *Hawk, I'm Your Brother* (Realistic Fiction, Native American, Caldecott Honor).

PROCEDURES: Review the setting, conflict, plot development, characterization, and theme already developed in the webs for *Hawk, I'm Your Brother.* Then ask the students to consider the significance of the author's title. Why did Baylor choose *Hawk, I'm Your Brother* for the title? What does the word *brother* imply? Is it an accurate description of Rudy Soto's relationship to the hawk? How are Rudy and the hawk alike? How are they different? Why did Rudy release the hawk? How do you think Rudy felt after releasing the hawk? How do you think the hawk felt after being released? What would you have done if you were Rudy Soto? How would you have reacted if you were the hawk?

Tell the students that an incident can be described in different ways by several people who have the same experience. The details they choose to describe, the feelings they experience, and their beliefs in the right or the wrong of an incident can vary depending on who the author chooses to tell the story. Consequently, the same story could change drastically depending on the point of view of the story teller. Ask the students to tell you whose point of view Baylor develops in *Hawk, I'm Your Brother.* How did they know that the story was told from Rudy's point of view? Ask them to consider how the story might be written if the author had chosen the hawk's point of view.

Ask the students to imagine that they are the hawk that Rudy captured. Have them write a story about what happened to them, beginning from the time that Rudy captured the hawk from the nest high on Santos Mountain.

Extended Books for Middle Elementary Students

The following books stimulate discussion about point of view, personal responses about point of view, and activities that encourage students to write stories from a specific point of view or to change the point of view developed by the author. As in the lower elementary grades, wordless books also can be used to help students choose and develop a point of view.

Wordless Books

MITSUMASA ANNO's *Anno's Britain, Anno's Italy,* and *Anno's Journey.* Students can create their own stories as a traveler goes through the various countries, meeting literary and historical characters along the way.

EMILY ARNOLD MCCULLY's *School.* Students can write the story from the point of view of the little mouse child, who follows his siblings to school; the siblings; the teacher; or the mother.

CHRIS VAN ALLSBURG's *The Mysteries of Harris Burdick.* A series of mystery and fantasy pictures encourages students to create their own stories.

Modern Fantasy

ROBERT C. O'BRIEN's *Mrs. Frisby and the Rats of NIMH* (Newbery Medal, Touchstone). The story is told from the viewpoint of the intelligent mice and rats. Some issues are related to human society that could be explored through considering contrasting points of view.

Realistic Fiction

BEVERLEY CLEARY's *Ramona Quimby, Age 8* (Newbery Honor). The story is told from the point of view of an eight-year-old girl. Students can discuss how her point of view is like or unlike their own.

JEAN CRAIGHEAD GEORGE's *My Side of the Mountain* (Newbery Honor) and *On the Far Side of the Mountain.* Both books are written from the point of view of Sam Gribley, who loves nature and survives in a mountain setting. In the second book, he must decide whether or not to let his beloved falcon go free. This book could motivate the writing of either story from the falcon's point of view.

MAVIS JUKES' *Like Jake and Me* (Newbery Honor). The story is told through the point of view of a boy who is adjusting to a stepfather. The story also could be written from the point of view of the stepfather or the mother.

Recreational Books for Middle Elementary Students

Modern Fantasy

RACHEL FIELD's *Hitty, Her First Hundred Years* (Newbery Medal)

PAUL FLEISCHMAN's *Graven Images* (Newbery Honor)

Realistic Fiction

C. S. ADLER's *Ghost Brother*

ELEANOR ESTES' *The Hundred Dresses* (Newbery Honor)

Core Books and Sample Lesson for Upper Elementary and Middle School Students

Before presenting this lesson, review point of view with the students. Even if they have not completed the previous lesson on *Hawk, I'm Your Brother,* this discussion and writing activity can be completed in the upper grades; this book can be used for both levels. Older students frequently provide interesting insights into the changing conflict, attitudes, and point of view.

LESSON ONE: To Develop An Appreciation and Understanding of Point of View

OBJECTIVES

To develop an appreciation for and an understanding of author's point of view.

To trace the changing point of view as a boy learns to respect the point of view of the eagles.

To write a story in which the storyteller changes viewpoint because of interaction with some form of animal life.

CORE BOOKS: William Mayne's *Antar and the Eagles* (Modern Fantasy), and several non-fictional books that develop accurate animal behavior.

PROCEDURES: This story does not include a transformation such as that developed in *Shoebag*. Instead, the main character is abducted by an eagle and transported to the eagle's mountain home. The boy, who is also afraid of heights, is prepared to accomplish a dangerous mission to rescue a lost egg that will save the eagles. His interaction with the eagles causes him to gradually see the world through their point of view.

Ask the students to identify incidents that reveal this changing point of view. For example:

1. Antar is annoyed because the eagles force him to accomplish certain actions by nipping his back and legs. He tells them that he cannot help his actions and that it is not fair (p. 31).

2. Antar thinks about escaping but believes that the only way the eagles will let him go is through his own death (p. 40).

3. Antar compares the eagles to school teachers—neither comparison is favorable (p. 45).

4. Antar describes the eagle, Garak, as the best teacher because with him he could share a joke. Antar learns eagle words and asks for things (pp. 55–56).

5. Antar compares human nature and eagle nature (p. 57).

6. As the eagles try to teach Antar to fly, Antar compares the characteristics of humans and eagles. Antar admits that the eagles are the greatest in the world and that they know many things (p. 63).

7. Antar learns about and grows to admire eagle wing signals, rules about wind, and dangers associated with smoke (p. 65).

8. Antar and the setting are described in eagle terms (pp. 71–73).

9. Antar agrees to try to accomplish the eagles' wishes (p. 75).

10. Antar describes himself through the point of view of the eagles and takes on eagle behavior when he interacts with humans (pp. 87–88).

11. During a crisis Antar reacts relying on eagle behavior (p. 102).

12. Antar returns to the eagles even though he could have walked home (p. 137).

13. Antar remains to nurture the young eagle (p. 146).

14. After Antar returns to his human home he does not forget the eagles and what they have taught him. A golden eagle feather becomes Antar's sign in the world (p. 166).

After students have identified these important incidents in the development of point of view, ask them to discuss the reasons for Antar's changing perspectives. Ask, "Why did Antar gradually take on the point of view of the eagles? How would the story change if Antar had remained with a human point of view? If you were Antar how do you think your point of view would have been influenced?"

After completing this discussion, encourage students to investigate animal behavior of their own choosing. Ask, "What would make you change your point of view? What information about an animal would you need to know to write a story from the point of view of the animal?" Allow the students to write their own stories in which humans learn to respect the point of view of animals.

Extended Books for Upper Elementary and Middle School Students

The books in this list provide sources for discussion about point of view. Many of the books also provide motivation for rewriting stories from the point of view of another character in the story.

Legends

SELINA HASTINGS' *Sir Gawain and the Loathly Lady.* The story is told from the chivalrous point of view of King Arthur and Sir Gawain. Students can retell the story from the point of view of the Black Knight, who challenges King Arthur, or from the point of view of one of the ladies of the court.

Realistic Fiction

NICHOLASA MOHR'S *Going Home* (Puerto Rican). The story is told from the point of view of a 12-year-old girl who experiences prejudice when she spends the summer with relatives in Puerto Rico. This is a good story to encourage a personal response in which students consider how they would respond to prejudice.

WALTER DEAN MYERS' *Scorpions* (Black, Newbery Honor). The story is told from the point of view of a boy who faces problems with a gang.

VIRGINIA DRIVING HAWK SNEVE'S *High Elk's Treasure* (Native American). The story is told from the point of view of a Native American who wants to expand the herd of palomino horses.

SUSAN FISHER STAPLES' *Shabanu, Daughter of the Wind* (Pakistani, Newbery Honor). The story is told from the point of view of a girl who faces an important decision. Will she uphold her family's honor even if it means personal servitude? Or will she rebel against her father's wishes, bring shame to her family, and betray her culture? The book encourages personal responses as students respond to Shabanu's conflict and consider what they would do in a similar situation.

Recreational Books for Upper Elementary and Middle School Students

Realistic Fiction

NINA BAWDEN'S *The Outside Child*

BETSY BYARS' *Bingo Brown and the Language of Love*

BARBARA CORCORAN'S *The Potato Kid*

WALTER FARLEY'S *The Black Stallion*

PAULA FOX'S *The Village by the Sea*

FRED GIPSON'S *Old Yeller* (Newbery Honor)

VIRGINIA HAMILTON'S *Cousins* (Black)

MARGUERITE HENRY's *King of the Wind* (Newbery Medal)
LOIS LOWRY's *Anastasia's Chosen Career*
KATHERINE PATERSON's *Come Sing, Jimmy Jo*
ZILPHA KEATLEY SNYDER's *Libby on Wednesday*
GARY SOTO's *Baseball in April and Other Stories* (Hispanic)
Historical Fiction
JOYCE ROCKWOOD's *Groundhog's Horse* (Native American)

REFERENCES

DAANE, M. C. (1990). A study of the understanding of metaphor in reading and the use of metaphor in writing by college freshmen. *Dissertation Abstracts International, 51,* 05A. (University Microfilms No. 90–25, 166)

DOLE, J., DUFFY, G., ROEHLER, L., & PEARSON, P. D. (1991). Moving from the old to the new: Research on reading comprehension instruction. *Review of Educational Research, 61,* 239–264.

EICHENBERG, F. (1990). Bell, book and candle. In *The Arbuthnot lectures 1980–1989.* Chicago: American Library Association.

FRYE, N., BAKER, S., & PERKINS, G. (1985). *The Harper handbook to literature.* New York: Harper & Row.

JANECZKO, P. B., selected by. (1990). *The place my words are looking for.* New York: Bradbury.

NORTON, D. E. (1989a). Developing the thought processes through modeling. Paper presented at the National Council of Teachers of English Conference, Colorado Springs, CO.

NORTON, D. E. (1989b). Personification in children's literature: Identifying, analyzing, and performing. *Classroom Practices in Teaching English, 24,* pp. 43–49.

SHANNON, G. (1989). *Arnold Lobel.* Boston: Twayne.

CHILDREN'S LITERATURE REFERENCES*

AARDEMA, VERNA. *Bringing the Rain to Kapiti Plain: A Nandi Tale.* Illustrated by Beatriz Vidal. New York: Dial, 1981 (I: 5–8).

_____. *Why Mosquitoes Buzz in People's Ears.* Illustrated by Leo and Diane Dillon. New York: Dial, 1975 (I: 5–9).

ACKERMAN, KAREN. *Song and Dance Man.* Illustrated by Stephen Gammell. New York: Knopf, 1988 (I: 3–8).

ADLER, C. S. *Ghost Brother.* New York: Clarion, 1990 (I: 9–12).

*I = Interest by age range

AESOP. *Aesop's Fables.* Illustrated by Heidi Holder. New York: Viking, 1981 (I: 9–12).

ALEXANDER, MARTHA. *Bobo's Dream.* New York: Dial, 1970 (I: 3–7).

AHLBERG, JANET & ALLEN AHLBERG. *Each Peach Pear Plum: An I-Spy Story.* New York: Viking, 1978 (I: 3–7).

AHNOLT, CATHERINE. *Truffles Is Sick.* Boston: Little, Brown, 1987 (I: 2–5).

ANNO, MITSUMASA, retold by. *Anno's Aesop: A Book of Fables by Aesop and Mr. Fox.* Illustrated by Mitsumasa Anno. New York: Orchard, 1989 (I: all).

_____. *Anno's Britain.* New York: Philomel, 1982 (I: all).

_____. *Anno's Italy.* New York: Collins, 1980 (I: all).

_____. *Anno's Journey.* New York: Philomel, 1978 (I: 6–12).

ASCH, FRANK & VLADIMIR VAGIN. *Here Comes the Cat!* New York: Scholastic, 1989 (I: all).

BAWDEN, NINA. *The Outside Child.* New York: Lothrop, Lee & Shepard, 1989 (I: 10+).

BAYLOR, BYRD. *Hawk, I'm Your Brother.* Illustrated by Peter Parnall. New York: Schribner's, 1976 (I: all).

_____. *Moonsong.* Illustrated by Ronald Himler. New York: Scribner's, 1982 (I: all).

_____. *The Desert is Theirs.* Illustrated by Peter Parnall. New York: Scribner's, 1975 (I: all).

BOND, MICHAEL. *A Bear Called Paddington.* Illustrated by Peggy Fortnum. Boston: Houghton Mifflin, 1960 (I: 6–9).

BRETT, JAN, retold by. *Beauty and the Beast.* New York: Clarion, 1989 (I: 8–12).

BRIGGS, RAYMOND. *The Snowman.* New York: Random, 1978 (I: 3–7).

BRITTAIN, BILL. *The Wish Giver.* Illustrated by Andrew Glass. New York: Harper & Row, 1983 (I: 8+).

BROWN, MARC. *Arthur's Baby.* Boston: Little, Brown, 1987 (I: 3–6).

BROWN, MARGARET WISE. *The Runaway Bunny.* Illustrated by Clement Hurd. New York: Harper & Row, 1972 (I: 2–7).

BROWNE, ANTHONY. *Gorilla*. New York: Watts, 1983 (I: 3–8).

BRYAN, ASHLEY. *Beat the Story-Drum Pum-Pum*. New York: Atheneum, 1980, (I: 6+).

BURTON, VIRGINIA LEE. *Katy and the Big Snow*. Boston: Houghton Mifflin, 1943, 1971 (I: 2–6).

———. *The Little House*. Boston: Houghton Mifflin, 1942 (I: 3–7).

BYARS, BETSY. *Bingo Brown and the Language of Love*. New York: Viking, 1989 (I: 9+).

CLEARY, BEVERLY. *Ramona Quimby, Age 8*. Illustrated by Alan Tiegreen. New York: Morrow, 1981 (I: 7–10).

COLE, JOANNA. (1982). *A Cat's Body*. Photographs by Jerome Wexler. New York: Morrow (I: 6–12).

——— & STEPHANIE CALMENSON. *Ready . . . Set . . . Read!: The Beginning Reader's Treasury*. New York: Doubleday, 1990 (I: 5–9).

COLLINGTON, PETER. *On Christmas Eve*. Knopf, 1990 (I: 5–8).

COOPER, SUSAN. *The Grey King*. New York: Atheneum, 1975 (I: 10+).

CORBETT, W. J. *Pentecost and the Chosen One*. New York: Delacorte, 1987 (I: 9+).

———. *The Song of Pentecost*. New York: Dutton, 1983 (I: 9+).

CORCORAN, BARBARA. *The Potato Kid*. New York: Atheneum, 1989 (I: 10+).

DALGLIESH, ALICE. *The Columbus Story*. Illustrated by Leo Politi. New York: Scribner's, 1955 (I: 5–8).

deBRUNHOFF, JEAN. *The Story of Babar*. New York: Random, 1933, 1961 (I: 3–9).

——— & LAURENT deBRUNHOFF. *Babar's Anniversary Album: 6 Favorite Stories*. New York: Random, 1981 (I: 3–9).

DURELL, ANN & MARILYN SACHS (eds.). *The Big Book of Peace*. New York: Dutton, 1990 (I: 8+).

DUVOISIN, ROGER. *Petunia*. New York: Knopf, 1950 (I: 3–6).

ENGEL, DIANA. *Josephina Hates Her Name*. New York: Morrow, 1989 (I: 5–8).

ERNST, LISA CAMPBELL. *Ginger Jumps*. New York: Bradbury, 1990 (I: 5–8).

ESTES, ELEANOR. *The Hundred Dresses*. Illustrated by Louis Slobodkin. New York: Scholastic, 1944, 1973 (I: 7–10).

FARLEY, WALTER. *The Black Stallion*. Illustrated by Keith Ward. New York: Random, 1944 (I: 8+).

FIELD, RACHEL. *Hitty, Her First Hundred Years*. Illustrated by Dorothy Lathrop. New York: Macmillan, 1929 (I: 8–10).

FLEISCHMAN, PAUL. *Graven Images*. New York: Harper & Row, 1982 (I: 8–10).

FLEISCHMAN, SID. *The Midnight Horse*. New York: Greenwillow, 1990 (I: 8+).

FOWLER, SUSI GREGG. *When Summer Ends*. Illustrated by Marisabina Russo. New York: Greenwillow, 1989 (I: 3–8),

FOX, PAULA. *The Village by the Sea*. New York: Watts, 1988 (I: 10+).

FRANK, RUDOLF. *No Hero for the Kaiser*, translated by Patricia Crampton. Illustrated by Klaus Steffens. New York: Lothrop, Lee & Shepard, 1986 (I: 10+).

GEORGE, JEAN CRAIGHEAD. *My Side of the Mountain*. New York: Dutton, 1959 (I: 10+).

———. *On the Far Side of the Mountain*. New York: Dutton, 1990 (I: 10+).

GIPSON, FRED. *Old Yeller*. Illustrated by Carl Burger. New York: Harper & Row, 1956 (I: 10+).

GOODALL, JOHN. *Paddy Under Water*. New York: Atheneum, 1982 (I: 5–9).

GRAHAME, KENNETH. *The Wind in the Willows*. Illustrated by E. H. Shepard. New York: Scribner's, 1908, 1940 (I: 7–12).

GRIFALCONI, ANN. *Darkness and the Butterfly*. Boston: Little, Brown, 1987 (I: 5–10).

HALE, SARA JOSEPHA. *Mary Had a Little Lamb*. New York: Scholastic, 1990 (I: 5–7).

HAMILTON, VIRGINIA. *Cousins*. New York: Philomel, 1990 (I: 10+).

HASTINGS, SELINA. *Sir Gawain and the Loathly Lady*. Illustrated by Juan Wijngaard. New York: Lothrop, Lee & Shepard, 1985 (I: 9–12).

HEIDE, FLORENCE PARRY & JUDITH HEIDE GILLILAND. *The Day of Ahmed's Secret*. Illustrated by Ted Lewin. New York: Lothrop, Lee & Shepard, 1990 (I: 5–9).

HENRY, MARGUERITE. *King of the Wind*. Illustrated by Wesley Dennis. Rand McNally, 1948, 1976 (I: 8–12).

HESS, LILO. *Diary of a Rabbit*. New York: Scribner's, 1982 (I: 9–12).

HOBAN, RUSSELL. *A Baby Sister for Frances*. Illustrated by Lillian Hoban. New York: Harper & Row, 1964 (I: 4–8).

———. *A Bargain for Frances*. Illustrated by Lillian Hoban. New York: Harper & Row, 1970 (I: 4–8).

———. *Best Friends for Frances*. Illustrated by Lillian Hoban. New York: Harper & Row, 1969 (I: 4–8).

———. *Bread and Jam for Frances*. Illustrated by Lillian Hoban. New York: Harper & Row, 1964 (I: 4–8).

HOBERMAN, MARY ANN. *Mr. and Mrs. Muddle*. Illustrated by Catharine O'Neill. Boston: Little, Brown, 1988 (I: 3–8).

HODGES, MARGARET. *Saint George and the Dragon*. Illustrated by Trina Schart Hyman. Boston: Little, Brown, 1984 (I: all).

HOFF, SYD. *Chester*. New York: Harper & Row, 1961 (I: 5–8).

———. *Sammy the Seal*. New York: Harper & Row, 1959 (I: 5–8).

HOOKS, WILLIAM H. *Circle of Fire*. New York: Atheneum, 1983 (I: 10+).

JAMES, MARY. *Shoebag*. New York: Scholastic, 1990 (I: 8–10).

JUKES, MAVIS. *Like Jake and Me*. Illustrated by Lloyd Bloom. New York: Knopf, 1984 (I: 6–9).

KIMMEL, ERIC A. *The Chanukkah Guest*. New York: Holiday, 1990 (I: 4–8).

KING-SMITH, DICK. *Martin's Mice*. Illustrated by Jez Alborough. New York: Crown, 1989 (I: 8–12).

KNUDSON, R. R. & MAY SWENSON, selected by. *American Sports Poems*. New York: Orchard, 1988 (I: 10+).

KRAUS, ROBERT. *Leo the Late Bloomer*. Illustrated by Jose and Ariane Aruego. New York: Windmill, 1971 (I: 2–6).

LASKY, KATHRYN. *Sugaring Time*. Photographs by Christopher Knight. New York: Macmillan, 1983 (I: all).

LAWSON, ROBERT. *Rabbit Hill*. New York: Viking, 1944 (I: 7–11).

LEGUIN, URSULA. *Catwings*. Illustrated by S. D. Schindler. New York: Watts, 1988 (I: 3–8).

———. *Catwings Return*. Illustrated by S. D. Schindler. New York: Watts, 1989 (I: 3–8).

LESTER, JULIUS. *Further Tales of Uncle Remus: The Misadventures of Brer Rabbit, Brer Fox, Brer Wolf, the Doodang and Other Creatures*. New York: Dial, 1990 (I: 8+).

LEWIN, HUGH. *Jafta*. Illustrated by Lisa Kopper. Minneapolis: Carolrhoda, 1983 (I: 3–7).

———. *Jafta's Mother*. Illustrated by Lisa Kopper. Minneapolis: Carolrhoda, 1983 (I: 3–7).

LEWIS, C. S. "Chronicles of Narnia," including *The Lion, the Witch and the Wardrobe*. New York: Macmillan, 1950 (I: 9+).

LINDBERGH, REEVE. *The Day the Goose Got Loose*. New York: Dial, 1990 (I: 3–7).

LIONNI, LEO. *Alexander and the Wind-Up Mouse*. New York: Pantheon, 1969 (I: 3–6).

———. *The Biggest House in the World*. New York: Pantheon, 1968 (I: 3–6).

———. *Swimmy*. New York: Pantheon, 1963 (I: 2–7).

———. *Tillie and the Wall*. New York: Knopf, 1989 (I: 2–7).

LIVINGSTON, MYRA COHN. *Space Songs*. Illustrated by Leonard Everett Fisher. New York: Holiday, 1988 (I: all).

LOBEL, ARNOLD. *Frog and Toad All Year*. New York: Harper & Row, 1976 (I: 5–8).

———. *Frog and Toad Are Friends*. New York: Harper & Row, 1970 (I: 5–8).

———. *Frog and Toad Together*. New York: Harper & Row, 1972 (I: 5–8)

———. *Grasshopper on the Road*. New York: Harper & Row, 1987 (I: 5–8).

———. *Owl at Home*. New York: Harper & Row, 1975 (I: 5–8).

———. *Uncle Elephant*. New York: Harper & Row, 1981 (I: 5–8).

LONGFELLOW, HENRY WADSWORTH. *Hiawatha*. Illustrated by Susan Jeffers. New York: Dutton, 1983 (I: all).

———. *Hiawatha's Childhood*. Illustrated by Errol LeCain. New York: Farrar, Straus & Giroux, 1984 (I: all).

LOWRY, LOIS. *Anastasia's Chosen Career*. Boston: Houghton Mifflin, 1987 (I: 10+).

MACDONALD, GEORGE. *At the Back of the North Wind*. Illustrated by Arthur Hughes. New York: Dutton, 1871, 1966 (I: 10+).

MARGOLIS, RICHARD. *Secrets of a Small Brother*. Illustrated by Donald Carrick. New York: Macmillan, 1984 (I: all).

MARSHAK, SAMUEL, retold by. *The Month-Brothers*. Translated by Thomas Whitney. Illustrated by Diane Stanley. New York: Morrow, 1983 (I: 8+).

MARSHALL, JAMES. *George and Martha One Fine Day*. Boston: Houghton Mifflin, 1978 (I: 3–8).

MATTHEWS, DOWNS. *Polar Bear Cubs*. Photographs by Dan Guravich. New York: Simon and Schuster, 1989 (I: 5–10).

MAYER, MERCER. *Frog Goes to Dinner*. New York: Dial, 1974 (I: 6–9).

MAYNE, WILLIAM. *Antar and the Eagles*. New York: Delacorte, 1990 (I: 8+).

MCCLOSKEY, ROBERT. *Time of Wonder*. New York: Viking, 1975 (I: 5–8).

MCCULLY, EMILY ARNOLD. *Picnic*. New York: Harper & Row, 1984 (I; 3–8).

———. *School*. New York: Harper & Row, 1987 (I: 3–8).

MILNE, A. A. *The House at Pooh Corner*. Illustrated by Ernest H. Shepard. New York: Dutton, 1928, 1956 (I: 6–10).

———. *Winnie-the-Pooh*. Illustrated by Ernest H. Shepard. New York: Dutton, 1926, 1954 (I: 6–10).

MOHR, NICHOLASA. *Going Home*. New York: Dial, 1986 (I: 10+).

MOORE, CLEMENT. *The Night Before Christmas*. Illustrated by Tomie De Paola. New York: Holiday, 1980 (I: all).

MYERS, WALTER DEAN. *Scorpions*. New York: Harper & Row, 1988 (I: 11+).

NOYES, ALFRED. *The Highwayman.* Illustrated by Charles Keeping. New York: Oxford, 1981 (I: 10+).

OAKLEY, GRAHAM. *The Church Mice in Action.* New York: Atheneum, 1982 (I: 5–10).

O'BRIEN, ROBERT C. *Mrs. Frisby and the Rats of NIMH.* Illustrated by Zena Berstein. New York: Atheneum, 1971 (I: 8–12).

PATERSON, KATHERINE. *Bridge to Terabithia.* Illustrated by Donna Diamond. New York: Crowell, 1977 (I: 10+).

_____. *Come Sing, Jimmy Jo.* New York: Dutton, 1985 (I: 10+).

PAULSEN, GARY. *Dogsong.* New York: Bradbury, 1988 (I: 10+).

PAXTON, TOM. *Belling the Cat and Other Aesop's Fables.* New York: Morrow, 1990 (I: 8+).

PEET, BILL. *The Gnats of Knotty Pine.* Boston: Houghton Mifflin, 1975 (I: 5–9).

POTTER, BEATRIX. *The Tale of Peter Rabbit.* New York: Warne, 1902 (I: 3–7).

PRELUTSKY, JACK (ed.). *The Random House Book of Poetry for Children.* Illustrated by Arnold Lobel. New York: Random, 1983 (I: all).

_____. *Something Big Has Been Here.* Illustrated by James Stevenson. New York: Greenwillow, 1990 (I: 8+).

PROVENSEN, ALICE & MARTIN PROVENSEN. *The Glorious Flight Across the Channel With Louis Bleriot, July 25, 1909.* New York: Viking, 1983 (I: all).

RAYNER, MARY. *Garth Pig and the Ice Cream Lady.* New York: Atheneum, 1977 (I: 5–9).

REY, HANS. *Curious George.* Boston: Houghton Mifflin, 1941, 1969 (I: 2–7).

ROCKWOOD, JOYCE. *Groundhog's Horse.* Illustrated by Victor Kalin. Orlando: Holt, Rinehart & Winston, 1978 (I: 8–12).

RYLANT, CYNTHIA. *Henry and Mudge.* Illustrated by Sucie Stevenson. New York: Bradbury, 1987. (I: 5–8).

_____. *Henry and Mudge and the Bedtime Thumps.* Illustrated by Sucie Stevenson. New York: Bradbury, 1991 (I: 5–8).

_____. *Henry and Mudge and the Forever Sea.* Illustrated by Sucie Stevenson. New York: Bradbury, 1989 (I: 5–8).

_____. *Henry and Mudge and the Happy Cat.* Illustrated by Sucie Stevenson. New York: Bradbury, 1990 (I: 5–8).

_____. *Henry and Mudge Get the Cold Shivers.* Illustrated by Sucie Stevenson. New York: Bradbury, 1989 (I: 5–8).

_____. *Henry and Mudge in the Green Time.* Illustrated by Sucie Stevenson. New York: Bradbury, 1987 (I: 5–8).

_____. *Henry and Mudge in the Sparkle Days.* Illustrated by Sucie Stevenson. New York: Bradbury, 1988 (I: 5–8).

_____. *Henry and Mudge in Puddle Trouble.* New York: Bradbury, 1987 (I: 5–8).

_____. *Henry and Mudge Under the Yellow Moon.* Illustrated by Sucie Stevenson. New York: Bradbury, 1987 (I: 5–8).

SCOTT, JACK DENTON. *The Book of the Pig.* Photographs by Ozzie Sweet. New York: Putnam, 1981 (I: 8–10).

SEREDY, KATE. *The White Stag.* New York: Viking, 1937 (I: 10+).

SEUSS, DR. *The Cat in the Hat.* New York: Random, 1957 (I: 4–7).

_____. *The Cat in the Hat Comes Back.* New York: Random, 1958 (I: 4–7).

_____. *Horton Hatches the Egg.* New York: Random, 1940, 1968 (I: 3–9).

SNEVE, VIRGINIA DRIVING HAWK. *High Elk's Treasure.* New York: Holiday, 1972 (I: 8–12).

SNYDER, ZILPHA KEATLEY. *Libby on Wednesday.* New York: Delacorte, 1990 (I: 10+).

SOTO, GARY. *Baseball in April and Other Stories.* Orlando: Harcourt, 1990 (I: 11+).

SPEARE, ELIZABETH GEORGE. *The Sign of the Beaver.* Boston: Houghton Mifflin, 1983 (I: 8–12).

STAPLES, SUSAN FISHER. *Shabanu, Daughter of the Wind.* New York: Knopf, 1989 (I: 10+).

STEVENSON, JAMES. *Monty.* New York: Greenwillow, 1979 (I: 5–9).

TAFURI, NANCY. *Have You Seen My Duckling?* New York: Greenwillow, 1984 (I: 2–7).

TAYLOR, MILDRED D. *Let the Circle be Unbroken.* New York: Dial, 1981 (I: 10+).

TOLKIEN, J. R. R. *Farmer Giles of Ham.* Illustrated by Pauline Baynes. Boston: Houghton Mifflin, 1978 (I: 7–10).

VAN ALLSBURG, CHRIS. *The Mysteries of Harris Burdick.* Boston: Houghton Mifflin, 1984 (I: all).

VAN LEEUWEN, JEAN. *More Tales of Amanda Pig* Illustrated by Ann Schweninger. New York: Dial, 1985 (I: 5–8).

_____. *Oliver and Amanda's Christmas.* Illustrated by Ann Schweninger. New York: Dial, (I: 5–8).

_____. *Oliver, Amanda, and Grandmother Pig.* Illustrated by Ann Schweninger. New York: Dial, 1987 (I: 5–8).

_____. *Oliver Pig at School.* Illustrated by Ann Schweninger. New York: Dial, 1990 (I: 5–8).

VINCENT, GABRIELLE. *Ernest and Celestine's Picnic.* New York: Greenwillow, 1982 (I: 3–7).

_____. *Feel Better, Ernest!* New York: Greenwillow, 1982 (I: 3–7).

_____. *Smile, Ernest and Celestine.* New York: Greenwillow, 1982 (I: 3–7).

VIORST, JUDITH. *If I Were in Charge of the World and Other Worries: Poems for Children and Their Parents.* Illustrated by Lynne Cherry. New York: Atheneum, 1981 (I: all).

WEBER, WILLIAM J. *Care of Uncommon Pets.* Orlando: Holt, Rinehart, & Winston, 1979 (I: all).

WELLS, ROSEMARY. *Timothy Goes to School.* New York: Dial, 1981 (I: 4–7).

WHITE, CLARENCE. *Cesar Chavez, Man of Courage.* Garrard, 1973 (I: 8+).

WHITE, E. B. *Charlotte's Web.* Illustrated by Garth Williams. New York: Harper & Row, 1952 (I: 7–11).

WIESNER, DAVID. *Free Fall.* New York: Lothrop, Lee & Shepard, 1988 (I: all).

WILLARD, NANCY. *A Visit to William Blake's Inn: Poems for Innocent and Experienced Travelers.* Illustrated by Alice and Martin Provensen. Orlando: Harcourt Brace Jovanovich, 1981 (I: all).

WILLIAMS, MARGERY. *The Velveteen Rabbit: Or How Toys Become Real.* Illustrated by William Nicholson. New York: Doubleday, 1958 (I: 6–9).

WILLIAMS, VERA B. *A Chair for My Mother.* New York: Greenwillow, 1982 (I: 3–7).

_____. *"More More More," Said the Baby: Three Love Stories.* New York: Greenwillow, 1990 (I: 2–7).

WISEMAN, BERNARD. *Morris Goes to School.* New York: Harper & Row, 1970 (I: 5–8).

_____. *Morris Has A Cold.* New York: Dodd, Mead, 1978 (I: 5–8).

WOOD, AUDREY. *Heckedy Peg.* Illustrated by Don Wood. Orlando: Harcourt Brace Jovanovich, 1987 (I: all).

_____. *King Bidgood's in the Bathtub.* Illustrated by Don Wood. Orlando: Harcourt Brace Jovanovich, 1985 (I: 6–9).

WORTH, VALERIE. *All the Small Poems.* Illustrated by Natalie Babbitt. New York: Farrar, Straus & Giroux, 1987 (I: all).

YOLEN, JANE. *The Hundredth Dove and Other Tales.* Illustrated by David Palladini. New York: Crowell, 1977 (I: 7–10).

YORINKS, ARTHUR. *Hey, Al.* Illustrated by Richard Egielski. New York: Farrar, Straus & Giroux, 1986 (I: all).

ZEMACH, HARVE. *Duffy and the Devil.* Illustrated by Margot Zemach. New York: Farrar, Straus & Giroux, 1977 (I: 8–12).

ZEMACH, MARGOT. *It Could Always Be Worse.* New York: Farrar, Straus & Giroux, 1977 (I: 5–9).

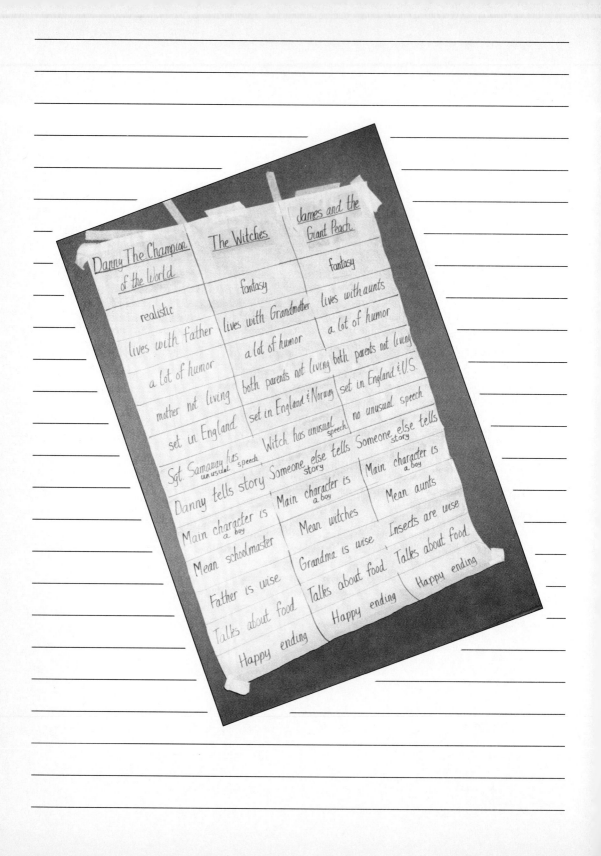

Danny The Champion of the World	The Witches	James and the Giant Peach
realistic	fantasy	fantasy
lives with father	lives with Grandmother	lives with aunts
a lot of humor	a lot of humor	a lot of humor
mother not living	both parents not living	both parents not living
set in England	set in England & Norway	set in England & U.S.
Sgt. Samaway has unusual speech	Witch has unusual speech	no unusual speech
Danny tells story	Someone else tells story	Someone else tells story
Main character is a boy	Main character is a boy	Main character is a boy
Mean schoolmaster	Mean witches	Mean aunts
Father is wise	Grandma is wise	Insects are wise
Talks about food	Talks about food	Talks about food
Happy ending	Happy ending	Happy ending

PART THREE

DEVELOPING UNDERSTANDING AND APPRECIATION OF LITERARY GENRE

Folklore
Modern Fantasy
Poetry
Realistic Fiction
Historical Fiction, Biography, and Informational Literature

CHAPTER 10

FOLKLORE

DEVELOPING UNDERSTANDING OF FOLKLORE
    Approaches that Develop Understanding of Folklore
    Core Books and Sample Lessons for Developing Understanding of Folklore
    Developing Folklore Units
    Units that Compare Different Versions of the Same Folktale
    Units that Investigate Folktales from One Country or Culture

The focus in this chapter and chapters 11–14 moves from literary elements to literary genres. According to Smith (1991) each type of literature presented to students has two important functions: "To develop a schema for that literary genre and to encourage the application of thinking skills in a variety of literary engagements" (p. 440). In previous chapters we referred to numerous genres as we discussed activities that help develop understanding and appreciation for areas such as plot, conflict, characterization, and setting. In the remaining chapters we will help students develop criteria for evaluating a genre, learn strategies for reading a genre, and explore units that can be developed around these genres. The units will encourage both efferent and aesthetic responses to literature, as well as integrate the various language arts and other content fields.

For example, a unit on folklore from a specific country encourages students to identify cultural foundations, appreciate the language and creativity of the people, explore settings developed through both the text and the illustrations, develop appreciation for values and beliefs, compare similarities across cultures, and write original stories. A unit on a folktale variant such as the "Cinderella" story encourages students to see similarities and differences among many cultures and to understand the cultural foundations found in variants within these common tales. A unit on modern fantasy helps students focus on the imagination and connect structures in folktales and literary fairy tales. A unit for older students traces the mythological foundations in the writings of fantasy authors such as J. R. R. Tolkien, C. S. Lewis, and Susan Cooper and encourages students to understand the connections between legend and mythology and high or heroic fantasy. Poetry units encourage students to appreciate the language and imagery created by poets and to write their own poetry. Students also can create biographies about the poets supported by the poetry of the poet.

As in the previous chapters, most of the lessons and units included both core books and extended books. The extended books may be used for group discussions, various independent activities, and recreational reading.

DEVELOPING UNDERSTANDING OF FOLKLORE

The folklore genre encompasses folktales, fables, myths, and legends. This literature, handed down through centuries by word of mouth, allows us to retain our cultural foundations and understand the foundations and beliefs of cultures that are similar or quite different from our own. Whether the stories first were told around campfires or in halls of large castles, the stories allowed family units and tribes to share their group traditions and values. On every continent around the globe, ancient peoples developed folktales, legends, and mythologies that speculated about human beginnings, attempted to explain the origins of the universe and other natural phenomena, emphasized ethical truths, and transmitted history from one generation to the next.

Early storytellers, whether they were known as bards, minstrels, or devisers of tales, knew how to tell stories with easily recognized settings, characters, and plot structures; language that might have encouraged the listeners to join in with the story, and themes that appealed to the people of the time. These characteristics still make folklore among the most loved literature. Our schema for the setting of a folktale is easily proven. All we need do is close our eyes and listen to, "Once upon a time . . ." Most of us visualize a castle or a deep mysterious woods. We can easily recognize the plot or the quest as the good characters overcome their evil foes.

When we think of folklore today, many of us remember the marvelous language in folktales such as that found in "Snow White and the Seven Dwarfs" as the evil stepmother asks: "Mirror, mirror on the wall, who is the fairest one of all?" We can join in with appreciation as the mirror answers: "You, Queen, are fairest in all this land. But over the hills, in the greenwood shade, where the seven dwarfs their home have made. Snow White is safely hidden, and she is fairer far, O Queen, to see." Or, our memories might recreate the rhythmical language in "Cinderella" as the unhappy girl goes to her mother's grave beneath the hazel tree and cries: "Shiver and quiver, little tree. Silver and gold throw over me." We may shudder at the warning when the pigeons on the same hazel tree call out the truth to the deceived prince: "Turn and look, turn and look. There's blood within the shoe. The shoe is much too small for her. The true bride waits for you." Activities developed around folklore should enhance our appreciation for the language and the story structure as well as our understanding of the cultural foundations of the folklore.

A list of some of the important understandings related to folklore (folktales, fables, myths, and legends) illustrates the rich instructional possibilities of the genre. For example, activities can be developed that emphasize these important understandings:

1. Folklore has been handed down through oral storytelling. The themes and characterizations reveal the ancient beliefs and values of the people.
2. The four major types of folklore are folktale, fable, legend, and myth. Each type has specific characteristics related to belief, setting, characterization, plot development, types of conflict, themes and values, style, and motifs.

3. The major folktale types are cumulative, beast, magic, humorous, pourquoi, and realistic tales.

4. Folklore is found in cultures from around the world. A knowledge of some of the people who wrote down the tales helps in the search for folklore from specific cultures. For example some of the leading retellers of the tales include: Joseph Jacobs and Howard Pyle (British); Charles Perrault (French); Brothers Grimm (German); Peter Asbjornsen and Jorgen Moe (Norwegian); Isaac Bashevis Singer and Alexander Pushkin (Jewish); Aesop, Thomas Bulfinch, and Padraic Colum (Greek); Edward Curtis, George Bird Grinnell, and John Bierhorst (Native American); Harold Courlander and Ashley Bryan (African); and Aleksandr Nikolaevich Afanasev (Russian).

5. Folklore influences other types of literature.

This list shows that folklore is not a simple subject. Understanding the different aspects of folklore can take many years. Teachers frequently ask, "What types of folklore and which understandings related to that folklore should be included at specific grade levels?" There are no concrete answers, but complexity differs among folktales, fables, legends, and myths. A scope and sequence for teaching folklore was developed after consulting with numerous teachers and school districts. Suggestions include types of folklore and related understandings that might be used with kindergarten through third grades, fourth through sixth grades, and seventh and eighth grades. The following scope and sequence shows how some of the important understandings can be developed into an instructional plan:

KINDERGARTEN THROUGH THIRD GRADES

1. Share, understand, and appreciate folktales.
2. Identify and appreciate the story elements associated with a folktale: Setting, plot, characterization, conflict, theme, motif, and style.
3. Understand how to read folktales.
4. Understand and appreciate the major types of folktales: cumulative, beast, magic, humorous, pourquoi, and realistic.
5. Appreciate and analyze the characteristics of folktales from a specific country. By third grade, take part in an in-depth study of folktales from one or two countries.
6. Share, understand, and appreciate fables.
7. Identify literary elements in fables.

FOURTH THROUGH SIXTH GRADES

1. Continue in-depth study of folktales from specific countries emphasizing such areas as values, themes, social studies, and geography.
2. Analyze variations of folktales found in different countries, speculate about causes of variations, and trace elements within the variations. This can be related to social studies and history.
3. Share, understand, and appreciate legends.
4. Identify story elements found in legends.
5. Analyze characteristics of legends from specific countries.
6. Compare and contrast characteristics of folktales and legends.

7. Share, understand, and appreciate myths. (Most teachers believe that an understanding of myth is more difficult than an understanding of legends. Consequently, the study of myth can be developed in the upper grades.)
8. Identify story elements found in myths.
9. Analyze characteristics of myths from specific countries.
10. Compare characteristics of folktale, legend, and myth.
11. Begin study of the relationships among folklore and other types of literature from one cultural group.

SEVENTH AND EIGHTH GRADES

1. Take part in an in-depth study of the characteristics of legends and myths.
2. Take part in an in-depth study of the relationships among mythology and literature from one or more cultural groups.

Approaches that Develop Understanding of Folklore

In this section we will focus on core lessons that can be used to clarify understandings and increase appreciation of folklore and on units that enhance students' cultural understandings. The first few core lessons can be used at several grade levels depending on the folklore selected for reading. The units are divided into lower elementary, middle elementary, and upper elementary and middle school categories.

Many of the instructional approaches described earlier in this text are excellent for developing understandings related to folklore. Some are especially good for developing understandings about literary genres and literary elements associated with folklore. Others are excellent for relating speaking, listening, reading, writing, and content areas such as social studies. All of the approaches either have been or will be developed within this text. A few examples of core lessons previously developed are shown in the following list. Many more folklore selections are listed under extended and recreational reading. The list shows a few of the instructional activities that can be used to develop an appreciation and an understanding of folklore.

1. Dramatization and other oral interpretations (Chapter 5 "Three Billy Goats Gruff").
2. Reading aloud and telling stories (Chapter 3, Highwater's *Anpao: An American Indian Odyssey*).
3. Diagraming plot structures (Chapter 5, "Three Billy Goats Gruff," Steptoe's *Mufaro's Beautiful Daughters*, Hastings' *Sir Gawain and the Loathly Lady*).
4. Relating vocabulary and plot development in the plot diagram (Chapter 3, De Paola's *The Legend of the Bluebonnet*, Brett's *Goldilocks and the Three Bears*, Hastings' *Sir Gawain and the Loathly Lady*).
5. Webbing literary elements of setting, characterization, conflict, and theme (Chapter 5, 6, 7, 8 Hastings' *Sir Gawain and the Loathly Lady*).
6. Identifying themes, motifs, and values in folktales, legends, and myths from different cultures.
7. Charting and comparing similarities and differences among folktales, fables, legends, and myths.

8. Charting and comparing different versions of the same folktale found in different cultures.

9. Analyzing folklore variations, identifying familiar theme and motif elements, identifying references to time and place, and providing reasons for cultural history and changes from the original versions.

10. Developing guidelines to help students read folktales, fables, legends, and myths.

11. Developing self-questioning strategies to help student comprehension (Chapter 2, Grimm's *Rumpelstiltskin*, Paterson's *The Tale of the Mandarin Ducks*, and San Souci's *The Talking Eggs: A Folktale from the American South*).

12. Developing self-questioning strategies that help students differentiate among folktales, fables, legends, and myths.

13. Responding to the vivid language and other elements in folklore through an artistic interpretation.

14. Analyzing the settings in highly illustrated folklore texts.

15. Gaining an understanding of art history through illustrations in folklore collections published during different time periods.

16. Writing creative stories that follow the structure and the characteristics of folktales, fables, legends, and myths.

17. Comparing "Touchstone" versions of folklore with other versions and retellings.

18. Comparing retellings of the same tale published in different time periods and considering possible reasons for the differences.

19. Comparing the traditional values in folklore with the values in contemporary fiction or poetry in the same culture. Considering reasons that values in two genres might be similar (Chapter 13).

20. Building bridges between folktales and literary fairy tales by comparing similarities in plot structures, settings, characterizations, themes, and motifs (Chapter 11).

21. Building bridges between fables and literary fables by comparing literary elements (Chapter 11).

22. Connecting mythology and legend with high fantasy by identifying foundations and comparing similarities in literary elements (Chapter 11).

23. Tracing literary allusions back to folklore (Chapter 8).

24. Tracing and considering the reasons that theme changes between some myths and legends and the high fantasy on which they are based. For example, shifting from the importance of fate to the importance of free will (Chapter 11).

25. Collecting examples of oral folklore from people in the community.

26. Relating the history of folklore with the history of music from a specific culture.

27. Using cues from the text and prior knowledge to make predictions (Chapter 2, Fox's *Hattie and the Fox*).

28. Developing understandings of symbolic interpretations (Chapter 7, Lang's *The Blue Fairy Book* and *The Red Fairy Book*, Grimm's *The Twelve Dancing Princesses and Other Tales From Grimm*, Perrault's *Complete Fairy Tales*, Onassis' *The Firebird and Other Russian Tales*, Liyi's *The Spring of Butterflies and Other Chinese Folk Tales*, Bierhorst's *The Monkey's Haircut and Other Stories Told by the Maya*, Lester's *The Knee-High Man and Other Tales*, Haviland's *North American Legends*, Grimm's *The Water of Life*).

29. Analyzing the development of themes (Chapter 8, *Aesop's Fables,* Grimm's *Little Red Riding Hood,* De Paolo's *The Legend of the Bluebonnet,* Goble's *Buffalo Woman,* Grimm's *Grimm's Household Tales,* or *The Complete Brothers Grimm Fairy Tales,* Grimm's *Dear Mili,* Highwater's *Anpao: An American Indian Odyssey*).

30. Developing units around folklore that encourage students to use many of the above approaches.

Core Books and Sample Lessons for Developing Understanding of Folklore

The following examples of core lessons can be used independently or as part of a unit. The lessons can be used at several different levels depending on the books chosen.

LESSON ONE: Developing Understandings About How to Read a Folktale

OBJECTIVES

To understand the story grammar associated with a folktale and to understand the unique characteristics of the setting, the characters, the plot, and the theme.

To develop and practice guidelines that will increase understanding when reading a folktale.

To write original tales that follow the folklore structure and to use the guidelines to evaluate the original writing.

CORE BOOKS: Individual folktale stories and anthologies that are appropriate for the grade level. For example, lower elementary: James Marshall's retelling of *Hansel and Gretel;* Arlene Mosel's *The Funny Little Woman* (Japanese, Caldecott Medal); and Anne Rockwell's *The Three Bears & 15 Other Stories.* Middle elementary: Grimm's *Snow-White and the Seven Dwarfs* (German, Caldecott Honor); Carole Kismaric's retelling of *The Rumor of Pavel and Paali: A Ukranian Folktale;* and Marianna Mayer's retelling of *The Twelve Dancing Princesses.* Upper elementary and middle school: Angela Carter's translation of *Sleeping Beauty & Other Favourite Fairy Tales* (French); C. S. Evans' retelling of *The Sleeping Beauty* (French); and Brothers Grimm *Household Tales* (Touchstone).

PROCEDURES: If previously used, this lesson can begin with a review of the common story grammars discussed in Chapter 2 and identified by Pearson (1984) and Barr and Sadow (1985). Students in the upper elementary and middle school can be introduced to the longer, more complex sequence of recurring actions identified in French and German tales by Favat (1977).

Ask the students to read or listen to two or three folktales. Ask them to think about the characteristics related to setting, characterization, plot, conflict, and theme that the stories have in common. For example, "What types of settings do the folktales have? How rapidly does the storyteller identify the nature of the characters and the problem? How would you describe the nature of the characters and their problems? What series of actions must the characters undertake to overcome the problem? Who, if anyone, helps the characters? What happens to the characters as a result of overcoming the problem? What message do you think the original storyteller is trying to get across? Could you infer this message by the actions that are rewarded and those that are punished?"

After they have read and discussed several examples of folktales, ask them to pretend that they are teachers helping students who have never read a folktale. Ask them to think about the role of the oral storyteller, the characteristics of a folktale, and the sequence of events. Ask them to think about how they gained meaning from the folktale and to identify what they thought about during each part of the tale and what they visualized as they were reading or listening to the folktales. Finally, ask them to list a sequence of events and questions they could ask themselves as they read the folktale. Have them evaluate whether their list of guidelines could help someone read and gain meaning from a folktale. Ask them to try using their own guidelines on a new folktale. (This sequence of events will require several days to accomplish.)

The following guidelines were developed with the help of a group of third- and fourth-grade students:

HOW I SHOULD READ A FOLKTALE

1. Try to picture the setting. Close my eyes. Can I see the deep, dark woods; the mountains covered with snow; or the castle? As soon as I hear, "Once upon a time," I should try to put myself back into the days of the storyteller and picture the setting in my mind.

2. As I read the first few paragraphs I should try to identify the characters and what they are like. Ask myself, "What are the characters like? Can I describe each character? Are they good or bad? What do they want? How do I think they will try to get what they want? Can I picture each of the characters in my mind?"

3. Try to identify the problem that must be overcome. Ask myself, "How do I think the characters might try to overcome the problem?"

4. As I read the folktale, I should identify the series of events that create the action and develop the conflict. Ask myself, "What is the series of events in the folktale?" I should remember that folktales often have three events and I should notice if the events happen in series of threes. Ask myself, "Who, if anyone, helps the characters? Which characters are helped? Why do they help the characters?"

5. As I reach the end of the story, I should notice what happens to make me think I am nearing the climax. Ask myself, "Am I right? What made me know I was near the climax?"

6. At the end of the story I should think about the message that the original storyteller was telling the people. Ask myself, "What could the message be? Do the characters, their actions, and the rewards or punishments support this message?"

Students should have many opportunities to apply their guidelines to their reading of folktales. The guidelines also can help students write stories following a folktale format. They now can evaluate their creative stories by applying their own guidelines as they read their stories from a reader's perspective rather than from the writer's perspective.

The same sequence can be developed in the upper grades with legends and myths. Students can read examples of each type of folklore, identify common elements within the folklore, and develop guidelines that will help them read legends or myths. Older students probably should begin with folktales if they have not already explored how to read folktales.

LESSON TWO: Differentiating Among Folktales, Fables, Myths, and Legends

OBJECTIVES

To identify the characteristics of folktales, fables, myths, and legends, and to identify the similarities and differences among each type of folklore.

To read additional folklore, to apply the characteristics, and to categorize the stories according to type of folklore.

To develop a series of questions that students can use to differentiate among folktales, fables, legends, and myths.

CORE BOOKS: Examples of each type of folklore. Folktales: Andrew Lang's *The Blue Fairy Book* (Touchstone); Liyi He's *The Spring of Butterflies and Other Chinese Folk Tales;* and Peter Christen Asbjornsen and Jorgen Moe's *Norwegian Folk Tales.* Fables: Aesop's *Aesop's Fables* and John Bierhorst's *Doctor Coyote: A Native American Aesop's Fables.* Legends: Nina Bawden's *William Tell;* Marcia Brown's *Backbone of the King: Story of Pakaa and His Son Ku;* and Howard Pyle's *The Story of King Arthur and His Knights* (Touchstone). Myths: Thomas Bulfinch's *Myths of Greece & Rome;* Padraic Colum's *The Golden Fleece and the Heroes Who Lived Before Achilles* (Newbery Honor, Touchstone); and Virginia Hamilton's *In the Beginning: Creation Stories from Around the World* (Newbery Honor).

PROCEDURES: This lesson is designed for students from the middle elementary grades through middle school. Younger students may differentiate between folktales and fables. This lesson will take several days to complete because students will need to read several examples of each type of folklore.

We will draw upon the definitions and guidelines for differentiating types of folklore developed by folklorist Bascom (1965). To begin the lesson place the chart from Figure 10.1 on the board, on a transparency, or on handouts. The chart should be empty except for the categories (Folktale, Fable, Myth, and Legend) and the top descriptors (Form and Examples, Belief, Time, Place, Attitude, and Principal Characters). Introduce the chart by telling the students that they are going to take the role of folklorists and try to categorize the various types of folklore: folktale, fable, myth, and legend. Explain to the students that one way folklorists such as Bascom categorize types of folklore is to analyze whether the original storytellers and their audiences considered the stories to be fiction or fact, to evaluate the time and place described in the setting, to question whether the stories have a secular or a sacred attitude, and to identify the natures of the principal characters. This lesson will require several days as students analyze each type of folklore and place examples on the chart.

Begin by reading several folktales. You can share with them and discuss Bascom's definition of *folktales:* Folktales are "prose narratives which are regarded as fiction. They are not considered as dogma or history, they may or may not have happened, and they are not taken seriously" (p. 4). Be sure that students understand that *dogma* is a set of established principles, beliefs, and opinions and that history is a recording of something that actually happened. This differentiation is important as the students analyze and discuss myths and legends. It also will be important later when they study the folklore of various cultures and begin to understand the importance of the folklore in providing cultural foundations. After reading several folktales, choose some that the students consider typical. Fill in the information on the chart using generalizations about most folktales and specific examples from a few folktales. For example, for the generalizations they might refer to Bascom's definition and write *fiction* in the Belief category. Next they might consider the time when the folktales take place. Ask the students, "Because many of the tales begin with 'Once upon a time,' how can we identify the time?" They might categorize these stories as some form of "Anytime." Next, ask the students to think about the locations. Ask, "Are specific countries and towns usually mentioned? How does the storyteller describe the place?" Because many of the folktales take place in an unnamed great forest, village, or castle, the students might categorize these stories with some form of "Anyplace." Next, the students should consider the attitudes of the storyteller, the audience, and the content of the stories. Are these attitudes secular or sacred? They should notice that most folktales are secular. Finally, they should identify the types of principal characters they find in folktales. For example, many have both human and nonhuman characters. They should place these designations on the chart. Finally, they should place examples from specific folktales on the chart and discuss how these examples fit into the listed definitions. The examples on the

FIGURE 10.1 Differentiating among characteristics of folktales, fables, myths, and legends.

Form and Examples	Belief	Time	Place	Attitude	Principal Characters
Folktale		*Anytime*	*Anyplace*		*Human or Nonhuman*
1. "Jack and the Beanstalk" (European)	fiction	"Once upon a time there was a poor widow"	"In a little cottage" "In a castle in the sky"	secular	giant human boy talking harp
2. "The Wonderful Brocade" (Chinese)	fiction	"Once upon a time"	"On the plain at the foot of a huge mountain"	secular	woman, three sons spirit maiden
Fable		*Anytime*	*Anyplace*		*Animal or Human*
1. "The Frogs Desiring a King" (Aesop)	fiction	"In the days of Old"	"in the Lakes"	secular/allegorical	frogs
2. "Doctor Coyote" (Aztec)	fiction	"One day"	in the country	secular/allegorical	coyote
Myth		*Remote Past*	*Other world or earlier world*		*Nonhuman*
1. "Nyambi the Creator" (African)	considered fact	"In the beginning"	early Earth	sacred (deities)	N-yam-bi the creator
2. "Cupid and Psyche" (Greek)	considered fact	remote past	early Earth, home of the gods	sacred (deities)	Venus—Greek goddess Cupid—her winged son
Legend		*Recent Past*	*World of today*		*Human*
1. "King Arthur" (European)	considered fact	recent past	Ancient Britain—but recognizable world of today	secular	King Arthur Knights of Round Table
2. "Paka'a and His Son Ku"	considered fact	recent past	Hawaii during ancient times—but recognizable world of today.	secular	royal guard attendant to the King

chart in Figure 10.1 were developed using this approach. Notice how specific examples are taken from each of the folktales. The original chart had many more examples from folktales as the students each added their own discoveries.

Continue the study of folklore characteristics by introducing and discussing fables. After reading several selections, students should be able to define *fables* as brief tales in which animal characters that talk and act like humans teach a moral lesson or explain something about human conduct. You can share a definition of *fables* such as that provided in *Funk & Wagnalls Standard Dictionary of Folklore, Mythology and Legend* (1972): "An animal tale with a moral; a short tale in which animals appear as characters, talking and acting like human beings, though usually keeping their animal traits, and having as its purpose the pointing out of a moral. The fable consequently has two parts: the narrative which exemplifies the moral, and the statement of the moral often appended in the form of a proverb" (p. 361).

Ask students to provide the general characteristics of a fable. These characteristics are closely related to the folktale (Figure 10.1). Students should understand, however, that fables are shorter and have stated morals. Older students also can discuss the allegorical purposes of the fables. Finally, place specific examples from fables on the chart. Before continuing this lesson, discuss the similarities and differences between folktales and fables. (Teachers who believe the students are not ready for the more complex legends and myths can conclude the lesson here.)

As the chart in Figure 10.1 shows, major differences exist between fictional folktales and fables and the more factual legends and myths. Remember that *factual* means the stories were considered to be true by the original storytellers and their audiences. It does not necessarily mean that the stories are considered true by today's readers.

You can introduce myth by relating and discussing Bascom's (1965) definition. Myths are "prose narratives which, in the society in which they are told, are considered to be truthful accounts of what happened in the remote past. They are accepted on faith; they are taught to be believed; and they can be cited as authority in answer to ignorance, doubt, or disbelief. Myths are the embodiment of dogma; they are usually sacred; and they are often associated with theology and ritual" (p. 4). This definition becomes important as older students read and discuss the mythological foundations of various cultural groups. They will discover that myths describe the origins of the world, natural phenomena such as thunder, human emotions, and various societal functions. Students also will discover that all cultures have important myths.

Share several myths with the students and ask them to identify the general characteristics on the chart. For example, students might refer to Bascom's definition and state that myths were considered fact by the original tellers and audience. When they analyze the settings for myths they will discover that the time is not "anytime" but rather the remote past often just before, during, or shortly after creation. The places are an earlier world such as Mount Olympus in Greek mythology. The settings might be in the sky, on Earth, or even in the underworld. The attitude of the stories is sacred because the principal characters are gods and goddesses such as Odin from Norse mythology or Aphrodite from Greek mythology. Have students place specific examples from the myths on the chart.

Finally, introduce, read, and discuss legends. You can share and discuss Bascom's (1965) definition of *legend:* Legends are "prose narratives which, like myths, are regarded as true by the narrator and his audience, but they are set in a period considered less remote, when the world was much as it is today. Legends are more often secular than sacred, and their principal characters are human" (p. 4). Students also should understand that legends often are more like history than are the other types of folklore. The legendary characters might actually have lived, although the tales probably are exaggerated. For example, legends from France tell about Joan of Arc while African legends report how the prophet Amakosa saved the Juba people from extinction. Some of the most famous legendary heroes include King Arthur and Robin Hood.

Share and discuss several examples of legends with the students. First fill in the general information on the chart and then ask them to provide specific examples. For example, for general information they might refer to Bascom's definition which states that legends are considered fact. They might support this definition by locating references to real people, such as William Tell, in both history and legend. Next they can consider the time of the legends such as 14th century Switzerland or early Britain during the age of chivalry. They should identify the time of a legend as the recent past, a past that we still recognize today. Similarly, legends take place in the world of today, in such settings as Sherwood Forest, the home of Robin Hood in England. Unlike the locations in folktales, the locations associated with legends usually are identified clearly. As Bascom states, the attitude of most legends is secular. Consequently, the principal characters are human beings such as the knights of the Round Table. Finally, ask the students to place specific examples from legends onto the chart. Then ask them to describe the differences between myths and legends and then among folktales, fables, myths, and legends.

This extended lesson easily can become a longer unit as students read numerous examples of folktales, fables, myths, and legends and defend their placement of each on the chart. They also can use the definitions and characteristics to write their own folktales, fables, myths, and legends.

As in the previous "How I Should Read a Folktale" lesson, students can use their considerable knowledge to develop questions they can ask themselves as they decide if a selection is folklore and if it should be categorized as folktale, fable, myth, or legend. The following questions were developed with the help of eighth-grade students:

QUESTIONS I CAN ASK MYSELF TO CATEGORIZE FOLKLORE

1. Was the tale passed down through the oral tradition? What is my evidence? Did I look for an original source in the end notes or within the title? Who wrote down the tale from an oral source?

2. Does the story follow a structure similar to that of other examples of folklore? How is it similar? What attracted my attention—the language, the plot, the characters, the theme?

3. Does the tale reflect an ancient culture, the land, and the problems of the storyteller and the audience? What is my evidence?

4. If the tale is identified as a folktale, does it meet the characteristics of a folktale? How do I know that it is fictitious? How would I classify the setting as "anytime" and "anyplace"? What makes the story secular? Who are the principal characters? Can I classify them as human or nonhuman?

5. If the tale is identified as a myth, does it meet the characteristics of myth? How do I know that the story was considered factual by the original teller and audience? How would I describe the setting as "the remote past" and "an earlier world"? What makes the story sacred? Can I classify the principal characters as gods or goddesses?

6. If the tale is identified as a legend, does it meet the characteristics of legend? How do I know that the story was considered factual by the original teller and audience? How would I describe the settings as "in the recent past" and "in a world like our world"? What makes the story secular? Can I classify the principal characters as human?

After students have developed their questions, allow them to use their questions as they read many examples of folktales, fables, myths, and legends.

LESSON THREE: Responding to the Vivid Language and Other Elements in Folklore Through Artistic Interpretations.

OBJECTIVE

To select passages that are particularly pleasing and to develop a personal response to those passages through art.

CORE BOOKS: Collect a wide variety of folktales, fables, myths, and legends with vivid language that appeals to students. Students can identify their own choices after reading the folktales. Although any collection of folklore can be used for this activity, the examples in this lesson are some student favorites: Wanda Gag's retelling of *Tales From Grimm;* Kevin Crossley-Holland's *British Folk Tales;* Robin Lister's *The Legend of King Arthur;* and Ingri and Edgar Parin D'Aulaire's *Norse Gods and Giants* (Touchstone).

PROCEDURES: Because folklore can be selected from a wide range of reading and listening levels, this lesson can be completed at any grade level. Younger students can listen to stories and select vivid passages to illustrate.

Begin the lesson by having the students read or listen to folktales, fables, myths, or legends. Remind the students that oral storytellers used language to appeal to their audiences. As they read or listen to these passages, ask the students to close their eyes and try to visualize the setting, the characters, or the conflict. Ask the students to select passages or sentences that particularly appeal to them. Ask them to think about the qualities of the writing, the characters, or the plot that they especially liked.

Encourage the students to share their favorite passages and then to draw pictures that reveal their aesthetic responses to the folklore. The following two passages were selected, discussed, and illustrated by students in the lower elementary grades after listening to and reading *Tales From Grimm:*

> Suddenly, into the vast green silence fell a ripple of sound so sweet, so gay, so silvery, that the children looked up in breathless wonder. A little white bird sat there in a tree; and when its beautiful song was ended, it spread its wings and fluttered away with anxious little chirps as though it wished to say, "Follow me! Follow me!" (p. 12, "Hansel and Gretel").
>
> 'Shake yourself, my little tree, Shower shiny clothes on me.' She had no sooner said this, when a dress fluttered down on her: a dress so heavenly fair that it must have been spun out of angels' dreams. A tiny crown, sparkling like a thousand dew drops, floated down and nestled in her hair; and two little golden slippers, set with dancing diamonds, fitted themselves neatly around her feet (p. 113, "Cinderella").

The following passages were selected, discussed, and illustrated by middle elementary students after listening to and reading *British Folk Tales:*

> It was an empty, oyster-and-pearl afternoon. The water lipped at the sand and sorted the shingle and lapped round the rock where the girl was sitting (p. 11, "Sea-Woman").
>
> Late one night, Patsy was walking home after playing at a dance in a neighbouring village. It wasn't too friendly a way, what with hanging rocks on either side of the road, and it wasn't too friendly a night—dungeon-dark and the November wind whistling sharp and out of tune (p. 17, "The Piper and the Pooka").
>
> It was a high and dry summer. The tall nettles behind the widow's cottage swayed and looked sorry for themselves. A silly warm wind chafed the elder leaves and the long grass (p. 24, "The Frog Prince").

The kitchen was a magic box, full of light and dancing shadows. Shafts of winter sunlight lanced the range and the dresser and the pail of milk, and the hawthorn tree shivered outside the window (p. 45, "Dathera Dad").

The following passages were selected and illustrated by middle and upper elementary students after reading *The Legend of King Arthur:*

My name is Merlin, a name to conjure with; Merlin the wizard; Merlin, King Arthur's friend. I live deep in a cave, a limestone treasure-house of water, rock and time. I sit beside a stream among the snow-white columns, formed where slowly stalagmites and stalactites have met. I sit where I have sat for centuries, sunk in soft cushions on my seat of stone. Like my books, which lie scattered about me, I am being slowly fossilized by the steady drip of time. Already my limbs are set in shining stone. My hair and beard have frosted hard. Even if I woke I could not move. For where is the ancient magic that might rescue me? (p. 5).

"Within moments two dragons had climbed out beside me. One was red, the other white. They were breathing fire in short bursts of flame which sizzled on the wet earth" (p. 13).

Upper elementary and middle school students undertook a similar activity using *Norse Gods and Giants.* They selected passages about the creation of the world in that cold climate and the giants who lived there. Passages such as the following were especially suited to artwork as students responded to the language and illustrated this world at the beginning of time:

Early in the morning of time there was no sand, no grass, no lapping wave. There was no earth, no sun, no moon, no stars. There was Niflheim, a waste of frozen fog, and Muspelheim, a place of raging flames. And in between the fog and fire there was a gaping pit—Ginungagap. For untold ages crackling embers from Muspelheim and crystals of ice from Niflheim whirled around in the dark and dismal pit (p. 12).

This collection of Norse myths has many other passages that appeal to readers and listeners.

Developing Folklore Units

Folklore units can be designed to develop both in-depth cultural understandings and cross-cultural comparisons. For example, when involved in units that stress cultural understanding, students can gain considerable information about a culture by studying in-depth the folktales, fables, legends, and myths associated with that culture. When involved in cross-cultural comparisons students can read numerous adaptations of story types found in various cultures and compare the similarities and differences across cultures.

Folklorists present strong arguments for developing cultural understanding through folklore. These arguments also reveal some of the objectives that should be developed in the folklore units. For example, Campbell (1988) identifies four functions of myth that are related to cultural understanding:

1. a mystical function that allows the people to experience the wonders of the universe
2. a cosmological dimension that identifies the shape of the universe
3. a sociological function that supports and validates a certain social order
4. a pedagogical function that tells the people how to live through different circumstances

These functions are important for students trying to understand their own culture or the cultures of other peoples.

Collectors of tales from various cultures support the strong relationships between traditional folklore and the culture. For example, Yep (1989) suggests that folktales offer strategies for living that are accepted by the culture. He states, "A culture defines its virtues and vices within its folktales.... Defining vices is as important as defining virtues" (p. 69). Yep argues that studying folktales provides an excellent way to understand the Chinese-American culture. Bierhorst (1976) argues just as strongly for using Native American traditional tales to learn about that culture. He states that within Native American myths, legends, and folktales the reader discovers what is important to the believer in that culture. The stories reveal how the people believed the world was created and given order, what problems and conflicts are found in the basic kinship unit, what actions are considered fair or foul in the society, and how members of the culture should progress through various life stages. Clearly, an in-depth study of the folklore of a culture can add to the social studies curriculum as well as to the literature and reading curriculums.

Educators also provide strong reasons for using folklore units to develop cultural understanding. Diakiw (1990) maintains that children's literature units can help develop global education and understanding of the world. One of the units that he recommends focuses on African folktales and then compares the tales with traditional tales from other cultures. Barnes (1991) recommends using traditional tales to make discoveries about cultural understandings and anthropological concepts. He maintains that even young students learn about the cultures of Native Americans, Asians, and Hispanics from the traditional and contemporary literature. I recommend a study of black, Native American, and Hispanic folk literature as a foundation for learning about a culture and validating the content of biography, poetry, and contemporary literature written by members of the cultural group (Norton, 1990).

Moss (1984) provides guidelines for developing units around literature: First, establish a set of goals and objectives. After the objectives are formulated and the focus is chosen, teachers should choose the core books. This collection should include books to be read aloud and discussed during group story sessions as well as books for independent reading. Next, teachers should develop the content for the story sessions that include reading and discussing core books. The stories introduced to the group should be in a "carefully planned sequence so that each new story is discussed in terms of those read previously. A series of questions is introduced to guide this comparative study of diverse tales and to foster the discovery of significant relationships, recurring patterns, and distinguishing characteristics. Such discoveries serve as the context for forming concepts, making inferences, and developing principles which can be used in subsequent experiences with literature (Moss, 1984, p. 5). Moss also recommends using books with related content for independent reading, turning literature discussions into backgrounds for creative writing, and using the unit to provide opportunities for creative expression through art, drama, dance, and music.

The following units develop comparative understandings as students analyze various versions of the same folktale and in-depth cultural understandings as they read and analyze several folklore selections from the same culture. Some of the books introduce the concepts with detailed discussions. Each unit includes a list of core books that can be used for whole-group reading and group discussions and additional books that can be used for independent reading. Each unit also provides suggestions for creative writing and other creative expression.

Units that Compare Different Versions of the Same Folktale

Studying variants of the same folktale found in different countries and cultures encourages students to develop understandings of cultural diffusion and common needs and problems. Numerous variants can be selected. For example, the "Cinderella," "Little Red Riding Hood," and "Hansel and Gretel" variants are found in cultures throughout the world. Units also can focus on how folktales change across time. Students can speculate about changes in attitudes, language, and illustrations. This last activity can be used to study art history. Scholarly books such as *Beauty and the Beast: Visions and Revisions of an Old Tale* (Hearne, 1989) suggest sources and focuses for a study of one tale over time.

UNIT ONE: Comparing Different Versions of "Cinderella"

OBJECTIVES

    To read and enjoy variations of the same folktale.

    To identify common elements within the folktales and discover how the culture is reflected in the tales.

    To discover that folktales are an excellent source of information about a culture.

    To become aware of cultural diffusion.

    To write a variant of a folktale that reflects students' own culture.

CORE BOOKS: A selection of tales should be chosen for group reading and discussions that reflect the Cinderella motif found in various cultures. Examples include Brothers Grimm's "Cinderella" (German), in *Household Tales;* Joseph Jacobs' "Tattercoats" (English), in Sutherland and Livingston's *The Scott, Foresman Anthology of Children's Literature* (1984); Charles Perrault's "Cinderella," (French), in Marcia Brown's *Cinderella* (Caldecott Medal) and *Perrault's Complete Fairy Tales;* Ann Nolan Clark's *In the Land of Small Dragon,* (Vietnamese); "The Indian Cinderella" (Native American), in Virginia Haviland's *North American Legends;* and William Hooks' *Moss Gown* (English). The last two are set in eastern North Carolina.

EXTENDED BOOKS FOR INDEPENDENT READING AND OTHER ASSIGNMENTS: For this related section choose as many additional "Cinderella" stories as you can locate. Some teachers prefer to encourage students to read the books independently and apply their understandings gained from the group discussions. Other teachers prefer to use these books for additional group work. Additional choices might include the following:

    SHIRLEY CLIMO'S *The Egyptian Cinderella*
    CHARLOTTE HUCK'S retelling of *Princess Furball* (English)
    AI-LING LOUIE'S *Yeh Shen: A Cinderella Story from China*
    JOHN STEPTOE'S *Mufaro's Beautiful Daughters: An African Tale* (Caldecott Honor)
    "Little Burnt Face" (Native American), in Sutherland and Livingston's *The Scott, Foresman Anthology of Children's Literature* (1984)
    LYNETTE DYER VUONG'S *The Brocaded Slipper* (Vietnamese)

PROCEDURES: To begin this unit tell the students that some folktales have common story types found in cultures throughout the world. These folktales are called *variants* because they have basic elements in common, but frequently differ in such areas as settings, names of characters, magical objects, tasks to be completed, and obstacles to be overcome.

After students have read several "Cinderella" stories, ask them to identify the common elements in the different versions, such as those retold by Grimm, Perrault, and Jacobs. Remind the students that the common elements should be general such as "The heroine has a lowly position in the family." After students have identified several common elements, begin the study of variants by reading the Brothers Grimm and French versions of "Cinderella" during the same class period. Ask the students to notice the common important elements in these tales and add them to the list they compiled earlier. Such a list might include the following:

1. The heroine has a lowly position in the family.
2. The heroine is persecuted by stepsisters or other members of the family.
3. The heroine accomplishes difficult tasks.
4. The heroine has an opportunity to meet a person who has great worth within the culture.
5. The heroine is kept from meeting the person of great worth because she lacks clothing to attend a function.
6. The heroine is helped by a supernatural being.
7. The heroine is warned to return by a certain time.
8. The person of great worth is attracted to the heroine.
9. There is a test for the rightful heroine.
10. The heroine passes the test and marries the person of great worth.

Next, ask the students to identify how each of these common elements are developed in the German and French tales. For example, in both tales the girl's lowly position is caused by the mother's death and the father's remarriage. There are some specific differences, however. For example, the girl in the German version receives her wishes from a bird on the tree on her mother's grave and the girl in the French version receives wishes from a fairy godmother. The endings are also different: The German version ends unhappily for the stepmother and stepsisters while the French version ends in forgiveness of the stepsisters and their marriage to noblemen.

After the students have identified common elements and specific examples across the German and French "Cinderella" tales, ask them to read or listen to variants from other cultures. During this activity they should identify the elements that are similar and those that are different. Why do the elements in the stories change? How are these changes related to the cultures in which the tales were told? They should analyze any illustrations for cultural information. For example, Clark's *In the Land of Small Dragon* develops considerable cultural background through the illustrations.

The Native American "Cinderella" variants are especially rich with cultural and setting information. For example, when reading or listening to "The Indian Cinderella" or "Little Burnt-Face" the students should identify the elements in the story that are common to the previously listed elements. Then ask them to identify the elements that reflect the Native American setting (woodlands) or the Native American culture. A list of Native American setting and cultural elements from "The Indian Cinderella" includes the following points:

1. The setting is on the Atlantic coast.
2. The person of great worth is Strong Wind, a great Indian warrior.

3. Strong Wind lives in a tent near the sea.
4. The heroine is one of three daughters of a great chief.
5. The test is to describe the invisible Strong Wind and the sled that he pulls across the sky.
6. The heroine patches her clothes with bits of birch bark.
7. The heroine passes the test and describes Strong Wind as pulling his sled with the rainbow and holding a bow string that is the Milky Way.
8. The heroine's raven hair is restored.
9. The heroine marries Strong Wind and helps him do great deeds.
10. The elder sisters are changed into aspen trees as punishment for their lies and cruelty.

This story has many of the "Cinderella" elements but is also set firmly in the culture of the Woodlands Indians. As do many Native American tales, the story has a close relationship with nature and the tale concludes with an answer to why something occurs in nature: The elder sisters who were changed into aspen trees still tremble when Strong Wind approaches because they fear his anger.

After reading and discussing numerous variants from various cultures, ask older students what they think would happen if the people who told the stories and listened to the stories moved to a new land. Ask, "Would they take their oral stories with them? How do you think the stories might change over the years to reflect different settings or cultures?" Encourage the students to speculate about such areas as differences in settings, occupations, foods, and activities. Tell the students that as they listen to or read *Moss Gown,* another variant of the "Cinderella" story, they should search for (a) Cinderella elements, (b) references to time and place, and (c) evidence of the European country the early storytellers came from. (If desired, students also can search for King Lear elements in this tale.)

Students should discover the following Cinderella elements:

1. The heroine, a generous young girl, has two greedy older sisters.
2. The heroine has a helper with supernatural powers.
3. The heroine has a gown that changes to rags at a specified time.
4. The heroine is given the hardest kitchen work.
5. An important person holds a dance.
6. The heroine cannot attend the dance because she lacks a dress.
7. A supernatural being casts a spell and provides a dress.
8. An order is given about the dress.
9. The important person dances only with the heroine.
10. The important person and the heroine are married.

The references to time and place include the following:

1. A great plantation
2. A house with eight marble columns
3. Fine fields
4. Riding and hunting in the mysterious swamp
5. Black-green cypress treetops
6. Gray Spanish moss
7. The word used to cast a spell is a French word used in the Carolinas
8. Important person holds a frolic

Students should discuss how these references to time and place reflect the new environment of the original storytellers. They also should identify where they think the story takes place. Students might identify the following evidence that shows that the original storytellers had English backgrounds: (a) Similarities to British "Tattercoats" include servants who mistreat the girl and a man of wealthy position who loves her even though she is dressed in rags, (b) activities such as riding and hunting are commonly found in England, and (c) King Lear elements reflect knowledge of English Shakespeare.

INDEPENDENT PROJECTS AND OTHER ACTIVITIES WITH THE CINDERELLA UNIT

Creative writing: Ask the students to pretend they are storytellers who are telling a variant of Cinderella that reflects their own culture, their school, or even their family. They should use the common Cinderella elements, but make the audience understand and picture the new culture.

Written personal response: Ask the students to choose a Cinderella variant and explain why they liked or disliked the plot and the characters.

Artistic response: Ask the students to choose a folktale variant that is not highly illustrated. Through their own illustrations, show the setting and other cultural references. Encourage them to research the area and the culture so they will be as accurate as possible.

Geography insights: Ask the students to point out on a map of the world the locations of the various Cinderella variants. Ask, "What does the map reveal about the importance of the Cinderella story?"

Creative drama: As a group project, ask the students to select several Cinderella characters from different cultures. Pretend that the characters are having a conversation. What information would the characters exchange? What questions would they ask each other? What advice would they give? Or, pretend that the more cruel members of the story or the supernatural beings could exchange ideas. What advice would they give?

Oral interviewing and collecting tales: Ask the students to interview people in their community, and ask them which Cinderella tale or tales they remember. Summarize the information to discover which Cinderella variant is the most popular in the community.

UNIT TWO: Comparing Variants of the "Little Red Riding Hood" Tale and Responding to the Illustrations

OBJECTIVES

To expand understanding of cultural contexts in folklore variants.

To compare the elements in the "Little Red Riding Hood" tale found in the versions of Perrault and Lang (French), Grimm (German), and Chang (Chinese).

To analyze the appropriateness of the illustrations for different versions of "Little Red Riding Hood."

CORE BOOKS: Two types of core books are used in this unit. The first type encourages students to analyze the variations: "Little Red Riding Hood" (French), in *Perrault's Complete Fairy Tales;* "The True History of Little Golden Hood" (French), in Andrew Lang's *The Red Fairy Book;* Trina Schart Hyman's retelling of Grimm's *Little Red Riding Hood* (German, Caldecott Honor); and "The Chinese Red Riding Hoods," in Sutherland and Livingston's *The Scott, Foresman Anthology of Children's Literature* (1984). The second type of core books encourages students to identify the possible source of each folktale and respond to the different illustrations in each version: Trina Schart Hyman's retelling of Grimm's *Little Red Riding Hood* (German, Caldecott Honor); James Marshall's retelling of *Red Riding Hood*

(German); Perrault's *Little Red Riding Hood,* illustrated by Sarah Moon (French) (the illustrations in this book are more appropriate for older students); and Ed Young's *Lon Po Po: A Red-Riding Hood Story from China* (Caldecott Medal).

PROCEDURES: Introduce this unit by explaining that the students will be reading another folktale with several variants. As the students read or listen to each of the stories in the first series of core books, ask them to compare the different versions of the tales according to specific events in the story and to similarities and differences in plot and characters, language and style, and morals stated in the stories.

Place the major categories for comparison on a chart similar to the one in Figure 10.2. Read each of the stories and ask the students to discuss and then place the appropriate information from each story on the chart. Continue this activity until all the variants have been read and discussed. Figure 10.2 illustrates some of the major similarities and differences found in the versions.

After completing a discussion of each of the variants, challenge the students to identify the country of origin for each of the books listed in the second series of "Little Red Riding Hood" variants. (The only one used in both series is the Hyman version.) To accomplish this task, cover the identity of the teller of the tale. Remind the students that each of the tales from the first series had characteristics that made it different from the rest. Ask, "What are some of the differences?" Encourage students to identify the differences in the endings between the German and French versions, as well as other specific differences. Ask, "Should these differences be reflected in the illustrations? For example, how might the endings of the stories cause the illustrations to differ between the German and French versions? How might we expect a happy or a sad ending to be reflected in the illustrations?"

Next, show each of the illustrated texts. Ask the students to respond to the illustrations in each of the books and to hypothesize about the origins of the story. They should give their reasons for choosing a specific location. For example, the more humorous nature of both Trina Schart Hyman's and James Marshall's illustrations create a lighter mood that seems appropriate for the German tale in which Little Red Riding Hood is rescued. Marshall's cartoon illustrations leave little doubt about the outcome of the story. In contrast, the stark and often frightening black-and-white photographs that accompany the French version create a mood that seems appropriate for the grimmer ending. The illustrations in *Lon Po Po: A Red-Riding Hood Story from China* show three girls and other cultural background information.

INDEPENDENT PROJECTS AND OTHER ACTIVITIES WITH THE LITTLE RED RIDING HOOD UNIT

Creative drama: Divide the class into smaller groups and have each group prepare one of the tales as a creative drama to share with the class.

Written personal responses: Ask the students to choose one of the variants of the folktales and describe their personal responses to the tale. Some students might choose to respond to the roles of the female characters in the different variants.

Responding through music: Encourage the students to identify music that seems appropriate for the different moods created by the text and illustrations in the illustrated versions from Germany, France, and China. Have groups of students prepare dramatic readings in which they show the illustrations and accompany the reading with music.

UNIT THREE: Comparing the Illustrations in Folklore Collections Published During Different Time Periods

OBJECTIVES

To encourage students to understand historical changes in illustrations and texts of folktales.

To respond to different types of illustrations.

To research the history of illustrations, early illustrators of folklore, or media used by artists.

CORE BOOKS: Use illustrated folklore collections published during different time periods. Many of the earlier texts are available in reissues. A series of earlier illustrated texts might

FIGURE 10.2 Comparing Variants of "Little Red Riding Hood."

Variants	French (Perrault)	German (Grimm)	Chinese (Chang)	French (Lang)
	"Little Red Riding Hood"	"Little Red Riding Hood"	"The Chinese Red Riding Hoods"	"The True History of Little Golden Hood"
What is taken to Grandmother?	Cake and pot of butter	Loaf of fresh bread, sweet butter, bottle of wine	(Not told) Mother visits Grandmother	Piece of cake
Where does Grandmother live?	In another village, "yonder by the mill"	In the woods "by the three big oak trees, right next to the blackberry hedge"	At the edge of the woods	At the other side of the wood, in the village, "near the windmill"
Who discovers wolf's deception?	No one	Huntsman	Felice, the oldest daughter	Grandmother, "The brave old dame"
What happens to Little Red Riding Hood?	Wicked wolf "leapt upon Little Red Riding Hood and gobbled her up"	She is eaten and then jumps out of the wolf after huntsman cuts wolf open	The three girls outwit the wolf	Wolf tries to eat her but she is saved by the magical hood that burns the wolf's throat
What happens to the wolf?	He eats Grandmother and Little Red Riding Hood and escapes	He is killed by the huntsman who skins the wolf and nails the pelt to the door	The girls drop him from a basket that is high up in a tree	Grandmother catches him in a sack, "runs and empties it in the well, where the vagabond, still howling, tumbles in and drowned"
Language sample	"Grandmother dear, what big teeth you have!" "The better to eat you with!"	"Please Grandmother, why do you have such big, sharp teeth?" "Those are to eat you up with, my dear!"	"Then Mayling felt the sharp claws of the wolf. Grammie, what are those sharp things?" "Go to sleep dear, they are just Grammie's nails."	"Oh! What a mouthful of great teeth you have, Grandmother!" "That's for crunching little children with!"
Moral stated	"From this story one learns that children, especially young lasses, pretty, courteous and well-bred, do very wrong to listen to strangers."	"I will never wander off the forest path again, as long as I live. I should have kept my promise to my mother."	"Lock the door and don't let anyone inside."	"She promised over and over again that she would never more stop to listen to a wolf, so that at last the mother forgave her."

include Jennifer Mulherine's *Favourite Fairy Tales,* illustrated by English illustrators of the 1700 and 1800s; Edmund Dulac's *The Sleeping Beauty and Other Fairy Tales,* first published in 1910; Edmund Dulac's *Fairy Book: Fairy Tales of the World,* 1916; C. S. Evans' retelling of *Cinderella,* illustrated by Arthur Rackham, published in the early 1900s; Howard Pyle's *The Story of King Arthur and His Knights,* 1902; Henry Gilbert's *Robin Hood & the Men of the Greenwood,* illustrated by Walter Crane, 1912. For a comparative study showing the possible changes in folklore illustrations, choose several books published with illustrations drawn in the 1980s and 1990s.

EXTENDED BOOKS FOR INDEPENDENT READING AND OTHER ASSIGNMENTS: Challenge the students to search home, school, and public libraries for examples of folklore published during different time periods.

PROCEDURES: Introduce the first series of illustrations for *Favourite Fairy Tales.* Point out to the students that the texts are from a late 18th century translation of Charles Perrault's *The Tales of Mother Goose.* The illustrations include the works of the great English illustrators of the 1700s and 1800s. As the students look at these illustrations, they gain an understanding about the published folktales that were available during this time. They also understand the tremendous gains that have been made in illustrated texts as the texts changed from crude woodcuts to full-color publications. Tell the students, "As you listen to the stories and look at these illustrations, try to place yourself into the audience for one of these folktales. Remember that mass printing is a new technique and that before this time many people did not believe that books should entertain their readers. Specifically, point out the engraving and 1742 wood cut in *Tales of Mother Goose,* Gustave Dore's 1862 illustrations for "Little Red Riding Hood," and Walter Crane's 1876 illustrations for "Little Red Riding Hood." Tell the students that Walter Crane illustrated more than 40 books, including numerous folktales. These books are credited with marking the beginning of the modern era in color illustrations. Notice that his illustrations suggest movement, detailed settings, and characterization. Also notice how Crane brings sweetness and innocence into the creation of the young maiden and both vitality and evil intent into his depiction of the wolf. Ask the students to respond to each of these earlier illustrations and to imagine what they would have felt like if they had been part of this early audience.

Introduce the illustrations in the two books illustrated by Edmund Dulac. In *The Sleeping Beauty and Other Fairy Tales,* ask the students to notice the elegant and romantic grandeur of the French court. Ask, "What message about French culture do you think the illustrator was portraying? What message about folktales is suggested in the illustrations?" In *Fairy Book: Fairy Tales of the World* ask students to respond to the strong cultural components in Dulac's illustrations. Ask, "What message is the illustrator offering about the importance of a cultural background for folktales?"

Share Arthur Rackham's black-and-white silhouette illustrations for *Cinderella.* Ask the students to compare the mood created by the silhouettes with that created by Dulac's elegant court. Share and discuss the illustrations for the early versions of the King Arthur and the Robin Hood legends. Compare the illustrations in folklore published in these earlier times with the illustrations in folklore published in the 1980s and 1990s. What are the differences? What changes have taken place over the last 100 years?

INDEPENDENT PROJECTS AND OTHER ACTIVITIES WITH THE FOLKLORE ILLUSTRATIONS UNIT

Creative writing: Encourage the students to pretend they are living in the 1800s, a time of few illustrated books. Those that are available are often illustrated with crude woodcuts. They have just been given one of Walter Crane's beautifully illustrated books. Have them write a story about themselves as they receive the book, experience their feelings, and share the book with others.

Researching illustrators or illustrations: Ask the students to choose one of the early illustrators of folklore and find out as much about the person as possible through library research. Why did the person illustrate folktales? What types of illustration did the person prefer? What books did the artist illustrate? Or, ask the students to choose one of the early media such as woodcuts, silhouettes, or other approaches and find out more about the medium and how it influenced early book illustrations.

Units that Investigate Folktales from One Country or Culture

Students can learn much about a culture through in-depth study of the folktales, fables, legends, and myths associated with that culture. To develop such a study, collect a variety of anthologies and single-volume tales from the culture. Studies can focus on specific Native American peoples or on the connections between African and black American folklore. After students have conducted a study of one culture, they can choose another culture and compare the similarities and differences between them.

The quotes by Campbell, Yep, and Bierhorst discussed earlier indicate how important folklore is in developing understandings of different peoples and their cultures. Therefore, as mentioned earlier, an in-depth study of the folklore of a culture can touch several curriculums, including social studies as well as literature and reading. For this study teachers should encourage students to read, analyze, and discuss numerous folklore collections from a single country or culture.

Research and experience supports the use of a sequence that begins with a study of the ancient literature of a culture and proceeds to the contemporary. For example, Ballinger (1984) and Dorris (1979) recommend a sequence of study of Native American literature that begins with broad oral traditions, narrows to specific tribal experiences as expressed in mythology, continues with biographical and autobiographical study of specific cultural areas, and concludes with a study of contemporary literature.

Norton (1990, 1991) adapts the sequence to children's literature and to black and Hispanic cultural studies as well as Native American studies.

The sequence of study begins with a broad awareness of myths, legends, and folktales from one cultural group (for example, Native American, African, or Aztec or Mayan). It narrows to the myths, legends, and folktales of specific peoples within the group (for example, Native American myths and legends from the Plains Indians, black folklore from the American South, or folklore from Mexico or the Hispanic Southwest that reflects interaction with other cultures). The sequence proceeds to autobiographies, biographies, and other informational literature about an earlier time in history, continues with historical fiction, and concludes with literature written for children by authors whose work represents that cultural group and contemporary time. The portions of these units covering folklore are in this chapter. Units on historical and contemporary works are in Chapters 13 and 14. Teachers can follow the sequence with another culture as students develop and build upon understandings.

UNIT ONE: Developing Appreciation for Native American Culture Through Folklore

OBJECTIVES

To develop appreciation for and understanding of the traditional Native American culture through a study of the ancient folklore.

To read, analyze, and discuss folklore that shows common features found in Native American folklore.

To read, analyze, and discuss folklore from at least one tribal area and to identify the values and beliefs found in that folklore.

To become involved in a storytelling experience around Native American folklore.

To create an aesthetic response to Native American folklore

CORE BOOKS: Books that illustrate the story types found in Native American folklore. Setting the world in order: Virginia Hamilton's *In the Beginning: Creation Stories from Around the World* (Native American selections, Newbery Honor). Family drama tales: Maurice Metayer's *Tales from the Igloo*. Trickster tales: Paul Goble's *Iktomi and the Boulder: A Plains Indian Story*. Crossing threshold tales: Paul Goble's *Buffalo Woman*. Books that reflect the values in folklore from specific tribal associations: Olaf Baker's *Where the Buffaloes Begin* (Caldecott Honor) and John Bierhorst's *The Ring in the Prairie, A Shawnee Legend* (Great Plains); Byrd Baylor's *A God on Every Mountain Top: Stories of Southwest Indian Mountains;* Frank Hamilton Cushing's *Zuni Folk Tales* (Southwestern); Edward Curtis' *The Girl Who Married a Ghost and Other Tales from the North American Indian;* and Christie Harris' *The Trouble With Adventurers* (Northwest Coast). Books for comparison of values: Tomie De Paola's *The Legend of the Bluebonnet* and Paul Goble's *Star Boy.*

EXTENDED BOOKS FOR INDEPENDENT READING AND OTHER

ASSIGNMENTS: The following books can be used for extended reading activities, independent reading, unit activities, and recreational reading.

They also can be used as core books.

Setting the World in Order

EMERSON AND DAVID COATSWORTH's *The Adventures of Nanabush: Ojibway Indian Stories*
BARBARA JUSTER ESBENSEN's *The Star Maiden*
JEAN GUARD MONROE AND RAY A. WILLIAMSON's *They Dance in the Sky: Native American Star Myths*

Family Drama

PAULA UNDERWOOD SPENCER's *Who Speaks for Wolf*

Trickster Tales

BERNICE ANDERSON's *Trickster Tales from Prairie Lodgefires*
PAUL GOBLE's *Iktomi and the Berries*
CHRISTIE HARRIS' *Mouse Woman and the Vanished Princesses*

Crossing Thresholds Tales

ELIZABETH CLEAVER's *The Enchanted Caribou*

Specific Tribal Associations and Tribal Areas

TOMIE DE PAOLA's *The Legend of the Indian Paintbrush* (Great Plains)
PAUL GOBLE's *Beyond the Ridge, Buffalo Woman, The Gift of the Sacred Dog,* and *Iktomi and the Berries* (Great Plains)

JOHN STEPTOE's *The Story of Jumping Mouse* (Great Plains, Caldecott Honor)

BETTY BAKER's *Rat is Dead and Ant Is Sad* (Pueblo, Southwest)

BYRD BAYLOR's *Moonsong* (Southwest)

CHRISTIE HARRIS' *Mouse Woman and the Vanished Princesses* (Northwest Coast)

GAIL ROBINSON's *Raven the Trickster: Legends of the North American Indians* (Northwest Coast)

JAMES WALLAS' *Kwakiutl Legends* (Northwest Coast)

JEAN GUARD MONROE AND RAY A. WILLIAMSON's *They Dance in the Sky: Native American Star Myths* (Collections)

VIRGINIA HAMILTON's *In the Beginning: Creation Stories from Around the World* (Collections)

VIRGINIA HAVILAND's *North American Legends* (Collections)

PROCEDURES: Introduce the unit on Native American traditional culture by showing the students a map of North America and discussing the diverse locations of Native American peoples. For example Bierhorst's *The Mythology of North America* (1985) shows the various mythological regions associated with Native Americans. *Atlas of Ancient America* (Coe, Snow, and Benson, 1986) provides detailed maps and information about the early Native American people and their cultures. Emphasize to the students that the Native American people were in North America long before Christopher Columbus arrived. Discuss photographs and illustrations of various Native American people. Tell the students that one of the best ways to make discoveries about the Native American people, their beliefs, and their values is to read and analyze their folklore.

Tell the students that they will be using Native American folklore to make discoveries about the people. First, they will listen to and read several tales to see if they can discover the four story types that folklorist Bierhorst (1985) claims are found in Native American folklore. Before the students begin this part of the unit, draw a web on the board with *Native American Story Types* written in the center. On the spokes of the web place *Setting the World in Order Tales, Family Drama Tales, Trickster Tales,* and *Crossing Thresholds Tales.*

Next, discuss the meaning of each of these types of tales. For example, tales that emphasize setting the world in order tell how the world was created, how certain animals came to Earth, and how social order was brought to the people. Family drama tales emphasize problems and dangers in the tribal unit or the nuclear family and comforts related to protection and food. Students need to understand that the family unit can be very broad. For example, the nuclear family in Native American folklore might refer to Earth as mother, sky as father, and humanity as children. Trickster tales represent what is considered fair and foul within the culture. Explain to the students that in the tales they will discover actions that are considered foolish and irresponsible, or wise and responsible. Just as in real life, the same trickster character can represent each of these vices and virtues. Finally, crossing thresholds tales show how characters progress through different stages of maturity. They might cross the threshold into adulthood, go into and out of the animal world, go into and out of death, or even progress from a life reflecting nature to one of culture.

Next, choose a tale from each of the four types listed in the core books for this unit. Read the story orally, discuss the type of tale the group thinks it is, and place the story on the web under the identified category. The students might decide that one story reflects more than one category. After this task has been completed with at least one book from each category, the students can read the remainder of the books independently. They can add those tales to the web and discuss why they believe each tale belongs in the chosen category. Figure 10.3 shows a web completed by upper elementary and middle school students.

FIGURE 10.3 Web of Native American story types.

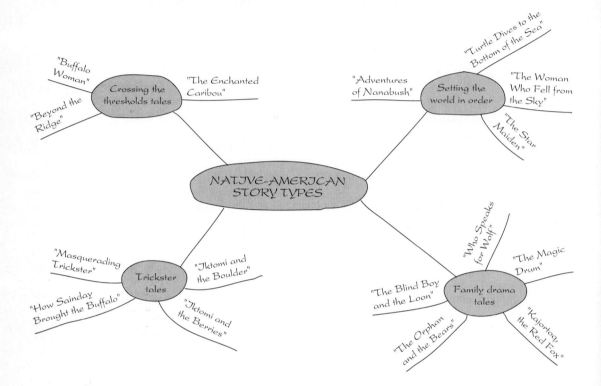

Before leaving this portion of the unit, summarize the students' knowledge to this point about Native American folklore and traditional Native American culture. Ask, "What is important to the people? What actions or beliefs are valued? What actions or beliefs are despised?"

Next, focus on the folklore of one tribal location such as the Great Plains, the Southwest, or the Northwest. (Numerous folklore collections are available from these areas.) Two types of activities are especially beneficial for developing students' cultural understandings related to the folklore: Webbing and charting. The teacher can use webbing to help students identify the culturally related information as well as the stories that reveal that information and charting to help students identify the values and beliefs of the people. These techniques are shown in Figures 10.4 and 10.5.

Draw a web on the board or on a transparency that focuses on the cultural and geographical information that can be gained from the folklore. In addition to providing information on the web, the students should identify evidence from the folklore that supports the cultural information and discuss how the evidence provides that support. Choose several of the tales to be used in a group activity as students read, discuss, and place information on the web. The remainder of the tales can be used for independent reading and filling in the web. After completing the web, summarize what has been learned about the Native American cultural values and beliefs.

Figure 10.4 exemplifies the type of web that has been developed with students in the upper elementary and middle grades. Notice that the webs for Native American, black (Fig-

FIGURE 10.4 Web of cultural values in Native American traditional tales.

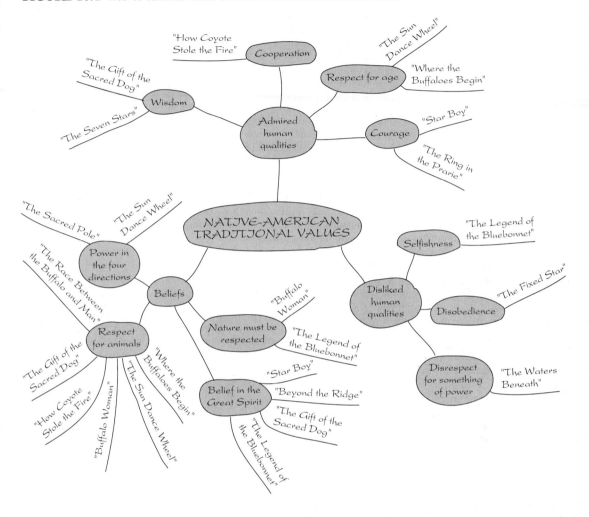

ures 10.6 and 10.8), and Hispanic (Figure 10.9) cultures include the same major listings. These similarities encourage students to make cross-cultural comparisons of important traditional beliefs and of admired and disliked human qualities.

Next, show the students how to verify the beliefs and values by developing a chart in which they identify and compare values found in numerous examples of Native American folklore (Norton, 1985). Print a chart that includes the following questions: What is the problem? What is desired? What are the personal characteristics of the heroes or heroines? What actions or values are rewarded or respected? What actions are punished or not respected? What rewards are given? Provide enough room on the chart for students to compare several examples of folklore. Read one of the tales, and fill in the information as a group activity. Later, students can complete this task as an independent activity. They should discuss their findings and draw some conclusions about the values found in Native American folklore. The chart in Figure 10.5 shows the comparisons between two folklore selections.

FIGURE 10.5 Values found in Native American folklore.

Questions for values identification and discussion	The Legend of the Bluebonnet (Comanche Indian)	Star Boy (Blackfeet Indian)
What reward is desired?	to end the drought and famine	to remove a scar
	to save the land and the people	to marry the chief's daughter
What actions are rewarded or admired?	sacrifice of a loved object to save the tribe	courage
		obedience to the Creator
	obedience to the will of the Great Spirit	
What actions are punished or despised?	selfishness	disobedience
	taking from the earth without giving back	cast out of Sky World and made unhappy; son's face is marked with scar
What rewards are given to the heroes, heroines, or great people?	Bluebonnets—beautiful flowers	scar removed
	a sign of forgiveness	married chief's daughter
	rain	happiness
	honored name change	life in Sky World after death
What are the personal characteristics of the heroes, heroines, or great people?	unselfishly loved her people	poor
	willing to give her most prized possession	courageous
		respect for wisdom of animals
		wisdom
		purity
		honoring the Creator

INDEPENDENT PROJECTS AND OTHER ACTIVITIES WITH THE NATIVE AMERICAN FOLKLORE UNIT

Oral story telling festival: Divide the students into groups and have each group select stories with similar themes and values and develop them as part of a Native American Storytelling Festival. Prepare the stories to share with the class.

Creative writing: Ask the students to choose a trickster or a hero character and create a story about the trickster's exploits.

Creative writing: Ask the students to choose a plant, a tree, an animal, or a rock formation that is native to their own environment. Have them write a story such as *The Legend of the Bluebonnet* or *The Legend of the Indian Paintbrush* to explain how and why it occurred. The stories should sound like Native American folklore and the students should illustrate them from a Native American perspective.

Creative writing: Ask the students to choose a current problem in the environment and write a story that speaks to the problem from a traditional Native American perspective. Remind them to think about the problems such as the one developed in *Who Speaks for Wolf.*

Aesthetic response through art: Ask the students to choose one of the non-illustrated stories and to illustrate it in a way that reflects their own emotional responses to the story and to the characters.

UNIT TWO: Developing Understanding and Appreciation of the Black Culture Through Folklore

OBJECTIVES

To develop understanding and appreciation of the traditional black culture through a study of folklore.

To read, analyze, and discuss folklore that shows common features found in African folklore and to analyze values and beliefs.

To read, analyze, and discuss Southern black folklore to identify the values and beliefs found in that folklore.

To become involved in a storytelling experience around black folklore.

To take part in a creative writing experience stimulated by black folklore.

To create an aesthetic response to black folklore.

CORE BOOKS: Books that illustrate the common types of stories in African folklore such as how the natural and tribal worlds began: "Wulbari the Creator" and "Nyambi the Creator" in Virginia Hamilton's *In the Beginning: Creation Stories from Around the World* (Newbery Honor). How animals and people got certain physical and spiritual traits: "How Animals Got Their Tails" and "Why Bush Cow and Elephant are Bad Friends" in Ashley Bryan's *Beat the Story-Drum, Pum-Pum* and "A Lesson for the Bat" in Barbara Walker's *The Dancing Palm Tree and Other Nigerian Folktales*. What values, beliefs, and cultural patterns are important, such as friendship: "Hen and Frog" in *Beat the Story-Drum, Pum-Pum*. Respect for oral storytelling: Gail Haley's *A Story, a Story*. Legitimate use of wit and trickery to dress the balance: Verna Aardema's *Who's in Rabbit's House*. Strict code concerning ownership and borrowing: Ashley Bryan's *The Cat's Purr*. Societal problems and solutions, such as tribal obligations: Verna Aardema's *Bringing the Rain to Kapiti Plain*. Stability in marriage: "The Husband Who Counted the Spoonfuls" in Ashley Bryan's *Beat the Story-Drum, Pum-Pum*. Respect for individuality: Jan Carew's *The Third Gift*. Respect for social and tribal customs: Ann Grifalconi's *The Village of Round and Square Houses* (Caldecott Honor). Books for comparing values identified in African folktales: Gail Haley's *A Story, a Story* and Jan Carew's *Children of the Sun* and *The Third Gift*. Books that include black American folklore such as Virginia Hamilton's *The People Could Fly: American Black Folktales*; Van Dyke Parks' adaptation of Joel Chandler Harris' *Jump! The Adventures of Brer Rabbit*; and Steve Sanfield's *The Adventures of High John the Conqueror*.

EXTENDED BOOKS FOR INDEPENDENT READING AND OTHER ASSIGNMENTS: These books can be used for extended reading activities, independent reading, unit activities, and recreational reading. They also can be used as core books.

Books that Illustrate African Folklore

VERNA AARDEMA's *What's So Funny, Ketu?*

ASHLEY BRYAN's *Lion and the Ostrich Chicks, and Other African Folk Tales*

HAROLD COURLANDER's *The Crest and the Hide: And Other African Stories of Heroes, Chiefs, Bards, Hunters, Sorcerers, and Common People*

ROSA GUY's *Mother Crocodile*

BARBARA KNUTSON's *How the Guinea Fowl Got Her Spots* and *Why the Crab Has No Head*

GERALD MCDERMOTT's *Anansi the Spider:* A Tale from the Ashanti

Books that Include Black American Folklore

VAN DYKE PARKS' adaptation of Joel Chandler Harris' *Jump Again! More Adventures of Brer Rabbit*

Julius Lester's *The Knee-High Man and Other Tales*
Julius Lester's adaptation of Joel Chandler Harris' *The Tales of Uncle Remus* and *Further Tales of Uncle Remus*
Patricia McKissack's *Flossie & the Fox*

PROCEDURES: Introduce the unit by showing and discussing a map of Africa. Point out the regions in Western Africa where many of the stories originated. For example, many of the stories are credited to the Yorubas and the Ashantis. Musgrove's (1976) *Ashanti to Zulu, African Traditions* includes a map locating specific peoples of Africa. Remind the students that the African people who were taken as slaves to the United States brought their oral folklore with them. On a globe show the route from Africa to the United States. Explain to the students that because of this movement of people the study of black folklore will begin by reading, discussing, and analyzing folklore from Africa and continue with the black folklore of the American South. Through this study the students will discover how the newer tales from the South combine a past culture, a new environment, and new experiences. Many of the same traditional values are found in folklore from both locations.

Oral language and storytelling are extremely important in traditional African culture. An enjoyable beginning to the study of African folklore might be to have students try to duplicate African storytelling styles. For example, after listening to the tape *The Dancing Granny and Other African Stories* (Bryan, 1985), ask the students to describe its vivid style and to visualize a storytelling experience. They will probably decide that rhythm is important and that the storytellers mimic the sounds of animals, change their voices to characterize both animal and human characters, develop dialogue, and encourage their listeners to interact with the story. Students also should be aware that African storytellers frequently add musical accompaniment with drums and other rhythm or string instruments such as thumb pianos. After listening to and discussing the oral storytelling style, ask students to choose several stories such as those found in Bryan's *Beat the Story-Drum, Pum-Pum* and to prepare them to reflect an appropriate storytelling style. They may use rhythm and string instruments.

Next, read and discuss an example of each of the types of African folklore listed in the core books. Ask the students to summarize what they have discovered about the culture after reading each of these tales. "What is important to the people? What qualities do they dislike? What qualities do they admire? What are the beliefs of the people?" Develop a web similar to the web shown for Native American traditional tales. Ask the students to fill in and discuss the appropriate information from the stories shared with the class and from additional tales they have read independently. Figure 10.6 illustrates a completed web. After completing the web, ask the students to summarize what they have learned about cultural values from the African traditional tales.

Next, complete a chart identifying and comparing values in African folklore. Complete one or two of these analyses together. Then ask the students to analyze additional folklore independently. After several tales are completed, ask the students to identify the values found in the chart. Which values are consistently developed in the African folktales? Figure 10.7 shows the values found in three African folktales.

Select several of the black American folktales and legends to be read and discussed as a group. Ask the students to listen carefully for any similarities and differences between African and black American folklore. Virginia Hamilton's *The People Could Fly: American Black Folktales* is an excellent introduction to this part of the unit because Hamilton divides the stories into specific types. The book also has a section on slave tales of freedom and a discussion about why this type of folktale was so important to the people. In *The Adventures of High John the Conqueror*, Steve Sanfield also interprets the reasons for some of the actions of this legendary hero. Share this information with the students and encourage them to offer personal responses to the stories.

FIGURE 10.6 Web of cultural values in African traditional tales.

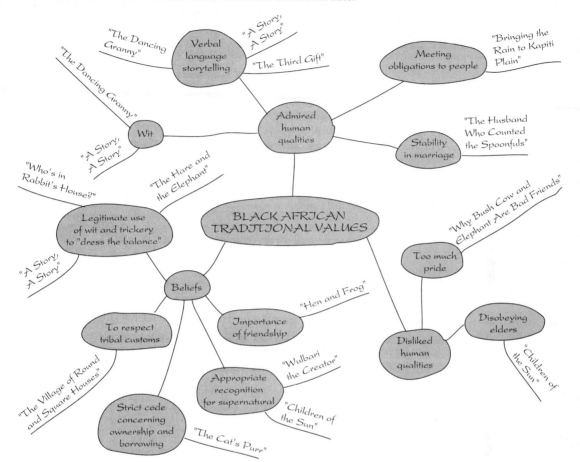

A web similar to the African cultural web can be developed using black American folklore. After the web is completed, ask the students to compare the information on the African and the black American cultural webs. What are the similarities? What are the differences? What might account for those similarities and differences? Figure 10.8 shows a black American cultural web.

Finally, have the students complete a chart showing the values in black American tales. Ask them to compare this chart with the chart of African values.

INDEPENDENT PROJECTS AND OTHER ACTIVITIES WITH THE BLACK FOLKLORE UNIT

Creative writing: Many African folktales are "why," or "pourquoi," stories that explain why animals have certain characteristics. Ask the students to choose an animal and develop their own story about why the animal has certain physical or behavioral characteristics. Encourage the students to use an African folktale style and illustrations for their stories.

FIGURE 10.7 Values found in African folklore.

Questions for values identification and discussion	A Story, a Story	The Third Gift	Children of the Sun
What reward is desired?	Stories from powerful sky god	Gift of wonders for people threatened with extinction	Peace Harmony
What actions are rewarded or admired?	Outwitting the leopard, the hornet, and the fairy	Climbing the highest mountain Using gifts wisely	Being good Searching for peace and harmony
What actions are punished or despised?			Disobeys father Haughtiness Rebelliousness Destroyed by great spirit
What rewards are given to the heroes, heroines, or great people?	Oral stories to delight the people	Gift of work Gift of beauty Gift of imagination Leader of people	Patience Life
What are the personal characteristics of the heroes, heroines, or great people?	Small old man Intelligence Verbal ability	Poets Bards Creators Leaders	Goodness Patience Desire to serve humanity

Creative writing: Other African and black American folktales are trickster tales in which the smaller animal must use its wits to outthink the larger or more powerful animal. Ask the students to identify a problem and create a trickster story in which a smaller animal uses its wits to trick the larger animal.

Creative drama: Verna Aardema's *Who's in Rabbit's House?* is introduced as a play. The illustrations show the Masai villagers waiting for the play to begin and the actors preparing the set, rehearsing their lines, and putting on their masks. Encourage the students to develop their own play complete with props and masks.

Personal response: Many black American folktales about slavery, such as *The People Could Fly,* create an emotional response in readers. Ask the students to write about their own feelings as they read this folktale. How did they feel about the characters, their problems, and their solutions? Some students might prefer responding through painting or drawing. How can they reveal their emotions through art? What colors would they use? How would they depict their emotions?

Library research: Music is an important part of both the African and black American culture. Ask students to trace the history and uses of music in these cultures.

Library research: Ask the students to choose one of the African groups depicted in the traditional oral stories. Have them research the group and describe any similarities and differences between the people depicted in the folklore and the people living in the 20th century.

Analyzing illustrations in folklore: Many versions of folklore have detailed illustrations showing the environment and the culture. Ask students to evaluate the illustrations for appropriate environmental and cultural information.

FIGURE 10.8 Web of black American traditional values.

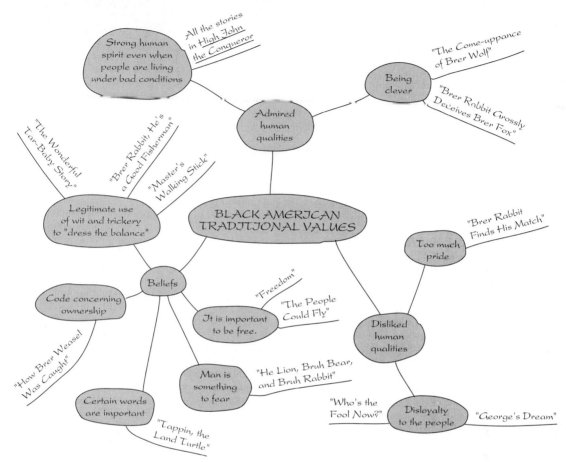

UNIT THREE: Developing Understanding and Appreciation of the Hispanic American Culture

OBJECTIVES

To develop understanding and appreciation of the traditional Hispanic culture through a study of folklore.

To read, analyze, and discuss ancient Aztec and Mayan folklore and to identify the values depicted in the folklore.

To understand the influence of cultural infusion on the people and their folklore and to read, analyze, and discuss folklore that reflects interaction with other cultures.

To analyze the cultural information in illustrations.

To respond to the vivid illustrations in highly illustrated versions of folklore.

CORE BOOKS: Books that provide examples of Aztec and Mayan folklore: John Bierhorst's *The Hungry Woman: Myths and Legends of the Aztecs* and *The Monkey's Haircut and Other*

Stories Told by the Maya. Comparisons between plots and illustrations in folklore and in Deborah Nourse Lattimore's *The Flame of Peace: A Tale of the Aztecs.* Poetry that reflects ancient culture: Toni de Gerez's adaptation of the ancient Toltec poem, *My Song Is a Piece of Jade.* Folklore that reflects interactions with other cultures: Verna Aardema's *The Riddle of the Drum: A Tale from Tizapan, Mexico;* John Bierhorst's *Doctor Coyote: A Native American Aesop's Fables;* Harriet Rohmer, Octavio Chow, and Morris Vidaure's *The Invisible Hunters;* and Jose Griego y Maestas and Rudolfo A. Anaya's *Cuentos: Tales from the Hispanic Southwest.* Folktales for comparison of values: Selections from M. A. Jagendorf and R. S. Boggs' *The King of the Mountains: A Treasury of Latin American Folk Stories.* Comparisons with African folklore: Verna Aardema's *What's So Funny, Ketu?*

EXTENDED BOOKS FOR INDEPENDENT READING AND OTHER

ASSIGNMENTS: The following books can be used for extended reading activities, independent reading, unit activities, and recreational reading. They also can be used as core books.

Aztec and Mayan Folklore

VIVIEN BLACKMORE's *Why Corn Is Golden: Stories About Plants*

FRANCISCO HINOJOSA's *The Old Lady Who Ate People*

MARCOS KURTYCZ AND ANA GARCIA KOBEH's *Tigers and Opossums: Animal Legends*

HARRIET ROHMER AND DORNMINSTER WILSON's *Mother Scorpion Country*

Interactions with Other Cultures

TOMIE DE PAOLA's *The Lady of Guadalupe*

JOHN BIERHORST's translation of *Spirit Child: A Story of the Nativity.*

PROCEDURES: Introduce the Hispanic Literature Unit by reading a quote by Griego y Maestas and Anaya (1980) that emphasizes the complexity of Hispanic literature and culture. The authors reinforce the importance of the traditional literature in understanding the culture and show the complexity of such a study: The tales "are a great part of the soul of our culture, and they reflect the values of our forefathers.... The stories reflect a history of thirteen centuries of infusing and blending from the Moors and Jews in Spain, to the Orientals in the Philippines, Africans in the Caribbean, and the Indians in America—be they Aztec, Apache or Pueblo" (p. 4). Discuss this quote and its implications with the students. Ask, "Would you expect to find influences of other cultures in the folklore? Why or why not?" Tell the students that they will began their study with the ancient folklore of the Aztec and the Mayan people and then proceed to the folklore that reflects the interaction with other cultures. Through this study they will be able to discover how folklore reflects early beliefs and values and how it infuses other cultures and values.

Show the students the locations of the Aztec and Mayan peoples on a map of Mexico and Central America. *Atlas of Ancient America* (Coe, Snow, & Benson, 1986) and *The Maya*, (Coe, 1984), include useful maps and information about these cultures. For additional background information, share and discuss R. J. Unstead's *An Aztec Town* (1980) and Deborah Nourse Lattimore's *The Flame of Peace: A Tale of the Aztecs.*

Read and discuss several selections of Aztec folklore such as those found in Bierhorst's *The Hungry Woman: Myths and Legends of the Aztecs.* After reading and discussing these tales, ask students to look again at the illustrations and text in *The Flame of Peace.* Ask, "What, if any, are the similarities between the folklore and the plot, characters, and illustrations in *The Flame of Peace: A Tale of the Aztecs?*"

Next, share and discuss several sources of Mayan folklore. Explain to the students that Bierhorst, in *The Monkey's Haircut and Other Stories Told by the Maya,* identifies several characteristics of Mayan folklore that emphasize cultural characteristics and values. As the students listen to these stories ask them to identify those characteristics and values. Bierhorst identifies the following: (a) cleverness, as shown by stories that include riddles, puns, double meanings, and tricksters; (b) culture, such as paying a bride service and being godparents; and (c) corn and farming practices. Students also should listen for and identify additional traditional values in the stories. Either share or have students read independently *The Old Lady Who Ate People, Mother Scorpion Country, Tigers and Opossums: Animal Legends,* and *Why Corn is Golden: Stories About Plants.* Have the students develop and discuss webs of the Aztec and Mayan folklore. Figure 10.9 illustrates a web developed around the cultural values discovered in Mayan folklore.

Before continuing to the study of the folklore that reflects interaction with other cultures, share and discuss Toni de Gerez's adaptation of the ancient Toltec poem, *My Song Is a Piece of Jade.* Ask the students to identify the values, characters, and mythological references in the folklore. Ask

FIGURE 10.9 Web of cultural values in Mayan traditional tales.

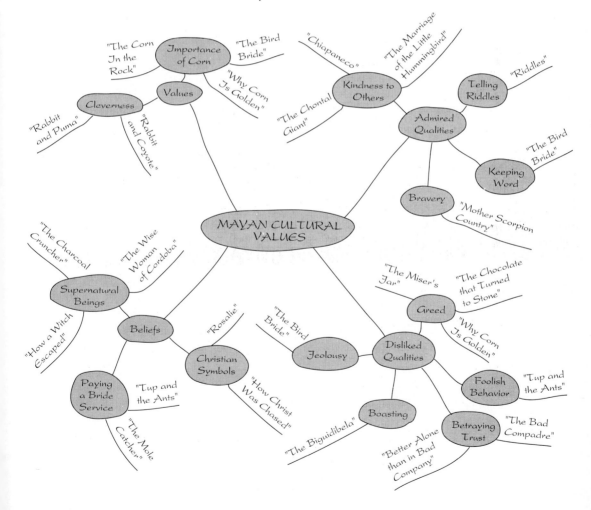

them to identify any additional information that the poetry reveals about the culture. Also, ask them to consider how and why a study of the traditional folklore foundations of the people makes this poem more interesting and understandable. If the students have unanswered questions about the poem, encourage them to research additional cultural references.

Next, introduce the series of folklore that reflects interactions with other cultures and even the clash of cultural values. Ask the students to consider at what point in history they would expect the greatest changes. Encourage the students to identify the arrival of Cortes and the Spanish as one of the greatest influences on the cultures and folklore. Ask them to think about how this occurrence changed the lives of the people and might have influenced their folktales, fables, myths, and legends.

Teachers should choose tales appropriate to the ages of their students. Some tales such as *The Riddle of the Drum: A Tale from Tizapan, Mexico* and *Doctor Coyote: A Native American Aesop's Fables* (retold from an Aztec manuscript), are easily analyzed according to the influence of physical setting and cultural architecture. Comparisons also can be made showing the influence of Spanish folktales and Aesop's fables.

Students can share and discuss what happens when cultures clash in *The Invisible Hunters,* and the interactions of the people and Christianity are found in *The Lady of Guadalupe* and *Spirit Child: A Story of the Nativity.* These books also develop strong cultural patterns through their illustrations.

Folktales in *Cuentos: Tales from the Hispanic Southwest* are especially good for identifying cultural values and the influence of other cultures. For example, share "The Man Who Knew the Language of the Animals," and ask students to identify the plot of the story. For this portion of the activity, they can draw plot structures such as those developed in Chapter 5. Next, ask the students to identify the values and beliefs stressed in the folktale and then compare it with a similar African folktale, *What's so Funny, Ketu.* Ask the students to draw a plot structure of the African tale and identify the emphasized values and beliefs. Next, ask them to identify the similarities and differences between the two tales. Ask, "What do you think the variants in this folktale reveal about the nature of the oral tradition? What do the similarities tell us about human values? How might the differences reflect cultural differences between the Hispanic and African peoples?" Develop a chart comparing the values in several selections of Hispanic folklore. The chart in Figure 10.10 shows the comparisons of two tales.

INDEPENDENT PROJECTS AND OTHER ACTIVITIES WITH THE HISPANIC FOLKLORE UNIT

Library research: Ask the students to research the early Aztec or Mayan cultures or one of the cultures that influenced the Hispanic culture. If they choose one of the cultures that influenced the Hispanic people, they should emphasize the time that the culture had the greatest influence and detail the influence.

Artistic investigations: The illustrations in many of the folklore texts reflect strong Hispanic influences. Some of the texts such as *The Old Lady Who Ate People,* illustrated by Leonel Maciel, and *Why Corn Is Golden: Stories about Plants,* illustrated by Sasana Martinez-Ostos, are illustrated by well-known Mexican artists. Investigate other works of these artists.

Creative writing: Ask the students to choose one of the Aesop's fables or another European folktale. Ask them to pretend that they heard this story from one of the early Spaniards who came to their country. Have them adapt the story to reflect their setting, culture, and beliefs.

Create a multicultural museum: Ask the students to create a museum that shows important information and artifacts from the traditional Native American, black, and Hispanic

FIGURE 10.10 Values found in Hispanic folklore.

Questions for values identification and discussion	"The Sacred Drum of Tepozteco" (Mexico)	"Pancho Villa and the Devil" (Mexico)
What reward is desired?	Protection of the people Wisdom Destiny to be a god	To fool the devil To show the devil Pancho Villa is smarter than the devil
What actions are rewarded or admired?	Wise counseling and under-standing Virtues	Fearlessness Extreme observation Going to church Wearing a cross
What actions are punished or despised?	Outward show does not demand respect Gathering an army and attacking the revered king and his people	Selling one's soul
What rewards are given to the he-roes, heroines, or great people?	Worshiped by the people People made him king and wor-shiped him as a god Love and respect	Going to heaven after death
What are the personal characteris-tics of the heroes, heroines, or great people?	Rich in wisdom and understanding Great strength Great speed Great hunter Successful counsel Rich in virtues	Stronger than others Knows everything Understands all things about men and animals Fearless

cultures that they have been studying. Divide the class into groups, with each group becoming curators of a specific section. Invite parents and friends to visit the museum with the students as guides.

Develop a multicultural festival: Ask the students to develop an introduction to their museum, including such activities as storytelling, musical features, slide shows, and guest experts.

REFERENCES

BALLINGER, F. (1984). A matter of emphasis: Teach-ing the 'literature' in Native American literature courses. *American Indian Culture and Research Journal, 8,* 1–12.

BARNES, B. (1991, January). Using children's liter-ature in the early anthropology curriculum. *Social Education,* pp. 17–18.

BARR, R. & SADOW, M. (1985). *Reading diagnosis for teachers.* New York: Longman.

BASCOM, W. (1965). The forms of folklore: Prose narratives. *Journal of American Folklore, 78,* 3–20.

BIERHORST, J. (1985). *The mythology of North Amer-ica.* New York: Morrow.

———. (1976). *The red swan: Myths and tales of the American Indians.* New York: Farrar, Straus & Giroux.

BRYAN, A. (1985). *The dancing granny and other Af-rican stories.* New York: Caedmon.

CAMPBELL, J. (1988). *The power of myth.* New York: Doubleday.

COE, M. (1984). *The Maya* (3rd ed.). New York: Thames and Hudson.

_____, SNOW, D. & BENSON, E. (1986). *Atlas of ancient America.* New York: Facts on File.

DIAKIW, J. (1990). Children's literature and global education: Understanding the developing world. *The Reading Teacher, 43,* pp. 296–300.

DORRIS, M. (1979). Native American literature in an ethnohistorical context. *College English, 41,* pp. 147–162.

FAVAT, F. A. (1977). *Child and tale: The origins of interest.* Urbana, IL: National Council of Teachers of English.

Funk & Wagnalls Standard Dictionary of Folklore, Mythology and Legend. (1972). New York: Harper & Row.

GRIEGO Y MAESTRAS, J. & ANAYA, R. A. (1980). *Cuentos: Tales from the Hispanic Southwest.* Santa Fe: Museum of New Mexico Press.

HEARNE, B. (1989). *Beauty and the beast: Visions and revisions of an old tale.* Chicago: University of Chicago Press.

MOSS, J. F. (1984). *Focus units in literature: A handbook for elementary school teachers.* Urbana, IL: National Council of Teachers of English.

MUSGROVE, MARGARET. (1976). *Ashanti to Zulu: African traditions.* Illustrated by Leo and Diane Dillon. New York: Dial.

NORTON, DONNA. (1985). *Language arts activities for children* (2nd ed.). Columbus, OH: Merrill.

_____. (1990). Teaching multicultural literature in the reading curriculum. *The Reading Teacher, 44.*

_____. (1991). Through the eyes of a child: An introduction to children's literature. Columbus, OH: Merrill.

PEARSON, P. D. (1984). "Asking questions about stories." In A. J. Harris & E. R. Sipay (Eds.), *Readings on reading instruction.* (pp. 274–283). New York: Longman.

SMITH, C. (1991). The role of different literary genres. *The Reading Teacher, 44,* 440–441.

SUTHERLAND, Z. & LIVINGSTON, M. C. (1984). *The Scott, Foresman anthology of children's literature.* Glenview, IL: Scott, Foresman.

UNSTEAD, R. J. (1980). *An Aztec town.* London: Hutchinson.

YEP, L. (1989). *The rainbow people.* New York: Harper & Row.

CHILDREN'S LITERATURE REFERENCES*

AARDEMA, VERNA. *Bringing the Rain to Kapiti Plain.* Illustrated by Beatriz Vidal. New York: Dial, 1981 (I: 5–8).

_____. *The Riddle of the Drum: A Tale from Tizipan, Mexico.* Illustrated by Tony Chen. New York: Four Winds, 1979 (I: 6–10).

_____. *What's So Funny, Ketu?* Illustrated by Marc Brown. New York: Dial, 1982 (I: all).

_____. *Who's in Rabbit's House.* Illustrated by Leo and Diane Dillon. New York: Dial, 1977 (I: 7+).

AESOP. *Aesop's Fables.* Illustrated by Heidi Holder. New York: Viking, 1981 (I: 9–12).

ANDERSON, BERNICE. *Trickster Tales from Prairie Lodgefires.* Illustrated by Frank Gee. Nashville: Abingdon, 1979 (I: all).

ASBJORNSEN, PETER CHRISTEN & JORGEN MOE. *Norwegian Folk Tales.* Illustrated by Erik Werenskiold and Theodor Kittelsen. New York: Viking, 1960 (I: all).

BAKER, BETTY. *Rat is Dead and Ant is Sad.* Illustrated by Mamoru Funai. New York: Harper & Row, 1981 (I: 6–8).

BAKER, OLAF. *Where the Buffaloes Begin.* Illustrated by Stephen Gammell. New York: Warne, 1981 (I: all).

BAWDEN, NINA. *William Tell.* Illustrated by Pascale Allamand. New York: Lothrop, Lee & Shepard, 1981 (I: 6–12).

BAYLOR, BYRD. *A God on Every Mountain Top: Stories of Southwest Indian Mountains.* Illustrated by Carol Brown. New York: Scribner's, 1981 (I: 6–10).

_____. *Moonsong.* Illustrated by Ronald Himler. New York: Scribner's, 1982 (I: all).

BIERHORST, JOHN. *Doctor Coyote: A Native American Aesop's Fables.* Illustrated by Wendy Watson. New York: Macmillan, 1987 (I: all).

_____. *The Ring in the Prairie, A Shawnee Legend.* Illustrated by Leo and Diane Dillon. New York: Dial, 1970 (I: all).

_____. *Spirit Child: A Story of the Nativity.* Illustrated by Barbara Cooney. New York: Morrow, 1984 (I: 8–12).

_____. *The Hungry Woman: Myths and Legends of the Aztecs.* New York: Morrow, 1984 (I: 12+).

_____. *The Monkey's Haircut and Other Stories Told by the Maya.* Illustrated by Robert Andrew Parker. New York: Morrow, 1986 (I: 8+).

BLACKMORE, VIVIEN. *Why Corn Is Golden: Stories About Plants.* Illustrated by Susana Martinez-Ostos. Boston: Little, Brown, 1984 (I: all).

BROWN, MARCIA. *Backbone of the King: Story of Pakaa and His Son Ku.* University of Hawaii Press, 1966 (I: all).

BRYAN, ASHLEY. *Beat the Story-Drum, Pum-Pum.* New York: Atheneum, 1980 (I: 6+).

_____. *The Cat's Purr.* New York: Atheneum, 1985 (I: 6+).

_____. *Lion and the Ostrich Chicks, and Other African Folktales.* New York: Atheneum, 1986 (I: 6+).

*I = Interest by age range

BULFINCH, THOMAS. *Myths of Greece & Rome*. New York: Penguin, 1981 (paperback) (I: 10+).

CAREW, JAN. *Children of the Sun*. Illustrated by Leo and Diane Dillon. Boston: Little, Brown, 1980 (I: 8+).

____. *The Third Gift*. Illustrated by Leo and Diane Dillon. Boston: Little, Brown, 1974 (I: 7+).

CARTER, ANGELA, translated by. *Sleeping Beauty & Other Favourite Fairy Tales*. Illustrated by Michael Foreman. London: Victor Gollanca, 1982 (I: 8+).

CLARK, ANN NOLAN. *In the Land of Small Dragon*. Illustrated by Tony Chen. New York: Viking, 1979. (I: 7–12).

CLEAVER, ELIZABETH. *The Enchanted Caribou*. New York: Atheneum, 1985 (I: 6–10).

CLIMO, SHIRLEY. *The Egyptian Cinderella*. Illustrated by Ruth Heller. New York: Crowell, 1989 (I: 7–9)

COATSWORTH, EMERSON, & DAVID COATSWORTH. *The Adventures of Nanabush: Ojibway Indian Stories*. Illustrated by Francis Kagige. New York: Atheneum, 1980 (I: 8+).

COLUM, PADRAIC. *The Golden Fleece and the Heroes Who Lived Before Achilles*. Illustrated by Willy Pogany. New York: Macmillan, 1921, 1949, 1962 (I: 9+).

COLUM, PADRAIC. *The Children of Odin*. Illustrated by Willy Pogany. New York: Macmillan, 1920, 1948 (I: 9+).

COURLANDER, HAROLD. *The Crest and the Hide: And Other African Stories of Heroes, Chiefs, Bards, Hunters, Sorcerers, and Common People*. Illustrated by Monica Vachula. New York: Coward, McCann, 1982 (I: 8+).

CROSSLEY-HOLLAND, KEVIN. *British Folk Tales*. New York: Watts, 1988 (I: 8+).

CURTIS, EDWARD. *The Girl Who Married a Ghost and Other Tales from the North American Indian*, edited by John Bierhorst. New York: Four Winds, 1978 (I: 9+).

CUSHING, FRANK HAMILTON. *Zuni Folk Tales*. University of Arizona Press, 1901, 1986, Adult source.

D'AULAIRE, INGRI & EDGAR PARIN D'AULAIRE. *Norse Gods and Giants*. New York: Doubleday, 1967 (I: 8–12).

DE GEREZ, TONI. *My Song Is a Piece of Jade*. Illustrated by William Stark. Boston: Little, Brown, 1981 (I: all).

DEPAOLA, TOMIE. *The Lady of Guadalupe*. New York: Holiday, 1980 (I: 8+).

____. *The Legend of the Bluebonnet*. New York: Putnam, 1983 (I: all).

____. *Legend of the Indian Paint Brush*. New York: Putnam, 1988 (I: all).

DULAC, EDMUND. *The Sleeping Beauty and Other Fairy Tales*. London: Hodder and Stoughton, 1910, 1981 (I: 8–12).

____. *Fairy Book: Fairy Tales of the World*. Hertfordshire, England: Omega, 1916, 1984 (I: 8–12).

ESBENSEN, BARBARA JUSTER. *The Star Maiden*. Illustrated by Helen K. Davie. Boston: Little, Brown, 1988 (I: all).

EVANS, C. S., retold by. *The Sleeping Beauty*. Illustrated by Arthur Rackham. London: Chancellor, 1920, 1987 (I: 8–12).

____. *Cinderella*. Illustrated by Arthur Rackham. New York: Penguin, 1919, 1978 (I: 8–12).

GAG, WANDA, retold by. *Tales from Grimm*. New York: Coward, 1936, 1964 (I: 3–8).

GILBERT, HENRY. *Robin Hood & the Men of the Greenwood*. Illustrated by Walter Crane. London: Bracken, 1912, 1985 (I: 10+).

GOBLE, PAUL. *Beyond the Ridge*. New York: Bradbury, 1989 (I: all).

____. *Buffalo Woman*. New York: Bradbury, 1984 (I: all).

____. *The Gift of the Sacred Dog*. New York: Bradbury, 1980 (I: all).

____. *Iktomi and the Berries*. New York: Watts, 1989 (I: 4–10).

____. *Iktomi and the Boulder: A Plains Indian Story*. New York: Watts, 1988 (I: 4–10).

____. *Star Boy*. New York: Bradbury, 1983 (I: all).

GRIEGO Y MAESTAS, JOSE & RUDOLFO A. ANAYA. *Cuentos: Tales from the Hispanic Southwest*. Santa Fe: Museum of New Mexico Press, 1980 (I: all).

GRIFALCONI, ANN. *The Village of Round and Square Houses*. Boston: Little, Brown, 1986 (I: 4–9).

GRIMM, BROTHERS. *Household Tales*. Illustrated by Mervyn Peake. New York: Schocken, 1973 (I: all).

____. *Little Red Riding Hood*, retold and illustrated by Trina Schart Hyman. New York: Holiday, 1983 (I: 6–9).

____. *Snow White and the Seven Dwarfs*, translated by Randall Jarrell. Illustrated by Nancy Ekholm Burket. New York: Farrar, Straus & Giroux, 1972 (I: 7–12).

GUY, ROSA. *Mother Crocodile*. Illustrated by John Steptoe. New York: Delacorte, 1981 (I: 5–9).

HALEY, GAIL. *A Story, a Story*. New York: Atheneum, 1970 (I: 6–10).

HAMILTON, VIRGINIA. *In the Beginning: Creation Stories from Around the World*. Illustrated by Barry Moser. Orlando: Harcourt Brace Jovanovich, 1980 (I: all).

____. *The People Could Fly: American Black Folktales*. Illustrated by Leo and Diane Dillon. New York: Knopf, 1985 (I: 9+).

HARRIS, CHRISTIE. *Mouse Woman and the Vanished Princesses*. Illustrated by Douglas Tait. New York: Atheneum, 1976 (I: 10+).

_____. *The Trouble with Adventurers*. Illustrated by Douglas Tait. New York: Atheneum, 1982 (I: 10 +).

HARRIS, JOEL CHANDLER. *Further Tales of Uncle Remus*, retold by Julius Lester. Illustrated by Jerry Pinkney. New York: Dial, 1990 (I: all).

_____. *Jump! The Adventures of Brer Rabbit*, adapted by Van Dyke Parks. Illustrated by Barry Moser. Orlando: Harcourt Brace Jovanovich, 1986 (I: all).

_____. *Jump Again! More Adventures of Brer Rabbit*, adapted by Van Dyke Parks. Illustrated by Barry Moser. Orlando: Harcourt Brace Jovanovich, 1987 (I: all).

_____. *The Tales of Uncle Remus*, retold by Julius Lester. Illustrated by Jerry Pinkney. New York: Dial, 1987 (I: all).

HAVILAND, VIRGINIA. *North American Legends*. Illustrated by Ann Stugnell. New York: Philomel, 1979 (I: all).

HE, LIYI. *The Spring of Butterflies and Other Chinese Folktales*. Illustrated by Pan Aiqing and Li Zhao. New York: Lothrop, Lee & Shepard, 1985 (I: all).

HINOJOSA, FRANCISCO. *The Old Lady Who Ate People*. Illustrated by Leonel Maciel. Boston: Little, Brown, 1984 (I: all).

HOOKS, WILLIAM H. *Moss Gown*. Illustrated by Donald Carrick. New York: Clarion, 1987 (I: 8 +).

HUCK, CHARLOTTE, retold by. *Princess Furball*. Illustrated by Anita Lobel. New York: Greenwillow, 1989 (I: 6 – 10).

JAGENDORF, M. A., & R. S. BOGGS. *The King of the Mountains: A Treasury of Latin American Folk Stories*. New York: Vanguard, 1960 (I: 9 +).

KISMARIC, CAROLE, retold by. *The Rumor of Pavel and Paali: A Ukranian Folktale*. Illustrated by Charles Mikolaycak. New York: Harper & Row, 1988 (I: 6 – 9).

KNUTSON, BARBARA. *How the Guinea Fowl Got Her Spots*. Minneapolis: Carolrhoda, 1990 (I: all).

_____. *Why the Crab Has No Head*. Minneapolis: Carolrhoda, 1987 (I: all).

KURTYCZ, MARCOS, & ANA GARCIA KOBEH. *Tigers and Opossums: Animal Legends*. Boston: Little, Brown, 1984 (I: all).

LANG, ANDREW. *The Blue Fairy Book*. Illustrated by H. J. Ford and G. P. Jacomb Hood. New York: Dover, 1889, 1965 (I: all).

_____. *The Red Fairy Book*. New York: Random, 1960 (I: all).

LATTIMORE, DEBORAH NOURSE. *The Flame of Peace: A Tale of the Aztecs*. New York: Harper & Row, 1987 (I: all).

LESTER, JULIUS. *The Knee-High Man and Other Tales*. Illustrated by Ralph Pinto. New York: Dial, 1972 (I: all).

LISTER, ROBIN. *The Legend of King Arthur*. Illustrated by Alan Baker. New York: Doubleday, 1988 (I: 8 +).

LOUIE, AI-LANG. *Yeh Shen: A Cinderella Story From China*. Illustrated by Ed Young. New York: Philomel, 1982 (I: 7 – 10).

MARSHALL, JAMES, retold by. *Hansel and Gretel*. New York: Dial, 1990 (I: 3 – 8).

_____. *Red Riding Hood*. New York: Dial, 1987 (I: 3 – 8).

MAYER, MARIANNA, retold by. *The Twelve Dancing Princesses*. Illustrated by K. Y. Craft. New York: Morrow, 1989 (I: 8 +).

McDERMOTT, GERALD. *Anasi the Spider: A Tale from the Ashanti*. Orlando: Holt, Rinehart & Winston, 1972 (I: 7 – 9).

McKISSACK, PATRICIA. *Flossie & the Fox*. Illustrated by Rachel Isadora. New York: Dial, 1986 (I: 3 – 8).

METAYER, MAURICE. *Tales from the Igloo*. Illustrated by Agnes Nanogak. Edmonton: Hurtig, 1972 (I: all).

MONROE, JEAN GUARD & RAY A. WILLIAMSON. *They Dance in the Sky: Native American Star Myths*. Illustrated by Edgar Steward. Boston: Houghton Mifflin, 1987 (I: 10 +).

MOSEL, ARLENE. *The Funny Little Woman*. Illustrated by Blair Lent. New York: Dutton, 1972 (I: 5 – 8).

MULHERINE, JENNIFER, edited by. *Favourite Fairy Tales*. New York: Granada, 1982 (I: 8 +).

PERRAULT, CHARLES. "Cinderella," retold and illustrated by Marcia Brown. New York: Scribner's, 1954 (I: all).

_____. *Little Red Riding Hood*. Illustrated by Sarah Moon. Mankato, Minn: Creative Education, 1983 (I: 8 +).

_____. *Perrault's Complete Fairy Tales*. Illustrated by W. Heath Robinson. New York: Dodd, Mead, 1961, 1982 (I: 8 +).

PYLE, HOWARD. *The Story of King Arthur and His Knights*. New York: Scribner's, 1903, 1978 (I: 12 +).

ROBINSON, GAIL. *Raven the Trickster: Legends of the North American Indians*. Illustrated by Joanna Troughton. New York: Atheneum, 1982 (I: 8 – 12).

ROCKWELL, ANNE. *The Three Bears & 15 Other Stories*. New York: Crowell, 1975 (I: 3 – 8).

ROHMER, HARRIET, OCTAVIO CHOW, & MORRIS VIDAURE. *The Invisible Hunters*. Illustrated by Joe Sa, San Francisco: Children's Press, 1987 (I: all).

_____. & DORNMINSTER WILSON. *Mother Scorpion Country*. Illustrated by Virginia Steams. San Francisco: Children's Press, 1987 (I: all).

SANFIELD, STEVE. *The Adventures of High John the Conqueror*. Illustrated by John Ward. New York: Watts, 1989 (I: 8 +).

SPENCER, PAULA UNDERWOOD. *Who Speaks for Wolf.* Illustrated by Frank Howell. Austin, TX: Tribe of Two Press, 1983 (I: all).

STEPTOE, JOHN. *Mufaro's Beautiful Daughters: An African Tale.* New York: Lothrop, Lee & Shepard, 1987 (I: all).

———. *The Story of Jumping Mouse.* New York: Lothrop, Lee & Shepard, 1984 (I: all).

VUONG, LYNETTE DYER. *The Brocaded Slipper.* Illustrated by Vo-Dinh Mai. Reading, MA: Addison-Wesley, 1982 (I: 8–12).

WALKER, BARBARA. *The Dancing Palm Tree and Other Nigerian Folktales.* Illustrated by Helen Siegl. Lubbock, TX: Texas Tech University Press, 1990 (I: all).

WALLAS, JAMES. *Kwakiutl Legends,* recorded by Pamela Whitacker. Vancouver: Hancock House, 1981 (I: all).

YOUNG, ED. *Lon Po Po: A Red-Riding Hood Story from China.* New York: Philomel, 1989 (I: all).

CHAPTER 11

MODERN FANTASY

DEVELOPING UNDERSTANDINGS OF MODERN FANTASY
    Approaches that Develop Understanding and Appreciation of Fantasy
    Core Books and Sample Lessons for Developing Understanding and
        Appreciation of Fantasy
    Developing Modern Fantasy Units

In many ways modern fantasy is similar to folklore: Both are certainly fantasy and some authors base their writing on styles, plots, and characters that closely resemble folklore. In fact, some of the stories, such as those created by Hans Christian Andersen, are called literary folktales or fairy tales. One of the major differences between a folktale and a literary folktale is authorship. Folktales were handed down for centuries through the oral tradition, while literary folktales were created by specific authors. These authors use similar structures but create original stories. Likewise, authors of some modern fantasy such as J. R. R. Tolkien and Susan Cooper build their elaborate fantasies on mythological and legendary foundations such as those found in Norse mythology and the Arthurian legends. These stories are called high, heroic, or epic fantasy because they have many of the characteristics of the earlier myths and legends.

The modern fantasy genre includes some of the most famous literature for children and young adults. More than one fourth of the books listed by the Children's Literature Association in *Touchstones: A List of Distinguished Children's Books* (1985) are modern fantasy. The stories range from Beatrix Potter's *The Tale of Peter Rabbit* and E. B. White's *Charlotte's Web* to the epic fantasy of J. R. R. Tolkien's *The Hobbit,* and the allegory of C. S. Lewis' "Narnia Series," for example, *The Lion, the Witch and the Wardrobe,* to the science fiction of Madeleine L'Engle's *A Wrinkle in Time.* In addition to being enjoyable, this literature challenges the intellect, reveals insights into human nature, stimulates the imagination, and nurtures the affective domain.

As would be expected in such a range, authors enrich their fantasies in many ways. They might personify their non-human characters; enhance settings, plots and characterizations with allegory, irony, and figurative language; develop and enrich their stories with traditional folklore elements; and rely on scientific probabilities to create the new worlds and plots found in science fiction. For some students, these techniques make fantasy an enjoyable and challenging genre. For other students, modern fantasy is difficult to appreciate and understand. Studies such as the one conducted by Swanton (1984) suggest that gifted students like modern fantasy, especially science fiction, because of the challenges the literature presents. While almost half of the books preferred by gifted students were classified as modern fantasy (29 percent science fiction, 18 percent other fantasy) none of the top choices of less able readers were similarly classified.

Because modern fantasy can be enjoyable for all readers, the differences in reading preferences are unfortunate. Instead of ignoring modern fantasy, however, teachers should encourage students to enjoy the genre by sharing the stories orally with them, encouraging them to read the stories independently, and using instructional techniques that help students appreciate and understand modern fantasy. In this section we will identify some of the important understandings to develop around modern fantasy, list approaches that develop those understandings, and develop core lessons and units around the modern fantasy genre.

DEVELOPING UNDERSTANDINGS OF MODERN FANTASY

As in folklore, a listing of the important understandings of modern fantasy suggests rich instructional possibilities. Activities and units can be developed to emphasize these important understandings:

1. Unlike realistic fiction, modern fantasy stories contain one or more altered elements, which render the story impossible in the world as we know it. For example, authors might create new worlds, animals that talk, or people with special powers.

2. While authors of modern fantasy can alter elements in their stories, they still must make their stories believable. Reader's should be able to suspend their disbelief, a crucial element of quality modern fantasy.

3. Authorities on modern fantasy such as Egoff (1988) categorize and describe several different types or branches of modern fantasy including epic fantasy (Tolkien's *The Hobbit*); enchanted realism (Philippa Pearce's *Tom's Midnight Garden*); stories of magic (E. Nesbit's *Melisande*); animal fantasies and beast tales (Kenneth Grahame's *The Wind in the Willows*); past-time fantasy (Lunn's *The Root Cellar*); science fiction fantasy (Dickinson's *The Weathermonger*); ghost stories (Joan Lowery Nixon's *Whispers From the Dead*); and light fantasy (Milne's *Winnie-the-Pooh*).

4. Because literary fairy tales have some of the same characteristics as folktales, students' schema for folktales can help them appreciate and understand literary fairy tales.

5. Because high or epic fantasies have some of the same characteristics as myths and legends, students' schema for myths and legends can help them appreciate and understand high fantasy.

6. Light fantasy or enchanted realism is characterized as fantasy that is light in tone, has a subtle mixture of real and make believe, focuses on personal development of the characters rather than on the forces of good and evil, and often includes humor and even satire.

7. High or epic fantasy is concerned with the unending battle between good and evil and is dominated by high purpose and worlds to be won or lost. The characters are frequently involved in battles for the common good.

This list illustrates the point that modern fantasy covers a wide range of literature and includes books appropriate for all grade levels. For example, the light fantasy and the animal stories are among children's earliest favorites. Many of the high or epic fantasies appeal to older students as well as to adults. As in folklore, the question of what types of fantasy and which understandings to include at specific grade levels has no concrete answer. The following suggested scope and sequence for fantasy was developed after consulting with numerous teachers and school districts. As you will notice, many of the types of activities and understandings are similar to those in folklore:

KINDERGARTEN THROUGH THIRD GRADE

1. Share, appreciate, discuss, and respond to appropriate selections of modern fantasy.
2. Identify and appreciate the story elements associated with literary fairy tales: Setting, plot, characterization, conflict, theme, motif, and style. Understand that story structures in literary fairy tales are similar to story structures in folktales.
3. Understand how to read fantasy.
4. Share, discuss, and respond to major elements in light fantasy.
5. Take part in enjoyable activities surrounding fantasy units.

FOURTH THROUGH SIXTH GRADES

1. Continue sharing, discussing, and responding to numerous examples of fantasy.
2. Analyze and evaluate author's ability to suspend disbelief.
3. Share, discuss, and respond to author's style in fantasy.
4. Share, discuss, and respond to high fantasy.
5. Identify legendary elements in high fantasy.
6. Analyze characteristics of high fantasy.
7. Compare and contrast characteristics of light and high fantasy.
8. Take part in enjoyable activities surrounding fantasy units.

SEVENTH THROUGH EIGHTH GRADES

1. Compare the motifs in and the mythological basis of Norse legend and mythology and the works of J. R. R. Tolkien; Welsh legend and mythology and the works of Lloyd Alexander; and English legend and mythology and the works of Susan Cooper.
2. Take part in an in-depth study of allusion, symbolism, and allegory in fantasy.

Approaches that Develop Understanding and Appreciation of Fantasy

This section focuses on core lessons and units that can be used to clarify understandings and increase appreciation of modern fantasy. The first few core lessons can be used at several grade levels depending on the fantasy selected for reading. The units are divided into lower elementary, middle elementary, and upper elementary and middle school categories.

Many of the instructional approaches described earlier in this text are excellent for developing understandings of modern fantasy. Other approaches are excellent for relating speaking, listening, reading, writing, and content areas such as social studies. In fact, many of the approaches already developed can be used in the fantasy units. A few examples of core lessons previously developed (and related books) are shown in the following list. Many more fantasy selections can be found in earlier chapters in the lists of extended and recreational books. The following approaches are developed either in previous chapters or in this chapter:

1. Visualizing descriptive settings (Ch. 3, Babbitt's *Tuck Everlasting*).

2. Writing poetry about characters (Ch. 3, Leaf's *The Story of Ferdinand*, Williams' *The Velveteen Rabbit or How Toys Become Real*).

3. Exploring and identifying person-against-society conflicts (Ch. 5, Burton's *The Little House*, Leaf's *The Story of Ferdinand*).

4. Exploring and identifying person-against-self conflicts (Ch. 5, Yorinks' *Hey, Al*).

5. Pantomiming characterization (Ch. 6, Potter's *The Tale of Peter Rabbit*).

6. Exploring the imagination through setting (Ch. 7, Lindgren's *The Wild Baby Goes to Sea*, Martin's *Will's Mammoth*, Ryder's *White Bear, Ice Bear*).

7. Interacting with and responding to music (Maxner's *Nicholas Cricket*).

8. Creating maps and illustrations for well-developed settings (Ch. 7, Lewis' *The Lion, the Witch and the Wardrobe* and Carroll's *Alice's Adventures in Wonderland*).

9. Responding to illustrations that create moods (Ch. 7, Scheer's *Rain Makes Applesauce*, Van Allsburg's *The Polar Express*).

10. Responding to personification (Ch. 9, Burton's *The Little House*, McCully's *Picnic*).

11. Modeling similes and figurative language (Ch. 9, Lionni's *Swimmy*, Brittain's *The Wish Giver*).

12. Charting comparisons between personified fantasy and nonfiction (Ch. 9, LeGuin's *Catwings*, O'Brien's *Mrs. Frisby and the Rats of NIMH*, King-Smith's *Martin's Mice*, Bond's *A Bear Called Paddington*, White's *Charlotte's Web*, and Lawson's *Rabbit Hill*).

13. Relating author's use of similes to the development of characterization (Ch. 9, Fleischman's *The Midnight Horse*).

14. Helping students understand various literary elements by introducing concepts through picture books and short stories (Ch 9, Corbett's *The Song of Pentecost*, MacDonald's *At the Back of the North Wind*, Oakley's *The Church Mice in Action*, Asch and Vagin's *Here Comes the Cat*).

15. Developing guidelines to help students read fantasies.

16. Writing creative stories that follow the structure and characteristics of fantasy.

17. Connecting folktales and literary fairy tales by comparing similarities in plot structures, settings, characterizations, themes, and motifs.

18. Connecting fables sand literary fables by comparing literary elements.

19. Connecting mythology and legend and high fantasy by identifying foundations and comparing similarities in literary elements.

20. Tracing and considering reasons that theme changes between some myths and legends and the high fantasy on which they are based. For example, shifting from the importance of fate to the importance of free will.

21. Using webbing and plot structures to understand and appreciate literary elements in fantasy.

22. Developing units around fantasy that encourage students to use many of the above approaches.

Core Books and Sample Lessons for Developing Understanding and Appreciation of Fantasy

The following core lessons can be used independently or as part of a unit. They also can be used at several different levels depending on the books chosen.

LESSON ONE: Developing Questions the Students Can Ask To Decide if a Book is Modern Fantasy

OBJECTIVES

> To identify the characteristics of modern fantasy.
>
> To develop a series of questions that students can use to decide whether a selection is modern fantasy.
>
> To read additional fantasy and apply the questions during independent reading.

CORE BOOKS: These core books represent fantasy and also are appropriate for the grade level. For lower elementary students: Ursula LeGuin's *Catwings.* Middle elementary: A. A. Milne's *Winnie-the-Pooh* (Touchstone). Upper elementary and middle school: Lloyd Alexander's *The Book of Three.*

EXTENDED BOOKS FOR INDEPENDENT READING AND RELATED ASSIGNMENTS: The following books have the same characteristics as the core books. They can be used as additional core books or to replace the core books. They also can be used for extended reading assignments and related discussions or for recreational reading. With the wordless books, students can identify fantasy elements in the illustrations.

> Lower Elementary
>
> Emily Arnold McCully's *School*
> Chris Van Allsburg's *The Wreck of the Zephyr* and *The Mysteries of Harris Burdick*
> David Wiesner's *Free Fall* (Caldecott Honor)
> Arthur Yorinks' *Hey, Al* (Caldecott Medal)
>
> Middle Elementary
>
> Lewis Carroll's *Alice's Adventures in Wonderland* (Touchstone)
> Philippa Pearce's *Tom's Midnight Garden* (Touchstone)
> E. B. White's *Charlotte's Web* (Touchstone, Newbery Honor)
>
> Upper Elementary and Middle School
>
> Margaret Anderson's *In the Keep of Time*
> Madeleine L'Engle's *A Wrinkle in Time* (Newbery Medal)

PROCEDURES: Begin by asking the students to identify several books that could be classified as fantasy. Ask, "What makes a story fantasy?" List and discuss their answers. Make sure that the students understand that a fantasy is a story that could not happen in the world as we know it. Discuss the idea that fantasy authors change something in their stories so that the stories could not take place in our world. For example, these changes might be in the settings, such as making up new worlds; in the characters, such as making them tiny or giving them special abilities; or in time, such as having the characters travel into the past or the future. Make sure that students understand that authors of fantasies do not have to make changes in all of these areas—many alter or manipulate only one element. Explain to the students that altering elements places considerable responsibility upon the authors. The authors must make us suspend our disbelief by developing the stories so carefully and including enough detail that we believe their worlds, plots, and characters could have existed in the times and places they describe.

If the students identify folklore selections as examples of fantasy, explain to them that many fantasies sound like folklore, but that a fantasy has an identified author. In contrast, folklore was handed down through the oral tradition and written down by someone as it was being told. Show the students how they can find this information on the title page of a book, in the endnotes, or in other parts of the book, such as the jacket cover.

Next, select a book that is appropriate for the grade level. Share the book with the students and ask them to consider what changes have been made—through either the text or the illustrations—from the world as they know it. (Many middle elementary, upper elementary, and middle school teachers also like to use the highly illustrated books listed for lower elementary students to encourage students to identify and discuss how fantasy is developed through illustrations.) After students have shared and discussed the fantasy elements in one book, share additional books or ask the students to read and respond to the fantasy elements independently. Ask them also to respond to how well they think the authors made them believe the story could happen, or caused them to suspend their disbelief.

For example, the following element identifications and responses to the book *Catwings* were completed with second-grade students:

The author changed the characters. The kittens were given wings so they could fly. The kittens and the mother cat could talk. The author made me think the story could happen because the mother cat dreamed that she wanted her kittens to be safe. I think that a mother would really want this. I think my Mom would do this. I thought giving kittens wings was a good way to make them safe. I liked the mother cat and the kittens. The story seemed real when the kittens flew away from real dangers. I liked the way the boy and the girl protected the kittens. I would like to protect kittens with wings, because people would hurt them.

Continue this type of activity, encouraging students to identify how the authors changed or manipulated the literary elements. Also, ask the students to determine whether they were able to suspend their disbelief and to consider the techniques the authors used to try to make them believe the stories really could happen.

After students have read, discussed, and responded to a variety of fantasy selections, ask them to develop a list of questions that they can use to decide whether a book is fantasy or if the fantasy is effective. For example, a group of fifth-grade students developed the following questions:

QUESTIONS I CAN ASK MYSELF WHEN I READ FANTASY

1. Did I look at the title page or at other notes to make sure the story is really a fantasy and not a folktale? Who is the author of the story?

2. What is the setting for the story? Is it like one in my real world? Why or why not? If the setting was changed, how was it changed? Can I describe the setting so I can picture it? How did the author try to make me believe there is such a place? Did the author succeed?

3. Who are the characters in the story? Are they like people or animals I know in the real world? Why or why not? If the characters are changed, how are they changed? Can I describe them? How did the author try to make me believe that the characters and what they can do are real? Did the author succeed?

4. What is the problem in the story? How is this problem overcome? Could I overcome the same problem in the same way? Why or why not? How did the author make me believe that this was a real problem? How did the author try to make me believe that the problem could be overcome in this way? Did the author succeed?

5. When does the story take place? Is the story in the past, the present, or the future? Do the characters travel between time periods? If the characters travel in time, how does the author try to make me believe that this is possible? If the story takes place in the future, how did the author make me believe in the future? Can I describe the future? Did the author succeed?

After the students have developed their questions, encourage them to use them as they read, discuss, and respond to several examples of fantasy.

LESSON TWO: Responding to Vivid Language and Other Elements in Fantasy Through Artistic Interpretations

OBJECTIVE

To select passages that are particularly pleasing and develop a personal response to those passages through art.

CORE BOOKS: Select and encourage students to choose fantasy with vivid, appealing language. Students can make their own choices after reading or listening to the fantasies. Although any fantasy can be used for this activity, the books in this lesson were student favorites: Beatrix Potter's *The Complete Tales of Beatrix Potter* (these tales also are available in individual texts); Hans Christian Andersen's *Hans Christian Andersen Eighty Fairy Tales;* and Susan Cooper's *The Dark Is Rising* (Newbery Honor).

EXTENDED BOOKS FOR INDEPENDENT READING AND RELATEDASSIGN-MENTS: Any favorite fantasy books chosen by the students.

PROCEDURES: Begin the lesson by encouraging students to read or listen to fantasy selections and select passages or sentences that particularly appeal to them. As they read or listen to these passages, ask the students to close their eyes and try to visualize the setting, the characters, or the conflict. Ask them to think about what qualities of writing, characterization or plot appealed to them.

Encourage the students to share passages that are especially appealing and then draw pictures that reflect their aesthetic responses to the fantasy. The following passages are examples of works selected, discussed, and illustrated by students in the lower elementary grades after listening to and reading *The Complete Tales of Beatrix Potter:*

> Little Benjamin said, "It spoils people's clothes to squeeze under a gate; the proper way to get in, is to climb down a pear tree." Peter fell down head first; but it was of no consequence, as the bed below was newly raked and quite soft ("The Tale of Benjamin Bunny," p. 59).
>
> In the time of swords and periwigs and full-skirted coats with flowered lappets—when gentlemen wore ruffles, and gold-laced waistcoats of paduasoy and taffeta—there lived a tailor in Gloucester ("The Tailor of Gloucester," p. 39).

The following passages are examples of works selected, discussed, and illustrated by middle elementary students after listening to and reading fantasy by Hans Christian Andersen in single volumes and in the anthology, *Hans Christian Andersen Eighty Fairy Tales:*

As darkness fell, coloured lanterns were lit, and the crew danced merrily on the deck. The little mermaid could not help thinking of the first time she came up out of the sea and gazed on just such a scene of joy and splendour. And now she joined in the dance, swerving and swooping as lightly as a swallow that avoids pursuit; and shouts of admiration greeted her on every side ("The Little Mermaid," p. 61).

Yes it certainly was lovely out in the country. Bathed in sunshine stood an old manor-house with a deep moat round it, and growing out of the wall down by the water were huge dock-leaves; the biggest of them were so tall that little children could stand upright underneath. The place was as tangled and twisty as the densest forest, and here it was that a duck was sitting on her nest. It was time for her to hatch out her little ducklings, but it was such a long job that she was beginning to lose patience. She hardly ever had a visitor; the other ducks thought more of swimming about in the moat than of coming and sitting under a dock-leaf just for the sake of a quack with her ("The Ugly Duckling," p. 107).

The following passages were selected and illustrated by middle and upper elementary students from *The Dark Is Rising:*

At the same moment, fire leaped up out of the fallen elm tree branch that Will had briefly lighted before, and flames cracked down from nowhere in a circle of searing white light all around Maggie Barnes, a circle of light higher than her head. She crouched down suddenly on the snow, cringing, her mouth slack with fear. The belt with the two linked Signs dropped out of her limp hand (p. 57).

The Rider's pale face flushed. He said softly, "The Dark is rising, Old One, and this time we do not propose that anything shall hinder its way. This is the time for our rising, and these next twelve months shall see us established at last. Tell them, all the Things of Power that they hope to possess we shall take from them, the grail and the harp and the Signs. We shall break your Circle before it can ever be joined. And none shall stop the Dark from rising!" (p. 118).

Encourage students to share their responses and their illustrations with the group.

LESSON THREE: Connecting Folktales and Literary Fairy Tales

OBJECTIVES

To develop the understanding that literary fairy tales have some of the same characteristics as folktales.

To read and analyze literary fairy tales that contain folktale elements.

To compare folktales from a specific culture and literary fairy tales that develop from that culture.

To compare the illustrations in folktales and literary fairy tales that have similar cultural settings.

To compare folktales and literary fairy tales through webs and plot structures.

To write a literary fairy tale that includes elements of folktales.

CORE BOOKS: Literary fairy tales that closely resemble folktales: Hans Christian Andersen's "The Wild Swans," in *Hans Christian Andersen Eighty Fairy Tales* (compare with German folktales); Eric Kimmel's *Hershel and the Hanukkah Goblins* (Caldecott Honor, compare with Jewish folktales); E. Nesbit's *Melisande* (compare with European folktales); Mwenye Hadithi's *Greedy Zebra* (compare with African pourquoi tales); and Keith Baker's *The Magic Fan* and Antonia Barber's *The Enchanter's Daughter* (compare with Asian folktales).

EXTENDED BOOKS FOR INDEPENDENT READING AND RELATED ASSIGNMENTS: These books or stories have the same characteristics as the core books. They can be used for independent comparisons or recreational reading:

"THUMBELINA" in *Hans Christian Andersen Eighty Fairy Tales* or use one of the highly illustrated texts (Compare with the German folktale "Tom Thumb."
JANE YOLEN's *The Faery Flag: Stories and Poems of Fantasy and the Supernatural, The Girl Who Cried Flowers,* and *The Hundredth Dove and Other Tales* (Compare with European folktales.)

PROCEDURES: This activity is appropriate for all grade levels. Students in the upper grades will analyze the stories and the illustrations with more sophisticated understandings of motif, theme, and symbolism. Students in the lower grades will identify fundamental similarities in plot structures and characterizations.

Introduce the lesson by reading one of the literary fairy tales to the students. Ask them to listen carefully and identify the genre. Most students probably will say the story either is or sounds like a folktale. Tell the students that it is a literary fairy tale, which we know because the author used a structure that is similar to that of a folktale. Explain to the students that literary fairy tales also have many of the same characteristics that they discovered when they read folktales. Review some of the characteristics related to time and place, types of characters, characteristics of plot development, style (similar to oral storytelling), and theme (such as good will overcome evil). Also tell the students that Hans Christian Andersen is credited with being one of the first persons to write literary fairy tales.

Tell the students that they will be listening or reading for the characteristics in several literary fairy tales that are similar to those of folktales. They then will compare the literary fairy tales with folktales depicting the same culture. Tell them they also should pay special attention to the illustrations in both the literary fairy tales and the folktales. They should evaluate whether the illustrations develop characteristics that are similar to those in the illustrations in folktales and if the illustrations depict the culture. This introductory activity will require several days.

Read one of the literary fairy tales together in class. (This can be the same literary fairy tale chosen as part of the introductory activity). Ask the students to identify all the elements that are similar to a folktale. They can place the plot on a plot diagram similar to one shown in Chapter 5. They also can compare the elements in the literary fairy tale with Bascome's definition for folktales (*see* Chapter 10).

Two different types of webs can be developed with the literary fairy tale. For example, a literary-elements web might focus on setting, characterization, conflict, and theme. Figure 11.1 shows a literary-elements web to accompany a literary fairy tale. Notice how closely the characteristics of setting, characters, conflict, and theme resemble those of oral folktales. Discuss these similarities with the students.

Another type of web is a cultural-values web similar to the webs developed around the cultural units under folktales. In this web encourage students to search the text and illustrations for information such as admired human qualities, disliked human qualities, and beliefs. Figure 11.2 shows a cultural values web developed around the same literary fairy tale as that shown in Figure 11.1. If students have previously studied the cultural values developed in the folklore of that culture, they can compare their analysis of the literary fairy tale and the cultural information gained from folklore. They should consider how closely the literary fairy tale develops some of the same cultural values as does the folklore.

Before proceeding to a different literary fairy tale, ask the students to compare the literary fairy tale with examples of folktales depicting that same culture. (Cultural comparisons are listed in the core book section of this lesson.) They can select several folktales and develop plot structures, literary webs, and cultural webs. Ask, "What, if any, are the similarities in the type

FIGURE 11.1 Literary-elements web for a literary fairy tale.

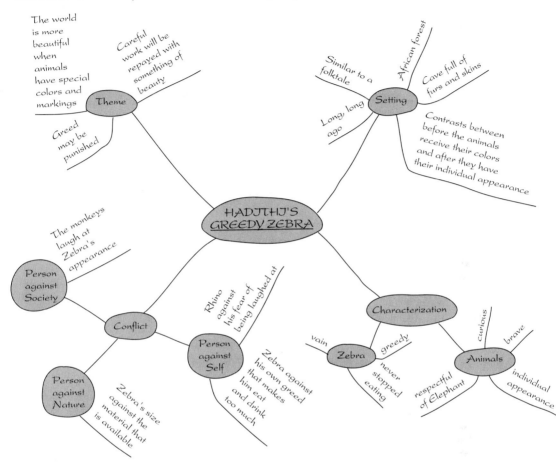

of plot structures, the settings, the characterizations, the conflict, the themes, and the cultural values? Did the authors follow the folklore structure for a folktale from that specific culture? What are some examples? Did the artists develop illustrations that depict the culture in similar ways as those developed in folktales? Explain your answer."

This activity can continue as a group activity, or students can read the remaining examples and do the comparisons independently. After students have read, analyzed, and responded to several literary fairy tales, ask them to create their own literary fairy tale that follows the structure and the characteristics of folklore from a specific culture. Encourage the students to illustrate their literary fairy tales.

Developing Modern Fantasy Units

Egoff (1988) develops strong reasons for developing units around modern fantasy when she states that fantasy has been "praised for its true reflection of reality and for its power to illuminate life's mysteries far beyond purportedly 'realistic' novels. It can transport us

FIGURE 11.2 Cultural-values web for a literary fairy tale.

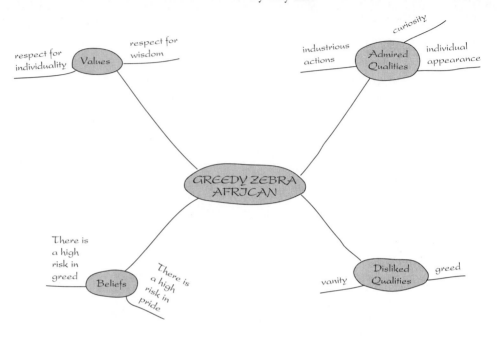

to another world, another time, or another dimension clearly separate and different from our own, or it can project the supernatural into the natural world" (p. 1).

Because of the range of available modern fantasy stories, units can be developed for any grade level. For example, in the lower elementary grades units can focus on favorite fantasy authors, themes such as the importance of love and friendship, animals, and responding to humor. Students in both lower and middle grades enjoy combining their interests in puppetry, creative drama, and fantasy. Such units combine the objectives associated with oral-language development, creative oral expression, literary responses, artistic expression, fantasy appreciation, and creative writing. Units centered on imaginary kingdoms, strange worlds, and eccentric characters fascinate students in the middle grades. Students in both the middle grades and upper elementary and middle school enjoy science fiction units. These units frequently integrate both science and social studies into the curriculum. Many emphasize important themes as characters face decisions that might be equally important in the world of today. Units in the upper elementary and middle school can focus on the mythological foundations of high fantasy and consider the important themes that connect the two forms of literature.

UNIT ONE: Developing an Appreciation of Fantasy Through Puppetry and Other Creative Interpretations in the Lower to Middle Elementary Grades

OBJECTIVES

To develop an appreciation of the fantasy genre.

To be involved in a puppetry production that increases aesthetic appreciation and language development.

To select fantasy that is appropriate for puppetry or other approaches.

To create and dramatize an original fantasy.

To respond to fantasy through an artistic interpretation.

CORE BOOKS: Select numerous books that are appropriate for puppetry or other creative productions. By providing a variety of books, students become involved in choosing stories they would like to dramatize. For puppetry, choose stories with action that can be shown through the movements and voices of the puppet characters, with plots that have a rapid pace and a clear structure; with plots the students will want to repeat, and with a moderate number of characters (too many characters on the stage at one time are impossible to manage).

Good selections for puppetry productions include stories from A. A. Milne's *Winnie-the-Pooh* (Touchstone); Beatrix Potter's *The Tale of Peter Rabbit* (Touchstone); stories from Hans Christian Andersen's *Hans Christian Andersen Eighty Fairy Tales,* such as "The Princess and the Pea" and "The Emperor's New Clothes" (Touchstone); selections from Carl Sandburg's *Rootabaga Stories;* stories from Rudyard Kipling's *Just So Stories* and *The Jungle Book* (Touchstone); E. Nesbit's *Melisande;* stories from Jane Yolen's *The Faery Flag: Stories and Poems of Fantasy and the Supernatural, The Girl Who Cried Flowers,* and *The Hundredth Dove and other Tales;* and Maurice Sendak's *Where the Wild Things Are* (Touchstone, Caldecott Medal).

EXTENDED BOOKS FOR INDEPENDENT READING AND OTHER ASSIGNMENTS:

After students have completed a puppetry project, teachers might want to give them experiences with other forms of creative drama or with artistic responses. The strange and curious worlds and the interesting characters in modern fantasy can stimulate students' artistic interpretations through such media as papier-mache, collage, murals, and shadowboxes. Any of the books or stories listed under core books can be used for these activities. Additional selections that are excellent for such group and individual activities include the following:

> KEITH BAKER's *The Magic Fan*
> LEWIS CARROLL's *Alice's Adventures in Wonderland* and *Through the Looking Glass* (Touchstone)
> ROALD DAHL's *James and the Giant Peach*
> RUMER GODDEN's *The Dolls' House*
> KENNETH GRAHAME's *The Wind in the Willows* (Touchstone)
> ROBERT LAWSON's *Rabbit Hill*
> C. S. LEWIS's *The Lion, the Witch and the Wardrobe* (Touchstone)
> MARY NORTON's *The Borrowers* (Touchstone)
> GEORGE SELDEN's *The Cricket in Times Square* (Newbery Honor)
> WILLIAM STEIG's *Abel's Island*
> E. B. WHITE's *Charolotte's Web* (Newbery Honor, Touchstone)

Highly illustrated fantasy picture storybooks that stimulate various artistic expressions include the following:

> EZRA JACK KEATS' *The Trip*
> LEO LIONNI's *Alexander and the Wind-Up Mouse* (Caldecott Honor) and *Swimmy* (Caldecott Honor)
> DAVID MACAULAY's *Black and White* (Caldecott Medal)
> PATRICIA C. McKISSACK *Mirandy and Brother Wind* (Black, Caldecott Honor)
> CHRIS VAN ALLSBURG's *The Garden of Abdul Gasazi* (Caldecott Honor), *Jumanji* (Caldecott Medal), and *The Polar Express* (Caldecott Medal)

MILDRED PITTS WALTER's *Brother to the Wind* (African)
DAVID WIESNER's *Free Fall* (Caldecott Honor)
AUDREY WOOD's *King Bidgood's in the Bathtub* (Caldecott Honor)
ARTHUR YORINKS' *Hey, Al* (Caldecott Medal)

PROCEDURES: Begin this unit by bringing some puppets into the classroom. Ask the students to share experiences they have had making puppets or watching puppet productions. Give them some additional background knowledge about puppetry. For example, tell them, "In Europe, puppet theaters are so elaborate that entire operas are performed by marionettes. The Japanese Banraku puppeteers perform classical drama, and the puppeteers in Thailand perform in the temple courtyards. In the United States puppets are especially popular on television. How many of you have watched the Muppets on 'Sesame Street' or the puppets in the Land of Make Believe on 'Mr. Rogers's Neighborhood'? Why do you think puppets are so popular around the world?"

Next, ask the students to consider what types of stories they think would lend themselves to good puppetry productions. You can tell them that the fantasy author Hans Christian Andersen created puppet plays from his own fantasies for the children of Copenhagen. Ask the students what characteristics these stories have that make them good for puppetry productions. Through discussion, encourage students to understand the importance of the characteristics listed under the core books.

Tell the students that they will be developing several puppet plays. For these plays they can use ideas they get from reading fantasy such as stories by Hans Christian Andersen. They will need to pick stories they think are enjoyable enough to present to an audience, identify which characters will become puppets, create their puppets, practice their puppet plays, and present the play to an audience. They even can create backdrops for the puppetry production.

Next, have the students choose the story they would like to use for their first puppetry production. Emphasize that because this is their first production, the story should be simple and the puppet characters should be made with simple materials. Tell them that after they have tried a few puppetry productions, they can make the productions and the puppets more elaborate. Encourage the students to select a short story for which they can make simple puppets out of paper plates or paper bags. Read the selected story to the group, ask the students to choose the characters they would like to be and, therefore, the puppets they would like to make. Have the students make simple paper-plate or paper-sack puppets. Divide the students into groups so that all students can take part in the production and use their puppets. Before putting on the production, you might want to reread the story. The students do not have to memorize their parts; instead they improvise, using their general knowledge of the story and the character. After the production is completed, discuss the process with the students. Ask them to reconsider the characteristics of a story that they think would make a good puppet production. Did their first production meet those characteristics?

Many students might want to try additional stories and more elaborate puppets. Explain to the students that they will have an opportunity to develop a puppetry festival in which they choose several related stories to present. For example, students could have a Winnie-The-Pooh Festival, a Beatrix Potter Festival, or a Jungle Book Festival. Longer books with chapters also can be used. For example, students could plan a Charlotte's Web Festival, a Wind in the Willows Festival, or an Alice in Wonderland Festival. The class can be divided into groups, with each group preparing a different story or chapter. Students enjoy such festivals because they can use the same puppets in different stories or chapters about the same characters. They also can create their own stories about these characters. After students have selected their story or series of stories for the next production, ask them to choose the characters they would like to create through puppetry. Directions for paper-plate puppets, paper-bag puppets, hand puppets, box puppets, sock puppets, cylinder puppets, molded-head puppets, rod puppets, humanette puppets, and a simple folding puppet stage are found in *The Effective Teaching of Language Arts* (Norton, 1989).

After the puppets are completed, the students should begin preparing for the actual production. First, a story should be read several times until the players know it thoroughly. However, as with the first production, students should not memorize their parts. Rather they should improvise dialogue after they thoroughly understand the story structure and have developed mental images of the characters and their personalities. Teachers need to help students plan who will be in the scene, what will happen in the scene, how the scene will move forward, and what the objective of the scene is. Many teachers encourage the students to pantomime the scene first, then repeat the scene and add sounds that express the characters' feelings. Finally, they improvise the scene using dialogue. This procedure can be repeated until the students develop the whole story or series of stories. Now the story or series of stories can be presented as a finished production. Throughout this production, students should have opportunities to be both performers and audience.

After students have developed a puppetry production motivated by specific literature, encourage them to create their own stories that are appropriate for puppetry. Students can add to the production roles by becoming writers, producers, and players.

INDEPENDENT PROJECTS AND OTHER ACTIVITIES WITH THE PUPPETRY UNIT

Library research: Ask students to research the development of different types of puppets, such as marionettes. They should discover how they are made, what type of productions they are used for, and the history of their usage.

Social studies: Have students research how puppets are used in a particular culture. For example, they could research Punch and Judy shows in England, Muppets in the United States, or Banraku puppets in Japan.

Artistic interpretations: Many additional artistic interpretations are possible with puppetry productions and modern fantasy. For example, students can create stage settings for their productions. These should be simple backgrounds that do not interfere with the movements of the puppets. Additional artistic interpretations that are especially appropriate for modern fantasy include papier-mache, collage, murals, shadowboxes, and paintings.

1. *Papier-mache:* To create papier-mache characters, cover lightweight structural forms with strips of newspaper or paper toweling that have been dipped into thinned wallpaper paste. The characters and settings in many fantasy stories make interesting subjects for papier-mache. For example, the queen's courtyard in Lewis's *The Lion, the Witch and the Wardrobe* includes the animals and other creatures that the queen has turned to stone. Papier-mache is an excellent medium for recreating the statues. The wild things in Sendak's *Where the Wild Things Are* and the characters from Carroll's *Alice's Adventures in Wonderland* are excellent papier-mache subjects.

2. *Collage:* Collage is a method of illustration in which artists glue different shapes and textures of materials onto a flat surface. These materials can include newspapers, tissue paper, twigs, leaves, fabrics, corrugated paper, buttons, and rope. Basically, anything that can be attached to a surface can be used to create the design and add texture to the illustration. Students might be motivated to create their own collage interpretations after reading books in which the illustrators use

total or partial collage techniques. Interesting collage illustrations are found in Lionni's *Alexander and the Wind-up Mouse* and *Swimmy.* Macaulay uses collage in a few of his illustrations in *Black and White.* After students have discussed the effect of collage illustrations, encourage them to use the technique to create their own collage interpretations of various fantasy settings. For example, the settings in Van Allsburg's *The Garden of Abdul Gasazi* lend themselves to collages because students can gather many natural materials to create the garden settings. The numerous animal characters and natural backgrounds in the Beatrix Potter books and in Kipling's *Just So Stories* and *The Jungle Book* also are excellent for collage interpretations. Scenes from Lawson's *Rabbit Hill* and Grahame's *The Wind in the Willows* also come to life through three-dimensional interpretations using many natural and man-made materials.

3. *Murals:* A mural is made by designing and creating a picture on a long piece of paper placed on the floor or long tables so that students can work together on the project. Consequently, students must plan together, decide on the responsibilities of each individual, and develop their appropriate segments. Teachers can use Wiesner's *Free Fall* to show a book in which the artist develops the quality and characteristics of a mural. Ask the students to look carefully at the illustrations in this wordless book and to note what happens to the illustrations after the boy goes to sleep. They should notice that the white side borders are no longer included. Instead, the pictures flow into the next double-page spread as if they were a continuous mural. If they took the book apart and taped the pages together, they would have a mural. Ask the students to respond to the effect of this mural quality in the book. Then ask them to choose a fantasy selection that they would like to use to create a mural. For example, the sequence of events in Dahl's *James and the Giant Peach* and in McKissack's *Mirandy and Brother Wind* would make interesting murals. Carroll's *Through the Looking Glass* provides both interesting backgrounds and unique characters. After the mural is completed students either can place it on the walls around the room, or turn it into a wordless book like *Free Fall.*

4. *Shadowboxes:* Shadowboxes are miniature recreations of settings and characters placed inside boxes or framed on shelves. Keats' *The Trip* can be used to show students how illustrators and authors use shadowboxes in fiction. In this story, the main character builds his old neighborhood in a box and then visits it in his imagination. Both picture storybooks and longer fantasies provide stimulation for shadowbox representations. For example, students can create a shadowbox for a setting in Van Allsburg's *Jumanji;* the garden in *The Garden of Abdul Gasazi;* the train, wilderness, or North Pole settings in *The Polar Express;* the apartment or the fantasy island in Yorinks' *Hey, Al;* the elaborate bathtub settings in Wood's *King Bidgood's in the Bathtub;* and the miniature rooms and little people in Norton's *The Borrowers* and Godden's *The Dolls' House.*

UNIT TWO: Responding to Contemporary Issues Through Science Fiction in the Middle to Upper Elementary Grades

OBJECTIVES

To develop an appreciation for science fiction.

To relate social studies and science fiction.

To relate science and science fiction.

To develop an understanding of the broad themes developed in science fiction and to relate those themes to issues in society, social studies, and science.

To write science fiction based on scientific probability.

To create a futuristic world.

CORE BOOKS: John Christopher's *The City of Gold and Lead, The Pool of Fire,* and *The White Mountains;* Virginia Hamilton's *The Gathering;* Monica Hughes' *Devil On My Back, The Dream Catcher, The Guardian of Isis, The Isis Pedlar,* and *The Keeper of the Isis Light;* H. M. Hoover's *Away Is A Strange Place To Be;* Alexander Key's *Escape to Witch Mountain;* and Madeleine L'Engle's *A Wrinkle in Time* (Newbery Medal).

EXTENDED BOOKS FOR INDEPENDENT READING AND OTHER ASSIGNMENTS:

PETER DICKINSON'S *Eva*
VIRGINIA HAMILTON'S *Dustland* and *Justice and Her Brothers*
MONICA HUGHES' *Ring-Rise Ring-Set*
MADELEINE L'ENGLE'S *A Swiftly Tilting Planet* and *A Wind in the Door*
ZILPHA KEATLEY SNYDER'S *Below the Root*

PROCEDURES: Begin this unit by asking students to discuss their previous experiences with science fiction, either through books they have read or films and television shows they have seen. Many students probably have seen television's "Star Trek" or the various "Star Wars" films. Ask, "When do most of these science fiction films take place? Where do they take place? Why do you think the writers place them in the future and in far distant galaxies? What types of problems do characters have in these future worlds? How do they solve them?"

Explain to the students that writers of science fiction rely on hypothesized scientific advancements and technology to create their plots. To achieve credibility, they provide detailed descriptions of this technology, portray characters who believe in the technology or the results of the technology, and create a world where science interacts with every area of society. Science fiction frequently takes place in a future world in which people travel to or live on distant planets, or on Earth usually in some future time. The authors of science fiction frequently hypothesize about the future of humanity and stress problem solving in future societies. Many of these stories help us consider important issues and "what ifs." They often consider such important issues as what if technology takes over people's lives, what if people lose their freedom of choice, or what if atomic wars make Earth uninhabitable?

Next, encourage the students to develop their own "what if" lists. For this activity they should consider the technology they know about, space travel and the NASA missions to various planets, the potential for colonizing planets, and the ecological issues facing today's world.

The books in the first list of core and independent reading include science fiction selections in which the authors contemplate the conflicts caused by inventions, machines, and computers; the problems resulting if society hinders free will; and the conflicts caused when people act inhumanely toward those who deviate from society's norms. The second group of books concentrates on the consequences of medical advances and environmental destruction.

Teachers have several choices when implementing this unit. They can choose one book on which to first focus the group reading, discussion, and projects. Then they can use the additional books for independent reading and additional projects. Or, they can begin by dividing the students into smaller interest groups and having each interest group choose an area such as futuristic mechanized societies, free choice in a controlled society, accepting those who are different, future environmental changes and possible destruction, and the role of medical advances in a future world and possible consequences of those advances. A group of students might choose to read futuristic books to discover what a city of the future might look like and how it would function. They would need to face such issues as transportation systems, sanitation systems, and urban growth. Each interest group should relate its study to both the science and social studies curriculums.

Following is a list of possible investigation and discussion topics, divided according to the important themes and topics found in the accompanying science fiction selections:

1. Influences on the world of inventions, machines, and computers: Christopher's *The City of Gold and Lead, The Pool of Fire,* and *The White Mountains;* Hamilton's *The Gathering;* and Hughes' *Devil On My Back.*

   a. Ask the students to consider changes in the world during the last 100 years as a result of inventions such as airplanes, automobiles, and computers. Encourage the students to speculate about a world without these inventions and a world in which any of these inventions could become too powerful. Have the students read one of the books and relate what happens in the futuristic world when technology becomes too powerful. What gives the inventions power? How do the people try to retain their freedom?

   b. Ask the students to think of a new invention, machine, or computer they have just heard about or to create their own. Encourage them to draw the invention, describe its purpose, and speculate what would happen if it became too powerful. Ask them to write a story in which the invention does become too powerful.

   c. Ask the students to trace the development of the conflicts and the themes in one of these science fiction books. What message about the future is the author presenting? Could this message come true? If the message about the future is dangerous for humanity, how can people respond so that this never happens? Are these conflicts and themes found in our society today? If so, how can we respond to these problems?

2. The role of free choice in controlled societies: Hughes' *The Dream Catcher, The Guardian of Isis,* and *The Isis Pedlar;* Hoover's *Away Is A Strange Place To Be.*

   a. Regarding these books, ask students to respond to the question, "Should society allow its members to have free will? What could happen if people do not strive to retain freedom of choice?"

   b. Ask students to trace the author's development of conflicts and themes in one of these books. What message does the author develop about freedom of choice? Is freedom of choice easily retained by the society in this book? Why or why not? Is freedom of choice easily retained by people living in our world? Why or why not? Encourage students to give examples in our current world in which people have to work or even fight to retain their freedoms.

   c. In *The Dream Catcher,* Hughes presents an interesting challenge when, after a destructive incident, she isolates a group of people who belong to the same profession in an Ark, a domed world created to protect these people. Ask students to speculate about some of the questions Hughes raises. For example, "When in an isolated situation such as the Arks, will people progress to higher levels of development or revert to a savage state? What environments, circumstances, and experiences might cause these reactions?" Another challenge from this book: "What would the Arks be like if each one were planned by different colleges on a university campus? How would they be different from each other 150 years after their development? Remember, none of the residents have interacted with anyone from the outside world. They brought with them their specified knowledge, their interests, and their abilities." Encourage students to choose a specific university college and speculate about what their world would look like if they were isolated from people with other interests for 150 years. Encourage students to write their own science fiction stories based on such circumstances and to draw an Ark that specific professional people might create.

3. Accepting those who are different: Hughes' *The Keeper of the Isis Light;* Key's *Escape To Witch Mountain;* and L'Engle's *A Wrinkle in Time.*
   a. Ask the students to speculate about one of the most important issues presented in these books. "How should people deal with those who are different? What could happen if society does not emphasize fellowship and love? Why are people who differ from those around them often misunderstood, feared, and even hated? How would interactions with people from other worlds be possible if people misunderstand, fear, and hate those who are different? Do such misunderstandings happen in our own world? How can people prevent such misunderstandings?"
   b. Ask the students to trace the conflicts and themes developed in one of the books. How did the author make them believe that these conflicts and themes are important?
   c. The main character in *The Keeper of the Isis Light* lives because she has physical adaptations that make it possible for her to survive on a harsh planet. The new people coming to the planet do not accept her because of these physical adaptations. As part of a science assignment, ask students to investigate the environmental characteristics of one of the known planets. Then ask them to create the physical adaptations that would allow a human to live on that planet. Now ask them to consider whether people would accept those differences. What would they need to do to remove the fear or mistrust from this experience?
   d. Students frequently have personal responses to the misunderstandings, fears, and hatred expressed toward the main characters in these books. Encourage the students to pretend they are one of these characters. How would they respond if they were Charles Wallace, whom people fear because he can communicate without speaking? How would they respond if they were the two alien children in *Escape to Witch Mountain* and criminals were trying to capture them to use their special powers? How would they respond if they were feared because they looked different from the new residents?

4. Environmental destruction influences a future earth or other planet: Hamilton's *Dustland* and *Justice and Her Brothers;* Hughes' *Ring-Rise Ring-Set;* and Snyder's *Below the Root.*
   a. This portion of the unit can be related closely to issues of ecology, pollution, and environmental destruction as the result of war. Ask students to search scientific journals, newspapers, and books to identify possible environmental problems that could influence Earth. What would happen to Earth if these problems are not resolved? What might happen to the people after environmental destruction? Ask the students to research ways that these environmental disasters could be prevented.
   b. Ask the students to trace the conflicts and themes in one of the books. Are there any parallels between these conflicts and themes and happenings in the world today? If so, what are they?
   c. Have students choose an environmental problem that could cause massive changes to human, animal, or plant life. Research how this problem might influence life and write a science fiction story that accounts for such changes.

d. Ask the students to pretend they are living in the world described in one of these books. Ask them to respond to the environment and the consequences of certain actions.

INDEPENDENT PROJECTS AND OTHER ACTIVITIES WITH THE SCIENCE FICTION UNIT

Artistic and architectural projects: Science fiction stories such as *Away Is A Strange Place To Be* often describe whole cities that are created on distant planets. Encourage the students to create their own model cities. Have them research known design possibilities and use their imaginations to develop a model of a futuristic city. They should consider such items as energy-efficient buildings, effective transportation systems, climate control that overcomes environmental problems, water and sanitation plants, homes with the latest technology, and recreational and cultural facilities.

Library resarch: Challenge the students to locate a planet or other celestial body that might support life if a controlled environment could be created. What factors would they need to overcome to support a colony?

Creative writing: In *A Wrinkle in Time* the characters tesseract—travel in the fifth dimension. The five dimensions are described as (1) a line, (2) a flat square, (3) a cube, (4) time, and (5) the square of time, a tesseract in which people can travel through space without going the long way around. Encourage students to write their own science fiction stories in which the characters have the ability to tesseract through space.

Create a spaceship: Travelers in science fiction often visit far distant galaxies in spaceships. Ask the students to draw or construct a model of a spaceship of the future. Ask them to compare their ship with the spaceships of today.

Library research: Encourage students to conduct library research on one of the early authors of science fiction such as Jules Verne or H. G. Wells. Why did these authors write science fiction? What topics and themes did they include in their books? How did they visualize the world of the future?

Comparing science fiction in films and books: Ask the students to compare the settings, plots, characters, and themes in a science fiction film with those of a science fiction book that covers similar content such as space travel or space colonization. What are the differences and similarities? How is believable science fiction developed in a film? How is believable science fiction developed in a book? What are the advantages of each form?

Develop a museum: Space travelers and colonists to distant planets might never return to Earth. Encourage the students to design and develop a museum that includes important elements they would want to remember from their Earth culture—for example, art, literature, history, scientific knowledge, geographical information, music, dance, films, theater, and architectural designs. Tell the students to select carefully because these examples might be the only way their children will learn about Earth.

UNIT THREE: Tracing Important Motifs Between Norse Legend and Mythology and Tolkien's Modern Fantasy in Upper Elementary and Middle School

OBJECTIVES

To read and enjoy high fantasy.

To develop an understanding that high-fantasy authors can develop their stories on mythological foundations.

To develop an understanding and appreciation of the important motifs in both Norse mythology and Tolkien's high fantasy.

To respond to the mythological foundations in high fantasy.

To take part in an independent study that traces the Arthurian legend in Susan Cooper's work.

CORE BOOKS: Several books can be used to identify important motifs in Norse mythology: Padraic Colum's *The Children of Odin;* Michael Harrison's *The Curse of the Ring;* Kevin Crossley-Holland's *The Faber Book of Northern Legends,* and *The Norse Myths;* J. R. R. Tolkien's *The Hobbit* (Touchstone), *The Lord of the Rings* trilogy, and *The Silmarillion. The Children of Odin, The Curse of the Ring,* and *The Hobbitt* (especially the illustrated versions) are considered easier literature than the others but still appropriate for higher grades.

EXTENDED BOOKS FOR INDEPENDENT READING AND OTHER ASSIGNMENTS: After students have completed a study of the mythological foundations in Tolkien's work, they can—in groups or independently—identify and analyze the Arthurian and Welsh legends in Susan Cooper's series *The Dark is Rising.* For this activity they will need several Arthurian legends and Cooper's *The Dark Is Rising* (Newbery Honor), *Greenwitch, The Grey King* (Newbery Medal), *Over Sea, Under Stone,* and *Silver on the Tree.* The reference book *Legends of the World,* edited by Richard Cavendish (1982), provides considerable background for this type of study.

PROCEDURES: Begin by reading and discussing one of the books of Norse mythology. Ask the students to identify important motifs or concepts found continually in the mythology. List the motifs as they are identified and then ask students to find examples of the motifs as they read the text. Students should be able to defend why they believe something is a motif and why a specific example should be placed under that motif.

Next, have them read and discuss one of Tolkien's texts. They should try to identify some of the same motifs and examples. After they complete this task, ask them to evaluate the role of Norse mythology in Tolkien's high fantasy. A group of middle school students found the following motifs and examples in Colum's *The Children of Odin.* Then they did the same with Tolkien's *The Hobbit.* Figure 11.3 shows a few examples of this comparison.

Students can make similar comparisons between Arthurian and Welsh legends and the legendary elements in *The Dark Is Rising* series. This comparison can be accomplished as an independent study or as a class activity. After students are familiar with Arthurian and Welsh legends, teachers can choose to divide the class into research groups according to each of the books in Cooper's series.

Some of the legendary elements in Cooper's work include the following:

1. In *Over Sea, Under Stone* Merrian is also Merlin of Arthurian and Welsh legend. He is introduced as a man of power, a legendary magician who suspends the laws of nature.

2. In *The Dark Is Rising* the prediction that the dark is rising is presented in the form of a poem; the hero is the seventh son of a seventh son; Merrian, like Merlin, can change shapes, create illusions, and see into the past and the future. Merlin, considered a prophet in Welsh tradition, is linked with Arthur.

3. In *The Grey King* the name of Arthur's hound, Cadall, is also the name of Arthur's son's dog and Arthur and his army sleep in a cave in Snowdonia until they are called in time of need. This is closely related to a Welsh legend that suggests that King

FIGURE 11.3 Comparison of motifs in Norse mythology and *The Hobbit*.

Common Motif	The Children of Odin	The Hobbit
1. Battle between good and evil to control humanity.	Battle between gods and giants.	Goblins vs. dwarfs
	Loki's betrayal of gods.	Bilbo vs. Gollum
		Bilbo vs. Smaug
		Smaug vs. Lake Men
		Battle of the Five Armies
	Evil forces lie to the East.	Evil forces lie to the East
	Evil forces are below the surface of the earth and good forces are above.	Goblins and Smaug live inside mountain.
	Wolves devour the sun and moon.	Threat of evil wolves
2. A dragon must be slain.	Dragon hoards treasure.	Smaug steals and hoards treasure
	Fafnir killed by sword with magical properties.	Smaug kills people
		Smaug killed by special arrow
	Fafnir killed by Sigurd, the greatest of heroes.	Smaug killed by greatest of Lake Men
3. The Ring is a symbol of power.	Engraved with runes, power of ancient written language	Ring gives power of invisibility.
		Ring changes personality of those who wear it
	Might possess soul of owner.	Bilbo and Gollum both want ring
	Sign of royalty	Dwarfs escape palace in barrels
	Symbolic circles	Circle of spider webs
4. Verbal contracts must be kept.	Sworn brotherhood	Bilbo makes contract with Gandalf to act as burglar
		Brotherhood between dwarfs
	Freya breaks promise to her husband and he leaves her	Gollum tries to break promise to Bilbo; Bilbo leaves Gollum
	Oath broken to giant who built Asgard's wall leads to downfall of the gods	Thorin's broken promise to Bilbo leads to Thorin's downfall
	Loki has to compensate Hreidmar for death of his son	The dwarfs have to compensate the lake people with treasure
5. Heroes make personal sacrifices for community	Odin sacrifices his eye to gain knowledge	Bilbo sacrifices his part of treasure to end fight and stop killing
	Sigmund sacrifices for honor	Bilbo sacrifices his way of life for adventure with dwarfs
6. The remote past was a golden age	Gods protected men	Gandalf protected dwarfs
	Aesthetic beauty of Asgard	Aesthetic beauty of Middle Earth
	Interactions between humans and gods	Interactions between humans and supernatural beings
		Birds and animals interacted with humans and dwarfs
	Transformations were possible	Transformations were possible
	Longevity for all	Longevity for all

Arthur was killed at Bwlch y Seathau (Pass of Arrows) in Snowdonia and buried at Carnedd (Cairn). According to this legend, Arthur and his army sleep in Ogof Llanciau Eryri (the Cave of the Young Men of Snowdonia).

4. *Silver on the Tree* contains references to Roman buildings as does Welsh legend; Arthur's sword and his ship Prydwen play important roles; the isle contains a house of glass where treasures of great power are kept; there is a lost land and City of Golden Island that has a magnificent palace with crystal walls; the Messianic Arthur rises when the need is greatest in the battle against evil; and a prophetic poem is used. References to the Messianic Arthur are popular in legend. In fact, one legend claims that his tomb contains the words: HIC IACET ARTHURUS REX QUODAM REXQUE FUTURUS ("Here lies Arthur, King once and King to be"). The relationships between Merlin and Arthur also are well developed in legend. Welsh sources claim that Merlin had a house of glass on the Isle of Bardsey and that he took to this isle the Thirteen Treasures of the Island of Britain. Important treasures or objects of power are important in *The Dark Is Rising* series. Legend also suggests that a drowned city lies beneath Cardigan Bay. Its ruler was entrusted with the care of the dykes to protect the kingdom, but he neglected his duties and a sudden rush of sea water drowned the land. A lost land and City of Golden Island are also important in Cooper's works.

INDEPENDENT PROJECTS AND OTHER ACTIVITIES WITH THE HIGH FANTASY UNIT

Library research: Ask the students to research a topic related to the mythological and legendary foundations of high fantasy. For example, they might choose to trace the importance of Merlin in both legend and fantasy. Or they might focus on objects of power and investigate their importance in high fantasy and legend.

Creative writing: Inspiration for the plots and characters in high fantasy can come from brief references in legends and myths. For example, when Lloyd Alexander was studying the Mabinogion, a collection of traditional Welsh legends, he was intrigued by the following quote: "And therefore, Amathaon ab Don, and Arawn, King of Annwn fought. And there was a man in that battle, unless his name were known he could not be overcome; and there was on the other side a woman called Achren, and unless her name were known her party would not be overcome. And Gwydion ab Don guessed the name of the man" (Tunnell and Jacobs, 1988). From this and additional research Alexander discovered the characters of Gwydion Son of Don, Arawn Death-Lord of Annuvin, Dallben the enchanter, and Hen Wen the oracular pig. He then created the immense battle between good and evil that is fought in the series "The Prydain Chronicles." Encourage the students to search for such intriguing characters or plot ideas. Ask them to write a fantasy around one of these characters or plot ideas. For example, what might happen if people had secret names? How would they try to retain their secret? What powers would they have because of their secret names?

Creative writing: Ask students to read several traditional folktales, legends, or myths from any culture and use ideas gained from the folklore to write a high fantasy. Pat O'Shea, for example, built *The Hounds of the Morrigan* on the foundations of Irish mythology and folktales. Ask the students to set their stories in the culture of the folklore they choose and to use characters that would be found in the folklore. They also can illustrate their stories to reflect the cultural settings.

Geography, social studies, and history: Ask the students to analyze the settings in the high fantasy of Tolkien or Cooper. Ask them to compare characteristics of the settings in the original myths or legends with the settings in the high fantasies. What are the similarities in such areas as climate, land formations, and seasons? What are the differences? Do any places in the world as we know it have these characteristics? Where are they located? Ask the students to analyze other cultural components and historical references. What similarities can be found in social structures and in other historical documentations? For example, students might investigate the historical references in both the Arthurian legends and in Cooper's high fantasies. Is there a basis on fact in either source? If there is, what information is factual?

Individual response: Ask the students to select a high fantasy character: on either the side of good or the side of evil. Ask the students to write a personal response to that character and that character's actions. Some students might prefer to choose opposing forces in the book and to respond to each of these characters. Ask them to cite specific examples that caused them to respond in certain ways. Ask them to consider what the author did to evoke those responses.

Individual response: Ask the students to consider the important themes and purposes in high fantasy. For example, these stories frequently develop themes around the constant battle between good and evil and the need to sacrifice for the common good. Ask the students to consider whether those themes are still important in the world of today. Ask them to write a personal response to the themes in a high fantasy. Through their personal responses they should consider whether the themes are important to them today.

REFERENCES

Cavendish, R. (Ed.)(1982). *Legends of the world.* New York: Schocken.

Children's Literature Association. (1985). *Touchstones: A list of distinguished children's books.* Lafayette, IN: Purdue University.

Egoff, Sheila. (1988). *Worlds within: Children's fantasy from the Middle Ages to today.* Chicago: American Library Association.

Norton, D. (1989). *The effective teaching of language arts.* Columbus: Merrill.

Swanton, S. (1984). Minds alive: What and why gifted students read for pleasure. *School Library Journal, 30,* 99–102.

Tunnell, M. O. & Jacobs, J. S. (1988). Alexander's chronicle of Prydain: Twenty years later. *School Library Journal, 34,* 27–31.

CHILDREN'S LITERATURE REFERENCES*

Alexander, Lloyd. *The Book of Three.* Orlando: Holt, Rinehart & Winston, 1964 (I: 10+).

Andersen, Hans Christian. *Hans Christian Andersen Eighty Fairy Tales.* New York: Pantheon, 1976, 1982 (I: all).

*I = Interest by age range

Anderson, Margaret. *In the Keep of Time.* New York: Knopf, 1977 (I: 9+).

Baker, Keith. *The Magic Fan.* San Diego: Harcourt Brace Jovanovich, 1989 (I: all).

Barber, Antonia. *The Enchanter's Daughter.* Illustrated by Errol Le Cain. New York: Farrar, Straus & Giroux, 1987 (I: all).

Carroll, Lewis. *Alice's Adventures in Wonderland.* Illustrated by John Tenniel. New York: Macmillan, 1866, 1984 (I: all).

_____. *Through the Looking Glass.* Illustrated by John Tenniel. New York: Macmillan, 1872, 1984 (I: 8+).

Christopher, John. *The City of Gold and Lead.* New York: Macmillan, 1967 (I: 10+).

_____. *The Pool of Fire.* New York: Macmillan, 1968 (I: 10+).

_____. *The White Mountains.* New York: Macmillan, 1967 (I: 10+).

Colum, Padraic. *The Children of Odin.* Illustrated by Willy Pogany. New York: Macmillan, 1920, 1948 (I: 9+). (Folklore)

Cooper, Susan. *The Dark Is Rising.* New York: Atheneum, 1973 (I: 10+).

_____. *Greenwitch.* New York: Atheneum, 1973 (I: 10+).

_____. *The Grey King.* New York: Atheneum, 1975 (I: 10+).

_____. *Over Sea, Under Stone.* Orlando: Harcourt Brace Jovanovich, 1965 (I: 10+).

_____. *Silver on the Tree.* New York: Atheneum, 1977, 1980 (I: 10+).

CROSSLEY-HOLLAND, KEVIN, edited by. *The Faber Book of Northern Legends.* (Folklore). Illustrated by Allan Howard. Boston: Faber and Faber, 1977, 1983 (I: 9+).

_____, retold by. *The Norse Myths.* (Folklore). New York: Pantheon, 1980 (I: 12+).

DAHL, ROALD. *James and the Giant Peach.* Illustrated by Nancy Ekholm Burkert. New York: Knopf, 1961 (I: 7–11).

DICKINSON, PETER. *Eva.* New York: Delacorte, 1989 (I: 10+).

_____. *The Weathermonger.* New York: Puffin, 1970.

GODDEN, RUMER. *The Dolls' House.* Illustrated by Tasha Tudor. New York: Viking, 1947, 1962 (I: 6–10).

GRAHAME, KENNETH. *The Wind in the Willows.* Illustrated by E. H. Shepard. New York: Scribner's, 1908, 1940 (I: 7–12).

HADITHI, MWENYE. *Greedy Zebra.* Illustrated by Adrienne Kennaway. Boston: Little, Brown, 1984 (I: 3–8).

HAMILTON, VIRGINIA. *Dustland.* New York: Greenwillow, 1980 (I: 10+).

_____. *The Gathering.* New York: Greenwillow, 1981 (I: 10+).

_____. *Justice and Her Brothers.* New York: Greenwillow, 1978 (I: 10+).

HARRISON, MICHAEL. *The Curse of the Ring.* (Folklore). Illustrated by Tudor Humphries. New York: Oxford, 1977 (I: 8+).

HOOVER, H. M. *Away Is A Strange Place To Be.* New York: Dutton, 1990 (I: 9–12).

HUGHES, MONICA. *Devil on My Back.* New York: Atheneum, 1985 (I: 9+).

_____. *The Dream Catcher.* New York: Atheneum, 1987 (I: 9+).

_____. *The Guardian of Isis.* New York: Atheneum, 1984 (I: 9+).

_____. *The Isis Pedlar.* New York: Atheneum, 1983 (I: 9+).

_____. *The Keeper of the Isis Light.* New York: Atheneum, 1984 (I: 9+).

_____. *Ring-Rise Ring-Set.* New York: Watts, 1982 (I: 9+).

KEATS, EZRA JACK. *The Trip.* New York: Greenwillow, 1978 (I: 3–8).

KEY, ALEXANDER. *Escape to Witch Mountain.* Illustrated by Leon Wisdom. Westminster, 1988 (I: 8–12).

KIMMEL, ERIC. *Hershel and the Hanukkah Goblins.* Illustrated by Trina Schart Hyman. New York: Holiday, 1989 (I: all).

KIPLING, RUDYARD. *Just So Stories.* New York: Doubleday, 1902, 1952 (I: 5–7).

_____. *The Jungle Book.* New York: Doubleday, 1894, 1964 (I: 8–12).

LAWSON, ROBERT. *Rabbit Hill.* New York: Viking, 1944 (I: 7–11).

LEGUIN, URSULA. *Catwings.* Illustrated by S. D. Schindler. New York: Watts, 1988 (I: 3–8).

L'ENGLE, MADELEINE. *A Swiftly Tilting Planet.* New York: Farrar, Straus & Giroux, 1978 (I: 9+).

_____. *A Wind in the Door.* New York: Farrar, Straus & Giroux, 1973 (I: 9+).

_____. *A Wrinkle in Time.* New York: Farrar, Straus & Giroux, 1962 (I: 9+).

LEWIS, C. S. *The Lion, the Witch and the Wardrobe.* Illustrated by Pauline Baynes. New York: Macmillan, 1950 (I: 9+).

LIONNI, LEO. *Alexander and the Wind-Up Mouse.* New York: Pantheon, 1969 (I: 3–6).

_____. *Swimmy.* New York: Pantheon, 1963 (I: 2–6).

LUNN, JANET. *The Root Cellar.* New York: Scribner's, 1983 (I: 10+).

MACAULAY, DAVID. *Black and White.* Boston: Houghton Mifflin, 1990 (I: all).

McCULLY, EMILY ARNOLD. *School.* New York: Harper & Row, 1987 (I: 3–8).

McKISSACK, PATRICIA C. *Mirandy and Brother Wind.* Illustrated by Jerry Pinkney. New York: Knopf, 1988 (I: all).

MILNE, A. A. *Winnie-The-Pooh.* Illustrated by Ernest H. Shepard. New York: Dutton, 1926, 1954 (I: 6–10).

NESBIT, E. *Melisande.* Illustrated by Patrick Lynch. San Diego: Harcourt Brace Jovanovich, 1989 (I: 7+).

NIXON, JOAN LOWERY. *Whispers from the Dead.* New York: Delacorte, 1989 (I: 10+).

NORTON, MARY. *The Borrowers.* Illustrated by Beth and Joe Krush. Orlando: Harcourt Brace Jovanovich, 1952 (I: 7–11).

O'SHEA, PAT. *The Hounds of the Morrigan.* New York: Holiday, 1986 (I: 10+).

PEARCE, PHILIPPA. *Tom's Midnight Garden.* New York: Lippincott, 1958 (I: 8–12).

POTTER, BEATRIX. *The Complete Tales of Beatrix Potter.* New York: Viking Penguin, 1989 (originals 1902–1930) (I: 5–9).

_____. *The Tale of Peter Rabbit.* New York: Warne, 1902 (I: 3–9).

SANDBURG, CARL. *Rootabaga Stories.* Illustrated by Maud and Miska Petersham. Orlando: Harcourt Brace Jovanovich, 1922, 1988 (I: 8–11).

SELDEN, GEORGE. *The Cricket in Times Square.* Illustrated by Garth Williams. New York: Farrar, Straus & Giroux, 1960 (I: 7–11).

SENDAK, MAURICE. *Where the Wild Things Are*. New York: Harper & Row, 1963 (I: 4–8).

SNYDER, ZILPHA KEATLEY. *Below the Root*. Illustrated by Alton Raible. New York: Atheneum, 1975 (I: 9+).

STEIG, WILLIAM. *Abel's Island*. New York: Farrar, Straus & Giroux, 1976, 1980 (I: 7–10).

TOLKIEN, J. R. R. *The Hobbit*. Boston: Houghton Mifflin, 1938 (I: 9–12).

_____. *The Lord of the Rings*. Boston: Houghton Mifflin, 1974 (I: 12+).

_____. *The Silmarillion*. Boston: Allen and Unwin, 1977, 1919 (Adult Source).

VAN ALLSBURG, CHRIS. *The Garden of Abdul Gasazi*. Boston: Houghton Mifflin, 1979 (I: 5–8).

_____. *Jumanji*. Boston: Houghton Mifflin, 1981 (I: 5–8).

_____. *The Mysteries of Harris Burdick*. Boston: Houghton Mifflin, 1984 (I: all).

_____. *The Polar Express*. Boston: Houghton Mifflin, 1985 (I: all).

_____. *The Wreck of the Zephyr*. Boston: Houghton Mifflin, 1983 (I: 5–8).

WALTER, MILDRED PITTS. *Brother to the Wind*. Illustrated by Diane and Leo Dillon. New York: Lothrop, Lee & Shepard, 1985 (I: all).

WHITE, E. B. *Charlotte's Web*. Illustrated by Garth Williams. New York: Harper & Row, 1952 (I: 7–12).

WIESNER, DAVID. *Free Fall*. New York: Lothrop, Lee & Shepard, 1988 (I: all).

WILLIAMS, MARGERY. *The Velveteen Rabbit: Or, How Toys Became Real*. Illustrated by William Nicholson. New York: Doubleday, 1958 (I: 6–9).

WOOD, AUDREY. *King Bidgood's in the Bathtub*. Illustrated by Don Wood. San Diego: Harcourt Brace Jovanovich, 1985 (I: 6–9).

YOLEN, JANE. *The Faery Flag: Stories and Poems of Fantasy and the Supernatural*. New York: Watts, 1989 (I: 7–10).

_____. *The Girl Who Cried Flowers*. Illustrated by David Palladini. New York: Crowell, 1974 (I: 7–10).

_____. *The Hundredth Dove and other Tales*. Illustrated by David Palladini. New York: Crowell, 1977 (I: 7–10).

YORINKS, ARTHUR. *Hey, Al*. Illustrated by Richard Egielski. New York: Farrar, Straus & Giroux, 1986 (I: all).

CHAPTER 12

POETRY

DEVELOPING UNDERSTANDINGS OF POETRY
  Approaches that Develop Understanding and Appreciation of Poetry
  Core Books and Sample Lessons for Developing Understanding and Appreciation
  of Poetry

Poetry is one of the more personal genres of literature for both the poet and the reader. Although the words are arranged in special forms, poetry has a touch of magic that lets carefully chosen words and sounds paint vivid pictures and allows the reader to hear, see, feel, and experience the world in new ways. Poets reveal their deep appreciation of the genre whenever they discuss their work or the work of others.

Janeczko (1990) shares the personal responses of poets Eve Merriam and Karla Kuskin. Merriam states, "Writing poetry is where my heart is," and describes her own experiences with and responses to poetry: "I devoured poetry of all kinds. . . . Sounds of words were enthralling: I was captivated by their musicality, and by the fact that you could have alliteration, so that if you said, 'Peter, Peter, Pumpkin Eater,' it was very funny. Or if you recited 'The Highwayman came riding, riding up to the old inn door,' it was exciting; you could hear a whole orchestra in your voice" (p. 65). Perhaps it is not surprising that Merriam's only rule for reading poetry is, "Please read a poem OUT LOUD" (p. 66).

Kuskin also discusses the importance of emphasizing sounds and rhythm when she writes poetry. She compares her points of view when she writes prose and when she writes poetry: "Writing prose makes me listen for stories. But if I am writing poetry I concentrate more on the rhythms and sounds of words, and on the details. The smallest observation can be the start of a poem" (p. 138).

The comments of both poets can guide teachers who are developing experiences around poetry. Students need many opportunities to listen to poetry and share their responses. They need to hear poetry read aloud, to read poetry aloud themselves, and to write poetry so they can have exciting experiences with words and sounds. The activities also should encourage students to discover rhythms and sounds in poetry and to see, hear, and feel the rhythms, sounds, and details in new ways. In this chapter we will emphasize several different activities that encourage students to interact with and respond to poetry. Some of these activities develop listening and appreciative abilities, some develop awareness and observational powers, and others develop creative writing abilities.

DEVELOPING UNDERSTANDINGS OF POETRY

The important understandings listed below suggest many enjoyable instructional possibilities:

1. Poetry is a personal form of literature that allows poets and readers to experience, see, hear, and feel the world in new ways. Students need many opportunities to experience and respond to different types of poetry. Personal emotional and physical reactions to poetry should be encouraged. Poetry should be shared for personal enjoyment.

2. Carefully selected words are important in poetry. Poets create pictures with words as artists create pictures with paints. These images allow readers to respond to the poetry.

3. Sound patterns also are important. Poems for young children should emphasize the sounds of language and encourage play with words. Students should have many opportunities to respond to such sound patterns as rhythm, rhyme, alliteration, assonance, and onomatopoeia.

4. The shape of a poem—the way the words are arranged on the page—can enhance meaning and create a significant visual effect.

5. Poetry has many different forms, such as lyric poetry, narrative poetry, ballads, limericks, concrete poems, free verse, and haiku. Students need opportunities to share different types of poetry and to understand that not all poetry has to rhyme.

6. Poetry selections need to be read several times. The reader can get something different out of the poem and develop new insights with each reading.

7. Students should have opportunities to write their own poetry, to expand their awareness and observational powers through writing. Reading and responding to good poetry is considered one of the best ways to stimulate poetry writing.

8. Teachers need to stimulate an interest in and a love for poetry by sharing many examples and allowing students to interact with poetry.

Approaches that Develop Understanding and Appreciation of Poetry

The approaches developed in this section will emphasize developing a love for poetry through such activities as listening to poetry, responding to rhythm and sounds, developing choral arrangements, and writing poetry. This section lists lessons developed around poetry in previous chapters and identifies the approaches that will be developed in this chapter:

1. Emphasizing repetitive language and descriptive words when reading rhymes aloud. (Ch. 3, Rosen's *We're Going on a Bear Hunt,* Rounds' *Old MacDonald Had a Farm* and *I Know An Old Lady Who Swallowed A Fly,* and Prelutsky's *Read-Aloud Rhymes for the Very Young.*)

2. Writing poetry that reflects characters, incidents, or themes in books. (Ch. 3, writing a cinquain, writing a diamante.)

3. Responding to moods in poetic texts and illustrations. (Ch. 7, Lindgren's *The Wild Baby Goes to Sea,* Merriam's *Halloween ABC,* Scheer's *Rain Makes Applesauce,* Lear and Nash's *The Scroobious Pip,* and Noyes's *The Highwayman.*)

4. Extending enjoyment of poetry through music. (Ch. 7, Crane's *The Baby's Opera,* Fox's *Go In and Out the Window: An Illustrated Songbook for Young People,* and Mahy's *17 Kings and 42 Elephants.*)

5. Identifying traditional mythological themes in the poetry of Native American authors. (Ch. 8, Highwater's *Moonsong Lullaby.*)

6. Developing appreciation for nature in a poem through personification, imagery, rhythm, and alliteration. (Ch. 9, Longfellow's *Hiawatha* and *Hiawatha's Childhood.*)

7. Developing appreciation for and understanding of point of view in poetry.

8. Listening to numerous examples of poetry.

9. Responding personally to the language and images in poetry.

10. Moving to the rhythms and sounds in poetry.

11. Dramatizing poetry.

12. Developing choral arrangements with poetry.

13. Developing an understanding of a poet by writing a biography of the poet using poetry as source material.

Many of these activities do not need to be developed as units or instructional activities—teachers simply can use them to share poetry with their students and let their students respond. The teacher's love of poetry is one of the best motivators for developing students' appreciation for poetry. Teachers also should use examples of poetry that fit particular occasions. For example, poems that express reactions to a beautiful spring day or to the first snowfall in winter, that explore moods on a dark rainy day, that tell about holidays, and that express feelings about birthdays and growing up.

Core Books and Sample Lessons For Developing Understanding and Appreciation of Poetry

The following core lessons can be used independently or as part of a unit. The lessons can be used at different grade levels depending on the poetry chosen.

LESSON ONE: Developing Understandings About What Poetry Is and How to Read Poetry

OBJECTIVES

To provide a personal definition for poetry.

To develop guidelines that will increase understandings and personal responses when reading poetry.

To stimulate the enjoyment of poetry through oral reading and listening experiences.

CORE BOOKS (these also can be used for extended reading and other independent reading activities): Eve Merriam's "How to Eat a Poem" and Naoshi Koriyama's "Unfolding Bud," in Stephen Dunning, Edward Lueders, and Hugh Smith's *Reflections on a Gift of Watermelon Pickle . . . and other Modern Verse* (Touchstone). Anthologies of poetry for lower to middle elementary students: Jack Prelutsky's *Read-Aloud Rhymes for the Very Young* and *The*

Random House Book of Poetry For Children. Anthologies for upper elementary and middle school students: Dunning, Lueders, and Smith's *Reflections on a Gift of Watermelon Pickle . . . and other Modern Verse*.

PROCEDURES: Begin this lesson by asking students, "What is poetry? When we say the word *poetry* what does it mean to you?" List the definitions offered by the students. (The definitions might differ depending on the students' positive or negative experiences with poetry. If they have negative comments, you might share some of the comments by and about poets in Janeczko's *The Place My Words Are Looking For* (1990) and Hopkins' *Pass the Poetry, Please!* (1987) Next read several poems from the anthologies. Encourage students to respond personally to the poems and to add to their definitions of *poetry*. They also might try to predict what definition one of the poets would give for poetry. Be sure the students note such characteristics of poetry as rhythm, vivid language, and imagery.

Next, tell the students that they will be listening to a poem that tells them how a poet thinks they should read and respond to a poem. Read Merriam's "How to Eat a Poem." Ask the students to respond to the visual images that Merriam presents. Ask, "What do you think she is telling us about how we should read a poem? How would her advice change the way you approach a poem? Do you think it is good advice? Why or why not?"

Next, read Koriyama's "Unfolding Bud." Ask the students to respond to the poet's viewpoint of poetry. "Why do you think the poet compares a poem to a flower bud? How does the bud change each time we look at it? What do you think the poet is telling us about how we should read a poem? Do you think it is good advice? Why or why not?"

After sharing and discussing numerous poems, ask the students to develop their own list of guidelines about how they think they should read poetry. The following list was developed with a group of fifth-grade students:

1. I should approach the poem as if I am experiencing a new adventure.
2. I should read the poem aloud several times to feel the language and to experience the rhythm of the sound patterns. I should notice how the rhythm makes me feel.
3. I should enjoy the magic of well-chosen words and try to see the world in a new way. I should close my eyes and picture the images.
4. I should decide for myself what the poem is saying to me.
5. I should think about how I responded to the poem. I should decide what the poet did to try to make me respond in a certain way, and if I thought the poet was successful.

Allow the students to try their guidelines for reading poetry by reading many more poetry selections. Ask the students to evaluate the effectiveness of their guidelines and to change their guidelines if necessary.

LESSON TWO: Differentiating Between Prose and Poetry

OBJECTIVES

To develop an understanding that prose and poetry are different forms of literature.

To use poetry to write prose.

To use prose to write poetry.

CORE BOOKS: (these also can be used for extended reading and other independent reading activities): Arnold Lobel's *The Random House Book of Mother Goose*, L. Frank Baum's *Mother Goose in Prose*, Tom Paxton's *Aesop's Fables* (retold in verse) and *Belling the Cat and Other Aesop's Fables* (retold in verse), and collections of Aesop's Fables told in prose.

PROCEDURES: Begin the lesson by reading several of the Mother Goose selections aloud. Ask the students to notice in what form the selections are written. Encourage them to notice that they are written as poetry and that many of them have poetic characteristics such as rhythm, rhyme, and alliteration. They also are written in lines and verses. Next, select a story from *Mother Goose in Prose* that was read earlier as a rhyme, such as "Little Bo-Peep," "The Cat and the Fiddle," or "Old King Cole." Ask the students to notice the characteristics of the prose forms of the stories. They should notice that the prose forms have the structure and characteristics of a story. Encourage the students to comment on the differences between poetry and prose. Ask, "Which form requires the most careful selection of single words? Which form relies more on the sounds of the language? Which form has a more detailed setting and plot? What are the advantages of each form of literature?"

After students have discussed the characteristics of and identified the advantages of each form of literature, allow them to use a prose story to form the ideas for a poem and to select a Mother Goose rhyme to turn into prose. Encourage the students to share their poetry and prose and to analyze some of the requirements for writing each type of literature.

Initiate a similar activity with the Aesop Fables. Read aloud the two retellings in verse form by Tom Paxton and several similar fables told through prose. Ask the students to compare the poetry and prose and to consider the advantages of each form. Then encourage them to choose an Aesop fable and retell it in poetry or to use the verse form and retell it as prose. Ask students to describe their thought processes as they approached each task.

LESSON THREE: Developing Personal Responses to Images, Language, and Feelings in Poetry

OBJECTIVES

To listen to poetry or read poetry orally and respond personally to it through art or journal entries.

To develop personal journals that include vivid language and appealing images.

CORE BOOKS (these also can be used for extended reading and other independent reading activities): Numerous poetry collections or anthologies. This lesson can be used at any grade level depending on the choices of literature. Lower and middle elementary students: Eric Carle's *Eric Carle's Animals Animals*, Eloise Greenfield's *Daydreamers* (Black); Nikki Grimes' *Something on My Mind* (Black); David McCord's *One At A Time* (Touchstone); and Shel Silverstein's *Where the Sidewalk Ends*. Upper elementary and middle school students: Sylvia Cassedy's *Roomrimes*; Richard J. Margolis' *Secrets of a Small Brother*; Cynthia Rylant's *Waiting to Waltz: A Childhood*; and Brenda Seabrooke's *Judy Scuppernong*. Both *Daydreamers* and *Something on My Mind* also can evoke interesting emotional responses with older students.

PROCEDURES: According to Rosenblatt (1980), students should have many opportunities to read poetry in which they focus on images, feelings, and ideas that give them the feeling that they have "lived through" the experience described in the poem. She maintains that teachers should encourage students to savor what they visualize, feel, think, and enjoy while hearing or reading poetry.

Encourage students to read orally, listen to, and read individually numerous poems. Allow them to select poems that are especially meaningful to them. Then have the students respond to the poems in which they particularly like the vivid images, the language, and the feelings. They can respond by drawing pictures of the images created by the poets' words or that reflect the emotions they felt in response to the poetry. Students can copy particularly responsive lines in their journals and identify how and why they responded to them. Older students in particular often share emotional responses if they have experienced feelings similar to those expressed by the poet. These emotional experiences can stimulate students to write their own poetry about their feelings.

LESSON FOUR: Moving to the Rhythms and Sounds of Poetry

OBJECTIVES

> To respond to the rhythms and sounds created by poetry.
>
> To feel the rhythm and sounds in poetry by becoming physically involved in the movement suggested by poetry.

CORE BOOKS (these also can be used for extended reading and other independent reading activities): This activity can be used with any grade level depending on the selection of poetry. Lower and middle elementary grades: Jump-rope rhymes, such as "Teddy Bear, Teddy Bear;" poems from Prelutsky's *Read-Aloud Rhymes for the Very Young,* such as Myra Cohn Livingston's "Just Watch" and Evelyn Beyer's "Jump or Jiggle;" and poems from Beatrice Schenk de Regniers' *Sing a Song of Popcorn,* such as Rhoda Bacmeister's "Galoshes," A. A. Milne's "The More It Snows," Robert Louis Stevenson's "The Swing," and Nancy Byrd Turner's "A Popcorn Song." Upper elementary and middle school students: Poems from Dunning, Lueders, and Smith's *Reflections on a Gift of Watermelon Pickle . . . and other Modern Verse* (Touchstone), such as Robert Hillyer's "Lullaby," Edwin A. Hoey's "Foul Shot," and Eve Merriam's "Cheers;" poems from Lillian Morrison's *Rhythm Road: Poems to Move To;* and poems from R. R. Knudson and May Swenson's *American Sports Poems.* Morrison's anthology contains poems appropriate for a wide range of students and can be used with all grades.

PROCEDURES: When working with younger students, begin this lesson with active poems such as jump-rope rhymes. Read the rhyme first, asking the students to listen to the rhythm and the sound of the rhyme. Then read the rhyme again, asking the students to join in with movement and words. Next, choose poems from the anthologies that encourage students to move in certain ways or to recreate the movements of animals, nature, or people. Read each poem several times while students feel the rhythm through their actions.

    With older students, teachers can begin this lesson by sharing and discussing some of Morrison's comments in the preface to *Rhythm Road: Poems to Move To.* For example, Morrison states the following:

> These poems are an invitation to what might be called a poetry workout. Reading them, we should be able to feel, in our pulse and in our muscles, the action described. Whether it is the twirl of a tarantella, the smooth glide of a Buick, the ticking of a watch, or the falling of a leaf, the poets have managed to suggest, and sometimes actually capture, the particular motion. They do this in many ways, not only by using accent, beat, and carefully placed pauses, and by controlling the speed, movement, and length of lines, but also by choosing and arranging their words and phrases so that the very sounds of the syllables resonate in us" (p. ix).

Select one of the poems in Morrison's anthology, read it orally, and ask the students to respond to the rhythm and the feelings of movement in the poem. Ask them to consider not only how they felt the movement but also what the poet did to make them feel that way. Then read the poem again and allow the students to move with the rhythm of the poem. This lesson can be repeated several times using different poetry selections.

LESSON FIVE: Dramatizing Poetry

OBJECTIVES

To encourage students to respond to the characters and situations in narrative poems.

To perform a dramatization motivated by poetry.

To write a sequel to a poem and perform the sequel.

CORE BOOKS (these also can be used for extended reading and other independent reading activities): A collection of narrative poems that can stimulate dramatization. This activity also can be used with any grade level depending on the narrative poems selected. Lower elementary grades: Edward Lear's *Hillary Knight's The Owl and the Pussy-Cat*; David McPhail's *The Dream Child*; Clement Moore's *The Night Before Christmas*; and Nancy Willard's *Night Story*. Middle and upper elementary students: Roy Gerrard's *Sir Cedric* and *Sir Francis Drake: His Daring Deeds*; Henry Wadsworth Longfellow's *Paul Revere's Ride*; and Nancy Willard's *The Voyage of the Ludgate Hill: Travels with Robert Louis Stevenson*. Upper elementary and middle school: Alfred Noyes' *The Highwayman* and Rudyard Kipling's *Gunga Din*.

PROCEDURES: Read one of the narrative poems orally to the students. Ask them to identify scenes that they would like to dramatize. They can use the scenes to stimulate additional ideas, create dialogue, and extend the story beyond what is developed in the narrative poem. For example, after reading McPhail's *The Dream Child* a group of first-grade students decided to dramatize the interactions between Dream Child and Tame Bear when the child teaches the frogs to hum, brings fruit to the hungry lion, visits Tame Bear's mother the queen, meets and tames the giants in the forest, and dances and makes friends with the apes. They first pantomimed the scenes as the teacher read the book aloud. They focused on the characterizations and actions of the various characters. Next, they thought of dialogue they could add during each of these interactions. Finally, they divided the class into groups according to scenes, improvised their scenes, and added dialogue they considered appropriate. They presented the dramatization several times so that students could try out different ideas and dialogues. Finally, they created a visit to the dream location for Dream Child and Tame Bear for the following night.

LESSON SIX: Choral Speaking Arrangements With Poetry

OBJECTIVES

To respond to poetry through an enjoyable group activity.

To interact with the rhythm and tempo in poetry through an oral presentation.

To experiment with choral speaking arrangements that heighten the enjoyment of a poem.

CORE BOOKS (these also can be used for extended reading and other independent reading activities): "The Yak," from Eric Carle's *Eric Carle's Animals Animals*; John Ciardi's *You Read to Me, Ill Read to You*; selections from Beatrice Schenk de Regniers' *Sing a Song of Popcorn*, such as "Arithmetic," "The Camel," "Four Seasons," "Five Little Squirrels," and "Who Has Seen the Wind?" Paul Fleischman's *I Am Phoenix: Poems for Two Voices* and *Joyful Noise: Poems for Two Voices* (Newbery Medal); David McCord's *One At A Time* (Touchstone); A. A. Milne's *When We Were Very Young*; Edward Lear's *Hillary Knight's The Owl and the Pussycat*; poems from Jack Prelutsky's *The Random House Book of Poetry for Children*, such as "Fog," and "The Myra Song"; Maurice Sendak's *Pierre: A Cautionary Tale*; and Robert Louis Stevenson's *A Child's Garden of Verses*.

PROCEDURES: Select poems that are appropriate for the grade level. For example, for students who cannot yet read, choose poems and rhymes that are simple enough to memorize. Poems and rhymes with refrains are especially appropriate for younger students because they can participate almost immediately in the activity. Allow students to help select and interpret the poetry. They should be allowed to experiment with different choral speaking arrangements and different combinations of voices. They also should have opportunities to be both performers and audience members.

Begin by allowing the students to explore the rhythm in poetry. For example, students can clap out fast and slow rhythms as the teacher reads the poems orally. Rhythm instruments can help students experiment with the rhythm and tempo in poetry such as David McCord's "The Pickety Fence," found in *One At A Time* and Robert Louis Stevenson's "From a Railway Carriage" found in *A Child's Garden of Verses*. (The movement activity described earlier is another way to introduce students to the importance of rhythm and tempo in poetry.)

Next, develop a series of experiences in which students can try out various types of choral arrangements before experimenting with their own interpretations. The following examples of arrangements are from *The Effective Teaching of Language Arts* (Norton, 1989):

1. *The refrain arrangement:* In this type of choral speaking, the teacher or a child reads or recites the body of a poem, and the rest of the class responds in unison with the refrain, or chorus. Three poems with refrains are *Pierre: A Cautionary Tale;* "The Wind," from *A Child's Garden of Verses;* and Jack Prelutsky's "The Yak," found in *Eric Carle's Animals, Animals.* The following example is based on the Mother Goose rhyme "A Jolly Old Pig."

Leader:	A jolly old pig once lived in a sty.
	And three little piggies had she,
	And she waddled about saying
Group:	"Grumph! grumph! grumph!"
Leader:	While the little ones said
Group:	"Wee! wee!"
Leader:	And she waddled about saying
Group:	"Grumph! grumph! grumph!"
Leader:	While the little ones said
Group:	"Wee! wee!"

2. *The line-a-child or line-a-group arrangement:* In this arrangement one child or a group of children reads one line, another child or group reads the next line, a third child or group reads the third line, and so forth. Poems that can be used for line arrangements are "Arithmetic," "Five Little Squirrels," "Four Seasons," from Beatrice Schenk de Regniers' *Sing a Song of Sixpence* and John Ciardi's "The Myra Song" from Jack Prelutsky's *The Random House Book of Poetry for Children*. This example is from the Mother Goose rhyme, "One, Two, Buckle My Shoe."

Group A:	One, two buckle my shoe
Group B:	Three, four, shut the door
Group C:	Five, six, pick up sticks
Group D:	Seven, eight, lay them straight
Group E:	Nine, ten, a good fat hen.

3. *Antiphonal or dialogue arrangements:* This involves alternate speaking by two groups. Boys' voices can be balanced against girls' voices, high voices against low voices, and so forth. Poems in which one line asks a question and the next answers it work well, such as Christina Rossetti's "Who Has Seen the Wind," in de Regniers' *Sing a Song*

of Popcorn; and A. A. Milne's "Puppy and I." Paul Fleischman's *I Am Phoenix: Poems for Two Voices* and *Joyful Noise: Poems for Two Voices* are especially good because the poems already are written in two parts. These poems are more complex, however, because the two voices frequently say different lines at the same time suggesting the sounds and movements of birds and insects. The following example is from the Mother Goose rhyme "Pussy-Cat, Pussy-Cat."

> **Group A:** Pussy-cat, Pussy-cat, where have you been?
> **Group B:** I've been to London to visit the Queen.
> **Group A:** Pussy-cat, Pussy-cat, what did you there?
> **Group B:** I frightened a little mouse under the chair.

4. *The cumulative arrangement:* This arrangement, also called the crescendo arrangement, is used when the poem builds to a climax. One group reads the first line, the first and second groups read the second line, and so forth, until the poem reaches its climax, at which time all the groups read together. Two examples of cumulative poems are *Hillary Knight's The Owl and the Pussy-Cat* and "Mummy Slept Late and Daddy Fixed Breakfast," from *You Read to Me, I'll Read to You.* Both of these examples can be read in a cumulative arrangement by six groups as the poems build to a climax. This example is from the Mother Goose rhyme "There Was a Crooked Man."

> **Group A:** There was a crooked man, and he went a crooked mile
> **Group A, B:** And he found a crooked sixpence against a crooked stile
> **Group A, B, C:** He bought a crooked cat, which caught a crooked mouse
> **Group A, B, C, D:** And they all lived together in a little crooked house.

5. *The unison arrangement:* In this arrangement, the entire group or class presents a whole selection together. This kind of presentation can be difficult because it often produces a sing-song effect. Good choices are shorter poems such as Sandburg's "Fog," in Prelutsky's *The Random House Book of Poetry for Children* or Ogden Nash's "The Camel" in de Regniers' *Sing a Song of Popcorn.* This arrangement of "A Big Black Cat" was written with the help of second-grade students:

> Whole Group: A big black cat walks down the street, meow, meow, meow.
> A big black cat with a long black tail, meow, meow, meow.
> He growls.
> He spats.
> He arches his back.
> The big black cat walks down the street, meow, meow, meow.

Older students also can experiment with the effects of grouping light, medium, and dark voices to add interest to poetry and literature interpretations. The following is one interpretation of "From a Railway Carriage," from *A Child's Garden of Verses:*

> High voice: Faster than fairies, faster than witches
> Medium voice: Bridges and houses, hedges and ditches
> Low voice: And charging along like troops in a battle
> Medium voice: All through the meadows the horses and cattle;
> All of the sights of the hill and the plain
> Low voice: Fly as thick as driving rain
> High voice: And ever again, in the wink of an eye, Painted stations whistle by.
> Medium voice: Here is a child who clambers and scrambles
> Low voice: All by himself and gathering brambles
> Medium voice: Here is a tramp who stands and gazes
> High voice: And here is the green for stringing the daisies!

Low voice: Here is a cart runaway in the road
Lumping along with man and load
High voice: And here is a mill and there is a river
All: Each a glimpse and gone forever!

After students have tried different types of choral arrangements, allow them to experiment with different arrangements of the same poem, present the arrangements, and discuss the effectiveness of each approach. They should consider the influence of voices and types of arrangements on the rhythm, tempo, feelings and moods expressed by the poems.

LESSON SEVEN: Identifying Poetry Collections and Individual Poems for Holidays, Occasions, and Specific Subjects

OBJECTIVES

To develop collections of poems that are enjoyable and appropriate for specific occasions and subjects.

To select poems with individual appeal and to consider what makes the poems appealing.

CORE BOOKS (these also can be used for extended reading and other independent reading activities): Anthologies in which the poems are grouped according to subject so that students can search for poems on specific topics. For example, Myra Cohn Livingston's *Christmas Poems* and *Celebrations* contain only holiday poems, and her *Space Songs* explores outer space; Nancy Larrick's *Mice Are Nice* contains only poems about mice. Large anthologies such as *The Book of a Thousand Poems: A Family Treasury* and Jack Prelutsky's *The Random House Book of Poetry for Children* are divided according to such subjects as nature, seasons, animals, and holidays.

PROCEDURES: Ask the students to join in a long-term project of developing a file of poems suitable for sharing during specific occasions or when you want to explore specific subjects. Some of these poems will be part of a class file, while other poems can be selected for students' individual files. Encourage students to share especially appealing poems with the class and to tell why they think that poem should be part of the class file. (Each student might have personal reasons for choosing the poems for their individual files, and they need not share those reasons with the class.) As the class file fills up, share the collected poems during appropriate occasions.

LESSON EIGHT: Developing Poetry Collections That Demonstrate Appealing Poetic Elements

OBJECTIVE

To select poems with interesting rhythm, rhyme, or other sound patterns; repetition; imagery; and shape.

CORE BOOKS (these also can be used for extended reading and other independent reading activities): Many of the books used during this longer-range activity will be poetry collections that students already have read, developed as choral arrangements, dramatized, or read independently. The following books are sources for this activity: Rhythm: Stephen Dunning, Edward Lueders, and Hugh Smith's *Reflections on a Gift of Watermelon Pickle . . . and other Modern Verse* (Touchstone); David McCord's *One At A Time;* and Henry Wadsworth Longfellow's *Hiawatha's Childhood.* Rhyme: Jack Prelutsky's *Something Big Has Been Here;* and Shel Silverstein's *Where the Sidewalk Ends.* Repetition: Arnold Lobel's *The Rose in My Garden* and Maurice Sendak's *Pierre: A Cautionary Tale.* Imagery: Toni de Gerez's *My Song Is A Piece of Jade: Poems of Ancient Mexico in English and Spanish* (Mexican); Dunning, Lueders, and

Smith's *Reflections on a Gift of Watermelon Pickle . . . and other Modern Verse;* Jamake Highwater's *Moonsong Lullaby* (Native American); and Edward Lear and Ogden Nash's *The Scroobious Pip.* Shape: Dunning, Lueders, and Smith's *Reflections on a Gift of Watermelon Pickle . . . and other Modern Verse* and McCord's *One At a Time.*

PROCEDURES: This lesson is similar to Lesson Seven but this time, the students will be identifying poems that they consider their favorites because they express a particularly interesting poetic element of rhythm, rhyme, repetition, imagery, or shape. Before asking students to locate these examples of poetry, share some of your favorite poems that highlight these elements.

The poems in Figure 12.1 were chosen by a group of fourth-grade students. The comments were made by students who selected the poetry and explained why they chose the selections.

FIGURE 12.1 Favorite poems for showing poetic elements.

Element	Poet	Poem	Comment
Rhythm:	Edwin Hoey	"Foul Shot," in *Reflections on a Gift of Watermelon Pickle*	I felt as if I were playing basketball.
	Eve Merriam	"Cheers," in *Reflections on a Gift of Watermelon Pickle*	It was exciting, like cheering for my team.
	David McCord	"The Pickety Fence," in *One at a Time*	I heard a stick hitting the fence.
	Henry Wadsworth Longfellow	"Hiawatha"	The drums were beating in the woods.
Rhyme:	Jack Prelutsky	"Twaddletalk Tuck," in *Something Big Has Been Here*	The rhyme sounded like nonsense and made me laugh.
	Shel Silverstein	"Ickle Me, Pickle Me, Tickle Me Too," in *Where the Sidewalk Ends*	The rhyme was a tongue twister and even rhymed in the middle of the poem.
Repetition:	Arnold Lobel	"The Rose in My Garden"	I enjoyed seeing each flower over and over.
	Maurice Sendak	"Pierre: A Cautionary Tale"	The repetition made me feel as if I were involved in the plot.
Imagery:	Toni de Gerez	"My Song Is a Piece of Jade"	I felt beautiful when I read the poem. I thought of things I would like to be.
	Edward Lear and Ogden Nash	"The Scroobius Pip"	I could picture all the parts of the funny animal.
	Jamake Highwater	"Moonsong Lullaby"	I felt as if I were living with nature a long time ago.
	Eve Merriam	"How to Eat a Poem"	I could taste the poem and feel the juice.
Shape:	William Smith	"Seal," in *Reflections on a Gift of Watermelon Pickle*	I could see the shape of the seal in the poem.
	David McCord	"The Grasshopper," in *One at a Time*	I could see and feel the grasshopper climbing slowly up the rope.

LESSON NINE: Creative Writing—Ideas for Stimulating Poetry Writing

OBJECTIVES

> To stimulate the imagination and develop awareness and observational powers.
>
> To develop an environment that stimulates an interest in poetry and poetry writing.
>
> To write poetry and collect the poetry in class files and individual books.

CORE BOOKS (these also can be used for extended reading and other independent reading activities): Fill the room with anthologies and highly illustrated editions of poetry. Books such as David McCord's *One At A Time* include sections on how to write certain types of poetry. Music selections can be used to stimulate feelings and motivate poetry writing. Art and poetry books such as Kenneth Koch and Kate Farrell's *Talking to the Sun* relate fine art and poetry.

PROCEDURES: Sharing many types of poetry with students is considered one of the best ways to introduce poetry writing. Poetry writing, like other types of writing, is best developed as students are motivated and stimulated through sharing ideas and through transcribing and revising written efforts in groups and with teacher guidance (Norton, 1989). Erdman and Gaetz (1988) found significant improvements in both the attitudes toward and the writing of poetry when they used a process approach to poetry. The ideas in the following list have been successful in many classrooms. As the students get involved in the activities, teachers can set up a composing and publishing center in which students can show their own works.

1. *Developing observational powers:* Read many nature poems and discuss the observational experiences that might have stimulated the poets. Before writing nature poems, take students for a walk during which they keep personal journals. Encourage them to notice small details and to list sight, sound, smell, and feeling words associated with the images they see. Ask the students to think of associations and comparisons as they are looking at specific features in nature. They might choose to draw images to remind them of specific features. Or bring animals or natural materials into the classroom and ask the students to carefully observe them. They should record their feelings and observations and then write a poem about the experience.

2. *Stimulate poetry writing through music and art:* Poets and authors frequently mention listening to music as a stimulus for writing. Provide opportunities during which students listen to music, either as a class activity or at a listening center, and write about their feelings and emotions as they listen to the music. Art and poetry also are closely related. Older students can read and discuss books such as *Talking to the Sun,* a collection of poems illustrated by reproductions from the Metropolitan Museum of Art. Ask the students to share their feelings about the art, the poetry, and the appropriateness of the art chosen to illustrate the poetry. Then ask students to select a piece of art that they particularly like and to write a poem that expresses their moods and feelings when they look at the art. Students can develop their own art and poetry anthologies. Younger students enjoy using their own artwork to stimulate poetry writing.

3. *Brainstorming descriptive words before writing cinquains and diamantes:* Before students write either type of poem, they should be encouraged to brainstorm the words they will use. For example, before they write a cinquain students should brainstorm descriptive words and action words. Before they write a diamante, they should brainstorm suggestions for contrasting nouns. (Chapter 3 presents the forms for writing cinquains and diamantes.)

LESSON TEN: Writing a Biography About a Poet

OBJECTIVES

> To select a poet and write a biography using his or her poetry to support the biographical information.
>
> To discover the personal nature of poetry.

CORE BOOKS (these also can be used for extended reading and other independent reading activities): Encourage students to select a favorite poet and then locate as many of his or her poems as possible. Some poets whose work is readily available include Arnold Adoff (Black); Byrd Baylor (Native American); Gwendolyn Brooks (Black); Lewis Carroll; John Ciardi; Aileen Fisher; Robert Frost; Eloise Greenfield (Black); Langston Hughes (Black): Edward Lear; Myra Cohn Livingston; David McCord; Eve Merriam; Jack Prelutsky; Shel Silverstein; Nancy Willard; and Valerie Worth.

PROCEDURES: This activity can be used with students from first grade through college. Students in the lower elementary grades can write their biographies as group stories or language experiences using group-shared poetry to stimulate the biography. The total group must select the same poet and listen to and discuss several of that poet's works. After listening to each poem, students can use the content, the mood, and the type of experiences the poet writes about to gather information and reach some conclusions about the poet.

Remind students that poetry is personal. Poets usually write about feelings and experiences that are meaningful to them. Also remind the students that a biography is a nonfiction story about a person. Ask the students to list the types of information they would expect to discover about a person from a biography. Ask, "What would someone want to know if they were writing your biography?" Discuss information such as personal experiences, family, likes and dislikes, accomplishments, and fears. Tell the students that they will be writing a biography about one of their favorite poets. The only information they have about the poet, however, is the poetry the person writes.

Choose one of the poets, such as Shel Silverstein, and ask the students, "What do you know about Mr. Silverstein from the poetry he writes? What type of poetry does he write? What kinds of experiences did he probably have as a child? Does he have a sense of humor? How did you figure that out from his poetry? Which poems would you use to support this information about Mr. Silverstein?" (Students usually enjoy this activity. A third-grade student wrote a biography about Shel Silverstein and concluded that it was the most interesting poetry assignment he had ever completed.)

Some students prefer writing about humorous poets, while other students prefer more serious poets. Just as a biographer supports information with documented facts, the students should support their statements with quotes from poetry and summaries obtained from poetry.

This assignment can be used to extend the multicultural study of folklore presented in Chapter 10. Students can select poets who represent a specific cultural group and investigate how the poetry reflects the traditional foundations of the poet.

REFERENCES

ERDMAN, M., & GAETZ, T. (1988). Using the process approach to teaching writing and poetry: An investigation of elementary student's attitudes. *Educational Research Quarterly, 12,* 51–56.

HOPKINS, L. B. (1987). *Pass the poetry please!* New York: Harper & Row.

JANECZKO, P. B. (1990). *The Place My Words Are Looking For: What Poets Say About and Through Their Work.* New York: Bradbury.

NORTON, DONNA E. *The Effective Teaching of Language Arts.* Columbus: Merrill/Macmillan, 1989.

ROSENBLATT, L. M. (1980). What facts does this poem teach you? *Language Arts, 57,* pp. 386–394.

CHILDREN'S LITERATURE REFERENCES*

BAUM, L. FRANK. *Mother Goose in Prose.* Illustrated by Maxfield Parrish. New York: Bounty, 1899, 1986 (I: 8+).

The Book of a Thousand Poems: A Family Treasury. New York: Bedrick, 1983 (I: all).

CARLE, ERIC. *Eric Carle's Animals Animals.* New York: Philomel, 1989 (I: 3–9).

CASSEDY, SYLVIA. *Roomrimes.* Illustrated by Michele Chessare. New York: Crowell, 1987 (I: 8+).

CIARDI, JOHN. *You Read to Me, I'll Read to You.* Illustrated by Edward Gorey. New York: Lippincott, 1962 (I: all).

DE GEREZ, TONI. *My Song Is a Piece of Jade: Poems of Ancient Mexico in English and Spanish.* Boston: Little, Brown, 1984 (I: all).

DE REGNIERS, BEATRICE SCHENK, et al., selected by. *Sing a Song of Popcorn.* New York: Scholastic, 1988 (I: 3–10).

DUNNING, STEPHEN, EDWARD LUEDERS, & HUGH SMITH, eds. *Reflections on a Gift of Watermelon Pickle . . . and other Modern Verse.* New York: Lothrop, Lee & Shepard, 1967 (I: 8+).

FLEISCHMAN, PAUL. *I Am Phoenix: Poems for Two Voices.* Illustrated by Ken Nutt. New York: Harper & Row, 1988 (I: 8+).

_____. *Joyful Noise: Poems for Two Voices.* Illustrated by Eric Beddows. New York: Harper & Row, 1988 (I: 8+).

GERRARD, ROY. *Sir Cedric.* New York: Farrar, Straus & Giroux, 1984 (I: 8+).

_____. *Sir Francis Drake: His Daring Deeds.* New York: Farrar, Straus & Giroux, 1988 (I: 8+).

GREENFIELD, ELOISE. *Daydreamers.* Illustrated by Tom Feelings. New York: Dial, 1981 (I: all).

GRIMES, NIKKI. *Something on My Mind.* Illustrated by Tom Feelings. New York: Dial, 1978 (I: all).

HIGHWATER, JAMAKE. *Moonsong Lullaby.* Photographs by Marcia Keegan. New York: Lothrop, Lee & Shepard, 1981 (I: all).

KIPLING, RUDYARD. *Gunga Din.* Illustrated by Robert Andrew Parker. Orlando: Harcourt Brace Jovanovich, 1987 (I: 10+).

KNUDSON, R. R., & MAY SWENSON, selected by. *American Sports Poems.* New York: Orchard, 1988 (I: 8+).

KOCH, KENNETH, & KATE FARREL (Eds.). *Talking to the Sun.* New York: Metropolitan Museum of Art/Holt, Rinehart & Winston, 1985 (I: 8+).

LARRICK, NANCY. *Mice Are Nice.* New York: Putnam, 1990 (I: 5–9).

LEAR, EDWARD. *Hillary Knight's the Owl and the Pussy-Cat.* Illustrated by Hillary Knight. New York: Macmillan, 1983 (I: 3–8).

_____ & OGDEN NASH. *The Scroobious Pip.* Illustrated by Nancy Burkert. New York: Harper & Row, 1968 (I: all).

LIVINGSTON, MYRA COHN, selected by. *Christmas Poems.* Illustrated by Trina Schart Hyman. New York: Holiday, 1984 (I: all).

_____. *Celebrations.* Illustrations by Leonard Everett Fisher. New York: Holiday, 1985 (I: all).

_____. *Space Songs.* New York: Holiday, 1988 (I: all).

LOBEL, ARNOLD. *The Random House Book of Mother Goose.* New York: Random, 1986 (I: 3–8).

_____. *The Rose in My Garden.* Illustrated by Anita Lobel. New York: Greenwillow, 1984 (I: 6–10).

LONGFELLOW, HENRY WADSWORTH. *Hiawatha.* Illustrated by Susan Jeffers. New York: Dutton, 1983 (I: all).

_____. *Hiawatha's Childhood.* Illustrated by Errol LeCain. New York: Farrar, Straus & Giroux, 1984 (I: all).

_____. *Paul Revere's Ride.* Illustrated by Ted Rand. New York: Dutton, 1990 (I: 5–8).

MARGOLIS, RICHARD J. *Secrets of a Small Brother.* Illustrated by Donald Carrick. New York: Macmillan, 1984 (I: 8+).

MCCORD, DAVID. *One At A Time.* Boston: Little, Brown, 1974 (I: all).

MCPHAIL, DAVID. *The Dream Child.* New York: Dutton, 1985 (I: 3–8).

MILNE, A. A. *When We Were Very Young.* Illustrated by Ernest Shepard. New York: Dutton, 1961 (I: 3–10).

*I = Interest by age range

Moore, Clement. *The Night Before Christmas.* Illustrated by Tomie dePaola. New York: Holiday, 1980 (I: 3–8).

Morrison, Lillian. *Rhythm Road: Poems to Move To.* New York: Lothrop, Lee & Shepard, 1988 (I: all).

Noyes, Alfred. *The Highwayman.* Illustrated by Charles Keeping. Oxford University Press, 1981 (I: 10+).

Paxton, Tom, retold by in verse. *Aesop's Fables.* Illustrated by Robert Rayevsky. New York: Morrow, 1988 (I: all).

———, retold by in verse. *Belling the Cat and Other Aesop's Fables.* Illustrated by Robert Rayevsky. New York: Morrow, 1990 (I: all).

Prelutsky, Jack, selected by. *Read-Aloud Rhymes for the Very Young.* Illustrated by Marc Brown. New York: Knopf, 1986 (I: 3–8).

——— (ed.). *The Random House Book of Poetry for Children.* Illustrated by Arnold Lobel. New York: Random, 1983 (I: all).

———. *Something Big Has Been Here.* Illustrated by James Stevenson. New York: Greenwillow, 1990 (I: 5–10).

Rylant, Cynthia. *Waiting to Waltz: A Childhood.* Illustrated by Stephen Gammell. New York: Bradbury, 1984 (I: 8+).

Seabrooke, Brenda. *Judy Scuppernong.* New York: Dutton, 1990 (I: 10+).

Sendak, Maurice. *Pierre: A Cautionary Tale.* New York: Harper & Row, 1962 (I: 3–8).

Silverstein, Shel. *Where the Sidewalk Ends.* New York: Harper & Row, 1974 (I: all).

Stevenson, Robert Louis. *A Child's Garden of Verses.* Longman's, 1885 (I: all).

Willard, Nancy. *Night Story.* Illustrated by Ilse Plume. Orlando: Harcourt Brace Jovanovich, 1986 (I: 3–8).

———. *The Voyage of the Ludgate Hill: Travels With Robert Louis Stevenson.* Illustrated by Alice and Martin Provensen. Orlando: Harcourt Brace Jovanovich, 1987 (I: 8+).

CHAPTER 13

REALISTIC FICTION

CONTEMPORARY REALISTIC FICTION
    Developing Understandings of Contemporary Realistic Fiction
    Approaches that Develop Understanding and Appreciation of Realistic Fiction
    Core Books and Sample Lessons for Developing Understanding and Appreciation of
     Realistic Fiction
    Developing Realistic Fiction Units

The focus in this chapter and in Chapter 14 is on the genres, with activities and units that help students develop criteria for evaluating and reading the genre and exploring numerous interrelationships through units. The units encourage both efferent and aesthetic responses to literature, as well as help students integrate the language arts and content fields.

In many ways the literature in this chapter and in Chapter 14 is different from the folklore and fantasy presented earlier. Instead of stories developed on fantastic happenings for which readers must suspend their disbelief, the stories in this chapter are based on realistic plots, characters, and settings that could and sometimes do exist in the world as we know it. The conflicts and the ways that characters overcome those conflicts must be possible in a realistic world. The characters must be believable in a realistic world. Careful research is required for some of this literature. For example, authors of historical fiction must ground their stories in historical happenings. Authors of biographies must make their stories as true to the characters of the people and the times as possible. Authors of informational books must research and present their topics clearly and reliably. Even authors of realistic fiction need to develop characters, plots, settings, and themes that are plausible in our world.

The nature of the literature in this chapter and the next encourages numerous interactions with different content areas. For example, students can authenticate historical fiction and biography as part of social studies or history. They can compare informational books on specific areas as part of science. Units can include several genres as students focus on important themes. For example, a multicultural unit developed in Chapter 14 focuses on the difficult times in history, and includes literature drawn from the historical fiction, biography, and nonfictional informational genres.

CONTEMPORARY REALISTIC FICTION

The words *realistic* and *fiction* used together can cause confusion for many students who do not understand the requirements of this type of fiction. Although the story structures might be quite similar, the fiction in modern fantasy and folklore is quite different from the stories developed in contemporary realistic fiction. Realistic fiction requires plots that focus on familiar, everyday problems, pleasures, and personal relationships and characters and settings that seem as real as those in the world we know. Students need to understand that the *fiction* in contemporary realistic fiction means that while the story did not really happen, it could have happened in the world as we know it. Characters must solve their problems through means that are possible for human characters. They cannot use magic and other special powers. Likewise, animal characters must behave in ways that we know are possible for animals. They must retain their animal characteristics and cannot talk or act like people.

The stories, problems, and themes in contemporary realistic fiction often are similar to those encountered by today's students. Consequently, these stories can evoke personal responses and help students face similar problems in their own lives. For example, realistic fiction themes for young readers frequently develop the importance of overcoming fear and meeting responsibilities. Themes in realistic fiction for older readers frequently emphasize the importance of developing self-esteem, overcoming fears, and being true to oneself. According to Bernstein (1989), reading about children who are facing emotional problems can help other children discharge repressed emotions and cope with fear, anger, or grief.

The problems faced by characters in realistic fiction also mirror the problems of contemporary society. Characters face problems such as divorce, violence, drug addiction, disability, minority social status, and desertion by non-caring parents and other members of society. As might be expected, certain realistic fiction topics and books create issues and prompt protests by groups who would like to censor what students read (Donelson, 1985; Meade, 1990; Shannon, 1989, and Silvey, 1988). However, if teachers have guidelines for selecting controversial fiction, they have a better chance of fighting censorship attempts. One of my undergraduate students, for example, used the guidelines presented in class to successfully meet a challenge to Katherine Paterson's *Bridge to Terabithia*. A parent wanted the book removed from the class reading list because of mild profanity. The student teacher successfully defended the book for its literary merit, especially the importance of themes (Norton, 1991). Naylor (1991) and Feldstein (1989) present additional recommendations for facing censorship issues.

Developing Understandings of Contemporary Realistic Fiction

Activities and units can be developed that emphasize each of these important understandings:

1. *Realistic fiction* means that the story did not actually take place, but that it could happen in our world. If the story happened exactly as stated, the book would be classified as biography or other nonfiction.

2. To create believable stories in realistic fiction, authors rely on relevant subjects, everyday occurrences, and realism.

3. To develop plots and conflicts in realistic fiction, authors might have the characters cope with problems that are similar to the problems in our world; some of these problems are difficult to face and overcome.

4. In realistic fiction, the people must act like real people and the animals must behave like real animals.

5. The settings must be in the world as we know it.

6. The themes in realistic fiction are usually important in contemporary life.

7. Like all good literature, realistic fiction should have conflicts that are integral to the plot, characters that develop throughout the story, and style that enhances plot and characterization.

Approaches that Develop Understanding and Appreciation of Realistic Fiction

Lessons developed in previous chapters are helpful when studying plot development, conflict, characterization, setting, theme, and author's style in realistic fiction. The following list identifies earlier lessons developed around realistic fiction. The list also includes new lessons and units that will be developed in this chapter.

1. Developing questioning strategies that focus on a taxonomy of comprehension. (Ch. 2, Cleary's *Dear Mr. Henshaw.*)

2. Developing questioning strategies that focus on the literary elements of plot, conflict, characterization, setting, and theme. (Ch. 2, Cleary's *Dear Mr. Henshaw.*)

3. Developing an understanding of person-against-nature conflict by identifying and responding to vivid descriptions. (Ch. 5, Sperry's *Call It Courage.*)

4. Developing an understanding of person-against-self conflict through personal responses to the conflict. (Ch 5, Sperry's *Call It Courage,* Fox's *One-Eyed Cat.*)

5. Webbing person-against-self, person-against-person, person-against-nature, and person-against-society conflict in a book. (Ch. 5, Baylor's *Hawk, I'm Your Brother.*)

6. Developing understanding of person-against-nature conflict by analyzing a character's problem-solving approaches. (Ch. 5, Paulsen's *Hatchet.*)

7. Drawing plot diagrams for person-against-self conflicts. (Ch. 5, Fox's *One-Eyed Cat.*)

8. Webbing characterization in a realistic fiction text. (Ch. 6, Grifalconi's *Darkness and the Butterfly,* Baylor's *Hawk, I'm Your Brother.*)

9. Developing understanding of characterization through symbolism. (Ch. 6, Voigt's *Dicey's Song.*)

10. Describing and writing descriptions of familiar settings. (Ch 7, Hest's *The Crack-of-Dawn Walkers,* Keats' *Goggles!,* Khalsa's *I Want A Dog,* Mark's *Fun,* Schwartz's *Annabelle Swift, Kindergartner.*)

11. Developing observational powers and responding to moods in illustrations and text. (Ch. 7, Flournoy's *The Patchwork Quilt.*)

12. Webbing settings in realistic fiction. (Ch 7, Grifalconi's *Darkness and the Butterfly,* Baylor's *Hawk, I'm Your Brother.*)

13. Developing understandings that settings create moods through texts and illustrations. (Ch. 7, Hendershot's *In Coal Country,* Yolen's *Owl Moon.*)

14. Comparing and contrasting symbolic settings in folktales and realistic fiction. (Ch. 7, Burnett's *The Secret Garden.*)

15. Tracing the emergence of theme in realistic fiction. (Ch. 8, Grifalconi's *Darkness and the Butterfly.*)

16. Webbing theme in realistic fiction. (Ch. 8, Baylor's *Hawk, I'm Your Brother.*)

17. Responding to similes developed through illustrations and text and illustrating meaningful similes in students' own lives. (Ch. 9, Lewin's *Jafta.*)

18. Responding to point of view by writing a story from a different point of view than the one developed by the author (Ch. 9, Baylor's *Hawk, I'm Your Brother.*)

19. Developing questioning strategies to decide if a story is realistic fiction.

20. Responding to realistic fiction during role playing and dramatizing.

21. Encouraging aesthetic responses to realistic fiction through writing.

22. Developing units around important themes in realistic fiction.

This chapter focuses on the last four approaches for developing appreciation and understanding of realistic fiction. The lessons developed in previous chapters can be used independently or as part of units to increase appreciation and understanding of realistic fiction. The activities already developed, such as webbing and diagramming plot structures, are excellent additions to units.

Core Books and Sample Lessons for Developing Understanding and Appreciation of Realistic Fiction

These core lessons can be used at several different grade levels depending on the books chosen. Each core lesson identifies books for students in lower elementary, middle elementary, and upper elementary and middle school grades. The lessons also can be used as part of a larger unit on realistic fiction.

LESSON ONE: Developing Questions the Students May Ask Themselves When Deciding if a Book is Contemporary Realistic Fiction

OBJECTIVES

To identify characteristics of contemporary realistic fiction.

To develop a series of questions that students can use to decide whether a selection is realistic fiction.

To read additional realistic fiction and to apply the questions during independent reading.

CORE BOOKS: The core and independent books for this lesson are divided for appropriate grade levels. The books suggested for this lesson include settings from different countries so that students do not conclude that "realistic" stories can occur only within their own environment. Lower elementary: Lisa Westberg Peters' *Good Morning, River!* Middle elementary: Catherine Stock's *Armien's Fishing Trip* (African). Upper elementary and middle school: Nicholasa Mohr's *Going Home* (Puerto Rican).

EXTENDED BOOKS FOR INDEPENDENT READING AND RELATED

ACTIVITIES: These books can be used for extended reading assignments and independent responses. Any of these books also can be used as core books.

Lower Elementary

Eve Bunting's *The Wednesday Surprise*

Florence Heide and Judith Heide Gilliland's *The Day of Ahmed's Secret* (Egyptian)

James Howe's *Pinkey and Rex Get Married*

Shirley Hughes' *The Big Concrete Lorry* (English)

MARISABINA RUSSO's *Waiting for Hannah*

CYNTHIA RYLANT's *The Relatives Came* (Caldecott Honor)

MARY STOLZ's *Storm in the Night* (Black)

COLIN THIELE's *Farmer Schulz's Ducks* (Australian)

THEODORE FARO GROSS's *Everyone Asked About You.* In this book students should decide which parts of the story are realistic fiction and which parts are fantasy.

Middle Elementary Grades

JUDY BLUME's *Fudge-A-Mania*

BEVERLY CLEARY's *Ramona Quimby, Age 8* (Newbery Honor)

INA FRIEDMAN's *How My Parents Learned to Eat* (Japanese)

MILDRED PITTS WALTER's *Justin and the Best Biscuits in the World* (Black)

Selected stories from ANN DURELL AND MARILYN SACHS' *The Big Book for Peace.* Students can decide which stories among the anthology are contemporary realistic fiction.

Upper Elementary and Middle School

KATHERINE PATERSON's *Bridge to Terabithia* (Newbery Honor)

JAN SLEPIAN's *The Broccoli Tapes*

SUZANNE FISHER STAPLES's *Shabanu, Daughter of the Wind* (Pakistani, Newbery Honor)

WALTER DEAN MYERS's *Scorpions* (Newbery Honor, Black)

For shorter picture books use any of the books listed for the lower grades.

PROCEDURES: Begin the lesson by asking students to identify several books that could be classified as contemporary realistic fiction. Ask, "What makes the book realistic? Why is the word *fiction* used along with realistic? (For older students add the term *contemporary* and discuss the idea that the stories are written to reflect the contemporary time period of the authors.) Could these stories happen in our world? Why or why not?" Make sure that students understand that *realistic* means that the story could happen in our world, but that *fiction* means that the story did not really take place.

Next, choose a book that is appropriate for the grade level. Share the book or a chapter from a longer book with the students and ask them to identify the settings, characters, conflicts or problems, and solutions that make the book realistic. For example, a group of second-grade students identified the following realistic points with *Good Morning, River!*:

Setting: The setting is in the country along a river. The book shows the different seasons and what it would be like to canoe and swim in the river. This setting could be in our world.

Characters: The characters are Katherine and Carl. She is a young girl and he is an older man. Everything they do and say could happen.

Conflicts or Problems: The older man becomes ill and leaves his home to stay with his sister. The girl is lonely without him. When the man returns to his home, his voice is too weak to call good morning to the river. This could happen. People are lonely when friends go away. Sometimes older people must be cared for.

Ways the Problems are Solved: The girl calls good morning to the river and an echo answers her. Both the girl and the older man are happy again. The problem could be solved in this way. Echoes do exist. One student said this was a realistic story because it reminds him of some things he does with his grandfather.

Next, ask the students to compare the characteristics of realistic fiction with the characteristics of modern fantasy that they developed in Chapter 11. Ask, "How do the two genres differ? What is different about the characters? The conflicts? The ways they can solve their problems? The settings?"

Continue sharing and reading independently additional realistic fiction books. After the students have read, discussed, and responded to several realistic fiction books, ask them to develop a list of questions that they can use to decide whether a book is realistic fiction and if the realistic fiction is effective. A group of fourth-grade students developed the following questions:

1. Did the author develop a setting that was possible in our world? Can I identify the setting and a place in the world where that setting could be? What made the setting seem real to me?

2. Did the author develop characters that could live in our world? Can I describe the characters? Do they sound like people who could live in my world? What made the characters seem real to me?

3. What were the problems and conflicts in the story? How did the author develop them? Could these problems and conflicts really happen? What made them seem real to me?

4. How did the characters solve their problems? Could these resolutions be possible in my world? What made the resolutions seem real to me?

5. Think about how I responded to the story. Why did I respond in certain ways? Did the realism affect the way I responded to the story?

LESSON TWO: Responding to Realistic Fiction Through Role Playing

According to child-development authorities, role playing fosters social development, increases problem-solving capabilities, and enhances creativity. Even very young children can benefit from role-playing activities by learning to understand how other people feel. Three-and 4-year olds can role play experiences around family life while 4-and-5-year olds can role play situations that increase and extend their interests beyond family and school and into the world around them. Shaffer (1989) provides guidelines that can help teachers select meaningful role-playing activities. He adapts Selman's stages of social perspective and describes characteristic student responses to others' perspectives. Understanding these typical responses can help the teacher in planning activities and observing or interacting with students during role playing. For example, 3-to-6-year olds are unaware of any perspective other than their own; 6-to-8-year olds recognize that people have perspectives different from their own; 8-to-10-year olds know that their points of view can conflict with others'; 10-to 12-year olds can consider their own and another person's point of view simultaneously; and 12-to-15-year olds attempt to understand another person's perspective by comparing it with that of the social system in which they operate.

OBJECTIVES

To respond to literature through a role-playing activity.

To be involved in a literature activity that encourages students to interact with the problem in the story.

To foster social development, increase problem solving, and enhance creativity.

CORE BOOKS: Teachers can choose the core books that have the appropriate problem-solving situations for their students. The remainder of the books can be used for extended reading, independent reading, and responses. Select books with characters who have interesting problem-solving situations, especially books in which characters can respond in different ways. Lower elementary: Patricia Gauch's *Christina Katerina and the Time She Quit the Family;* Mavis Jukes' *Like Jake and Me* (Newbery Honor); Phyllis Naylor's *Keeping A Christ-*

mas Secret; William Steig's *Spinky Sulks;* Roni Schotter's *Captain Snap and the Children of Vinegar Lane;* Mildred Pitts Walter's *Two and Too Much* (Black); Vera Williams' *A Chair for My Mother* (Caldecott Honor).

Lower and middle elementary: Jeannie Baker's *Where the Forest Meets the Sea,* Dayal Khalsa's *I Want a Dog,* Sharon Bell Mathis' *The Hundred Penny Box* (Black, Newbery Honor), Jane Madsen and Diane Bockoras' *Please Don't Tease Me....;* and Theodore Taylor's *The Trouble With Tuck.*

Upper elementary and middle school: Carol Lea Benjamin's *The Wicked Stepdog;* Judy Blume's *Blubber;* Betsy Byars' *The Summer of the Swans;* Beverly Cleary's *Dear Mr. Henshaw* (Newbery Medal); Janet Taylor Lisle's *Afternoon of the Elves* (Newbery Honor); and Nicholasa Mohr's *Felitia* and *Going Home* (Puerto Rico).

PROCEDURES: Sutherland and Arbuthnot (1991) recommend the following procedures for role playing: First, encourage students to think about what will happen next in the story, to consider how the story might end, and to identify with the characters. Second, ask students to describe the characters, and then play those roles. Third, ask the audience to observe and decide if the solution is a realistic one. Fourth, ask the students who are role playing to decide what they will do to practice dialogue. Encourage them to describe the staging they will use. Fifth, have the students role play the situation with each student playing the character that he or she represents. The focus is on solving a problem, not on acting. Sixth, engage the players, and the audience, in a discussion of the role playing, the consequences of the actions, and any alternative behaviors. Next, have the role players try new interpretations based on the ideas generated from the discussion. Finally, encourage students to assess the outcomes and determine the best ways to deal with the problems.

The role-playing situations can be stimulated by the problems in whole books, portions of books, or even chapters of longer books. The following problems and related core books have been used for role-playing activities and discussions:

Family Life

Gauch's *Christina Katerina and the Time She Quit the Family.* Problem: What should happen in a family when a child wants to do only what pleases her and not what would make her part of the family?

Jukes' *Like Jake and Me.* Problem: How should a stepfather and his new son adjust to each other?

Naylor's *Keeping A Christmas Secret.* Problem: How can a child redeem himself when he reveals an important family secret? How should the rest of the family respond? Steig's *Spinky Sulks.* Problem: What should happen when a sulky boy discovers that his family really is trying to help him?

Walter's *Two and Too Much.* Problem: What type of interaction should take place when a 7-year old is asked to take care of his 2-year-old sister?

Interpersonal Relationships

Madsen and Bockoras' *Please Don't Tease Me....*Problem: How should people respond to a child with physical disabilities who asks for understanding? What should the child do and say to receive that understanding?

Mathis' *The Hundred Penny Box.* Problem: How should a boy respond when he makes friends with his great-great aunt and tries to explain her feelings about an old box of pennies to his mother? How should the aunt and the mother interact with each other?

Schotter's *Captain Snap and the Children of Vinegar Lane.* Problem: How should children act and talk when they want to make friends with a lonely older man? How should the man respond to the children?

Making Difficult Decisions

Baker's *Where the Forest Meets the Sea.* Problem: How can difficult ecological decisions be made so that the forest and seashore will be protected? How should the boy let his grandfather know that he understands the problem?

Khalsa's *I Want A Dog.* Problem: How can you convince your family that you are responsible enough to own a pet?

Taylor's *The Trouble With Tuck.* Problem: How should a family respond when their dog goes blind?

Family Disturbances

Benjamin's *The Wicked Stepdog.* Problem: How should a girl, her father, and her new stepmother act when her father remarries? What can they each do to accept each other?

Cleary's *Dear Mr. Henshaw.* Problem: How can a boy overcome his problems related to his parents' divorce? What should the mother, the father, and the boy say to each other? How can the parents help the boy understand what has happened to his family?

Lisle's *Afternoon of the Elves.* Problem: How should a family try to survive when a parent is mentally or physically incompetent? How can a friend help in this situation?

Accepting Others and Overcoming Prejudice

Blume's *Blubber.* Problem: How can students show sensitivity toward a student who is overweight?

Byars' *The Summer of the Swans.* Problem: How should a sister and society respond to a mentally retarded child?

Mohr's *Felitia* and *Going Home.* Problem: In the first book, how can prejudice toward a Puerto Rican girl in New York be overcome? In the second book, how can the same girl overcome prejudice against a Puerto Rican American girl when she visits Puerto Rico?

LESSON THREE: Encouraging Aesthetic Responses to Realistic Fiction Through Writing and Art

OBJECTIVES

To interact with literature through an activity that stimulates an aesthetic response.

To enhance writing through a response to literature.

To enhance creativity through an artistic response to literature.

CORE BOOKS: These are not divided into core books and extended reading and independent reading books because the lesson develops several types of aesthetic responses that are appropriate for any of the books listed. This activity can be accomplished at any grade level depending on the books chosen. The lesson also can be used with a core book shared with the class or with books chosen for independent reading. Lower elementary: Valerie Flournoy's *The Patchwork Quilt* (Black), constructing a quilt brings a family together; Shirley Hughes' *Dogger,* a young boy loses his favorite stuffed dog and his sister makes it possible for him to get it back; Miska Miles' *Annie and the Old One* (Newbery Honor, Native American), a girl believes that she can prevent her beloved grandmother's death; Barbara Ann Porte's *Harry in Trouble,* a young boy keeps losing his library card; and Ian Wallace's *Chin Chiang and the Dragon's Dance* (Asian), a boy longs to dance the dragon dance but is afraid he will shame his grandfather.

Middle elementary: C. S. Adler's *Ghost Brother,* a 12-year-old boy tries to live up to the image of his older brother who was killed in an accident; Betsy Byars' *Bingo Brown, Gypsy Lover,* a sixth-grade boy experiences his first romance; Eloise Greenfield's *Sister* (Black), a girl reviews the memories written by her sister; and Virginia Hamilton's *Zeely* (Black), a girl believes her neighbor is a Watusi queen.

Upper elementary and middle school: Jean Craighead George's *Julie of the Wolves* (Eskimo, Newbery Medal), a girl survives on the North Slope of Alaska with the help of wolves and *On the Far Side of the Mountain,* a boy faces challenges when he lives alone in the mountains; Paula Fox's *One-Eyed Cat* (Newbery Honor), an 11-year-old boy shoots a cat and then must face his guilt; Virginia Hamilton's *The Planet of Junior Brown* (Black, Newbery Honor), three outcasts from society create their own world in a secret basement room in a schoolhouse; Katherine Paterson's *Come Sing, Jimmy Jo,* an 11-year-old boy makes self-discoveries through his musical gift; Suzanne Fisher Staples' *Shabanu, Daughter of the Wind* (Newbery Honor), a female tries to fight against restrictive family and cultural rules in Pakistan; Cynthia Voigt's *A Solitary Blue* (Newbery Honor), a boy develops a loving relationship with his father after he faces his mother's desertion; and Laurence Yep's *Child of the Owl* (Asian American), a girl learns to respect her heritage and to look deep inside herself. Many of the books listed for the middle grades also are appropriate.

PROCEDURES: Describe several different types of written and artistic aesthetic responses that the students can use to accompany a book. Then either read a book to the students and let them choose an aesthetic response or allow them to read a book independently and choose an aesthetic response. Students or teachers can choose one of the following aesthetic responses (Many, 1990):

1. Students keep free-association journals in which they write comments about the literature as students read or listen to their books. These journals can include such topics as emotions students are feeling, questions they would like to ask the characters or the authors, reactions to the characters and plot situations, personal memories that the book stimulates, responses to vivid language, reactions to point of view, and overall judgments about the books.

2. Students use focused responses in which they respond to the following probes after completing a book.
   a. Write an emotional response to this book. Discuss the emotions you felt while reading and tell what made you feel this way.
   b. List the associations that came to mind as you read this book. This should be a simple list of people, places, or incidents of which you were reminded as you read. It might be someone you know, or something you have read about, or something you have seen in a movie or on television.
   c. Think of a feature that sticks in your mind after reading this book. It can be an image, a phrase, a motif, a theme, anything that is called to mind as you think about this book. Then try to explain why it was important to you.

3. Students use their choice of response to a book, such as dramatizing a favorite scene, painting a picture, creating a diorama, writing a poem from a character's point of view, making a film, writing a sequel to the book, designing a mural, telling a friend about the book, talking about the book into a tape recorder, keeping a diary while reading, discussing the book in a small group, designing a book poster, and sharing your responses to the book with your teacher in a one-to-one discussion.

Developing Realistic Fiction Units

This section presents two units developed around important themes in realistic fiction. The first unit, designed for students in the lower elementary grades, focuses on literature that develops the importance of friendship with humans and animals, and possible types of friendships from peer friendships to family friendships to friendships that cross age or other barriers. The second unit, depending on the books chosen, can be used with students from middle elementary grades through middle school. The unit focuses on the important themes of personal and physical survival.

UNIT ONE: Friendship Themes in Literature

OBJECTIVES

> To develop an understanding and appreciation of various types of friendship themes in literature.
>
> To increase social consciousness.
>
> To develop personal responses to the themes of friendship in literature.
>
> To identify characteristics of friends.
>
> To identify commonalties across books with friendship as the theme.
>
> To write a creative story about friendship.

CORE BOOKS: These books are divided according to specific themes of friendship. Friendship across generations: Karen Ackerman's *Song and Dance Man* (Caldecott Medal); Eve Bunting's *The Wednesday Surprise;* and Mary Stolz's *Storm in the Night* (Black). Friendship between peers: Evaline Ness's *Sam, Bangs & Moonshine* (Caldecott Medal) and Bernard Waber's *Ira Says Goodbye.* Other types of friendships: Shirley Hughes's *Dogger* and Keiko Narahashi's *I Have A Friend.*

EXTENDED BOOKS FOR INDEPENDENT READING AND RELATED ACTIVITIES: These books are divided according to the same themes as the core books. The books may be used for additional core books, extended reading activities, independent reading, and additional projects.

> Friendship Across Generations
>
> SID FLEISCHMAN's *The Scarebird*
> VALERIE FLOURNOY's *The Patchwork Quilt* (Black)
> MEM FOX's *Night Noises*
> ANN GRIFALCONI's *Darkness and the Butterfly* (African)
> HELEN V. GRIFFITH's *Grandaddy's Place*
> AMY HEST's *The Crack-of-Dawn Walkers* and *The Purple Coat*
> LISA WESTBERG PETERS' *Good Morning, River!*
> KAREN T. TAHA's *A Gift for Tia Rosa* (Hispanic)
>
> Friendship Between Peers
>
> PETER DESBARATS' *Gabriele and Selena*
> THEODORE FARO GROSS's *Everyone Asked About You*
> KEVIN HENKES' *Jessica*
> JAMES HOWE's *Pinky and Rex Get Married*
> STEVEN KELLOGG's *Best Friends*
> JEANNE PETERSON's *I Have a Sister, My Sister Is Deaf*
> MARGARET WILD's *Mr. Nick's Knitting*
>
> Other Types of Friendships
>
> DONALD HALL's *The Man Who Lived Alone*
> AMY SCHWARTZ's *Oma and Bobo*

PROCEDURES: Ask students to tell you what friendship means to them. "What kinds of people can be friends? How do you know when people are friends? How would you describe a good friend? How are good friends different from other people? How does one become a friend? Is it easy to be a friend? Why or why not? Does a friend have to be a person? Why do you think it is important to have friends? What other types of friends could we have? How would you know that they are your friends?" Write their responses on the board, a chart, or a transparency. These responses will be used later in the unit to compare their understandings about friendship with the characters and plots in the books.

After the students have discussed friendship and shared their experiences, tell them that they will be listening to and reading many books about different types of friendships. They will be trying to find out what books about friendships have in common and to discover the qualities of a friend as developed in books. They then will compare those qualities with the qualities that they identified at the beginning of the unit.

Begin by reading orally one of the books from the Friendships-across-generations category. As you read the book, ask the students to listen for signs of friendship in the story. For example, if you begin with *Song and Dance Man* ask the students, "Do you think that Grandpa and his grandchildren are friends? How do you know they are friends? How do these friends act toward each other? How would you describe them when they are together? What are the qualities of a friend as developed by this author?" Ask the students to respond personally to the friendship developed by the author and artist. "Was the friendship between Grandpa and his grandchildren believable? How did the author and the illustrator make you believe that the friendship was real? Would you like to have a friend like Grandpa? If Grandpa was your friend what would you want to do with him? How would you respond to him? If you were one of the children, how would you describe the most important quality of a friend? If you were Grandpa, would you like to have friends like the grandchildren? If you were Grandpa, what other things would you like to do with your friends? If you were Grandpa, how would you describe the most important quality of a friend?"

Develop a list on the board, a chart, or a transparency on which the students can summarize their discoveries about friendship in this book and other books that they read in this unit. Figure 13.1 shows a chart developed with second-grade students after reading several of the books from each of the friendship categories.

Continue reading and discussing additional selections from the friendships-across-generations category. Use a similar discussion approach as the one described for *Song and Dance Man*. Be sure that the students provide characteristics of friendship in the book and give a personal response to those friendships. Encourage students to read independently some of the books from this category and to add their discoveries to the findings about friendship across generations.

Next, choose a book from the friendship-between-peers category. Before reading the book orally, ask the students to consider how friendships between people of the same age might be the same as or different from the friendships between people of different ages. Ask, "If there are problems between friends of the same age, how would these problems be different from those in the previous section? Would the solutions be the same?" Encourage the students to compare the characteristics of friendships between people of different ages and between people of the same age. Ask them to think about how they would approach developing a friendship with someone their own age versus someone who is not their own age. Could they have different responsibilities in the two types of friendships?

Now read a book orally such as *Sam, Bangs and Moonshine*. Ask the students to listen for signs and characteristics of friendship as well as responsibilities associated with friendship developed in the story. After reading the book ask the students, "By the end of the book, do

FIGURE 13.1 Characteristics of friendship in literature.

Book	Characteristics of Friends
	Friendships Between Children and Older People
Song and Dance Man	They are happy together. They look forward to visits. They love to listen to stories. Grandpa gives hugs.
The Wednesday Surprise	They like to work together. They cooperate. Grandma gives hugs. They are happy together. They are proud of each other.
Storm in the Night	They understand each other. They don't tease about fear. They trust each other.
	Friendships Between Peers
Ira Says Goodbye	They do many things together. They miss each other when one is away. They stay friends even when one moves.
Sam, Bangs & Moonshine	Thomas trusted his friend. Friends worry about you. Sam learned not to lie to her friend because her lies could hurt him.
	Other Types of Friendships
Dogger	Dave takes the toy dog everywhere. Dave misses the toy when it is gone. Dave is happy when the toy is found.
I Have A Friend	Shadow goes everywhere with boy. Shadow keeps boy's dreams a secret.

you think that Sam and Thomas were good friends? Why or why not? How did their friendship change during the story? How would you describe each of these friends? Which of these characters learned the most about friendship? What did that character discover? What are the qualities of a friend as developed by this author?" Then ask the students to respond personally to the theme of friendship developed by the author. "Was the friendship between Sam and her cat, Bangs, believable? How did the author make you believe it was real? Was the friendship between Sam and Thomas believable? How did the author make you believe it was real? Would you like to be Thomas's friend? Why or why not? Would you like to be Sam's friend at the beginning of the story? Would you like to be Sam's friend at the end of the story? Why? What message about friendship do you think the author was trying to develop? Was the message important to you?"

Add to the chart a summary of characteristics about friendship from this book. Read orally several more books from this category and discuss the qualities and characteristics of friendship as well as the problems in each book. Encourage students to read additional books independently and summarize their findings on the chart. Compare the characteristics of friendships in books from these first two categories and discuss the reasons for similarities and differences.

Finally, read a book orally from the other-types-of-friendships category. Follow the same procedures as described in the previous sections. Ask students to summarize their findings on the chart and draw some conclusions about the nature of friendships and the problems associated with developing and maintaining friendships.

INDEPENDENT PROJECTS AND OTHER ACTIVITIES WITH THE FRIENDSHIP UNIT

Identifying themes related to friendship: Using the lesson on developing theme in *Darkness and the Butterfly* in Chapter 8 as a model, develop a lesson in which students identify themes related to friendship. Ask the students to support their findings through such proof as the illustrations, the character's actions, the character's thoughts, the way the story ends, and the way the author might tell the reader.

Developing plot diagrams of the stories: Using the lesson on developing plot diagrams in "Three Billy Goats Gruff" or *Darkness and the Butterfly* in Chapter 5 as a model, develop a lesson in which students draw the plot structures of any of the books in this unit.

Webbing literary elements: Ask the students to develop a literary web for any of the books in this unit. Have them pay particular attention to the characteristics of the characters in the story.

Creative writing: Ask the students to develop a guide for friendship. The guide can include do's and don'ts for creating friendships, characteristics of friends, advice for developing and maintaining friendships, and short stories and poems about friendships.

Role playing: Choose several of the stories that include problems that must be solved by friends. Develop a role-playing activity in which the students demonstrate various ways for solving the problems.

Responding to themes about friendship through art: Ask students to develop an artistic interpretation that shows their feelings about the three categories of friendship books developed in this unit: Friendships across generations, friendship between peers, and other types of friendships. Develop a bulletin-board display that shows the three types of books read in the unit.

Creative writing: Ask students to choose their favorite book from the unit and to write a sequel to the book. Or they can choose a book with an ending they did not like and write a new ending.

UNIT TWO: Survival Themes in Literature

OBJECTIVES

To increase enjoyment of reading through survival literature.

To analyze the plot structures common in survival literature.

To analyze the characteristics of settings common in survival literature.

To develop an appreciation for the characters developed in survival literature.

To identify similarities in themes in literature that develops plots around personal and physical survival.

To integrate the study of science and geography into the study of survival literature.

To integrate the study of current affairs into the study of survival literature.

To use knowledge gained from the study of Native American folklore to analyze the traditional foundations in contemporary Native American survival literature.

To stimulate creative writing through survival themes.

To develop personal responses to the characters and the situations developed in survival literature.

CORE BOOKS: These are not divided into core books and extended reading and independent reading books because teachers and students may choose any of the books as core books and others as independent-reading books. The books listed in this unit are divided into five types of survival literature. Teachers can choose to include as many of these topics as they believe are appropriate for the students in their classes. Topics such as survival in wilderness and survival on islands also integrate well with geography and science. Survival of one's heritage can be integrated with a study of Native American folklore. Survival in a dangerous world and survival in inner-city life can be related to a study of current events. (The last two topics are more appropriate for middle school students.)

Survival in the Wilderness

Jean Craighead George's *Julie of the Wolves* (Newbery Medal). An Eskimo girl lost on the North Slope of Alaska survives with the help of wolves.

My Side of the Mountain (Newbery Honor). In the Catskill Mountains, a boy creates a home inside a rotted-out tree and survives off the land.

On the Far Side of the Mountain. In a sequel to the previous book, Sam Gribley continues living in the mountains.

River Rats, Inc. Two boys survive in a canyon in Southwestern United States.

Gary Paulsen's *Hatchet* (Newbery Honor). A boy experiences physical and emotional survival in the Canadian wilderness.

Survival at Sea or on Islands

Scott O'Dell's *Island of the Blue Dolphins* (Newbery Medal). Twelve-year-old Karana survives alone for 18 years before a ship takes her to the California mainland.

Gary Paulsen's *The Voyage of the Frog.* A boy is caught alone in a fierce storm at sea and must survive in a small sail boat.

Armstrong Sperry's *Call It Courage* (Newbery Medal). A Polynesian boy faces his fear of the sea alone in an outrigger canoe.

Theodore Taylor's *The Cay.* A blind American boy is stranded on a Caribbean cay with a West Indian.

Johann David Wyss's *The Swiss Family Robinson.* In a classic story, a family is shipwrecked and must survive on an island.

Survival of One's Heritage

Jean Craighead George's *The Talking Earth.* A Seminole Indian girl searches for her legendary heritage in the solitude of the Big Cypress Swamp.

Dennis Haseley's *The Scared One.* A Native American boy's ancient heritage helps him face and overcome fear and ridicule.

Jamake Highwater's *Legend Days.* Traditional omens, powers, and visions play an important role in the life of a Northern Plains Indian.

Scott O'Dell's *Black Star, Bright Dawn.* An Eskimo girl enters the Iditarod Trail Sled Dog Race in Alaska where she learns to depend on her dogs, herself, and the strength of her Eskimo heritage.

Gary Paulsen's *Dogsong* (Newbery Honor). Traditional dreams and visions become part of the learning experience as an Eskimo boy faces a 1,400 mile dog sled trek in the isolated ice and tundra.

White Deer of Autumn's *Ceremony—In the Circle of Life.* A nine-year-old boy discovers his ancestor's beliefs as he faces the destruction of earth around his city home.

Survival in an Inner-City Reality

VIRGINIA HAMILTON's *The Planet of Junior Brown* (Newbery Honor). Three outcasts from
society create their own world in a secret basement room.

FELICE HOLMAN's *Secret City, U.S.A.* A 13-year-old boy turns an abandoned house in the
ghetto into a shelter for the homeless.

Slake's Limbo. A teenage misfit finds refuge in a subway cave in New York City.

WALTER DEAN MYERS' *It Ain't All for Nothin*. After his grandmother dies, a boy's life
changes drastically when he enters his father's world of crime and neglect.

Scorpions (Newbery Honor). A boy becomes involved with a gang, and his best friend
tries to stop his actions.

Survival in a Dangerous World

GILLIAN CROSS's *On the Edge*. In a gripping story, an English boy is kidnapped by terrorists in an effort to prevent his journalist mother from revealing an assassination plot.

LOIS DUNCAN's *Don't Look Behind You*. A family must move and develop a new identity
when the father's life is threatened.

ROSEMARY HARRIS's *Zed*. An 8-year-old boy is held by terrorists in London.

SUSAN LOWRY RARDIN's *Captives in a Foreign Land*. Six American children are held
hostage.

JAMES WATSON's *Talking in Whispers*. In a political thriller, a boy survives against an
oppressive military government.

PROCEDURES: There are several ways of approaching this unit depending on students'
grade levels and reading abilities, and teachers' desires to relate the unit to various content
areas. Many teachers prefer first selecting one of the survival areas, then choosing a book to
read and be discussed by all the students. After the core book has been read and discussed, they
divide the class into interest groups. The students in each group identify survival categories in
which they will read additional books independently; discuss them in small-group settings;
complete independent projects; draw conclusions about survival themes and the characteristics
of people who survive; and compare the plots, conflicts, characterizations, and settings with
those of the core book read as a group. Other teachers prefer to concentrate both group and
individual efforts on one survival category and to discuss how the literature in that category
can be related to a study of science, geography, or current events. The discussion topics and
independent projects provide sources for activities that can accompany either approach.

Begin the unit by asking students to identify the different circumstances in which people
might be required to survive alone or in small groups. What types of things could happen to
them that would force them to survive without the help of their families or other adults and
the conveniences they are used to? Make a list of the students' ideas. Next to each circumstance
ask the students to identify the setting that the survivor would need to face and the characteristics of that setting that would require survival skills. Ask the students to think about
individuals who might be forced to survive alone in a strange environment. Ask, "Would those
individuals change as a result of the experience? How do you think they would change?"

Finally, list the survival categories that will be used as part of this unit. Place the category
or categories on the board. Introduce each category by discussing the meaning of each. Allow
students to brainstorm about special requirements and knowledge needed by survivors in each
category. List these survival needs or special requirements on the board under each category.
Ask the students to suggest some ways that authors might develop stories in each of these
categories so that readers believe the main character really is facing a survival problem.

Ask the students to help you develop a list of evaluative criteria, questions and discussion
topics that they could use as they read and analyze the survival themes in various books. Tell

the students that they will use their list as they read and discuss the first book together. If necessary, they will add to the list as they progress through the first book. Then they will use the same topics as they read a book independently. Remind the students that an author needs to develop a detailed, believable setting; a plot and conflict that the reader believes is important to the story; characterization that changes as the characters overcome problems; themes that relate to the story and important experiences in people's lives; and a writing style that encourages readers to visualize and interact with the experiences. A group of upper elementary and middle school students helped develop the following questions and discussion topics. (These students had had considerable experience interacting with and evaluating literary elements in literature.)

1. Setting must be very important in survival stories, especially if the survival is in the wilderness or on an island. Notice whether the author develops the setting so that we understand why the setting is causing problems. What techniques does the author use to make me believe that the setting is causing a problem? Find some examples of setting that I think are good and tell why I think they are good. Close my eyes and try to see the setting and imagine why the character is in danger. How would I react if I were in that setting? Did I believe that the setting was causing danger?

2. What are the main conflicts in the story? Try to identify the major types of conflict that the character faces. Remember that a book can have up to four kinds of conflict. Try to describe that conflict so that I know it is important to the person's survival. What techniques does the author use to make me believe each type of conflict? Can I describe the conflict? Can I tell why the conflict is important to the person? Try to web the conflicts in the story. Are the conflicts well developed?

3. Can I identify the important incidents in the story and place them on a plot structure? Try to draw a plot structure that introduces the problem and shows the increasing action, climax, and resolution in the story.

4. Characterization must be well developed if the story tells how and why a character survives. Describe the character at the beginning of the book. What techniques does the author use to make me understand the character? Trace how the character changes in the book. What causes these changes? Describe the character at the end of the book. Are these changes reasonable? Do I believe in this character? If I believe in the character, why? Describe how the character overcame the conflict. Do I believe this is possible? Did I like the end of the story? Why or why not?

5. Survival stories should have important themes. Try to identify the main themes in the book. How does the author develop the themes? Identify places in the story that support the themes? Are these themes also important to me? What do the themes say about people?

6. Look for words and vivid descriptions that make the story exciting and enjoyable. How does the author use language to improve the story? What do I like about the author's language? What does the language make me think about? Try to find examples of language for myself and to share with the class.

Place the students' list of evaluative criteria, questions, and discussion topics on charts that can be seen easily throughout the room. Next, introduce the core book that will be read and discussed by all of the students. Read and discuss one or two chapters each day. Encourage the students to use their guidelines during reading and discussion. After the book has been completed, ask the students to summarize their new knowledge about survival stories and to evaluate the effectiveness of the book. Ask them to evaluate their own guiding questions. "Do our questions cover the main topics in this survival book? Are there any other topics that should be added?"

At this point students either can divide into interest groups to pursue different survival categories or read additional books from the same category. Many of the following independent projects and other activities can be used with either approach.

INDEPENDENT PROJECTS AND OTHER ACTIVITIES WITH THE SURVIVAL UNIT

Responding to author's style: Do the activity that accompanies *Call It Courage* in Chapter 5. Develop understanding of person-against-nature conflict by identifying and responding to vivid descriptions in Sperry's text. Do the activity that accompanies *Hatchet* in Chapter 5. Develop understanding of person-against-nature conflict by analyzing a character's problem-solving approaches.

Relating different genres: Relate the books in the survival-of-one's-heritage category to those in the traditional Native American unit in Chapter 10. The books in this unit can be used as an extension of the traditional Native American literature unit. Use the information gained about the values and beliefs expressed in the traditional folklore to analyze the importance of such beliefs and values in contemporary realistic fiction. For example, the values and beliefs developed in the contemporary story *Ceremony—In the Circle of Life* are almost identical to the values in the Comanche *The Legend of the Bluebonnet.* Likewise, the rest of the stories all emphasize the importance of retaining traditional cultural beliefs in a modern world. Students can identify these traditional Native American beliefs in modern literature. The contemporary survival stories, however, show how difficult this is for Native Americans, who frequently are torn between the cultural values of two worlds.

Comparing the story structures in survival stories and high fantasy: Many of the contemporary realistic fiction survival stories are similar in plot structure to the quest tales in legends and heroic high fantasy. Ask students to identify two similar stories from the different genres and compare the similarities. It might be helpful if they develop plot structures and literary webs for the two books.

Integrating survival stories with science and geography: Using the survival-in-the-wilderness or survival-at-sea-or-on-islands books, develop a web that identifies the important geographical and scientific concepts stressed in the book. For example, develop a web for each location with the words *Important Survival Knowledge* in the center and *Geography, Natural Food Sources, Seasonal Weather, Clothing, Medical Care,* and *Shelter* on the spokes. Finish the web by identifying the details from the book that relate to each of these categories. Authenticate the information in the survival book by comparing it with information in nonfictional information sources.

Integrating survival stories with science and geography: After completing the Survival-in-the-Wilderness or Survival-at-Sea-or-on-Islands categories, create an island or wilderness survival center. Using the web categories identified in the previous activity, have the students develop displays that demonstrate each type of survival knowledge.

Integrating survival stories with current events: While reading the Survival-in-an-Inner-City-Reality or Survival-in-a-Dangerous-World books, identify related survival instances found in current newspaper, magazine, and television articles. Compare a current incident with an incident developed in one of the books. Describe the similarities and differences. How would you describe the two conflicts and the people involved in those conflicts? What are the chances of resolution of the conflicts and survival in the current event?

Comparative studies and library research: Ask the students to identify an author who has written more than one selection of survival literature such as Jean Craighead George, Felice Holman, Walter Dean Myers, Scott O'Dell, or Gary Paulsen. Ask them to read at least two survival books by this author and compare the similarities in the two books. Then ask the students to conduct library research to discover any reasons that the authors might write their type of survival literature.

Creative writing: Ask the students to choose a survival topic that interests them and to write their own survival story. They can write their story in any form. Some students might choose the diary format used by Jean Craighead George in *My Side of the Mountain*. Or, they might choose a story for which they would have preferred a different ending and write a new ending. Or, as George does for *On the Other Side of the Mountain*, they might write a sequel to one of the survival stories.

Personal response through art: The settings in survival stories often are described vividly. Ask the students to choose such a setting and respond to it through art. They should consider the mood of the setting as well as any dangers and benefits gained from the setting.

Personal response through writing: Ask the students to keep a free-association journal and to respond to the various aspects of a survival book as they read. For example, they can write down questions, have a dialogue with the character or the author, describe an emotional response to an incident or a setting, or evaluate the techniques that the author used to try to convince them that the survival story could happen.

REFERENCES

BERNSTEIN, J. E. (1989). Bibliotherapy: How books can help young children cope. In M. K. Rudman (Ed.), *Children's Literature: Resource for the Classroom* (pp. 159–173). Norwood, MA: Christopher Gordon.

DONELSON, K. (1985). Almost 13 years of book protests—Now what? *School Library Journal, 31,* 93–98.

FELDSTEIN, BARBARA. "Selection as a Means of Diffusing Censorship." In *Children's Literature: Resource for the Classroom,* edited by Masha Kabakow Rudman. Norwood, Mass: Christopher Gordon, 1989, 139–158.

MANY, J. (1990, November). *Encouraging aesthetic responses to literature.* Paper presented at the GTE Conference on Children's Literature and Literacy. College Station: Texas A&M University.

MEADE, J. (1991, November/December). A war of words. *Teacher,* pp. 37–45.

NAYLOR, ALICE. "Perspectives on Censorship." In *Children and Books,* eighth edition, by Zena Sutherland and May Hill Arbuthnot. New York: Harper Collins, 1991.

NORTON, D. E. (1991). *Through the eyes of a child: An introduction to children's literature* (3rd ed.). Columbus, OH: Merrill.

SHAFFER, D. R. (1989). *Developmental psychology: Childhood and adolescence* (2nd ed.). Pacific Grove, CA: Brooks/Cole.

SHANNON, P. (1989). Overt and covert censorship of children's books. *The New Advocate, 2,* pp. 97–104.

SILVEY, A. (1988, January/February). The goats. *The Horn Book* p. 23.

SUTHERLAND, Z. & ARBUTHNOT, M. H. (1991). *Children and books* (8th ed.). New York: Harper Collins.

CHILDREN'S LITERATURE REFERENCES*

ACKERMAN, KAREN. *Song and Dance Man.* Illustrated by Stephen Gammell. New York: Knopf, 1988 (I: 3–8).

ADLER, C. S. *Ghost Brother.* New York: Clarion, 1990 (I: 9–12).

BAKER, JEANNIE. *Where the Forest Meets the Sea.* New York: Greenwillow, 1988 (I: 4–10).

BENJAMIN, CAROL LEA. *The Wicked Stepdog.* New York: Crowell, 1982 (I: 9–12).

BLUME, JUDY. *Blubber.* New York: Bradbury, 1974 (I: 10+).

*I = Interest by age range

_____. *Fudge-A-Mania.* Dutton, 1990 (I: 8–12).

BUNTING, EVE. *The Wednesday Surprise.* Illustrated by Donald Carrick. New York: Clarion, 1989 (I: 5–8).

BYARS, BETSY. *Bingo Brown, Gypsy Lover,* New York: Viking, 1990 (I: 9–12).

_____. *The Summer of the Swans.* Illustrated by Ted CoConis. New York: Viking, 1970 (I: 8–12).

CLEARY, BEVERLY. *Dear Mr. Henshaw.* Illustrated by Paul O. Zelinsky. New York: Morrow, 1983 (I: 9–12).

_____. *Ramona Quimby, Age 8.* New York: Morrow, 1981 (I: 7–10).

CROSS, GILLIAN. *On the Edge.* New York: Holiday, 1985 (I: 10 +).

DESBARATS, PETER. *Gabriele and Selena.* Illustrated by Nancy Grossman. Orlando: Harcourt Brace Jovanovich, 1968 (I: 5–8).

DUNCAN, LOIS. *Don't Look Behind You.* New York: Delacorte, 1989 (I: 12 +).

DURELL, ANN & MARILYN SACHS, edited by. *The Big Book for Peace.* New York: Dutton, 1990 (I: all).

FLEISHMAN, SID. *The Scarebird.* Illustrated by Peter Sis. New York: Greenwillow, 1988 (I: 5–9).

FLOURNOY, VALERIE. *The Patchwork Quilt.* Illustrated by Jerry Pinkney. New York: Dial, 1985 (I: 5–8).

FOX, MEM. *Night Noises.* Illustrated by Terry Denton. New York: Harcourt Brace Jovanovich, 1989 (I: 5–8).

FOX, PAULA. *One-Eyed Cat.* New York: Bradbury, 1984 (I: 10 +).

FRIEDMAN, INA. *How My Parents Learned to Eat.* Illustrated by Allen Say. Boston: Houghton Mifflin, 1984 (I: 5–10).

GAUCH, PATRICIA. *Christina Katerina and the Time She Quit the Family.* Illustrated by Elise Primavera. New York: Putnam's, 1987 (I: 4–8).

GEORGE, JEAN CRAIGHEAD. *Julie of the Wolves.* Illustrated by John Schoenher. New York: Harper & Row, 1972 (I: 10 +).

_____. *My Side of the Mountain.* New York: Dutton, 1959 (I: 10 +).

_____. *On the Far Side of the Mountain.* New York: Dutton, 1990 (I: 10 +).

_____. *River Rats, Inc.* New York: Dutton, 1979 (I: 10 +).

_____. *The Talking Earth.* New York: Harper & Row, 1983 (I: 10 +).

GREENFIELD, ELOISE. *Sister.* Illustrated by Moneta Barnett. New York: Crowell, 1974 (I: 8–12).

GRIFALCONI, ANN. *Darkness and the Butterfly.* Boston: Little, Brown, 1987 (I: 4–8).

GRIFFITH, HELEN V. *Grandaddy's Place.* Illustrated by James Stevenson. New York: Greenwillow, 1987 (I: 5–8).

GROSS, THEODORE FARO. *Everyone Asked About You.* New York: Philomel, 1990 (I: 5–8).

HALL, DONALD. *The Man Who Lived Alone.* Illustrated by Mary Azarian. Boston: Bodine, 1928, 1984 (I: all).

HAMILTON, VIRGINIA. *The Planet of Junior Brown.* New York: Macmillan, 1971 (I: 12 +).

_____. *Zeely.* Illustrated by Symeon Shimin. New York: Macmillan, 1967 (I: 8–12).

HARRIS, ROSEMARY. *Zed.* New York: Faber & Faber, 1982 (I: 12 +).

HASELEY, DENNIS. *The Scared One.* Illustrated by Deborah Howland. Warne, 1983 (I: 5–8).

HEIDE, FLORENCE & JUDITH HEIDE GILLILAND. *The Day of Ahmed's Secret.* Illustrated by Ted Lewin. New York: Lothrop, Lee & Shepard, 1990 (I: 5–9).

HENKES, KEVIN. *Jessica.* New York: Greenwillow, 1989 (I: 5–8).

HEST, AMY. *The Crack-of-Dawn Walkers.* Illustrated by Amy Schwartz. New York: Macmillan, 1984 (I: 5–8).

_____. *The Purple Coat.* Illustrated by Amy Schwartz. New York: Macmillan, 1988 (I: 5–8).

HIGHWATER, JAMAKE. *Legend Days.* New York: Harper & Row, 1984 (I: 12 +).

HOLMAN, FELICE. *Secret City, U.S.A.* New York: Scribner's, 1990 (I: 12 +).

_____. *Slake's Limbo.* New York: Scribner's, 1974 (I: 12 +).

HOWE, JAMES. *Pinky and Rex Get Married.* New York: Atheneum, 1990 (I: 5–9).

HUGHES, SHIRLEY. *Dogger.* London: Bodley, 1977 (I: 3–8).

_____. *The Big Concrete Lorry.* New York: Lothrop, Lee & Shepard, 1990 (I: 6–8).

JUKES, MAVIS. *Like Jake and Me.* Illustrated by Lloyd Bloom. New York: Knopf, 1984 (I: 6–9).

KELLOGG, STEVEN. *Best Friends.* New York: Dial, 1986 (I: 5–8).

KHALSA, DAYAL. *I Want a Dog.* Clarkson, 1987 (I: 4–7).

LISLE, JANET TAYLOR. *Afternoon of the Elves.* New York: Orchard 1989 (I: 10 +).

MADSEN, JANE & DIANE BOCKORAS. *Please Don't Tease Me....* Illustrated by Kathleen T. Brinko. Judson, 1983 (I: 6–9).

MATHIS, SHARON BELL. *The Hundred Penny Box.* Illustrated by Leo and Diane Dillon. New York: Viking, 1975 (I: 6–9).

MILES, MISKA. *Annie and the Old One.* Illustrated by Peter Parnall. Boston: Little, Brown, 1971 (I: 6–8).

MOHR, NICHOLASA. *Felitia.* Illustrated by Ray Cruz. New York: Dial, 1979 (I: 9–12).

_____. *Going Home.* New York: Dial, 1986 (I: 10 +).

MYERS, WALTER DEAN. *It Ain't All for Nothin.* New York: Viking, 1978 (I: 10+).

_____. *Scorpions.* New York: Harper & Row, 1988 (I: 10+).

NARAHASHI, KEIKO. *I Have A Friend.* New York: Macmillan, 1987 (I: 3–7).

NAYLOR, PHYLLIS. *Keeping A Christmas Secret.* Illustrated by Lena Schiffman. New York: Atheneum, 1989 (I: 5–8).

NESS, EVALINE. *Sam, Bangs & Moonshine.* New York: Holt, Rinehart and Winston, 1966 (I: 5–9).

O'DELL, SCOTT. *Black Star, Bright Dawn.* Boston: Houghton Mifflin, 1988 (I: 8+).

_____. *Island of the Blue Dolphins.* Boston: Houghton Mifflin, 1960 (I: 8+).

PATERSON, KATHERINE. *Bridge to Terabithia.* Illustrated by Donna Diamond. New York: Crowell, 1977 (I: 10–14).

_____. *Come Sing, Jimmy Jo.* New York: Dutton, 1985 (I: 10+).

PAULSEN, GARY. *Dogsong.* New York: Bradbury, 1985 (I: 10+).

_____. *Hatchet.* New York: Bradbury, 1987 (I: 10+).

_____. *The Voyage of the Frog.* New York: Watts, 1989 (I: 10+).

PETERS, LISA WESTBERG. *Good Morning, River!* Illustrated by Deborah Kogan Ray. Boston: Little, Brown, 1990 (I: 5–8).

PETERSON, JEANNE. *I Have a Sister, My Sister Is Deaf.* Illustrated by Deborah Ray. New York: Harper & Row, 1977 (I: 3–8).

PORTE, BARBARA ANN. *Harry in Trouble.* Illustrated by Yossi Abolafia. New York: Greenwillow, 1989 (I: 3–8).

RARDIN, SUSAN LOWRY. *Captives in a Foreign Land.* Boston: Houghton Mifflin, 1984 (I: 10+).

RUSSO, MARISABINA. *Waiting for Hannah.* New York: Greenwillow, 1989 (I: 5–8).

RYLANT, CYNTHIA. *The Relatives Came.* Illustrated by Stephen Gammell. New York: Bradbury, 1985 (I: 5–8).

SCHOTTER, RONI. *Captain Snap and the Children of Vinegar Lane.* Illustrated by Marcia Sewell. New York: Orchard, 1989 (I: 5–9).

SCHWARTZ, AMY. *Oma and Bobo.* New York: Bradbury, 1987 (I: 5–9).

SLEPIAN, JAN. *The Broccoli Tapes.* New York: Philomel, 1989 (I: 10+).

SPERRY, ARMSTRONG. *Call It Courage.* New York: Macmillan, 1940 (I: 9–13).

STAPLES, SUZANNE FISHER. *Shabanu, Daughter of the Wind.* New York: Knopf, 1989 (I: 10+).

STEIG, WILLIAM. *Spinky Sulks.* New York: Farrar, Straus & Giroux, 1988 (I: 3–8).

STOCK, CATHERINE. *Armien's Fishing Trip.* New York: Morrow, 1990 (I: 6–9).

STOLZ, MARY. *Storm in the Night.* Illustrated by Pat Cummings. New York: Harper & Row, 1988 (I: 5–8).

TAHA, KAREN T. *A Gift for Tia Rosa.* Illustrated by Dee deRosa. Minneapolis: Dillon, 1986 (I: 5–9).

TAYLOR, THEODORE. *The Cay.* New York: Doubleday, 1969 (I: 10+).

_____. *The Trouble With Tuck.* New York: Doubleday, 1981 (I: 6–10).

THIELE, COLIN. *Farmer Schulz's Ducks.* Illustrated by Mary Milton. New York: Harper & Row, 1986 (I: 5–10).

VOIGT, CYNTHIA. *A Solitary Blue.* New York: Atheneum, 1983 (I: 10+).

WABER, BERNARD. *Ira Says Goodbye.* Boston: Houghton, Mifflin, 1988 (I: 3–8).

WALLACE, IAN. *Chin Chiang and the Dragon's Dance.* New York: Atheneum, 1984 (I: all).

WALTER, MILDRED PITTS. *Justin and the Best Biscuits in the World.* New York: Lothrop, Lee & Shepard, 1985 (I: 7–10).

_____. *Two and Too Much.* Illustrated by Pat Cummings. New York: Bradbury, 1990 (I: 5–9).

WATSON, JAMES. *Talking in Whispers.* Victor Gollancz, 1983 (I: 12+).

WHITE DEER OF AUTUMN. *Ceremony—In the Circle of Life.* Illustrated by Daniel San Souci. Raintree, 1983 (I: all).

WILD, MARGARET. *Mr. Nick's Knitting.* Illustrated by Dee Huxley. Orlando: Harcourt Brace Jovanovich, 1989 (I: 4–8).

WILLIAMS, VERA. *A Chair for My Mother.* New York: Greenwillow, 1982 (I: 3–7).

WYSS, JOHANN DAVID. *The Swiss Family Robinson.* Illustrated by Lynd Ward. Grosset & Dunlap, 1949 (I: 10+).

YEP, LAURENCE. *Child of the Owl.* New York: Harper & Row, 1977 (I: 10+).

CHAPTER 14

HISTORICAL FICTION, BIOGRAPHY, AND INFORMATIONAL LITERATURE

HISTORICAL FICTION
    Developing Understandings of Historical Fiction
    Approaches that Develop Understanding and Appreciation of Historical Fiction
    Core Books and Sample Lessons for Developing Understanding and Appreciation of
        Historical Fiction
BIOGRAPHY
    Developing Understandings of Biography
    Approaches that Develop Understanding and Appreciation of Biography
    Core Books and Sample Lessons for Developing Understanding and Appreciation
        of Biography
INFORMATIONAL LITERATURE
    Developing Understandings of Informational Literature
    Approaches that Develop Understanding and Appreciation of Informational
        Literature
    Core Books and Sample Lessons for Developing Understanding and Appreciation of
        Informational Literature
    Developing Units Using Historical Fiction, Biography, and Informational Literature

HISTORICAL FICTION

Historical fiction is similar to contemporary realistic fiction, except that the stories are set in the past rather than in the contemporary world. The settings and the types of conflicts must be authentic for the particular time period. As in contemporary realistic fiction, the stories did not actually happen, but the main characters must be developed so that they express values and beliefs that are realistic for the time period. Authors of historical fiction frequently state that they base their characters and plots on real people and events in history. The stories have enough fictional information, however, that they are not considered biographies or other types of nonfiction.

Historical fiction has many values for students of today. They can relive the past vicariously as they follow the adventures of heroes and heroines across different time periods. They can gain understandings about their own heritage and the heritages of other cultures. They can learn about the people, values, beliefs, hardships, and physical surroundings that were common for a particular time period. They begin to see the sweep of history and the interrelationships that help explain human changes.

Historical fiction also lends itself to exciting lessons and units. For example, this chapter includes lessons that encourage students to authenticate historical fiction through such techniques as verifying with nonfictional sources, interviewing people who can evaluate characters and incidents from the past, and researching other documentation. We will use recurring themes in historical fiction to develop units that encourage students to understand the sweep of history. Within the units, we will relate historical fiction to music, art, and history.

Developing Understandings of Historical Fiction

The following list shows the understandings that students need to evaluate, appreciate, and understand historical fiction:

1. The term *historical fiction* means that the story is placed in an authentic setting in the past; fiction means that the story did not happen, but it needs to be written with enough authenticity that it could have happened.
2. The setting must be authentic in every detail and integral to the story.

3. Authors develop credible plots and conflicts in historical fiction by developing stories that reflect the experiences, conflicts, and resolutions characteristic of the times.

4. Many historical fiction books feature person-against-society conflicts, which must be developed so that readers understand the nature and values of the society and the people who are in conflict with that society.

5. Authors must develop characters whose actions, beliefs, and values are realistic for the time periods.

6. Many of the themes in historical fiction are relevant to human understanding and are as important today as they were during the historical time period.

7. The authors' style should enhance the mood and clarify the conflicts, characterizations, settings, and themes.

8. Authors of historical fiction usually conduct considerable research before writing their stories.

9. Historical fiction allows readers to travel vicariously back in history and interact with the people of the time; through historical fiction readers discover the sweep of history.

Approaches that Develop Understanding and Appreciation of Historical Fiction

Lessons and units should be developed that help students appreciate these important understandings of historical fiction. The following list identifies lessons that have been developed around historical fiction in previous chapters. The list also includes new lessons and units that will be developed in this chapter.

1. Webbing a pioneer America unit to include pioneer environment, education, entertainment, and values. (Ch. 2, numerous pioneer books are listed)

2. Webbing literary elements in historical fiction. (Ch. 2, Slepian's *Risk N'Roses*)

3. Writing poetry to extend understandings of characters in historical fiction. (Ch. 3, MacLachlan's *Sarah, Plain and Tall*, Forbes's *Johnny Tremain*)

4. Expanding vocabulary through individualized word cards. (Ch. 3, Frank's *No Hero for the Kaiser*)

5. Encouraging an aesthetic response to person-against-society conflict through dramatization, art, and writing. (Ch. 5, Speare's *The Witch of Blackbird Pond*)

6. Analyzing an artist's ability to reflect person-against-society conflict through illustrations. (Ch. 5, Carrick's *Stay Away from Simon!*)

7. Modeling the inferring of characterization. (Ch. 6, MacLachlan's *Sarah, Plain and Tall*)

8. Modeling understanding figurative language in historical fiction. (Ch. 9, Frank's *No Hero for the Kaiser*)

9. Developing questioning strategies to decide whether a story is historical fiction.

10. Responding to historical fiction through dramatizations and role playing.

11. Creating a day in the life of a child in another time period.

12. Developing units that relate the important themes across time periods in historical fiction; develop the ability to authenticate historical fiction through nonfictional sources; respond to historical fiction through writing, art, and music; and integrate the social studies and history curriculum.

This chapter focuses on the last four approaches for developing understanding and appreciation of realistic fiction. The unit listed in No. 12 will be developed at the end of the chapter because it also uses the nonfictional sources of biography and informational literature. The activities already developed, such as modeling and webbing, are excellent additions to lessons and units.

Core Books and Sample Lessons for Developing Understanding and Appreciation of Historical Fiction

These core lessons can be used at several different grade levels depending on the books chosen. They also can be incorporated into longer units on historical fiction.

LESSON ONE: Developing Questioning Strategies to Decide if a Story is Historical Fiction

OBJECTIVES

To identify characteristics of historical fiction.

To develop a series of questions that students can use to decide whether a selection is historical fiction.

To read additional historical fiction and to apply the questions during independent reading.

CORE BOOKS: Select books that represent historical fiction and are appropriate for the grade level. If the title is not obvious, the time period and setting are listed for identification. Lower elementary: Alice Dalgliesh's *The Courage of Sarah Noble* (1707, American wilderness, Newbery Honor). Middle elementary: Laura Ingalls Wilder's *Little House on the Prairie* (pioneer Kansas, Touchstone). Upper elementary and middle school: Joan Blos's *A Gathering of Days: A New England Girl's Journal, 1830–32* (Newbery Medal).

EXTENDED BOOKS FOR INDEPENDENT READING AND RELATED ACTIVITIES: These books also can be used as core books.

Lower Elementary

SIBYL HANCOCK's *Old Blue.* An 1878 trail drive.

ELLEN HOWARD's *Edith Herself.* A girl with epilepsy learns to value herself in the 1890s.

KERRY RAINES LYDON's *A Birthday for Blue.* A pioneer boy spends his seventh birthday in a covered wagon.

F. N. MONJO's *The Drinking Gourd* ("I-Can-Read" Book). A story about the Underground Railroad.

Middle Elementary

CAROL RYRIE BRINK's *Caddie Woodlawn* (Newbery Medal). The Wisconsin frontier in 1864.

CAROL CARRICK's *Stay Away from Simon!* A mentally retarded boy and a snowstorm in New England in the early 1800s help two children realize that people with disabilities can have great worth.

MARGUERITE DEANGELI's *The Door in the Wall* (Newbery Medal). A boy overcomes the consequences of a mysterious ailment in England during the time of Edward III.

VIRGINIA HAMILTON's *The Bells of Christmas* (Black). Christmas in Ohio in 1890.

Upper and Middle Elementary

Avi's *The Fighting Ground.* A 13-year-old boy experiences the reality of war during the American Revolution.

Kathryn Lasky's *The Night Journey.* A girl escapes from Czarist Russia in 1900.

Farley Mowat's *Lost in the Barrens.* A Cree Indian boy and his friend are lost in northern Canada.

Scott O'Dell's *Carlota* (Spanish). A Spanish-American girl fights beside her father during the Mexican War in early California.

Mary Stolz's *Bartholomew Fair.* A group of people in 1597 London attend a fair that changes their lives.

PROCEDURES: Begin by asking students to identify several books that they think could be classified as historical fiction. Ask, "What do you think makes a book historical? What does the author need to do to make you believe it is historical? What makes it fiction?" Make sure that students understand that historical fiction is set in real time periods and that the stories did not really happen, but they could have. Also make sure they understand that readers should be able to visualize and feel the time period.

Next, choose a book that is appropriate for the grade level. Share the book, or a chapter from a longer book, with the students and ask them to identify and respond to the settings, the characters, the conflicts or problems, and the solutions that make the books historical fiction and that relate to the historical time period. Ask them to look for any clues in the author's notes that would indicate whether the book is historical fiction. For example, a group of sixth-grade students identified the following historical fiction points in the first two chapters of *A Gathering of Days:*

Setting: The first diary entry is dated Sunday, October 17, 1830. The location is identified as Meredith, New Hampshire. The details described by Catherine identify characteristics of the setting. For example, Father goes to Boston to buy provisions for the months ahead. That probably means it is not easy to get to Boston and they have to store provisions for a long time. Later the neighbor's sister travels by coach and rides on the wagon seat. The family uses torches to see at night. This means that they did not have cars and electric lights. The descriptions of cooking sound as if they took place a long time ago. Catherine had to raise the pot from the fire. The author identifies a book, *Godey's Lady's Books,* that was used to get ideas for the latest fashions. The descriptions of the family's actions are from an earlier time: They go to church twice a day on the Sabbath. They are excited about getting store sweets wrapped in paper. Father tells stories after supper. The neighbor plays the fiddle. All of these details make us understand what life must have been like in 1830.

Characters: Catherine Cabot Hall is age 13 years, 7 months, and 8 days. She takes care of the family because her mother died of fever. In earlier times people often died of fever. Catherine is proud of her cooking and wants to take care of the family for a long time. She makes a special dress for Thanksgiving by adding a new lace collar to her Sabbath dress. She does not complain because she has so few clothes. Women were expected to take care of the house and family during earlier times. This role is shown again when a neighbor makes a point about his unmarried sister. Maybe Catherine's best friend is going to have a harder life. When she is 15, she is to be sent to Lowell, Massachusetts, to work in the mills. Catherine feels sorry for her friend's family because they are poor.

Conflict: Father and the neighbor argue about what to do if they find a runaway bound boy. Should they help him or turn him in? Advertisements in the *Courier* are described that report bound boys who run away. This indicates an earlier time because people are no longer bound for work.

Proof for historical fiction from author's notes: The author describes how she became interested in a restored house and barn at the end of a dirt road north of Meredith, New Hampshire. She then tells how much of her story is true: "I started with a handful of facts, an amateur's interest in the history of the region, and an intention to reconstruct life as it was when the house was new. To do this I worked with documents and books and newspapers of the region, visited museums and small collections, and even explored old graveyards in search of further clues. Some of the journal's episodes are freely adapted from sources consulted, among them the teacher's bodily ouster and the Count of Meredith's surprising and stylish return. But little by little the figures I imagined became more real than the rest" (p. 145).

The students discussed their evidence that the story was historical fiction and shared their personal responses to the settings and the characters. They discussed the author's reasons for writing the story and the research she needed to conduct to develop her setting and characters. They were especially interested in Blos's comment that her make-believe characters came alive for her as she researched and wrote the story. This point later became a focal point for the group as they evaluated various authors' abilities to create believable historical fiction and tried to write their own historical fiction.

After students have identified and responded to the historical fiction points in several books, ask them to develop a list of questions that they can use when they are deciding whether a book is historical fiction or evaluating the effectiveness of the historical fiction. The same group of sixth graders developed the following list:

1. Did I look for any notes by the author that tell me if the story is historical fiction? Where did the author get this story idea? What research did the author do? Did the author know anyone who had a similar experience?

2. Did the author make me see and feel the setting? I should close my eyes and try to see some of the details. Can I identify the time and place of the setting? I should look for hints in the book that let me know about the time and place.

3. Can I describe the characters, their beliefs, and their values? Do these descriptions, beliefs, and values seem right for what I know about the time period? Does the way that the characters speak seem right for the time period? What words do they use that make me believe I am hearing real people? I should try to imagine that I can hear their conversations. Does this conversation sound right for the time?

4. What is the conflict in the story? Would this conflict have happened during that time period? How do the characters overcome the conflict? Is this solution appropriate for the time period? Did I believe the conflict was really happening? I should try to describe each type of conflict and think about why each character experiences that conflict.

Allow students to read several historical fiction selections independently and apply their questions and evaluations. These questions and evaluations also can be used as part of a longer unit.

LESSON TWO: Responding to Historical Fiction Through Dramatizations and Role Playing

OBJECTIVES

To make history come alive through dramatizations.

To interact with historical fiction during a dramatization and to "feel" the time period.

To empathize with characters and their problems.

To develop an understanding of the conflicts that occurred in specific time periods.

CORE BOOKS (these also can be used for extended reading and other independent reading activities): Choose books with vivid scenes and characterizations. Historical fiction is filled with dramas, conflicts, and motivations that can be used for dramatizations or role playing. The activity can be used at any grade level if appropriate books are chosen. The following books and time periods are listed according to levels. Lower elementary: Brett Harvey's *Cassie's Journey: Going West in the 1860s,* the story of a wagon train; Elizabeth Howard's *Chita's Christmas Tree* (Black), set in early Baltimore; Arnold Lobel's *On the Day Peter Stuyvesant Sailed Into Town,* a story about the New Amsterdam colony; and Carla Stevens' *Anna, Grandpa, and the Big Storm,* set in New York City in 1888.

Middle elementary: Byrd Baylor's *The Best Town in the World* set in a small pioneer town; Zibby Oneal's *A Long Way to Go*, women's suffrage during World War I; and Mildred Taylor's *The Gold Cadillac* (Black), racial prejudice in 1950.

Upper elementary and middle school: Joan Lingard's *Tug of War,* a Latvian family in World War II; Janet Lunn's *Shadow in Hawthorn Bay* set in 1800s Canada; Elizabeth George Speare's *The Witch of Blackbird Pond* (Newbery Medal), set in colonial New England; and Mildred Taylor's *Roll of Thunder, Hear My Cry* (Black, Newbery Medal), prejudice in rural Mississippi.

PROCEDURES: Encourage the students to choose scenes, interesting dialogues, or stimulating ideas that can be expanded. The following dramatization and role-playing ideas were developed around the core books for this lesson:

Cassie's Journey: Going West in the 1860s: Dramatize a scene in which Cassie has an exciting experience as she travels in the covered wagon, or role play a conversation she has with her father as she sits beside him on the wagon seat.

Chita's Christmas Tree: Choose one of the scenes described in the book, such as Christmas Eve, and dramatize the family celebration.

On the Day Peter Stuyvesant Sailed Into Town: Dramatize Peter walking through the town, giving his comments, and his orders. Role play the colonists' reactions to Mr. Stuyvesant coming to town.

Anna, Grandpa, and the Big Storm: Dramatize the people caught in the blizzard, or role play possible conversations between Anna and her grandfather.

The Best Town in the World: Dramatize the activities associated with a scene described in the text and illustrations. For example, dramatize the activities associated with a picnic celebration in the days when a picnic was a major social event, or role play conversations between people in the general store.

A Long Way to Go: Dramatize a gathering in which women are arguing for their right to vote, or role play the dialogue between someone who supports women's suffrage and someone who does not.

The Gold Cadillac: Dramatize a scene that shows that love and unity can help families overcome terrible experiences, or role play the disbelief expressed by the younger family members when they experience discrimination for the first time.

Tug of War: Dramatize several of the major incidents that show what happens when Hugo and his family are separated and then must flee from advancing Russians during World War II, or role play Hugo's dilemma as he chooses whether to go to Canada with his own family or to stay in Europe with the family that cared for him.

Shadow in Hawthorn Bay: Dramatize several of the major incidents as the Scottish girl leaves her home to try to find and help her cousin in Canada, or role play the various reactions to her second sight as expressed by those in Scotland who believe in her ability and those in Canada who are fearful of her powers.

The Witch of Blackbird Pond: Dramatize the trial in which Kit is accused of witchcraft, or role play the conversations between Kit and Hannah Tupper.

Roll of Thunder, Hear My Cry: Dramatize the school scene in which Cassie and her brother excitedly await their new schoolbooks, only to receive worn, dirty castoffs from the white elementary school, or role play any of the warm family interactions that help the family members develop their self-esteem.

LESSON THREE: Creating a Day in the Life of a _____ Child

OBJECTIVES

To read historical fiction and to pick out details that could be used to recreate a day in the life of a person living during that time period.

To do additional research to identify details related to areas such as settings, reading materials, entertainment, and other activities.

To empathize with characters and make the characters come to life.

CORE BOOKS (these also can be used for extended reading and other independent reading activities): Choose interesting literature selections with enough detail so that students can recreate the typical life of a child living during that time. This activity is appropriate for any grade level depending on the literature chosen and the complexity of the research used to develop additional details of the time period.

Lower elementary: Barbara Brenner's *Wagon Wheels* (Easy to Read), set in pioneer America; Tomie de Paola's *An Early American Christmas,* set in New England during the 1800s; Donald Hall's *Ox-Cart Man* (Caldecott Medal), set in New England in the 1800s; and Robert McCloskey's *Lentil,* set in Alto, Ohio in the early 1800s.

Middle elementary: Robert Cormier's *Other Bells for Us to Ring,* set in America during World War II; Marguerite DeAngeli's *The Door in the Wall* (Newbery Medal), set in England during the time of Edward III; and Laura Ingalls Wilder's *Little House in the Big Woods* (Touchstone), pioneer Wisconsin.

Upper elementary and middle school: Patricia Clapp's *Constance: A Story of Early Plymouth,* a story about the Plymouth Colony; Esther Forbes's *Johnny Tremain* (Newbery Medal, Touchstone), set in Boston during the Revolutionary War; Uri Orlev's *Island on Bird Street,* set in Warsaw during World War II; and Elizabeth George Speare's *The Sign of the Beaver* (Newbery Medal), set in New England during the frontier days.

PROCEDURES: These books cover various historical times including the Middle Ages and castle life in Europe, Colonial America, Pioneer America on several frontiers, and World War II in the United States and in Warsaw. Some of the books, such as *Little House in the Big Woods,* reflect happy times in supportive families, while other books such as *Island on Bird Street* develop the frightening circumstances surrounding Jewish survival during the Holocaust.

Choose a core book and a time period that the students would like to use to recreate a day in the life of someone in that time period. As the students read or listen to the book, ask them to note details that can be used to recreate the day. For example, they should try to describe the surroundings so that the setting can be as authentic as possible. They should notice how the people dress and talk, what they talk about, what they do for work and entertainment, what they read or listen to, where they go and how they get there, what they eat, how they get and cook their food, how they are educated, what problems they face, and how they try to solve those problems. Many of the characters mention specific music that they listen to, stories they hear, or books they read. In some of the books, such as *Other Bells for Us to Ring,* the characters listen to specific radio programs.

Encourage the students to select several incidents that they can recreate. For example, *Little House in the Big Woods* includes numerous descriptions of both work and entertainment that can be recreated: Making butter; visiting the general store; and square dancing to the folksongs "Buffalo Gals," "The Irish Washerwoman," and "The Arkansas Traveler." Pa also plays and sings "Pop Goes the Weasel," "Rock of Ages," and "Yankee Doodle." The students also can recreate the stories that Pa tells.

After students have selected several incidents to recreate, teachers and students should conduct additional research sources to add authenticity and detail to their dramatization. For example, Bingham and Scholt's *Fifteen Centuries of Children's Literature: An Annotated Chronology of British and American Works in Historical Context* (1980) can be consulted to find literature that would have been read during that time period. Likewise, *The Oxford Book of Children's Verse* (Opie & Opie, 1984), presents poetry in the order in which it was written from Medieval times through the 20th century. Fox's *Go In and Out the Window* (1987) and Larrick's *Songs from Mother Goose* (1989) are sources of music sung during earlier time periods. *The Foxfire Book* (Wigginton, 1972) describes how pioneers preserved fruits and vegetables and made various necessities. The first Newbery Medal winner, Hendrik Willem Van Loon's nonfictional *The Story of Mankind,* can provide historical background for the time period.

Finally, encourage the students to make their day as authentic as possible. They can develop an appropriate setting for the characters, dress like the characters, talk like the characters, act like the characters, and solve problems of the characters.

BIOGRAPHY

A biography is a nonfictional story that tells about characters who actually lived. The setting must describe real places where the people lived; the events in the plot must really have happened. When evaluating biography, readers are concerned with accuracy, with characterization that reflects the many sides of the biographical character, with whether the subject makes a statement about humanity—for good or ill—that students should be aware of, and with the quality of the author's research. If the biography is an illustrated story for younger readers, the illustrations must be as accurate as possible.

Another requirement makes writing biographies for children more difficult than writing other forms of literature: Authors must balance the requirement for accuracy with the requirement for an appealing narrative. This is especially true when writing biographies for younger students. Consequently, critics such as Girard describe children's biographies as "The Truth With Some Stretchers" (1988). Current biographers however, are developing stories that rely on accuracy as well as more candid portrayals of their biographical characters (Norton, 1991).

Developing Understandings of Biography

Activities and units can be developed that emphasize each of these important understandings:

1. Biography is a genre of literature in which an author develops the life of a person who actually lived or is living today.

2. The details in a biography, including dates, places, and names should be accurate; they should be able to be authenticated through other nonfictional sources.

3. The settings in biography must be the actual places in which the biographical character lived; the settings must be accurate.

4. The characterization, one of the most important aspects of a biography, should reflect several sides of the person.

5. The plot in the biography must actually have happened.

6. Because biographical authors have a considerable responsibility in researching their subjects, they should use primary sources and list the sources they used to obtain their information.

Approaches that Develop Understanding and Appreciation of Biography

The list of important understandings highlights some of the considerations that students should make when they read, respond to, and evaluate biography. As can historical fiction, the study of biographical characters can be integrated with other content areas as students make discoveries about science, history, politics, exploration, art, music, and literature by reading about leaders in the fields. Students can discover the human qualities that make men and women special by reading about common people who overcame great obstacles. The following approaches include lessons that were developed in previous chapters and lessons and units that will be developed in this chapter.

1. Analyzing the reasons for an author's understanding of person-against-nature conflicts in his realistic fiction by analyzing important instances in his life as revealed through his autobiography. (Ch. 5, Paulsen's *Woodsong.*)

2. Modeling inferring of characterization in biography. (Ch. 6, Fritz's *The Great Little Madison.*)

3. Drawing time lines of important instances in a biographical character's life (Ch. 7, Freedman's *Franklin Delano Roosevelt.*)

4. Developing self-questioning strategies that help students decide whether a story is a biography and evaluate the effectiveness of the biography.

5. Giving an oral presentation to the class in which students try to convince the class that a biographical character is real.

6. Comparing biographies of the same character written by different authors and researching the authenticity of the biographies.

7. Developing personal responses to biographical characters through writing, role playing, and art.

8. Gaining experience writing biographies through such approaches as choosing a supporting character in a biography and writing about that character, writing about someone known to the students, and writing about someone they do not know.

9. Comparing a biography written about an author and the writings of that author.

10. Developing units that integrate historical fiction, biography, and other nonfictional sources.

This chapter focuses on lessons and units that develop the approaches listed in No. 4–10. The approaches developed in previous chapters can be used for the study of biography and can be added to units.

Core Books and Sample Lessons for Developing Understanding and Appreciation of Biography

These core lessons can be used at several different grade levels depending on the books chosen. Each core lesson identifies books for students in lower elementary, middle elementary, and upper elementary and middle school. The lessons also can be used as part of larger units on biography.

LESSON ONE: Developing Questions Students Can Ask When Deciding Whether a Book is Biography or When Evaluating a Biography

OBJECTIVES

To develop questions that students can ask themselves to decide whether a book is biography.

To develop questions that students can use to evaluate biography.

To read additional biography and apply the questions during independent reading.

CORE BOOKS: For lower elementary students, choose highly illustrated biographies: Jean Fritz's *Why Don't You Get a Horse, Sam Adams?* Middle elementary: Jean Fritz's *Make Way for Sam Houston.* Upper elementary and middle school: Polly Schoyer Brooks' *Queen Eleanor: Independent Spirit of the Medieval World.*

EXTENDED BOOKS FOR INDEPENDENT READING AND RELATED ACTIVITIES: The following books also can be used as core books. For shorter biographies, use any of the books listed for the lower grades.

Lower Elementary

ALICE DALGLIESH's *The Columbus Story*

JAMES T. DEKAY's *Meet Martin Luther King, Jr.* (Black)

OPHELIA SETTLE EGYPT's *James Weldon Johnson* (Black)

Middle Elementary

ALIKI's *The King's Day: Louis XIV of France*

ROBERT QUACKENBUSH's *Mark Twain? What Kind of a Name Is That? A Story of Samuel Langhorne Clemens*

DIANE STANLEY AND PETER VENNEMA's *Shaka: King of the Zulus* (Black)

Upper Elementary and Middle School

JEAN FRITZ's *Stonewall*

PATRICIA LAUBER's *Lost Star: The Story of Amelia Earhart*

BETSY LEE's *Charles Eastman, The Story of an American Indian* (Native American)

PROCEDURES: Ask students to identify books that could be classified as biography. Ask, "What makes the book a biography?" Make sure students understand that a biography is a nonfictional story about a real person who lived or is living. Then ask the students to compare a historical fiction book such as Dalgliesh's *The Courage of Sarah Noble* and a biography such as Fritz's *Why Don't You Get a Horse, Sam Adams?* Ask, "What are the similarities in the books?

What are the differences in the books?" Make sure students understand that the historical fiction is based on authentic historical settings and problems but the stories and people did not exist. In contrast, biography is based on real people, real settings, and problems and conflicts that actually happened.

Next, choose a book that is appropriate for the grade level. Share the book, or a chapter from a longer book, with the students and ask them to identify the people, the settings, the conflicts, and the author's writing and research that makes the book biographical. A group of fourth-grade students identified the following biographical points using the first chapter and the author's notes from Fritz's *Make Way for Sam Houston:*

> *Characters:* In the first chapter the author identifies the main character, Sam Houston. The author describes Houston's feelings toward school, his heroes, and his early life. The author describes why Houston understood the Cherokee Indians and identifies other people who influenced his life: The Cherokee chief, John Jolly, Gen. Andrew Jackson, and John C. Calhoun, the secretary of war. When Fritz tells humorous things about Sam Houston, she makes us believe he was a real person. All of the people mentioned are real people who actually lived.
>
> *Settings:* The author identifies many dates and places, such as the date of Houston's birth (March 2, 1793). The author states that at this time the Revolutionary War had been over for 12 years. More dates are given, such as on March 27, 1814, Houston was in the army with Gen. Andrew Jackson. The first chapter describes how Houston moved to Tennessee and later lived with the Cherokees. The author identifies battles such as the Battle of Horseshoe Bend and the Battle of New Orleans. All these dates, locations, and battles can be checked. They make the biography seem real.
>
> *Conflicts of the time period:* The major conflicts are wars and moving the Cherokee Indians. Sam Houston joins the army in 1813 to fight with Gen. Andrew Jackson against England in the War of 1812. Two battles are described along with Houston's injury at the Battle of Horseshoe Bend. The winning of the Battle of New Orleans made Andrew Jackson a national hero. Sam Houston persuaded his friends the Cherokee Indians to move west. All of these conflicts are part of history.
>
> *Author's writing and research:* The author identifies the sources she used to write her biography. These include letters and papers written by Sam Houston and a scrapbook he collected. The author identifies 24 books and 11 articles she used for research. A map shows many of the places discussed in the book. The biography probably is more accurate because the author used these sources. We can use some of these sources to do our own research.

Encourage the students to discuss the importance of these characteristics and how each characteristic can add to the authenticity of a biography. Ask them to consider which of the characteristics make the biographies more meaningful and vivid to them. They can read and respond to the remainder of *Make Way for Sam Houston* and read several additional biographies. Next, ask the students to develop a list of questions that they can use to decide whether a book is biography or evaluate the effectiveness of the biography. The same group of fourth-grade students developed the following list:

1. Who is the biographical character? Did all the people in the book actually live? What techniques did the author use to make me believe the characters are real? I should try to picture the characters. Did the author make me believe in the characters? Why or why not?

2. Where does the biography take place? What dates and places does the author use? Are these dates and places authentic for the character's life? I should try to picture the settings. Can I check other sources to see if the dates and places are accurate? If I am not sure, I should check these sources.

3. What problems does the biographical character face? How does the author make sure I understand those problems? Are the problems authentic for the biographical character and the time period? I should ask myself, "How can I check if these problems are accurate?"

4. What research did the author do to support the actions and dialogue in the biography? Can I identify sources that would reveal accurate information? I should ask myself, "Do I think the author did enough research before writing this biography? Should the author have done more research? What would this research be?"

LESSON TWO: Giving an Oral Presentation to Convince the Class that a Biographical Character Is Real

OBJECTIVES

To respond to biographical characters by choosing an incident in their lives that seems particularly believable to the students.

To prepare a convincing oral presentation that argues for the reality of a biographical character.

To evaluate and identify effective authors' techniques.

CORE BOOKS (these also can be used for extended reading and other independent reading activities): Select biographies in which the authors develop believable characterizations. This lesson can be used at any grade level depending on the materials chosen. Also, any biographies recommended in previous or subsequent lessons can be used.

For lower elementary students: Ruth Franchere's *Cesar Chavez* (Hispanic); Bill Gutman's *The Picture Life of Reggie Jackson* (Black); John Jakes's *Susanna of the Alamo;* and Joe Lasker's *The Great Alexander the Great.*

For middle elementary students: Lillian Gish and Selma G. Lanes's *An Actor's Life for Me!;* Jane Goodsell's *Daniel Inouye* (Japanese American) and *Eleanor Roosevelt;* and Ruth Belov Gross's *True Stories About Abraham Lincoln.*

For upper elementary and middle school students: Jean Fritz's *The Great Little Madison;* Virginia Hamilton's *Anthony Burns: The Defeat and Triumph of a Fugitive Slave* (Black); Albert Marrin's *Hitler;* and Milton Meltzer's *Dorothea Lange, Life Through the Camera.*

PROCEDURES: Ask the students to choose a main or supporting character from a biography and give a short oral presentation in which they make the class believe the biographical character is real. They can tell anecdotes or use photographs from the biography, argue about the research capabilities of the author, or support something that happened from the story with another nonfictional source. Or, if the author did not convince the students that the biographical character was real, they can try to make the class believe that their biographical character could not be real, offering reasons that the author did not develop a believable character. For example, a middle elementary student retold the anecdotes developed in *An Actor's Life for Me!* arguing that the anecdotes made Gish seem like a real person. The student said her father told similar stories about her grandfather, which made her grandfather seem real to her.

LESSON THREE: Comparing Biographies of the Same Biographical Characters

OBJECTIVES

To compare biographies of the same biographical characters written by different authors.

To evaluate and research the authenticity of the biographies.

To evaluate the effectiveness of different biographies written about the same person.

To analyze personal responses to different biographies written about the same person.

CORE BOOKS (these also can be used for extended reading and other independent reading activities): Choose as many biographies written about the same person as possible. The books in this section are divided into biographical subjects rather than grade levels—teachers can choose the books that are appropriate for their grades. Students in the upper grades can read, analyze, and evaluate both the easier and the more difficult books. This list includes older as well as more recent biographies about the same person. Older students can make interesting comparisons across time as well as across authors. Several biographies are available about the following people:

Christopher Columbus

ALICE DALGLIESH's *The Columbus Story.* A picture book biography covers Columbus's first voyage.

INGRI AND EDGAR PARIN D'AULAIRE's *Columbus.* A highly illustrated biography.

JEAN FRITZ's *Where Do You Think You're Going, Christopher Columbus?* This biography covers the four voyages of Columbus.

DAVID GOODNOUGH's *Christopher Columbus.* An illustrated life story of Columbus.

NANCY SMILER LEVINSON's *Christopher Columbus: Voyager to the Unknown.* This biography includes the current controversy over Columbus's exact location for his landing.

MILTON MELTZER's *Columbus and the World Around Him.* The author uses primary sources to develop a well-supported biography.

PETER AND CONNIE ROOP's *I, Columbus: My Journal, 1492–3.* The text includes passages from Columbus's journal.

PIERO VENTURA's *Christopher Columbus.* A highly illustrated picture biography.

Abraham Lincoln

INGRI AND EDGAR PARIN D'AULAIRE's *Abraham Lincoln* (Caldecott Medal). A highly illustrated biography.

RUSSELL FREEDMAN's *Lincoln: A Photobiography* (Newbery Medal). A carefully documented biography.

RUTH BELOV GROSS's *True Stories About Abraham Lincoln.* A series of short stories emphasize aspects of Lincoln's life, especially his early years.

CARL SANDBURG's *Abe Lincoln Grows Up.* The biography covers the first 19 years of Lincoln's life.

Eleanor Roosevelt

MARGARET DAVIDSON's *The Story of Eleanor Roosevelt.* A well-developed biography of Roosevelt's life.

JANE GOODSELL's *Eleanor Roosevelt.* This biography develops Roosevelt's life as a shy child, as well as her years in the White House and her work after her husband's death.

ELLIOT ROOSEVELT's *Eleanor Roosevelt, with Love.* This biography tells about Roosevelt's life through the viewpoint of her son.

SHARON WHITNEY's *Eleanor Roosevelt.* This biography follows the life of Roosevelt from childhood through work with the United Nations.

Franklin D. Roosevelt

Russell Freedman's *Franklin Delano Roosevelt*. The biography covers Roosevelt's life from his youth, through his early political career and presidency.

Catherine Owens Peare's *The FDR Story*. The biography covers Roosevelt's political accomplishments.

Barbara Silberdick's *Franklin D. Roosevelt, Gallant President*. This biography focuses on Roosevelt's accomplishments.

Martin Luther King, Jr.

James DeKay's *Meet Martin Luther King, Jr.* An illustrated biography that stresses the magnitude of King's work and his reasons for fighting injustice.

James Haskin's *The Life and Death of Martin Luther King, Jr.* The biography covers the life of the Civil Rights leader.

Lillie Patterson's *Martin Luther King, Jr. and the Freedom Movement*. The biography tells of King's nonviolent struggles against segregation.

Benjamin Franklin

James Daugherty's *Poor Richard*. The biography covers Franklin's life and activities.

Jean Fritz's *What's the Big Idea, Ben Franklin?* A biography of the inventor, ambassador, and coauthor of the Declaration of Independence.

Milton Meltzer's *Benjamin Franklin: The New American*. A carefully documented biography of the American statesman.

Multiple biographies also can be found about individuals such as Mary McLeod Bethune, Daniel Boone, Rachel Carson, Cesar Chavez, Samuel Langhorne Clemens, Leonardo Da Vinci, Emily Dickinson, Frederick Douglass, Eleanor of Aquitaine, Galileo Galilei, Langston Hughes, Andrew Jackson, Thomas Jefferson, Joan of Arc, Winnie Mandela, William Penn, Pocahontas, Beatrix Potter, Jackie Robinson, Harriet Tubman, and George Washington.

PROCEDURES: This comparative activity can be accomplished as a group or as an individual activity. If it is developed as a group project, divide the students into groups according to a biographical character. If this is an individual activity students should choose a subject that has at least two biographies to compare.

Introduce the activity by telling students that biographers have both responsibilities and choices when they develop their stories. The settings, dates, characterizations, and actions must be authentic. The authenticity usually can be checked by referring to other sources or comparing two or three biographies. Biographers also choose the portion of a person's life on which to focus, the activities they wish to reveal, and the various sides of the character that they want to develop. Sometimes authors even have purposes for writing biographies, which can color the work if the author interprets actions in certain ways or leaves out portions of the subject's life that do not support the biographer's view. Ask the students to consider how they would write a biography about someone they like very much and someone whose ideas they do not believe in. Choose a well-known public figure. Ask the students, "How would you write a biography to reflect that you like or support the work of the character? How would you write a biography if you do not like or support the work of the character? What incidents would you put in your biography? What incidents would you leave out?"

Next, ask students either in groups or individually to read several biographies and compare their reactions, the authenticity of the details, and the authors' purposes for writing the biographies. Students can follow these guidelines when comparing two or more biographies:

1. Compare the introductions to the biography. How does each author attract your interest to the biographical character? Which approach is more effective? Why?

2. Draw and label the life-line of each biographical character. Compare the life-lines in several biographies of the same character. How are the life-lines the same? How are they different? What could account for the differences?

3. Identify the focus of each author. Why might each author have developed that particular focus? What portion of the character's life is developed? What information is included? What information is left out? Why might each author have included or left out that information? Is the author's point of view positive, negative, or neutral toward the biographical character? How can you tell?

4. How does each author develop characterization? What techniques does each author use to make readers believe in the reality of the biographical characters? Which author is more successful at developing characterization? Why? Which character created a more personal response in the reader? What caused that response?

5. Identify the specific details of time and place. Notice and compare the dates of specific occurrences and the places where actions occurred. Do the biographies agree? If not, how can you decide which biography is accurate? Try to identify the biography that is the most accurate for time and place.

6. Compare the major conflicts in the biographies. Does each biography emphasize the same conflicts? What techniques do the authors use to let readers understand the conflicts faced by the character? Which author is the most successful at developing conflict? What makes that author successful?

7. Identify the themes in each biography. Are the themes similar in each work? Try to account for any differences in theme.

8. Identify and compare the research support listed by the different biographers. How would you compare the quality of the research? Which biography is best supported by research?

9. Summarize the results of the comparisons. Is one biography superior? Or does each biography have specific strengths and weaknesses? Pretend you are writing a book review or recommending one of the biographies to a friend. Which would you recommend? Why?

LESSON FOUR: Developing Personal Responses to Biographical Characters Through Writing, Role Playing, and Art

OBJECTIVES

To develop an aesthetic response to biographical characters.

To empathize with a biographical character and respond to that character through writing.

To understand the conflicts faced by a biographical character and to respond to those conflicts through role playing.

To develop an emotional response through art.

CORE BOOKS (these also can be used for extended reading and other independent reading activities): Biographies in which students can interact with the emotional experiences, motives, and action of the characters. This activity can be used with any grade level depending on the books chosen.

    Lower elementary: Alice Dalgliesh's *The Columbus Story;* John Jakes' *Susanna of the Alamo;* and Bernard Wolf's *In This Proud Land: The Story of a Mexican Family.*

Middle elementary: Wyatt Blassingame's *Thor Heyerdahl: Viking Scientist;* Lillian Gish and Selma G. Lanes's *An Actor's Life for Me!;* and Fay Stanley's *The Last Princess: The Story of Princess Ka'iulani of Hawai'i.*

Upper elementary and middle school: Jean Fritz's *Traitor: The Case of Benedict Arnold;* Carol Ann Pearce's *Amelia Earhart;* Johanna Reiss's *The Upstairs Room;* Sidney Rosen's *Galileo and the Magic Numbers;* and Elizabeth Yates's *Amos Fortune, Free Man* (Newbery Medal).

PROCEDURES: Select a book to share orally or for students to read independently. They may choose to respond to the biographical character through writing, role playing, or art. For example, some students who have read *The Upstairs Room* have responded to the girl's fears in writing. They have written journal entries as if they are the girl, written characterizations about the people who helped them, and written their reactions when they went back to the house after the war. They have role played the interactions among members of the family, the girls, and the Nazis who search the house. They have drawn pictures to show what they would feel and visualize if they were hidden in a small closet. Through art, they have traced their various feelings as they interacted with the biographical characters.

The other books have equal potential for interesting, individual responses. For example lower elementary students, after reading Dalgliesh's *The Columbus Story,* respond to the call for adventure when the author states, "Mystery, danger, adventure—what exciting worlds! (p. 3). They frequently describe how they would react to such a call for adventure. Through art, they illustrate what they think the mystery, danger, and adventure might be. In Jakes' *Susanna of the Alamo* students respond to the danger and the responsibility of being in the Alamo and taking an important message away from the battle. Students enjoy role playing their interactions with the various characters. Many students develop diaries that cover the time of the biography. After reading Wolf's *In This Proud Land: The Story of a Mexican Family,* students respond to the photographs and the text as a family from the Rio Grande Valley travels to Minnesota for summer employment.

Students in the middle elementary grades frequently respond to Blassingame's *Thor Heyerdahl: Viking Scientist* by describing what might have happened if they had been on the Kon Tiki as it sailed 4,000 miles from Peru to the Polynesian islands. This biography is excellent for art interpretations. In Gish and Lanes' *An Actor's Life for Me!* students respond to the excitement and loneliness of Gish's life as a young actress away from her family. Many students enjoy placing themselves in similar circumstances and describing their emotional reactions. Other students enjoy role playing an early acting experience. In Stanley's *The Last Princess: The Story of Princess Ka'iulani of Hawai'i* students respond to the life experiences of this young girl.

Many of the books listed for upper elementary and middle school students develop strong personal responses. For example, after reading Fritz's *Traitor: The Case of Benedict Arnold* students respond to the characterization as Arnold changes from a man called "the bravest of the brave" to "the veriest villain of centuries past" and role play his support for the British cause during the Revolutionary War. Some students contrast their possible feelings toward Arnold from the British and the American points of view. Pearce's *Amelia Earhart* develops interesting responses as students debate whether Earhart should try her various flights and then hypothesize about what happened on her final flight. Interesting diaries reveal how students might respond if they were Earhart on her last flight. Rosen's *Galileo and the Magic Numbers* encourages students to respond to Galileo's elation as he studies the craters of the moon through his improved telescope and to his bitterness when he is charged with heresy, forced to recant his position, and imprisoned. Exciting role-playing scenes can develop as students place themselves in the various roles. In Yates's *Amos Fortune, Free Man,* students respond to this slave's struggle as he works for his freedom in America.

LESSON FIVE: Writing Biographies

OBJECTIVES

> To apply the knowledge gained from reading, analyzing, and evaluating biographies to the writing of biographies.
>
> To develop interviewing skills that can be helpful when writing a biography about someone the students know.
>
> To research the background of a character and write a biography about that character.

CORE BOOKS: All the biographies listed in the previous lessons can be used in this lesson and for independent reading. Students should use those works to summarize important information about writing biographies and to identify supporting characters that could be subjects for biographies.

PROCEDURES: Ask the students to choose a person they know, such as a family member, a neighbor, or a classmate. Have the class brainstorm information they would need to know and questioning techniques they might use to gather information about that person. After the questions and techniques are identified, role play the interviewing experiences. Ask the students to consider other sources of information such as school yearbooks, newspaper articles, photograph albums, journals, courthouse documents, and people who know the person. Ask the students to select an interesting anecdote, a personal characteristic, or an experience that would make an interesting short biography and have them compose a rough draft of the biographical character. Share the rough draft with a group of their peers. Have the group consider how the character was made to seem real. Ask, "Are there any other techniques that you could use to improve understanding of the character?" Have the students organize the introduction, body, and conclusion. Ask, "Does each part reinforce the qualities or the experiences you are emphasizing?" Continue the rewriting process until the stories seem like biographies of real and interesting people.

Ask the students to find out more about one of the supporting characters developed in a biography and write a short biography from the viewpoint of that character. They should include the original main character in their biography, but give that character a supporting role. For example, actress Mary Pickford appears in *An Actor's Life For Me!,* and could be the focus of a student biography. Lillian Gish, the main character in the original biography, would be a supporting character in the student biography. Likewise, either Andrew Jackson or John C. Calhoun, supporting characters in *Make Way for Sam Houston,* can be the main character in a student biography.

Ask the students to write a biography about a person they do not know. They should choose a subject that will require library research and other documentation. Ask them to consider possible sources of information and how they will gather that information. Be sure they choose a character about whom there is sufficient source material. Ask the students to choose an interesting period in that person's life and to accumulate as many reference materials as they can find. For example, they can search for speeches and writings by the person, reproductions of the front page of a newspaper that might have been available at that time, biographies and autobiographies, newspaper and magazine articles about the person, letters, diaries, and so forth. Have them write a biography that uses the facts to support a person's possible thoughts, actions and associations. They should make the readers believe that the person is real. As they are writing, they should share the biographies with their editing group and with the teacher during conferences.

LESSON SIX: Comparing Autobiographies and Biographies and the Creative Works of the Characters

OBJECTIVES

To compare characterizations in autobiographies with those in works developed by that author.

To analyze motivations and relationships in two types of writing.

To discover why authors might write certain types of literature.

To discover why illustrators might draw certain types of illustrations.

CORE BOOKS (these also can be used for extended reading and other independent reading activities): The books chosen for this lesson are all autobiographies or biographies written by or about well-known children's authors or illustrators.

For lower elementary students: Bill Peet's *Bill Peet: An Autobiography* (Caldecott Honor); For middle elementary, upper elementary, and middle school students: Angelica Shirley Carpenter and Jean Shirley's *Frances Hodgson Burnett: Beyond the Secret Garden* (Biography); Beverly Cleary's *A Girl from Yamhill: A Memoir* (Autobiography); Martin Fido's *Rudyard Kipling: An Illustrated Biography;* Eloise Greenfield and Lessie Jones Little's *Childtimes: A Three-Generation Memoir* (Autobiography, Black); Trina Schart Hyman's *Self-Portrait: Trina Schart Hyman;* Milton Meltzer's *Starting from Home: A Writer's Beginnings* (Autobiography); Elizabeth Yates's *My Diary, My World* and *My Widening World* (Autobiographies); and Margot Zemach's *Self-Portrait, Margot Zemach.*

PROCEDURES: Choose an autobiography or biography of one of the authors or illustrators whose works interest the students. Collect as many of those works as you can locate in the library. Tell the students that they will be listening to or reading the autobiography or biography to try to discover information about the author or illustrator. For example, if they read *Bill Peet: An Autobiography,* they will make discoveries about the author and illustrator of humorous picture storybooks written for younger children. Carpenter and Shirley's *Frances Hodgson Burnett: Beyond the Secret Garden* will give them a glimpse of the author of the classic book about a girl and a boy who find that discovering and working in a locked garden allows them to overcome their problems. Cleary's *A Girl from Yamhill: A Memoir* is about the author of contemporary realistic fiction about such characters as Ramona, Henry, and Beezus. She tells about her early life through high school. Fido's *Rudyard Kipling: An Illustrated Biography* will let students discover the fantasy author who set his stories in India. Greenfield and Little's *Childtimes: A Three-Generation Memoir* reveals insights about the author of poetry and contemporary realistic fiction. Through Hyman's *Self-Portrait: Trina Schart Hyman* students can discover information about the life of the award-winning artist of many picture storybooks. Meltzer's *Starting from Home: A Writer's Beginning* allows students to learn more about the author of biographies such as *Benjamin Franklin: The New American; Columbus and the World Around Him; Dorothea Lange, Life Through the Camera;* and *George Washington and the Birth of Our Nation.* Yates's *My Diary, My World* and *My Widening World* help students understand the author of *Amos Fortune, Free Man.* Zemach's *Self-Portrait, Margot Zemach* provides information about the illustrator of many folktales. Ask them to list any information that reveals insights into the author's or illustrator's motivations or purposes for writing or painting.

For this activity, students can use Cianciolo's (1985) findings when she analyzed the comments about good writing expressed by various children's authors. Ask students if they can find some of these qualities in the works they are reading:

1. Good writers must be good readers.
2. Good writers care intensely about language and are sensitive to it.
3. Good writers are well educated.
4. Good writers are alert observers.
5. Good writers are storytellers and enjoy stories told by others.
6. Good writers are compulsive writers.

Finally, ask the students to read or listen to several books written or illustrated by the autobiographical or biographical subjects. Ask them to identify any commonalities between the two sources. What evidence do they find that suggests why an author writes in a certain way or writes about certain subjects or themes? What important experiences might have motivated them to write or illustrate?

INFORMATIONAL LITERATURE

Informational books provide opportunities for students to gain new knowledge about the world. Through informational books students learn to value the scientific method, become self-reliant as they investigate many topics, develop critical reading and thinking skills, expand their vocabularies, enhance their curiosity, and enjoy new hobbies. Because informational books can be found in many content areas, they play an important part in the school curriculum. Consequently, students should be encouraged to discover the important characteristics of informational literature and learn how to read the books.

Developing Understandings of Informational Literature

Activities and units can be developed that emphasize these important understandings:

1. All facts in information books must be accurate.
2. The author should be qualified to write a book on the particular subject.
3. Facts should be distinguished clearly from theories.
4. Significant facts should not be omitted.
5. If the subject is controversial, differing views should be presented.
6. The information should be as up-to-date as possible. Consequently, copyright dates are important for certain types of informational books.
7. Informational authors should not use anthropomorphism (giving human thoughts, motives, or emotions to animals or plants).
8. The illustrations should be accurate and add to the clarity of the text.
9. The organization of the book should be logical for the subject matter.
10. Informational books should have organizational aids if needed to help readers find important information.
11. Well-written informational books should encourage students to become involved in the subject and to solve problems logically.

Approaches that Develop Understanding and Appreciation of Informational Literature

The approaches for developing understanding and appreciation of informational books differ from the approaches for the other genres. The approaches are more similar to those used for teaching reading in the areas of science, social studies, and history. For example, teaching students to use context clues, use parts of a book, analyze the author's organization, and evaluate the nonfictional information and the author's qualifications are all important when developing understandings of informational books. The following approaches were developed in previous chapters or will be developed in this chapter:

1. Expanding vocabulary through individualized dictionaries. (Ch. 3, Dodd's *Wheel Away!*).

2. Expanding vocabulary through context clues. (Ch. 3, Selsam and Hunt's *A First Look at Animals With Horns,* Lauber's *The News About Dinosaurs,* Fischer-Nagel's *The Life of the Honeybee,* Johnson's *Potatoes,* Matthew's *Polar Bear Cubs,* Goodall's *The Chimpanzee Family Book,* Emberley's *City Sounds,* the Roops' *Seasons of the Cranes,* Simon's *Storms,* Sattler and Gallant's *The Book of Eagles,* Gallant's *Before the Sun Dies: The Story of Evolution,* McLaughlin's *Dragonflies*).

3. Expanding vocabulary by webbing vocabulary associated with units and themes. (Ch. 3, vocabulary associated with seasonal unit using Rockwell's *First Comes Spring,* Fowler's *When Summer Ends,* and Aragon's *Winter Harvest*).

4. Expanding vocabulary through semantic feature analysis. (Ch. 3, Lauber's *Volcano: The Eruption and Healing of Mount St. Helens*).

5. Describing and writing descriptions of familiar settings. (Ch. 7, Selsam and Hunt's *Keep Looking!,* Garland's *My Cousin Katie,* George's *Box Turtle at Long Pond*).

6. Analyzing settings that create geographical backgrounds. (Ch. 7, Baer's *This Is the Way We Go to School, A Book About Children Around the World*).

7. Comparing characteristics of personified animals in fantasy with characteristics of animals in nonfictional sources. (Ch. 9, Cole's *A Cat's Body,* Weber's *Care of Uncommon Pets,* Matthews's *Polar Bear Cubs,* Scott's *The Book of the Pig,* and Hess's *Diary of a Rabbit*).

8. Using previously developed approaches, such as webbing, to identify relationships in books.

9. Developing self-questioning strategies to decide whether a book is nonfiction informational literature and to evaluate the informational book.

10. Teaching students to use the parts of an informational book including index, table of contents, related readings, and glossary.

11. Helping students read for understanding by analyzing how the author organizes the work to present information.

12. Writing content journals and personal responses to informational literature.

13. Incorporating nonfiction informational literature into units developed for the various content areas.

14. Using nonfiction informational materials to authenticate historical fiction and biography.

This section will focus on the approaches listed in Nos. 9–14. The previous approaches should be added to lessons and extended units using informational literature. Informational materials can be related to various content fields in more ways than can be discussed in this chapter, but teachers should be aware of some of the recommendations of experts in the area of content reading. For example, Roehler and Duffy (1989) state that for content area teachers to develop conceptual understandings among their students instruction must have the following five characteristics: "Conceptual learning occurs when meanings about content area knowledge are (1) gradually constructed, (2) by the learners, (3) through a series of interactions with the content, (4) with new information integrated with old information (5) so that the result in conscious awareness of what is being learned, when it will be useful, and how to use it effectively" (p. 116). Hayes and Peters (1989) outline approaches such as concept mapping and accessing prior knowledge that are successful in providing reading instruction in the social studies classroom. Ogle (1989) presents study techniques that increase students' success in the content areas. For example, she suggests developing strategy sheets on which the students list what they know, what they want to find out, and what they learned and still need to learn; using multiple sources of materials; developing a repertoire of strategies; and developing self-awareness in which students are conscious of their own learning and the achievement of their objectives.

Core Books and Sample Lessons for Developing Understanding and Appreciation of Informational Literature

These core lessons can be used at several different grade levels depending on the books chosen. Books are listed lower elementary, middle elementary, and upper elementary and middle school students. The core lessons can be used as individual lessons or extended into units.

LESSON ONE: Developing Self-Questioning Strategies to Decide Whether a Book Is Non-fiction Informational Literature and to Evaluate the Informational Book

OBJECTIVES

To identify characteristics of nonfiction informational literature.

To develop a series of questions that students can use to decide whether a selection is informational literature and to evaluate that literature.

To read additional informational literature and apply the questions during independent reading.

CORE BOOKS: Select several books that represent informational literature and that are appropriate for the grade level. The books for lower grades are mostly highly illustrated informational books. Lower elementary: Joan Anderson's *The First Thanksgiving Feast* and Barbara Bash's *Desert Giant: The World of the Saguaro Cactus*. Middle elementary: Heiderose Fischer-Nagel and Andreas Fischer-Nagel's *Life of the Honey Bee* and Laurence Pringle's *Global Warming: Assessing the Greenhouse Threat*. Upper elementary and middle school: Nathan Aaseng's *Better Mousetraps: Product Improvements that Led to Success* and Rhoda Blumberg's *Commodore Perry in the Land of the Shogun* (Newbery Honor).

EXTENDED BOOKS FOR INDEPENDENT READING AND RELATED ACTIVITIES: The following books also can be chosen as core books.

Lower Elementary

MILLICENT E. SELSAM's *The Amazing Dandelion.* The life cycle of the dandelion is depicted in text and photographs.

MILLICENT E. SELSAM AND JOYCE HUNT's *A First Look at Bird Nests* and *A First Look at Caterpillars.* These are part of series of books in which the authors introduce various animals and insects through illustrations and text.

ANGELA WILKES' *My First Activity Book* and *My First Nature Book.* Through illustrations and text, these books provide detailed directions for various projects.

Middle Elementary

CAROLINE ARNOLD's *Saving the Peregrine Falcon.* The author discusses several ways that people are trying to save the falcon from extinction.

ROBERT D. BALLARD's *Exploring the Titanic.* Traces the history of the ship and its discovery in the ocean.

GINNY JOHNSTON AND JUDY CUTCHINS' *Windows on Wildlife.* The text and illustrations show how realistic habitats are created in zoos, wildlife parks, and aquariums.

Upper Elementary and Middle School

NANCY O'KEEFE BOLICK AND SALLIE G. RANDOLPH's *Shaker Inventions.* Explores the Shaker culture and the inventions created by the people.

HILDA SIMON's *Sight and Seeing: A World of Light and Color.* Shows how human and animal eyes function.

PROCEDURES: Ask students to identify books or subjects for books that could be classified as nonfiction informational books. Ask, "What makes the book nonfiction? What does *informational* mean when you are identifying literature?" Make sure that the students understand that everything in an informational book is nonfictional. They also should understand that informational books can be written about many subjects such as life cycles of animals, history, plants, hobbies, and geography. Ask, "Do authors of informational books have any responsibilities to the reader? What are these responsibilities? What happens if an author gives wrong information in one of these books?" Make sure that the students understand that the information should be as accurate and as up-to-date as possible because it helps them gain knowledge about the world.

Next, choose a book that is appropriate for the grade level. Share the book, or a chapter from a longer book, with the students and ask them to identify the characteristics that make the book informational. For example, a group of middle elementary students identified the following points from *Global Warming: Assessing the Greenhouse Threat:*

Facts are accurate: The author gives a lot of information about changing climates. He defines the greenhouse effect and the carbon cycle. He shows photographs of real things that cause greenhouse gasses. He shows photographs of what happens when the sea rises. He traces changing weather patterns. He tells how countries and people are trying to reduce greenhouse gasses. The information seemed to be real because he talked about things that we hear on television. The photographs made us believe that he was giving nonfictional information. When the author writes about things that have not happened yet he uses the word *could.*

Qualifications of the author to write the book: The author is a scientist. He has written more than 60 books about scientific subjects. Many of his books are about the environment. His qualifications sound right for this book.

Illustrations should make us understand the subject: Colored photographs show examples. The author adds captions so that we know what the photographs show. The drawings are labeled so that we know what each part means. A map shows what could happen to Florida if the sea level rises 25 feet. A computer model of a world map shows what could happen to the world if carbon dioxide is doubled. These photographs and illustrations help us understand the text.

Are the materials up-to-date? The copyright date on the book is 1990, so it is as up-to-date as possible. If new information comes out about the greenhouse effect and the author writes an updated edition, we will use the later book.

The organization should aid understanding: The book goes from what we know now to what is causing the problem to what will happen if nothing is done to how we can prevent global warming. This organization helps us understand the problem and presents the author's argument.

Did we become involved in the subject? The author made us realize that our lives might change if we do not do something about global warming. We believed there was a real problem that we would do something about.

Did the author use any devices to help readers find information? A table of contents listed what was in the book. A glossary helped define words. An index showed where to find subjects.

Continue sharing and reading informational books. After the students have read, responded to, discussed, and evaluated several informational books, ask them to develop a list of questions that they can use to decide whether a book is informational or to evaluate the effectiveness of the book. The same middle elementary students developed the following questions:

1. Can I identify the subject matter? Is the subject informational? Did the author present accurate facts? I should try to list some of these facts. Do these facts match other facts that I know about the subject? How did the author let me know the facts were accurate? What proof did the author give?

2. Does the book contain the author's qualifications? Are these qualifications important for the subject of the book? Why or why not? Do I think that this author can write a book of this subject? Why or why not?

3. Did the author try to help me understand the subject through the illustrations? Are the illustrations labeled so that I understand what they are? Did the illustrations help me picture the subject of the book? Why or why not?

4. I should think about the subject and decide if the date when the author wrote the book is important for that subject. Can I identify when the book was written? I should look at the copyright date of the book. Has new information been discovered since the book was written? How would this new information change the book?

5. Is the book well organized for the subject? How did the organization help me understand the subject? Could the book have been better organized? How?

6. As I read the book I should see if I am becoming involved in the subject. Did the author make me believe that it was important? How did the author try to interest me in the subject? How did the author try to get me involved? Did the author succeed? Why or why not?

7. I should look for aids that could help me read the book and understand the subject. What aids did the author use? Did I use the aids? Why or why not?

LESSON TWO: Teaching Students to Use the Parts of an Informational Book: Table of Contents, Index, Glossary, and Further Readings

OBJECTIVES

To develop the ability to use the table of contents, index, glossary, and further readings list provided by the authors of informational books.

To develop an understanding of the importance of various parts of an informational book.

CORE BOOKS: (these also can be used for extended reading and other independent reading activities): Locate a group of books in which the authors provide various aids to help students find information in the books. This lesson differs with the grade level. Books for lower elementary students usually do not contain many aids. For lower elementary students: Millicent E. Selsam and Joyce Hunt's "A First Look At" series, including *A First Look at Seals, Sea Lions, and Walruses.*

For middle and upper elementary and middle school students: Books that include at least three of the aids, such as Rhoda Blumberg's *The Incredible Journey of Lewis & Clark;* Franklyn Branley's *Mysteries of Outer Space;* Margery and Howard Facklam's *Changes in the Wind: Earth's Shifting Climate;* Roy A. Gallant's *Before the Sun Dies: The Story of Evolution;* James Jespersen and Jane Fitz-Randolph's *From Quarks to Quasars: A Tour of the Universe;* Kathryn Lasky's *Traces of Life: The Origins of Humankind;* Dorothy Hinshaw Patent's *Appaloosa Horses;* Laurence Pringle's *Saving Our Wildlife;* Joyce Pope's *Kenneth Lilly's Animals;* and Helen Roney Sattler's *Giraffes, the Sentinels of the Savannas.*

PROCEDURES: Select core books that use the appropriate aids. For lower elementary students any of Selsam and Hunt's "A First Look At" series use simple indexes. In *A First Look at Seals, Sea Lions, and Walruses,* the authors list the seals, sea lions, and walruses presented in the book and the pages on which each may be found.

The aids increase in books for middle and upper elementary and middle school students. The subject matter and the lessons on using aids can be related to other content areas. For example, Rhoda Blumberg's *The Incredible Journey of Lewis & Clark* describes exploration of the west and includes maps showing the journey and clarifying the text. Branley's *Mysteries of Outer Space* uses a question-and-answer format to explore major questions about space. Facklam's *Changes in the Wind: Earth's Shifting Climate* discusses changes in climate. Gallant's *Before the Sun Dies: The Story of Evolution* presents theories and scientific thinking about the Earth. Jespersen and Fitz-Randolph's *From Quarks to Quasars: A Tour of the Universe* describes how scientists have conducted research and contributed to knowledge of the universe. Lasky's *Traces of Life: The Origins of Humankind* presents a history of humanoid research. Patent's *Appaloosa Horses* traces the origins of and describes the characteristics of Appaloosas. Pringle's *Saving Our Wildlife* discusses how people are trying to save our wildlife. Pope's *Kenneth Lilly's Animals* discusses animals according to geographic regions. Sattler's *Giraffes, the Sentinels of the Savannas* discusses the physical characteristics, habits, and natural environment of giraffes.

Introduce and describe each of the aids found in informational books. Discuss with the students the purposes for the aids and how they help improve students' understanding of the subject. After each aid is introduced and discussed encourage students to use that aid in an informational book. For example, when developing an understanding of the table of contents ask students to do tasks such as:

Find the chapter describing how giraffes can detect moving objects from a mile away in Sattler's *Giraffes, the Sentinels of the Savannas* (Chapter 7, pp. 21–25).

Find the chapter in which scientists use ice to discover how much carbon dioxide was in the atmosphere hundreds of years ago in Facklam's *Changes in the Wind: Earth's Shifting Climate* (Chapter 7, pp. 62–71).

When developing an understanding of the index ask students to do tasks such as:

Identify Jonathan Leakey (pp. 89–90).

When developing an understanding of the glossary ask students to do tasks such as:

Describe a leopard in terms of a horse in Patent's *Appaloosa Horses* (p. 71).

When developing an understanding of further readings found in informational books ask the students to do tasks such as:

Go to the library and check out at least one of the books listed in the further readings section of Pringle's *Saving Our Wildlife* (pp. 61–62).

 LESSON THREE: Helping Students Read for Understanding by Analyzing the Organization of an Informational Book

OBJECTIVES

To identify the organizational formats of informational books.

To identify, read, and discuss the advantages of formats such as question-answer; problem-effect-cause-solutions; chronological order of a life cycle, steps in an experiment, or chronological order of time and location.

To identify, read, and discuss the advantages of paragraphs that proceed from the main idea to supporting details.

To write organizational formats that include one of these structures.

CORE BOOKS: Choose informational books in which authors use definite organizational patterns. For core lessons, select books with obvious structures. Question-and-answer format: Seymour Simon's *New Questions and Answers About Dinosaurs*. Problem-effect-cause-solution format: Laurence Pringle's *Global Warming: Assessing the Greenhouse Threat*. Chronological-order format: Peter and Connie Roop's *Seasons of the Cranes*. Books with paragraphs that proceed from main idea to supporting details: Helen Roney Sattler's *Giraffes, the Sentinels of the Savannas*.

EXTENDED BOOKS FOR INDEPENDENT READING AND RELATED ACTIVITIES: These books also can be chosen as core books. They have the same formats as the core books. Students can use any of the informational books in their library to search for similar books.

Question-and-Answer Format

FRANKLYN BRANLEY's *Mysteries of Outer Space*

DAVID AND MARYMAE KLEIN's *How Do You Know It's True? Sifting Sense From Nonsense*

Problem-Effect-Cause-Solution Format

THOMAS CAJACOB AND TERESA BURTON's *Close to the Wild: Siberian Tigers in a Zoo*

Chronological-Order Format

RHODA BLUMBERG's *The Incredible Journey of Lewis & Clark*

SYLVIA JOHNSON's *Potatoes*

Main Idea to Supporting Details

SEYMOUR SIMON's *Meet the Giant Snakes*

PROCEDURES: Introduce the organizational format by drawing diagrams of each. Discuss each format and the advantage of using it in informational literature. Ask the students to identify some subjects in which understandings could be improved if the format were used. Have the students identify information from the text that shows which format is used by the author. The following examples illustrate each of the formats:

QUESTION-AND-ANSWER
Simon's New Questions and Answers About Dinosaurs

Question	"What are dinosaurs"?
Answer	"A group of reptiles that first appeared over 225 million years ago." (p. 4)
Question	"How are dinosaurs different from other reptiles?"
Answer	"Dinosaurs had straight thighbones, and their hips held their legs directly underneath the body." (p. 7)

PROBLEM-EFFECT-CAUSE-SOLUTION
Pringle's Global Warming: Assessing the Greenhouse Threat

Problem	Global warming will harm weather patterns, plants, and people.
Effect of Problem	Climates will change.
	A greenhouse effect will develop that might not support life.
Cause of Problem	Human activities release gasses that trap more heat in the atmosphere.
Possible Solutions to the Problem	Prepare for effects of warming by using conservation.
	Reduce greenhouse gasses.
	Reforest the Earth.

CHRONOLOGICAL ORDER
The Roops' Seasons of the Cranes

First	In spring the cranes return to Canada.
	The female crane lays her eggs.
	The baby cranes hatch and grow.
Second	In summer the baby cranes feed and grow.
	The baby cranes learn to fly.
Third	In fall the cranes fly to Aransas National Wildlife Refuge in Texas.
Fourth	In winter the cranes secure their territory.
	The young crane learns to be independent.

MAIN IDEA TO DETAILS
Sattler's Giraffes

Main Idea	A baby giraffe is vulnerable to attack while the mother feeds.
Important Details	It cannot run fast enough to outrun a predator.
	It must hide in the tall grass while the mother eats.
	It is camouflaged by dark spots on a creamy background.

Continue this activity by asking students to find additional examples of organizational formats in informational books and to evaluate the effectiveness of each format. Finally, encourage the students to use these different formats in their own writing.

LESSON FOUR: Writing Content Journals and Developing Personal Responses to Informational Literature

OBJECTIVES

To write informally about scientific topics and other content-related topics in a journal.

To respond to informational literature through writing activities and art.

To encourage an emotional response to an issue in an informational book.

CORE BOOKS: Any informational book can be used for this activity as well as for independent reading. Books that deal with ecology or endangered species work well because they usually encourage emotional responses.

PROCEDURES

Writing content journals: Encourage students to write in their journals everything they know about a subject before they read the book. When they finish the book, have them write what they learned from the book; what misconceptions, if any, were changed after reading the book; and any questions they would like to have answered.

Writing personal responses to informational literature: Ask the students to pretend they are the author of an informational book they have just read. Ask them to describe the audience they pictured for their book. How did they spark the interest of the readers and make them understand the subject? Were they successful? Or, ask the students to pretend they are the author of the book and describe their purpose for writing the book. What decisions did they have to make as they wrote the book? Do they think they were successful? If they could rewrite the book, how would they change it?

Responding to issues in informational books through writing or art: Ask the students to choose a book to which they reacted strongly. Maybe the book discussed the need for conservation, the danger to some animal, or the threat of nuclear war. Ask them to choose an activity such as writing a letter to the author or drawing a poster to inform people about the problem.

Debating issues discovered through informational literature: Many informational books focus on controversial issues. Encourage students to choose teams, do additional research, and present their viewpoints as debates.

Developing Units Using Historical Fiction, Biography, and Informational Literature

The units in this section combine literature from historical fiction, biography, and informational books. The three genres are especially effective in units that integrate social studies and history. Both biographies and informational books can be used to help students authenticate the settings, the themes, and the values expressed in historical fiction. For example, without nonfiction informational books students would not be able to authenticate the plots and the characters in historical fiction stories set during the Civil War. Likewise, without informational books students would not be able to decide whether a biographical writer is presenting accurate information.

The first and second units in this section are an extension of the units developed in Chapter 10, which focused on analyzing the values and beliefs in Native American, black, and Hispanic literature. In these units students expand their understandings of the cultures by searching for evidence of traditional philosophy, values, and beliefs in historical fiction and biographies. They use nonfiction informational sources to identify the historical events and to evaluate the authenticity of the historical fiction and biographical writings. The third unit developed in this section focuses on some of the recurring themes found in history.

UNIT ONE: Multicultural Study of Native American Historical Fiction, Biography, and Informational Literature

OBJECTIVES

To analyze the role of traditional values in historical fiction and biography.

To evaluate the settings, conflicts, characterizations, themes, and authors' styles in historical fiction.

To authenticate historical fiction and biography by referring to historical events in informational books.

To provide a personal response to the characters and the situations developed in historical fiction, biography, and informational literature.

To compare the information in and responses to historical fiction, biography, and informational literature with information in and responses to a film about Native Americans.

CORE BOOKS: Jan Hudson's *Sweetgrass* (Historical Fiction, Canadian Library Association's Book of the Year Award), the story of a Blackfoot girl who experiences a smallpox epidemic in 1837; Dorothy Nafus Morrison's *Chief Sarah: Sarah Winnemucca's Fight for Indian Rights* (Biography), the story of the 1800s leader of the Paiute people. Brent Ashabranner's *Morning Star, Black Sun: The Northern Cheyenne Indians and America's Energy Crisis* (Informational).

EXTENDED BOOKS FOR INDEPENDENT READING AND RELATED ACTIVITIES: Any of the following books also can be used as core books.

Historical Fiction

FARLEY MOWAT's *Lost in the Barrens* (Canadian Library Association's Book of the Year Award). A survival story in which a Cree Indian boy and his friend are lost in northern Canada.

SCOTT O'DELL's *Sing Down the Moon* (Newbery Honor). A young Navaho girl describes the forced march of her people in 1846.

ELIZABETH GEORGE SPEARE's *The Sign of the Beaver* (Newbery Honor). The story of a white boy who survives in the 1700s Maine wilderness with the help of his Penobscot Indian friend.

Biography

RUSSELL FREEDMAN's *Indian Chiefs*. Short biographies of Native American chiefs of the 1800s.

ROSE SOBOL's *Woman Chief*. A story about Lonesome Star, a chief of the Crow Indians.

Informational Books

BRENT ASHABRANNER's *To Live in Two Worlds: American Indian Youth Today*. Stories from several young people.

RUSSELL FREEDMAN's *Buffalo Hunt*. The text and illustrations show the importance of the buffalo to the Great Plains Indians.

ARLENE HIRSCHFELDER's *Happily May I Walk: American Indians and Alaska Natives Today*. The book discusses topics such as reservations, performing artists, and sports.

ALBERT MARRIN's *War Clouds in the West: Indians & Cavalrymen, 1860–1890*. A history of the conflict in the West.

ALICE HERMINA POATGIETER'S *Indian Legacy: Native American Influences on World Life and Culture*. A discussion of Native North and South American contributions to democratic attitudes, agriculture, and culture.

PROCEDURES: Review and discuss the maps presented during the study of Native American folklore. Review the discoveries made during the unit on Native American folklore in Chapter 10. Make a large copy of the Map of the West in 1840 shown in Freedman's *Indian Chiefs*, p. 7. Show the students pictures of the prairies and the mountains as they would have looked in the 1700s and early 1800s. Pictures of large buffalo herds would be especially important. In contrast, share pictures of the same areas after the settlers built towns and the miners came into the mountains. Ask the students, "How would you feel if you were a member of a group who hunted buffalo and loved the land and saw settlers and hunters kill the buffalo and force you off your land?" Encourage the students to give their personal responses.

Tell the students that in this unit they will be reading historical fiction set during the time when many Native Americans experienced great changes in their lives. They also will read biographies of Native American leaders who tried to solve the problems related to the changes. To analyze the accuracy of these books, the students will read several informational books to see if the authors have developed authentic settings.

Select a historical fiction book to share with the group. (The students can do this first series of activities around a single book and then read the additional selections and add them to their analyses and discussions.) This activity encourages students to identify and evaluate the important literary elements found in historical fiction. First, place the shell of the chart in Figure 14.1 on the blackboard or on transparencies. Review the importance of each of these elements in historical fiction: Setting, conflict, characterization, theme, and language and authors' style. Use the chart as a discussion guide while the students identify examples under each category and discuss the effectiveness of the authors' techniques to create believable elements for Native American historical fiction. Figure 14.1 shows examples of those elements.

As each example is identified and placed on the chart, ask the students to consider why this is a good (or bad) example to be used in a book reflecting the Native American culture. After the students have completed the task with one of the books, they can divide in groups with each group selecting a different book or they can complete the readings independently.

After they have completed their analysis of the literary elements in the historical fiction, ask the students to look carefully at the conflicts developed in these books. Ask, "Do you think these conflicts were authentic for the time period? Why or why not? How could we find out? Do you think the settings and the characterizations were accurate for the time period? Why or why not? How could we find out?"

Next, ask the students to remember the beliefs and values they learned about when they read the Native American folklore. Ask, "Can you identify any beliefs and values that also are shown in the historical fiction? Which ones are important in historical fiction?" If the students developed a web of the Native American traditional values, review the web and encourage them to identify such important beliefs as respect for nature, respect for animals, and belief in the Great Spirit. Ask, "Did we find these beliefs in the historical fiction? What are the examples? Did any of the characters show the admired human qualities of respect for age, cooperation, and wisdom or show that they disliked the human qualities of selfishness and disrespect?" Ask the students to identify examples of these qualities from historical fiction. Ask, "Would we expect characters to experience conflict if they find themselves in situations in which these beliefs are not respected?" Ask the students to look at the themes they identified in the historical fiction. Ask, "Do these themes relate to the traditional beliefs and values found in Native American literature?" Ask the students to place themselves in the position of a character who is in conflict with a strong belief or value. Ask, "How would you respond in

FIGURE 14.1 Evaluating historical fiction about Native Americans.

Literary category	Criteria for evaluation	Books	Examples and authors' techniques
Setting	Must be authentic and encourage readers to understand time, place, and conflict.	Mowat's *Lost in the Barrens*	Author creates person-against-nature conflict by describing foaming rapids, searching for food, and preparing for winter.
		O'Dell's *Sing Down the Moon*	Author develops conflict by contrasting beautiful and peaceful Canyon de Chelly with harsh, dry Fort Sumner.
Conflict	Must reflect the times and attitudes of the people.	Hudson's *Sweetgrass*	Sweetgrass fights to save her family from the smallpox epidemic of 1837. This epidemic really happened.
		Speare's *The Sign of the Beaver*	The author describes the setting that is an enemy of the inexperienced white boy and a friend to the Penobscot Indians. A person-against-society conflict develops for the Indians because they must move west to get away from the settlers.
Characterization	The character's actions, beliefs, values must be true to the time period without depending on stereotypes.	Hudson's *Sweetgrass*	The author develops Sweetgrass' emotions and concerns about growing up. The girl's actions show that she values her tribe and believes in their values.
Theme	Theme should be worthwhile, as relevant today as in the historical time. The Native American culture, values, and beliefs should be respected.	Mowat's *Lost in the Barrens*	Working together is important for survival. The theme is developed as a white boy and a Cree boy struggle to survive.
		O'Dell's *Sing Down the Moon*	The loss of spiritual hope might be the greatest tragedy. Hatred and prejudice are destructive. The themes are developed as the Navaho try to survive the march to Fort Sumner.
		Hudson's *Sweetgrass*	It is important to have moral obligations toward others. It is important to keep one's dreams. It is important to respect one's family and one's tribe.
Language and authors' style	Language should be authentic for the time without relying on too many colorful terms. Style should vividly depict setting, characters, and culture.	Hudson's *Sweetgrass*	The author uses figurative language and prairie symbolism to describe Sweetgrass—when picking strawberries, "Her little hands pulled at them as daintily as a deer plucking grass in a meadow."

that situation?" Tell the students they are using the beliefs and values found in traditional Native American folklore to authenticate some of the beliefs and values found in the historical fiction. Tell them they also will search for these traditional values in biographies. Then they will use informational books to authenticate the settings, conflicts, and characterizations.

Next, select one of the biographies listed in the core and independent books. Tell the students that they will be searching for evidence of the values and beliefs found in the traditional folklore, themes similar to those found in traditional folklore and historical fiction, and sources of conflict that might relate to the traditional values and the historical fiction. Finally, they will use nonfiction informational books to try to identify the historical events and to evaluate the authenticity of the biographies. Place the shell of the chart in Figure 14.2 on the board or on a transparency to guide the reading and discussions. The chart in Figure 14.2 includes examples from the literature.

After students have finished reading one of the biographies, encourage them to read the remaining biographies in groups or independently and to identify the important information. After they have identified the sources of conflict in several biographies, ask them to read several informational books to try to verify the conflicts and the settings found in the biographies. (They also can use the informational books to verify the accuracy of the settings and the conflicts in the historical fiction.)

Several of the informational books present facts about Native Americans today. Ask the students to consider how their lives are different from the lives of the people living in the 1800s. Ask them to pay special attention to any of the conflicts identified by Native Americans today. Ask the students to think about why these conflicts might be important today. Ask, "Which of these conflicts are similar to the ones you have read about in earlier times? Why do you think the people are experiencing these conflicts?"

INDEPENDENT PROJECTS AND OTHER ACTIVITIES WITH THE MULTICULTURAL UNIT

Personal responses: Ask students to respond through writing or art to the characters and conflicts they find in historical fiction and biographies.

FIGURE 14.2 Analyzing biography about Native Americans.

Literature example	Evidence of values and beliefs from folklore and historical fiction	Sources of conflict	Historical events and evaluation
Morrison's *Chief Sarah*	Sarah expected people to follow the rules of Indian courtesy such as respecting the chief of the people.	Person-against-society as the miners destroyed the Paiute lands to get silver. The Paiutes then were hungry.	1855 — The Numa and the settlers made a treaty of friendship.
	Promises were important to Sarah.	People were moved from the open lands of the Great Basin to a reservation.	Pyramid Lake War — Paiutes
	Sarah began each day by facing sunrise and praying to the Spirit-Father.	Sarah worried about the suffering of her people.	Reservation established at Pyramid lake.
	Values respected: Cooperation, respect for nature, respect for wisdom of elders.		Sarah went to Boston to argue for Indian rights.
			Sarah established first Indian School taught by Indians.

Comparative study of literature and film: Encourage the students to use the knowledge they have gained about the Native American culture through literature to analyze the film "Dances With Wolves." Ask the students to respond to the themes, characterizations, setting, and conflicts developed in the film. Ask them to consider differences in their personal responses between literature and film. How do their responses differ? What makes the difference? Ask the students to identify one of the historical fiction or biography selections about Native Americans that they believe would make a good film. Ask the students to describe the locations they would use, the plot they would emphasize, and the characters who would be in the film. Ask the students to consider how they would change the book to meet the requirements of a movie screen.

Library research: Have the students, in groups or individually, select one of the Native American tribes identified on Freedman's map and research that tribe. Ask them to present a report on their findings.

Art interpretations: Ask the students to draw the settings in one of these books. For example, they could draw the contrasting settings in *Sing Down the Moon* as the people leave the beautiful Canyon de Chelly and move to the harsh reality of Fort Sumner.

Dramatizations and role playing: Have the students choose a dynamic scene from one of the books and present the scene as a dramatization, or role play the possible conversations. For example, they could dramatize a scene in which Chief Sarah argues for the rights of her people or role play the possible dialogue between Chief Sarah and one of her adversaries.

Library research: Read one of the sources listed in the bibliography of *Chief Sarah* or in the further readings section of *Morning Star, Black Sun* or *War Clouds in the West*. What additional insights can be gained from these sources? How did the authors use this information in their books?

Library research: Ask the students to develop a time line illustrating the contributions of Native Americans in history.

Creative writing: Choose a historical fiction text or a biography. Write a sequel to the story. Choose a time period in the future and write about the characters and their conflicts during this new time period.

Literature extension: Ask the students to read several works by a Native American author such as Byrd Baylor, Jamake Highwater, or Virginia Driving Hawk Sneve. Have them analyze the types of stories that the authors chose to write. Ask them to consider how their author develops a cultural perspective and to respond personally to the literature.

UNIT TWO: Multicultural Study of Black Historical Fiction, Biography, and Informational Literature

OBJECTIVES

To analyze the role of African traditional values in historical fiction and biography.

To evaluate the settings, conflicts, characterizations, themes, and authors' style in historical fiction depicting the black culture.

To authenticate historical fiction and biographies by referring to historical events in informational books.

To provide a personal response to the characters and the situations developed in historical fiction, biographies, and informational literature.

CORE BOOKS: Two time periods are reflected in the core and independent books. Strong historical fiction and biographies have been written about overcoming problems associated with slavery and about the fight for civil rights in the 1900s. Teachers can use both periods or focus on one. James and Christopher Collier's *Jump Ship to Freedom* (Historical Fiction), the story of a slave who obtains his freedom and that of his mother; Jeri Ferris's *Go Free or Die: A Story of Harriet Tubman* (Biography), Tubman's experiences during slavery and the Underground Railroad; and Milton Meltzer's *The Black Americans: A History in Their Own Words, 1619–1983* (Informational), includes writings of many people from different times.

EXTENDED BOOKS FOR INDEPENDENT READING AND RELATED ACTIVITIES: Any of these books can be used as core books.

Historical Fiction

PAULA FOX's *The Slave Dancer* (Newbery Medal). The story of a fife player in 1840 who experiences the misery of the slave trade.

BELINDA HURMENCE's *A Girl Called Boy.* This book includes a time-warp experience, but most of it is set in North Carolina during the 1850s.

F. N. MONJO's *The Drinking Gourd* ("I-Can-Read" Book). A story about the Underground Railroad.

MILDRED TAYLOR's *Roll of Thunder, Hear My Cry* (Newbery Medal). The story of a black Mississippi family in 1933 as they retain their pride through humiliating and frightening situations.

MILDRED TAYLOR's *Let the Circle Be Unbroken.* The sequel to *Roll of Thunder, Hear My Cry.*

MILDRED TAYLOR's *The Gold Cadillac.* A black family experiences racial prejudice as they drive an expensive car through the segregated South.

Biography

OSSIE DAVIS's *Langston: A Play.* Scenes from Langston Hughes's life in play format.

VIRGINIA HAMILTON's *Anthony Burns: The Defeat and Triumph of a Fugitive Slave.* The story of an escaped slave whose trial caused riots in Boston.

LILLIE PATTERSON's *Martin Luther King, Jr. and the Freedom Movement.* Begins with an account of the 1955–1956 bus boycott in Montgomery, Alabama, and explores King's leadership in the civil rights movement.

GLENNETTE TILLIE TURNER's *Take a Walk in Their Shoes.* Short biographies and skits about 14 black Americans.

ELIZABETH YATES's *Amos Fortune, Free Man* (Newbery Medal). The story of a free African man who is taken into slavery in America and works for his freedom.

Informational Books

VERONICA FREEMAN ELLIS's *Afro-Bets First Book About Africa.* Explores the natural, social, and political history of Africa.

JAMES HASKINS's *Black Theater in America.* Traces the contributions of black writers, actors, and musicians from minstrel shows through contemporary protest plays and drama.

PROCEDURES: Prepare the school environment by collecting pictures that show the various stages in black history from freedom in Africa to slavery in earlier America to the contributions of contemporary politicians, authors, and musicians. Ask the students to bring to class any examples of music, writing, and art that reflects the black culture.

Introduce one of the historical fiction books. Explain to older students that authors who write about slavery face special problems. How accurately should historical fiction reflect the attitudes and circumstances of the times. Should authors use terms of the period that are considered insensitive and offensive today? For example, tell the students, "In the authors' note in *Jump Ship to Freedom,* James and Christopher Collier consider the use of the word *nigger.* Although the word is considered offensive today, would avoiding it in a novel about slavery distort history? The Colliers chose to use the term to illustrate their main character's change in attitude as he develops self-respect and self-confidence and to highlight the social attitudes of the other characters in the book. In *Jump Ship to Freedom,* those who use the word express racial bias toward blacks, and those who do not are concerned with the rights and self-respect of all humans. As older students read Collier's book, ask them to trace the use of the word and how the authors use it to develop conflict and characterization. Ask them if they think the authors were successful in depicting conflict, characterization, and changes in attitude. After students have read the book, ask them to debate the issue of using controversial words in historical fiction.

Use the same discussion and analysis structure as that shown in Figure 14.1 for evaluating historical fiction about Native Americans. Ask the students to identify and discuss examples of setting, conflicts, characterizations, theme, and authors' style. Follow a similar discussion procedure as the one described for Native American historical fiction.

After the students have read, responded to, and discussed several historical fiction selections, introduce the biographies. Tell the students that as they read each biography they will be searching for evidence of the values and beliefs found in traditional folklore, themes that are similar to those found in traditional folklore and historical fiction, and sources of conflict that might relate to the traditional values and the historical fiction. Finally, they will use nonfiction informational books to try to identify the historical events and evaluate the authenticity of the biographies. Place a shell of the chart in Figure 14.2 on the board or on a transparency to guide the reading and discussions.

For example, when they use this chart to analyze *Go Free or Die: A Story of Harriet Tubman,* they will find the following evidence of values and beliefs found in both traditional folklore and in historical fiction:

1. The themes developed by the author show that freedom is worth risking one's life for and we must help others obtain their freedom.
2. The values developed by the characters and their actions show that obligations to family and others are important, wit and trickery might be needed to influence the balance of power, responsibility is important, and expressing gratitude is essential.

Students will discover that the sources of conflict are person against society as Harriet fights to free blacks and combat injustice. When they look to various nonfiction informational sources to identify the historical events, they will discover:

1. The setting is in America from the mid-1800s to the end of the Civil War.
2. The story is based on facts about slavery, the Underground Railroad, the 1850 Fugitive Slave Act, and the 1863 Emancipation Proclamation.
3. They will discover that Tubman freed more than 300 slaves in 10 years.

Either in groups or individually, ask the students to read and analyze additional biographies. Use the chart in Figure 14.2 to structure their analyses and discussions. After the students have read biographies about contemporary people, ask them to consider any similarities between the themes, values, and conflicts. Ask the students to think about why these themes, values, and person-against-society conflicts might be important in the lives of people today.

INDEPENDENT PROJECTS AND OTHER ACTIVITIES WITH THE MULTICULTURAL UNIT

Creative dramatizations and role playing: Have the students choose a scene and present it as a dramatization, or choose an issue and role play the various responses that people might have as they try to decide the issue. Have students choose one of the books, such as *Langston: A Play* or *Take a Walk in Their Shoes,* and read it as a "readers theatre" presentation or perform one of the skits.

Dramatic readings: Have students read the poetry of Langston Hughes and prepare several of the poems as dramatic readings to share with the class.

Library research: Ask students to choose one of the African countries from which slaves were sent to America. Compare the country during the time of slavery with the country today.

Personal responses through writing and art: Ask students to keep a writing journal and to respond to what happens to the characters in the historical fiction or biographical stories. For example, in *A Girl Called Boy,* they can respond to both the beliefs of the contemporary girl and what happens to her when she experiences slavery. They also can create a collage that expresses their feelings as a historical character faces and overcomes conflict.

Personal responses through dialogue: Have the students choose an incident in the life of a contemporary worker for civil rights, such as Martin Luther King, Jr., and ask them to pretend they can have a conversation with the person. What would they talk about? What questions would they ask? What advice might they give the person?

Library research: Ask the students to compare the objectives of the earlier civil rights movement with the objectives of current black leaders such as Jesse Jackson. Are the objectives the same? How are they different? What might cause the similarities and the differences?

Library research: After reading a book such as *Black Theater in America,* ask the students to write a short biography on a black artist.

Developing interviewing techniques: Ask the students to interview people about the contributions of a person who worked for the civil rights movement.

Library research: Ask the students to research and develop a timeline illustrating the contributions of black Americans.

Library research: After reading a biography about a black athlete, ask students to research and discuss records set by the athlete.

Literature expansion: Ask the students to read several works of a black author such as Virginia Hamilton, Eloise Greenfield, John Steptoe, Tom Feelings, Ossie Davis, Langston Hughes, Mildred Taylor, or Walter Dean Myers. Have them analyze the types of stories they write, consider how these authors develop a cultural perspective in their works, and respond personally to their works.

Artistic expansion: Ask the students to choose a black illustrator such as Leo Dillon, Tom Feelings, Jerry Pinkney, or John Steptoe. Have the students analyze the types of illustrations these artists create and the stories they choose to illustrate. Ask the students to consider how these illustrators develop cultural perspectives in their works and to respond personally to their illustrations.

UNIT THREE: Overcoming Obstacles and Hardships

The theme for this unit is based on the quote by Thomas Paine: "These are the times that try men's souls." This quote was used frequently during the 1991 Persian Gulf War. During debates over the war, Shanker (1991) wrote an editorial arguing that students need to understand the implications of history so that they can understand and debate the issues of today. Instead, the debate, "which was one of the high points in our recent history, showed how exciting—and even essential—it can be to apply ideas to events and grope for solutions. It would be a good thing for our kids to be prepared for that, too" (p. 9E). It is the hope that teachers using this unit will encourage students to apply ideas and grope for solutions.

OBJECTIVES

To understand the sweep of history.

To identify themes in historical fiction and biography depicting different time periods and to develop an understanding about why certain themes are found in different time periods.

To understand qualities in characters that allow them to overcome obstacles.

To authenticate historical fiction through nonfiction informational sources.

To understand that heroes in history are not just the "great" people; ordinary people also can be heroes.

To debate issues that have perplexed people across time.

To relate art and music to difficult times in history.

CORE BOOKS: These books are not divided between core and extended or independent reading books because teachers will want to choose books that are appropriate for specific grade levels. The selection of core or independent books also depends on how teachers decide to develop this unit as described in the procedures. The books chosen for this unit cover some major time periods in which people have had to overcome tremendous obstacles, and have shown great courage. The core books include historical fiction, biography, and informational books and feature important themes such as the willingness to face hardships for religious, political, or personal freedom; the need to retain moral obligations; and the belief that family love and loyalty help people endure or survive catastrophic experiences. The list of books includes books for different reading levels. Although many of these books are written for older students, some of the biographies written by Jean Fritz are appropriate for younger students.

The American Revolution and Writing the Constitution

Historical Fiction

Patricia Clapp's *I'm Deborah Sampson: A Soldier in the War of the Revolution*. Deborah disguises herself as a man and fights in the Revolutionary War.

Esther Forbes's *Johnny Tremain* (Newbery Medal, Touchstone). Through Johnny's observations, actions, and thoughts, the author emphasizes the issues of the times, the values of the people, and the feelings about freedom.

Biography

Jean Fritz's *Traitor: The Case of Benedict Arnold*. The life of the man who chose the British cause in the American Revolution.

Where Was Patrick Henry on the 29th of May? A humorous telling of incidents in Patrick Henry's youth and political career.

Will You Sign Here, John Hancock? The rise to fame of a Revolutionary War hero.

Milton Meltzer's *Benjamin Franklin: The New American*. A carefully documented biography of the statesman.

Milton Meltzer's *George Washington and the Birth of Our Nation*. A comprehensive biography traces Washington's life through his years of leadership.

Selma R. Williams's *Demeter's Daughters: The Women Who Founded America, 1587–1787*. Biographical sketches of great women of Colonial and revolutionary America.

Informational Books

Doris and Harold Faber's *We the People: The Story of the United States Constitution Since 1787*. Discusses the writing of the Constitution and subsequent changes in the document.

DORIS AND HAROLD FABER'S *The Birth of a Nation: The Early Years of the United States*. Covers major events in early United States history.

MILTON MELTZER'S *The American Revolutionaries: A History in Their Own Words, 1750– 1800*. A collection of letters, diaries, interviews, and speeches.

JUDITH ST. GEORGE'S *The White House: Cornerstone of a Nation*. Begins in 1791 with planning the White House and progresses through events of the next two centuries. This may be used during any of the time periods.

The Civil War

Historical Fiction

JAMES AND CHRISTOPHER COLLIER'S *Jump Ship to Freedom*. Depicts the inhumanity of slavery and the personal courage needed to overcome prejudice and persecution.

JANET HICKMAN'S *Zoar Blue*. The young men of a Zoar, Ohio, religious group experience personal and religious conflicts when they fight in the war.

IRENE HUNT'S *Across Five Aprils* (Newbery Honor). A family is in conflict when sons fight for different sides in the war.

F. N. MONJO'S *The Drinking Gourd*. A family helps a fugitive slave family escape.

CAROLYN REEDER'S *Shades of Gray*. A boy encounters pacifism.

Biography

RAE BAINS' *Harriet Tubman: The Road to Freedom*. An illustrated version of Tubman's experiences with the Underground Railroad.

RUSSELL FREEDMAN'S *Lincoln: A Photobiography* (Newbery Medal). A carefully documented life of Lincoln.

RUTH BELOV GROSS'S *True Stories About Abraham Lincoln*. A series of short stories that emphasize various aspects of Lincoln's life.

VIRGINIA HAMILTON'S *Anthony Burns: The Defeat and Triumph of A Fugitive Slave*. The story of an escaped slave whose trial caused riots in Boston.

DOUGLAS MILLER'S *Frederick Douglass and the Fight for Freedom*. The life of the black leader who escaped slavery to become a political leader.

JOHN ANTHONY SCOTT AND ROBERT ALAN SCOTT'S *John Brown of Harper's Ferry*. A biography of the abolitionist.

Informational Books

MILTON MELTZER'S *Voices from the Civil War*. Excerpts from speeches, diaries, and letters.

DELIA RAY'S *A Nation Torn: The Story of How the Civil War Began*. The author focuses on the events leading up to the Civil War.

Early 20th Century and Social Conflicts, World War I, and the Great Depression

Historical Fiction

RUDOLPH FRANK'S *No Hero for the Kaiser*. In a book banned by Hitler, a boy refuses to be used by the German High Command.

CONSTANCE GREENE'S *Dotty's Suitcase*. Set during the Depression.

WILLIAM HOOKS *Circle of Fire*. Consequences of hatred and prejudice in a conflict between Gypsies and the Ku Klux Klan.

MILDRED TAYLOR'S *Roll of Thunder, Hear My Cry* (Newbery Medal). The author explores racial prejudice and strong family ties in the early 20th century.

CRYSTAL THRASHER'S *A Taste of Daylight*. During the Depression, a girl and her family move from the country to the city.

Biography

RUSSELL FREEDMAN's *Franklin Delano Roosevelt*. The biography contains several chapters about Roosevelt during the Depression. Emphasis is on the New Deal and such reforms as Works Progress Administration, Society Security, and Civilian Conservation Corps.

World War II

Historical Fiction

MARIAN BAUER's *Rain of Fire*. A 12-year-old boy discovers the complexity and the cruel reality of war through his brother who is a veteran.

ROBERT CORMIER's *Other Bells for Us to Ring*. Set in America during the war.

BARBARA GEHRTS's *Don't Say A Word*. A family discovers the dangers of living in Germany during the war.

PETER HARTLING's *Crutches*. A boy and a crippled man search for the boy's mother in post-war Vienna.

JOAN LINGARD's *Tug of War*. A family is separated as they leave Latvia before the Russian invasion.

LOIS LOWRY's *Number the Stars* (Newbery Medal). In 1943 Copenhagen, the Danes try to save their Jewish citizens.

MARIE McSWIGAN's *Snow Treasure*. Norwegian children use their sleds to help take $9 million in gold bullion past German sentries.

URI ORLEV's *The Island on Bird Street*. A 12-year-old Jewish boy survives in the Warsaw ghetto.

KIT PEARSON's *The Sky is Falling*. Two young children are sent from England to Canada during the war.

JOHANNA REISS's *The Upstairs Room*. A Jewish girl hides from the Nazis during the war.

YOSHIKO UCHIDA's *Journey Home*. A Japanese American family returns to California after being held in an internment camp.

JANE YOLEN's *The Devil's Arithmetic*. This story contains a time-warp, which makes it a fantasy. Emphasize the part of the story that takes place in a concentration camp.

Biography

MICHAEL FOREMAN's *War Boy: A Country Childhood*. A well-known illustrator tells about his boyhood experiences growing up in England during the bombings.

RUSSELL FREEDMAN's *Franklin Delano Roosevelt*. Several chapters focus on Roosevelt's presidency during the war.

ALBERT MARRIN's *Hitler*. Emphasizes Hitler's rise to power, his victories, and his final defeat.

ALBERT MARRIN's *Stalin: Russia's Man of Steel*. Emphasizes how Stalin shaped Russia.

ELLIOTT ROOSEVELT's *Eleanor Roosevelt, with Love*. The biography includes Eleanor Roosevelt's work during the war.

SHARON WHITNEY's *Eleanor Roosevelt*. Several chapters focus on war-time experiences.

Informational Books

DANIEL DAVIS's *Behind Barbed Wire: The Imprisonment of Japanese Americans During World War II*. Tells about the internment of Japanese Americans and how their lives were altered.

MILTON MELTZER's *Rescue: The Story of How Gentiles Saved Jews in the Holocaust*. Stories of heroism.

BARBARA ROGASKY's *Smoke and Ashes: The Story of the Holocaust*. A history of the 1933–1945 Holocaust.

The Civil Rights Movement

Biography

ARNOLD ADOFF's *Malcolm X.* Stresses how and why Malcolm X urged black Americans to be proud of their heritage and themselves.

JAMES T. DEKAY's *Meet Martin Luther King, Jr.* This biography stresses the magnitude of King's work and his reasons for fighting injustice.

ELOISE GREENFIELD's *Rosa Parks.* A biography about the woman who refused to give up her bus seat in Montgomery, Alabama.

JAMES HASKINS' *The Life and Death of Martin Luther King, Jr.* The biography covers the life of the civil rights leader.

PATRICIA MCKISSACK's *Jesse Jackson.* A biography of the political leader emphasizes his accomplishments.

JUDIE MILLS' *John F. Kennedy.* The biography includes details of Kennedy's involvement with the civil rights movement. A detailed index allows students to find specific topics related to civil rights.

LILLIE PATTERSON's *Martin Luther King, Jr. and the Freedom Movement.* The emphasis is on King's nonviolent struggles against segregation.

Informational Books

JAMES HASKINS' *Black Theater in America.* Includes contemporary protest plays written by black authors.

PATRICIA AND FREDERICK MCKISSACK's *A Long Hard Journey: The Story of the Pullman Porter.* A history of the porters who formed the first American black-controlled union.

MILTON MELTZER's *The Black Americans: A History in Their Own Words, 1619–1983.* The last portion of the book emphasizes the struggle for equality among black Americans.

PROCEDURES: Begin the unit by exploring with the students how much they know about the topic of the unit. Write on the board, "These are the times that try men's and women's souls." Ask the students to identify some of these times in history. (You might remind them that at the time of the Persian Gulf War, President Bush used the quote, "These are the times that try men's souls," first spoken by the Revolutionary War hero, Thomas Paine. By using this quote President Bush was implying similarities between the two time periods.) Encourage students to brainstorm times in history that could qualify as "trying." Ask them to identify what was happening during those times and to consider how people living then tried to solve their problems. Encourage the students to consider why an understanding of history is important to them.

Tell the students that we can discover more about these time periods by reading biographies about people who lived then, reading historical fiction that shows us the important conflicts and how people solved their problems, and reading informational books that provide details about a historical period. By reading all of these sources, we start to develop an understanding of history and to realize why people often quote someone who lived a long time ago. Explain to the students that they will be placing themselves in these time periods. They will be applying ideas, debating issues, and groping for solutions to some of the major problems that faced people then and probably still face people today. They also will be using their own abilities to evaluate the accuracy of the stories. By the time they are finished with the unit they will be able to identify characteristics of people who can overcome obstacles.

Teachers can approach this unit several ways. Some prefer to read, analyze, and discuss the literature of one time period with their whole class. They draw conclusions about that time period, and proceed to another time period. Then they compare the time periods as the students read, analyze, and discuss literature from the second time period. Other teachers prefer approaches that can help students understand, authenticate, and respond to literature from a particular time period. Then the teachers divide their students in time-period interest groups. The students in this approach do considerable independent and group research, meet in smaller discussion groups, and then bring their findings to the whole class. Whichever approach is used, students should search for conflicts and issues found during each time period, identify and consider the importance of themes developed during each time period, identify characteristics of people who overcome obstacles, and identify the historical events taking place. The suggested activities for this unit can be used for either approach. Specific activities, such as webbing, are developed with a book for a specific time period, but the approach can be used during the study of any time periods.

Activities to accompany the American Revolution and writing the Constitution:

1. *Authenticating historical fiction:* As students read *Johnny Tremain* or *I'm Deborah Sampson: A Soldier in the War of the Revolution,* ask them to become "history detectives" and note details of the setting including dates, place names, descriptions of streets, houses, clothing, transportation, working conditions, organizational names, weather, and battles or other events such as the Boston Tea Party. Ask them to identify issues that are important to the people. Ask them to identify real people who provide the background for the story such as well-known figures who lived during the American Revolution. After they have noted this information for the historical fiction, ask them to think about how they could verify the authenticity of these background facts, types of conflicts, issues, and background characters. Encourage the students to use biographies and other nonfiction informational books to authenticate the accuracy of the historical fiction. A group of sixth-grade students who participated in this activity even checked old almanacs and called the weather bureau to determine weather conditions in a specific location. Finally, ask the students to give an oral report on their findings.

2. *Researching a well-known figure:* Ask the students to choose one of the well-known characters identified in *Johnny Tremain*—make sure it is a figure about whom there is sufficient source material. Divide the students into small research groups, each to work on a different aspect of that person's life. Next, have the students accumulate as many reference materials as possible: Biographies, information about the person's home, speeches or writings by the person, information about the person's childhood, and reproductions of newspapers available at that time. Have each group develop a composite picture of the historical figure during the chosen period; this should include possible thoughts, writings, actions, associations, and concerns. After students research their character, have them give their research to the group. Students could develop "Days in the life of _____," and present their information as dramatizations. Finally, they can compare their findings with a biography written about that figure.

3. *Dramatizing, role playing, and debating:* Encourage the students to choose a vivid scene from historical fiction, biography, or informational literature and develop the scene as a dramatization. For example, they could dramatize the Boston Tea Party, Paul Revere's ride, or a meeting of the Boston Observers. Or have students select an issue developed in historical fiction or biography, such as "Should the colonies separate from England or stay loyal to the British crown?" Have them develop a debate that reflects both sides of this issue.

4. *Identifying important themes and characterizations:* For example, in both the historical fiction selections, students will discover that the characters believe political freedom is worth fighting for. They also will discover that strong beliefs require strong commitments. Ask the students to identify proof that these are important themes in both historical fiction and biography of this time period. Then ask the students to consider why these themes were important during this time period. Ask the students to identify characteristics of both historical fiction characters and biographical characters that allow them to overcome the obstacles they face. Finally, ask the students to consider if these themes and characteristics are still important today. Why or why not?

5. *Responding to characters and issues:* Ask the students to select a historical or biographical character and describe how they responded to the obstacles the person faced and how the person overcame those obstacles. Ask them to consider how they might have reacted if they were that person.

6. *Researching music of the Revolutionary War era:* Ask the students to present examples of this music to the class. They also should consider how the music reflects the issues of the times.

Activities to accompany the Civil War:

1. *Authenticating historical fiction:* The historical fiction selections in this section cover many different issues. Share with students that the historical fiction covers serious moral issues such as slavery and helping fugitive slaves escape, religious convictions that prevent going to war, and families divided because of the conflict between the North and South. Divide the students into research groups according to each of these topics and have the students read the corresponding historical fiction. Ask them to note both details that depict the settings such as dates, place names, and events and issues that develop the conflicts in the stories. Using biographies and nonfiction information books, ask the students to authenticate the historical fiction.

2. *Responding to historical fiction and biography:* The stories in this section frequently evoke personal responses in the students. Encourage students to keep journals as they read biographies or historical fiction. Ask them to identify the issues, the occurrences, and the characterizations that created an emotional response and to describe how they responded.

3. *Creative writing:* Ask students to select a secondary character in a biography or historical fiction selection who does not agree with the primary character. Have them choose an issue that concerns the main character and write a response to the issue from the point of view of the secondary character.

4. *Library research:* Ask the students to research an important battle in the Civil War or an important act, such as the Fugitive Slave Act or the Emancipation Proclamation. Have the students present an oral report to the class.

5. *Evaluating techniques of biographical authors:* Freedman uses many excellent techniques in his writing of *Lincoln: A Photobiography.* Ask the students to respond to the effectiveness of each technique and to consider what they learn about Lincoln through the author's approaches: (a) He introduces each chapter with quotations from Lincoln's writing, (b) he separates legend about Lincoln from facts, (c) he supports his text with photographs of documents, (d) he includes photographs of Lincoln and important settings, (e) he includes photographs of posters that were found during that period, (f) he supports the text with numerous references.

6. *Researching the importance of music:* Ask the students to identify music that was important during the Civil War. The music can include protest songs against slavery or songs of the troops and other people living during this time. Ask the students to share the music and to relate it to the themes and events of the time.

7. *Identifying important themes and characterizations:* Ask students to support the themes found in the historical fiction and the biographies by describing how the authors make these themes important to the readers. For example, important themes found in both historical fiction and biographies include moral obligations must be met even at the risk of one's life or freedom; moral sense does not depend on skin color, but rather on what is inside a person; take pride in yourself and your accomplishments; prejudice and hatred are destructive forces; humans will search for freedom; personal conscience might not allow humans to kill other humans; strong family ties help people persevere; and the Union must be preserved. Next, ask the students to describe the characteristics of people who overcome obstacles. Finally, ask the students to consider whether these themes and characteristics are still important today. Why or why not?

8. *Debating the important issues of the time period:* The issues and themes developed in the literature of this time are strong and vivid. Select an issue and debate the issue from the roles of the opposing forces.

9. *Responding to issues and writing editorials:* Ask the students to choose an issue and write an editorial for the newspaper that reflects the opinion of someone living during that period. Then write another editorial from the perspective of someone looking back on history. What would you tell the people that might make it easier for them to solve their problems?

Activities to accompany the early 20th century:

1. *Webbing setting, characterization, conflict, theme, and author's style:* Use the web of Frank's *No Hero For The Kaiser* (Figure 14.3) and nonfiction informational sources to authenticate the settings, characterizations, conflicts, themes, and author's style that would be accurate for a story set in Poland and Germany during World War I.

2. *Researching your town:* Ask the students to research their town as it was during either World War I or the Depression. They should search old newspapers, locate old family albums and letters, and research documents at the courthouse or historical society. They can interview people who lived through the Depression or who can remember family stories about the Depression. They can include radio shows that people listened to, music that was played, comic strips that were read, and responses to political speeches and candidates. They can document their report with photographs and information from other sources. One group of students recreated their town in miniature as it looked during an earlier period.

3. *Comparing home towns and historical fiction towns:* If the students researched their town during the Depression, ask them to use this information to compare their town and the details of the time with those in Greene's *Dotty's Suitcase* or Thrasher's *A Taste of Daylight.*

4. *Researching Roosevelt's New Deal:* Ask students to research one of Roosevelt's programs under the New Deal. They might choose the Works Progress Administration, Social Security, or the Civilian Conservation Corps. Ask them to identify the goals of the programs, the need for the programs, any issues that surrounded the programs, and the consequences of the programs.

FIGURE 14.3 Literary web of *No Hero For The Kaiser.*

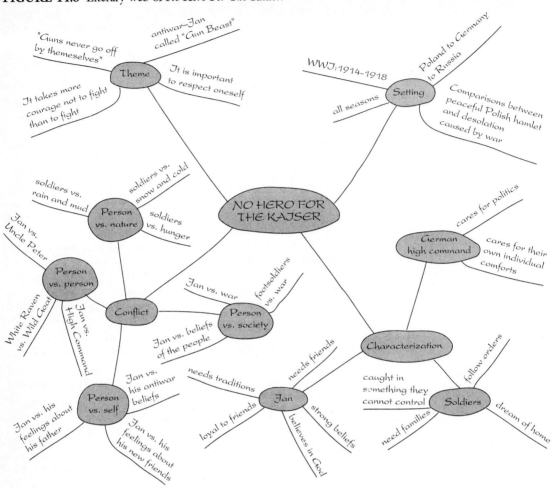

5. *Debating the issues:* Ask the students to debate one of the issues around either World War I or the Depression.

6. *Identifying important themes:* Students will find that themes around the Depression emphasize that humans will strive for survival of body and spirit; people cannot survive without spirit; prejudice and discrimination are destructive forces; a bond develops between people who experience injustice; and monetary wealth does not create a rich life. Ask students to find support for the themes and to identify characteristics of people who overcome obstacles. Finally, ask the students if these themes and characteristics are still important today. Why or why not?

7. *Researching the music of the time period:* Ask students to research and share the music that was popular during World War I and the Depression. They also should share how the music relates to the themes and conflicts of the time period.

Activities to accompany a study of World War II:

1. *Authenticating historical fiction:* The fiction written around World War II can be divided into several categories. Stories such as *Crutches, Don't Say a Word, Snow Treasure,* and *Tug of War* take place in Europe and describe the experiences of people and families as they are caught in the war. Stories such as *The Devil's Arithmetic, Number the Stars, The Island on Bird Street,* and *The Upstairs Room* focus on the experiences of Jewish families as they try to survive the Holocaust. Stories such as *Rain of Fire, Other Bells for Us to Ring, The Sky Is Falling,* and *Journey Home* focus on experiences in the United States and Canada. Divide the students into groups according to the types of stories found in the historical fiction of this period. Ask each group to authenticate the settings, the conflicts, the issues, and the characterizations developed in the stories. They can use biography, informational literature, newspaper and magazine articles, and interviews. Have each group report their findings to the class. The class then should compare the themes and conflicts found in these different categories. They also can compare the survival techniques developed by the characters.

2. *Describing your town during World War II:* Ask the students to research their own town during this time period. They should investigate newspapers, interview people who lived there, search for family albums and letters, and research courthouse records and records at the historical society. Ask the students to create a museum that reflects their town during the war. The museum could include items such as gas and food rationing stamps, newspaper articles about soldiers from the town and people who worked for the war effort, newspaper editorials that expressed various sides of the issues, music that would be played during the time period, radio shows that people would have listened to, and photographs that show people from the town during that time.

3. *Developing a list of questions:* Identify people living in or near your town who lived through World War II. They might have lived in Europe during the War, experienced or known people who experienced the Holocaust, been a soldier in the war, or remember growing up in the United States or Canada during the war. After reading several historical fiction stories, biographies, or informational books, ask the students to develop a list of questions that they would like to ask someone who lived through the experiences in the books. Encourage the students to focus their questions on the types of experiences this person had. Invite the person to come to class and answer questions. If the person cannot visit the class, a tape recording of the interview is an acceptable alternative. One class that did this activity actually found people living in their community who had experienced each of these situations. The students developed four different lists of questions, interviewed the people, and had the opportunity to listen to the experiences that each person remembered. Finally, they used these responses to further evaluate the effectiveness and accuracy of the historical fiction and biographies they had read.

4. *Responding to biography through creative writing:* After reading *War Boy: A Country Childhood,* encourage the students to respond to Foreman's remembrances as if they were living in England during the bombings. How would they have reacted to Foreman's experiences? What was their emotional response as Foreman described his young life? Ask the students to use information they have gained from the nonfiction information sources and create an illustrated book about themselves as if they were living during the time period and in that setting.

5. *Responding to literature through journal writing:* Many stories, such as those that take place during the Holocaust, create emotional responses in students. Ask them to keep a personal journal as they read one of these books and respond to the characters, their conflicts, the dangers, and their ways of solving problems.

6. *Dramatization:* These stories are filled with moments well suited to dramatization, role playing, and debate. For example, encourage students to select instances in Roosevelt's life in which he had to make decisions that influenced history. They can debate the issues surrounding Roosevelt's early choice of a hands-off policy toward events overseas as Hitler and Hirohito were gaining power, expanding their military, and dominating other countries. They can debate possible responses to and consequences of the Neutrality Act of 1935, which prohibited Americans from shipping arms to nations at war. They can dramatize or debate the discussions that must have gone into the decision to begin the nation's first peacetime draft on October 29, 1940. They might role play different politicians responding to the issues associated with the draft. They can role play various conversations between Roosevelt and Churchill, as Churchill tries to win the support of the American president. They can recreate a fireside chat in which Roosevelt reports to the people over radio. They can dramatize and role play the interactions of Churchill, Roosevelt, and Stalin at the Big Three Conference in Yalta in February 1945.

7. *Comparing Issues Between World War II and the Persian Gulf War:* After students have debated the issues that faced Roosevelt, Congress, and the American people before and during World War II, ask them to investigate the issues that faced Congress as it prepared to debate the war in the Persian Gulf. Ask them to investigate the attitudes of the American president and the American people. Have them recreate a portion of the debate that was held in Congress. After they have completed their research and their debate, ask the students to compare the issues and the resolution of the issues during World War II and the Persian Gulf War.

8. *Identifying themes and characterizations:* As students read the historical fiction and biographies written about World War II, ask them to identify important themes, how authors develop those themes, and why those themes were important during the time period. For example, they will find that humans seek freedom from religious and political persecution; prejudice and hatred are destructive forces; moral obligations and personal conscience are strong human forces; freedom is worth fighting for; and family love and loyalty help people endure or survive catastrophic experiences. Ask them to identify characteristics of people that help them survive. Finally, ask the students to consider if these themes and characterizations are still important today. Why or why not?

9. *Researching the music of World War II:* Ask the students to research and share the music that was popular during the time period. As they share the music, they should relate it to the important themes and conflicts of the period.

10. *Expanding a study of the Holocaust and genocide:* Teachers of older students might wish to expand their students' understandings of the Holocaust, the various issues around genocide, and the history of genocide within various cultures. A special issue of *Social Education,* edited by Parsons and Totten (1991), presents discussion topics, related literature, and units that focus on this topic.

Activities to accompany a study of the civil rights movement:

1. *Authenticating biographies of people who were active in the civil rights movement:* Ask students to read several biographies written about Martin Luther King, Jr. Ask them to note dates, details of settings, details related to characters, and issues that

the characters were facing. When possible compare the same information as developed in the different biographies. Ask them to list the similarities and differences they find in all the biographies. Then ask them to consider their responses to the similarities or differences, and to use nonfiction informational sources to research the differences.

2. *Debating the issues:* Ask the students to identify one of the issues and the people who might have had opposing opinions. Have them develop a debate that explores these issues.

3. *Responding to characters and issues:* This is another area in which students might have strong personal responses. For example, as they read *Rosa Parks* they can explain their emotional reactions to the situation in the bus when she refuses to give up her seat. They may place themselves in her place and think about how they would respond if they were forbidden to be in a certain location.

4. *Preparing a dramatization:* Select one of the biographical incidents during the civil rights movement and prepare the incident as a "You Are There" television presentation. Ask the students to research the incident, the roles of the people who took part in the situation, and the responses of people who might have been bystanders or in an audience. Have the students recreate the incident as a television presentation with an announcer who reports the news and characters who recreate the scene. They should try to make the setting as believable as possible.

5. *Creating hypothetical conversations:* Ask students to think about the conversations that might take place between people who were involved in fights for freedom during the Civil War, during the civil rights movement, and during the 1990s. Ask students to recreate meetings between people who lived during these different time periods. Have them use their knowledge of the different time periods and the people who were involved in the issues to create conversations. For example, what might Frederick Douglass and Martin Luther King, Jr. say to each other? What would Abraham Lincoln and John F. Kennedy discuss about their work for freedom and civil rights? What advice would Martin Luther King, Jr. give Barbara Jordan or Jesse Jackson? What would they tell him about the current efforts for civil rights? How would King respond to the current efforts? Students can develop the conversations as discussions in which the audience also asks questions.

6. *Research the music associated with the civil rights movement:* Ask the students to research and share the music that was played during the civil rights movement. Have the students relate the music to the themes and issues of the time period.

7. *Identifying important themes and characterizations in the literature of the civil rights movement:* As students read the literature, ask them to identify the important themes developed by the authors. For example they will discover that humans will seek freedom from political and social persecution; prejudice is difficult to overcome; prejudice and hatred are destructive forces; moral sense does not depend on skin color, but rather on what is inside a person; and take pride in yourself and your accomplishments. Ask the students to identify how authors develop these important themes and why the themes are important during this time period. Ask the students to identify characteristics of people who survive obstacles during this time period. Finally, ask the students to consider if these themes and characterizations are still important today. Why or why not?

Some comparative activities that can be used across time periods:

1. *Comparing themes:* After the students have identified the themes for each of these periods, ask them to note any similar themes. Ask them to consider why the themes were important during all of these time periods that featured major

difficulties. What do each of these time periods have in common? Are these themes important for us today? Why or why not? What lessons might we learn from these themes?

2. *Comparing characterizations:* After the students have identified characterizations associated with people who survive and overcome great obstacles during different time periods, ask them to develop a list of common human characteristics that allow people to overcome obstacles. Are these characteristics important for us today? Why or why not? What lessons might we learn from these characteristics?

3. *Developing guidelines from our historical perspective:* Ask the students to consider the problems, the outcomes of the problems, how people tried to solve the problems, and the issues that recur over time. If they could develop some guidelines for the world, what would they be? Have students prepare a dramatization in which they present their guidelines to the United Nations.

4. *Creating a montage or mural of history:* Encourage the students to choose vivid pictures that represent each time period or to create their own illustrations and create a montage or mural that shows the sweep of history over these important time periods.

5. *Creating a slide presentation:* Encourage the students to take slides of pictures, magazine illustrations, and even current incidents that reflect the feelings of the time periods. Put these together with music in a presentation that emphasizes the issues and the themes found during each time period. The students can add narration if they choose. Present the slide show to an audience.

REFERENCES

BINGHAM, J. & SCHOLT, G. (1980). *Fifteen centuries of children's literature: An annotated chronology of British and American works in historical context.* Westport, CT: Greenwood.

CIANCIOLO, P. (1985, December). Reading literature, and writing from writers' perspectives. *English Journal, 74,* 65–69.

FOX, D. (1987). *Go in and out the window.* New York: Metropolitan Museum of Art/Henry Holt.

HAYES, B. & PETERS, C. (1989). The role of reading instruction in the social studies classroom. In D. Lapp, J. Flood, & N. Farnam (Eds.), *Content area reading and learning: Instructional strategies* (pp. 152–178). Englewood Cliffs: Prentice Hall.

GIRARD, L. (1988, July/August). The truth with some stretchers. *The Horn Book,* pp. 464–469.

LARRICK, N. compiled by. (1989). *Songs from Mother Goose.* Illustrated by Robin Spowart. New York: Harper & Row.

NORTON, D. E. (1991). *Through the eyes of a child: An introduction to children's literature* (3rd ed.). Columbus, OH: Merrill.

OGLE, D. (1989). Study techniques that ensure content area reading success. In D. Lapp, J. Flood, & N. Farnam (Eds.), *Content area reading and learning: Instructional strategies* (pp. 225–234). Englewood Cliffs, NJ: Prentice Hall.

OPIE, I. & OPIE, P. selected by. (1984). *The Oxford book of children's verse.* New York: Oxford University Press.

PARSONS, W. & TOTTEN, S. edited by. (1991). Teaching about genocide. *Social Education, 55,* 84–132.

ROEHLER, L. R. & DUFFY, G. G. (1989). The content area teacher's instructional role: A cognitive mediational view. In D. Lapp, J. Flood, & N. Farnam (Eds.), *Content area reading and learning: Instructional strategies* (pp. 115–122). Englewood Cliffs: Prentice Hall.

SHANKER, A. (1991, January 20). Debating war in the Persian Gulf and . . . the uses of history. *The New York Times,* p. 9E.

WIGGINTON, E. (1972). *The Foxfire book.* New York: Doubleday.

CHILDREN'S LITERATURE REFERENCES*

Historical Fiction

AMES, MILDRED. *Grandpa Jake and the Grand Christmas* New York: Scribners, 1990 (I: 9–12).

*I = Interest by age range

AVI. *The Fighting Ground.* Philadelphia: Lippincott, 1984 (I: 10+).

BAUER, MARIAN. *Rain of Fire.* New York: Clarion, 1983 (I: 10+).

BAYLOR, BYRD. *The Best Town in the World.* Illustrated by Ronald Himler. New York: Scribner's, 1983 (I: all).

BLOS, JOAN. *A Gathering of Days: A New England Girl's Journal, 1830–32.* New York: Scribner's, 1979 (I: 8–14).

BRENNER, BARBARA. *Wagon Wheels.* Illustrated by Don Bolognese. New York: Harper & Row, 1978. (I: 6–9).

BRINK, CAROL RYRIE. *Caddie Woodlawn.* Illustrated by Trina Schart Hyman. New York: Macmillan, 1935, 1973 (I: 8–12).

CARRICK, CAROL. *Stay Away from Simon!* Illustrated by Donald Carrick. New York: Clarion, 1985 (I: 7–10).

CLAPP, PATRICIA. *Constance: A Story of Early Plymouth.* New York: Lothrop, Lee & Shepard, 1968 (I: 12+).

———. *I'm Deborah Sampson: A Soldier in the War of the Revolution.* New York: Lothrop, Lee & Shepard, 1977 (I: 9+).

COLLIER, JAMES, & CHRISTOPHER COLLIER. *Jump Ship to Freedom.* New York: Delacorte, 1981 (I: 10+).

CORMIER, ROBERT. *Other Bells for Us to Ring.* New York: Delacorte, 1990 (I: 8–12).

DALGLIESH, ALICE. *The Courage of Sarah Noble.* Illustrated by Leonard Weisgard. New York: Scribner's, 1954 (I: 6–9).

DEANGELI, MARGUERITE. *The Door in the Wall.* New York: Doubleday, 1949 (I: 8–12).

DE PAOLA, TOMIE. *An Early American Christmas.* New York: Holiday, 1987 (I: 4–7).

FORBES, ESTHER. *Johnny Tremain.* Illustrated by Lynd Ward. Boston: Houghton Mifflin, 1943 (I: 10–14).

FOX, PAULA. *The Slave Dancer.* Illustrated by Eros Keith. New York: Bradbury, 1973 (I: 12+).

FRANK, RUDOLF. *No Hero for the Kaiser,* translated by Patricia Crampton. Illustrated by Klaus Steffens. New York: Lothrop, Lee & Shepard, 1986 (I: 10+).

GEHRTS, BARBARA. *Don't Say A Word,* translated by Elizabeth Crawford. New York: Macmillan, 1987 (I: 12+).

GREENE, CONSTANCE. *Dotty's Suitcase.* New York: Viking, 1980 (I: 8–12).

HALL, DONALD. *Ox-Cart Man.* Illustrated by Barbara Cooney. New York: Viking, 1987 (I: 3–8).

HAMILTON, VIRGINIA. *The Bells of Christmas.* Illustrated by Lambert Davis. Orlando: Harcourt Brace Jovanovich, 1989 (I: 8+).

HANCOCK, SIBYL. *Old Blue.* Illustrated by Erick Ingraham. New York: Putnam, 1980 (I: 7–9).

HARTLING, PETER. *Crutches.* New York: Lothrop, Lee & Shepard, 1989 (I: 10+).

HARVEY, BRETT. *Cassie's Journey: Going West in the 1860s.* Illustrated by Deborah Kogan Ray. New York: Holiday, 1988 (I: 7–9).

HICKMAN, JANET. *Zoar Blue.* New York: Macmillan, 1978 (I: 9–12).

HOOKS, WILLIAM. *Circle of Fire.* New York: Atheneum, 1983 (I: 10+).

HOWARD, ELIZABETH. *Chita's Christmas Tree.* Illustrated by Floyd Cooper. New York: Bradbury, 1989 (I: 4–8).

HOWARD, ELLEN. *Edith Herself.* New York: Atheneum, 1987 (I: 7–10).

HUDSON, JAN. *Sweetgrass.* New York: Philomel, 1989 (I: 10+).

HUNT, IRENE. *Across Five Aprils.* New York: Follett, 1964 (I: 10+).

HURMENCE, BELINDA. *A Girl Called Boy.* Boston: Houghton Mifflin, 1982 (I: 10+). (Technically this is a modern fantasy, but use the 1853 slave experience.)

LASKY, KATHRYN. *The Night Journey.* Illustrated by Trina Schart Hyman. New York: Warne, 1981 (I: 10+).

LINGARD, JOAN. *Tug of War.* New York: Dutton, 1989 (I: 10+).

LOBEL, ARNOLD. *On the Day Peter Stuyvesant Sailed Into Town.* New York: Harper & Row, 1971 (I: 4–8).

LOWRY, LOIS. *Number the Stars.* Boston: Houghton Mifflin, 1989 (I: 10+).

LUNN, JANET. *Shadow in Hawthorn Bay.* New York: Scribner's, 1986 (I: 10+).

LYDON, KERRY RAINES. *A Birthday for Blue.* Illustrated by Michael Hayes Albert. Niles, IL: Whitman, 1989 (I: 5–8).

McCLOSKEY, ROBERT. *Lentil.* New York: Viking, 1940 (I: 4–9).

McSWIGAN, MARIE. *Snow Treasure.* Illustrated by Mary Reardon. New York: Dutton, 1942 (I: 8–12).

MONJO, F. N. *The Drinking Gourd.* Illustrated by Fred Brenner. New York: Harper & Row, 1970 (I: 7–9).

MOWAT, FARLEY. *Lost in the Barrens.* Illustrated by Charles Geer. McClelland & Steward, 1966, 1984 (I: 9+).

O'DELL, SCOTT. *Carlota.* Boston: Houghton Mifflin, 1981 (I: 10+).

———. *Sing Down the Moon.* Boston: Houghton Mifflin, 1970 (I: 10+).

ONEAL, ZIBBY. *A Long Way to Go.* Illustrated by Michael Dooling. New York: Viking, 1990 (I: 8–12).

ORLEV, URI. *The Island on Bird Street.* Translated by Hillel Halkin. Boston: Houghton Mifflin, 1984 (I: 10+).

PEARSON, KIT. *The Sky is Falling.* New York: Viking, 1990 (I: 9–12).

REEDER, CAROLYN. *Shades of Gray.* New York: Macmillan, 1989 (I: 10+).

REISS, JOHANNA. *The Upstairs Room.* New York: Crowell, 1972 (I: 10+).

SPEARE, ELIZABETH GEORGE. *The Sign of the Beaver.* Boston: Houghton Mifflin, 1983 (I: 10+).

———. *The Witch of Blackbird Pond.* Boston: Houghton Mifflin, 1958 (I: 9–14).

STEVENS, CARLA. *Anna, Grandpa, and the Big Storm.* Illustrated by Margot Tomes. Houghton Mifflin, 1982 (I: 6–9).

STOLZ, MARY. *Bartholomew Fair.* New York: Greenwillow, 1990 (I: 10+).

TAYLOR, MILDRED. *The Gold Cadillac.* Illustrated by Michael Hays. New York: Dial, 1987 (I: 8–10).

———. *Let the Circle Be Unbroken.* New York: Dial, 1981 (I: 10+).

———. *Roll of Thunder, Hear My Cry.* Illustrated by Jerry Pinckney. New York: Dial, 1976 (I: 10+).

THRASHER, CRYSTAL. *A Taste of Daylight.* New York: Atheneum, 1984 (I: 10+).

UCHIDA, YOSHIKO. *Journey Home.* Illustrated by Charles Robinson. New York: Atheneum, 1978 (I: 10+).

WILDER, LAURA INGALLS. *Little House in the Big Woods.* Illustrated by Garth Williams. New York: Harper & Row, 1932, 1953 (I: 8–12).

———. *Little House on the Prairie.* Illustrated by Garth Williams. New York: Harper & Row, 1935, 1953 (I: 8–12).

YOLEN, JANE. *The Devil's Arithmetic.* New York: Viking/Kestrel, 1988 (I: 8+). (This is technically a time-warp fantasy, but the major part of the story takes place in a concentration camp.)

Biography

ADOFF, ARNOLD. *Malcolm X.* New York: Crowell, 1979 (I: 7–12).

ALIKI. *The King's Day: Louis XIV of France.* New York: Crowell, 1989 (I: 8+).

BAINS, RAE. *Harriet Tubman: The Road to Freedom.* Illustrated by Larry Johnson. Mahwah, NJ: Troll, 1982 (I: 8–12).

BLASSINGAME, WYATT. *Thor Heyerdahl: Viking Scientist.* Elsevier-Dutton, 1979 (I: 8+).

BROOKS, POLLY SCHOYER. *Queen Eleanor: Independent Spirit of the Medieval World.* Philadelphia: Lippincott, 1983 (I: 10+).

CARPENTER, ANGELICA SHIRLEY & JEAN SHIRLEY. *Frances Hodgson Burnett: Beyond the Secret Garden.* Lerner, 1990 (I: 10+).

CLEARY, BEVERLY. *A Girl from Yamhill: A Memoir.* New York: Morrow, 1988 (I: 8+).

DALGLIESH, ALICE. *The Columbus Story.* Illustrated by Leo Politi. New York: Scribner's, 1955 (I: 5–8).

DAUGHERTY, JAMES. *Poor Richard.* New York: Viking, 1941 (I: 12+).

D'AULAIRE, INGRI & EDGAR PARIN D'AULAIRE. *Abraham Lincoln.* New York: Doubleday, 1939, 1957 (I: 8–11).

———. *Columbus.* New York: Doubleday, 1955 (I: 7–10).

DAVIDSON, MARGARET. *The Story of Eleanor Roosevelt.* New York: Four Winds, 1969 (I: 9–12).

DAVIS, OSSIE. *Langston: A Play.* New York: Delacorte, 1982 (I: 10+).

DEKAY, JAMES T. *Meet Martin Luther King, Jr.* Illustrated by Ted Burwell. New York: Random, 1969 (I: 7–9).

EGYPT, OPHELIA SETTLE. *James Weldon Johnson.* Illustrated by Moneta Barnett. New York: Crowell, 1974 (I: 5–9).

FERRIS, JERI. *Go Free or Die: A Story of Harriet Tubman.* Minneapolis: Carolrhoda, 1988 (I: 7+).

FIDO, MARTIN. *Rudyard Kipling: An Illustrated Biography.* New York: Harper & Row, 1987 (I: 10+).

FOREMAN, MICHAEL. *War Boy: A Country Childhood.* Arcade, 1990 (I: 8+).

FRANCHERE, RUTH. *Cesar Chavez.* Illustrated by Earl Thollander. New York: Crowell (I: 7–9).

FREEDMAN, RUSSELL. *Franklin Delano Roosevelt.* New York: Clarion, 1990 (I: 9+).

———. *Indian Chiefs.* New York: Holiday, 1987 (I: 10+).

———. *Lincoln: A Photobiography.* New York: Clarion, 1987 (I: 8+).

FRITZ, JEAN. *The Great Little Madison.* New York: Putnam, 1989 (I: 9+).

———. *Make Way for Sam Houston.* Illustrated by Elise Primavera. New York: Putnam, 1986 (I: 9+).

———. *Stonewall.* Illustrated by Stephen Gamell. New York: Putnam, 1979 (I: 10+).

———. *Traitor: The Case of Benedict Arnold.* New York: Putnam, 1981 (I: 8+).

———. *What's the Big Idea, Ben Franklin?* Illustrated by Margot Tomes. New York: Coward, McCann, 1978 (I: 7–10).

———. *Where Do You Think You're Going, Christopher Columbus?* Illustrated by Margot Tomes. New York: Putnam, 1980 (I: 7–12).

———. *Where Was Patrick Henry on the 29th of May?* Illustrated by Margot Tomes. New York: Coward, McCann, 1975 (I: 7–10).

———. *Why Don't You Get a Horse, Sam Adams?* Illustrated by Trina Schart Hyman. New York: Coward, McCann, 1974 (I: 7–10).

_____. *Will You Sign Here, John Hancock?* Illustrated by Trina Schart Hyman. New York: Coward, McCann, 1976 (I: 7–10).

GISH, LILLIAN. As told to Selma G. Lanes. *An Actor's Life for Me!* Illustrated by Patricia Lincoln. New York: Viking, 1987 (I: 8 +).

GOODNOUGH, DAVID. *Christopher Columbus.* Illustrated by Burt Dodson. Mahwah, NJ: Troll, 1979 (I: 8–12).

GOODSELL, JANE. *Daniel Inouye.* New York: Crowell, 1977 (I: 7–10).

_____. *Eleanor Roosevelt.* Illustrated by Wendell Minor, New York: Crowell, 1970 (I: 7–10).

GREENFIELD, ELOISE. *Rosa Parks.* Illustrated by Eric Marlow. New York: Crowell, 1974 (I: 8–12).

_____. & LESSIE JONES LITTLE. *Childtimes: A Three-Generation Memoir.* New York: Crowell, 1979 (I: 10 +).

GROSS, RUTH BELOV. *True Stories About Abraham Lincoln.* Illustrated by Jill Kastner. New York: Lothrop, Lee & Shepard, 1990 (I: 7–10).

GUTMAN, BILL. *The Picture Life of Reggie Jackson.* New York: Watts, 1978 (I: 5–8).

HAMILTON, VIRGINIA. *Anthony Burns: The Defeat and Triumph of a Fugitive Slave.* New York: Knopf, 1988 (I: 10 +).

HASKINS, JAMES. *The Life and Death of Martin Luther King, Jr.* New York: Lothrop, Lee & Shepard, 1977 (I: 10 +).

HYMAN, TRINA SCHART. *Self-Portrait: Trina Schart Hyman.* Reading: MA: Addison-Wesley, 1981 (I: 9 +).

JAKES, JOHN. *Susanna of the Alamo.* Illustrated by Paul Bacon. Orlando: Harcourt Brace Jovanovich, 1986 (I: 7–12).

LASKER, JOE. *The Great Alexander the Great.* New York: Viking, 1983 (I: 6–9).

LAUBER, PATRICIA. *Lost Star: The Story of Amelia Earhart.* New York: Scholastic, 1988 (I: 10 +).

LEE, BETSY. *Charles Eastman, The Story of an American Indian.* Minneapolis: Dillon, 1979 (I: 8–12).

LEVINSON, NANCY SMILER. *Christopher Columbus: Voyager to the Unknown.* New York: Lodestar, 1990 (I: 10 +).

MARRIN, ALBERT. *Hitler.* New York: Viking, 1987 (I: 10 +).

_____. *Stalin: Russia's Man of Steel.* New York: Viking, 1988 (I: 10 +).

McKISSACK, PATRICIA. *Jesse Jackson.* New York: Scholastic, 1989 (I: 8 +).

MELTZER, MILTON. *Benjamin Franklin: The New American.* New York: Watts, 1988 (I: 10 +).

_____. *Columbus and the World Around Him.* New York: Watts, 1990 (I: 11 +).

_____. *Dorothea Lange, Life Through the Camera.* New York: Viking, 1985 (I: 10 +).

_____. *George Washington and the Birth of Our Nation.* New York: Watts, 1986 (I: 10 +).

_____. *Starting From Home: A Writer's Beginnings.* New York: Viking Kestrel, 1988 (I: 10 +).

MILLER, DOUGLAS. *Frederick Douglass and the Fight for Freedom.* Facts on File, 1988 (I: 10 +).

MILLS, JUDIE. *John F. Kennedy.* New York: Watts, 1988 (I: 12 +).

MORRISON, DOROTHY NAFUS. *Chief Sarah: Sarah Winnemucca's Fight for Indian Rights.* New York: Atheneum, 1980 (I: 10 +).

PATTERSON, LILLIE. *Martin Luther King, Jr. and the Freedom Movement.* Facts on File, 1989 (I: 10 +).

PEARCE, CAROL ANN. *Amelia Earhart.* Facts on File, 1988 (I: 8 +).

PEARE, CATHERINE OWENS. *The FDR Story.* New York: Crowell, 1962 (I: 12 +).

PEET, BILL. *Bill Peet: An Autobiography.* Boston: Houghton Mifflin, 1989 (I: all).

QUACKENBUSH, ROBERT. *Mark Twain? What Kind of a Name Is That? A Story of Samuel Langhorne Clemens.* Prentice-Hall, 1984 (I: 7–10).

REISS, JOHANNA. *The Upstairs Room.* New York: Crowell, 1972 (I: 11 +).

ROOP, PETER & CONNIE ROOP, edited by. *I, Columbus: My Journal, 1492–3.* Walker, 1990 (I: all).

ROOSEVELT, ELLIOT. *Eleanor Roosevelt, with Love.* New York: Dutton, 1984 (I: 10 +).

ROSEN, SIDNEY. *Galileo and the Magic Numbers.* Illustrated by Harie Stein. Boston: Little, Brown, 1958 (I: 10 +).

SANDBURG, CARL. *Abe Lincoln Grows Up.* Illustrated by James Daugherty. Orlando: Harcourt Brace Jovanovich, 1926, 1954 (I: 10 +).

SCOTT, JOHN ANTHONY, & ROBERT ALAN SCOTT. *John Brown of Harper's Ferry.* Facts on File, 1988 (I: 10 +).

SILBERDICK, BARBARA. *Franklin D. Roosevelt, Gallant President.* Feinberg, 1981 (I: 9–12).

SOBOL, ROSE. *Woman Chief.* New York: Dell, 1976 (I: 8 +).

STANLEY DIANE, & PETER VENNEMA. *Shaka: King of the Zulus.* New York: Morrow, 1988 (I: 8 +).

STANLEY, FAY. *The Last Princess: The Story of Princess Ka'iulani of Hawai'i.* Illustrated by Diane Stanley. New York: Four Winds, 1991 (I: 8–12).

TURNER, GLENNETTE TILLIE. *Take a Walk in Their Shoes.* Cobblehill Books, 1989 (I: 8 +).

VENTURA, PIERO. Based on text by Gian Paolo Ceserani. *Christopher Columbus.* New York: Random, 1978 (I: all).

WHITNEY, SHARON. *Eleanor Roosevelt*. New York: Watts, 1982 (I: 10+).

WILLIAMS, SELMA R. *Demeter's Daughters: The Women Who Founded America 1587–1787*. New York: Atheneum, 1976 (I: 12+).

WOLF, BERNARD. *In This Proud Land: The Story of a Mexican Family*. Philadelphia: Lippincott, 1978 (I: all).

YATES, ELIZABETH. *Amos Fortune, Free Man*. Illustrated by Nora S. Unwin. New York: Dutton, 1950 (I: 10+).

_____. *My Diary, My World*. Philadelphia: Westminster, 1983 (I: 10+).

_____. *My Widening World*. Philadelphia: Westminster, 1983 (I: 10+).

ZEMACH, MARGOT. *Self-Portrait, Margot Zemach*. Reading, MA: Addison-Wesley, 1978 (I: all).

Informational Books

AASENG, NATHAN. *Better Mousetraps: Product Improvements That Led to Success*. Minneapolis: Lerner, 1990 (I: 10+).

ANDERSON, JOAN. *The First Thanksgiving Feast*. Photographs by George Ancona. New York: Clarion, 1984 (I: 6–9).

ARNOLD, CAROLINE. *Saving the Peregrine Falcon*. Photographs by Richard R. Hewett. Minneapolis: Carolrhoda, 1985 (I: 8–12).

ASHABRANNER, BRENT. *To Live in Two Worlds: American Indian Youth Today*. Photographs by Paul Conklin. New York: Dodd, Mead, 1984 (I: 10+).

_____. *Morning Star, Black Sun: The Northern Cheyenne Indians and America's Energy Crisis*. Photographs by Paul Conklin. New York: Dodd, Mead, 1982 (I: 10+).

BALLARD, ROBERT. D. *Exploring the Titanic*. New York: Scholastic, 1988 (I: 8+).

BASH, BARBARA. *Desert Giant: The World of the Saguaro Cactus*. Boston: Sierra Club/Little, Brown, 1989 (I: 5–9).

BLUMBERG, RHODA. *Commodore Perry in the Land of the Shogun*. New York: Lothrop, Lee & Shepard, 1985 (I: 9+).

_____. *The Incredible Journey of Lewis & Clark*. New York: Lothrop, Lee & Shepard, 1987 (I: 9+).

BOLICK, NANCY O'KEEFE & SALLIE G. RANDOLPH. *Shaker Inventions*. Illustrated by Melissa Francisco. New York: Walker, 1990 (I: 11+).

BRANLEY, FRANKLYN. *Mysteries of Outer Space*. Illustrated by Sally J. Bensusen. New York: Dutton, 1985 (I: 9+).

CAJACOB, THOMAS, & TERESA BURTON. *Close to the Wild: Siberian Tigers in a Zoo*. Minneapolis: Carolrhoda, 1986 (I: 7–10).

DAVIS, DANIEL. *Behind Barbed Wire: The Imprisonment of Japanese Americans During World War II*. New York: Dutton, 1982 (I: 10+).

ELLIS, VERONICA FREEMAN. *Afro-Bets First Book About Africa*. Just Us Books, 1990 (I: 8–12).

FABER, DORIS, & HAROLD FABER. *The Birth of a Nation: The Early Years of the United States*. New York: Scribner's, 1989 (I: 10+).

_____. *We the People: The Story of the United States Constitution Since 1787*. New York: Scribner's, 1987 (I: 10+).

FACKLAM, MARGERY, & HOWARD FACKLAM. *Changes in the Wind: Earth's Shifting Climate*. Orlando: Harcourt Brace Jovanovich, 1986 (I: 10+).

FISCHER-NAGEL, HEIDEROSE, & ANDREAS FISCHER-NAGEL. *Life of the Honey Bee*. Minneapolis: Carolrhoda, 1986 (I: 6–10).

FREEDMAN, RUSSELL. *Buffalo Hunt*. New York: Holiday, 1988 (I: 8+).

GALLANT, ROY A. *Before the Sun Dies: The Story of Evolution*. New York: Macmillan, 1989 (I: 10+).

HASKINS, JAMES. *Black Theater in America*. New York: Crowell, 1982 (I: 10+).

HIRSCHFELDER, ARLENE. *Happily May I Walk: American Indians and Alaska Natives Today*. New York: Scribner's, 1986 (I: 10+).

JESPERSEN, JAMES, & JANE FITZ-RANDOLPH. *From Quarks to Quasars: A Tour of the Universe*. New York: Atheneum, 1987 (I: 10+).

JOHNSTON, GINNY, & JUDY CUTCHINS. *Windows on Wildlife*. New York: Morrow, 1990 (I: 8–11).

JOHNSON, SYLVIA. *Potatoes*. Photographs by Masaharu Suzuki. Minneapolis: Lerner, 1984 (I: 8+).

KLEIN, DAVID, & MARYMAE KLINE. *How Do You Know It's True? Sifting Sense from Nonsense*. New York: Scribner's, 1984 (I: 12+).

LASKY, KATHRYN. *Traces of Life: The Origins of Humankind*. Illustrated by Whitney Powell. New York: Morrow, 1990 (I: 10+).

MARRIN, ALBERT. *War Clouds in the West: Indians & Cavalrymen, 1860–1890*. New York: Atheneum, 1984 (I: 10+).

McKISSACK, PATRICIA & FREDERICK McKISSACK. *A Long Hard Journey: The Story of the Pullman Porter*. New York: Walker, 1989 (I: 10+).

MELTZER, MILTON. *The American Revolutionaries: A History in Their Own Worlds, 1750–1800*. New York: Crowell, 1987 (I: 10+).

_____. *The Black Americans: A History in Their Own Words, 1619–1983*. New York: Crowell, 1984 (I: 10+).

_____. *Rescue: The Story of How Gentiles Saved Jews in the Holocaust*. New York: Harper & Row, 1988 (I: 10+).

_____. *Voices from the Civil War.* New York: Crowell, 1989 (I: 10+).

PATENT, DOROTHY HINSHAW. *Appaloosa Horses.* Photographs by William Munoz. New York: Holiday, 1988 (I: 8–12).

POATGIETER, ALICE HERMINA. *Indian Legacy: Native American Influences on World Life and Culture.* Messner, 1981 (I: 10+).

POPE, JOYCE. *Kenneth Lilly's Animals.* Illustrated by Kenneth Lilly. New York: Lothrop, Lee & Shepard, 1988 (I: all).

PRINGLE, LAURENCE. *Global Warming: Assessing the Greenhouse Threat.* New York: Arcade, 1990 (I: 8+).

_____. *Saving Our Wildlife.* Hillside, NJ: Enslow, 1990 (I: 9+).

RAY, DELIA. *A Nation Torn: The Story of How the Civil War Began.* New York: Lodestar, 1990 (I: 10+).

ROGASKY, BARBARA. *Smoke and Ashes: The Story of the Holocaust.* New York: Holiday, 1988 (I: 10+).

ROOP, PETER, & CONNIE ROOP. *Seasons of the Cranes.* New York: Walker, 1989 (I: 8+).

SATTLER, HELEN RONEY. *Giraffes, the Sentinels of the Savannas.* New York: Lothrop, Lee & Shepard, 1990 (I: 9+).

SELSAM, MILLICENT E. *The Amazing Dandelion.* Photographs by Jerome Wexler. New York: Morrow, 1977 (I: 7–10).

_____ & JOYCE HUNT. *A First Look at Bird Nests.* Illustrated by Harriet Springer. New York: Walker, 1985 (I: 5–8).

_____. *A First Look at Caterpillars.* Illustrated by Harriet Springer. New York: Walker, 1987 (I: 5–8).

_____. *A First Look At Seals, Sea Lions, and Walruses.* Illustrated by Harriet Springer. New York: Walker, 1988 (I: 5–8).

SIMON, SEYMOUR. *Meet the Giant Snakes.* Illustrated by Harriet Springer. New York: Walker, 1979 (I: 7–10).

_____. *New Questions and Answers About the Dinosaurs.* Illustrated by Jennifer Dewey. New York: Morrow, 1990 (I: 9–12).

SIMON, HILDA. *Sight and Seeing: A World of Light and Color.* New York: Philomel, 1983 (I: 10+).

ST. GEORGE, JUDITH. *The White House: Cornerstone of a Nation.* New York: Putnam's, 1990 (I: 8+).

VAN LOON, HENDRIK WILLEM. *The Story of Mankind.* New York: Liveright, 1921, 1984 (I: all).

WILKES, ANGELA. *My First Activity Book.* New York: Knopf, 1990 (I: 6–10).

_____. *My First Nature Book.* New York: Knopf, 1990 (I: 6–10).

AUTHOR INDEX

Aardema, Verna, 197, 250, 303, 306, 308, 310
Aaseng, Nathan, 402
Ackerman, Karen, 187, 260, 369, 370
Adler, C. S., 174, 263, 367
Adoff, Arnold, 148, 356, 420
Aesop, 220, 255, 278, 283
Afanasyev, Alexander Nikolayevich, 147, 196, 278
Ahlberg, Allen, 243
Ahlberg, Janet, 243
Ahnolt, Catherine, 243
Aiken, Joan, 207
Alcock, Vivien, 207
Aldridge, James, 181
Alexander, Lloyd, 50, 146, 206, 320, 322
Alexander, Martha, 133, 259
Aliki, 391
Anaya, Rudolfo A., 308, 310
Andersen, Hans Christian, 133, 146, 147, 166, 198, 218, 223, 224, 225, 318, 324–25, 326, 329, 330
Anderson, Bernice, 298
Anderson, Joan, 402
Anderson, Margaret, 322
Anderson, R., 4, 60
Anders, P., 61, 88–89
Anno, Misumasa, 255, 263
Anthony, H., 41
Aragon, Jane Chelsea, 84, 401
Arbuthnot, M. H., 46, 126, 366
Archambault, John, 64
Arnold, Caroline, 403
Arnold, M., 5
Aruego, Jose, 191
Asbjornsen, Peter, 196, 278, 283
Asch, Frank, 255, 256, 321
Ashabranner, Brent, 157, 409, 413
Avi, 385
Aylesworth, Jim, 79

Babbitt, Natalie, 65, 179, 255, 321
Bacmeister, Rhoda, 349

Baer, Edith, 193, 401
Bains, Rae, 418
Baker, Betty, 299
Baker, Jeannie, 366, 367
Baker, Keith, 42, 325, 329
Baker, Olaf, 224, 298
Baker, S., 255, 256
Ballard, Robert D., 403
Ballinger, F., 297
Banachek, Linda, 71
Barber, Antonia, 325
Barnes, B. R., 7, 48, 289
Barracca, Debra, 190
Barracca, Sal, 190
Barrie, James, 197
Barr, R., 38, 281
Barton, Byron, 78, 79
Bascom, W., 283, 285, 326
Bash, Barbara, 402
Bauer, Marion Dane, 151, 152, 153, 156, 157, 229, 419, 425
Baum, L. Frank, 197, 347, 348
Bawden, Nina, 229, 265, 283
Baylor, Byrd, 129, 144–45, 172, 174, 196, 198, 221, 222, 223, 250, 256, 262, 298, 299, 356, 362, 363, 387, 413
Beatty, Patricia, 158
Belpré, Pura, 197
Benchley, Nathaniel, 134
Benjamin, Carol Lea, 366, 367
Benson, E., 299, 308
Benson, Kathleen, 87
Bernstein, J. E., 361
Beyer, Evelyn, 349
Bierhorst, John, 194, 278, 280, 283, 289, 297, 298, 299, 307–9, 310
Bingham, J., 389
Blachowicz, C., 90–91
Blackmore, Vivien, 308
Black, Sheila, 207
Blassingame, Wyatt, 397
Blos, Joan, 384, 385–86
Blumberg, Rhoda, 402, 405, 406

Blume, Judy, 50, 146, 158, 224, 364, 366
Bockoras, Diane, 366
Boggs, R. S., 197, 308
Bolick, Nancy O'Keefe, 403
Bond, Michael, 198, 244, 321
Bond, Nancy, 207
Bos, C., 61, 88–89
Boston, Lucy M., 147
Branley, Franklin, 80, 405, 406
Branscum, Robbie, 206
Brenner, Barbara, 388
Brett, Jan, 81, 129–30, 218, 255, 256, 279
Briggs, Raymond, 259
Brink, Carol Ryrie, 10, 197, 224, 384
Brittain, Bill, 65, 207, 245–47, 255, 256, 321
Brooks, Bruce, 180
Brooks, Gwendolyn, 356
Brooks, Polly Schoyer, 207, 391
Brown, Marc, 190, 243
Brown, Marcia, 137, 199, 229, 283, 290
Brown, Margaret Wise, 168, 190, 243
Brown, Tricia, 218–19
Browne, Anthony, 242
Bryan, Ashley, 250, 278, 303, 304
Bulfinch, Thomas, 278, 283
Bunting, Eve, 85, 137, 138, 146, 167, 363, 369
Burnett, Francis Hodgson, 47, 165, 180, 202, 204, 229, 362
Burnford, Sheila, 146
Burns, P., 107
Burton, Teresa, 406
Burton, Virginia Lee, 68, 142, 143, 237–38, 242, 321
Buscaglia, Leo, 70
Byars, Betsy, 147, 174, 180, 206, 265, 366

Cajacob, Thomas, 406
Calfee, R., 58–59

California State Department of Education, 4, 9
Callen, Larry, 224
Calmenson, Stephanie, 260
Cameron, Eleanor, 173
Campbell, J., 288, 297
Carew, Jan, 146, 303, 306
Carle, Eric, 348, 350, 351
Carpenter, Angelica Shirley, 399
Carr, E., 60–61
Carrick, Carol, 146, 153, 154, 224, 383, 384
Carroll, Lewis, 67, 109–10, 186, 197, 321, 322, 329, 331, 332, 356
Carter, Angela, 281
Cassedy, Sylvia, 348
Cavendish, Richard, 337
Cazet, Denys, 85, 140, 219
Cendrars, Blaise, 65
Chase, Richard, 87
Cheetham, Ann, 157
Chetwin, Grace, 133
Choate, J., 74
Chow, Octavio, 308, 310
Christopher, John, 156, 157, 229, 333, 334
Cianciolo, P. J., 46, 127, 399–400
Ciardi, John, 350, 351, 352, 356
Clapp, Patricia, 158, 388, 417, 421
Clark, Ann Nolan, 158, 290, 291
Cleary, Beverly, 50, 68, 87, 147, 173, 174, 198, 224, 263, 362, 364, 366, 367, 399
Cleaver, Bill, 158
Cleaver, Elizabeth, 298
Cleaver, Vera, 158
Climo, Shirley, 290
Clymer, Eleanor, 158
Coatsworth, David, 197, 298
Coatsworth, Emerson, 197, 298
Cobb, Vicki, 80
Coe, M., 299, 308
Cohen, C. L., 141
Cole, Brock, 180, 229
Cole, Joanna, 80, 244, 260
Collier, Christopher, 229, 414–15, 418
Collier, James, 229, 414–15, 418
Collington, Peter, 116, 130, 131–32, 259
Collodi, Carlo, 146
Colt, J., 8–9
Colum, Padraic, 87, 278, 283, 337, 338
Conger, David, 197
Conrad, Pam, 181
Cooney, Barbara, 191
Cooney, Nancy Evans, 188, 189
Cooper, Susan, 134, 257, 276, 318, 320, 324, 325, 337, 339, 340

Corbett, W. J., 255, 257, 321
Corcoran, Barbara, 265
Cormier, Robert, 388, 419, 425
Courlander, Harold, 87, 278, 303
Cousins, Lucy, 64
Crane, Walter, 189, 296, 346
Cresswell, Helen, 197
Crews, Donald, 71
Cross, Gillian, 208, 374
Crossley-Holland, Kevin, 174, 197, 337
Cullinan, B., 46, 126
Curtis, Edward, 278, 298
Cushing, Frank Hamilton, 222, 298
Cutchins, Judy, 403

Daane, M. C., 236
Dahl, Roald, 147, 329, 332
Dalgleish, Alice, 198, 224, 249, 384, 391, 394, 396
Daniels, J. P., 45
Daugherty, James, 395
D'Aulaire, Edgar Parin, 287, 288, 394
D'Aulaire, Ingri, 287, 288, 394
Davidson, Margaret, 224, 394
Davis, Daniel, 419
Davis, Ossie, 414, 416
Davis, S., 127
DeAngeli, Marguerite, 146, 174, 384, 388
Debarats, Peter, 369
DeBrunhoff, Jean, 242
De Gerez, Toni, 308, 309–10, 353
DeKay, James, 147, 391, 395, 420
Delton, Judy, 197
De Paola, Tomie, 64, 76–78, 81–84, 129, 169, 191, 219, 220–21, 224, 279, 281, 298, 308, 310, 376, 388
De Regniers, Beatrice Schenk, 349, 350, 351–52
Dewey, Ariane, 147, 191
Dewey, John, 6
Diakiw, J. Y., 187, 289
Dickinson, Peter, 319, 333
Dillon, Leo, 416
Dodds, Dayle Ann, 71, 401
Dole, J., 253
Donelson, K., 361
Dore, Gustave, 296
Dorris, M., 297
Dowden, Anne Ophelia, 109
Drescher, Henrik, 116
Dressel, J. H., 46
Dronka, P., 14
Drum, P., 58–59
Duffy, G. G., 169, 253, 401
Dulac, Edmund, 296
Duncan, Lois, 374

Dunning, Stephen, 48, 346, 347, 349, 353–54
Durell, Ann, 255, 364
Durkin, D., 13
Duvoisin, Roger, 243

Egoff, Sheila, 319, 327–28
Egypt, Ophelia Settle, 391
Eichenberg, F., 258
Ellis, Veronica Freeman, 414
Emberley, Rebecca, 78, 401
Engel, Diana, 243
Enright, Elizabeth, 174
Erdman, M., 355
Ernst, Lisa Campbell, 85, 134, 242
Esbensen, Barbara Juster, 298
Estes, Eleanor, 263
Evans, C. S., 281, 296

Faber, Doris, 417, 418
Faber, Harold, 417, 418
Facklam, Howard, 89–90, 405, 406
Facklam, Margery, 89–90, 405, 406
Fairbanks, M., 59–60
Farley, Walter, 265
Farr, R., 99, 108
Farrell, Kate, 355
Fatio, Louise, 191
Favat, F. A., 281
Feelings, Tom, 416
Feldstein, Barbara, 361
Ferris, Jeri, 147, 224, 414, 415
Fiderer, A., 45
Fido, Martin, 399
Field, Rachel, 263
Fife, Dale, 158
Fischer-Nagel, Andreas, 75–76, 90, 401, 402
Fischer-Nagel, Heiderose, 75–76, 90, 401, 402
Fishel, C. T., 11
Fisher, Aileen, 356
Fitz-Randolph, Jane, 405
Fleischman, Paul, 158, 263, 350, 352
Fleischman, Sid, 167, 219, 247–48, 321, 369
Fleming, Ian, 146
Flournoy, Valerie, 188, 219, 362, 367, 369
Forbes, Esther, 48, 69, 126, 383, 388, 417, 421
Ford, Alice, 197
Foreman, Michael, 419, 425
Fowler, Susi Gregg, 84, 187, 401
Fox, Dan, 189, 346, 389
Fox, Mem, 41–42, 64, 280, 369
Fox, Paula, 70, 151, 152, 156, 158, 208, 224, 265, 362, 368, 414
Franchere, Ruth, 148, 393

Frank, Rudolf, 72–73, 252–55, 418, 423, 424
Frederick, H. V., 49
Freedman, Russell, 201–2, 390, 394, 395, 409, 410, 418, 419, 422
Freppon, P. A., 5
Freud, Sigmund, 6
Friedman, Ina, 85, 364
Friedman, Russell, 69
Fritz, Jean, 68, 89, 148, 175–77, 197, 224, 390, 417
Frost, Robert, 356
Frye, Northrop, 6, 255, 256

Gaetz, T., 355
Gag, Wanda, 189, 287
Galdone, Paul, 64, 132
Gallant, Roy, 79–80, 401, 405
Gallenkamp, Charles, 89
Gardner, M., 12
Gardner, Martin, 67
Garfield, Leon, 158, 207
Garland, Michael, 187, 401
Garner, Alan, 147, 207
Gauch, Patricia, 365, 366
Gehrts, Barbara, 419, 425
George, Jean Craighead, 70, 147, 157, 180, 208, 263, 368, 373, 377
George, William, 187, 401
Gerhardt, L., 49
Gibbons, Gail, 72
Gilbert, C., 47
Gilbert, Henry, 296
Gillespie, J., 47
Gilliland, Judith Heide, 260, 363
Ginsburg, Mirra, 132
Gipson, Fred, 174, 265
Girard, L., 389
Giroux, H., 13
Gish, Lillian, 393, 397, 398
Goble, Paul, 137–38, 220, 281, 298
Godden, Rumer, 329, 332
Goodall, Jane, 78, 401
Goodall, John, 259
Goodnough, David, 394
Goodsell, Jane, 207, 393, 394
Goor, Nancy, 80, 150
Goor, Ron, 80, 150
Grahame, Kenneth, 47, 67, 249, 319, 329, 332
Greenaway, Kate, 47
Greene, Constance, 146, 224, 418, 423
Greenfield, Eloise, 147, 198, 224, 348, 356, 367, 399, 416, 420, 427
Griego y Maestas, Jose, 308, 310
Grifalconi, Ann, 129, 132, 133, 167, 168, 189–90, 215, 217–18, 303, 362, 369

Griffith, Helen V., 169, 191, 224, 369
Grimes, Nikki, 348
Grimm, Brothers, 39, 47, 132, 146, 198, 202, 204, 216–17, 219, 224, 225, 278, 280, 281, 290, 293
Grimm, Wilhelm, 225–26
Grinnell, George Bird, 278
Gripe, Maria, 157
Gross, Ruth Belov, 393, 394, 418
Gross, Theodore Faro, 364, 369
Grove, Vicki, 181
Guadalupi, G., 200, 201
Gutman, Bill, 393
Guy, Rosa, 303

Hadithi, Mwenye, 219, 325, 327
Haggard, M. R., 73, 84
Hale, Sara Josepha, 260
Haley, Gail E., 198, 303, 306
Hall, Donald, 137, 138, 369, 388
Hall, Lynn, 208
Hamilton, Virginia, 70, 87, 147, 158, 181, 198, 206, 207, 224, 228, 265, 283, 298, 299, 303, 304, 306, 333, 334, 335, 367, 368, 374, 384, 393, 416, 418
Hancock, Sibyl, 197, 384
Harris, Christie, 298, 299
Harris, Joel Chandler, 303
Harris, Rosemary, 374
Harrison, Michael, 337
Hartling, Peter, 419, 425
Harvey, Brett, 10, 387
Haseley, Dennis, 146, 373
Haskins, James, 395, 414, 416, 420
Haskins, Jima, 87
Hastings, Selina, 61, 84, 85, 86, 129, 148, 149, 155–56, 179, 180, 205–6, 227, 228, 265, 279
Hautzig, Esther, 158
Haviland, Virginia, 194, 280, 290, 291–92, 299
Hayes, B., 402
Hearne, B., 46, 290
Heide, Florence Parry, 260, 363
Hendershot, Judith, 198, 362
Henkes, Kevin, 369
Henry, Marguerite, 266
Hepler, S., 46, 126
Herman, P., 60
Hess, Lilo, 244, 401
Hest, Amy, 85, 187, 369
Heyer, Marilee, 147, 224
Hickman, J., 46, 126
Hickman, Janet, 147, 207, 229, 418
Hiebert, E. H., 4, 8–9
Highwater, Jamake, 66, 226–27, 279, 281, 346, 354, 373, 413

Hillocks, G., 44
Hillyer, Robert, 349
Hinojosa, Francisco, 134, 308, 309
Hirschfelder, Arlene, 409
Hirsh, E. D., 4
Hoban, Russell, 134, 168, 242
Hoban, Tana, 61, 72
Hoberman, Mary Ann, 64, 243
Hodges, Margaret, 84, 87, 148, 149, 256
Hoey, Edwin A., 349
Hoff, Syd, 260
Hogrogian, Nonny, 224
Holder, Heidi, 220, 255
Holling, Holling Clancy, 150
Holloway, K., 13
Holman, Felice, 374, 377
Honig, William, 4
Hooks, William, 158, 229, 290, 292–93, 418
Hoover, H. M., 333, 334, 336
Hopkins, L. B., 347
Howard, Elizabeth, 387
Howard, Ellen, 174, 224, 384
Howe, James, 363, 369
Huck, C., 46, 126
Huck, Charlotte, 290
Hudson, Jan, 67, 409
Hughes, Langston, 356, 416
Hughes, Monica, 157, 333, 334–35
Hughes, Shirley, 167, 169, 219, 363, 367, 369
Hunt, Irene, 418
Hunt, Joyce, 75, 187, 401, 403, 405
Hurmence, Belinda, 414, 416
Hutchins, Pat, 71–72, 116, 191
Hyman, Trina Schart, 216, 293, 294, 399

Ike, Jane, 147
Isele, Elizabeth, 198
Ishii, Momoko, 222
Ivemey, John, 64

Jacobs, J. S., 339
Jacobs, Joseph, 278
Jagendorf, M. A., 197, 308
Jakes, John, 148, 393, 396
James, Mary, 261–62
Janeczko, P. B., 236, 344, 347
Jeffers, Susan, 191, 250–52
Jespersen, James, 405
Johns, J., 107
Johnson, A. E., 194
Johnson, Sylvia, 75, 76, 401, 406
Johnston, Ginny, 403
Johnston, Tony, 134
Jones, T., 49
Jukes, Mavis, 167, 263, 365, 366

Kaye, D. B., 60
Keats, Ezra Jack, 85, 133, 166, 167, 169, 187, 188–89, 191, 329, 332, 362
Keith, Harold, 207
Keller, Beverly, 174
Keller, Holly, 191
Kellogg, Stephen, 369
Kerr, Judith, 158
Key, Alexander, 147, 333, 335
Khalsa, Dayal, 85, 187, 362, 366, 367
Kherdian, David, 207
Kimmel, Eric A., 224, 258, 259, 325
King-Smith, Dick, 244, 321
Kinsey-Warnock, Natalie, 197
Kipling, Rudyard, 147, 198, 229, 332, 350
Kismaric, Carole, 147, 281
Klause, Annette Curtis, 206
Klein, David, 406
Klein, Marymae, 406
Kline, Suzy, 174
Knudson, R. R., 257, 349
Knutson, Barbara, 303
Kobeh, Ann Garcia, 308, 309
Koch, Kenneth, 355
Konigsburg, E. L., 68
Konopak, B. C., 45
Koriyama, Naoshi, 346, 347
Kraus, Robert, 242
Krumgold, Joseph, 69
Kurtycz, Marcos, 308, 309
Kuskin, Karla, 344

Lagerlöf, Selma, 146
Lamme, L. L., 62–63, 187
Lampman, Evelyn, 207
Lanes, Selma G., 393, 397, 398
Lang, Andrew, 194, 280, 283, 293
Larrick, Nancy, 353, 389
Lasker, Joe, 393
Lasky, Kathryn, 80, 229, 249, 257, 385, 405
Lattimore, Deborah Nourse, 308
Lauber, Patricia, 61, 80, 89, 150, 391, 401
Lavies, Bianca, 80
Lawson, Robert, 197, 224, 244, 321, 329, 332
Leaf, Munro, 68, 142, 143, 219, 321
Lear, Edward, 65–66, 346, 350, 352, 354, 356
LeCain, Errol, 146, 250–52
Lee, Betsy, 148, 197, 391
LeGuin, Ursula K., 206, 244, 321, 323
Lehr, S., 215
L'Engle, Madeleine, 229, 318, 322, 333, 335, 336

Lester, Julius, 87, 194, 257, 280, 304
Levine-Provost, Gail, 181
Levinson, Nancy Smiler, 87, 394
Lewin, Hugh, 238–39, 243, 363
Lewis, C. S., 50, 68, 193–94, 206, 229, 255, 276, 318, 321, 329, 331
Lewis, Naomi, 194
Lindbergh, Reeve, 258–59
Lindgren, Barbro, 189, 321, 346
Lingard, Joan, 387, 419, 425
Lionni, Leo, 68, 219, 239–41, 242, 243, 321, 329, 332
Lipson, M. Y., 99–100, 101–2, 103
Lisle, Janet Taylor, 180, 206, 366, 367
Lister, Robin, 287, 288
Little, Jean, 174, 224
Little, Lessie Jones, 399
Livingston, Myra Cohn, 250, 290, 293, 349, 353, 356
Liyi, He, 194, 280, 283
Lobel, Arnold, 43, 64, 129, 216, 236–37, 242, 260, 347, 353, 387
Lollyd, David, 134
London, Jack, 50
Longfellow, Henry Wadsworth, 250–52, 353
Louie, Ai-lang, 290
Lowry, Lois, 126, 147, 174, 181, 266, 419, 425
Lueders, Edward, 48, 346, 347, 349, 353–54
Lukens, R. J., 126, 214
Lunn, Janet, 157, 229, 319, 387
Luskay, J., 4
Lydon, Kerry Raines, 384
Lyon, George Ella, 207

Macaulay, David, 329
MacDonald, George, 255, 321
Maciel, Leonel, 310
MacLachlan, Patricia, 10, 68, 164, 169, 170–72, 174, 383
Madsen, Jane, 366
Mahy, Margaret, 189, 346
Manguel, A., 200, 201
Many, J., 118, 368
Margolis, Richard, 249, 348
Mark, Jan, 187, 362
Marrin, Albert, 393, 409, 413, 419
Marshak, Samuel, 219, 249
Marshall, James, 133, 134, 243, 281, 293–94
Martin, Bill, Jr., 64
Martin, M. A., 45
Martin, Rafe, 189, 321
Martin, S. H., 45
Martinez-Ostos, 310

Maruki, Toshi, 198, 199
Marzano, J., 60, 61–62, 63
Marzano, R., 60, 61–62, 63
Mathers, Petra, 85
Mathews, J., 98–99
Mathis, Sharon Bell, 223, 366
Matthews, D., 47
Matthews, Downs, 78, 150, 244, 401
Maxner, Joyce, 189, 321
Mayer, Marianna, 134, 281
Mayer, Mercer, 116, 133, 147, 191, 259
Mayne, William, 264
Mazer, Norma Fox, 158
McCaffrey, Anne, 158
McCloskey, Robert, 47, 191, 242, 388
McCord, David, 348, 350, 351, 353, 354, 355, 356
McCracken, M., 43
McCracken, R., 43
McCullough, C., 74
McCully, Emily Arnold, 114–15, 166–67, 191, 237, 238, 260, 263, 321, 322
McDermott, Gerald, 303
McKeown, M., 60
McKinley, Robin, 87, 157, 180
McKissack, Frederick, 420
McKissack, Patricia, 68, 304, 329, 420
McLaughlin, Molly, 80, 401
McMillan, Bruce, 72
McNamara, J. F., 119
McPhail, David, 192, 350
McSwigan, Marie, 147, 419, 425
Meade, J., 14, 361
Melling, O. R., 147
Meltzer, Milton, 87, 393, 394, 395, 399, 414, 417, 418, 419, 420
Merriam, Eve, 126, 192, 236, 344, 346, 347, 349, 356
Metayer, Maurice, 197, 298
Meyer, Carolyn, 89
Miles, Miska, 219, 367
Miller, Douglas, 87, 207, 418
Miller, M., 4
Mills, Judie, 207
Milne, A. A., 249, 250, 319, 322, 329, 349, 350, 352
Moe, A., 107
Moe, Jorgen, 196, 278, 283
Moeri, Louise, 10
Mohr, Nicholasa, 146, 157, 229, 265, 363, 366, 367
Monjo, F. N., 384, 414, 418
Monroe, Jean Guard, 298, 299
Monson, D., 5–7
Montgomery, L. M., 47
Moone, Sarah, 294

Moore, Clement, 191, 243, 350
Morrison, Dorothy Nafus, 409, 412, 413
Morrison, Lillian, 349
Mosel, Arlene, 281
Moss, J. F., 289
Mowat, Farley, 385, 409
Mulherine, Jennifer, 296
Musgrove, Margaret, 304
Myers, Walter Dean, 181, 229, 265, 364, 374, 377, 416

Nagy, W., 60
Narahashi, Keiko, 369
Nash, Ogden, 198, 199, 346, 350, 352, 354
National Commission on Social Studies in the Schools, 7
National Council of Teachers of English, 14
National Endowment for the Humanities, 13
Naylor, Alice, 361
Naylor, Phyllis Reynolds, 133, 365–66
Nesbit, E., 319, 325, 329
Ness, Evaline, 168, 369, 370–71
Newman, Robert, 208
Nhuong, Huynh Quang, 158
Nixon, Hershell, 80
Nixon, Joan Lowery, 80, 319
Noll, Sally, 72
Norton, D. E., 6, 46, 49, 119, 126, 169, 226, 237, 289, 297, 301, 331, 355, 361, 389
Norton, Mary, 68, 198, 329, 332
Noyes, Alfred, 198, 199–200, 256, 346, 350

Oakley, Graham, 250, 255, 256, 321
O'Brien, Robert, 244, 263, 321
O'Dell, Scott, 69, 156, 157, 208, 373, 377, 385, 409, 413
Ogle, D., 402
Onassis, Jacqueline, 194, 280
Oneal, Zibby, 387
Opie, Iona, 64, 389
Opie, Peter, 64, 389
Orlev, Uri, 69, 181, 388, 419, 425
Ormerod, Jan, 134
O'Shea, Pat, 339
Otsuka, Yuzo, 223

Park, Barbara, 174
Parks, Van Dyke, 224, 303
Parsons, W., 426
Patent, Dorothy Hinshaw, 80, 405, 406
Paterson, Katherine, 40, 111, 157, 180, 181, 206, 229, 266, 280, 361, 364, 368

Patterson, Lillie, 87, 208, 395, 414
Paulsen, Gary, 126, 150–51, 257, 362, 373, 376, 377, 390
Paxton, Tom, 255, 347, 348
Pearce, A. M., 46
Pearce, Carol Ann, 87, 148, 397
Pearce, Philippa, 229, 319, 322
Peare, Catherine Owens, 395
Pearson, Kit, 419, 425
Pearson, P. D., 38, 253, 281
Peet, Bill, 243, 399
Pelgrom, Els, 207
Pellowski, Anne, 224
People for the American Way, 14
Perkins, G., 255, 256
Perrault, Charles, 47, 198, 199, 278, 280, 290, 293, 294, 296
Perrine, L., 165, 178, 214–15, 216
Peters, C., 402
Peters, C. W., 100
Peters, Lisa Westberg, 191, 363, 364, 369
Peterson, Jeanne, 369
Petry, Ann, 156, 157, 229
Phillips, Betty Lou, 224
Phipson, Joan, 158, 229
Pikulski, J. J., 98, 104, 107
Pinkney, Jerry, 416
Piper, D., 48
Piper, Watty, 219
Poatgieter, Alice Hermina, 410
Polacco, Patricia, 192
Pomerantz, Charlotte, 219
Pope, Joyce, 405
Porte, Barbara Ann, 367
Potter, Beatrix, 133, 164, 166, 167, 168, 257, 258, 259, 318, 321, 324, 329, 332
Powell, J. S., 60
Prago, Albert, 158
Prelutsky, Jack, 64, 249, 250, 345, 346–47, 349, 350, 351, 352, 353, 356
Pringle, Laurence, 80, 90, 401, 402, 405, 407
Pritchard, R., 99, 108
Provensen, Alice, 175, 191, 243
Provensen, Martin, 191, 243
Provost, Gary, 181
Purdy, Carol, 219
Purves, A., 5–7, 13, 15, 127
Pushkin, Alexander, 278
Putka, G., 4, 13
Pyle, Howard, 278, 283, 296

Quackenbush, Robert, 391

Rabe, Berniece, 147
Rackham, Arthur, 296
Rakes, T., 74

Randolph, Sallie G., 403
Ransome, Arthur, 134
Raphael, T., 41
Rardin, Susan Lowry, 374
Raskin, Ellen, 208
Ray, Delia, 418
Rayner, Mary, 243
Reeder, Carolyn, 158, 418
Reiss, Johanna, 229, 397, 419, 425
Rey, Hans, 68, 243
Rice, Eve, 85
Robertson, Keith, 208
Robinson, Gail, 299
Rockwell, Anne, 42, 72, 84, 133, 281, 401
Rockwood, Joyce, 147, 266
Rodgers, Mary, 147
Roe, B., 107
Roehler, L. R., 169, 253, 402
Rogasky, Barbara, 202, 204, 419
Rogers, T., 127
Rohmer, Harriet, 308, 310
Roop, Connie, 79, 394, 401, 406, 407
Roop, Peter, 79, 394, 401, 406, 407
Roosevelt, Elliott, 87, 394, 419
Rosenblatt, L. M., 6, 348
Rosen, Michael, 42, 43, 63, 345
Rosen, Sidney, 397
Rossetti, Christina, 350, 351–52
Rothman, R., 14
Rounds, Glen, 43, 64, 345
Ruddell, R., 59
Rudman, M. K., 46, 126–27
Russo, Marisabina, 364
Ryder, Joanne, 189, 321
Rylant, Cynthia, 137, 138, 151, 152, 153, 192, 242, 260, 348, 364

Sachs, Marilyn, 224, 255, 364
Sadler, Catherine Edwards, 113, 114, 115
Sadow, M., 38, 281
Sager, C., 44
St. George, Judith, 89, 418
Sandburg, Carl, 206, 329, 350, 352, 394
Sandin, Joan, 224
Sanfield, Steve, 87, 303, 304
San Souci, Robert D., 40, 68, 280
Sattler, Helen Roney, 72, 79, 81, 90, 401, 405, 406, 407
Scheer, Julian, 198, 199, 321, 346
Scholt, G., 389
Schotter, Roni, 169, 366
Schwartz, Amy, 169, 187, 362, 369
Scott, J., 4
Scott, Jack Denton, 81, 244, 401
Scott, John Anthony, 418
Scott, Robert Alan, 418
Seabrooke, Brenda, 348

Sebesta, S., 49–50
Selden, George, 68, 173, 329
Selsam, Millicent, 75, 81, 187, 401, 403, 405
Sendak, Maurice, 68, 191, 226, 329, 331, 350, 351, 353
Seredy, Kate, 229, 257
Seuss, Dr., 134, 191, 242, 243, 260
Shaffer, D. R., 365
Shanker, A., 416
Shannon, G., 237
Shannon, P., 361
Sherman, Josepha, 146
Shirley, Jean, 399
Siegel, Beatrice, 87
Silberdick, Barbara, 395
Silvaroli, N., 107
Silverstein, Shel, 224, 348, 353, 356
Silvey, A., 361
Simon, Seymour, 79, 80, 150, 401, 406, 407
Simon, Hilda, 403
Simonsen, S., 38–41
Singer, H., 38–41
Singer, Isaac Bashevis, 134, 223, 278
Sis, Peter, 219
Slepian, Jan, 364, 383
Slote, Alfred, 181
Smith, C., 276
Smith, Hugh, 48, 346, 347, 349, 353–54
Sneve, Virginia Driving Hawk, 158, 265, 413
Snow, D., 299, 308
Snyder, Dianne, 68, 134
Snyder, Zilpha Keatley, 266, 333, 335
Sobol, Rose, 87, 409
Soter, A., 127
Soto, Gary, 266
Speare, Elizabeth George, 153, 154–55, 156, 181, 207, 229, 256–57, 383, 387, 388, 409
Spencer, Paula Underwood, 298
Sperry, Armstrong, 11, 65, 70, 137, 138–39, 140, 141–42, 362, 373, 376
Stahl, S., 59–60
Stamm, Claus, 112, 113
Stanley, Diane, 391
Stanley, Fay, 397
Staples, Suzanne Fisher, 265, 364, 368
Stefoff, Rebecca, 207
Steig, William, 329, 366
Steptoe, John, 134, 135, 136, 168, 219, 223, 279, 290, 299, 416
Sternberg, R. J., 60
Stevens, Carla, 387
Stevenson, James, 243
Stevenson, Robert Louis, 349, 350, 351, 352–53

Stewig, J., 126
Stock, Catherine, 363
Stolz, Mary, 364, 369, 385
Sutcliff, Rosemary, 87, 158, 207
Sutherland, Z., 46, 126, 290, 293, 366
Swanton, S., 50, 318
Swenson, May, 257, 349
Swope, J. W., 45

Tafuri, Nancy, 260
Taha, Karen T., 369
Taylor, Mildred D., 147, 156, 229, 387, 414, 416, 418
Taylor, Sydney, 224
Taylor, Theodore, 366, 367, 373
Tejima, Keizaburo, 137, 138
Thiele, Colin, 364
Thompson, E. H., 45
Thrasher, Crystal, 418, 423
Tolkien, J. R. R., 50, 186, 200, 250, 276, 318, 319, 320, 337, 338, 340
Tompkins, G., 42
Toth, L., 49
Totten, S., 426
Trelease, J., 47
Tuck, Jay, 87
Tulley, M. A., 99, 108
Tunnell, M. O., 339
Turner, Glennette Tillie, 414, 416
Tway, E., 48

Uchida, Yoshiko, 158, 229, 419, 425
Unstead, R. J., 308

Vagin, Vladimir, 255, 256, 321
Valencia, S., 98, 104–5
Van Allsburg, Chris, 42, 116, 133, 191, 198, 199, 263, 321, 322, 329, 332
Van Leeuwen, Jean, 260
Van Loon, Hendrik Willem, 389
Vennema, Peter, 391
Ventura, Piero, 394
Vergara, Norma, 87
Verne, Jules, 336
Vidaure, Morris, 308, 310
Vincent, Gabrielle, 169, 242
Viorst, Judith, 68, 250
Voigt, Cynthia, 70, 164, 177–79, 362, 368
Vuong, Lynette Dyer, 290

Waber, Bernard, 369
Walker, Barbara K., 197, 303
Wallace, Ian, 218, 367
Wallas, James, 299
Walter, Mildred Pitts, 85, 134, 223, 330, 364, 366

Ward, Lynd, 191
Watson, D., 127
Watson, James, 374
Weber, M., 42
Weber, William J., 244, 401
Weiss, Nicki, 43
Wells, H. G., 336
Wells, Rosemary, 68, 134, 243
Westall, Robert, 207
Weston, L. H., 215
Whipple, Laura, 64
White, Clarence, 224
White, E. B., 47, 68, 173, 223, 318, 321, 322, 329
White Deer of Autumn, 373, 376
Whitney, Sharon, 394, 419
Wiesner, David, 116, 260, 322, 330, 332
Wiessler, J., 14
Wigginton, E., 389
Wild, Margaret, 369
Wilder, Laura Ingalls, 10, 48, 126, 147, 198, 224, 384, 388, 389
Wilkes, Angela, 403
Wilkinson, I., 4
Will, George, 6
Willard, Nancy, 257, 350, 356
Williams, Margery, 70, 218, 242, 321
Williams, Selma R., 417
Williams, Vera B., 169, 260, 366
Williamson, Ray A., 298, 299
Wilson, Dornminster, 308
Wiseman, Bernard, 260
Wisniewski, David, 147
Wixson, K. K., 60–61, 107–8
Wojciechowska, Maia, 70, 181
Wolf, Bernard, 168, 396
Wood, Audrey, 191, 255, 256, 260, 330, 332
Woods, M. L., 107
Worth, Valerie, 250, 356
Wyss, Johann David, 373

Yagawa, Sumiko, 146, 222, 223
Yashima, Taro, 153–54, 218
Yates, Elizabeth, 397, 399, 414
Yep, Laurence, 157, 207, 208, 228, 289, 297, 368
Yolen, Jane, 142, 143–44, 198, 199, 224, 250, 326, 329, 362, 419, 425
Yorinks, Arthur, 140–41, 218, 255, 256, 321, 322, 330, 332
Young, Ed, 134, 294

Zarrillo, J., 12
Zemach, Harve, 224, 250
Zemach, Margot, 198, 260, 399
Zimmerman, Baruch, 147
Zolotow, Charlotte, 168, 191

SUBJECT INDEX

A Apple Pie (Greenaway), 47
Abe Lincoln Grows Up (Sandburg), 394
Abel's Island (Steig), 329
Abraham Lincoln (D'Aulaire), 394
Acorn Quest, The (Yolen), 224
Across Five Aprils (Hunt), 418
Actor's Life for Me!, An (Gish & Lanes), 393, 397, 398
Adventures of High John the Conqueror, The (Sanfield), 87, 303, 304
Adventures of Johnny May, The (Branscum), 206
Adventures of Nanabush, The: Ojibway Indian Stories (Coatsworth & Coatsworth), 197, 298
Adventures of Pinocchio, The: Tale of a Puppet (Collodi), 146
Adventures of Taxi Dog, The (Barracca), 190
Aesop's Fables (Aesop), 220, 255, 283
Aesop's Fables (Paxton), 347, 348
Aesthetic responses, 20–21. *See also* Drama activities; Writing activities
  and assessment, 117–19
  and author's style, 247, 256
  and characterization, 166, 179
  and contemporary realistic fiction, 367–68, 372, 377
  and fantasy, 324–25, 328–32, 336
  and folklore, 287–88, 293, 302, 306, 310
  and historical fiction, biography and informational literature, 396–97, 408, 412, 413, 416, 428
  and plot development, 139, 142, 143–44, 153, 155
  poetry, 348–49
  and setting, 187, 188, 189, 195
Afro-Bets First Book About Africa (Ellis), 414
Afternoon of the Elves (Lisle), 180, 206, 366, 367

After the Rain (Mazer), 158
Agnes Cecilia (Gripe), 157
Alexander and the Terrible, Horrible, No Good, Very Bad Day (Viorst), 68
Alexander and the Wind-up Mouse (Lionni), 242, 329, 332
Alfie Gives a Hand (Hughes), 169
Alice's Adventures in Wonderland (Carroll), 67, 194, 197, 321, 322, 329, 331
All-of-a-Kind Family (Taylor), 224
All the Small Poems (Worth), 250
Amazing Dandelion, The (Selsam), 403
Amelia Earhart (Pearce), 87, 148, 397
American Revolutionaries: A History in Their Own Words, 1750–1800 (Meltzer), 418
American Sports Poems (Knudson & Swenson), 257, 349
Amos Fortune, Free Man (Yates), 397, 414
Analytic Reading Inventory, 107
Analytic structure, 6
Anansi the Spider: A Tale from the Ashanti (McDermott), 303
Anastasia Krupnik (Lowry), 147
Anastasia on Her Own (Lowry), 174
Anastasia's Chosen Career (Lowry), 266
. . . And Now Miguel (Krumgold), 69
And Then There Was One: The Mysteries of Extinction (Facklam & Facklam), 89–90
And to Think That I Saw It on Mulberry Street (Seuss), 191
Angel and the Soldier Boy, The (Collington), 116, 130, 131–32
Angel's Mother's Wedding (Delton), 197
Animal, The Vegetable, and John D. Jones, The (Byars), 147
Anna, Grandpa, and the Big Storm (Stevens), 387

Annabelle Swift, Kindergartner (Schwartz), 169, 187, 362
Anna's Silent World (Wolf), 168
Anne of Green Gables (Montgomery), 47
Annie and the Old One (Miles), 219, 367
Anno's Aesop: A Book of Fables by Aesop and Mr. Fox (Anno), 255
Anno's Britain (Anno), 263
Anno's Italy (Anno), 263
Anno's Journey (Anno), 263
Annotated Alice, The (Gardner), 67
Anpao: An American Indian Odyssey (Highwater), 66, 226–27, 279, 281
Antar and the Eagles (Mayne), 264–65
Anthony Burns: The Defeat and Triumph of a Fugitive Slave (Hamilton), 87, 393, 414, 418
Appaloosa Horses (Patent), 405, 406
Appreciation questions, 36
"Arithmetic," 350, 351
Armien's Fishing Trip (Stock), 363
Art activities. *See* Aesthetic responses
Arthur's Baby (Brown), 190, 243
Ashanti to Zulu, African Traditions (Musgrove), 304
Assessment, 98–120
  cloze techniques, 108–10
  instructional environment, 99–104
  students, 104–19
  webbing, 110–14
Atlas of Ancient America (Coe, Snow & Benson), 308
At the Back of the North Wind (MacDonald), 255, 321
Author's style, 236–57
  lower elementary grades, 237–43
  middle elementary grades, 243–50
  questioning strategies, 37–38
  upper elementary and middle school, 250–57

Away Is A Strange Place To Be (Hoover), 333, 334, 336
Aztec Town, A (Unstead), 308

Babar's Anniversary Album: 6 Favorite Stories (deBrunhoff), 242
Baby Sister for Frances, A (Hoban), 242
Baby's Opera, The (Crane), 189, 346
Backbone of the King: Story of Pakuu and His Son (Brown), 229, 283
Badger and the Magic Fan, The (Johnston), 134
Bag of Moonshine, A (Garner), 147
Bagthorpes Unlimited (Cresswell), 197
Balancing Girl, The (Rabe), 147
Bargain for Frances, A (Hoban), 242
Barrett's Taxonomy of Comprehension, 34–35
Bartholomew Fair (Stolz), 385
Basal readers, 5, 10, 13, 58–59, 126–27
Baseball in April and Other Stories (Soto), 266
Basic Reading Inventory, 107
Bear Called Paddington, A (Bond), 198, 244, 321
Beat the Story-Drum, Pum-Pum (Bryan), 250, 303, 304
Beauty and the Beast (Brett), 218, 255
Beauty and the Beast: Visions and Revisions of an Old Tale (Hearne), 290
Becoming a Nation of Readers (Anderson, Hiebert, Scott & Wilkinson), 4
Before the Sun Dies: The Story of Evolution (Gallant), 79–80, 401, 405
Behind Barbed Wire: The Imprisonment of Japanese Americans During World War II (Davis), 419
Belling the Cat and Other Aesop's Fables (Paxton), 255, 347
Bells of Christmas, The (Hamilton), 198, 224, 384
Below the Root (Snyder), 333, 335
Benjamin Franklin: The New American (Meltzer), 395, 417
Best Books for Children (Gillespie & Gilbert), 47
Best Friends (Kellogg), 369
Best Friends for Frances (Hoban), 168, 242
Best Town in the World, The (Baylor), 24, 387
Better Mousetraps: Product Improvements that Led to Success (Aaseng), 402
Beyond the Divide (Lasky), 229
Beyond the Ridge (Goble), 298
"Big Black Cat, A," 352

Big Book for Peace, The (Durell & Sachs), 255, 364
Big Concrete Lorry, The (Hughes), 363
Biggest Bear, The (Ward), 191
Biggest House in the World, The (Lionni), 243
Bill Peet: An Autobiography (Peet), 399
Bingo Brown, Gypsy Lover (Byars), 174, 367
Bingo Brown and the Language of Love (Byars), 265
Biography, 389–400, 408–28. *See also specific books*
   and multicultural understanding, 409–16
   and setting, 201–2, 203
Birthday for Blue, A (Lydon), 384
Birth of a Nation: The Early Years of the United States (Faber and Faber), 418
Black Americans, The: A History in Their Own Words (Meltzer), 414, 420
Black and White (Macaulay), 329
Black Cauldron, The (Alexander), 206
Blacks, 303–7, 413–15. *See also* Multicultural understanding; *specific books*
Black Stallion, The (Farley), 265
Black Star, Bright Dawn (O'Dell), 208, 373
Black Theater in America (Haskins), 414, 416, 420
Blubber (Blume), 146, 366, 367
Blue Fairy Book, The (Lang), 194, 280, 283
Bobo's Dream (Alexander), 133, 259
Booklist, 47, 126
Book of a Thousand Poems, The: A Family Treasury, 353
Book of Eagles, The (Sattler & Gallant), 79, 401
Book of the Pig, The (Scott), 244, 401
Book of Three, The (Alexander), 206, 322
Borrowed Children (Lyon), 207
Borrowers, The (Norton), 68, 329, 332
Borrowers Afloat, The (Norton), 198
Box and Cox (Chetwin), 133
Box Turtle at Long Pond (George), 187, 401
Boy, A Dog, and A Frog, A (Mayer), 116, 191
Boy, A Dog, A Frog, and A Friend, A (Mayer), 191
Boy of the Three-Year Nap, The (Snyder), 68, 134
Bread and Jam for Frances (Hoban), 242
Bridge to Terabithia (Paterson), 180, 206, 229, 361, 364

Bringing the Rain to Kapiti Plain: A Nandi Tale (Aardema), 250, 303
British Folk Tales (Crossley-Holland), 197, 287
Brocaded Slipper, The (Vuong), 290
Broccoli Tapes, The (Slepian), 364
Bronze Bow, The (Speare), 207, 229
Brother to the Wind (Walter), 85, 223, 330
Buck Stops Here, The: The Presidents of the United States (Provensen), 175
Buffalo Hunt (Freedman), 409
Buffalo Woman (Goble), 220, 281, 298
Bulletin of the Center for Children's Books, 47

Caddie Woodlawn (Brink), 10, 28, 197, 224, 384
Caldecott Medal and Honor Awards, 47, 48. *See also specific books*
Call It Courage (Sperry), 11, 65, 70, 129, 137, 138–39, 140, 141–42, 362, 373, 376
"Camel, The" (Nash), 350, 352
Canada Geese Quilt, The (Kinsey-Warnock), 197
Canadian Library Award, 47. *See also specific books*
Canterbury Tales (Chaucer), 24
Canterbury Tales (Cohen), 24
Canterbury Tales, The (Hastings), 24
Captain Snap and the Children of Vinegar Lane (Schotter), 169, 366
Captive, The (O'Dell), 157
Captives in a Foreign Land (Rardin), 374
Care of Uncommon Pets (Weber), 244, 401
Carlota (O'Dell), 385
Carnegie Medal, 47, 48. *See also specific books*
Case of the Baker Street Irregular, The (Newman), 208
Case of the Vanishing Corpse, The (Newman), 208
Cassie's Journey: Going West in the 1860s (Harvey), 10, 387
Castle (Macaulay), 24
Castle of Llyr, The (Alexander), 206
Cat in the Hat, The (Seuss), 134, 242, 260
Cat in the Hat Comes Back, The (Seuss), 134, 242, 260
Cat's Body, A (Cole), 244, 401
Cat's Purr, The (Bryan), 303
Catwings (LeGuin), 244, 321, 322, 323
Catwings Return (LeGuin), 244
Cay, The (Taylor), 373

Celebrations (Livingston), 353
Censorship, 13–14, 361
Ceremony—In the Circle of Life (White Deer of Autumn), 373, 376
Cesar Chavez (Franchere), 148, 393
Cesar Chavez, Man of Courage (White), 224
Chair for My Mother, A (Williams), 169, 260, 366
Changes, Changes (Hutchins), 116
Changes in the Wind: Earth's Shifting Climate (Facklam & Facklam), 405, 406
Chanukkah Guest, The (Kimmel), 258, 259
Chanukkah Tree, The (Kimmel), 30
Characterization, 164–81
    and author's style, 247–48
    and historical fiction, biography, and informational literature, 423, 426, 427, 428
    lower elementary grades, 165–69
    middle elementary grades, 169–75
    questioning strategies, 37
    upper elementary and middle school, 175–81
Charles Eastman: The Story of an American Indian (Lee), 148, 197, 391
Charlotte's Web (White), 47, 68, 194, 223, 244, 318, 321, 322, 329
"Cheers" (Merriam), 349
Chester (Hoff), 260
Chief Sarah: Sarah Winnemucca's Fight for Indian Rights (Morrison), 409, 412, 413
Child of the Owl (Yep), 228, 368
Children and Books (Sutherland & Arbuthnot), 46, 126
Children of Odin, The (Colum), 337, 338
Children of the Sun (Carew), 303, 306
Children's Book Award, 47. *See also specific books*
Children's Choices list, 49–51
Children's Literature (Huck, Hepler, & Hickman), 46
Children's Literature: An Issues Approach (Rudman), 46
Children's Literature in the Elementary School (Huck, Hepler, & Hickman), 126
Child's Garden of Verses, A (Stevenson), 350, 351, 352–53
Childtimes: A Three-Generation Memoir (Little), 399
Chimpanzee Family Book, The (Goodall), 78, 401
Chin Chiang and the Dragon's Dance (Wallace), 218, 367
Chita's Christmas Tree (Howard), 387
Chitty Chitty Bang Bang (Fleming), 146

Choosing Books for Children: A Commonsense Guide (Hearne), 46
Choral arrangements, 251, 350–53
Christina Katerina and the Time She Quit the Family (Gauch), 365, 366
Christmas Poems (Livingston), 353
Christopher Columbus (Goodnough), 394
Christopher Columbus (Ventura), 394
Christopher Columbus: Voyager to the Unknown (Levinson), 87, 394
"Chronicles of Narnia, The" (Lewis), 255, 318. *See also specific books*
Church Mice in Action, The (Oakley), 250, 255, 256, 321
Cinderella (Brown), 198
Cinderella (Evans), 296
Cinderella (Perrault), 198
Cinquain, 67–69
Circle of Fire (Hook), 158, 229, 418
City of Gold and Lead, The (Christopher), 157, 333, 334
City Sounds (Emberley), 78, 401
Classroom Reading Inventory, 107
Close to the Wild: Siberian Tigers in a Zoo (Cajacob & Burton), 406
Clover & the Bee, The: A Book of Pollination (Dowden), 109
Cloze techniques, 108–10
Cognitive structure, 6
Columbus (D'Aulaire), 394
Columbus and the World Around Him (Meltzer), 394
Columbus Story, The (Dalgleish), 250, 391, 394, 396
Come Sing, Jimmy Jo (Paterson), 181, 266, 368
Commodore Perry in the Land of the Shogun (Blumberg), 402
Comparisons, 76–78
Complete Brothers Grimm Fairy Tales (Grimm), 225, 281
Complete Tales of Beatrix Potter, The (Potter), 324
Conflict. *See* Plot development
Constance: A Story of Early Plymouth (Clapp), 388
Contemporary realistic fiction, 360–77. *See also specific books*
    understanding, 361–68
    units, 368–77
Content areas, integration with literature, 25–26, 360, 376. *See also* Informational literature
    and contemporary realistic fiction, 376
    and fantasy, 331, 332–36, 340
Context clues, 22, 74–81
Core literature, 9–10, 43–44
    author's style, 237, 238, 239, 244, 245, 247, 249, 250, 252, 255
    biography, 391, 393, 394, 396–97, 409, 413–14, 417–20

characterization, 166, 167, 170
contemporary realistic fiction, 363, 365–66, 367, 369, 373–74
fantasy, 322, 324, 325, 329, 333, 337
folklore, 281, 283, 287, 290, 293–94, 295–96, 298, 303
historical fiction, 384, 387, 409, 413–14, 417–20
informational literature, 402, 405, 406, 408, 409, 413–14, 417–20
plot development, 129–30, 132, 134, 137, 140, 142, 144, 148, 150, 151, 153, 155
poetry, 346–47, 348, 349, 350, 353–54, 355, 356
point of view, 258, 261, 262, 264
setting, 187, 188–89
theme, 216, 217, 220, 221, 225, 226, 227
Coretta Scott King Award, 47. *See also specific books*
Could Be Worse! (Stevenson), 30
Courage of Sarah Noble, The (Dalgliesh), 28, 198, 224, 384, 391
Cousins (Hamilton), 265
Cracker Jackson (Byars), 180
Crack-of-Dawn Walkers, The (Hest), 187, 362, 369
Crane Wife, The (Yagawa), 146, 222, 223
Crest and the Hide, The: And Other African Stories of Heroes, Chiefs, Bards, Hunters, Sorcerers, and Common People (Courlander), 87, 303
Cricket in Times Square, The (Selden), 68, 329
Critical Handbook of Children's Literature, A (Lukens), 126
Crow Boy (Yashima), 153–54, 218
Crutches (Hartling), 419, 425
Cuentos: Tales from the Hispanic Southwest (Griego y Maestas & Anaya), 308, 310
Cultural Literacy: What Every American Needs to Know (Hirsch), 4
Cumulative files, 106
Curious George (Rey), 68, 243
Curse of the Ring, The (Harrison), 337
Cybil War, The (Byars), 206

Daddy Is A Monster . . . Sometimes (Steptoe), 168
"Dances With Wolves," 413
Dancing Granny, The, and Other African Stories (Bryan), 304
Dancing Palm Tree, The, and Other Nigerian Folktales (Walker), 197, 303
Danger from Below: Earthquakes-Past, Present and Future (Simon), 80

Daniel Inouye (Goodsell), 207, 393
Danza! (Hall), 208
Dark is Rising, The (Cooper), 324, 325, 337, 339
Darkness and the Butterfly (Grifalconi), 31, 129, 132, 133, 167, 168, 189–90, 215, 217–18, 362, 369
David and Max (Provost & Levine-Provost), 181
Daydreamers (Greenfield), 348
Day of Ahmed's Secret, The (Heide & Gilliland), 260, 363
Day the Goose Got Loose, The (Lindbergh), 258–59
Dear Mili (Grimm), 225–26, 281
Dear Mr. Henshaw (Cleary), 34–38, 68, 362, 366
December Rose, The (Garfield), 158, 207
Definitions, 75–76
Demeter's Daughters: The Women Who Founded America, 1587–1787 (Williams), 417
Desert Giant: The World of the Saguaro Cactus (Bash), 402
Desert Is Theirs, The (Baylor), 256
Destination Unknown (Fife), 158
Devil on My Back, The (Hughes), 333, 334
Devil's Arithmetic, The (Yolen), 142, 143–44, 419, 425
Devil with the Three Golden Hairs, The (Grimm), 224
Diamante, 69–70
Diary of a Rabbit (Hess), 244, 401
Dicey's Song (Voigt), 70, 164, 177–79, 362
Dictionaries, individualized, 71–74
Dictionary of Imaginary Places, The (Manguel & Guadelupi), 200, 201
Different Dragons (Little), 174, 224
Direct instruction. *See* Teacher-led activities
Discovery learning strategies, 25
Doctor Coyote: A Native American Aesop's Fables (Bierhorst), 283, 308, 310
Dr. Dredd's Wagon of Wonders (Brittain), 207
Dogger (Hughes), 167, 219, 367, 369
Dogsong (Paulsen), 257, 373
Doll's House, The (Godden), 329, 332
Don't Look Behind You (Duncan), 374
Don't Say a Word (Gehrt), 419, 425
Door in the Wall, The (DeAngeli), 146, 174, 384, 388
Dorothea Lange, Life Through the Camera (Meltzer), 393
Dotty's Suitcase (Greene), 224, 418, 423

Dragonflies (McLaughlin), 80, 401
Dragonsong (McCaffrey), 158
Dragonwings (Yep), 157, 207, 228
Drama activities
  and author's style, 238, 239
  and contemporary realistic fiction, 365–67, 372
  and folklore, 293, 294, 306
  and historical fiction, biography and informational literature, 386–89, 415–16, 421, 426, 427
  and plot development, 130–31, 135, 155
  and poetry, 350
  and setting, 200
Dream Catcher, The (Hughes), 333, 334–35
Dream Child, The (McPhails), 192, 350
Drinking Gourd, The (Monjo), 384, 414, 418
Duffy and the Devil (Zemach), 224, 250
Dustland (Hamilton), 206, 333, 335

Each Peach Pear Plum: An I-Spy Story (Ahlberg & Ahlberg), 243
Early American Christmas, An (de Paola), 191, 388
Ears of Louis, The (Greene), 146
East of the Sun and West of the Moon (Mayer), 147
Edith Herself (Howard), 174, 224, 384
"Education Secretary Bennett's Suggested Reading List for Elementary-School Pupils," 6
Edward Lear's The Scroobious Pip (Nash), 198, 199
Effective Teaching of Language Arts, The (Norton), 49, 51–52, 117, 331, 351
Efferent reading, 20–21
Egyptian Cinderella, The (Climo), 290
18th Emergency, The (Byars), 147
Eleanor Roosevelt (Goodsell), 393, 394
Eleanor Roosevelt (Whitney), 394, 419
Eleanor Roosevelt, With Love (Roosevelt), 87, 394, 419
Elidor (Garner), 207
Empty Window, The (Bunting), 146
Enchanted Caribou, The (Cleaver), 298
Enchanter's Daughter, The (Barber), 325
Endless Steppe, The: A Girl in Exile (Hautzig), 158
Enemy at Green Knowe, An (Boston), 147
English-Language Arts Framework for California Public Schools:

Kindergarten Through Grade Twelve (California State Department of Education), 9
Eric Carle's Animals Animals (Whipple), 64, 348, 350
Ernest and Celestine's Picnic (Vincent), 169, 242
Escape to Witch Mountain (Key), 333, 335
Eva (Dickinson), 333
Evaluation questions, 36
Everyone Asked About You (Gross), 364, 369
Evil Spell, The (McCully), 114–15
Exactly the Opposite (Hoban), 72
Exploring the Titanic (Ballard), 403
Extended literature, 10
  author's style, 242–43, 249–50, 256–57
  biography, 391, 409–10, 414
  characterization, 167–68, 172–74, 179–81
  contemporary realistic fiction, 363–64, 369
  fantasy, 322, 329–30, 333, 337
  folklore, 290, 296, 298–99, 303–4
  historical fiction, 384–85, 409–10, 414
  informational literature, 403, 406, 409–10, 414
  plot development, 132–33, 145–47, 156–57
  point of view, 259–60, 262–63, 265
  setting, 190–91, 196–97, 206–7, 227–29
  theme, 218–19, 221–23

Faber Book of Northern Legends, The (Crossley-Holland), 337
Fables, 216, 282–86
Fables (Lobel), 216
Facts and Fictions of Minna Pratt, The (MacLachlan), 174
Faery Flag, The: Stories and Poems of Fantasy and the Supernatural (Yolen), 326, 329
Fairy Book: Fairy Tales of the World (Dulac), 296
Fall of Freddie the Leaf, The (Buscaglia), 70
Familiar expressions, 78–79
Fantasy, 318–40. *See also specific books*
  and contemporary realistic fiction, 376
  understanding, 322–27
  units, 327–40
Farmer Giles of Ham (Tolkien), 250
Farmer Schulz's Ducks (Thiele), 364
Farthest Shore, The (LeGuin), 206
Fastest Friend in the West, The (Grove), 181

Favourite Fairy Tales (Mulherine), 296
FDR Story, The (Peare), 395
Feel Better, Ernest! (Vincent), 169, 242
Felita (Mohr), 146, 229, 366, 367
Ferdinand Magellan and the Discovery of the World Ocean (Stefoff), 207
Fifteen Centuries of Children's Literature: An Annotated Chronology of British and American Works in Historical Context (Bingham & Scholt), 389
Fighting Ground, The (Avi), 385
Figurative language, 66–67. *See also* Author's style
Fine White Dust, A (Rylant), 151, 152, 153
Firebird, The, and Other Russian Fairy Tales (Onassis), 194, 280
First Comes Spring (Rockwell), 72, 84, 401
First Look at Animals that Eat Other Animals, A (Selsam & Hunt), 75
First Look at Animals With Horns, A (Selsam & Hunt), 75, 401
First Look at Bird Nests, A (Selsam & Hunt), 75, 403
First Look at Caterpillars, A (Selsam & Hunt), 75, 403
First Look at Seals, Sea Lions, and Walruses, A (Selsam & Hunt), 75, 405
First Thanksgiving Feast, The (Anderson), 402
"Fish" (Hoberman), 64
Fish in His Pocket, A (Cazet), 31, 85, 140, 219
"Five Little Squirrels," 350, 351
Flame of Peace, The: A Tale of the Aztecs (Lattimore), 308
Flap Your Wings and Try (Pomerantz), 219
Flossie & the Fox (McKissack), 304
Focus units. *See* Units
"Fog" (Sandburg), 350, 352
Folklore, 276–311. *See also specific books*
    black, 303–7
    comparisons, 290–97
    and fantasy, 325–27
    Native American, 298–302, 410, 412
    and plot development, 134–36
    and setting, 194–95
    and theme, 216–17, 220–21, 225–26
    understanding, 281–88
Fool and the Fish, The: A Tale from Russia (Afanasyev), 147
Fool of the World and the Flying Ship, The (Ransome), 134
Forgotten Door, The (Key), 147

For Love of Reading: A Parent's Guide to Encouraging Young Readers from Infancy Through Age 5 (Rudmand & Pearce), 46
"Foul Shot" (Hoey), 349
"Four Seasons," 350, 351
Fox and the Cat, The: Animal Tales from Grimm (Crossley-Holland), 197
Foxfire Book, The (Wigginton), 389
Fox's Dream (Tejima), 137, 138
Frances Hodgson Burnett: Beyond the Secret Garden (Shirley), 399
Franklin Delano Roosevelt (Freedman), 201–2, 203, 390, 395, 419
Franklin D. Roosevelt, Gallant President (Silberdick), 395
Frederick Douglas and the Fight for Freedom (Miller), 87, 207, 418
Free-choice activities, 25
Free Fall (Wiesner), 116, 260, 322, 330, 332
Freight Train (Crews), 71
Frog, Where Are You? (Mayer), 191
Frog and Toad All Year (Lobel), 242, 260
Frog and Toad Are Friends (Lobel), 242
Frog and Toad Together (Lobel), 242
Frog Goes to Dinner (Mayer), 133, 191, 259
Frog Prince, The (Ormerod & Lollyd), 134
Frog Princess, The (Isele), 198
"From a Railway Carriage" (Stevenson), 351, 352–53
From Quarks to Quasars: A Tour of the Universe (Jespersen & Fitz-Randolph), 405
From the Mixed-Up Files of Mrs. Basil E. Frankweiler (Konigsburg), 68
Fudge-A-Mania (Blume), 364
Fun (Mark), 187, 362
Funk & Wagnalls Standard Dictionary of Folklore, Mythology and Legend, 285
Funny Little Woman, The (Mosel), 281
Further Tales of Uncle Remus: The Misadventures of Brer Rabbit, Brer Fox, Brer Wolf, the Doodang and Other Creatures (Lester), 257, 304

Gabriele and Selena (Desbarats), 369
Galaxies (Simon), 80
"Galoshes" (Bacmeister), 349
Garden of Abdul Gasazi, The (Van Allsburg), 3, 191, 329, 332
Garth Pig and the Ice Cream Lady (Rayner), 243
Gathering, The (Hamilton), 206, 333, 334

Gathering of Days, A: A New England Girl's Journal, 1830-32 (Blos), 28, 29, 384, 385–86
Generative structure, 6
George and Martha One Fine Day (Marshall), 243
George Washington and the Birth of Our Nation (Meltzer), 87, 417
Geraldine's Big Snow (Keller), 191
Get-Away Car, The (Clymer), 158
Ghost Abbey (Westall), 207
Ghost Brother (Adler), 174, 263, 367
Ghost's Hour, Spook's Hour (Bunting), 137, 138
Gift for Tia Rosa, A (Taha), 369
Gift of the Sacred Dog, The (Goble), 298
Ginger Jumps (Ernst), 134, 242
Giraffes, the Sentinels of the Savannas (Sattler), 90, 405, 406, 407
Girl Called Boy, A (Hurmence), 414, 416
Girl from Yamhill, A: A Memoir (Cleary), 87, 399
Girl Who Cried Flowers, The (Yolen), 326, 329
Girl Who Loved Wild Horses, The (Goble), 137–38
Girl Who Married a Ghost, The, and Other Tales from the North American Indian (Curtis), 298
Giving Tree, The (Silverstein), 224
Global Warming: Assessing the Greenhouse Threat (Pringle), 402, 403–4, 406
Glorious Flight Across the Channel With Louis Bleriot, July 25, 1909 (Provensen & Provensen), 243
Gnats of Knotty Pine, The (Peet), 243
Goats, The (Coles), 180, 229
God on Every Mountain Top, A: Stories of Southwest Indian Mountains (Baylor), 298
Go Free or Die: A Story of Harriet Tubman (Ferris), 147, 224, 414, 415
Goggles! (Keats), 133, 187, 362
Go In and Out the Window: An Illustrated Songbook for Young People (Fox), 189, 346, 389
Going Home (Mohr), 157, 229, 265, 363, 366, 367
Golda Meir Story, The (Davidson), 224
Gold Cadillac, The (Taylor), 147, 387, 414
Golden Fleece, The (Colum), 87
Golden Fleece, The, and the Heroes Who Lived Before Achilles (Colum), 283
Goldilocks and the Three Bears (Brett), 81, 82, 83, 129–30, 279

Goldilocks and the Three Bears (Marshall), 134
Good Morning, River! (Peters), 191, 363, 364, 369
Gorilla (Browne), 242
Grandaddy's Place (Griffith), 169, 191, 369
Grasshopper on the Road (Lobel), 242, 260
Graven Images (Fleischman), 263
Great Alexander the Great, The (Lasker), 393
Great Gilly Hopkins, The (Paterson), 181
Great Little Madison, The (Fritz), 175–77, 224, 390, 393
Great White Man-Eating Shark, The: A Cautionary Tale (Mahy), 30
Greedy Zebra (Hadithi), 219, 325, 327
Greenwitch (Cooper), 337
Grey King, The (Cooper), 257, 337, 339
Grimm's Household Tales (Grimm), 281
Groundhog's Horse (Rockwood), 147, 266
Guardian of Isis, The (Hughes), 157, 333, 334
Gunga Din (Kipling), 350

Halloween ABC (Merriam), 192, 346
Hang Tough, Paul Mather (Slote), 181
Hans Christian Andersen: Eighty Fairy Tales (Andersen), 225, 324–25, 326, 329
Hansel and Gretel (Grimm), 219
Hansel and Gretel (Marshall), 133, 281
Happily May I Walk: American Indians and Alaska Natives Today (Hirschfelder), 409
Happy Lion, The (Fatio), 191
Harriet Tubman: The Road to Freedom (Bains), 418
Harry in Trouble (Porte), 367
Hatchet (Paulsen), 126, 150–51, 362, 373, 376
Hattie and the Fox (Fox), 41–43, 280
Have You Seen My Duckling? (Tafuri), 260
Hawk, I'm Your Brother (Baylor), 129, 144–45, 172, 174, 196, 221, 222, 223, 262, 362, 363
Heckedy Peg (Wood), 255, 256
Hello, Amigos! (Brown), 218–19
Henry and Mudge (Rylant), 242
Henry and Mudge and the Bedtime Thumps (Rylant), 242
Henry and Mudge and the Forever Sea (Rylant), 242, 260
Henry and Mudge and the Happy Cat (Rylant), 242

Henry and Mudge Get the Cold Shivers (Rylant), 242, 260
Henry and Mudge in Puddle Trouble (Rylant), 242
Henry and Mudge in the Green Time (Rylant), 242
Henry and Mudge in the Sparkle Days (Rylant), 242, 260
Henry and Mudge Under the Yellow Moon (Rylant), 242
Herbie Jones and the Monster Ball (Kline), 174
Here a Chick, There a Chick (McMillan), 72
Here Comes the Cat! (Yagin), 255, 256, 321
Hero and the Crown, The (McKinley), 157, 180
Heroes of Puerto Rico (Tuck & Vergara), 87
Hershel and the Hanukkah Goblins (Kimmel), 224, 325
Hey, Al (Yorinks), 140–41, 146, 218, 255, 256, 322, 330, 332
Hiawatha (Longfellow), 250–52, 346
Hiawatha's Childhood (Longfellow), 250–52, 346, 353
High Elk's Treasure (Sneve), 158, 265
High Interest, Easy Reading (Matthews), 47
High King, The (Alexander), 206
Highwayman, The (Noyes), 198, 199–200, 256, 346, 350
Hillary Knight's The Owl and the Pussycat (Lear), 350, 352
Hiroshima No Pika (Maruki), 198, 199
Hispanic culture, 307–11
Historical fiction, 382–89, 408–28. *See also specific books*
    and multicultural understanding, 409–16
    and schema theory, 24
Historical structure, 5–6
Hitler (Marrin), 393, 419
Hitty, Her First Hundred Years (Fields), 263
Hobbit, The (Tolkien), 186, 200–201, 318, 337, 338
Hornbook, 126
Horton Hatches the Egg (Seuss), 243
Hounds of the Morrigan, The (O'Shea), 339
House at Pooh Corner, The (Milne), 250
Household Tales (Grimm), 281, 290
House of Dies Drear, The (Hamilton), 158, 206, 228
How Do You Know It's True? Sifting Sense From Nonsense (Klein), 406
How Many Miles to Babylon? (Fox), 224

How My Parents Learned to Eat (Friedman), 85, 364
How the Guinea Fowl Got Her Spots (Knutson), 303
"How to Eat a Poem" (Merriam), 346, 347
Hundred Dresses, The (Estes), 263
Hundred Penny Box, The (Mathis), 223, 366
Hundredth Dove, The, and Other Tales (Yolen), 250, 326, 329
Hungry Woman, The: Myths and Legends of the Aztecs (Bierhorst), 307, 308

I, Columbus: My Journal, 1492–3 (Roop & Roop), 394
I Am Phoenix: Poems for Two Voices (Fleischman), 350, 352
If I Ran the Zoo (Seuss), 30
If I Were in Charge of the World and Other Worries: Poems for Children and Their Parents (Viorst), 250
I Have A Friend (Narahashi), 369
I Have a Sister, My Sister is Deaf (Peterson), 369
I Know An Old Lady Who Swallowed a Fly (Rounds), 30, 43, 64, 345
Iktomi and the Boulder: A Plains Indian Story (Goble), 298
Illinois Public Act 84–126, 13
Illustrations, 127
    and author's style, 236–37, 238, 239, 251–52, 255–56
    and characterization, 178
    folklore, 294–97, 306, 308, 326
    and multicultural understanding, 416
    and plot development, 136–38, 139–41, 142–43, 150, 152, 153–54
    and schema theory, 24
    and setting, 187, 188, 192, 193–94, 199–200
    and theme, 215
    and vocabulary development, 65–66
    and whole text reading, 31
I'm Deborah Sampson: A Soldier in the War of the Revolution (Clapp), 158, 417, 421
Imogene's Antlers (Small), 30
In Coal Country (Hendershot), 198, 199, 362
Incredible Journey, The (Burnford), 146
Incredible Journey of Lewis & Clark, The (Blumberg), 405, 406
Incredible Painting of Felix Clousseau, The (Agee), 30
Independent reading, 8–9, 25, 60–61. *See also* Recreational reading groups; Sustained Silent Reading; Uninterrupted

Independent reading *continued*
Sustained Silent Reading
Indian Chiefs (Freedman), 409, 410
Indian Legacy: Native American Influences on World Life and Culture (Poatgieter), 410
Individualized dictionaries, 71–74
Inferences, 44
Inferential questions, 35–36
Informal Reading Inventories (IRIs), 107
Informational literature, 400–428.
    See also specific books
    and multicultural understanding, 409–16
    understanding, 400–408
In Search of a Sandhill Crane (Robertson), 208
Instructional environment, assessment, 99–104
Interactive strategies, 25
Interest inventory, 51–52, 105
In the Beginning: Creation Stories from Around the World (Hamilton), 228, 283, 298, 299, 303
In the Keep of Time (Anderson), 322
In the Land of the Small Dragon (Clark), 290, 291
In This Proud Land: The Story of a Mexican Family (Wolf), 396, 397
Invisible Hunters, The (Rohmer, Chow & Vidaure), 308, 310
Ira Says Goodbye (Waber), 369
IRIs. (Informal Reading Inventories), 107
Isis Pedlar, The (Hughes), 157, 333, 334
Island Boy (Cooney), 191
Island of the Blue Dolphins (O'Dell), 157, 373
Island on Bird Street, The (Orlev), 69, 181, 388, 419, 425
It Ain't All for Nothin (Myers), 374
It Could Always Be Worse: A Yiddish Folktale (Zemach), 30, 198, 260
I Want a Dog (Khalsa), 85, 187, 362, 366, 367
I Want to Be an Astronaut (Barton), 79

Jack Jouett's Ride (Haley), 198
Jack Tales, The (Chase), 87
Jacob Have I Loved (Paterson), 157
Jafta (Lewin), 238–39, 363
Jafta's Mother (Lewin), 243
James and the Giant Peach (Dahl), 147, 329, 332
James Weldon Johnson (Egypt), 391
Japanese Fairy Tale, A (Zimmerman), 147
Jesse Jackson (McKissack), 420
Jessica (Henkes), 369

John Brown of Harper's Ferry (Scott & Scott), 418
John F. Kennedy (Mills), 207, 420
John James Audubon (Ford), 197
Johnny Tremain (Forbes), 48, 69, 126, 383, 388, 417, 421
Josephina Hates Her Name (Engel), 243
Journal writing, 408, 422, 426
    and author's style, 249
    and comprehension, 45
    and poetry, 348–49
    and vocabulary development, 70–71
Journey Home (Uchida), 158, 229, 419, 425
Journey to Topaz (Uchida), 229
Joyful Noise: Poems for Two Voices (Fleischman), 350, 352
Judy Scuppernong (Seabrooke), 348
Julie of the Wolves (George), 157, 180, 368, 373
Jumanji (Van Allsburg), 133, 329, 332
Jump Again! More Adventures of Brer Rabbit (Parks), 303
"Jump or Jiggle" (Beyer), 349
Jump Ship to Freedom (Collier & Collier), 229, 414–15, 418
Jump! The Adventures of Brer Rabbit (Parks), 224, 303
Jungle Book, The (Kipling), 147, 198, 229, 329, 332
Jungle Sounds (Emberley), 78
Junius Over Far (Hamilton), 228
Jupiter (Simon), 80
Just So Stories (Kipling), 329, 332
"Just Watch" (Livingston), 349
Justice and Her Brothers (Hamilton), 206, 333, 335
Justin and the Best Biscuits in the World (Walter), 364

Kate Greenaway Award, 47, 48. *See also specific books*
Katy and the Big Snow (Burton), 242
Keep Looking! (Selsam & Hunt), 187, 401
Keeper of the Isis Light, The (Hughes), 157, 333, 335
Keeping a Christmas Secret (Naylor), 133, 365–66
Kid in the Red Jacket, The (Park), 174
King Bidgood's in the Bathtub (Wood), 191, 260, 330, 332
King of the Mountains, The: A Treasury of Latin American Folk Stories (Jagendorf and Boggs), 197, 308
King of the Wind (Henry), 266
King's Day, The: Louis XIV of France (Aliki), 391

Knee-High Man, The, and Other Tales (Lester), 280, 304
Kwakiutl Legends (Wallas), 299

Lady Ellen Grae (Cleaver), 158
Lady of Guadalupe, The (de Paola), 224, 308, 310
Land I Lost, The: Adventures of a Boy in Vietnam (Nhuong), 158
Langston: A Play (Davis), 414, 416
Language Arts, 47
Last Princess, The: The Story of Princess Ka'iulani of Hawaii (Stanley), 397
Least of All (Purdy), 219
Legend Days (Highwater), 226, 227, 373
Legend of King Arthur, The (Lister), 287, 288
Legend of the Bluebonnet, The (de Paola), 76–78, 81–84, 220–21, 279, 281, 298, 302, 376
Legend of the Christmas Rose, The (Lagerlöf), 146
Legend of the Indian Paintbrush, The (de Paola), 298
Legends, 282–86
Legends of the World (Cavendish), 337
Lentil (McCloskey), 388
Leo the Late Bloomer (Kraus), 242
Let the Circle Be Unbroken (Taylor), 229, 414
Libby on Wednesday (Snyder), 266
Library research activities and contemporary realistic fiction, 377
    and fantasy, 331, 336, 339
    and folklore, 306, 310
    and historical fiction, biography, and informational literature, 398, 413, 416, 421, 422, 425
    and setting, 193, 202
Life and Death of Martin Luther King, Jr., The (Haskin), 395, 420
Life of the Honeybee, The (Fischer-Nagel), 75–76, 90, 401, 402
Like Jake and Me (Jukes), 167, 263, 365, 366
Lillian Wald of Henry Street (Siegel), 87
Lincoln: A Photobiography (Friedman), 69, 394, 418, 422
Lion, The Witch, and the Wardrobe, The (Lewis), 68, 193–94, 206, 229, 318, 321, 329, 331
Lion and the Ostrich Chicks, And Other African Folk Tales (Bryan), 303
Literal-level questions, 35
Literary elements, 126–29. *See also specific literary elements*
Literature and the Child (Cullinan), 46

Literature-based instruction history,
     5–8
  instructional formats, 8–10
  new interest in, 4–5
  objectives, 14–15
  program development, 12–14
  reading program choices, 10–12
Literature comprehension, 18–52
  assessment, 106–7, 110–12,
     114–16
  efferent and aesthetic responses,
     19–21
  literature selection, 46–52
  research, 22–23
  scientific approaches, 23–44
  and writing activities, 45–46
Literature selection, 46–52. See also
     specific subjects
Little Dog Laughed, The, and other
     Nursery Rhymes (Cousins), 64
Little Engine That Could, The (Piper),
     219
Little Giants (Simon), 80
Little House, The (Burton), 31, 68,
     142, 143, 237–38, 321
Little House in the Big Woods (Wilder),
     10, 28, 29, 126, 224, 388, 389
Little House on the Prairie (Wilder),
     384
"Little House" series (Wilder), 48.
     See also specific books
Little Lame Prince, The (Wells), 68, 134
Little Red Riding Hood (Grimm),
     216–17, 281, 293
Little Red Riding Hood (Perrault), 294
Lon Po Po: A Red-Riding Hood Story
     from China (Young), 134, 294
Long Hard Journey, A: The Story of the
     Pullman Porter (McKissack), 420
Long Journey from Space, The (Simon),
     80
Long Way to a New Land, The
     (Sandin), 224
Long Way to Go, A (Oneal), 387
Long Winter, The (Wilder), 147, 198
Lorax, The (Seuss), 142
Lord of the Rings trilogy (Tolkien), 337
Lost in the Barrens (Mowat), 385, 409
Lost Star: The Story of Amelia Earhart
     (Lauber), 391
Louie (Keats), 169
Lower elementary grades author's
     style, 237–43
  characterization, 165–69
  fantasy, 320
  folklore, 278
  plot development, 129–34
  point of view, 258–60
  setting, 187–91
  theme, 216–19
  vocabulary development, 63–64, 68
"Lullaby" (Hillyer), 349

Machines at Work (Barton), 78
Magic Fan, The (Baker), 42, 325, 329
Make Way for Ducklings (McCloskey),
     47, 191
Make Way for Sam Houston (Fritz),
     391, 392–93, 398
Malcolm X (Adoff), 148, 420
Man Who Lived Alone, The (Hall),
     369
Many Lands, Many Stories: Asian
     Folktales for Children (Conger),
     197
Mark Twain? What Kind of a Name Is
     That? A Story of Samuel
     Langhorne Clemens
     (Quackenbush), 391
Martin Luther King, Jr. and the
     Freedom Movement (Patterson),
     87, 208, 395, 414, 420
Martin's Mice (King-Smith), 244, 321
Mary Had a Little Lamb (Hale), 260
Matchlock Gun, The (Edmond), 28
Maya, The (Coe), 308
Mazel and Shlimazel, or the Milk of the
     Lioness (Singer), 134, 223
M.C. Higgins the Great (Hamilton),
     228
Meaning. See Literature
     comprehension
Meet Martin Luther King, Jr.
     (DeKay), 147, 391, 395, 420
Meet the Giant Snakes (Simon), 406
Melisande (Nesbit), 319, 325, 329
Meteor! (Polacco), 30, 192
Mice Are Nice (Larrick), 353
Middle elementary grades author's
     style, 243–50
  characterization, 169–75
  fantasy, 320
  folklore, 278–79
  plot development, 134–48
  point of view, 260–63
  setting, 191–98
  theme, 219–24
  vocabulary development, 64–66,
     68
Midnight Horse, The (Fleischman),
     247–48, 321
Mike Mulligan and His Steam Shovel
     (Burton), 68
Millions of Cats (Gag), 189
Mirandy and Brother Wind
     (McKissack), 68, 329, 332
Modeling, 32, 34
  and author's style, 239–41,
     245–47, 252–55
  and characterization, 165, 169–72,
     173, 175–77
Monkey's Haircut, The, and Other
     Stories Told by the Maya
     (Bierhorst), 194, 280, 307–9
Monsters (Hoban), 134

Month-Brothers, The (Marshak), 219,
     249
Monty (Stevenson), 243
Moonlight Man, The (Fox), 158
Moonsong (Baylor), 250, 299
Moonsong Lullaby (Highwater), 226,
     227, 346, 354
"More It Snows, The" (Milne), 349
"More More More," Said the Baby
     (Williams), 260
More Tales of Amanda Pig (Van
     Leeuwen), 260
Morning Star, Black Sun: The
     Northern Cheyenne Indians and
     America's Energy Crisis
     (Ashabrenner), 409, 413
Morris Goes to School (Wiseman), 260
Morris Has a Cold (Wiseman), 260
Moss Gown (Hooks), 290, 292–93
Mother Crocodile (Guy), 308
Mother Goose in Prose (Baum), 347,
     348
Mother Goose rhymes, 64. See also
     specific books
Mother Scorpion Country (Rohmer &
     Wilson), 308
Mouse Woman and the Vanished
     Princesses (Harris), 298, 299
Moves Make the Man, The (Brooks),
     180
Mr. and Mrs. Muddle (Hoberman),
     243
Mr. Nick's Knitting (Wild), 369
Mr. Rabbit and the Lovely Present
     (Zolotow), 191
Mrs. Frisby and the Rats of NIMH
     (O'Brien), 244, 263, 321
Mufaro's Beautiful Daughters: An
     African Tale (Steptoe), 134, 135,
     136, 223, 279, 290
Multicultural understanding and
     folklore, 288–311
  and historical fiction, biography,
     and informational literature,
     409–16
  and literature selection, 48–49
  and units, 26, 27–28
"Mummy Slept Late and Daddy
     Fixed Breakfast," 352
Music and folklore, 294
  and historical fiction, biography,
     and informational literature, 422,
     423, 424, 426, 427
  and setting, 189, 192, 200
My Cousin Katie (Garland), 187, 401
My Daniel (Conrad), 181
My Diary (Yates), 399
My First Activity Book (Wilkes), 403
My First Nature Book (Wilkes), 403
My Grandson Lew (Zolotow), 168
My Prairie Year: Based on the Diary of
     Eleanor Plaisted (Harvey), 24

"Myra Song, The" (Ciardi), 350, 351

My Side of the Mountain (George), 147, 263, 373, 377

My Song Is a Piece of Jade: Poems of Ancient Mexico in English and Spanish (de Gerez), 308, 309–10, 353

Mysteries of Harris Burdick, The (Van Allsburg), 116, 263

Mysteries of Outer Space (Branley), 405, 406

Mystery of the Ancient Maya, The (Meyer & Gallenkamp), 89

Myths, 282–86

Myths of Greece & Rome (Bulfinch), 283

My Widening World (Yates), 399

My World (Yates), 399

Nana Upstairs & Nana Downstairs (de Paola), 219

Nation Torn, A: The Story of How the Civil War Began (Ray), 418

Native Americans, 27–28, 66–67, 298–302, 376, 409–13. See also Folklore; Multicultural understanding; specific books

New Advocate, The, 47

Newbery Medal and Honor Awards, 47, 48. See also specific books

New Questions and Answers About Dinosaurs (Simon), 406, 407

New Read-Aloud Handbook, The (Trelease), 47

News About Dinosaurs, The (Lauber), 75, 89, 401

Nicholas Cricket (Maxner), 189, 321

Night Before Christmas, The (Moore), 191, 243, 350

Nightingale, The (Andersen), 198, 224

Night Journey, The (Lasky), 385

Night Noises (Fox), 64, 369

Night Story (Willard), 350

No Beasts! No Children! (Keller), 174

No Hero for the Kaiser (Frank), 72–73, 252–55, 383, 418, 423, 424

No Such Things (Peet), 30

Norse Gods and Giants (D'Aulaire & D'Aulaire), 287, 288

Norse Myths, The (Crossley-Holland), 337

North American Legends (Haviland), 194, 280, 290, 291–92, 299

Norwegian Folk Tales (Asbjornsen & Moe), 196, 283

Number the Stars (Lowry), 126, 419, 425

Of Colors and Things (Hoban), 61

Old Blue (Hancock), 197, 384

Old Lady Who Ate People, The (Hinojosa), 134, 308

Old MacDonald Had a Farm (Rounds), 43, 64, 345

Old Yeller (Gipson), 174, 265

Oliver, Amanda, and Grandmother Pig (Van Leeuwen), 260

Oliver and Amanda's Christmas (Van Leeuwen), 260

Oliver Button Is A Sissy (de Paola), 169

Oma and Bobo (Schwartz), 369

Once in Puerto Rico (Belprβéβ), 197

On Christmas Eve (Collington), 259

One At A Time (McCord), 348, 351, 353, 354, 355

One Crow: A Counting Rhyme (Aylesworth), 79

One-Eyed Cat (Fox), 70, 151, 152, 156, 362, 368

One Frog Too Many (Mayer), 191

One Morning in Maine (McCloskey), 191

On My Honor (Bauer), 151, 152, 153, 156, 157, 229

On the Day Peter Stuyvesant Sailed Into Town (Lobel), 387

On the Edge (Cross), 208, 374

On the Far Side of the Mountain (George), 263, 368, 373, 377

Oral language activities. See Reading aloud

Ordinary Jack (Cresswell), 197

Oscar Otter (Benchley), 134

Other Bells for Us to Ring (Cormier), 388, 419, 425

Other Way to Listen, The (Baylor), 198

Outlaws of Sherwood, The (McKinley), 87

Outside Child, The (Bawden), 265

Over Sea, Under Stone (Cooper), 337

Owl at Home (Lobel), 242, 260

Owl Moon (Yolen), 198, 199, 362

Ox-Cart Man, The (Hall), 137, 138, 388

Oxford Book of Children's Verse, The (Opie & Opie), 389

Paddington Abroad (Bond), 198

Paddle to the Sea (Hollings), 150

Paddy Under Water (Goodall), 259

Parent surveys, 106

Pass the Poetry, Please! (Hopkins), 347

Patchwork Quilt, The (Flournoy), 188, 219, 362, 367, 369

Path of the Pale Horse (Fleischman), 158

Paul Revere's Ride (Longfellow), 350

Paul Robeson: The Life and Times of a Free Black Man (Hamilton), 207

Pentecost and the Chosen One (Corbett), 257

People Could Fly, The (Hamilton), 228, 303, 304, 306

Perrault's Complete Fairy Tales (Johnson), 194, 280, 290, 293, 294

Personal responses. See Aesthetic responses; Writing activities

Personification, 237–38, 243–45, 250–52

Peter Pan (Barrie), 197

Peter's Chair (Keats), 85, 168

Peter's Pockets (Rice), 85

Pet Show! (Keats), 191

Petunia (Duvoisin), 243

"Pickety Fence, The" (McCord), 351

Picnic (McCully), 116, 237, 238, 260, 321

Picture books. See Illustrations

Picture Books for Children (Cianciolo), 46

Picture Life of Reggie Jackson, The (Gutman), 393

Picture Story of Nancy Lopez, The (Phillips), 224

Pierre: A Cautionary Tale (Sendak), 350, 351, 353

Pinky and Rex Get Married (Howe), 363, 369

Pit, The (Cheetham), 157

Place My Words Are Looking For, The (Janeczko), 347

Planet of Junior Brown, The (Hamilton), 70, 181, 368, 374

Please Don't Tease Me... (Madsen & Bockoras), 366

Plot development, 129–58
  and assessment, 114–16
  and contemporary realistic fiction, 376
  lower elementary grades, 129–34
  middle elementary grades, 134–48
  questioning strategies, 37, 38–41
  upper elementary and middle school, 148–58
  and vocabulary development, 81–84

Plot diagrams and comprehension, 114–16
  and contemporary realistic fiction, 372
  and plot development, 130, 131–32, 133, 135–36, 141, 144, 149, 152
  and vocabulary development, 81–84

Poetry, 344–56. See also specific books
  and author's style, 250–52
  and vocabulary development, 67–70

Point of view, 257–66

Polar Bear Cubs (Matthews), 78, 150, 244, 401

Polar Express, The (Van Allsburg), 198, 199, 321, 329, 332

Pompeii: Exploring a Roman Ghost Town (Goor & Goor), 150
Pool of Fire, The (Christopher), 157, 333, 334
Poor Richard (Daugherty), 395
"Popcorn Song, A" (Turner), 349
Portfolio approach to assessment, 98–99, 104–5
Potato Kid, The (Corcoran), 265
Potatoes (Johnson), 75, 76, 401, 406
Prediction, 41–43, 64
Prereading activities, 24, 25
Previous knowledge, 79–80. *See also* Schema theory; Semantic feature analysis
Princess Furball (Huck), 290
Psychological structure, 6
Puppetry, 328–32
"Puppy and I" (Milne), 352
Purple Coat, The (Hest), 85, 369

Queen Eleanor: Independent Spirit of the Medieval World (Brooks), 207, 391
Questioning strategies, 21, 24
and comprehension, 34–41
contemporary realistic fiction, 363–65, 373–74
fantasy, 323–24
folklore, 286
historical fiction, biography, and informational literature, 384–86, 391–93, 402–4

Rabbit Hill (Lawson), 197, 224, 244, 321, 329, 332
Rabble Starkey (Lowry), 181
Rain Makes Applesauce (Scheer), 198, 199, 321, 346
Rain of Fire (Bauer), 419, 425
Rainbow People, The (Yep), 228
Rainbow Rhino (Sis), 219
Rainbow Writing (Merriam), 126
Ralph S. Mouse (Cleary), 198
Ramona and Her Father (Cleary), 147
Ramona and Her Mother (Cleary), 174, 224
"Ramona" books (Cleary), 68. *See also specific books*
Ramona Quimby, Age 8 (Cleary), 147, 263, 364
Random House Book of Mother Goose, The (Lobel), 64, 129, 347
Random House Book of Poetry for Children, The (Prelutsky), 64, 249, 347, 350, 352, 353
Rat is Dead and Ant is Sad (Baker), 299
Raven the Trickster: Legends of the North American Indians (Robinson), 299

Read-Aloud Rhymes for the Very Young (Prelutsky), 64, 345, 346, 349
Reading aloud and comprehension, 18, 42, 44
and folklore, 299, 302
and poetry, 251, 347, 350–53
and schema theory, 23
and vocabulary development, 62–67
Reading is Fundamental (RIF), 29
Reading levels, 44
Reading Teacher, The, 47
Reading Today (Miller & Luskay), 4–5
Ready...Set...Read!: The Beginning Reader's Treasury (Cole & Calmenson), 260
Realistic fiction. *See* Contemporary realistic fiction; Historical fiction
Recommended Readings in Literature: Kindergarten Through Grade Eight (California State Department of Education), 4, 9
Recreational literature, 10
author's style, 243, 250, 260
characterization, 168–69, 174, 181
plot development, 134, 147–48, 157–58
point of view, 265–66
setting, 191, 197–98, 207–8
theme, 219, 224
Recreational reading groups, 29–31, 50
Red Fairy Book, The (Lang), 194, 280, 293
Red Riding Hood (Grimm), 293–94
Red Shoes, The (Andersen), 146
Reflections on a Gift of Watermelon Pickle . . . And Other Modern Verse (Dunning, Lueders, & Smith), 48, 346, 347, 349, 353–54
Regards to the Man in the Moon (Keats), 191
Relatives Came, The (Rylant), 364
Rescue: The Story of How Gentiles Saved Jews in the Holocaust (Meltzer), 419
Rhythm Road: Poems to Move To (Morrison), 349
Riddle of the Drum, The: A Tale from Tizapβáβn, Mexico (Aardema), 197, 308, 310
RIF (Reading is Fundamental), 29
Rifles for Watie (Keith), 207
Ring in the Prairie, The, A Shawnee Legend (Bierhorst), 298
Ring-Rise Ring-Set (Hughes), 333, 335
Risk N'Roses (Slepian), 383
River Rats, Inc. (George), 208
Road from Home, The: The Story of an Armenian Girl (Kheridian), 207
Robin Hood & the Men of the Greenwood (Gilbert), 296

Role playing. *See* Drama activities
Roll of Thunder, Hear My Cry (Taylor), 156, 229, 387, 388, 414, 418
Roomrimes (Cassedy), 348
Rootabaga Stories (Sandburg), 206, 329
Rosa Parks (Greenfield), 147, 224, 420, 427
Roscoe's Leap (Cross), 208
Rose in My Garden, The (Lobel), 43, 353
Round & Round & Round (Hoban), 61
Rudyard Kipling: An Illustrated Biography (Fido), 399
Rumor of Pavel and Paali, The: A Ukrainian Folktale (Kismaric), 147, 281
Rumpelstiltskin (Grimm), 39, 198, 280
Runaway Bunny, The (Brown), 168, 190, 243
Running Wild (Griffiths), 224
Russian Folk Tales (Afanasev), 196

Saint George and the Dragon (Hodges), 84, 87, 148–49, 256
Sam, Bangs & Moonshine (Ness), 168, 369, 370–71
Sammy the Seal (Hoff), 260
Sarah, Plain and Tall (MacLachlan), 10, 24, 68, 164, 169, 170–72, 383
Saturn (Simon), 80
Save Queen of Sheba (Moeri), 10
Saving Our Wildlife (Pringle), 90, 401, 405, 407
Saving the Peregrine Falcon (Arnold), 403
Scarebird, The (Fleischman), 167, 219, 369
Scared One, The (Haseley), 146, 373
Schema theory, 22, 23–25, 32, 89
School (McCully), 116, 166–67, 191, 263, 322
School Library Journal, The, 47, 126
Scorpions (Myers), 181, 229, 265, 364, 374
Scott, Foresman Anthology of Children's Literature, The (Sutherland & Livingston), 290, 293
Scroobious Pip, The (Lear), 65–66, 346, 354
Sea Glass (Yep), 228
Seasons of the Cranes (Roop), 79, 401, 406, 407
Secret City, U.S.A. (Holman), 374
Secret Garden, The (Burnett), 47, 165, 180, 202, 204, 229, 362
Secrets of a Small Brother (Margolis), 249, 348

Self-Portrait, Margot Zemach (Zemach), 399

Self-Portrait: Trina Schart Hyman (Hyman), 399

Semantic feature analysis, 88–90

Semantic mapping. *See* Webbing

Serpent's Children, The (Yep), 208

Setting, 186–208
  lower elementary grades, 187–91
  middle elementary grades, 191–98
  questioning strategies, 36–37
  upper elementary and middle school, 198–208

17 Kings and 42 Elephants (Mahy), 30, 189, 346

Shabanu, Daughter of the Wind (Staples), 265, 364, 368

Shades of Gray (Reeder), 158, 418

Shadow (Cendrars), 65, 66, 137

Shadow in Hawthorn Bay (Lunn), 156, 157, 229, 387

Shadow of a Bull (Wojciechowska), 70, 181

Shaka: King of the Zulus (Stanley & Vennema), 391

Shaker Inventions (Bolick & Randolph), 403

Shapes, Shapes, Shapes (Hoban), 61

Shh! We're Writing the Constitution (Fritz), 89

Shoebag (James), 261–62

Sight and Seeing: A World of Light and Color (Simon), 403

Sign of the Beaver, The (Speare), 181, 256–57, 388, 409

Silmarillion, The (Tolkien), 337

Silver Cow, The: A Welsh Tale (Cooper), 134

Silver Kiss, The (Klause), 206

Silver on the Tree (Cooper), 337, 339

Similes, 238–41, 245–48

Sing a Song of Popcorn (de Regniers), 349, 350, 351–52

Sing Down the Moon (O'Dell), 69, 156, 157, 409, 413

Singing Stone, The (Melling), 147

Sir Cedric (Gerrard), 350

Sir Francis Drake: His Daring Deeds (Gerrard), 350

Sir Gawain and the Loathly Lady (Hastings), 61, 84, 85, 86, 129, 148–49, 155–56, 179, 180, 205–6, 227, 228, 265, 279

Sister (Greenfield), 367

Sitting Bull and the Battle of the Little Bighorn (Black), 207

Sky is Falling, The (Pearson), 419, 425

Slake's Limbo (Holman), 374

Slave Dancer, The (Fox), 414

Sleeping Beauty, The (Evans), 281

Sleeping Beauty & Other Favourite Fairy Tales (Carter), 281

Sleeping Beauty, The, and Other Fairy Tales (Dulac), 296

Smallest Dinosaurs, The (Simon), 80

Small-group interactions, 8–9

Smile, Ernest and Celestine (Vincent), 169, 242

Smoke and Ashes: The Story of the Holocaust (Rogasky), 419

Snake In, Snake Out (Banachek), 71

Snow Queen, The (Andersen), 146

Snow Treasure (McSwigan), 147, 419, 425

Snow White and the Seven Dwarfs (Grimm), 198, 281

Snowman, The (Briggs), 259

Snowy Day, The (Keats), 166

Social Education, 47

Social Education (Parsons & Totten), 426

Solitary Blue, A (Voigt), 70, 164, 179, 368

Something Big Has Been Here (Prelutsky), 64, 250, 353

Something on My Mind (Grimes), 348

Song and Dance Man (Ackerman), 187, 260, 369, 370

Song for a Dark Queen (Sutcliff), 158

Song of Pentecost, The (Corbett), 255, 321

Songs from Mother Goose (Larrick), 389

Sorrow's Song (Callen), 224

Space Challenge: The Story of Guion Bluford (Haskins & Benson), 87

Space Songs (Livingston), 250, 353

Spinky Sulks (Steig), 366

Spirit Child: A Story of the Nativity (Bierhorst), 308, 310

Spring of Butterflies, The, and Other Chinese Folk Tales (Liyi), 194, 280, 283

Stalin: Russia's Man of Steel (Marrin), 419

Standardized tests, 98

Star Boy (Goble), 298, 302

Star Maiden, The (Esbensen), 298

Starting from Home: A Writer's Beginnings (Meltzer), 399

State Goals for Learning and Sample Learning Objectives: Language Arts (State of Illinois), 14

Stay Away from Simon! (Carrick), 146, 153, 224, 383, 384

Steadfast Tin Soldier, The (Andersen), 223

Stone Walkers, The (Alcock), 207

Stonewall (Fritz), 391

Storm (Crossley-Holland), 174

Storm in the Night (Stolz), 364, 369

Storms (Simon), 79, 80, 150, 401

Story, A Story, A (Haley), 303, 306

Story grammar, 38–41

Story of Babar, The (deBrunhoff), 242

Story of Eleanor Roosevelt, The (Davidson), 394

Story of Ferdinand, The (Leaf), 68, 142, 143, 219, 321

Story of Jumping Mouse, The (Steptoe), 219, 299

Story of King Arthur and His Knights, The (Pyle), 283, 296

Story of Mankind, The (Van Loon), 389

Strangers in Their Own Land: A History of Mexican-Americans (Prago), 158

String in the Harp, A (Bond), 207

Stuart Little (White), 68

Student interests, 49–52, 105–6

Student involvement, 27, 38–41, 60, 100–101. *See also specific topics*

Style. *See* Author's style

Sugaring Time (Lasky), 249, 257

Suho and the White Horse: A Legend of Mongolia (Otsuka), 223

Summaries, 78

Summer of the Swans, The (Byars), 366

Summer Switch (Rodgers), 147

Sun Horse, Moon Horse (Sutcliff), 207

Susanna of the Alamo (Jakes), 148, 393, 396, 397

Sustained Silent Reading, 8. *See also* Uninterrupted Sustained Silent Reading

Sweetgrass (Hudson), 67, 409

Swiftly Tilting Planet, A (L'Engle), 229, 333

Swimmy (Lionni), 68, 219, 239–41, 321, 332

"Swing, The" (Stevenson), 349

Swiss Family Robinson, The (Wyss), 373

Sword and the Circle, The (Sutcliff), 87

Symbolism and characterization, 177–79
  and setting, 194–95, 202, 204–5

Synonyms, 80–81

Tail Feathers from Mother Goose: The Opie Rhyme Book (Opie), 64

Take a Walk in Their Shoes (Turner), 414, 416

Tale of Mrs. Tiggy-Winkle, The (Potter), 168

Tale of Peter Rabbit, The (Potter), 133, 164, 257, 258, 318, 321, 329

Tale of Squirrel Nutkin, The (Potter), 167

Tale of the Mandarin Ducks, The (Paterson), 40, 111, 112, 280

Tales From Grimm (Gag), 287

Tales from the Igloo (Metayer), 197, 298

Tales of a Fourth Grade Nothing (Blume), 224

Tales of Mother Goose (Perrault), 296
Tales of Uncle Remus, The (Lester), 87, 304
Talking Earth, The (George), 70, 373
Talking Eggs, The: A Folktale from the American South (San Souci), 40–41, 68, 280
Talking in Whispers (Watson), 374
Talking to the Sun (Koch & Farrell), 355
Taran Wanderer (Alexander), 206
Taste of Daylight, A (Thrasher), 418, 423
Teacher behaviors, 103–4
Teacher-led activities, 8–9, 25, 43–44, 59–60. *See also specific topics and activities*
"Teaching Multicultural Literature in the Reading Curriculum," 49
"Teddy Bear, Teddy Bear," 349
Tehanu: The Last Book of Earthsea (LeGuin), 206
Theme, 214–29
  and contemporary realistic fiction, 372
  and historical fiction, biography, and informational literature, 423, 424, 426, 427–28
  lower elementary grades, 216–19
  middle elementary grades, 219–24
  questioning strategies, 37
  upper elementary and middle school, 225–29
Theodor and Mr. Balbini (Mathers), 85
There's a Nightmare in My Closet (Mayer), 133
They Dance in the Sky: Native American Star Myths (Munroe & Williamson), 298, 299
Thimble Summer (Enright), 174
Third Gift, The (Carew), 146, 303, 306
This Is the Way We Go to School: A Book About Children Around the World (Baer), 193, 401
Thor Heyerdahl: Viking Scientist (Blassingame), 397
Three Bears, The (Galdone), 132
Three Bears, The, and 15 Other Stories (Rockwell), 42, 133, 281
Three Bears Rhyme Book, The (Yolen), 64
Three Blind Mice (Ivemey), 64
Three Jovial Huntsmen (Jeffers), 191
Three Strong Women: A Tale From Japan (Stamm), 112, 113
Through the Eyes of A Child: An Introduction to Children's Literature (Norton), 46, 49, 126
Through the Looking Glass, and What Alice Found There (Carroll), 67, 109–10, 329, 332
Thunder God's Son, The (Dewey), 147

Tiger Eyes (Blume), 158
Tigers and Opossums: Animal Legends (Kurtycz & Kobeh), 308, 309
Tillie and the Wall (Lionni), 242
Time of Wonder (McCloskey), 242
Timothy Goes to School (Wells), 243
Tituba of Salem Village (Petry), 156, 157, 229
To Live in Two Worlds: American Indian Youth Today (Ashabranner), 157, 409
Tombs of Atuan (LeGuin), 206
Tomie de Paola's Mother Goose (de Paola), 64, 129
Tom's Midnight Garden (Pearce), 229, 319, 322
Tongue-Cut Sparrow, The (Ishii), 222
To Stand Against the Wind (Clark), 158
Touchstones: A List of Distinguished Children's Books (Children's Literature Association), 6, 47–48, 318. *See also specific books*
Town Cats, The, and Other Tales (Alexander), 146
Traces of Life: The Origins of Humankind (Lasky), 405
Trains (Gibbons), 72
Train Whistles (Sattler), 72
Traitor: The Case of Benedict Arnold (Fritz), 397, 417
Treasure Mountain: Folktales from Southern China (Sadler), 113, 114, 115
Trickster Tales from Prairie Lodgefires (Anderson), 298
Trip, The (Keats), 188–89, 329, 332
Trouble With Adventurers, The (Harris), 298
Trouble With Tuck, The (Taylor), 366, 367
True Stories About Abraham Lincoln (Gross), 393, 394, 418
True Story of Spit MacPhee, The (Aldridge), 181
Truffles Is Sick (Ahnolt), 243
Tuck Everlasting (Babbitt), 65, 66, 179, 321
Tug of War (Lingard), 24, 387, 419, 425
Twelve Dancing Princesses, The (Mayer), 134, 281
Twelve Dancing Princesses, The, and Other Tales From Grimm (Lewis), 194, 280
Two and Too Much (Walter), 134, 366
Two Greedy Bears (Ginsburg), 132

Ugly Duckling, The (Andersen), 133, 166, 218
Umbrella Day, The (Cooney), 188, 189

Uncle Elephant (Lobel), 242, 260
Under the Sunday Tree (Greenfield), 198
"Unfolding Bud" (Koriyama), 346, 347
Uninterrupted Sustained Silent Reading (USSR), 25, 29
Units, 25–29, 84–88. *See also specific topics*
Up and Down on the Merry-Go-Round (Archambault), 64
Upper elementary and middle school author's style, 250–57
  characterization, 175–81
  fantasy, 320
  folklore, 279
  plot development, 148–58
  point of view, 263–66
  setting, 198–208
  theme, 225–29
  vocabulary development, 66–67, 69
Upstairs Room, The (Reiss), 229, 397, 419, 425
USSR (Uninterrupted Sustained Silent Reading), 25, 29

Values clarification, 27
Vassilisa the Wise: A Tale of Medieval Russia (Sherman), 146
Velveteen Rabbit, The, or How Toys Become Real (Williams), 70, 218, 242, 321
Village by the Sea, The (Fox), 208, 265
Village of Round and Square Houses, The (Grifalconi), 303
Visit to William Blake's Inn, A: Poems for Innocent and Experienced Travelers (Willard), 257
Vocabulary development, 58–91
  assessment, 110, 113–14
  context clues, 74–81
  reading aloud, 62–67
  research conclusions, 58–61
  semantic feature analysis, 88–90
  webbing, 81–88
  writing activities, 67–74
Voices from the Civil War (Meltzer), 418
Volcano: The Eruption and Healing of Mount St. Helens (Lauber), 61, 89, 150, 401
Volcanoes (Simon), 80
Voyage of the Frog, The (Paulsen), 373
Voyage of the Ludgate Hill, The: Travels with Robert Louis Stevenson (Willard), 350

Wagon Wheels (Brenner), 388
Wait for Me, Watch for Me, Eula Bee (Beatty), 28, 158
Waiting for Hannah (Russo), 364

Waiting to Waltz: A Childhood (Rylant), 348

War Boy: A Country Childhood (Foreman), 419, 425

War Clouds in the West: Indians & Cavalrymen, 1860–1890 (Marrin), 409, 413

Warrior and the Wise Man, The (Wisniewski), 147

Watcher in the Garden, The (Phipson), 158, 229

Watch Where You Go (Noll), 72

Water of Life, The (Grimm), 146, 202, 204, 280

Weathermonger, The (Dickinson), 319

Weaving of a Dream, The (Heyer), 147, 224

Webbing, 32, 33

  and assessment, 110–14

  and author's style, 251, 252

  and characterization, 167, 172, 179, 180

  and contemporary realistic fiction, 372, 376

  and fantasy, 326–27

  and folklore, 299, 300–301, 305, 307, 309

  and historical fiction, biography, and informational literature, 423, 424

  and plot development, 144–45, 155–56

  and setting, 189–90, 195–96, 205–6

  and thematic units, 27, 28

  and theme, 221, 222, 227, 228

  and vocabulary development, 81–88

Wednesday Surprise, The (Bunting), 85, 167, 363, 369

We Hide, You Seek (Aruego & Dewey), 191

We're Going on a Bear Hunt (Rosen), 42, 43, 63–64, 345

Westing Game, The (Raskin), 208

We the People: The Story of the United States Constitution Since 1787 (Faber & Faber), 417

What Game Shall We Play? (Hutchins), 71–72

What's in Fox's Sack? An Old English Tale (Galdone), 132

What's So Funny, Ketu? (Aardema), 303, 308, 310

What's the Big Idea, Ben Franklin? (Fritz), 68, 395

Wheel Away! (Dodds), 71, 401

When Bluebell Sang (Ernst), 85

When Hitler Stole Pink Rabbit (Kerr), 158

When I Was Young in the Mountains (Rylant), 137, 138, 192

When Summer Ends (Fowler), 84, 187, 401

When We Were Very Young (Milne), 350

Where Does the Brown Bear Go? (Weiss), 43

Where Do You Think You're Going, Christopher Columbus? (Fritz), 197, 394

Where the Buffaloes Begin (Baker), 224, 298

Where the Forest Meets the Sea (Baker), 366, 367

Where the Sidewalk Ends (Silverstein), 348, 353

Where the Wild Things Are (Sendak), 68, 191, 329, 331

Where Was Patrick Henry on the 29th of May? (Fritz), 68, 417

Whispers From the Dead (Nixon), 319

White Bear, Ice Bear (Ryder), 189, 321

White Captives (Lampman), 207

White House, The: Cornerstone of a Nation (St. George), 89, 418

White Mountains, The (Christopher), 156, 229, 333, 334

White Stag, The (Seredy), 229, 257

"Who Has Seen the Wind?" (Rossetti), 350, 351–52

Who's in Rabbit's House (Aardema), 303, 306

Who Speaks for Wolf (Spencer), 298

Why Corn is Golden: Stories About Plants (Blackmore), 308, 309

Why Don't You Get a Horse, Sam Adams? (Fritz), 148, 391

Why Mosquitoes Buzz in People's Ears (Aardema), 250

Why the Crab Has No Head (Knutson), 303

Wicked Stepdog, The (Benjamin), 366, 367

Wild Baby Goes to Sea, The (Lindgren), 189, 321, 346

Wild Swans, The (Andersen), 147

William's Doll (Zolotow), 168

William Tell (Bawden), 229, 283

Will's Mammoth (Martin), 189, 321

Will You Sign Here, John Hancock? (Fritz), 417

"Wind, The" (Stevenson), 351

Wind Blew, The (Hutchins), 191

Winding Valley Farm: Annie's Story (Pellowski), 224

Wind in the Door, A (L'Engle), 333

Wind in the Willows, The (Grahame), 47, 67, 249, 319, 329, 332

Windows on Wildlife (Johnston & Cutchins), 403

Winnie-the-Pooh (Milne), 249, 319, 322, 329

Winter Harvest (Aragon), 84, 401

Winter When Time Was Frozen, The (Pelgrom), 207

Wish Giver, The (Brittain), 65, 245–47, 255, 256, 321

Witch of Blackbird Pond, The (Speare), 153, 154–55, 156, 229, 383, 387, 388

Wizard of Earthsea, A (LeGuin), 206

Wizard of Oz, The (Baum), 197

Wolf and the Seven Little Kids, The (Grimm), 132

Wolves of Willoughby Chase, The (Aiken), 207

Woman Chief (Sobol), 87, 409

Woodsong (Paulsen), 150, 151, 390

Wordless books, 116–17

Wreck of the Zephyr, The (Van Allsburg), 322

Wrinkle in Time, A (L'Engle), 229, 318, 322, 333, 335, 336

Writing activities. *See also* Aesthetic responses

  and assessment, 116–17

  and author's style, 238, 247, 248, 249

  and characterization, 166–67, 171

  and comprehension, 45–46

  and contemporary realistic fiction, 372, 377

  and fantasy, 336, 339, 340

  and folklore, 226, 282, 293, 294, 296–97, 302, 305–6, 310

  and historical fiction, biography, and informational literature, 397, 398, 408, 413, 416, 422, 425, 426

  and plot development, 132, 142, 143, 151

  and poetry, 67–70, 347–49, 355, 356

  and point of view, 259, 262, 265

  and setting, 187, 201, 204–5

  and theme, 226

  and vocabulary development, 67–74

"Yak, The" (Prelutsky), 350, 351

Year at Maple Hill Farm, The (Provensen & Provensen), 191

Yeh Shen: A Cinderella Story from China (Louie), 290

Yellow Umbrella, The (Drescher), 116

You Read to Me, I'll Read to You (Ciardi), 350, 352

Z Was Zapped, The (Van Allsburg), 42

Zed (Harris), 374

Zeely (Hamilton), 147, 224, 367

Zoar Blue (Hickman), 147, 207, 229, 418

Zuni Folk Tales (Cushing), 222, 298

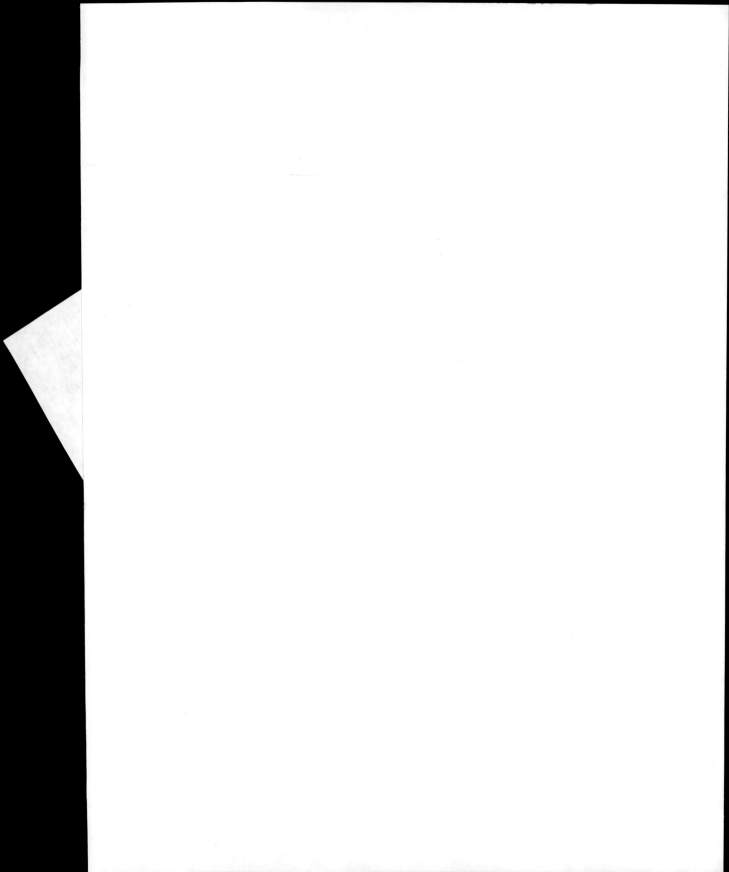

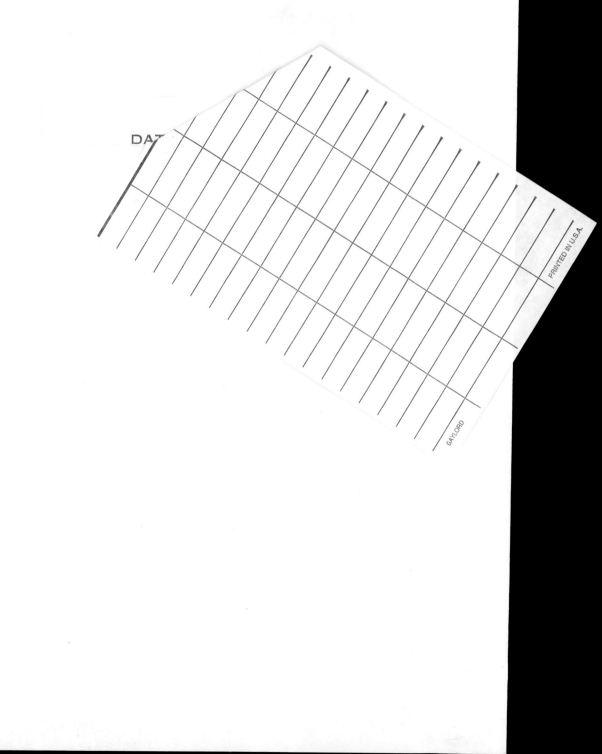

DAT

GAYLORD   PRINTED IN U.S.A.